Readings from *Classical* Rhetoric

Edited by
Patricia P. Matsen
Philip Rollinson
Marion Sousa

Southern Illinois University Press
Carbondale and Edwardsville

Designed by Shannon M. McIntyre
Production supervised by Natalia Nadraga
93   3

Library of Congress Cataloging-in-Publication Data

Readings from classical rhetoric / edited by Patricia P. Matsen, Philip
    Rollinson, Marion Sousa.
        p. cm.
    Includes bibliographical references.
    1. Rhetoric, Ancient. 2. Classical literature—Translations into
English. 3. English literature—Translations from classical
languages. I. Matsen, Patricia P., 1933–   . II. Rollinson,
Philip B. III. Sousa, Marion, 1941 Sept. 11–
PA3637.R5R4 1990
808'.048—dc20   89-36897
                                                                     CIP

ISBN 0-8093-1592-0
ISBN 0-8093-1593-9 (pbk.)

The paper used in this publication meets the minimum requirements of American National
Standard for Information Sciences —Permanence of Paper for Printed Library Materials,
ANSI Z39.48-1984.♾

Contents

Preface

A lthough most of us are probably not aware of it, we still formally express our ideas, whether orally or in writing, according to principles that were first developed by the Greeks and Romans. Oratory defined the intellectual life of the Greeks and Romans, and their intellectual descendants made classical rhetoric the basis of education for many generations.

Since the relevance of classical rhetoric has been increasingly recognized, we decided to gather together representative selections from the most important ancient sources. We thought that making these excerpts available in a single anthology would be the best way to provide a detailed overview of classical rhetoric in the words of the ancient authorities themselves. (Perhaps we should pause to explain the predominance of the masculine pronoun in these texts. The orator is usually referred to in the masculine gender because the arenas in which classical rhetoric was practiced were open only to free male citizens. Although we might wish that oratorical opportunities had been equally extended to women during ancient times, we have copied the texts as history has preserved them.)

We have extended the traditional canon beyond the normal one so as to include representatives of all the writings having to do with rhetoric that were composed before the fall of Rome. Thus the first selections from Homer and the early historians represent the pretechnical era of rhetoric. At the end of our period, the fourth-century excerpt from Basil illustrates how rhetoric came to be used in the Byzantine east, while the fifth-century selections from Augustine show how rhetoric was adapted to western Christianity in the closing years of the Roman era.

The recent interest in orality and literacy influenced our first selections from Homer, Herodotus, and Thucydides. Although we have no desire to take any particular position on the controversial orality/literacy issue, we include excerpts that reflect a rich repertoire of speeches and debates. In the introductions to each of these authors, we also point out some of the techniques they used to represent oratory in the relatively new technology of writing.

Modern scholarship has recognized that the sophists deserve much more respect than Plato ever gave them. Because this research tends to confirm the continuing influence of the sophists, we include a new translation of Gorgias' important encomium on Helen of Troy. We also present a new translation—the first in English since 1919—of the essay on composition written by the sophist Alcidamas. In this polemic Alcidamas argues that writing hinders the ability to compose and deliver extemporaneous speeches.

In general, we have attempted to extract from the works of Plato, Aristotle, Cicero, and the rest of our authorities those selections that touch most directly upon rhetorical theory and practice. In making these choices, we have tried to include the most significant passages: Aristotle on *topoi*, one of Cicero's most influential discussions of style, Quintilian's argument for the orator as a good man, and so forth. Furthermore, we have attempted to capture the important excerpts that illustrate original techniques, methods, and approaches, such as the application of Hermagoras' *staseis* in Cicero and the formulary directions for invention in the *Rhetorica ad Herennium*.

Finally, we have edited our selections so as to avoid repetition and duplication. We chose, for example, to present the complete section on delivery from the *Rhetorica ad Herennium*, but we do not repeat Quintilian's treatment of the same topic. Similarly, we use Quintilian's complete treatment of memory, because it is more detailed, developed, and comprehensive than the earlier discussion of memory in the *ad Herennium*.

The order of our selections is chronological, up to a point. Following the selection from Tacitus, which discusses the changes in rhetoric from the Roman Republic to the Silver Age, we decided it would be easier to group the entries according to topics. Thus the excerpts from Theon, Nicolaus, and Aphthonius are together because they all wrote versions of *progymnasmata*. The introductions to the *Progymnasmata* by Theon and Nicolaus are here translated into English for the first time. Since these are the only discussions extant from antiquity concerning the purpose of these rhetorical exercises, we think that they add an important contemporary dimension to an overview of educational rhetoric. We also group Dionysius, Demetrius, Longinus, and Hermogenes together since all four of these writers discuss style.

Our final chapter returns to the chronological framework insofar as we have included excerpts from the third, fourth, and fifth centuries. As might be expected, however, these selections represent the extremely divergent streams that classical rhetoric was to follow. Menander Rhetor tells contemporary sophists how to formulate an impromptu speech; specifically, an encomium of a provincial governor. On the other hand, Basil and Augustine explain how Christians can use rhetoric for their own education and in sermons.

We have tried to organize and present these selections so that they are easily accessible. To accompany each author, there is a short introduction and as many notes as we thought would be of help to readers without overloading them with background information. It is our hope that these selections will enable any interested person to comprehend the scope and significance of rhetoric in antiquity.

We offer our thanks to Kenney Withers, director of Southern Illinois University Press, for his interest and support, and to Carol A. Burns, manuscript editor for Southern Illinois University Press, whose expertise went beyond mere matters of spelling, punctuation, and format and led to the clarification of our ideas in many places.

Readings from *Classical* Rhetoric

1

Early Figures

Homer, Herodotus, and Thucydides knew that men's deeds, without men's words, are dead. In the selections that follow, Achilleus, Agamemnon, Otanes, Megabyzus, Darius, Cleon, and Diodotus all have this in common: they are men debating. Men debating are men thinking. The great question of how men best govern themselves underlies each of these debates.

The debate in the assembly of the Achaians (*Iliad* 1.53–305) opens with the critical issue of how best to appease Phoibos Apollo, who has sent the plague that is devastating the army of the Achaians. With the help of the prophet Kalchas, a decision is quickly reached to send the captive woman Chryseis back to her father Chryses, the priest of Apollo. However, Agamemnon's demand for an immediate replacement for Chryseis provokes Achilleus to challenge the authority of Agamemnon. When Agamemnon says that he will take Achilleus' prize of honor, the woman Briseis, a quarrel breaks out between the two heroes. This contest of words grows more and more abusive until Nestor intervenes and stops it.

The angry words of Achilleus and Agamemnon consist of improvised emotional charge and countercharge more than of reasoned argument. The speech of Nestor (254–84), on the other hand, is well constructed. He states the question at issue. The quarrel must stop. If it continues, it will only be to the advantage of the Trojans (254–58). Nestor then validates his credentials as a persuader on the basis of his great age and his previous experience as a settler of disputes (259–73). Finally, he closes his speech by arguing for a compromise (274–84). Each warrior must back off. Agamemnon must not take Achilleus' prize. Achilleus must not challenge Agamemnon's authority. Although Agamemnon is the greater in authority, Achilleus is the greater fighter. Therefore, each must respect the other if the Achaians are to prevail over the Trojans.

Herodotus' three Persians show much more skill at rhetorical techniques than do Homer's heroes. Each speaker argues his case succinctly. The arguments used in proof or refutation are both philosophical (what is the effect of power on human beings?) and practical (which system of governance does the least harm?). In fact, taken as a whole, the debate is a minilesson in political science, for one finds in these speeches the perennial major commonplaces with which to argue the relative merits of democracy, oligarchy, and monarchy.

In the more than four hundred years from Homer to Herodotus, Greece, and particularly Athens, developed from an oral, preliterate society governed by an aristocracy to an increasingly literate and democratic society in which every citizen could participate in public debate. Public debate develops public rhetorical consciousness and the awareness that a mastery of rhetorical techniques can help an individual as well as a state to acquire power over others.

Thucydides' brilliant and masterful recreation of the debate at Athens over the fate of the Mytilenaeans adds to the question of the nature of democracy the issue of the effect of professional oratory on public decision making. The first two sections of Cleon's speech (37–38) and Diodotus' reply (42–43) deal with this question. The arguments presented in these sections warrant close study and comparison.

For example, Cleon blames the Athenians: "It is your wont to be spectators of words and hearers of deeds, forming your judgment of future enterprises according as able speakers represent them to be feasible, but as regards accomplished facts, not counting what has been done more credible, because you have seen it, than what you have heard, you are swayed in judgment by those who have made an eloquent invective." To this, Diodotus replies: "As for words, whoever contends that they are not to be guides of our actions is either dull of wit or has some private interest at stake—dull, if he thinks it possible by any other means to throw light on that which still belongs to the dim and distant future; self-interested, if, wishing to put through a discreditable measure, he realizes that while he cannot speak well in a bad cause, he can at least slander well and thus intimidate both his opponents and his hearers."

The question at issue, however, is whether it is good for the state to put the Mytilenaeans to death. In these sections (39, 40 and 44–48), the reader will find familiar and contemporary the commonplaces employed by the speakers in arguing *for* (Cleon) and *against* (Diodotus) the death penalty—for example, the idea that the death penalty is/is not a guarantee against further crime (revolt of other allies).

These scenes of rhetoric in action from Homer, Herodotus, and Thucydides are presented as a prologue to the theoretical sections that follow.

Homer

Before the invention of the alphabet gave us the *Iliad* and the *Odyssey*, there was Greek literature. Generations of singers *(aoidoi)* had sung tales of the Trojan War and other exploits of Greeks of the heroic age. That these tales could be passed down from generation to generation was due to the use the Greek oral epic made of an exacting verse form, the dactylic hexameter, and of repetition of formulas, phrase patterns, themes, and motifs.[1] These were the bard's building blocks, and they enabled him to compose his verses extemporaneously and, we may suppose, to change his tale as he went along in response to his audience.

Homer was able to manipulate the fixed and uniform diction and the content of the oral tradition within which he had to work so as to produce a tale that is full of vigor and realism. This vitality is due in large measure to the extensive use of direct discourse. For example, 373 of the 611 lines of *Iliad* 1 are in direct discourse. There are thirty-five speeches varying in length from two to forty-eight lines each. Homer's characters are no strangers to the art of speaking. George Kennedy writes: "Techniques of rhetorical theory are already evident in the speeches of the Homeric poems to such a degree that later antiquity found formal rhetoric everywhere in Homer and on the basis of *Iliad* 15, 283 f., even conjured up a picture of practice declamations among the Homeric heroes."[2]

In the first book of the *Iliad* we find debates, appeals, threats, and prayers. The god Hephaistos is the subject of his own *chreia* or generalization illustrated by an anecdote (589–94). As many teachers of rhetoric later observed, Homer was also a master of *prosōpopoeia* or dramatization. Book 1 of the *Iliad* is a good illustration of this.

1. Richmond Lattimore provides handy explanations and examples of Homeric verse and repetitions in the introduction to his translation of the *Iliad*, 37–40. See also M. M. Willcock's introduction to his edition of the Greek text, xix–xxii. That the Homeric poems are composed in a traditional oral, formulaic style was the discovery of Milman Parry. Seth L. Schein gives a good general discussion of Parry's work and of developments in the study of heroic narrative since Parry, 1–44.

2. *Persuasion*, 35.

Iliad

Book 1 *feudal system (kings)*

1   Sing, goddess, the anger of Peleus' son Achilleus
and its devastation, which put pains thousandfold upon the
     Achaians,
hurled in their multitudes to the house of Hades strong souls
of heroes, but gave their bodies to be the delicate feasting

5   of dogs, of all birds, and the will of Zeus was accomplished
since that time when first there stood in division of conflict
Atreus' son the lord of men and brilliant Achilleus.
     What god was it then set them together in bitter collision?
Zeus' son and Leto's, Apollo, who in anger at the king drove

10   the foul pestilence along the host, and the people perished,
since Atreus' son had dishonoured Chryses, priest of Apollo,
when he came beside the fast ships of the Achaians to ransom
back his daughter, carrying gifts beyond count and holding
in his hands wound on a staff of gold the ribbons of Apollo

15   who strikes from afar, and supplicated all the Achaians,
but above all Atreus' two sons, the marshals of the people:
'Sons of Atreus and you other strong-greaved Achaians,
to you may the gods grant who have their homes on Olympos
Priam's city to be plundered and a fair homecoming thereafter,

20   but may you give me back my own daughter and take the ransom,
giving honour to Zeus' son who strikes from afar, Apollo.'
     Then all the rest of the Achaians cried out in favour
that the priest be respected and the shining ransom be taken;
yet this pleased not the heart of Atreus' son Agamemnon,

25   but harshly he drove him away with a strong order upon him:
'Never let me find you again, old sir, near our hollow
ships, neither lingering now nor coming again hereafter,
for fear your staff and the god's ribbons help you no longer.
The girl I will not give back; sooner will old age come upon her

30   in my own house, in Argos, far from her own land, going
up and down by the loom and being in my bed as my companion.
So go now, do not make me angry; so you will be safer.'
     So he spoke, and the old man in terror obeyed him
and went silently away beside the murmuring sea beach

35   Over and over the old man prayed as he walked in solitude
to King Apollo, whom Leto of the lovely hair bore: 'Hear me,
lord of the silver bow who set your power about Chryse
and Killa the sacrosanct, who are lord in strength over Tenedos,
Smintheus, if ever it pleased your heart that I built your temple,

if ever it pleased you that I burned all the rich thigh pieces   40
of bulls, of goats, then bring to pass this wish I pray for:
let your arrows make the Danaans pay for my tears shed.'
    So he spoke in prayer, and Phoibos Apollo heard him,
and strode down along the pinnacles of Olympos, angered
in his heart, carrying across his shoulders the bow and the hooded   45
quiver; and the shafts clashed on the shoulders of the god walking
angrily. He came as night comes down and knelt then
apart and opposite the ships and let go an arrow.
Terrible was the clash that rose from the bow of silver.
First he went after the mules and the circling hounds, then let go   50
a tearing arrow against the men themselves and struck them.
The corpse fires burned everywhere and did not stop burning.
    Nine days up and down the host ranged the god's arrows,
but on the tenth Achilleus called the people to assembly;
a thing put into his mind by the goddess of the white arms, Hera,   55
who had pity upon the Danaans when she saw them dying.
Now when they were all assembled in one place together,
Achilleus of the swift feet stood up among them and spoke forth:
'Son of Atreus, I believe now that straggling backwards
we must make our way home if we can even escape death,   60
if fighting now must crush the Achaians and the plague likewise.
No, come, let us ask some holy man, some prophet,
even an interpreter of dreams, since a dream also
comes from Zeus, who can tell why Phoibos Apollo is so angry,
if for the sake of some vow, some hecatomb he blames us,   65
if given the fragrant smoke of lambs, of he goats, somehow
he can be made willing to beat the bane aside from us.'
    He spoke thus and sat down again, and among them stood up
Kalchas, Thestor's son, far the best of the bird interpreters,
who knew all things that were, the things to come and the things past,   70
who guided into the land of Ilion the ships of the Achaians
through that seercraft of his own that Phoibos Apollo gave him.
He in kind intention toward all stood forth and addressed them:
'You have bidden me, Achilleus beloved of Zeus, to explain to
you this anger of Apollo the lord who strikes from afar. Then   75
I will speak; yet make me a promise and swear before me
readily by word and work of your hands to defend me,
since I believe I shall make a man angry who holds great kingship
over the men of Argos, and all the Achaians obey him.
For a king when he is angry with a man beneath him is too strong,   80
and suppose even for the day itself he swallow down his anger,
he still keeps bitterness that remains until its fulfilment
deep in his chest. Speak forth then, tell me if you will protect me.'
    Then in answer again spoke Achilleus of the swift feet:
'Speak, interpreting whatever you know, and fear nothing.   85

arete— virtue

In the name of Apollo beloved of Zeus to whom you, Kalchas,
make your prayers when you interpret the gods' will to the Danaans,
no man so long as I am alive above earth and see daylight
shall lay the weight of his hands on you beside the hollow ships,
90   not one of all the Danaans, even if you mean Agamemnon,
who now claims to be far the greatest of all the Achaians.'
    At this the blameless seer took courage again and spoke forth:
'No, it is not for the sake of some vow or hecatomb he blames us,
but for the sake of his priest whom Agamemnon dishonoured
95   and would not give him back his daughter nor accept the ransom.
Therefore the archer sent griefs against us and will send them
still, nor sooner thrust back the shameful plague from the Danaans
until we give the glancing-eyed girl back to her father
without price, without ransom, and lead also a blessed hecatomb
100   to Chryse; thus we might propitiate and persuade him.'
    He spoke thus and sat down again, and among them stood up
Atreus' son the hero wide-ruling Agamemnon
raging, the heart within filled black to the brim with anger
from beneath, but his two eyes showed like fire in their blazing.
105   First of all he eyed Kalchas bitterly and spoke to him:
'Seer of evil: never yet have you told me a good thing.
Always the evil things are dear to your heart to prophesy,
but nothing excellent have you said nor ever accomplished.
Now once more you make divination to the Danaans, argue
110   forth your reason why he who strikes from afar afflicts them,
because I for the sake of the girl Chryseis would not take
the shining ransom; and indeed I wish greatly to have her
in my own house; since I like her better than Klytaimestra
my own wife, for in truth she is no way inferior,
115   neither in build nor stature nor wit, not in accomplishment.
Still I am willing to give her back, if such is the best way.
I myself desire that my people be safe, not perish.
Find me then some prize that shall be my own, lest I only
among the Argives go without, since that were unfitting;
120   you are all witnesses to this thing, that my prize goes elsewhere.'
    Then in answer again spoke brilliant swift-footed Achilleus:
'Son of Atreus, most lordly, greediest for gain of all men,
how shall the great-hearted Achaians give you a prize now?
there is no great store of things lying about I know of.
125   But what we took from the cities by storm has been distributed;
it is unbecoming for the people to call back things once given.
No, for the present give the girl back to the god; we Achaians
thrice and four times over will repay you, if ever Zeus gives
into our hands the strong-walled citadel of Troy to be plundered.'
130   Then in answer again spoke powerful Agamemnon:
'Not that way, good fighter though you be, godlike Achilleus,

strive to cheat, for you will not deceive, you will not persuade me.
What do you want? To keep your own prize and have me sit here
lacking one? Are you ordering me to give this girl back?
Either the great-hearted Achaians shall give me a new prize   135
chosen according to my desire to atone for the girl lost,
or else if they will not give me one I myself shall take her,
your own prize, or that of Aias, or that of Odysseus,
going myself in person; and he whom I visit will be bitter.
Still, these are things we shall deliberate again hereafter.   140
Come, now, we must haul a black ship down to the bright sea,
and assemble rowers enough for it, and put on board it
the hecatomb, and the girl herself, Chryseis of the fair cheeks,
and let there be one responsible man in charge of her,
either Aias or Idomeneus or brilliant Odysseus,   145
or you yourself, son of Peleus, most terrifying of all men,
to reconcile by accomplishing sacrifice the archer,'
   Then looking darkly at him Achilleus of the swift feet spoke:
'O wrapped in shamelessness, with your mind forever on profit,
how shall any one of the Achaians readily obey you   150
either to go on a journey or to fight men strongly in battle?
I for my part did not come here for the sake of the Trojan
spearmen to fight against them, since to me they have done nothing.
Never yet have they driven away my cattle or my horses,
never in Phthia where the soil is rich and men grow great did they   155
spoil my harvest, since indeed there is much that lies between us,
the shadowy mountains and the echoing sea; but for your sake,
o great shamelessness, we followed, to do you favour,
you with the dog's eyes, to win your honour and Menelaos'
from the Trojans. You forget all this or else you care nothing.   160
And now my prize you threaten in person to strip from me,
for whom I laboured much, the gift of the sons of the Achaians.
Never, when the Achaians sack some well-founded citadel
of the Trojans, do I have a prize that is equal to your prize.
Always the greater part of the painful fighting is the work of   165
my hands; but when the time comes to distribute the booty
yours is far the greater reward, and I with some small thing
yet dear to me go back to my ships when I am weary with fighting.
Now I am returning to Phthia, since it is much better
to go home again with my curved ships, and I am minded no longer   170
to stay here dishonoured and pile up your wealth and your luxury.'
   Then answered him in turn the lord of men Agamemnon:
'Run away by all means if your heart drives you. I will not
entreat you to stay here for my sake. There are others with me
who will do me honour, and above all Zeus of the counsels.   175
To me you are the most hateful of all the kings whom the gods love.
Forever quarrelling is dear to your heart, and wars and battles;

and if you are very strong indeed, that is a god's gift.
Go home then with your own ships and your own companions,
180   be king over the Myrmidons. I care nothing about you.
I take no account of your anger. But here is my threat to you.
Even as Phoibos Apollo is taking away my Chryseis.
I shall convey her back in my own ship, with my own
followers; but I shall take the fair-cheeked Briseis,
185   your prize, I myself going to your shelter, that you may learn well
how much greater I am than you, and another man may shrink back
from likening himself to me and contending against me.'
    So he spoke. And the anger came on Peleus' son, and within
his shaggy breast the heart was divided two ways, pondering
190   whether to draw from beside his thigh the sharp sword, driving
away all those who stood between and kill the son of Atreus,
or else to check the spleen within and keep down his anger.
Now as he weighed in mind and spirit these two courses
and was drawing from its scabbard the great sword, Athene descended
195   from the sky. For Hera the goddess of the white arms sent her,
who loved both men equally in her heart and cared for them.
The goddess standing behind Peleus' son caught him by the fair hair,
appearing to him only, for no man of the others saw her.
Achilleus in amazement turned about, and straightway
200   knew Pallas Athene and the terrible eyes shining.
He uttered winged words and addressed her: 'Why have you come now,
o child of Zeus of the aegis, once more? Is it that you may see
the outrageousness of the son of Atreus Agamemnon?
Yet will I tell you this thing, and I think it shall be accomplished.
205   By such acts of arrogance he may even lose his own life.'
    Then in answer the goddess grey-eyed Athene spoke to him:
'I have come down to stay your anger—but will you obey me?—
from the sky; and the goddess of the white arms Hera sent me,
who loves both of you equally in her heart and cares for you.
210   Come then, do not take your sword in your hand, keep clear of fighting,
though indeed with words you may abuse him, and it will be that way.
And this also will I tell you and it will be a thing accomplished.
Some day three times over such shining gifts shall be given you
by reason of this outrage. Hold your hand then, and obey us.'
215   Then in answer again spoke Achilleus of the swift feet:
'Goddess, it is necessary that I obey the word of you two,
angry though I am in my heart. So it will be better.
If any man obeys the gods, they listen to him also.'
    He spoke, and laid his heavy hand on the silver sword hilt
220   and thrust the great blade back into the scabbard nor disobeyed
the word of Athene. And she went back again to Olympos
to the house of Zeus of the aegis with the other divinities.
    But Peleus' son once again in words of derision

spoke to Atreides, and did not yet let go of his anger:
'You wine sack, with a dog's eyes, with a deer's heart. Never   225
once have you taken courage in your heart to arm with your people
for battle or go into ambuscade with the best of the Achaians.
No, for in such things you see death. Far better to your mind
is it, all along the widespread host of the Achaians
to take away the gifts of any man who speaks up against you.   230
King who feed on your people, since you rule nonentities;
otherwise, son of Atreus, this were your last outrage.
But I will tell you this and swear a great oath upon it:
in the name of this sceptre, which never again will bear leaf nor
branch, now that it has left behind the cut stump in the mountains,   235
nor shall it ever blossom again, since the bronze blade stripped
bark and leafage, and now at last the sons of the Achaians
carry it in their hands in state when they administer
the justice of Zeus. And this shall be a great oath before you:
some day longing for Achilleus will come to the sons of the Achaians,   240
all of them. Then stricken at heart though you be, you will be able
to do nothing, when in their numbers before man-slaughtering Hektor
they drop and die. And then you will eat out the heart within you
in sorrow, that you did no honour to the best of the Achaians.'
   Thus spoke Peleus' son and dashed to the ground the sceptre   245
studded with golden nails, and sat down again. But Atreides
raged still on the other side, and between them Nestor
the fair-spoken rose up, the lucid speaker of Pylos,
from whose lips the streams of words ran sweeter than honey.
In his time two generations of mortal men had perished,   250
those who had grown up with him and they who had been born to
these in sacred Pylos, and he was king in the third age.
He in kind intention toward both stood forth and addressed them:
'Oh, for shame. Great sorrow comes on the land of Achaia.
Now might Priam and the sons of Priam in truth be happy,   255
and all the rest of the Trojans be visited in their hearts with gladness,
were they to hear all this wherein you two are quarrelling,
you, who surpass all Danaans in council, in fighting.
Yet be persuaded. Both of you are younger than I am.
Yes, and in my time I have dealt with better men than   260
you are, and never once did they disregard me. Never
yet have I seen nor shall see again such men as these were,
men like Peirithoös, and Dryas, shepherd of the people,
Kaineus and Exadios, godlike Polyphemos,
or Theseus, Aigeus' son, in the likeness of the immortals.   265
These were the strongest generation of earth-born mortals,
the strongest, and they fought against the strongest, the beast men
living within the mountains, and terribly they destroyed them.
I was of the company of these men, coming from Pylos,

270   a long way from a distant land, since they had summoned me.
        And I fought single-handed, yet against such men no one
        of the mortals now alive upon earth could do battle. And also
        these listened to the counsels I gave and heeded my bidding.
        Do you also obey, since to be persuaded is better.
275   You, great man that you are, yet do not take the girl away
        but let her be, a prize as the sons of the Achaians gave her
        first. Nor, son of Peleus, think to match your strength with
        the king, since never equal with the rest is the portion of honour
        of the sceptred king to whom Zeus gives magnificence. Even
280   though you are the stronger man, and the mother who bore you was
            immortal,
        yet is this man greater who is lord over more than you rule.
        Son of Atreus, give up your anger; even I entreat you
        to give over your bitterness against Achilleus, he who
        stands as a great bulwark of battle over all the Achaians.'
285   Then in answer again spoke powerful Agamemnon:
        'Yes, old sir, all this you have said is fair and orderly.
        Yet here is a man who wishes to be above all others,
        who wishes to hold power over all, and to be lord of
        all, and give them their orders, yet I think one will not obey him.
290   And if the everlasting gods have made him a spearman,
        yet they have not given him the right to speak abusively.'
            Then looking at him darkly brilliant Achilleus answered him:
        'So must I be called of no account and a coward
        if I must carry out every order you may happen to give me.
295   Tell other men to do these things, but give me no more
        commands, since I for my part have no intention to obey you.
        And put away in your thoughts this other thing I tell you.
        With my hands I will not fight for the girl's sake, neither
        with you nor any other man, since you take her away who gave her.
300   But of all the other things that are mine beside my fast black
        ship, you shall take nothing away against my pleasure.
        Come, then, only try it, that these others may see also;
        instantly your own black blood will stain my spearpoint.'
            So these two after battling in words of contention
305   stood up, and broke the assembly beside the ships of the Achaians.
        Peleus' son went back to his balanced ships and his shelter
        with Patroklos, Menoitios' son, and his own companions.
        But the son of Atreus drew a fast ship down to the water
        and allotted into it twenty rowers and put on board it
310   the hecatomb for the god and Chryseis of the fair cheeks
        leading her by the hand. And in charge went crafty Odysseus.
            These then putting out went over the ways of the water
        while Atreus' son told his people to wash off their defilement.
        And they washed it away and threw the washings into the salt sea.

Then they accomplished perfect hecatombs to Apollo,   315
of bulls and goats along the beach of the barren salt sea.
The savour of the burning swept in circles up to the bright sky.
    Thus these were busy about the army. But Agamemnon
did not give up his anger and the first threat he made to Achilleus,
but to Talthybios he gave his orders and Eurybates   320
who were heralds and hard-working henchmen to him: 'Go now
to the shelter of Peleus' son Achilleus, to bring back
Briseis of the fair cheeks leading her by the hand. And if he
will not give her, I must come in person to take her
with many men behind me, and it will be the worse for him.'   325
    He spoke and sent them forth with this strong order upon them.
They went against their will beside the beach of the barren
salt sea, and came to the shelters and the ships of the Myrmidons.
The man himself they found beside his shelter and his black ship
sitting. And Achilleus took no joy at all when he saw them.   330
These two terrified and in awe of the king stood waiting
quietly, and did not speak a word at all nor question him.
But he knew the whole matter in his own heart, and spoke first:
'Welcome, heralds, messengers of Zeus and of mortals
Draw near. You are not to blame in my sight, but Agamemnon   335
who sent the two of you here for the sake of the girl Briseis.
Go then, illustrious Patroklos, and bring the girl forth
and give her to these to be taken away. Yet let them be witnesses
in the sight of the blessed gods, in the sight of mortal
men, and of this cruel king, if ever hereafter   340
there shall be need of me to beat back the shameful destruction
from the rest. For surely in ruinous heart he makes sacrifice
and has not wit enough to look behind and before him
that the Achaians fighting beside their ships shall not perish.'
    So he spoke, and Patroklos obeyed his beloved companion.   345
He led forth from the hut Briseis of the fair cheeks and gave her
to be taken away; and they walked back beside the ships of the Achaians,
and the woman all unwilling went with them still. But Achilleus
weeping went and sat in sorrow apart from his companions
beside the beach of the grey sea looking out on the infinite water.   350
Many times stretching forth his hands he called on his mother:
'Since, my mother, you bore me to be a man with a short life,
therefore Zeus of the loud thunder on Olympos should grant me
honour at least. But now he has given me not even a little.
Now the son of Atreus, powerful Agamemnon,   355
has dishonoured me, since he has taken away my prize and keeps it.'
    So he spoke in tears and the lady his mother heard him
as she sat in the depths of the sea at the side of her aged father,
and lightly she emerged like a mist from the grey water.
She came and sat beside him as he wept, and stroked him   360

with her hand and called him by name and spoke to him: 'Why then,
child, do you lament? What sorrow has come to your heart now?
Tell me, do not hide it in your mind, and thus we shall both know.'
   Sighing heavily Achilleus of the swift feet answered her:

365 'You know; since you know why must I tell you all this?
We went against Thebe, the sacred city of Eëtion,
and the city we sacked, and carried everything back to this place,
and the sons of the Achaians made a fair distribution
and for Atreus' son they chose out Chryseis of the fair cheeks.

370 Then Chryses, priest of him who strikes from afar, Apollo,
came beside the fast ships of the bronze-armoured Achaians to ransom
back his daughter, carrying gifts beyond count and holding
in his hands wound on a staff of gold the ribbons of Apollo
who strikes from afar, and supplicated all the Achaians,

375 but above all Atreus' two sons, the marshals of the people.
Then all the rest of the Achaians cried out in favour
that the priest be respected and the shining ransom be taken;
yet this pleased not the heart of Atreus' son Agamemnon,
but harshly he sent him away with a strong order upon him.

380 The old man went back again in anger, but Apollo
listened to his prayer, since he was very dear to him, and let go
the wicked arrow against the Argives. And now the people
were dying one after another while the god's shafts ranged
everywhere along the wide host of the Achaians, till the seer

385 knowing well the truth interpreted the designs of the archer.
It was I first of all urged then the god's appeasement;
and the anger took hold of Atreus' son, and in speed standing
he uttered his threat against me, and now it is a thing accomplished.
For the girl the glancing-eyed Achaians are taking to Chryse

390 in a fast ship, also carrying to the king presents. But even
now the heralds went away from my shelter leading
Briseus' daughter, whom the sons of the Achaians gave me.
You then, if you have power to, protect your own son, going
to Olympos and supplicating Zeus, if ever before now

395 either by word you comforted Zeus' heart or by action.
Since it is many times in my father's halls I have heard you
making claims, when you said you only among the immortals
beat aside shameful destruction from Kronos' son the dark-misted,
that time when all the other Olympians sought to bind him,

400 Hera and Poseidon and Pallas Athene. Then you,
goddess, went and set him free from his shackles, summoning
in speed the creature of the hundred hands to tall Olympos,
that creature the gods name Briareus, but all men
Aigaios' son, but he is far greater in strength than his father.

405 He rejoicing in the glory of it sat down by Kronion,
and the rest of the blessed gods were frightened and gave up binding him.

Sit beside him and take his knees and remind him of these things
now, if perhaps he might be willing to help the Trojans,
and pin the Achaians back against the ships and the water,
dying, so that thus they may all have profit of their own king,   410
that Atreus' son wide-ruling Agamemnon may recognize
his madness, that he did no honour to the best of the Achaians.'
    Thetis answered him then letting the tears fall: 'Ah me,
my child. Your birth was bitterness. Why did I raise you?
If only you could sit by your ships untroubled, not weeping,   415
since indeed your lifetime is to be short, of no length.
Now it has befallen that your life must be brief and bitter
beyond all men's. To a bad destiny I bore you in my chambers.
But I will go to cloud-dark Olympos and ask this
thing of Zeus who delights in the thunder. Perhaps he will do it.   420
Do you therefore continuing to sit by your swift ships
be angry at the Achaians and stay away from all fighting.
For Zeus went to the blameless Aithiopians at the Ocean
yesterday to feast, and the rest of the gods went with him.
On the twelfth day he will be coming back to Olympos,   425
and then I will go for your sake to the house of Zeus, bronze-founded,
and take him by the knees and I think I can persuade him.'
    So speaking she went away from that place and left him
sorrowing in his heart for the sake of the fair-girdled woman
whom they were taking by force against his will. But Odysseus   430
meanwhile drew near to Chryse conveying the sacred hecatomb.
These when they were inside the many-hollowed harbour
took down and gathered together the sails and stowed them in the black
    ship,
let down mast by the forestays, and settled it into the mast crutch
easily, and rowed her in with oars to the mooring.   435
They threw over the anchor stones and made fast the stern cables
and themselves stepped out on to the break of the sea beach,
and led forth the hecatomb to the archer Apollo,
and Chryseis herself stepped forth from the sea-going vessel.
Odysseus of the many designs guided her to the altar   440
and left her in her father's arms and spoke a word to him:
'Chryses, I was sent here by the lord of men Agamemnon
to lead back your daughter and accomplish a sacred hecatomb
to Apollo on behalf of the Danaans, that we may propitiate
the lord who has heaped unhappiness and tears on the Argives.'   445
    He spoke, and left her in his arms. And he received gladly
his beloved child. And the men arranged the sacred hecatomb
for the god in orderly fashion around the strong-founded altar.
Next they washed their hands and took up the scattering barley.
Standing among them with lifted arms Chryses prayed in a great voice: 450
'Hear me, lord of the silver bow, who set your power about

Chryse and Killa the sacrosanct, who are lord in strength over
Tenedos; if once before you listened to my prayers
and did me honour and smote strongly the host of the Achaians,
455   so one more time bring to pass the wish that I pray for.
Beat aside at last the shameful plague from the Danaans.'
    So he spoke in prayer, and Phoibos Apollo heard him.
And when all had made prayer and flung down the scattering barley
first they drew back the victims' heads and slaughtered them and skinned
    them,
460   and cut away the meat from the thighs and wrapped them in fat,
making a double fold, and laid shreds of flesh upon them.
The old man burned these on a cleft stick and poured the gleaming
wine over, while the young men with forks in their hands stood about
    him.
But when they had burned the thigh pieces and tasted the vitals,
465   they cut all the remainder into pieces and spitted them
and roasted all carefully and took off the pieces.
Then after they had finished the work and got the feast ready
they feasted, nor was any man's hunger denied a fair portion.
But when they had put away their desire for eating and drinking,
470   the young men filled the mixing bowls with pure wine, passing
a portion to all, when they had offered drink in the goblets.
All day long they propitiated the god with singing,
chanting a splendid hymn to Apollo, these young Achaians,
singing to the one who works from afar, who listened in gladness.
475   Afterwards when the sun went down and darkness came onward
they lay down and slept beside the ship's stern cables.
But when the young Dawn showed again with her rosy fingers,
they put forth to sea toward the wide camp of the Achaians.
And Apollo who works from afar sent them a favouring stern wind.
480   They set up the mast again and spread on it the white sails,
and the wind blew into the middle of the sail, and at the cutwater
a blue wave rose and sang strongly as the ship went onward.
She ran swiftly cutting across the swell her pathway.
But when they had come back to the wide camp of the Achaians
485   they hauled the black ship up on the mainland, high up
on the sand, and underneath her they fixed the long props.
Afterwards they scattered to their own ships and their shelters.
    But that other still sat in anger beside his swift ships,
Peleus' son divinely born, Achilleus of the swift feet.
490   Never now would he go to assemblies where men win glory,
never more into battle, but continued to waste his heart out
sitting there, though he longed always for the clamour and fighting.
    But when the twelfth dawn after this day appeared, the gods who
live forever came back to Olympos all in a body
495   and Zeus led them; nor did Thetis forget the entreaties

of her son, but she emerged from the sea's waves early
in the morning and went up to the tall sky and Olympos.
She found Kronos' broad-browed son apart from the others
sitting upon the highest peak of rugged Olympos.
She came and sat beside him with her left hand embracing   500
his knees, but took him underneath the chin with her right hand
and spoke in supplication to lord Zeus son of Kronos:
'Father Zeus, if ever before in word or action
I did you favour among the immortals, now grant what I ask for.
Now give honour to my son short-lived beyond all other   505
mortals. Since even now the lord of men Agamemnon
dishonours him, who has taken away his prize and keeps it.
Zeus of the counsels, lord of Olympos, now do him honour.
So long put strength into the Trojans, until the Achaians
give my son his rights, and his honour is increased among them.'   510
        She spoke thus. But Zeus who gathers the clouds made no answer
but sat in silence a long time. And Thetis, as she had taken
his knees, clung fast to them and urged once more her question:
'Bend your head and promise me to accomplish this thing,
or else refuse it, you have nothing to fear, that I may know   515
by how much I am the most dishonoured of all gods.'
        Deeply disturbed Zeus who gathers the clouds answered her:
'This is a disastrous matter when you set me in conflict
with Hera, and she troubles me with recriminations.
Since even as things are, forever among the immortals   520
she is at me and speaks of how I help the Trojans in battle.
Even so, go back again now, go away, for fear she
see us. I will look to these things that they be accomplished.
See then, I will bend my head that you may believe me.
For this among the immortal gods is the mightiest witness   525
I can give, and nothing I do shall be vain nor revocable
nor a thing unfulfilled when I bend my head in assent to it.'
        He spoke, the son of Kronos, and nodded his head with the dark brows,
and the immortally anointed hair of the great god
swept from his divine head, and all Olympos was shaken.   530
        So these two who had made their plans separated, and Thetis
leapt down again from shining Olympos into the sea's depth,
but Zeus went back to his own house, and all the gods rose up
from their chairs to greet the coming of their father, not one had courage
to keep his place as the father advanced, but stood up to greet him.   535
Thus he took his place on the throne; yet Hera was not
ignorant, having seen how he had been plotting counsels
with Thetis the silver-footed, the daughter of the sea's ancient,
and at once she spoke revilingly to Zeus son of Kronos:
'Treacherous one, what god has been plotting counsels with you?   540
Always it is dear to your heart in my absence to think of

secret things and decide upon them. Never have you patience
frankly to speak forth to me the thing that you purpose.'
   Then to her the father of gods and men made answer:
545 'Hera, do not go on hoping that you will hear all my
thoughts, since these will be too hard for you, though you are my wife.
Any thought that it is right for you to listen to, no one
neither man nor any immortal shall hear it before you.
But anything that apart from the rest of the gods I wish to
550 plan, do not always question each detail nor probe me.'
   Then the goddess the ox-eyed lady Hera answered:
'Majesty, son of Kronos, what sort of thing have you spoken?
Truly too much in time past I have not questioned nor probed you,
but you are entirely free to think out whatever pleases you.
555 Now, though, I am terrible afraid you were won over
by Thetis the silver-footed, the daughter of the sea's ancient.
For early in the morning she sat beside you and took your
knees, and I think you bowed your head in assent to do honour
to Achilleus, and to destroy many beside the ships of the Achaians.'
560   Then in return Zeus who gathers the clouds made answer:
'Dear lady, I never escape you, you are always full of suspicion.
Yet thus you can accomplish nothing surely, but be more
distant from my heart than ever, and it will be the worse for you.
If what you say is true, then that is the way I wish it.
565 But go then, sit down in silence, and do as I tell you,
for fear all the gods, as many as are on Olympos, can do nothing
if I come close and lay my unconquerable hands upon you.'
   He spoke, and the goddess the ox-eyed lady Hera was frightened
and went and sat down in silence wrenching her heart to obedience,
570 and all the Uranian gods in the house of Zeus were troubled.
Hephaistos the renowned smith rose up to speak among them,
to bring comfort to his beloved mother, Hera of the white arms:
'This will be a disastrous matter and not endurable
if you two are to quarrel thus for the sake of mortals
575 and bring brawling among the gods. There will be no pleasure
in the stately feast at all, since vile things will be uppermost.
And I entreat my mother, though she herself understands it,
to be ingratiating toward our father Zeus, that no longer
our father may scold her and break up the quiet of our feasting.
580 For if the Olympian who handles the lightning should be minded
to hurl us out of our places, he is far too strong for any.
Do you therefore approach him again with words made gentle,
and at once the Olympian will be gracious again to us.'
   He spoke, and springing to his feet put a two-handled goblet
585 into his mother's hands and spoke again to her once more:
'Have patience, my mother, and endure it, though you be saddened,
for fear that, dear as you are, I see you before my own eyes

struck down, and then sorry though I be I shall not be able
to do anything. It is too hard to fight against the Olympian.
There was a time once before now I was minded to help you,   590
and he caught me by the foot and threw me from the magic threshold,
and all day long I dropped helpless, and about sunset
I landed in Lemnos, and there was not much life left in me.
After that fall it was the Sintian men who took care of me.'
 He spoke, and the goddess of the white arms Hera smiled at him,   595
and smiling she accepted the goblet out of her son's hand.
Thereafter beginning from the left he poured drinks for the other
gods, dipping up from the mixing bowl the sweet nectar.
But among the blessed immortals uncontrollable laughter
went up as they saw Hephaistos bustling about the palace.   600
 Thus thereafter the whole day long until the sun went under
they feasted, nor was anyone's hunger denied a fair portion,
nor denied the beautifully wrought lyre in the hands of Apollo
nor the antiphonal sweet sound of the Muses singing.
 Afterwards when the light of the flaming sun went under   605
they went away each one to sleep in his home where
for each one the far-renowned strong-handed Hephaistos
had build a house by means of his craftsmanship and cunning.
Zeus the Olympian and lord of the lightning went to
his own bed, where always he lay when sweet sleep came on him.   610
Going up to the bed he slept and Hera of the gold throne beside him.

Herodotus

Herodotus is important as an oral stylist, his rhetorical position falling between the roles of Homer and Thucydides, "between the largely oral and the indubitably literate."[1] Herodotus was born in the late 480s and died during the early part of the Peloponnesian War. Although an Ionian, he was familiar with the currents of sophistic and democratic thought of midcentury Athens, for he visited and gave readings of his work at Athens during the leadership of Pericles. He then moved to, and probably died at, Thurii, a panhellenic city in Italy founded by Pericles in 444–443 B.C.

How Greece defended herself against the menance of Persia is the central theme of Herodotus' *Persian Wars*. The debates that he inserted into his narrative of events show that he understood rhetorical techniques, though he probably picked up these techniques by observation rather than by training. The selection which we present here (3.80–83) is a debate explaining Persian monarchy, but the speakers express their ideas in terms of Greek political philosophy. The three speakers in turn advocate democracy (Otanes), aristocracy (Megabyzus), and monarchy (Darius). Each speech is a straightforward example of deliberative oratory: exhortation, dissuasion, the expedient.

1. Lang, 52.

The Persian Wars

When the tumult was abated, and five days had passed, the rebels against the 3.80
Magians[1] held a council on the whole state of affairs, at which words were uttered
which to some Greeks seem incredible; but there is no doubt that they were
spoken. Otanes was for giving the government to the whole body of the Persian
people. "I hold," he said, "that we must make an end of monarchy; there is no
pleasure or advantage in it. You have seen to what lengths went the insolence of
Cambyses,[2] and you have borne your share of the insolence of the Magian.[3] What
right order is there to be found in monarchy, when the ruler can do what he will,
nor be held to account for it? Give this power to the best man on earth, and it
would stir him to unwonted thoughts. The advantage which he holds breeds
insolence, and nature makes all men jealous. This double cause is the root of all
evil in him; sated with power he will do many reckless deeds, some from
insolence, some from jealousy. For whereas an absolute ruler, as having all that
heart can desire, should rightly be jealous of no man, yet it is contrariwise with
him in his dealing with his countrymen; he is jealous of the safety of the good,
and glad of the safety of the evil; and no man is so ready to believe calumny. Of all
men he is the most inconsistent; accord him but just honour, and he is displeased
that you make him not your first care; make him such, and he damns you for a
flatterer. But I have yet worse to say of him than that; he turns the laws of the land
upside down, he rapes women, he puts high and low to death. But the virtue of a
multitude's rule lies first in its excellent name, which signifies equality before the
law; and secondly, in that it does none of the things that a monarch does. All
offices are assigned by lot, and the holders are accountable for what they do
herein; and the general assembly arbitrates on all counsels. Therefore I declare
my opinion, that we make an end of monarchy and increase the power of the
multitude, seeing that all good lies in the many."

Such was the judgment of Otanes: but Megabyzus' counsel was to make a   81
ruling oligarchy. "I agree," said he, "to all that Otanes says against the rule of one;
but when he bids you give the power to the multitude, his judgment falls short of
the best. Nothing is more foolish and violent than a useless mob; to save ourselves
from the insolence of a despot by changing it for the insolence of the unbridled
commonalty—that were unbearable indeed. Whatever the despot does, he does
with knowledge; but the people have not even that; how can they have knowledge,
who have neither learnt nor for themselves seen what is best, but ever rush
headlong and drive blindly onward, like a river in spate? Let those stand for
democracy who wish ill to Persia; but let us choose a company of the best men and

Reprinted by permission of the publishers and The Loeb Classical Library from Herodotus [The
Persian Wars] (3.80–83), vol. 2, trans. A.D. Godley, Cambridge, Mass.: Harvard University Press,
1957.

1. The Magians were the priests of Ahura Mazda.
2. Cambyses lost his wits before he died in 522 B.C.
3. The Magian had posed as Cambyses' dead brother, Smerdis, and had usurped the throne of
Persia. When Hystaspes, the next in line to the throne, did not attempt to overthrow the false Smerdis,
Darius, the son of Hystaspes, then conspired with six nobles and killed the usurper.

invest these with the power. For we ourselves shall be of that company; and where we have the best men, there 'tis like that we shall have the best counsels."

82 Such was the judgment of Megabyzus. Darius was the third to declare his opinion. "Methinks," said he, "Megabyzus speaks rightly concerning democracy, but not so concerning oligarchy. For the choice lying between these three, and each of them, democracy, oligarchy and monarchy being supposed to be the best of its kind, I hold that monarchy is by far the most excellent. Nothing can be found better than the rule of the one best man; his judgment being like to himself, he will govern the multitude with perfect wisdom, and best conceal plans made for the defeat of enemies. But in an oligarchy, the desire of many to do the state good service ofttimes engenders bitter enmity among them; for each one wishing to be chief of all and to make his counsels prevail, violent enmity is the outcome, enmity brings faction and faction bloodshed; and the end of bloodshed is monarchy; whereby it is shown that this fashion of government is the best. Again, the rule of the commonalty must of necessity engender evil-mindedness; and when evil-mindedness in public matters is engendered, bad men are not divided by enmity but united by close friendship; for they that would do evil to the commonwealth conspire together to do it. This continues till someone rises to champion the people's cause and makes an end of such evil-doing. He therefore becomes the people's idol, and being their idol is made their monarch; so his case also proves that monarchy is the best government. But (to conclude the whole matter in one word) tell me, whence and by whose gift came our freedom—from the commonalty or an oligarchy or a single ruler? I hold therefore, that as the rule of one man gave us freedom, so that rule we should preserve; and, moreover, that we should not repeal the good laws of our fathers; that were ill done."

83 Having to judge between these three opinions, four of the seven declared for the last.[4] Then Otanes, his proposal to give the Persians equality being defeated, thus spoke among them all: "Friends and partisans! seeing that it is plain that one of us must be made king (whether by lot, or by our suffering the people of Persia to choose whom they will, or in some other way), know that I will not enter the lists with you; I desire neither to rule nor to be ruled; but if I waive my claim to be king, I make this condition, that neither I nor any of my posterity shall be subject to any one of you." To these terms the six others agreed; Otanes took no part in the contest but stood aside; and to this day his house (and none other in Persia) remains free, nor is compelled to render any unwilling obedience, so long as it transgresses no Persian law.[5]

---

4. In chapters 84–87, Herodotus tells how Darius was elected king by means of a clever trick.
5. "The special position of the house of Otanes seems to be a fact, but was probably of earlier date," according to How and Wells, 1:279.

Thucydides

The historian Thucydides (ca. 460–400 B.C.) understood the techniques of rhetoric as taught by Gorgias and the other sophists, and he used these techniques carefully in order to emphasize the underlying thought of the speeches in his *Peloponnesian Wars*. In the speeches, historical and rhetorical truth come together. Thucydides' own words reveal that he was well aware of the rhetorical problem of the historian: "With reference to the speeches in this history, some were delivered before the war began, others while it was going on; some I heard myself, others I got from various quarters; it was in all cases difficult to carry them word for word in one's memory, so my habit has been to make the speakers say what was in my opinion demanded of them by the various occasions, of course adhering as closely as possible to the general sense of what they really said" (1.22, Crawley trans.). The writing of speeches suitable to the character of the speaker and the occasion is, of course, an important problem in the composition of all literature.

The subject of the selection that we present here (3.36–50) is the debate in the assembly at Athens in the summer of 427 B.C. whether to reconsider the decision made the day before to put to death all the male Mytilenaeans and to enslave their women and children. Cleon speaks against reconsideration, and Diodotus opposes Cleon. These speeches, in which each speaker obtains a focus in thought similar to that of his opponent by means of concentrating on the single argument of what is expedient, are masterpieces of antithesis.

The Peloponnesian War

3.36   When Salaethus and the others arrived at Athens, the Athenians at once put Salaethus to death, although he offered among other things to induce the Peloponnesians to abandon Plataea, which was still under siege;[1] as to the others they held a debate, and under the impulse of anger finally determined to put to death, not only the Mytilenaeans who were there in Athens, but also all who were of adult age, and to enslave their women and children. The general charge which they brought against them was that they had made this revolt in spite of the fact that they were not held in subjection like the other allies; and what contributed not least to their fury was that the Peloponnesian fleet had dared to venture over to Ionia to their support; for from this they thought the revolt had been made after long deliberation. Accordingly they sent a trireme to Paches[2] to announce what had been determined upon, and bidding him to despatch the Mytilenaeans with all haste; but on the very next day a feeling of repentance came over them and they began to reflect that the design which they had formed was cruel and monstrous, to destroy a whole city instead of merely those who were guilty. And when this became known to the Mytilenaean envoys who were present and their Athenian supporters, they induced those in authority to bring the question before the people again; and they found less difficulty in persuading them because it was evident to them also that the greater part of the citizens wished that another opportunity should be given them to consider the matter. A meeting of the assembly was held immediately, at which various opinions were expressed by the several speakers. One of these was Cleon son of Cleaenetus, who had been successful in carrying the earlier motion to put the Mytilenaeans to death. He was not only the most violent of the citizens, but at that time had by far the greatest influence with the people. He now came forward a second time and spoke as follows:

37   "On many other occasions in the past I have realized that a democracy is incompetent to govern others, but more than ever to-day, when I observe your change of heart concerning the Mytilenaeans. The fact is that, because your daily life is unaffected by fear and intrigue in your relations to each other, you have the same attitude towards your allies also, and you forget that whenever you are led into error by their representations or yield out of pity, your weakness involves you in danger and does not win the gratitude of your allies. For you do not reflect that the empire you hold is a despotism imposed upon subjects who, for their part, do intrigue against you and submit to your rule against their will, who render obedience, not because of any kindnesses you may do them to your own hurt, but because of such superiority as you may have established by reason of your strength rather than of their goodwill. But quite the most alarming thing is, if nothing we

Reprinted by permission of the publishers and The Loeb Classical Library from Thucydides *[The Peloponnesian War]* (3.36–50), vol. 2, trans. Charles Forster Smith, Cambridge, Mass.: Harvard University Press, 1965.

1. Salaethus was the Lacedaemonian sent secretly into Mytilene at the end of 428 B.C. to tell the besieged Mytilenaeans that Peloponnesian help was on the way. That help did not arrive.
2. Paches was the admiral in charge of the Athenian fleet operating off the coast of Asia Minor.

have resolved upon shall be settled once for all, and if we shall refuse to recognize that a state which has inferior laws that are inviolable is stronger than one whose laws are good but without authority; that ignorance combined with self-restraint is more serviceable than cleverness combined with recklessness; and that simpler people for the most part make better citizens than the more shrewd. The latter always want to show that they are wiser than the laws, and to dominate all public discussions, as if there could never be weightier questions on which to declare their opinions, and as a consequence of such conduct they generally bring their states to ruin; the former, on the contrary, mistrusting their own insight, are content to be less enlightened than the laws and less competent than others to criticise the words of an able speaker, but being impartial judges rather than interested contestants they generally prosper. Thus, then, we ought to act and not be so excited by eloquence and combat of wits as to advise the Athenian people contrary to our own judgment.

"As for me, I have not changed my opinion, and I wonder at those who propose   38 to debate again the question of the Mytilenaeans and thus interpose delay, which is in the interest of those who have done the wrong; for thus the edge of the victim's wrath is duller when he proceeds against the offender, whereas the vengeance that follows upon the very heels of the outrage exacts a punishment that most nearly matches the offence. And I wonder, too, who will answer me and undertake to prove that the wrong-doings of the Mytilenaeans are beneficial to us but that our misfortunes prove injurious to our allies. Manifestly he must either have such confidence in his powers of speech as to undertake to show that what is universally accepted as true has not been established, or else, incited by gain, will by an elaborate display of specious oratory attempt to mislead you. But in contests of that kind the city bestows the prizes upon others, while she herself undergoes all the risks. And you are yourselves to blame, for your management of these contests is wrong. It is your wont to be spectators of words and hearers of deeds, forming your judgment of future enterprises according as able speakers represent them to be feasible, but as regards accomplished facts, not counting what has been done more credible, because you have seen it, than what you have heard, you are swayed in judgment by those who have made an eloquent invective. You are adepts not only at being deceived by novel proposals but also at refusing to follow approved advice, slaves as you are of each new paradox and scorners of what is familiar. Each of you wishes above all to be an orator himself, or, failing that, to vie with those dealers in paradox by seeming not to lag behind them in wit but to applaud a smart saying before it is out of the speaker's mouth; you are as quick to forestall what is said as you are slow to foresee what will come of it. You seek, one might say, a world quite unlike that in which we live, but give too little heed to that which is at hand. In a word, you are in thrall to the pleasures of the ear and are more like men who sit as spectators at exhibitions of sophists than men who take counsel for the welfare of the state.

"And it is from these ways that I seek to turn you when I attempt to prove that   39 Mytilene has done you more injury than any single state. I can make allowance for men who resorted to revolt because they were unable to bear your rule or because they were compelled by your enemies to do so; but men who inhabited a fortified island and had no fear of our enemies except by sea, and even there were not without the protection of a force of their own triremes, who moreover were independent and were treated by us with the highest consideration, when these men have acted thus, what else is it but conspiracy and rebellion rather than revolt—for revolt is the work of those who suffer oppression—and a deliberate attempt by taking their stand on the side of our bitterest enemies to bring about our destruction? And yet this is assuredly a more heinous thing than if they had gone to war against us by themselves for the acquisition of power. The calamities of their neighbours who had already revolted from us and been subdued proved no warning to them; nor did the good fortune which they enjoyed make them hesitate to take the perilous step; on the contrary, becoming over-confident as to the future, and conceiving hopes which, though greater than their powers, were less than their ambition, they took up arms, presuming to put might before right; for the moment they thought they should prove superior they attacked us unprovoked. And indeed it is the rule, that such states as come to unexpected prosperity most fully and most suddenly, do turn to insolence, whereas men generally find success less precarious when it comes in accordance with reasonable calculations than when it surpasses expectation, and more easily, as it seems, they repel adversity than maintain prosperity. But the Mytilenaeans from the first ought never to have been treated by us with any more consideration than our other allies, and then they would not have broken out into such insolence; for it is human nature in any case to be contemptuous of those who pay court but to admire those who will not yield.

"Let them be punished, therefore, even now, in a manner befitting their crime, and do not put the blame upon the aristocrats and exonerate the common people. For they all alike attacked you, even the commons, who, if they had taken our side, might now have been reinstated in their city; but they thought there was less risk in sharing the dangers of the oligarchs, and so joined them in the revolt. Consider, moreover, your allies: if you inflict upon those who wilfully revolt no greater punishment than upon those who revolt under compulsion from our foes, which of them, think you, will not revolt on a slight pretext, when the alternatives are liberty if he succeeds or a fate not irreparable if he fails? We, on the other hand, shall have to risk our money and our lives against each separate state, and when we succeed we shall recover a ruined state and be deprived for the future of its revenue, the source of our strength, whereas if we fail we shall be adding fresh enemies to those we have already, and when we should be resisting our present foes we shall be fighting our own allies.

40   "We must not, therefore, hold out to them any hope, either to be secured by eloquence or purchased by money, that they will be excused on the plea that their error was human. For their act was no unintentional injury but a deliberate plot; and it is that which is unintentional which is excusable. Therefore, I still protest, as I have from the first, that you should not reverse your former decision or be led into error by pity, delight in eloquence, or clemency, the three influences most prejudicial to a ruling state. For compassion may rightly be bestowed upon those who are likewise compassionate and not upon those who will show no pity in return but of necessity are always enemies. As to the orators who charm by their

eloquence, they will have other opportunities of display in matters of less importance, and not where the city for a brief pleasure will pay a heavy penalty while they themselves get a fine fee for their fine speaking. And clemency would better be reserved for those who will afterwards be faithful allies than be shown to those who remain just what they were before and no whit the less our enemies.

"I can sum up what I have to say in a word. If you take my advice, you will do not only what is just to the Mytilenaeans but also at the same time what is expedient for us; but if you decide otherwise, you will not win their gratitude but will rather bring a just condemnation upon yourselves; for if these people had a right to secede, it would follow that you are wrong in exercising dominion. But if, right or wrong, you are still resolved to maintain it, then you must punish these people in defiance of equity as your interests require; or else you must give up your empire and in discreet safety practise the fine virtues you preach. Resolve also to punish them with the same penalty that has already been voted, and that those who have escaped the plot shall not appear to have less feeling than those who framed it, bearing in mind what they would probably have done to you had they won the victory, especially since they were the aggressors. Indeed it is generally those who wrong another without cause that follow him up to destroy him utterly, perceiving the danger that threatens from an enemy who is left alive; for one who has been needlessly injured is more dangerous if he escape than an avowed enemy who expects to give and take.

"Do not, then, be traitors to your own cause, but recalling as nearly as possible how you felt when they made you suffer and how you would then have given anything to crush them, now pay them back. Do not become tender-hearted at the sight of their present distress, nor unmindful of the danger that so lately hung over you, but chastise them as they deserve, and give to your other allies plain warning that whoever revolts shall be punished with death. For if they realise this, the less will you have to neglect your enemies and fight against your own allies."

Such was Cleon's speech. After him Diodotus son of Eucrates, who in the   41
earlier meeting had been the principal speaker against putting the Mytilenaeans to death, came forward now also and spoke as follows:

"I have no fault to find with those who have proposed a reconsideration of the   42
question of the Mytilenaeans, nor do I commend those who object to repeated deliberation on matters of the greatest moment; on the contrary, I believe the two things most opposed to good counsel are haste and passion, of which the one is wont to keep company with folly, the other with an undisciplined and shallow mind. As for words, whoever contends that they are not to be guides of our actions is either dull of wit or has some private interest at stake—dull, if he thinks it possible by any other means to throw light on that which still belongs to the dim and distant future; self-interested, if, wishing to put through a discreditable measure, he realizes that while he cannot speak well in a bad cause, he can at least slander well and thus intimidate both his opponents and his hearers. Most dangerous of all, however, are precisely those who charge a speaker beforehand with being bribed to make a display of rhetoric. For if they merely imputed ignorance, the speaker who failed to carry his audience might go his way with the repute of being dull but not dishonest; when, however, the charge is dishonesty,

the speaker who succeeds becomes an object of suspicion, whereas if he fails he is regarded as not only dull but dishonest as well. And all this is a detriment to the state, which is thus robbed of its counsellors through fear. Indeed it would prosper most if its citizens of this stamp had no eloquence at all, for then the people would be least likely to blunder through their influence. But the good citizen ought to show himself a better speaker, not by trying to browbeat those who will oppose him but by fair argument; and while the wise city should not indeed confer fresh honours upon the man whose advice is most often salutary, it certainly should not detract from those which he already has, and as for him whose suggestion does not meet with approval, so far from punishing him, it should not even treat him with disrespect. For then it would be least likely that a successful speaker, with a view to being counted worthy of still greater honours, would speak insincerely and for the purpose of winning favour and that the unsuccessful speaker would employ the same means, by courting favour in his turn in an effort to win the multitude to himself.

43   "But we pursue the opposite course, and, moreover, if a man be even suspected of corruption, albeit he give the best counsel, we conceive a grudge against him because of the dubious surmise that he is corrupt and thus deprive the state of an indubitable advantage. And it has come to such a pass that good advice frankly given is regarded with just as much suspicion as the bad, and that, in consequence, a speaker who wants to carry the most dangerous measures must resort to deceit in order to win the people to his views, precisely as the man whose proposals are good must lie in order to be believed. And because of this excessive cleverness Athens is the only state where a man cannot do a good service to his country openly and without deceiving it; for whenever he openly offers you something good you requite him by suspecting that in some way he will secretly profit by it. Yet even so, in view of the very great interests at stake, and in so grave a matter, we who advise must regard it as our duty to look somewhat further ahead than you who give matters only a brief consideration, especially since we are responsible advisers, while you are irresponsible listeners. Indeed, if not only those who gave advice but also those who followed it had to suffer alike, you would show greater prudence in your decisions; but as it is, whenever you meet with a reverse you give way to your first impulse and punish your adviser for his single error of judgment instead of yourselves, the multitude who shared in the error.

44   "But I have come forward neither as an advocate of the Mytilenaeans in opposition to Cleon nor as their accuser. For the question for us to consider, if we are sensible, is not what wrong they have done, but what is the wise course for us. For no matter how guilty I show them to be, I shall not on that account bid you to put them to death, unless it is to our advantage; and if I show that they have some claim for forgiveness, I shall not on that account advise you to spare their lives, if this should prove clearly not to be for the good of the state. In my opinion we are deliberating about the future rather than the present. And as for the point which Cleon especially maintains, that it will be to our future advantage to inflict the penalty of death, to the end that revolts may be less frequent, I also in the interest of our future prosperity emphatically maintain the contrary. And I beg you not to

be led by the speciousness of his argument to reject the practical advantages in mine. For embittered as you are toward the Mytilenaeans, you may perhaps be attracted by his argument, based as it is on the more legal aspects of the case; we are, however, not engaged in a law-suit with them, so as to be concerned about the question of right and wrong; but we are deliberating about them, to determine what policy will make them useful to us.

"Now the death-penalty has been prescribed in various states for many offences   45
which are not so serious as this is, nay, for minor ones; but nevertheless men are so ·
inspired by hope as to take the risk; indeed, no one ever yet has entered upon a
perilous enterprise with the conviction that this plot was condemned to failure.
And as to states, what one that was meditating revolt ever took the decisive step in
the belief that the resources at hand, whether its own or contributed by its allies,
were inadequate for success? All men are by nature prone to err, both in private
and in public life, and there is no law which will prevent them; in fact, mankind
has run the whole gamut of penalties, making them more and more severe, in the
hope that the transgressions of evil-doers might be abated. It is probable that in
ancient times the penalties prescribed for the greatest offences were relatively
mild, but as transgressions still occurred, in course of time the penalty was
seldom less than death. But even so there is still transgression. Either, then, some
terror more dreadful than death must be discovered, or we must own that death at
least is no prevention. Nay, men are lured into hazardous enterprises by the
constraint of poverty, which makes them bold, by the insolence and pride of
affluence, which makes them greedy, and by the various passions engendered in
the other conditions of human life as these are severally mastered by some mighty
and irresistible impulse. Then, too, Hope and Desire are everywhere; Desire
leads, Hope attends; Desire contrives the plan, Hope suggests the facility of
fortune; the two passions are most baneful, and being unseen phantoms prevail
over seen dangers. Besides these, fortune contributes in no less degree to urge
men on; for she sometimes presents herself unexpectedly and thus tempts men to
take risks even when their resources are inadequate, and states even more than ·
men, inasmuch as the stake is the greatest of all — their own freedom or empire
over others — and the individual, when supported by the whole people, unreasonably overestimates his own strength. In a word, it is impossible, and a mark of
extreme simplicity, for anyone to imagine that when human nature is wholehear-
tedly bent on any undertaking it can be diverted from it by rigorous laws or by any
other terror.

"We must not, therefore, so pin our faith to the penalty of death as a guarantee   46
against revolt as to make the wrong decision, or lead our rebellious subjects to
believe that there will be no chance for them to repent and in the briefest time
possible put an end to their error. Consider now: according to your present policy
if a city has revolted and then realizes that it will fail, it may come to terms while
still able to pay the indemnity and to keep up its tribute in the future; but, in the
other case, what city, think you, will not prepare itself more thoroughly than now,
and hold out in siege to the last extremity, if it makes no difference whether it
capitulates quickly or at its leisure? And as for us, how can we fail to suffer loss,
incurring the expense of besieging a city because it will not surrender, and, if we

capture it, recovering one that is ruined, and losing thereafter the revenue from it—the source of our strength against our enemies? We must not, therefore, be such rigorous judges of the delinquents as to suffer harm ourselves, but we must rather see how for the time to come, by punishing moderately, we may have at our service dependent cities that are strong in material resources; and we must deem it proper to protect ourselves against revolts, not by the terror of our laws, but rather by the vigilance of our administration. At present we do just the opposite: whenever a free people that is forced into subjection revolts, as it naturally will, in order to recover its independence, we think that, as soon as we have subdued it, we must punish it severely. We ought, on the contrary, instead of rigorously chastising free peoples when they revolt, to watch them rigorously before they revolt, and thus forestall their even thinking of such a thing; and when we have subdued a revolt, we ought to put the blame on as few as possible.

47   "And do you consider, too, how great a mistake you would make in another point also by following Cleon's advice. At the present time the populace of all the cities is well disposed to you, and either does not join with the aristocrats in revolting, or, if forced to do so, is hostile from the beginning to those who stirred up the revolt; and so, when you go to war, you have the populace of the rebellious city as your allies. If, however, you destroy the populace in Mytilene, which took no part in the revolt, and which voluntarily put the city into your hands as soon as it got hold of arms, in the first place you will be guilty of killing your benefactors, and, in the second place, you will bring about what the influential men most wish: the next time they instigate a revolt among our allies they will at once have the populace on their side, because you will have published it abroad that the same punishment is ordained for the innocent and for the guilty. Why, even if they were guilty, you should pretend not know it, to the end that the only class that is still friendly to us may not become hostile. And it is, I think, far more conducive to the maintenance of our dominion, that we should willingly submit to be wronged, than that we should destroy, however justly, those whom we ought not to destroy. And whereas Cleon claims that this punishment combines justice and expediency, it appears that in such a policy the two cannot be combined.

48   "Do you, then, recognize that mine is the better course, and without being unduly swayed by either pity or clemency—for neither would I have you influenced by such motives—but simply weighing the considerations I have urged, accede to my proposal: pass sentence at your leisure upon the Mytilenaeans whom Paches sent here as guilty, but let the rest dwell in peace. Such a course will be best for the future, and will cause alarm among our enemies at once; for he who is wise in counsel is stronger against the foe than he who recklessly rushes on with brute force."

49   Such was the speech of Diodotus. And after these opinions had been maintained with nearly equal force, the one against the other, the Athenians, in spite of the reaction, experienced such a conflict of opinion that in the show of hands they were about equally divided; but the view of Diodotus prevailed. They then immediately despatched a second trireme with all haste, hoping that the first trireme, which had the start by about a day and a night, might not arrive first and the city be found destroyed. The Mytilenaean envoys provided wine and barley

for the crew and promised a large reward if they should arrive in time; and such was their haste on the voyage that they kept on rowing as they ate their barley-cakes, kneaded with wine and oil, and took turns at sleeping and rowing. And since by good fortune no contrary wind arose, and the earlier ship was sailing in no hurry on so horrible a business, while the second pressed on it the manner described, although the former did in fact arrive first, so that Paches had just time enough to read the decree and was about to execute the orders, the second put in close after it and prevented the destruction of the city. By just so much did Mytilene escape its peril.

The rest of the men, however, whom Paches had sent to Athens as chief authors of the revolt, numbering somewhat more than a thousand, were put to death by the Athenians on the motion of Cleon. They also pulled down the wall of Mytilene and took possession of the Mytilenaean fleet. Afterwards, instead of imposing a tribute upon the Lesbians, they divided all the land except that of the Methymnaeans into three thousand allotments, and reserving three hundred of these as sacred to the gods they sent out Athenian colonists, chosen by lot, to occupy the rest. With these the Lesbians made an arrangement to pay a rental of two minas a year for each lot, they themselves to cultivate the land. The Athenians also took possession of all the towns on the mainland which the Mytilenaeans controlled, and these were thereafter subject to the Athenians. Such was the course of events at Lesbos.

50

2

Greek Rhetoric

I n the fifth and fourth centuries B.C., rhetoric became a professional discipline. In this section we look first at sophistic rhetoric as represented by Gorgias, Alcidamas, and Isocrates. Next, we examine Plato's reaction to the rhetorical techniques of the sophists. Finally, we see how Aristotle advanced the theoretical study of rhetoric.

The older generation of sophists were the "visiting professors" of their day, and they traveled widely over the Greek world. However, they all came to Periclean Athens and made this city the center of their movement for some sixty years, beginning in the middle of the fifth century. Plato has given us vivid portraits of such persons as Hippias, Prodicus, Protagoras, and Gorgias.

The term *sophistēs* (skilled person) was an honorable word that was applied to all the sages of ancient Greece, including Homer and Hesiod. In fact, the classical sophists saw themselves continuing the tradition of the poets as the teachers of the Greeks.

Up to the age of fourteen years, Athenian boys went to school and studied four basic subjects: *grammatikē* (language), *mousikē* (literature), *logistikē* (arithmetic), and *gumnastikē* (athletics). The education that the sophists offered went beyond these subjects to train young men for a career in public life. A career in politics demands that a person be capable of speaking in public, so the art of persuasive speaking was an important part of a young Athenian's career training.

Thus, in addition to whatever subjects they may have taught, the sophists were teachers of rhetoric and composition. There were two distinct methods of instruction in rhetorical composition employed by the sophists, and these do not seem to have overlapped. In the concluding chapter of *On Sophistical Refutations*, Aristotle seems to say that some sophists taught by means of the setting forth of rules, that is, by theoretical instruction *(technē)*.

Those who discovered the beginnings of rhetoric carried them forward quite a little way, whereas the famous modern professors of the art, entering into the heritage, so to speak, of a long series of predecessors who had gradually advanced it, have brought it to its present perfection—Tisias following the first inventors, Thrasymachus following Tisias, Theodorus following Thrasymachus, while numerous others have made numerous contributions; hence it is no wonder that the art possesses a certain amplitude. (183b)

This gradual building upon the work of predecessors produced handbooks. None of the early rhetorical handbooks have survived, but we can get a good general idea of their contents from Plato's description in *Phaedrus*, 266d5–267d. The late fourth-century *Rhetorica ad Alexandrum* stands in the tradition of these early sophistic handbooks.

In the same chapter of *On Sophistical Refutations*, Aristotle also says that the training method employed by the sophists who taught disputation (eristic) resembled that of Gorgias in that they made their students learn speeches by heart. Whether Gorgias made his pupils memorize entire speeches as part of their training is a matter of dispute among modern scholars. However, sophists did produce specimen speeches for their students to study and imitate. We have examples of such speeches in the display speeches *Helen* and *Palamades* by Gorgias, and in the *tetralogies* of Antiphon (480–411 B.C.). These were specimen court speeches.

A passage in Cicero (*Brutus* 46–47) suggests that some sophists prepared collections of commonplaces to be memorized by students to use in constructing arguments extemporaneously. Plato gives us an amusing picture of this method of composition in the *Menexenus*.

MENEXENUS. Do you think that you yourself could speak [the funeral oration], if it should be necessary, and the Council should choose you?

SOCRATES. It is no amazing thing even for me to be able to speak, because I have for my teacher she who is not at all ordinary in the matter of rhetoric, but who has produced many other excellent orators, and one who is very distinguished among the Hellenes, Perikles, the son of Xanthippos.

MENEXENUS. Who is this? Obviously you mean Aspasia.

SOCRATES. Yes, I do, and Konnos, the son of Metrobios. For these are my two instructors, he of literature, and she of rhetoric. So, now, it is no amazing thing for a man nourished in this way to be clever at speaking. But even one who was trained in a manner inferior to me, trained in literature by Lampros and in rhetoric by Antiphon the Rhamnousian, could nonetheless be popular when praising Athenians among Athenians.

MENEXENUS. And what could you say, if it should be necessary for you to speak?

SOCRATES. Perhaps nothing issuing from myself. But even yesterday I listened to Aspasia recite from beginning to end a funeral speech about these very things. For she had heard the very things which you are talking about, that the Athenians were about to choose the person to speak. Then she went through such things as are fitting to say. Some things she made up on the spot, but others she had thought of beforehand earlier when, it seems to me, she was composing the funeral oration which Perikles spoke, gluing together some things left over from that speech (235e1–236b6, trans. Patricia P. Matsen).

Gorgias' *Helen* is a fine example of an *epideixis*, or lecture, designed for the purpose of showing off its author's rhetorical talents. In the *Helen*, Gorgias lists a number of possibilities and does away with each one of them. This is the apagogic method of arguing. The primary stylistic device employed by Gorgias is antithesis. Antithesis is a real crowd pleaser, and used with the apagogic method of argumentation, its effects can be bewitching. Gorgias is a poet who writes in prose.

In his essay *Concerning Those Who Write Written Speeches, or Concerning Sophists*, Alcidamas argues that the ability to speak extemporaneously is the true rhetoric, writing being a sham art done for the sake of amusement—and anyone can write. Improvised speech is effective because it speaks to the opportunity or the right moment in time (*kairos*). Thus, written compositions have no validity for solving the immediate problems of everyday life.

Isocrates is a sophist in a class all by himself. Neither a philosopher nor a politician in the modern sense, Isocrates was the quintessential educator. In *Against the Sophists* (391 B.C.), he sets forth his educational program in contrast to his contemporaries who merely teach skills. He maintains that the moral growth of his pupils is more important to society than their facility for public speaking. The *Antidosis* (353 B.C.), written toward the end of his long life, is his defense of his life's work. In it he still holds to his position that the good orator or writer of discourses must also be a good person.

Isocrates is praised in one of Plato's dialogues that treats sophistry and rhetoric. At the end of the *Phaedrus*, Socrates appeals for the development of a higher rhetoric, incorporating his own dialectical focus, which will be committed to persuading people of only the truth. This may well be a conciliatory allusion to the Isocratean position that philosophy does not change people's behavior because it does not use persuasion, since Socrates is made to predict here that Isocrates will probably bring rhetoric to that higher plane.

Almost everything else about sophistry and rhetoric in Plato is critical and negative. Three of the dialogues, the *Protagoras*, *Theaetetus*, and *Sophist*, critique sophistry, while two, the *Phaedrus* and *Gorgias*, treat rhetoric. We have selected excerpts from the last two.

In the *Phaedrus*, Socrates objects to the pronounced tendency in current rhetorical practice to trivialize meaning; he prefers his own method of dialectic.

The *Gorgias* contains a one-sided attack on rhetoric, which is characterized by a series of false dichotomies presented by Socrates but never answered in the dialogue. Sophistry becomes sham legislation and rhetoric sham justice. No interlocutor is allowed to point out the obvious fact that one is not either a persuasive counterfeiter of real knowledge or an unpersuasive purveyor of the truth. The opposite of both is clearly possible. One can be the essence of integrity and knowledge and be a persuasive speaker, and lies can be proposed in the most unpersuasive ways imaginable. Similarly, the radical teaching in this dialogue that it is better to suffer evil unjustly than to be unjust and avoid punishment is never allowed to be corrected by the obvious truth that it is still possible to be just and not to suffer wrongly. Socrates concedes only one use for rhetoric—in legal prosecution but not in defense (480, 504).

Aristotle responded very differently to rhetoric. He was not bothered by it or hostile to it, and his discussion in the *Rhetoric* revolutionized the treatment of the subject. Aristotle's understanding of rhetoric is based on its position in his whole scheme of the kinds of knowledge: theoretical (e.g., metaphysics), practical (e.g., ethics), or productive, that is, guides to the creation of useful or artistic objects (e.g., poetics and rhetoric). Rhetoric is also related to analytics (later called logic by the Stoics), which is a special knowledge of the *logos*, a tool or instrument of inquiry into the various sciences. Instead of viewing speeches quantitatively and linearly (introduction, narration, proof, and conclusion), Aristotle treats their qualitative, functional components—invention, arrangement, style, and delivery.

Gorgias

The quintessential sophist, Gorgias (ca. 480–375 B.C.) became an instant phenomenon when he arrived at Athens in 427 as an ambassador from his native Leontini in Sicily. Having studied under both Tisias and the philosopher Empedocles, Gorgias was the first orator to develop and teach a distinctive style of speaking. According to Philostratus, his speeches, which attracted huge crowds, were characterized by "virile and energetic style, . . . daring and unusual expressions, . . . and by his habit of breaking off his clauses and making sudden transitions, by which devices a speech gains in sweetness and sublimity" (1.9). Furthermore, the traveling orator won admiration for his ability to speak extemporaneously on any subject proposed by his audience. Gorgias was frequently invited to speak at the Olympic games and other religious festivals; after his *Pythian Oration*, the Greeks installed a solid gold statue of him in the temple of Apollo at Delphi.

Although the Gorgianic style eventually came to be criticized as bombastic, during Gorgias' lifetime he was honored for his original contributions to rhetoric. Borrowing various features from Greek tragedy and poetry, he incorporated them into his speeches. Gorgias used metaphor and paradox heavily, but his most famous trademarks were certain figures of speech or *schemata*. These included equally balanced clauses *(isocolon)*, the joining of contrasting ideas *(antithesis)*, the parallel structure of successive clauses *(parison)*, and the rhyming of word endings *(homoeoteleuton)*.

Because of these unique features, the challenges of translating Gorgias' *Helen* are overwhelming. LaRue Van Hook tried to render faithfully what he termed the "florid and frigid original,"[1] whereas D M. Macdowell made a more literal translation for his Greek classes at the University of Glasgow. These two versions could be viewed as opposite ends of the scale. Van Hook's translation of section 7, for example, says: "But if by violence she was defeated and unlawfully she was treated and to her injustice was meted, clearly her violator as a terrifier was importunate, while she, translated and violated, was unfortunate." On the other hand, MacDowell's translation of the same sentence simply says: "But if she was seized by force and unlawfully violated and unjustly assaulted, clearly the man who seized or assaulted did wrong, and the woman who was seized or was assaulted suffered misfortune."

George A. Kennedy's new translation, which appears here for the first time, tries to convey both style and substance. Besides the Gorgianic figures, there is much else of interest in this short speech. For example, as MacDowell says, "Gorgias's arrangement of topics is remarkably orderly and well-signposted."[2] Furthermore, the encomium of *Helen* shows Gorgias' interest in argumentation; he makes his point by systematically refuting a series of possible alternatives.

A good example of epideictic oratory, the *Helen* is supposed to have been Gorgias' showpiece or demonstration speech, which he delivered to attract students. The nominal goal of the speech is to defend the legendary Helen against the charge of abandoning her Greek husband Menelaus and going to Troy with her lover Paris (Alexander). However, the oration also cleverly sets forth Gorgias' philosophy of rhetoric: persuasion is a powerful force that can bewitch and deceive the unwary.

1. 122.
2. 17.

Helen

1   *[Proeminon]* Fairest ornament *[kosmos]* to a city is a goodly army and to a body beauty and to a soul wisdom and to an action virtue and to speech truth, but their opposites are unbefitting. Man and woman and speech and deed and city and object should be honored with praise if praiseworthy, but on the unworthy blame should be laid; for it is equal error and ignorance to blame the praiseworthy and to

2   praise the blameworthy. It is the function of a single speaker both to prove the needful rightly and to disprove the wrongly spoken. Thus I shall refute those who rebuke Helen, a woman about whom there is univocal and unanimous testimony among those who have believed the poets, and whose ill-omened name has become a memorial of disasters. I wish by giving some logic to language to free the accused of blame and to show that her critics are lying and to demonstrate the truth and to put an end to ignorance.

3   *[Narration]* Now that by nature and birth the woman who is the subject of this speech was preeminent among preeminent men and women, this is not unclear, not even to a few. For it is clear that Leda was her mother, while as a father she had in fact a god, though allegedly a mortal, the latter Tyndareus, the former Zeus; and of these the one seemed her father because he *was* and the other was disproved because he was only *said* to be; and one was the greatest of men, the other the lord

4   of all. Born from such parents she possessed god-like beauty, which getting and not forgetting she preserved. On many did she work the greatest passions of love, and by her one body she brought together many bodies of men greatly minded for great deeds. Some had the greatness of wealth, some the glory of ancient noblesse, some the vigor of personal prowess, some the power of acquired knowledge. And all came because of a passion that loved conquest and a love of honor that was

5   unconquered. Who he was and why and how he (Paris) sailed away taking Helen as his love, I shall not say; for to tell the knowing what they know is believable but not enjoyable. Having now exceeded the time already allotted for my introduction, I shall proceed to my intended speech and shall propose the causes for which Helen's voyage to Troy was likely *[eikos]* to have taken place.

6   *[Proposition]* For by Fate's will and gods' wishes and Necessity's decrees she did what she did, or by force reduced, or by words seduced, or by love induced.

       [Proof] Now if for the first reason (the gods), the responsible one should rightly be held responsible: it is impossible to prevent a god's predetermination by human premeditation, since by nature the stronger force is not prevented by the weaker but the weaker is ruled and driven by the stronger; the stronger leads, the weaker follows. But god is stronger than man in force and in wisdom and in other ways. If, therefore, by fate and god the cause had been decreed, Helen must of all disgrace be freed.

7   But if she was seized by force and illegally assaulted and unjustly insulted, it is clear that the assailant as insulter did the wrong and the assailed as insulted suffered wrongly. It is right for the barbarian who laid barbarous hands on her by

word and law and deed to meet with blame in word, disenfranchisement in law, and punishment in deed, while she who was seized and deprived of her country and bereft of her friends, — how should she not be pitied rather than pilloried? He did dread deeds; she suffered them. Her it is just to pity; him to hate.

But if speech persuaded her and deceived her soul, not even to this is it difficult   8
to make answer and to banish blame, as follows. Speech is a powerful lord that with the smallest and most invisible body accomplishes most god-like works. It can banish fear and remove grief and instill pleasure and enhance pity. I shall show how this is so. It is necessary for it to seem so as well in the opinion of my   9
hearers. All poetry I regard and name as speech having metre. On those who hear it come fearful shuddering and tearful pity and grievous longing as the soul, through words, experiences some experience of its own at others' good fortune and ill fortune. Listen as I turn from one argument to another.

Divine sweetness transmitted through words is inductive of pleasure, reductive   [10]
of pain. Thus by entering into the opinion of the soul the force of incantation is wont to beguile and persuade and alter it by witchcraft, and the two arts of witchcraft and magic are errors of the soul and deceivers of opinion. How many   11
speakers on how many subjects have persuaded others and continue to persuade by molding false speech? If everyone, on every subject, had memory of the past and knowledge of the present and foresight of the future, speech would not do what it does, but as things are it is easy neither to remember the past nor consider the present nor predict the future; so that on most subjects most people take opinion as counselor to the soul. But opinion, being slippery and insecure, casts those relying on it into slippery and insecure fortune. What is there to prevent the   12
conclusion that Helen too, when still young, was carried off by speech just as if constrained by force? Her mind was swept away by persuasion, and persuasion has the same power as necessity, although it may bring shame. For speech, by persuading the soul that it persuaded, constrained her both to obey what was said and to approve what was done. The persuader, as user of force, did wrong; the persuaded, forced by speech, is unreasonably blamed. To understand that   13
persuasion, joining with speech, is wont to stamp the soul as it wishes one must study, first, the words of astronomers who, substituting opinion for opinion, removing one and instilling another, make incredible and unclear things appear true to the eyes of opinion [e.g., by demonstrating that the world is round]; second, forceful speeches in public debate, where one side of the argument pleases a large crowd and persuades by being written with art even though not spoken with the truth; third, the verbal wrangling of philosophers in which too a swiftness of thought is exhibited, making confidence in opinion easily changed.   14
The power of speech has the same effect on the condition of the soul as the application of drugs to the state of bodies, for just as different drugs dispell different fluids from the body, and some bring an end to disease but others end life, so also some speeches cause pain, some pleasure, some fear; some instill courage, some drug and bewitch the soul with a kind of evil persuasion.

Thus it has been explained that if she was persuaded by speech she did no   15
wrong but was unfortunate. I shall now go on to the fourth cause in a fourth discourse. If it was love that did these things it will not be difficult to escape the

charge of error that is alleged. For we see not what we wish but what each of us has
16   experienced: through sight the soul is stamped in diverse ways. Whenever men at
war, enemy against enemy, buckle up in the armaments of bronze and iron,
whether in defense or offense, when their sight beholds the scene it is alarmed and
causes alarm in the soul, so that often they flee in terror from future danger as
though it were present. Obedience to law is strongly brought home by fear derived
from sight which, coming upon people, made them desire both what is judged
17   seemly by law and thought good by the mind, but as soon as they have seen
terrible sights they abandon the thought of the moment. Thus discipline is
extinguished and fear drives out the concept. Many fall victim to imaginary
diseases and dreadful pains and hard-to-cure mental aberrations; thus does sight
engrave on the mind images of things seen. Any many terrors remain, and those
18   that remain are very like things that have been said. Moreover, whenever pictures
of many colors and figures create a perfect image of a single figure and form they
delight the sight. How much does the production of statues and the workmanship
of artifacts furnish pleasurable sight to the eyes! Thus it is natural for the sight
sometimes to grieve, sometimes to delight. Much love and desire for many
19   objects is created in many minds. If then the eye of Helen, pleased by the body of
Alexander (Paris), gave to her soul an eagerness and response in love, what
wonder? If love, a god, prevails over the divine power of the gods, how could a
lesser one be able to reject and refuse it? But if love is a human disease and an
ignorance of the soul it should not be blamed as a mistake but regarded as a
misfortune. For she (Helen) went (with Paris) caught by the nets around her soul,
not by the wishes of her mind, and by the necessity of love, not by the devices of
art.
20   [*Epilogue*] How then can blame of Helen be thought just? Whether she did
what she did by falling in love or persuaded by speech or seized by violence or
forced by divine necessity, she is completely acquitted. By speech I have removed
disgrace from a woman. I have abided by the principle I posed at the start of my
speech: I have tried to refute the injustice of defamation and the ignorance of
allegation. I wished to write a speech that would be Helen's celebration and my
own recreation.

Alcidamas

Ancient testimony tells us that the fourth-century B.C. rhetorician and sophist Alcidamas was born at Elaea in Aeolis. He was a student of Gorgias and a rival of Isocrates. Among his many writings were said to be an encomium on death and an encomium on the courtesan Nais. Many of his compositions were still available to the twelfth-century polymath John Tzetzes. Now, however, only two complete works remain extant under his name, and of these only the one we present here is considered genuine.

The following essay receives its title from a description of its contents: "peri tōn tous graptous logous graphontōn ē peri sophistōn" (concerning those who write written speeches, or concerning sophists). The essay is polemic, probably aimed at Gorgias' most famous follower, the logographer Isocrates. Alcidamas stresses the usefulness in all areas of public life of the power of rough-and-ready improvised speech based on wide knowledge, compared to the power of the performance of a fixed text full of the refinements of language.

Aristotle thought that Alcidamas' style was frigid and his use of metaphor inept (*Rhetoric* 1406a4).

Concerning Those Who Write Written Speeches,
or Concerning Sophists

1   Since indeed some of those who are called sophists have neglected inquiry and training and are without experience of being able to speak in like manner with common men, but practicing written speeches and through books demonstrating their own skill they give themselves airs and have high thoughts, and possessing a small fraction of rhetorical skill they dispute about the whole art, for this reason I

2   shall attempt to make an accusation against written speeches, not as considering their skill alien from my own, but as having higher thoughts for reasons of another kind, and thinking it to be right to practice writing as secondary business to speaking, and having suspected that those who spend their life upon this very thing have fallen far short of both rhetoric and philosophy, and believing that much more justly would they be addressed as writers than as sophists.

3   First, therefore, one might disparage writing on the grounds that it is a thing easy to attack, easy to do, and easily accessible to ordinary natural ability. For to speak on the spot fairly well concerning whatever turns up, and to employ a quick abundance of arguments and words, and to follow the opportunity of affairs and the desires of men in a well-aimed manner and to speak the appropriate speech is

4   characteristic neither of every natural ability nor of ordinary training; but even for the untrained it would be a natural and easy thing to write at great length and to revise at leisure, and having set before oneself the written compositions of the sophists of old, to gather together arguments from many places into the same place, and to imitate the successes of things well said, and to revise some things for oneself from the advice of common men, and to prune and rewrite other

5   things after having meditated many times in oneself. All good and beautiful things are scarce and difficult and accustomed to come into being through labors, but low and common things have their acquisition easy; therefore since writing is more at hand to us than speaking, we might reasonably think also the acquisition of it of less worth.

6   Next, no thinking person would doubt that the skilled at speaking, with little changing of the habit of their soul, could write speeches pretty well, but no one would believe that those who are trained to write could also speak from the same skill. For it is reasonable that those who complete the difficult parts of their tasks, whenever they change the direction of their intelligence to the easier parts, handle the completing of their affairs in a resourceful manner; but for those who are trained for easy things, the care bestowed upon the more difficult becomes repelling and steep. And one might understand this from the following examples.

7   For the one who is able to lift a large burden would easily approach and handle the lighter ones, but the one who uses all his strength to lift light objects would be able to carry none of the heavier things. And again the footswift runner would easily be able to accompany the slower ones, but the slow one would not be able to run on the same course with the swifter ones. And yet in addition to these, the one who is able with good aim to hurl his javelin or shoot with his bow distant objects

A new translation from the Greek by Patricia P. Matsen, 1989.

will also easily hit those close at hand, but it is not yet evident whether the one who knows how to hit things near will also be able to hit things distant. In the same way, of course, also concerning words, it is clear that the one who uses them well on the spot will with time and leisure for writing be an important speech writer; but it is no secret that the one who engages himself in writing as a serious occupation, when going over to improvised words, will have his thought full of perplexity, digression, and confusion.

But I also think that speaking is ever and continually useful for the life of men, but the skill of writing seldom becomes seasonable to it. For who does not know that to speak on the spot is a necessary thing for those who speak in the public assembly, for those who go to law, and for those who make private transactions; and often unexpectedly opportunities for actions fall in one's way, at which times those who are silent will seem to be contemptible, but we see those who speak being honored by the others as if having intelligence that is godlike. For whenever it is necessary to warn those who are erring or to console the unfortunate or to calm the desperate or to refute charges the moment that they have been brought, at that time the power of speaking is able to act as an ally to men's need; but writing requires leisure and makes the delays longer than the opportunities; for the opportunities demand that help be swift in time of contests, but writing completes its speeches at leisure and slowly. And so what thinking person would strive after this skill that falls so much short of the opportunities? But how is it not ridiculous, if while the herald is saying in invitation, "Who of the citizens wishes to speak?," or while the water of the water clock in the courtroom is already running out, the orator should proceed to his tablet in order to compose and to learn his speech? For indeed if we were absolute rulers of states, it would be in our power both to assemble the courts and to make resolutions concerning common matters with the result that after we had written our speeches, then we could summon the rest of the citizens to hear them. But since others are in charge of these things, would it not be foolish for us to propose a different kind of training for speeches? In fact, those speeches that have been brought to completion with respect to their words and resemble poetic compositions more than speeches (having rejected that which is both spontaneous and more like actualities, but seeming to have been fabricated and put together with practice) fill the thoughts of the listeners with disbelief and ill will. Now the greatest proof of it is this: those who compose speeches for the courts avoid refinements and imitate the expressions of those who speak offhand, and then they seem to write most beautifully whenever they provide speeches that least resemble those that have been written. And since even for the logographers this is an object of reasonableness, whenever they imitate those who speak offhand, how ought not we to give our highest regard to that part of training from which we shall have an easy relationship with this class of speeches?

But I think that also on account of this it is a worthwhile thing to reject written speeches, because they make the life of their practitioners uneven. For to know written speeches concerning all matters belongs by nature to the impossible; but whenever one improvises some things and models other things it is necessary that the speech, being composed of dissimilar elements, will cause blame to the

8

9

10

11

12

13

14

speaker, because some parts seem to resemble closely the playing of a part on the stage and the recitation of epic poetry, but other parts appear low and common as compared with the precision of the former.

15   And it is a wonderful thing for the one who claims to say something about culture and who promises to train others to be able to display his own skill if he holds a tablet or a book. But if he does not have these, he becomes no better than those without training. And, if time is allowed, he can bring forth a speech. However, when it is a question of an immediate proposal, he is completely at a loss. Thus it is a terrible thing to profess methods of making speeches but to appear without even having the smallest faculty for speaking. Indeed the practice

16   of writing offers the most difficulty for speaking. For someone who is accustomed to work out his speeches little by little and to compose his phrases with precision and proportion is also accustomed to complete his expression by using movement of thought that is slow. Therefore this man, when he extemporizes, must act in a manner contrary to his habits, have his thought full of difficulty and confusion, be displeased at all things, and like a bad orator with a weak voice, never use his

17   soul's ready wit relaxed to speak in a smoothly flowing and generous manner. But just as those who have been freed from chains after long periods of time are not able to walk like other men and their posture displays those figures and rhythms with which it was necessary for them to move while chained, in the same manner writing, by causing the passages for thought to be slow and by making the practice of speaking reverse its habits, also places the soul in chains and totally obstructs the flow of impromptu speech.

18   And I think that the learning of written speeches is difficult, the remembering laborious, and the forgetting disgraceful in the contests. For all would agree that small matters are more difficult than large ones to learn and call to mind, and many matters are more difficult than a few. Therefore in respect to the arguments that one uses while extemporizing, it is necessary only to hold the thought and to make it clear on the spot by means of the words; but in the written speeches it is necessary to learn and remember the words exactly as they hold together the

19   arguments. Now there are in speeches a few great arguments, but many common words and phrases that little differ from one another, and each of the arguments is made clear once only, but we are forced to use the same words many times; therefore, of some things the remembering is easy, but for others the memory

20   becomes hard to recover and the learning hard to guard. Furthermore, moments of forgetfulness in respect to extemporaneous speaking keep their disgrace hidden. For when the expression is relaxed and the words have not been smoothed together with precision, if therefore one of the arguments should also escape, it is not a difficult thing for the orator to pass over that subject, and by taking hold of the adjacent arguments to invest his speech with no disgrace, but also, if later he shall recall those points that escaped him, it is an easy thing to reveal them.

21   But it is necessary that perplexity and digression and searching be born in those who speak things that are written, if as a result of the contest, they leave out and alter even some small thing, and they must stop for long periods and often divide their speech with intervals of silence and make their perplexity misshapen, ridiculous, and hard to meet.

But I also think that those who extemporize deal with the desires of their   22
listeners better than those who speak things that are written. For those who
laboriously work out their writings for a long time before the contests sometimes
miss their opportunities; indeed either they incur the enmity of their listeners by
speaking at greater length than they desire, or while men are still willing to listen,
they stop their speeches beforehand.

For it is a difficult thing, and perhaps an impossible thing, for human   23
forethought to attain to the future so as to foresee exactly how the minds of the
listeners will react to the lengths of the things being spoken. But in extemporaneous speaking, it is in the power of the speaker to control his words by paying
attention to the effects of his words, both to cut short their lengths and to clarify at
greater lengths matters that have been examined briefly.

Moreover, apart from this, we see that both cannot even use in like manner the   24
arguments that issue from the contests themselves. For it is an easy thing for those
who are speaking unwritten material to position any argument that they may take
from their opponents or one that may have issued from their own intense
thinking. For with their words they make all things clear immediately, nor when
they say more things than have been examined do they anywhere cause their
speech to be inconsistent and confused. But for those who contest by means of   25
written speeches, if then any thought apart from the prepared one be given, it is a
difficult thing to fit in and use suitably. For the refinements of the working out of
words do not allow the spontaneous, but one must either make no use at all of
arguments given by luck, or if one does use them, he must dissolve and destroy the
arrangements of the words, and by speaking some things with precision and other
things at random, make their expression disturbed and discordant. And yet what   26
person with good sense would follow such a practice that by its employment both
gets in the way of spontaneous good effects and, worse luck, offers its aid to the
opponents? For while the other skills are accustomed to draw the life of human
beings toward the better thing, this one presents a hindrance even to spontaneous
advantages.   27

But I think that it is not even right for the written products to be called speeches
but, so to speak, images and shapes and copies of speeches, and we could
reasonably hold the same opinion against them that indeed we also hold against
the bronze statues of men, the stone statues of gods, and paintings of animals. For
even as these are copies of true bodies and have enjoyment at the time of their
viewing but offer no service to the life of human beings, in the same manner the   28
written speech, being subject to one form and arrangement, has some effects on
the emotions when viewed from a book, but because of its being immovable, it
offers no benefit at the critical times to those who have acquired it. But even as
true bodies, which are much inferior in comeliness to beautiful statues, offer
many times as many benefits in the case of their works, so also the speech that is
spoken on the spot from the process of thought itself is animate and lives and
accompanies actions and is made like the true bodies, but that which has been
written, having its nature similar to an image of a speech, has no share in every
activity.

Now perhaps one might say that it is absurd to make accusation against the art   29 of writing and to present openly his proofs through this medium and to raise prejudices beforehand against this occupation through which he is preparing himself to be highly esteemed in the judgment of the Hellenes and, furthermore, for him, while busy with the pursuit of knowledge, to praise extemporary speeches and to consider luck more serviceable than forethought and those who

30   speak at random more prudent than those who write with preparation. But, first, I have spoken these words not altogether rejecting the art of writing but considering it to be inferior to the art of extemporaneous speaking and thinking that the most care ought to be given to the ability to speak; next, I am using writing not considering it the greatest thing for this purpose but in order that I may prove to those who exalt themselves with this art that by laboring at small things we shall

31   be able to hide from sight and destroy their arguments. And in addition to these things, I am engaging in writing also for the sake of the set speeches that are produced for the crowds. For by that method I am encouraging those who meet us [Alcidamas] often to gain experience of us whenever we are able to speak opportunely and harmoniously concerning every proposal. But if there are those who have come up to the lectures after an interval and have never before met us, I am attempting to make some display of my writings to them. For since they are accustomed to listen to the written speeches of others, perhaps they would form an opinion against us less than is our due if they should hear us speaking

32   extemporaneously. But apart from these things, signs also of the improvement that reasonably is born in the process of thought are most visible to observe from written speeches. For whether we are now extemporizing better than before is not an easy thing to decide. For the remembering of speeches that have been spoken beforehand becomes difficult, but it is an easy thing for men looking down into writings just as in a mirror to view the improvements of the soul. Moreover, because we are eager to leave behind also memorials of ourselves and to gratify our love of honor, we are putting our hand to writing speeches.

33   And yet it is not even worthwhile to believe that by preferring the art of extemporizing to that of writing I encourage speaking at random. For, on the one hand, orators ought to handle arguments and arrangement with forethought, but on the other hand, they ought to extemporize in respect of the setting forth of words. For the refinements of written speeches surrender their advantage when

34   measured against the timeliness of impromptu explanations. Now he who desires to become a powerful orator but is not a competent writer of speeches, and who wishes to make good use of opportunities rather than to use words in order to speak precisely, and who hastens to have the good will of his hearers as an ally rather than their ill will as an antagonist, and who furthermore also wishes to make his thought relaxed, his remembering easy, and his forgetting concealed, and who is eager to acquire skill for speeches commensurate with his life's need, would he not reasonably make active always and continually his practice of extemporizing, and when cultivating writing as an amusement and a bywork be judged to be rational by those who are rational?

Isocrates

Isocrates (436–338 B.C.) was influenced by his teachers, the sophists Prodicus and Gorgias, and also by his acquaintance with Socrates. Like Socrates, he shunned the limelight; in fact, Isocrates suffered from extreme shyness and never delivered any of his speeches in public. During the early part of his career, he supported himself by working as a logographer, a professional writer of speeches for those who needed to deliver them in court.[1]

Like Gorgias, however, Isocrates believed that oratory should build patriotism. Furthermore, Isocrates shared Gorgias' concern with style. By taking the flamboyant, poetical features of the Gorgianic style and modifying them to suit his subject matter, Isocrates originated the stately, periodic style that has descended to us through Cicero.

The sophists of the time were traveling teachers, and there was as yet no definite curriculum for higher education. Isocrates set out to change this by opening a school of rhetoric in Athens around 393 B.C. Even though he charged a high tuition, required his students to remain for three or four years, and accepted fewer than nine pupils at a time, Isocrates' school was an immediate success. In fact, it lasted for more than fifty years, turning out students who consistently won the top prizes in oratorical contests, and who became legislators, philosophers, and historians. Isocrates' most famous students included Plato's nephew Speusippos, the general Timotheus, the historians Theopompos and Ephoros, and three of Plutarch's canon of the ten best Attic orators: Lycurgus, Isaeus, and Hypercides. (Actually, during his lifetime, Isocrates' influence was greater than that of either Plato or Aristotle.)[2]

In a program centered on the highest ideals of rhetoric, Isocrates taught oratory, composition, history, citizenship, culture, and morality. These subjects, which were later adopted by Quintilian, became the foundation for the liberal arts education as we know it today.

Against the Sophists was a polemic written by Isocrates to explain the rationale for his newly opened school. He begins by inveighing against two types of teachers: the Eristics, who disputed about theoretical and ethical matters, and the sophists, who offered a rote training in the techniques of political debate. Unlike these people, Isocrates provided a broad-based education, but here he makes it clear that even this could do no more than improve upon the student's natural ability. *Against the Sophists*, then, is Isocrates' plea for truth in educational advertising. The selection we reprint is the second half of the extant text, in which Isocrates sets forth his own educational philosophy.

Thirty-five years after *Against the Sophists*, Isocrates wrote the *Antidosis*, a discourse in which he defends his philosophy of education. The title takes its name from a type of suit which Athenian citizens could bring if they felt they had been unfairly taxed. Under Athenian law, the wealthiest citizens had to bear the heaviest civic duties, such as equipping a warship for battle and paying its expenses for one year. Isocrates had recently been assigned such a burden and had protested it in an actual *antidosis*. When

---

1. See, for example, Isocrates' "Against Callimachus" or "Trapeziticus" in *Isocrates*, trans. George Norlin, vol. 3, Loeb Classical Library (1929; reprint, Cambridge: Harvard University Press, 1982).
2. Grube, 11.

the verdict went against him he was surprised and hurt; he felt that he had been misunderstood by the Athenian citizens. To set the record straight, Isocrates then wrote this *Antidosis*, in which he pretends to speak in his own defense against the charge of collecting large amounts of money to train young men in the art of winning lawsuits deviously. In the discourse, the supposed plaintiff's name is Lysimachus.

The selections we reprint are from the second half of the text, where Isocrates defends the policies and practices he has put into effect at his school.

Against the Sophists

However, if it is my duty not only to rebuke others, but also to set forth my own 14
views, I think all intelligent people will agree with me that while many of those
who have pursued philosophy have remained in private life, others, on the other
hand, who have never taken lessons from any one of the sophists have become
able orators and statesmen. For ability, whether in speech or in any other activity,
is found in those who are well endowed by nature and have been schooled by
practical experience. Formal training makes such men more skillful and more 15
resourceful in discovering the possibilities of a subject; for it teaches them to take
from a readier source the topics which they otherwise hit upon in haphazard
fashion. But it cannot fully fashion men who are without natural aptitude into
good debaters or writers, although it is capable of leading them on to self-
improvement and to a greater degree of intelligence on many subjects.

But I desire, now that I have gone this far, to speak more clearly on these 16
matters. For I hold that to obtain a knowledge of the elements out of which we
make and compose all discourses is not so very difficult if anyone entrusts
himself, not to those who make rash promises, but to those who have some
knowledge of these things. But to choose from these elements those which should
be employed for each subject, to join them together, to arrange them properly,
and also, not to miss what the occasion demands but appropriately to adorn the
whole speech with striking thoughts and to clothe it in flowing and melodious
phrase—these things, I hold, require much study and are the task of a vigorous
and imaginative mind: for this, the student must not only have the requisite
aptitude but he must learn the different kinds of discourse and practise himself in
their use; and the teacher, for his part, must so expound the principles of the art
with the utmost possible exactness as to leave out nothing that can be taught, and, 18
for the rest, he must in himself set such an example of oratory that the students
who have taken form under his instruction and are able to pattern after him will,
from the outset, show in their speaking a degree of grace and charm which is not
found in others. When all of these requisites are found together, then the devotees
of philosophy will achieve complete success; but according as any one of the
things which I have mentioned is lacking, to this extent must their disciples of
necessity fall below the mark.

Now as for the sophists who have lately sprung up and have very recently 19
embraced these pretensions, even though they flourish at the moment, they will
all, I am sure, come round to this position. But there remain to be considered
those who lived before our time and did not scruple to write the so-called arts of
oratory.[1] These must not be dismissed without rebuke, since they professed to
teach how to conduct law-suits, picking out the most discredited of terms, which
the enemies, not the champions, of this discipline might have been expected to

Reprinted by permission of the publishers and The Loeb Classical Library from Isocrates, *Against the
Sophists* (14–22), vol. 2, trans. George Norlin, Cambridge, Mass.: Harvard University Press, 1982.

1. For example, Corax and Tisias.

20   employ—and that too although this facility, in so far as it can be taught, is of no greater aid to forensic than to all other discourse. But they were much worse than those who dabble in disputation; for although the latter expounded such captious theories that were anyone to cleave to them in practice he would at once be in all manner of trouble, they did, at any rate, make professions of virtue and sobriety in their teaching, whereas the former, although exhorting others to study political discourse, neglected all the good things which this study affords, and became nothing more than professors of meddlesomeness and greed.

21   And yet those who desire to follow the true precepts of this discipline may, if they will, be helped more speedily towards honesty of character than towards facility in oratory. And let no one suppose that I claim that just living can be taught; for, in a word, I hold that there does not exist an art of the kind which can implant sobriety and justice in depraved natures. Nevertheless, I do think that the study of political discourse can help more than any other thing to stimulate and form such qualities of character.

22   But in order that I may not appear to be breaking down the pretensions of others while myself making greater claims than are within my powers, I believe that the very arguments by which I myself was convinced will make it clear to others also that these things are true.

Antidosis

In my treatment of the art of discourse, I desire, like the genealogists, to start at the beginning. It is acknowledged that the nature of man is compounded of two parts, the physical and the mental, and no one would deny that of these two the mind comes first and is of greater worth; for it is the function of the mind to decide both on personal and on public questions, and of the body to be servant to the judgements of the mind. Since this is so, certain of our ancestors, long before our time, seeing that many arts *[technai]* had been devised for other things, while none had been prescribed for the body and for the mind, invented and bequeathed to us two disciplines: physical training for the body, of which gymnastics is a part, and, for the mind, philosophy, which I am going to explain. These are twin arts— parallel and complementary—by which their masters prepare the mind to become more intelligent and the body to become more serviceable, not separating sharply the two kinds of education, but using similar methods of instruction, exercise, and other forms of discipline.

For when they take their pupils in hand, the physical trainers instruct their followers in the postures which have been devised for bodily contests, while the teachers of philosophy impart all the forms of discourse in which the mind *[logos]* expresses itself. Then, when they have made them familiar and thoroughly conversant with these lessons, they set them at exercises, habituate them to work, and require them to combine in practice the particular things which they have learned, in order that they may grasp them more firmly and bring their theories *[doxai]* into closer touch with the occasions for applying them—I say "theories," for no system of knowledge can possibly cover these occasions, since in all cases they elude our science. Yet those who most apply their minds to them and are able to discern the consequences which for the most part grow out of them, will most often meet these occasions in the right way.

Watching over them and training them in this manner, both the teachers of gymnastic and the teachers of discourse are able to advance their pupils to a point where they are better men and where they are stronger in their thinking or in the use of their bodies. However, neither class of teachers is in possession of a science *[epistēmē]* by which they can make capable athletes or capable orators out of whomsoever they please. They can contribute in some degree to these results, but these powers are never found in their perfection save in those who excel by virtue both of talent and of training.

I have given you now some impression of what philosophy is. But I think that you will get a still clearer idea of its powers if I tell you what professions I make to those who want to become my pupils. I say to them that if they are to excel in oratory or in managing affairs or in any line of work, they must, first of all, have a natural aptitude for that which they have elected to do; secondly, they must submit to training and master the knowledge of their particular subject, whatever

180

181

182

183

184

185

186
187

Reprinted by permission of the publishers and The Loeb Classical Library from Isocrates, *Antidosis* (180–257, 274–280, 293–296), vol. 2, trans. George Norlin, Cambridge, Mass.: Harvard University Press, 1982.

188 it may be in each case; and, finally, they must become versed and practised in the use and application of their art; for only on these conditions can they become fully competent and pre-eminent in any line of endeavour. In this process, master and pupil each has his place; no one but the pupil can furnish the necessary capacity; no one but the master, the ability to impart knowledge; while both have a part in the exercises of practical application: for the master must painstakingly direct his pupil, and the latter must rigidly follow the master's instructions.

189 Now these observations apply to any and all the arts. If anyone, ignoring the other arts, were to ask me which of these factors has the greatest power in the education of an orator I should answer that natural ability is paramount and comes before all else. For given a man with a mind which is capable of finding out and learning the truth and of working hard and remembering what it learns, and also with a voice and a clarity of utterance which are able to captivate the

190 audience, not only by what he says, but by the music of his words, and, finally, with an assurance which is not an expression of bravado, but which, tempered by sobriety, so fortifies the spirit that he is no less at ease in addressing all his fellow-citizens than in reflecting to himself—who does not know that such a man might, without the advantage of an elaborate education and with only a superficial and

191 common training, be an orator such as has never, perhaps, been seen among the Hellenes? Again, we know that men who are less generously endowed by nature but excel in experience and practice, not only improve upon themselves, but surpass others who, though highly gifted, have been too negligent of their talents. It follows, therefore, that either one of these factors may produce an able speaker or an able man of affairs, but both of them combined in the same person might produce a man incomparable among his fellows.

192 These, then, are my views as to the relative importance of native ability and practice. I cannot, however, make a like claim for education [*paideia*]; its powers are not equal nor comparable to theirs. For if one should take lessons in all the principles of oratory and master them with the greatest thoroughness, he might, perhaps, become a more pleasing speaker than most, but let him stand up before the crowd and lack one thing only, namely, assurance, and he would not be able to utter a word.

193 But let no one of you think that before you I belittle my pretensions, while when I address those who desire to become my pupils I claim every power for my teaching; for it was to avoid just such a charge as this that, when I entered upon my profession, I wrote and published a discourse in which you will find that I

194 attack those who make pretensions which are unwarranted, and set forth my own ideas. Now I am not going to quote from it my criticisms of others; for they are too long for the present occasion; but I shall attempt to repeat to you that part in which I express my own views. I begin at this point. . . . [See *Against the Sophists* 14–18.]

195 Now this quotation is of a more finished style than what has been said before, but its meaning is the same, and this ought to be taken by you as a convincing proof of my honesty; for you see that I did not brag and make big promises when I was young only to speak modestly for my philosophy now that I have reaped the harvest of my labours and am an old man, but that, on the contrary, I speak in the

same terms both when I was at the height of my career and now when I am ready to retire from it, both when I had no thought of danger and now when I stand in jeopardy, and both in addressing those who wanted to become my pupils and now in addressing those who are to vote upon my fate. I do not see, therefore, how the sincerity and honesty of my professions could be more clearly shown.

Let this quotation, then, add its weight to what I have said before. I do not, however, delude myself as to the people who are ill disposed towards my teaching: nothing of what I have said so far is enough to disabuse them of this feeling; and it will take many arguments of all sorts to convert them to a different opinion from that which they now hold. Accordingly I must not leave off expounding and speaking until I shall accomplish one of two things — until I have persuaded them to change their views or have proved that the slanders and charges which they repeat against me are false. 196 197

These charges are of two kinds. Some of them say that the profession of the sophist is nothing but sham and chicane, maintaining that no kind of education has ever been discovered which can improve a man's ability to speak or his capacity for handling affairs, and that those who excel in these respects owe their superiority to natural gifts; while others acknowledge that men who take this training are more able, but complain that they are corrupted and demoralized by it, alleging that when they gain the power to do so, they scheme to get other people's property. 198

Now there is not a sound or true word in either complaint, as I am very confident that I can prove to everyone. First of all I would have you note, in the case of those who assert that education is a sham, that they quite obviously talk rubbish themselves; for while they ridicule it as powerless to help us — nothing but humbug and chicane — at the same time they demand that my pupils show improvement from the moment they come to me; that when they have been with me a few days, they must be abler and wiser in speech than those who have the advantage over them both in years and in experience; and that when they have been with me no more than a year, they must all be good and finished orators; nor must the indolent be a whit less accomplished than the industrious, nor they who are lacking in ability than those who are blessed with vigorous minds. These are the requirements they set up, and yet they have never heard me make such promises, nor have they ever seen like results in the other arts and disciplines. On the contrary, all knowledge yields itself up to us only after great effort on our part, and we are by no means all equally capable of working out in practice what we learn. Nay, from all our schools only two or three students turn out to be real champions, the rest retiring from their studies into private life. 199 200 201

And yet how can we fail to deny intelligence to those who have the effrontery to demand powers which are not found in the recognized arts of this which they declare is not an art and who expect greater advantages to come from an art in which they do not believe than from arts which they regard as thoroughly perfected? Men of intelligence ought not to form contrary judgements about similar things nor refuse to recognize a discipline which accomplishes the same results as most of the arts. For who among you does not know that most of those who have sat under the sophists have not been duped nor affected as these men 202 203 204 claim, but that some of them have been turned out competent champions and others able teachers; while those who have preferred to live in private have become more gracious in their social intercourse than before, and keener judges of discourses and more prudent counsellors than most? How then is it possible to scorn a discipline which is able to make of those who have taken advantage of it men of that kind?

205   Furthermore, this also will be agreed to by all men, namely, that in all the arts and crafts we regard those as the most skilled who turn out pupils who all work as
206   far as possible in the same manner. Now it will be seen that this is the case with philosophy. For all who have been under a true and intelligent guide will be found to have a power of speech so similar that it is evident to everyone that they have shared the same training. And yet, had not a common habit and a common technique of training been instilled into them, it is inconceivable that they should have taken on this likeness.

207   Again, every one of you could name many of your schoolfellows who when they were boys seemed to be the dullest among their companions, but who, growing older, outstripped them farther in intelligence and in speech than they had lagged behind them when they were boys. From this fact you can best judge what training can do; for it is evident that when they were young they all possessed such mental powers as they were born with, but as they grew to be men, these outstripped the others and changed places with them in intelligence, because their companions lived dissolutely and softly, while they gave heed to their own
208   opportunities and to their own welfare. But when people succeed in making progress through their own diligence alone, how can they fail to improve in a much greater degree both over themselves and over others if they put themselves under a master who is mature, of great experience, and learned not only in what has been handed down to him but in what he has discovered for himself?

209   But there remain still other reasons why everyone may well be astonished at the ignorance in men who venture so blindly to condemn philosophy. For, in the first place, they know that pains and industry give proficiency in all other activities and
210   arts, yet deny that they have any such power in the training of the intellect; secondly, they admit that no physical weakness is so hopeless that it cannot be improved by exercise and effort, but they do not believe that our minds, which are naturally superior to our bodies, can be made more serviceable through educa-
211   tion and suitable training; again, they observe that some people possess the art of training horses and dogs and most other animals by which they make them more spirited, gentle or intelligent, as the case may be, yet they do not think that any education has been discovered for training human nature, such as can improve
212   men in any of those respects in which we improve the beasts. Nay, so great is the misfortune which they impute to us all, that while they would acknowledge that it is by our mental powers that every creature is improved and made more useful, yet they have the hardihood to claim that we ourselves, who are endowed with an intelligence through which we render all creatures of greater worth, cannot help
213   each other to advance in excellence. But most absurd of all, they behold in the shows which are held year after year lions which are more gentle toward their trainers than some people are toward their benefactors, and bears which dance

about and wrestle and imitate our skill, and yet they are not able to judge even   214
from these instances the power which education and training have, nor can they
see that human nature will respond more promptly than the animals to the
benefits of education. In truth, I cannot make up my mind which should astonish
us the more — the gentleness which is implanted in the fiercest of wild beasts or the
brutishness which resides in the souls of such men.

One might say more upon this head, but if I say too much on questions about   215
which most men are agreed, I fear you may suspect that I have little to say on
questions which are in dispute. Therefore I shall leave this subject and turn my
attention to a class of people who do not, to be sure, contemn philosophy but
condemn it much more bitterly since they attribute the iniquities of those who
profess to be sophists, but in practice are far different, to those whose ways have
nothing in common with them. But I am speaking, not in behalf of all those who   216
pretend to be able to educate the young, but in behalf of those only who have
justly earned this reputation, and I think that I shall convince you that my
accusers have shot very wide of the truth if only you are willing to hear me to the
end.

In the first place, then, we must determine what are the objects which make   217
people venture to do evil; for if we define these correctly, you will be better able to
make up your minds whether the charges which have been made against us are
true or false. Well then, I maintain that everyone does everything which he does
for the sake of pleasure or gain or honour; for I observe that no desire springs up in
men save for these objects. If this be so, it only remains to consider which of these   218
objects we should attain by corrupting the young.

Do you suppose it would give us pleasure to see or hear that our pupils were bad
and in evil repute with their fellow-citizens? And who is so insensate that he
would not be distressed to have such things reported about himself? But surely we   219
could not expect to be admired nor to enjoy great honour for sending out disciples
of that sort; on the contrary, we should be much more despised and hated than
those who are charged with other forms of villainy. And, mark you, even if we
could shut our eyes to these consequences, we could not gain the most money by
directing a training of that character; for, I suppose, all men are aware that a   220
sophist reaps his finest and his largest reward when his pupils prove to be
honourable and intelligent and highly esteemed by their fellow-citizens, since
pupils of that sort inspire many with the desire to enjoy his teaching, while those
who are depraved repel even those who were formerly minded to join his classes.
Who, then, could be blind to the more profitable course, when there is so vast a
difference between the two?

Perhaps, however, some might venture to reply that many men, because of   221
their incontinence, are not amenable to reason, but neglect their true interests
and rush on in the pursuit of pleasure. I grant you that many men in general and
some who pretend to be sophists are of this nature. Nevertheless, no one even of   222
their number is so incontinent as to desire his pupils also to show the same lack of
control; for he would not be able to share in the pleasures which they might enjoy
as the result of their incontinence, while he would bring down upon his own head
most of the evil repute which would result from their depravity.

223   Again, whom would they corrupt and what manner of people would they get as pupils? For this is worth inquiring into. Would they get those who are already perverse and vicious? And who, pray, would make an effort to learn from another what his own nature teaches him? Would they, then, get those who are honest and ambitious to lead a useful life? But no such person would deign to speak with men who are evil in their words and in their deeds.

224   I should like to ask those who disapprove of me what they think about the students who cross the sea from Sicily, from the Pontus, and from other parts of the world in order to enjoy my instruction. Do they think that they voyage to Athens because of the dearth of evil-minded men at home? But anywhere on

225   earth anyone can find no lack of men willing to aid him in depravity and crime. Do they think, then, that they come here in order to become intriguers and sycophants, at great expense to themselves? But, in the first place, people of this mind are much more inclined to lay hold of other people's property than to part with anything of their own; and, in the next place, who would pay out money to learn depravity, since it is easy to be depraved at no expense whatever, whenever one is so inclined? For there is no need of taking lessons in evil-doing; all that a man has to do is to set his hands to it.

226   No, it is evident that these students cross the sea and pay out money and go to all manner of trouble because they think that they themselves will be the better for it and that the teachers here are much more intelligent than those in their own countries. This ought to fill all Athenians with pride and make them appreciate at their worth those who have given to the city this reputation.

227   But, in fact, some of our people are extremely unreasonable. They know that neither the strangers who come here nor the men who preside over their education occupy themselves with anything harmful, but that they are, on the contrary, the most unofficious and the most peaceable of all who live in Athens, giving their

228   minds to their own affairs and confining their intercourse to each other, and living, furthermore, day by day in the greatest simplicity and decorum, taking their pleasures in discourse — not the kind of discourse which is employed in petty litigation nor that which is offensive to anyone, but the kind which has the approbation of all men. Nevertheless, although they know all this about them, they do not refrain from traducing them and saying that they engage in this

229   training in order that they may defeat the ends of justice in the courts and win their own advantage. And yet who that engages in the practice of injustice and of evil-doing would be willing to live more continently than the rest? Whom have these traducers ever seen reserving and treasuring up their depravities for future use instead of indulging from the first the evil instincts present in their nature?

230   But, apart from these considerations, if it be true that cleverness in speech results in plotting against other people's property, we should expect all able

231   speakers to be intriguers and sycophants;[1] for the same cause produces in every instance the same effect. In fact, however, you will find that among our public men who are living to-day or who have but lately passed away those who give most

---

1. Sycophants were demagogues who attempted to fatten the treasury by bringing false indictments against wealthy Athenian citizens (see *Antidosis* 20–28).

study to the art of words are the best of the statesmen who come before you on the rostrum, and, furthermore, that among the ancients it was the greatest and the most illustrious orators who brought to the city most of her blessings.

First of all was Solon. For when he was placed at the head of the people, he gave 232 them laws, set their affairs in order, and constituted the government of the city so wisely that even now Athens is well satisfied with the polity which was organized by him. Next, Cleisthenes, after he had been driven from Athens by the tyrants, succeeded by his eloquence in persuading the Amphictyons to lend him money from the treasury of Apollo, and thus restored the people to power, expelled the tyrants, and established that democracy to which the world of Hellas owes its greatest blessings. After him, Themistocles, placed at the head of our forces in the 233 Persian War, counselled our ancestors to abandon the city (and who could have persuaded them to do this but a man of surpassing eloquence?), and so advanced their circumstances that at the price of being homeless for a few days they became for a long period of time the masters of the Hellenes. Finally, Pericles, because he 234 was both a good leader of the people and an excellent orator, so adorned the city with temples, monuments, and other objects of beauty, that even to-day visitors who come to Athens think her worthy of ruling not only the Hellenes, but all the world; and, more than this, he stored away in the Acropolis a sum of not less than 235 ten thousand talents. And of these men who carried out such great enterprises not one neglected the art of discourse; nay, so much more did they apply their minds to eloquence than to other things, that Solon was named one of the seven sophists and was given the title which is now dishonoured and on trial here; and Pericles studied under two of the sophists, Anaxagoras of Clazomenae and Damon, the latter in his day reputed to be the wisest among the Athenians. Could one, then, 236 show more clearly than by these examples that the powers of eloquence do not turn men into evil-doers? No, but, on the other hand, those who are evil from their birth, like my accuser, will, I doubt not, continue to the end indulging their depravity both in words and in deeds.

But I can show you also where you may see, if you desire, the names of our 237 trouble-makers and of the men who are really liable to the charges which these people apply to the sophists. They are published by law on the tablets which the magistrates set up: public offenders and sycophants have their names published by the Thesmothetae; malefactors and their instigators, by the Eleven; and private offenders and authors of unjust complaints by the Forty.[2] In these lists you will 238 find the names of this fellow[3] and his friends recorded many times, but you will not find my name nor that of anyone of my profession published in a single one of them. On the contrary, you will find that we so order our own affairs as to stand in 239 no need of your lawsuits. And yet, when men keep clear of these troubles, when they live decently and have had no part in any disgraceful act, why do you not give them their due of praise instead of subjecting them to trial? For it is evident that the principles which we instill into our students are such as we practise in our own lives.

2. The Thesmothetae, the Eleven, and the Forty were the three judicial bodies that adjudicated cases involving, respectively, state offenses, major crimes, and small claims.
3. Lysimachus.

240   Now you will appreciate even more clearly from the things which I am going to say that I am far from being a corrupter of our youth. For if I were guilty of this, Lysimachus would not be the one to be incensed in their behalf, nor anyone of his kind, but you would see the fathers and relatives of my pupils up in arms,
241   framing writs and seeking to bring me to justice. But instead of that they bring their sons to me and are ready to pay me money, and are rejoiced when they see them spending their days in my society, while the sycophants are the men who speak evil of me and hale me into court. And who more than these sycophants would like to see many of our citizens corrupted and depraved, since they know that when they live among such characters they wield great power, whereas when
242   they fall into the hands of honourable and intelligent men, they are doomed to destruction? Therefore these men are wise in seeking to do away with all studies which they consider will make men better, and so render them more intolerant of the depravities and intrigues of the sycophants. It is well for you, however, to take the opposite course and regard those pursuits as the best to which you see that these men are most inimical.

243   But I now find myself in a curious position; for I am going to be frank even if some will say that I shift my ground too easily. A little while ago I said that many good men had been misled about philosophy, and are consequently harshly disposed toward it. Now, however, I have assumed that the arguments which I have presented are so plain and evident to all that no one, it seems to me, can misapprehend its power or accuse me of corrupting my disciples or have any such
244   feeling as I imputed to them a little while ago. Nevertheless, if I am to speak the truth and say what has now come into my mind, I am of the opinion that while all those who are envious of my success covet the ability to think and speak well, yet they themselves neglect to cultivate it, some because they are indolent, some
245   because they discredit their own powers, and some on other pretexts (and these are legion); but when other men take great pains and show a desire to attain what they themselves covet, then they grow irritated, jealous, perturbed in spirit, and are much in the same state of mind as lovers are. Indeed, how could one more aptly
246   explain their condition? They envy the good fortune of those who are able to use words eloquently; yet they reproach the youth who aspire to win this distinction. There is no one of them who would not pray the gods to bestow the power of eloquence upon himself, first of all, and failing that, upon his sons and his own
247   kin; yet when men strive through work and study to accomplish for themselves what these people would like to have as a gift from the gods, they accuse them of going utterly astray. At one moment they make believe to mock at them as dupes and victims; and then again, for no reason at all, they change about and denounce
248   them as adepts in grasping their own advantage. When any danger threatens the city, they seek counsel from those who can speak best upon the question at issue and act upon their advice; but when men devote their efforts to preparing themselves to serve the state in just such crises, they think it proper to traduce them. And they reproach the Thebans and our other enemies for their ignorance; yet when men seek by every means to escape from that malady, they never cease maligning them.

But as a symptom, not only of their confusion of mind, but of their contempt   249
for the gods, they recognize that Persuasion is one of the gods, and they observe
that the city makes sacrifices to her every year,[4] but when men aspire to share the
power which the goddess possesses, they claim that such aspirants are being
corrupted, as though their desire were for some evil thing. But what is most   250
astonishing of all is that while they would grant that the mind is superior to the
body, nevertheless, in spite of this opinion, they look with greater favour upon
training in gymnastics than upon the study of philosophy. And yet how unreasonable it is to give higher praise to those who cultivate the less than to those who
cultivate the greater thing, and that too when everyone knows it was not through
excellence of body that Athens ever accomplished any noteworthy thing, but that
through wisdom of men she became the most prosperous and the greatest of
Hellenic states.

It would be possible to bring together many more contradictions than the above   251
in the views of these people, but that is a task for those who are younger than I and
who are free from anxiety about the present occasion. For example, one might put
the following questions on this very subject: Suppose the case of men who, having
inherited large fortunes from their ancestors, used their wealth, not to render
themselves serviceable to the state, but to outrage their fellow-citizens and to
dishonour their sons and their wives; would anyone venture to put the blame upon
the authors of their wealth instead of demanding that the offenders themselves be   252
punished? Again, suppose the case of men who, having mastered the art of war,
did not use their skill against the enemy, but rose up and slew many of their fellow-
citizens; or suppose the case of men who, having been trained to perfection in the
art of boxing or of the pancration, kept away from the games and fell foul of the
passers-by; would anyone withhold praise from their instructors instead of putting
to death those who turned their lessons to an evil use?

We ought, therefore, to think of the art of discourse just as we think of the other   253
arts, and not to form opposite judgements about similar things, nor show
ourselves intolerant toward that power which, of all the faculties which belong to
the nature of man, is the source of most of our blessings. For in the other powers
which we possess, as I have already said on a former occasion, we are in no respect
superior to other living creatures; nay, we are inferior to many in swiftness and in
strength and in other resources; but, because there has been implanted in us the   254
power to persuade each other and to make clear to each other whatever we desire,
not only have we escaped the life of wild beasts, but we have come together and
founded cities and made laws and invented arts; and, generally speaking, there is
no institution devised by man which the power of speech has not helped us to   255
establish. For this it is which has laid down laws concerning things just and
unjust, and things honourable and base; and if it were not for these ordinances we
should not be able to live with one another. It is by this also that we confute the

4. Isocrates refers to a well-known fact: "The people of Athens made yearly sacrifices to the statue of
the goddess Persuasion, whose worship was said to have been established in the city by Theseus" (Dixon,
7). See also Pausanias 1.22.3.

bad and extol the good. Through this we educate the ignorant and appraise the wise; for the power to speak well is taken as the surest index of a sound understanding, and discourse which is true and lawful and just is the outward

256 image of a good and faithful soul. With this faculty we both contend against others on matters which are open to dispute and seek light for ourselves on things which are unknown; for the same arguments which we use in persuading others when we speak in public, we employ also when we deliberate in our own thoughts; and, while we call eloquent those who are able to speak before a crowd,

257 we regard as sage those who most skillfully debate their problems in their own minds. And, if there is need to speak in brief summary of this power, we shall find that none of the things which are done with intelligence take place without the help of speech, but that in all our actions as well as in all our thoughts speech is our guide, and is most employed by those who have the most wisdom.

274   I consider that the kind of art which can implant honesty and justice in depraved natures has never existed and does not now exist, and that people who

275 profess that power will grow weary and cease from their vain pretensions before such an education is ever found. But I do hold that people can become better and worthier if they conceive an ambition to speak well, if they become possessed of the desire to be able to persuade their hearers, and, finally, if they set their hearts on seizing their advantage—I do not mean "advantage" in the sense given to that

276 word by the empty-minded, but advantage in the true meaning of that term; and that this is so I think I shall presently make clear.

For, in the first place, when anyone elects to speak or write discourses which are worthy of praise and honour, it is not conceivable that he will support causes which are unjust or petty or devoted to private quarrels, and not rather those

277 which are great and honourable, devoted to the welfare of man and our common good; for if he fails to find causes of this character, he will accomplish nothing to the purpose. In the second place, he will select from all the actions of men which bear upon his subject those examples which are the most illustrious and the most edifying; and, habituating himself to contemplate and appraise such examples, he will feel their influence not only in the preparation of a given discourse but in all the actions of his life. It follows, then, that the power to speak well and think right will reward the man who approaches the art of discourse with love of wisdom and love of honour.

278 Furthermore, mark you, the man who wishes to persuade people will not be negligent as to the matter of character; no, on the contrary, he will apply himself above all to establish a most honourable name among his fellow-citizens; for who does not know that words carry greater conviction when spoken by men of good repute than when spoken by men who live under a cloud, and that the argument which is made by a man's life is of more weight than that which is furnished by words? Therefore, the stronger a man's desire to persuade his hearers, the more zealously will he strive to be honourable and to have the esteem of his fellow citizens.

279 And let no one of you suppose that while all other people realize how much the scales of persuasion incline in favour of one who has the approval of his judges,

the devotees of philosophy alone are blind to the power of good will. In fact, they appreciate this even more thoroughly than others, and they know, furthermore,   280 that probabilities and proofs and all forms of persuasion support only the points in a case to which they are severally applied, whereas an honourable reputation not only lends greater persuasiveness to the words of the man who possesses it, but adds greater lustre to his deeds, and is, therefore, more zealously to be sought after by men of intelligence than anything else in the world.

Therefore, it behooves all men to want to have many of their youth engaged in   293 training to become speakers, and you Athenians most of all. For you, yourselves, are pre-eminent and superior to the rest of the world, not in your application to the business of war, nor because you govern yourselves more excellently or preserve the laws handed down to you by your ancestors more faithfully than others, but in those qualities by which the nature of man rises above the other animals, and the   294 race of the Hellenes above the barbarians, namely, in the fact that you have been educated as have been no other people in wisdom and in speech. So, then, nothing more absurd could happen than for you to declare by your votes that students who desire to excel their companions in those very qualities in which you excel mankind, are being corrupted, and to visit any misfortune upon them for availing themselves of an education in which you have become the leaders of the world.

For you must not lose sight of the fact that Athens is looked upon as having   295 become a school for the education of all able orators and teachers of oratory. And naturally so; for people observe that she holds forth the greatest prizes for those who have this ability, that she offers the greatest number and variety of fields of exercise to those who have chosen to enter contests of this character and want to   296 train for them, and that, furthermore, everyone obtains here that practical experience which more than any other thing imparts ability to speak; and, in addition to these advantages, they consider that the catholicity and moderation of our speech, as well as our flexibility of mind and love of letters, contribute in no small degree to the education of the orator. Therefore they suppose, and not without just reason, that all clever speakers are the disciples of Athens.

Plato

Plato (ca. 429–347 B.C.) founded his famous Academy in Athens around 387 B.C.. The excerpts from the *Gorgias* and the *Phaedrus* presented here show how greatly Plato disagreed with his rival educator, Isocrates, about the nature and the place of rhetoric in the education of men for life in the polis.

In the *Gorgias*, the sophist Gorgias serves as a sort of figurehead for the dialogue. The real theme is Gorgias' profession, the teaching of rhetoric. We present here only the opening scenes of the *Gorgias*, in which Socrates seeks from Gorgias an answer to his question concerning the nature of rhetoric, namely, "About which of the things which exist *[tōn ontōn]* is it a science *[epistēmē]?*"[1] The selection ends with Socrates dividing the arts *(technai)* into eight parts and showing that both sophistic and rhetoric are sham arts, mere "flatteries," in relation to the care of the soul, just as cooking and cosmetology are sham arts in relation to the care of the body. Sophistic and rhetoric, like cooking and cosmetology, he says, aim at pleasure rather than at that which is good for the soul.

In the *Phaedrus*, Socrates and Phaedrus discuss a speech written by Lysias, the well-known logographer, in which he proposed that one should yield to a nonlover rather than to a lover. Phaedrus reads the speech to Socrates, and Socrates criticizes it for being repetitious and for using the inventions of others (235–36). Then, using the same thesis, Socrates composes his own speech. Afterwards, saying that he has committed an impious act by his attack on Eros, he recants and makes a second speech in praise of Love. In his second speech, Socrates praises Love as both divine madness and divine blessing. This speech includes the famous description of the soul as a charioteer who drives two horses.

In our selection we present only the concluding portion of the *Phaedrus*, that which follows the second speech of Socrates. In this part, Socrates presents a reformed, or philosophical, rhetoric based on a mutual search for truth (dialectic) instead of on arguments from probability (oratory). Socrates also rejects the written word as an effective teaching method on grounds similar to those on which rhetoric was rejected in the *Gorgias*.[2]

---

1. This question (449D), here literally translated, appears to be an ironic echo of the title of Gorgias' treatise *On the Nonexistent Or On Nature*. For the contents of this treatise, see Sprague, 42–46.

2. Before Plato's day, "writing was considered as an aid to speaking rather than a substitute for it. . . . By Plato's time the position was already changing, and at this transitional stage the relationship between spoken and written *logos* became a subject of lively argument. . . . [There is] evidence of a controversy, in Plato's own time, between the upholders of the spoken and of the written word. With Plato's rival Isocrates oratory itself became a purely written medium. . . . Opposed to him was Alcidamas, who maintained that speeches should not be written down at all, even for subsequent delivery, but should be improvised as the *kairos* [occasion] of the moment demanded. This he argued in a work *On those who compose written speeches* which has survived, and there are striking resemblances between its language and that of the *Phaedrus*, too close to be fortuitous" (Guthrie, 4: 58–59).

Sophists - oriented to public affairs
Socrates sets a trap

Gorgias

CALLICLES. This is how they say you should take part in warfare and battle,   447A
Socrates.

SOCRATES. What, have we arrived at the latter end of a feast, as the saying
goes?

CALLICLES. Yes, and a very charming feast: for Gorgias has just given us a fine
and varied display.

SOCRATES. Well, Chaerepho here is to blame, Callicles: for he compelled us to
loiter in the market place.

CHAEREPHO. 'Tis no matter, Socrates: for I can supply the remedy too. Gorgias   B
is a friend of mine, and will treat us to another display, now, if you want, or if
not, later.

CALLICLES. What, Chaerepho? Is Socrates anxious to hear Gorgias?

CHAEREPHO. That is the very reason why we are here.

CALLICLES. Any time you like to come home with me, then: for Gorgias is
staying with me and will give you an exhibition.

SOCRATES. Most kind of you, Callicles: but would he also be willing to   C
converse with us? I want to learn from him what is the scope of his art and
just what he professes and teaches. As for the exhibition, let him give us
that, as you suggest, on some other occasion.

CALLICLES. There's nothing like asking him, Socrates: for that was one feature
of his display. He bade any one of the company present just now ask any
question he pleased, and said he would answer all such questions.

SOCRATES. Splendid! Chaerepho, ask him.

CHAEREPHO. Ask him what?

SOCRATES. Who he is.   D

CHAEREPHO. What do you mean?

SOCRATES. Well, supposing he were a maker of shoes, he would surely answer
you that he was a cobbler: you see what I mean, do you not?

CHAEREPHO. I see: and I will ask him. Tell me, Gorgias, is Callicles right in
saying that you profess to answer any question you are asked?

GORGIAS. He is right, Chaerepho: that is the very statement I made just now,   448A
and I assure you that nobody has asked me a new question these many years.

CHAEREPHO. You must indeed be ready with your answers, Gorgias.

GORGIAS. You are at liberty to make the experiment, Chaerepho.

POLUS. Yes indeed: and upon me, if you wish, Chaerepho: for Gorgias, I think,
is played out: he has already spoken at great length.

CHAEREPHO. Why, Polus, do you think you could answer better than Gorgias?

POLUS. What does that matter, if it is well enough for you?   B

CHAEREPHO. Not at all: but since you want to, you may answer.

POLUS. Proceed.

Reprinted by permission of the publishers from Plato, *Gorgias* (447A–465E), in *Plato: Socratic
Dialogues*, ed. and trans. W. D. Woodhead, general ed. Raymond Klibansky, Walton-on-Thames:
Thomas Nelson and Sons, 1953.

CHAEREPHO. I will. If Gorgias were an expert in the same art as his brother Herodicus, what should we rightly call him? By the same professional name as his brother?

POLUS. Assuredly.

CHAEREPHO. Then we should be correct in calling him a doctor?

POLUS. Yes.

CHAEREPHO. And if he were skilled in the same art as Aristophon, son of Aglaophon, or Aristophon's brother, what should we rightly call him?

C   POLUS. Obviously a painter.

CHAEREPHO. But, as it is, in what craft is he expert, and by what name should we correctly call him?

POLUS. There are many arts, Chaerepho, among mankind experimentally devised by experience: for experience guides our life along the path of art, inexperience along the path of chance. And in each of these different arts different men partake in different ways, the best men following the best arts. And Gorgias here is one of the best and partakes in the noblest of arts.

D   SOCRATES. It is plain, Gorgias, that Polus is well equipped to make speeches: but he fails to accomplish what he promised to Chaerepho.

GORGIAS. Pray, how is that, Socrates?

SOCRATES. It seems that he does not quite answer the question asked.

GORGIAS. Well, if you prefer it, you may ask him yourself.

SOCRATES. No, not if you are ready to answer instead: I would much rather question you. For it is obvious from what Polus has said that he is much better versed in what is called rhetoric than in dialogue.

E   POLUS. How is that, Socrates?

SOCRATES. Why, Polus, because when Chaerepho asks in what art Gorgias is proficient, you praise his art as though someone were attacking it, but neglect to answer what it is.

POLUS. Did I not answer that it was the noblest of arts?

SOCRATES. Certainly. But no one is asking in what kind of art Gorgias is engaged but what it actually is and what we should call Gorgias. On the

449A   lines laid down before by Chaerepho, when you answered correctly and briefly, tell us now in similar manner what this art is and what name we must give to Gorgias. Or rather, Gorgias, tell us yourself in what art you are expert and what we should call you.

GORGIAS. The art of Rhetoric, Socrates.

SOCRATES. Then we must call you a rhetorician?

GORGIAS. Yes, and a good one, Socrates, if you really want to call me what, in Homer's expression, I boast myself to be.

SOCRATES. That is what I want.

GORGIAS. Then call me so.

B   SOCRATES. Are we to say that you can make rhetoricians of others also?

GORGIAS. That is the profession I make both here and elsewhere.

SOCRATES. Would you be willing, Gorgias, to continue our present method of conversing by question and answer, postponing to some other occasion lengthy discourses of the type begun by Polus? You must not, however, disappoint us in your promise but show yourself ready to answer the question briefly.

GORGIAS. There are certain answers, Socrates, that must necessarily be given at length: however, I will attempt to answer as briefly as possible. For that too is one of the claims I make, that nobody could give the same answers more briefly than I.   C

SOCRATES. That is what I want, Gorgias: give me an exhibition of this brevity of yours, and reserve a lengthy discourse for another time.

GORGIAS. I will do so, and you will admit you have never heard a speaker more concise.

SOCRATES. Well then: you claim that you are an expert in the art of rhetoric and that you can make rhetoricians of others. Now just what is the scope of rhetoric? Weaving, for example, has to do with the making of garments: you agree?   D

GORGIAS. Yes.

SOCRATES. And music with composing melodies?

GORGIAS. Yes.

SOCRATES. By Hera, Gorgias, I marvel at your answers: they could not be briefer.

GORGIAS. Yes, I think I succeed pretty well, Socrates.

SOCRATES. Good: and now answer in the same way about rhetoric: what is the field of this science?

GORGIAS. Words.

SOCRATES. Of what kind, Gorgias? Those that reveal to the sick what treatment will restore their health?   E

GORGIAS. No.

SOCRATES. Then rhetoric is not concerned with every kind of words.

GORGIAS. Certainly not.

SOCRATES. Yet it makes men able to speak.

GORGIAS. Yes.

SOCRATES. And able to think also about the matter of their discourse?

GORGIAS. Of course.

SOCRATES. Now does not the science of medicine, which we have just mentioned, make men able to think and to speak about their patients?   450A

GORGIAS. Assuredly.

SOCRATES. Then medicine also, it seems, is concerned with words.

GORGIAS. Yes.

SOCRATES. Words about diseases?

GORGIAS. Certainly.

SOCRATES. And is not gymnastic concerned with words that relate to good or bad bodily condition?

GORGIAS. Undoubtedly.

SOCRATES. And so it is with the other arts also, Gorgias: each of them is concerned with words that have to do with its own subject-matter.   B

GORGIAS. Evidently.

SOCRATES. Then, as the other arts have to do with words, why do you not call them by the name of 'rhetoric', since you call rhetoric any art that is concerned with words?

GORGIAS. Because all the knowledge of the other arts is in general, Socrates, concerned with manual crafts and similar activities, whereas rhetoric deals with no such manual product but all its activity and all that it accomplishes is through the medium of words. Therefore I claim that the art of rhetoric has to do with words, and maintain that my claim is correct.

SOCRATES. I wonder whether I understand the kind of thing you wish to call it. But I shall soon know more clearly. Answer me this: we admit, do we not, the existence of arts?

GORGIAS. Yes.

SOCRATES. Among the various arts there are, I think, some that consist for the most part of action and have little need of words; and some in fact have no need, but their function can be achieved in silence, as for instance painting and sculpture and many others. I fancy it is with such arts that you say rhetoric has no concern, is it not?

GORGIAS. You are entirely right in your opinion, Socrates.

SOCRATES. But there are other arts that secure their result entirely through words and have practically no need, or very little need, of action: arithmetic, for instance, and calculation and geometry and the game of draughts and many other arts, some of which involve almost as many words as actions, and many of them far more, their whole achievement and effect in general being due to words. It is to this kind of art, I believe, that you assign rhetoric.

GORGIAS. You are right.

SOCRATES. But I do not imagine that you intend to call any of these aforementioned arts rhetoric, though your actual expression was that 'the art which secures its effect through words is rhetoric', and anyone who wished to make trouble in our debate might object: 'Then you call arithmetic rhetoric, Gorgias?' But I do not think you mean by rhetoric either arithmetic or geometry.

451A   GORGIAS. You are right, Socrates, and your supposition is quite correct.

SOCRATES. Come then, and complete for yourself the answer for which I asked. Since rhetoric is one of those arts that for the most part employ words, and since there are other such arts also, try to tell me what is the field of that particular art securing its effect through words which is called rhetoric. Suppose that somebody should ask me about any of the arts recently mentioned: 'Socrates, what is the art of arithmetic?' I should reply, as you did just now, that it is one of the arts which secure their effect through speech: and if he should further inquire, 'in what field?' I should reply, that of the odd and the even, however great their respective numbers might be. And if he should next inquire, 'What art do you call calculation?' I should say that this art too is one of those that secure their entire effect through words: and if he should further demand 'in what field?' I should reply, like the mover of an amendment in the Assembly, that in details 'hereinbefore mentioned' the art of calculation resembles arithmetic — for its field is the same, the even and the odd—but that calculation differs in this respect, that it investigates how the odd and the even are related both to themselves and to each other in regard to number. And if anyone should ask about astronomy and, when I said that this science too secures its effect entirely through words, should demand: 'What is the field of discourses relating to astronomy, Socrates?'—I should reply, the movement of the stars, the sun, and the moon, and their relative speed.

GORGIAS. Your statement, Socrates, is quite correct.

SOCRATES. And now let us have your reply, Gorgias. Rhetoric is one of the arts that achieve and fulfill their function entirely through words, is it not? D

GORGIAS. That is so.

SOCRATES. Tell me then in what field. What is the subject matter of the words employed by rhetoric?

GORGIAS. The greatest and noblest of human affairs, Socrates.

SOCRATES. But, Gorgias, what you are now saying is disputable and not yet clear. I think you must have heard men singing at drinking parties the familiar song in which they enumerate our blessings, health being the first, beauty the second, and third, as the composer of the song claims, wealth obtained without dishonesty. E

GORGIAS. I have heard it. But what is the point of your remark?

SOCRATES. Suppose the men who produce the blessings praised by the author of that song should suddenly appear, the doctor, the trainer, and the business man, and the doctor should speak first and say: 'Socrates, Gorgias is deceiving you: it is not his craft, but mine, that is concerned with the greatest blessing to mankind'. If I were to ask him, 'Who are you that make such a claim?' he would, I suppose, answer that he was a physician. 'Then what do you mean? Is the product of your art the greatest blessing of all?' 'Of course', he would doubtless reply; 'health, Socrates! What greater blessing has man than health?' And then suppose that after him the physical trainer should say: 'I too should be surprised if Gorgias could display to you a blessing greater than mine.' I should say to him in turn: 'And who are you, my good fellow, and what is your function?' 'A trainer', he would answer, 'and my task is to make men strong and beautiful of body.' And after the trainer the business man would speak, in utter contempt, I imagine, of all others: 'Pray consider, Socrates, whether you believe there is any greater blessing than wealth, whether in the pocket of Gorgias or of any other man.' 'What?' we should say to him, 'is that what you make?' 'Yes', he would reply. 'And who are you?' 'A business man.' 'Then', we shall say, 'do you judge wealth to be the greatest blessing for man?' 'Of course', he will answer. 'And yet Gorgias here insists that his art produces greater benefits than yours', we shall say. It is obvious then that he will next inquire: 'And what is this benefit? Let Gorgias tell us.' And so come, Gorgias: imagine you are questioned by these men and by myself as well, and answer what it is you claim to be the greatest blessing to man, and claim also to produce. 452A

452A

B

C

D

GORGIAS. Something, Socrates, that is in very truth the greatest boon: for it brings freedom to mankind in general and to each man dominion over others in his own country.

E   SOCRATES. And what exactly do you mean by that?

GORGIAS. I mean the power to convince by your words the judges in court, the senators in council, the people in the assembly or in any other gathering of a citizen body. And yet possessed of such power you will make the doctor, you will make the trainer your slave: and your business man will prove to be making money, not for himself, but for another, for you who can speak and persuade multitudes.

453A   SOCRATES. Now at last, Gorgias, you have revealed most precisely, it seems to me, what art you consider rhetoric to be: and if I understand you aright, you assert that rhetoric is a creator of persuasion, and that all its activity is concerned with this, and this is its sum and substance. Can you state any wider scope for rhetoric than to produce persuasion in the soul of the hearer?

GORGIAS. By no means, Socrates: I think you define it adequately: for that is its sum and substance.

B   SOCRATES. Then listen, Gorgias. I am convinced, you may be sure, that if there is any man who in a discussion with another is anxious to know just what is the real subject under discussion, I am such a man: and I am confident that you are too.

GORGIAS. What then, Socrates?

SOCRATES. I will tell you. Just what that persuasion is which you claim is produced by rhetoric, and with what subjects it deals, I assure you, I do not know: but I have a suspicion as to what persuasion you mean, and its field. Yet I shall ask you none the less what you mean by the conviction produced

C   by rhetoric and what is its province. And why shall I ask you instead of speaking myself, when I have this suspicion? Not for your sake, but because I am anxious that the argument should so proceed as to clarify to the utmost the matter under discussion. Consider whether I am right in asking you that further question: if I had asked you what kind of painter Zeuxis was and you had answered, a painter of living creatures, might I not with justice ask you, what kind of living creatures, and where they may be found?

GORGIAS. Certainly.

D   SOCRATES. And the reason is that there are other painters with many other living subjects?

GORGIAS. Yes.

SOCRATES. Whereas, if Zeuxis had been the only painter, yours would have been a good answer?

GORGIAS. Certainly.

SOCRATES. Then come, tell me about rhetoric. Do you think that rhetoric alone produces persuasion or do other arts as well? What I mean is this: when a man teaches a subject, does he persuade where he teaches, or not?

GORGIAS. One cannot deny that, Socrates: certainly he persuades.

E   SOCRATES. Let us take once more the same arts as we discussed just now. Arithmetic and the arithmetician teach us, do they not, the properties of a number?

GORGIAS. Certainly.

SOCRATES. And consequently persuade us?

GORGIAS. Yes.

SOCRATES. Then arithmetic is also a creator of persuasion?

GORGIAS. Evidently.

SOCRATES. Now, if anyone should ask us what kind of persuasion and in what field, we shall answer him, I suppose, that which teaches about the odd and the even in all their quantities: and we shall be able to prove that all the other arts just mentioned are creators of persuasion and name the type and the field, shall we not? 454A

GORGIAS. Yes.

SOCRATES. Then rhetoric is not the only creator of persuasion.

GORGIAS. That is true

SOCRATES. Then since other arts besides rhetoric produce this result, we should be justified in asking next, as in the case of the painter, of what kind of persuasion is rhetoric the art, and what is its province? Do you not think that is a fair question to ask next? B

GORGIAS. I do.

SOCRATES. Then answer, Gorgias, since you share my opinion.

GORGIAS. The kind of persuasion employed in the lawcourts and other gatherings, Socrates, as I said just now, and concerned with right and wrong.

SOCRATES. I suspected too, Gorgias, that you meant this kind of persuasion, with such a province: it is merely that you may not be surprised if a little later I ask you the same kind of question, though the answer seems clear to me: yet I may repeat it—for, as I said, I am questioning you, not for your own sake, but in order that the argument may be carried forward consecutively, and that we may not form the habit of suspecting and anticipating each other's views, but that you may complete your own statements as you please, in accordance with your initial plan. C

GORGIAS. I think your method is right, Socrates.

SOCRATES. Then let us consider the next point. Is there a state which you call 'having learned'?

GORGIAS. There is.

SOCRATES. And such a thing as 'having believed'?

GORGIAS. There is.

SOCRATES. Now do you think that to have learned and to have believed, or knowledge and belief, are one and the same or different? D

GORGIAS. I consider them different, Socrates.

SOCRATES. You are right; and you can prove it thus: if anybody were to say to you, 'Can there be both a false belief and a true, Gorgias?' you would, I think, say that there is.

GORGIAS. Yes.

SOCRATES. But can there be both a false and a true knowledge?

GORGIAS. By no means.

SOCRATES. Then it is obvious that knowledge and belief are not the same.

GORGIAS. You are right.

E   SOCRATES. But both those who have learned and those who believe have been persuaded.

GORGIAS. That is so.

SOCRATES. Shall we lay it down then that there are two forms of persuasion, the one producing belief without knowledge, the other knowledge?

GORGIAS. Certainly.

SOCRATES. Now which kind of conviction about right and wrong is produced in the lawcourts and other gatherings by rhetoric? That which issues in belief without knowledge, or that which issues in knowledge?

GORGIAS. Evidently, Socrates, that which issues in belief.

455A   SOCRATES. Then rhetoric apparently is a creator of a conviction that is persuasive but not instructive about right and wrong.

Contradiction

GORGIAS. Yes.

SOCRATES. Then the rhetorician too does not instruct courts and other assemblies about right and wrong, but is able only to persuade them: for surely he could not instruct so large a gathering in a short time about matters so important.

GORGIAS. No indeed.

SOCRATES. Well then, let us see just exactly what we are saying about rhetoric:

B   for I cannot myself yet understand what I mean. Whenever there is a gathering in the city to choose doctors or shipwrights or any other professional group, surely the rhetorician will not then give his advice: for it is obvious that in each such choice it is the real expert who must be selected. And when it is a question about the building of walls or equipment of harbours or dockyards, we consult, not the rhetoricians, but the master builders: and again when we need advice about a choice of generals or some tactical formation against the enemy or the occupation of positions, mili-

C   tary experts will advise us, not rhetoricians: or what do you say, Gorgias, about such matters? Since you claim yourself to be a rhetorician and to make rhetoricians of others, it is right to examine you on the qualities of your art. And so, imagine that my interest is on your behalf: for perhaps some of those present are anxious to become your disciples—there are some, I know, quite a number, in fact—who would be bashful perhaps

D   about questioning you. And so, just imagine that when I inquire, they too are asking: 'What shall we gain, Gorgias, if we associate with you? On what subjects shall we be able to advise the city, about right and wrong alone, or the subjects just mentioned by Socrates?' Try to answer them, then.

GORGIAS. Well, Socrates, I will try to reveal to you clearly the full scope of rhetoric: for you have shown me the path excellently. You know, of course,

E   that your dockyards and the walls of Athens and her harbour equipment are due to the advice, partly of Themistocles, partly of Pericles, not to that of architects.

SOCRATES. That is what they say, Gorgias, about Themistocles: and Pericles I myself heard when he recommended the building of the middle wall.

456A   GORGIAS. And when any of the choices you mentioned just now is in question,

Socrates, you see that it is the orators who give advice and carry their motions.

SOCRATES. That is what surprises me, Gorgias, and that is why I asked you long since what is the scope of rhetoric. When so looked at, it seems to me to possess almost superhuman importance.

GORGIAS. Ah, if only you knew all, Socrates, and realised that rhetoric includes practically all other faculties under her control. And I will give you good proof of this. I have often, along with my brother and with other physicians, visited one of their patients who refused to drink his medicine or submit to the surgeon's knife or cautery: and when the doctor was unable to persuade them, I did so, by no other art but rhetoric. And I claim too that, if a rhetorician and a doctor visited any city you like to name and they had to contend in argument before the assembly or any other gathering as to which of the two should be chosen as doctor, the doctor would be nowhere, but the man who could speak would be chosen, if he so wished. And if he should compete against any other craftsman whatever, the rhetorician rather than any other would persuade the people to choose him: for there is no subject on which a rhetorician would not speak more persuasively than any other craftsman, before a crowd. Such then is the scope and character of rhetoric: but it should be used, Socrates, like every other competitive art. We must not employ other competitive arts against one and all merely because we have learned boxing or mixed fighting or weapon combat, so that we are stronger than our friends and foes: we must not, I say, for this reason strike our friends or wound or kill them. No indeed, and if a man who is physically sound has attended the wrestling school and has become a good boxer, and then strikes his father or mother or any other of his kinsmen or friends, we must not for this reason detest or banish from our cities the physical trainers or drill instructors. For they imparted this instruction for just employment against enemies or wrong-doers, in self-defence not aggression: but such people perversely employ their strength and skill in the wrong way. And so the teachers are not guilty, and the craft is not for this reason evil or to blame, but rather, in my opinion, those who make improper use of it. And the same argument applies also to rhetoric. The rhetorician is competent to speak against anybody on any subject, and to prove himself more convincing before a crowd on practically every topic he wishes: but he should not any the more rob the doctors—or any other craftsmen either—of their reputation, merely because he has this power: one should make proper use of rhetoric as of athletic gifts. And if a man becomes a rhetorician and makes a wrongful use of this faculty and craft, you must not, in my opinion, detest and banish his teacher from the city. For he imparted it for a good use, but the pupil abuses it. And therefore it is the man who abuses it whom we should rightly detest and banish and put to death, not his instructor.

SOCRATES. I think, Gorgias, that, like myself, you have had much experience in discussions and must have observed that speakers can seldom define the topic of debate and after mutual instruction and enlightenment bring the meeting to a close: but if they are in dispute and one insists that the other's statements are incorrect or obscure, they grow angry and imagine their opponent speaks with malice toward them, being more anxious for verbal victory than to investigate the subject under discussion. And finally some of them part in the most disgraceful fashion, after uttering and listening to

E such abusive language that their audience are disgusted with themselves for having deigned to give ear to such fellows. Now why do I say this? Because, it seems to me, what you are now saying is not quite consistent or in tune with what you said at first about rhetoric. But I am afraid to cross-examine you, for fear you might think my pertinacity is directed against you, and not

458A to the clarification of the matter in question. Now, if you are the same kind of man as I am, I should be glad to question you: if not, I will let you alone. And what kind of man am I? One of those who would gladly be refuted if anything I say is not true, and would gladly refute another who says what is not true, but would be no less happy to be refuted myself than to refute: for I consider that a greater benefit, inasmuch as it is a greater boon to be delivered from the worst of evils oneself than to deliver another. And I

B believe there is no worse evil for man than a false opinion about the subject of our present discussion. If you then are the same kind of man as I am, let us continue: but if you feel that we should drop the matter, then let us say goodbye to the argument and dismiss it.

GORGIAS. No, I claim to be myself the type of man you indicate: but perhaps we ought to have been thinking of our audience. For quite a time ago before your arrival I gave a long display to the company present, and now, perhaps, if we continue our debate, it will be a prolonged affair. So we should

C consider the convenience of our audience, in case we are detaining here some who are anxious to be doing something else.

CHAEREPHO. You can hear for yourselves, Gorgias and Socrates, the protests of the company, who are eager to hear whatever you have to say: as for me, heaven forbid I should have any engagement so pressing as to desert a conversation of such a character and between such interlocutors for however profitable an occupation.

D CALLICLES. Indeed, Chaerepho, I too have listened to many a debate: but I think I have never enjoyed one so much as this. I shall be delighted in fact if you are ready to talk all day long.

SOCRATES. Well, I have no objections to offer, if Gorgias is willing.

GORGIAS. After all this, Socrates, it would be disgraceful of me to refuse, when I personally volunteered to meet any question that might be put. But if

E those present agree, carry on the conversation and ask what you will.

SOCRATES. Then listen, Gorgias, to what surprises me in your statement: for perhaps you were right and I misunderstood you. You claim you can make a rhetorician of any man who wishes to learn from you?

GORGIAS. Yes.

SOCRATES. With the result that he would be convincing about any subject before a crowd, not through instruction but by persuasion?

459A GORGIAS. Certainly.

SOCRATES. Well, you said just now that a rhetorician will be more persuasive than a doctor regarding health.

GORGIAS. Yes, I said so, before a crowd.

SOCRATES. And before a crowd means among the ignorant: for surely, among those who know, he will not be more convincing than the doctor.

GORGIAS. That is quite true.

SOCRATES. Then if he is more persuasive than the doctor, he is more persuasive than the man who knows?

GORGIAS. Certainly.

SOCRATES. Though not himself a doctor.   B

GORGIAS. Yes.

SOCRATES. And he who is not a doctor is surely ignorant of what a doctor knows.

GORGIAS. Obviously.

SOCRATES. Therefore when the rhetorician is more convincing than the doctor, the ignorant is more convincing among the ignorant than the expert. Is that our conclusion, or is something else?

GORGIAS. That is the conclusion, in this instance.

SOCRATES. Is not the position of the rhetorician and of rhetoric the same with respect to other arts also? It has no need to know the truth about things but   C merely to discover a technique of persuasion, so as to appear among the ignorant to have more knowledge than the expert?

GORGIAS. But is not this a great comfort, Socrates, to be able without learning any other arts but this one, to prove in no way inferior to the specialists?

SOCRATES. Whether or not the rhetorician is inferior to other craftsmen for this reason, we will consider later, if the question should prove relevant: but now let us first investigate whether the relation of the rhetorician to right   D and wrong, the noble and the base, the just and the unjust is the same as it is to health and the objects of the other arts—whether he does not know what is right or wrong, noble or base, just or unjust, but has contrived a technique of persuasion in these matters, so that, though ignorant, he appears among the ignorant to know better than the expert. Or must your   E prospective pupil in rhetoric have such knowledge and bring it with him when he comes to you? And if he is ignorant, will you, his teacher of rhetoric, teach your pupil none of these things—for that is not your concern—but make him appear before the crowd to have such knowledge, when he has it not, and appear to be a good man, when he is not? Or will you be utterly unable to teach him rhetoric if he does not beforehand know the truth about these matters? How do we stand here, Gorgias? In heaven's name, reveal, as you promised just now, the true power of rhetoric.   460A

GORGIAS. Well, Socrates, I suppose that if he does not possess this knowledge, he can learn these things also from me.

SOCRATES. Stop one moment! What you say is right. If you make a rhetorician of any man, he must already have knowledge of right and wrong either by previous acquaintance or by learning it from you.

GORGIAS. Certainly.

B   SOCRATES. Now is not the man who has learned the art of carpentry a carpenter?

GORGIAS. Yes.

SOCRATES. And he who has learned the art of music a musician?

GORGIAS. Yes.

SOCRATES. And he who has learned medicine a physician? And so too on the same principle, the man who has learned anything becomes in each case such as his knowledge makes him?

GORGIAS. Certainly.

SOCRATES. Then according to this principle he who has learned justice is just.

GORGIAS. Most assuredly.

SOCRATES. And the just man, I suppose, does just acts?

GORGIAS. Yes.

C   SOCRATES. Now the rhetorician must necessarily be just, and the just man must wish to do just actions?

GORGIAS. Evidently.

SOCRATES. Then the just man will never wish to do injustice?

GORGIAS. Necessarily.

SOCRATES. And our argument demands that the rhetorician be just?

GORGIAS. Yes.

SOCRATES. Then the rhetorician will never wish to do wrong?

GORGIAS. Evidently not.

D   SOCRATES. Now do you remember saying a short while ago that we should not blame our trainers or expel them from our cities, if a boxer practises his art in a wrongful manner and does injury, and so too if a rhetorician makes wrongful use of his rhetoric, we should not censure or banish his instructor but rather the guilty man who wrongly employs rhetoric? Was this said or not?

GORGIAS. It was said.

E   SOCRATES. But now it is clear that this same rhetorician would never do wrong, is it not?

GORGIAS. It is clear.

SOCRATES. And in our earlier discussion, Gorgias, it was stated that rhetoric is concerned with words that deal, not with the odd and even, but with right and wrong. Is that so?

GORGIAS. Yes.

SOCRATES. Now at the time when you stated this, I considered that rhetoric could never be a thing of evil, since its discourse is always concerned with
461A   justice: but when a little later you said that the rhetorician might actually make an evil use of rhetoric, I was surprised, and considering that what was said was inconsistent, I spoke as I did, saying that if, like myself, you thought it of value to be refuted, it was worth while pursuing the conversation: but if not, we should let it drop. And as a result of our subsequent review you can see for yourself it is admitted that the rhetorician is
B   incapable of making a wrong use of rhetoric and unwilling to do wrong. Now, by the dog, Gorgias, it will need no short discussion to settle

satisfactorily where the truth lies.

POLUS. What, Socrates? Is what you are saying your true opinion about rhetoric? Or do you imagine just because Gorgias was ashamed not to admit that the rhetorician will know the just also and the honourable and the good, and that, if any man came to him without this knowledge, he himself would instruct him, and then, as a result, I suppose, of this admission a contradiction arose in the argument—which is just what you love and you yourself steer the argument in that direction—why, who do you think will deny that he himself knows the right and will teach it to others? But it is the height of bad taste to lead discussions into such channels.

C

SOCRATES. My noble friend Polus, the very reason why we acquire friends and children is that when we ourselves grow old and make slips, you younger people present may set us right both in actions and in words. And now if Gorgias and I are tripping anywhere in our argument, here you are to lend a helping hand—it is only right that you should do so—and if you think that any of our admissions are at fault, I am willing to retract whatever you desire, provided that you observe one condition.

D

POLUS. What is that?

SOCRATES. That you restrain that exuberance, Polus, which you set out to use at first.

POLUS. What? May I not speak at what length I please?

SOCRATES. It would indeed be hard on you, my good friend, if, on coming to Athens, the one spot in Greece where there is the utmost freedom of speech, you alone should be denied it. But look at my side. Would it not be hard on me also, if I may not go away and refuse to listen, when you speak at length and will not answer the question? But if you have any interest in what has been said and wish to set it right, then, as I said just now, retract whatever you please, question and answer in turn, as Gorgias and I did, and refute me and be refuted. For you say, to be sure, that you know what Gorgias knows, do you not?

E

462A

POLUS. I do.

SOCRATES. And do you not also bid anyone at any time to ask you what he will, since you know how to answer?

POLUS. Certainly.

SOCRATES. Then do whichever of the two you choose now, question or answer.

B

POLUS. Well then, I will do so. Answer me, Socrates: since Gorgias seems to you at a loss regarding the nature of rhetoric, what do you say it is?

SOCRATES. Are you asking what art I hold it to be?

POLUS. I am.

SOCRATES. To tell you the truth, Polus, no art at all.

POLUS. But what do you think rhetoric is?

SOCRATES. Something of which you claim to have made an art in your treatise which I recently read.

C

POLUS. What do you mean?

SOCRATES. I call it a kind of routine.

POLUS. Then you think rhetoric is a routine?

SOCRATES. Subject to your approval, I do.

POLUS. What kind of routine?

SOCRATES. One that produces gratification and pleasure.

POLUS. Then you do not think rhetoric a fine thing, if it can produce gratification among men?

D   SOCRATES. What, Polus? Have you already learned from me what I consider rhetoric to be, that you proceed to ask if I do not think it a fine thing?

POLUS. Have I not learned that you call it a kind of routine?

SOCRATES. Well, since you prize gratification so highly will you gratify me to a small extent?

POLUS. I will.

SOCRATES. Then ask me what kind of art I consider cookery.

POLUS. I will. What art is cookery?

SOCRATES. No art, Polus.

POLUS. Then what is it? Tell me.

SOCRATES. In my opinion, a kind of routine.

POLUS. Tell me, what routine?

E   SOCRATES. One that produces gratification and pleasure, I claim, Polus.

POLUS. Then cookery and rhetoric are identical?

SOCRATES. By no means: but each is a part of the same activity.

POLUS. And what is that?

SOCRATES. I am afraid it may sound unmannerly to tell the truth: and I hesitate for fear that Gorgias may think I am caricaturing his profession.

463A   For my part, I do not know whether this is the rhetoric that Gorgias practises: for we reached no definite conclusion in our recent argument as to his opinion: but what I mean by rhetoric is part of an activity that is not very reputable.

GORGIAS. What is it, Socrates? Tell us and feel no scruples about me.

SOCRATES. Well then, Gorgias, the activity as a whole, it seems to me, is not an art, but the occupation of a shrewd and enterprising spirit, and of one

B   naturally skilled in its dealings with men: and in sum and substance I call it 'flattery'. Now it seems to me that there are many other parts of this activity, one of which is cookery. This is considered an art, but in my judgment is no art, only a routine and a knack. And rhetoric I call another part of this general activity, and beautification, and sophistic—four parts with four distinct objects. Now if Polus wishes to question me, let him do so: for he

C   has not yet ascertained what part of flattery I call rhetoric. He does not realise that I have not yet answered him, but proceeds to ask if I do not think it something fine. But I shall not answer whether I consider rhetoric a fine thing or a bad until I have first answered what it is. For that is not right, Polus. Then if you wish to question me, ask me what part of flattery I claim rhetoric to be.

POLUS. I will then: answer, what part?

D   SOCRATES. I wonder whether you will understand my answer. Rhetoric in my opinion is the semblance of a part of politics.

POLUS. Well then do you call it good or bad?

SOCRATES. Bad—for evil things I call bad—if I must answer you as though you already understood what I mean.

GORGIAS. Why, Socrates, even I myself do not grasp your meaning.

SOCRATES. Naturally enough, Gorgias: for I have not yet clarified my statement. But Polus here, like a foal, is young and flighty.   E

GORGIAS. Well, let him alone, and tell me what you mean by saying that rhetoric is the semblance of a part of politics.

SOCRATES. I will try to explain to you my conception of rhetoric: and if it is wrong, Polus will refute me. You admit the existence of bodies and souls?

GORGIAS. Of course   464A

SOCRATES. And do you not consider that there is a healthy condition for each?

GORGIAS. I do.

SOCRATES. And a condition of apparent, but not real health? For example: many people appear to be healthy of body, and no one could perceive they are not so, except a doctor or some physical trainer.

GORGIAS. That is true.

SOCRATES. There exists, I maintain, both in body and in soul, a condition which creates an impression of good health in each case, although it is false.

GORGIAS. That is so.   B

SOCRATES. Let me see now if I can explain more clearly what I mean. To the pair, body and soul, there correspond two arts: that concerned with the soul I call the political art: to the single art that relates to the body I cannot give a name off-hand, but this single art that cares for the body comprises two parts, gymnastic and medicine: and in the political art what corresponds to gymnastic is legislation, while the counterpart of medicine is justice. Now   C
in each case the two arts encroach upon each other, since their fields are the same, medicine upon gymnastic, and justice upon legislation: nevertheless there is a difference between them. There are then these four arts which always minister to what is best, one pair for the body, the other for the soul. But flattery perceiving this—I do not say by knowledge but by conjecture— has divided herself also into four branches, and insinuating herself into the   D
guise of each of these parts, pretends to be that which she impersonates: and having no thought for what is best, she regularly uses pleasure as a bait to catch folly and deceives it into believing that she is of supreme worth. Thus it is that cookery has impersonated medicine and pretends to know the best foods for the body, so that, if a cook and a doctor had to contend in the presence of children or of men as senseless as children, which of the two, doctor or cook, was an expert in wholesome and bad food, the doctor would   E
starve to death. This then I call a form of flattery, and I claim that this kind   465A
of thing is bad—I am now addressing you, Polus—because it aims at what is pleasant, ignoring the good: and I insist that it is not an art but a routine, because it can produce no principle in virtue of which it offers what it does, nor explain the nature thereof, and consequently is unable to point to the cause of each thing it offers. And I refuse the name of art to anything irrational. But if you have any objections to lodge, I am willing to submit to

further examination.

B

Cookery then, as I say, is a form of flattery that corresponds to medicine: and in the same way gymnastic is personated by beautification, a mischievous, deceitful, mean, and ignoble activity, which cheats us by shapes and colours, by smoothing and draping, thereby causing people to take on an alien charm to the neglect of the natural beauty produced by exercise.

C

To be brief, then, I will express myself in the language of geometricians—for by now perhaps you may follow me: sophistic is to legislation what beautification is to gymnastic; and rhetoric to justice what cookery is to medicine. But, as I say, while there is this natural distinction between them, yet because they are closely related, sophist and rhetorician, working in the same sphere and upon the same subject matter, tend to be confused with each other, and they know not what to make of each other, nor do

D

others know what to make of them. For if the body was under the control, not of the soul, but of itself, and if cookery and medicine were not investigated and distinguished by the soul, but the body instead gave the verdict, weighing them by the bodily pleasures they offered, then the principle of Anaxagoras would everywhere hold good—that is something you know about, my dear Polus—and all things would be mingled in indiscriminate confusion, and medicine and health and cookery would be indistinguishable.

E

Well, now you have heard my conception of rhetoric: it is the counterpart in the soul of what cookery is to the body.

Phaedrus

PHAEDRUS. And I have this long while been filled with admiration for your 257C
speech as a far finer achievement than the one you made before. It makes
me afraid that I shall find Lysias cutting a poor figure, if he proves to be
willing to compete with another speech of his own. The fact is that only the
other day, my dear good sir, one of our politicians was railing at him and
reproaching him on this very score, constantly dubbing him a 'speech-
writer'; so possibly we shall find him desisting from further composition to
preserve his reputation.

SOCRATES. What a ridiculous line to take, young man! And how utterly you D
misjudge our friend, if you suppose him to be such a timid creature! Am I
to believe you really do think that the person you speak of meant his raillery
as a reproach?

PHAEDRUS. He gave me that impression, Socrates; and of course you know as
well as I do that the men of greatest influence and dignity in political life are
reluctant to write speeches and bequeath to posterity compositions of their
own, for fear of the verdict of later ages, which might pronounce them
Sophists.

SOCRATES. Phaedrus, you are unaware that the expression 'Pleasant Bend'
comes from the long bend in the Nile. [1] and besides the matter of the Bend E
you are unaware that the proudest of politicians have the strongest desire to
write speeches and bequeath compositions; why, whenever they write a
speech, they are so pleased to have admirers that they put in a special clause
at the beginning with the names of the persons who admire the speech in
question.

PHAEDRUS. What do you mean? I don't understand.

SOCRATES. You don't understand that when a politician begins a composition 258A
the first thing he writes is the name of his admirer.

PHAEDRUS. Is it?

SOCRATES. Yes, he says maybe 'Resolved by the Council' or 'by the People' or
by both: and then 'Proposed by so-and-so'—a pompous piece of self-
advertisement on the part of the author; after which he proceeds with what
he has to say, showing off his own wisdom to his admirers, sometimes in a
very lengthy composition. This sort of thing amounts, don't you think, to
composing a speech?

PHAEDRUS. Yes, I think it does. B

SOCRATES. Then if the speech holds its ground, the author quits the scene
rejoicing; but if it is blotted out, and he loses his status as a recognised
speech-writer, he goes into mourning, and his friends with him.

PHAEDRUS. Quite so.

Reprinted by permission of the publishers from Plato, *Phaedrus* (257C–279C), trans. R. Hackforth, Cambridge: Cambridge University Press, 1952.

1. This saying comes from a Greek proverb: it means that a pleasant expression can sometimes be used in place of a harsh one.

SOCRATES. Which clearly implies that their attitude to the profession is not one of disdain, but of admiration.

PHAEDRUS. To be sure.

C SOCRATES. Tell me then: when an orator, or a king, succeeds in acquiring the power of a Lycurgus, a Solon or a Darius, and so winning immortality among his people as a speech-writer, doesn't he deem himself a peer of the gods while still living, and do not people of later ages hold the same opinion of him when they contemplate his writings?

PHAEDRUS. Yes, indeed.

SOCRATES. Then do you suppose that anyone of that type, whoever he might be, and whatever his animosity towards Lysias, could reproach him simply on the ground that he writes?

PHAEDRUS. What you say certainly makes that improbable; for apparently he would be reproaching what he wanted to do himself.

D SOCRATES. Then the conclusion is obvious, that there is nothing shameful in the mere writing of speeches.

PHAEDRUS. Of course.

SOCRATES. But in speaking and writing shamefully and badly, instead of as one should, that is where the shame comes in, I take it.

PHAEDRUS. Clearly.

SOCRATES. Then what is the nature of good writing and bad? Is it incumbent on us, Phaedrus, to examine Lysias on this point, and all such as have written or mean to write anything at all, whether in the field of public affairs or private, whether in the verse of the poet or the plain speech of prose?

E PHAEDRUS. Is it incumbent! Why, life itself would hardly be worth living save for pleasures like this: certainly not for those pleasures that involve previous pain, as do almost all concerned with the body, which for that reason are rightly called slavish.

SOCRATES. Well, I suppose we can spare the time; and I think too that the cicadas overhead, singing after their wont in the hot sun and conversing

259A with one another, don't fail to observe us as well. So if they were to see us two behaving like ordinary folk at midday, not conversing but dozing lazy-minded under their spell, they would very properly have the laugh of us, taking us for a pair of slaves that had invaded their retreat like sheep, to have their midday sleep beside the spring. If however they see us conversing and

B steering clear of their bewitching siren-song, they might feel respect for us and grant us that boon which heaven permits them to confer upon mortals.

PHAEDRUS. Oh, what is that? I don't think I have heard of it.

SOCRATES. Surely it is unbecoming in a devotee of the Muses not to have heard of a thing like that! The story is that once upon a time these creatures were men — men of an age before there were any Muses: and that when the latter came into the world, and music made its appearance, some of the

C people of those days were so thrilled with pleasure that they went on singing, and quite forgot to eat and drink until they actually died without noticing it. From them in due course sprang the race of cicadas, to which the Muses have granted the boon of needing no sustenance right from their birth, but of singing from the very first, without food or drink, until the day of their death: after which they go and report to the Muses how they severally are paid honour amongst mankind, and by whom. So for those whom they report as having honoured Terpsichore in the dance they win that Muse's favour; for those that have worshipped in the rites of love the favour of Erato; and so with all the others, according to the nature of the worship paid to each. To the eldest, Calliope, and to her next sister Urania, they tell of those who live a life of philosophy and so do honour to the music of those twain whose theme is the heavens and all the story of gods and men, and whose song is the noblest of them all.

Thus there is every reason for us not to yield to slumber in the noontide, but to pursue our talk.

PHAEDRUS. Of course we must pursue it.

SOCRATES. Well, the subject we proposed for inquiry just now was the nature of good and bad speaking and writing: so we are to inquire into that.

PHAEDRUS. Plainly.

SOCRATES. Then does not a good and successful discourse presuppose a knowledge in the mind of the speaker of the truth about his subject?

PHAEDRUS. As to that, dear Socrates, what I have heard is that the intending orator is under no necessity of understanding what is truly just, but only what is likely to be thought just by the body of men who are to give judgment; nor need he know what is truly good or noble, but what will be thought so; since it is on the latter, not the former, that persuasion depends.

SOCRATES. 'Not to be lightly rejected', Phaedrus, is any word of the wise; perhaps they are right: one has to see. And in particular this present assertion must not be dismissed.

PHAEDRUS. I agree.

SOCRATES. Well, here is my suggestion for discussion.

PHAEDRUS. Yes?

SOCRATES. Suppose I tried to persuade you to acquire a horse to use in battle against the enemy, and suppose that neither of us knew what a horse was, but I knew this much about you, that Phaedrus believes a horse to be that tame animal which possesses the largest ears.

PHAEDRUS. A ridiculous thing to suppose, Socrates.

SOCRATES. Wait a moment: suppose I continued to urge upon you in all seriousness, with a studied encomium of a donkey, that it was what I called it, a horse: that it was highly important for you to possess the creature, both at home and in the field: that it was just the animal to ride on into battle, and that it was handy, into the bargain, for carrying your equipment and so forth.

PHAEDRUS. To go to that length would be utterly ridiculous.

SOCRATES. Well, isn't it better to be a ridiculous friend than a clever enemy?

PHAEDRUS. I suppose it is.

SOCRATES. Then when a master of oratory, who is ignorant of good and evil, employs his power of persuasion on a community as ignorant as himself, not by extolling a miserable donkey as being really a horse, but by extolling evil as being really good: and when by studying the beliefs of the masses he persuades them to do evil instead of good, what kind of crop do you think his oratory is likely to reap from the seed thus sown?

PHAEDRUS. A pretty poor one.

SOCRATES. Well now, my good friend, have we been too scurrilous in our abuse of the art of speech? Might it not retort: 'Why do you extraordinary people talk such nonsense? I never insist on ignorance of the truth on the part of one who would learn to speak; on the contrary, if my advice goes for anything, it is that he should only resort to me after he has come into possession of truth; what I do however pride myself on is that without my aid knowledge of what is true will get a man no nearer to mastering the art of persuasion.'

PHAEDRUS. And will not such a retort be just?

SOCRATES. Yes, if the arguments advanced against oratory sustain its claim to be an art. In point of fact, I fancy I can hear certain arguments advancing, and protesting that the claim is false, that it is no art, but a knack that has nothing to do with art: inasmuch as there is, as the Spartans put it, no 'soothfast' art of speech, nor assuredly will there ever be one, without a grasp of truth.

261A   PHAEDRUS. We must have these arguments, Socrates. Come, bring them up before us, and examine their purport.

SOCRATES. Come hither then, you worthy creatures, and impress upon Phaedrus, who is so blessed in his offspring, that unless he gets on with his philosophy he will never get on as a speaker on any subject; and let Phaedrus be your respondent.

PHAEDRUS. I await their questions.

SOCRATES. Must not the art of rhetoric, taken as a whole, be a kind of influencing of the mind by means of words, not only in courts of law and other public gatherings, but in private places also? And must it not be the same art that is concerned with great issues and small, its right employment commanding no more respect when dealing with important matters than with unimportant? Is that what you have been told about it?

PHAEDRUS. No indeed, not exactly that: it is principally, I should say, to lawsuits that an art of speaking and writing is applied—and of course to public harangues also. I know of no wider application.

SOCRATES. What? Are you acquainted only with the 'Arts' or manuals of oratory by Nestor and Odysseus, which they composed in their leisure hours at Troy? Have you never heard of the work of Palamedes?

PHAEDRUS. No, upon my word, nor of Nestor either; unless you are casting Gorgias for the role of Nestor, with Odysseus played by Thrasymachus, or maybe Theodorus.[2]

SOCRATES. Perhaps I am. But anyway we may let them be, and do you tell me, what is it that the contending parties in lawcourts do? Do they not in

2. Theodorus and Thrasymachus were famous teachers of rhetoric.

fact contend with words, or how else should we put it?

PHAEDRUS. That is just what they do.

SOCRATES. About what is just and unjust?

PHAEDRUS. Yes.

SOCRATES. And he who possesses the art of doing this can make the same thing appear to the same people now just, now unjust, at will?   D

PHAEDRUS. To be sure.

SOCRATES. And in public harangues, no doubt, he can make the same things seem to the community now good, and now the reverse of good?

PHAEDRUS. Just so.

SOCRATES. Then can we fail to see that the Palamedes of Elea[3] has an art of speaking, such that he can make the same things appear to his audience like and unlike, or one and many, or again at rest and in motion?

PHAEDRUS. Indeed he can.

SOCRATES. So contending with words is a practice found not only in lawsuits and public harangues but, it seems, wherever men speak we find this single art, if indeed it is an art, which enables people to make out everything to be like everything else, within the limits of possible comparison, and to expose the corresponding attempts of others who disguise what they are doing.   E

PHAEDRUS. How so, pray?

SOCRATES. I think that will become clear if we put the following question. Are we misled when the difference between two things is wide, or narrow?

PHAEDRUS. When it is narrow.   262A

SOCRATES. Well then, if you shift your ground little by little, you are more likely to pass undetected from so-and-so to its opposite than if you do so at one bound.

PHAEDRUS. Of course.

SOCRATES. It follows that anyone who intends to mislead another, without being misled himself, must discern precisely the degree of resemblance and dissimilarity between this and that.

PHAEDRUS. Yes, that is essential.

SOCRATES. Then if he does not know the truth about a given thing, how is he going to discern the degree of resemblance between that unknown thing and other things?

PHAEDRUS. It will be impossible.   B

SOCRATES. Well now, when people hold beliefs contrary to fact, and are misled, it is plain that the error has crept into their minds through the suggestion of some similarity or other.

PHAEDRUS. That certainly does happen.

SOCRATES. But can anyone possibly master the art of using similarities for the purpose of bringing people round, and leading them away from the truth about this or that to the opposite of the truth, or again can anyone

---

3. Palamades, like his contemporary, Odysseus, was noted for his cleverness. The "Palamades of Elea" refers to Zeno, the Eleatic philosopher.

possibly avoid this happening to himself, unless he has knowledge of what the thing in question really is?

PHAEDRUS. No, never.

C SOCRATES. It would seem to follow, my friend, that the art of speech displayed by one who has gone chasing after beliefs, instead of knowing the truth, will be a comical sort of art, in fact no art at all.

PHAEDRUS. I dare say.

SOCRATES. Then would you like to observe some instances of what I call the presence and absence of art in that speech of Lysias which you are carrying, and in those which I have delivered?

PHAEDRUS. Yes, by all means: at present our discussion is somewhat abstract, for want of adequate illustrations.

D SOCRATES. Why, as to that it seems a stroke of luck that in the two speeches we have a sort of illustration of the way in which one who knows the truth can mislead his audience by playing an oratorical joke on them. I myself, Phaedrus, put that down to the local deities, or perhaps those mouthpieces of the Muses that are chirping over our heads have vouchsafed us their inspiration; for of course I don't lay claim to any oratorical skill myself.

PHAEDRUS. I dare say that is so: but please explain your point.

SOCRATES. Well, come along: read the beginning of Lysias's speech.

E PHAEDRUS. 'You know how I am situated, and I have told you that I think it to our advantage that the thing should be done. Now I claim that I should not be refused what I ask simply because I am not your lover. Lovers repent when —'

SOCRATES. Stop. Our business is to indicate where the speaker is at fault, and shows absence of art, isn't it?

263A PHAEDRUS. Yes.

SOCRATES. Well now, is not the following assertion obviously true, that there are some words about which we all agree, and others about which we are at variance?

PHAEDRUS. I think I grasp your meaning, but you might make it still plainer.

SOCRATES. When someone utters the word 'iron' or 'silver', we all have the same object before our minds, haven't we?

PHAEDRUS. Certainly.

SOCRATES. But what about the words 'just' and 'good'? Don't we diverge, and dispute not only with one another but with our own selves?

PHAEDRUS. Yes indeed.

B SOCRATES. So in some cases we agree, and in others we don't.

PHAEDRUS. Quite so.

SOCRATES. Now in which of the cases are we more apt to be misled, and in which is rhetoric more effective?

PHAEDRUS. Plainly in the case where we fluctuate.

SOCRATES. Then the intending student of the art of rhetoric ought, in the first place, to make a systematic division of words, and get hold of some mark distinguishing the two kinds of words, those namely in the use of which the multitude are bound to fluctuate, and those in which they are not.

PHAEDRUS. To grasp that, Socrates, would certainly be an excellent piece of discernment.   C

SOCRATES. And secondly, I take it, when he comes across a particular word he must realise what it is, and be swift to perceive which of the two kinds the thing he proposes to discuss really belongs to.

PHAEDRUS. To be sure.

SOCRATES. Well then, shall we reckon love as one of the disputed terms, or as one of the other sort?

PHAEDRUS. As a disputed term, surely. Otherwise can you suppose it would have been possible for you to say of it what you said just now, namely that it is harmful both to the beloved and the lover, and then to turn round and say that it is really the greatest of goods?

SOCRATES. An excellent point. But now tell me this, for thanks to my inspired   D
condition I can't quite remember: did I define love at the beginning of my speech?

PHAEDRUS. Yes indeed, and immensely thorough you were about it.

SOCRATES. Upon my word, you rate the Nymphs of Achelous and Pan, son of Hermes, much higher as artists in oratory than Lysias, son of Cephalus. Or am I quite wrong? Did Lysias at the beginning of his discourse on love compel us to conceive of it as a certain definite entity, with a meaning he   E
had himself decided upon? And did he proceed to bring all his subsequent remarks, from first to last, into line with that meaning? Shall we read his first words once again?

PHAEDRUS. If you like; but what you are looking for isn't there.

SOCRATES. Read it out, so that I can listen to the author himself.

PHAEDRUS. 'You know how I am situated, and I have told you that I think it   264A
to our advantage that the thing should be done. Now I claim that I should not be refused what I ask simply because I am not your lover. Lovers, when their craving is at an end, repent of such benefits as they have conferred.'

SOCRATES. No: he doesn't seem to get anywhere near what we are looking for: he goes about it like a man swimming on his back, in reverse, and starts from the end instead of the beginning; his opening words are what the lover would naturally say to his boy only when he had finished. Or am I quite wrong, dear Phaedrus?

PHAEDRUS. I grant you, Socrates, that the substance of his address is really a   B
peroration.

SOCRATES. And to pass to other points: doesn't his matter strike you as thrown out at haphazard? Do you find any cogent reason for his next remark, or indeed any of his remarks, occupying the place it does? I myself, in my ignorance, thought that the writer, with a fine abandon, put down just what came into his head. Can you find any cogent principle of composition which he observed in setting down his observations in this particular order?

PHAEDRUS. You flatter me in supposing that I am competent to see into his mind with all that accuracy.   C

SOCRATES. Well, there is one point at least which I think you will admit, namely that any discourse ought to be constructed like a living creature, with its own body, as it were; it must not lack either head or feet; it must have a middle and extremities so composed as to suit each other and the whole work.

PHAEDRUS. Of course.

SOCRATES. Then ask yourself whether that is or is not the case with your friend's speech. You will find that it is just like the epitaph said to have been carved on the tomb of Midas the Phrygian.

D   PHAEDRUS. What is that, and what's wrong with it?

SOCRATES. It runs like this:

> A maid of bronze I stand on Midas' tomb,
> So long as waters flow and trees grow tall,
> Abiding here on his lamented grave,
> I tell the traveller Midas here is laid.[4]

E   I expect you to notice that it makes no difference what order the lines come in.

PHAEDRUS. Socrates, you are making a joke of our speech!

SOCRATES. Well, to avoid distressing you, let us say no more of that—though indeed I think it provides many examples which it would be profitable to notice, provided one were chary of imitating them—and let us pass to the other speeches; for they, I think, presented a certain feature which everyone desirous of examining oratory would do well to observe.

265A   PHAEDRUS. To what do you refer?

SOCRATES. They were of opposite purport, one maintaining that the lover should be favoured, the other the non-lover.

PHAEDRUS. Yes, they did so very manfully.

SOCRATES. I thought you were going to say—and with truth—madly; but that reminds me of what I was about to ask. We said, did we not, that love is a sort of madness?

PHAEDRUS. Yes.

SOCRATES. And that there are two kinds of madness, one resulting from human ailments, the other from a divine disturbance of our conventions of conduct.

B   PHAEDRUS. Quite so.

SOCRATES. And in the divine kind we distinguished four types, ascribing them to four gods: the inspiration of the prophet to Apollo, that of the mystic to Dionysus, that of the poet to the Muses, and a fourth type which we declared to be the highest, the madness of the lover, to Aphrodite and Eros; moreover we painted, after a fashion, a picture of the lover's experience, in which perhaps we attained some degree of truth, though we may well have sometimes gone astray; the blend resulting in a discourse which had some

C   claim to plausibility, or shall we say a mythical hymn of praise, in due religious language, a festal celebration of my master and yours too, Phaedrus, that god of love who watches over the young and fair.

PHAEDRUS. It certainly gave me great pleasure to listen to it.

---

4. This epigram can be found in Diogenes Laertius 1.90.

SOCRATES. Then let us take one feature of it, the way in which the discourse contrived to pass from censure to encomium.

PHAEDRUS. Well now, what do you make of that?

SOCRATES. For the most part I think our festal hymn has really been just a festive entertainment, but we did casually allude to a certain pair of procedures, and it would be very agreeable if we could seize their significance in a scientific fashion.

PHAEDRUS. What procedures do you mean?

SOCRATES. The first is that in which we bring a dispersed plurality under a single form, seeing it all together: the purpose being to define so-and-so, and thus to make plain whatever may be chosen as the topic for exposition. For example, take the definition given just now of love: whether it was right or wrong, at all events it was that which enabled our discourse to achieve lucidity and consistency.

PHAEDRUS. And what is the second procedure you speak of, Socrates?

SOCRATES. The reverse of the other, whereby we are enabled to divide into forms, following the objective articulation; we are not to attempt to hack off parts like a clumsy butcher, but to take example from our two recent speeches. The single general form which they postulated was irrationality; next, on the analogy of a single natural body with its pairs of like-named members, right arm or leg, as we say, and left, they conceived of madness as a single objective form existing in human beings: wherefore the first speech divided off a part on the left, and continued to make divisions, never desisting until it discovered one particular part bearing the name of 'sinister' love, on which it very properly poured abuse. The other speech conducted us to the forms of madness which lay on the right-hand side, and upon discovering a type of love that shared its name with the other but was divine, displayed it to our view and extolled it as the source of the greatest goods that can befall us.

PHAEDRUS. That is perfectly true.

SOCRATES. Believe me, Phaedrus, I am myself a lover of these divisions and collections, that I may gain the power to speak and to think; and whenever I deem another man able to discern an objective unity and plurality, I follow 'in his footsteps where he leadeth as a god'. Furthermore—whether I am right or wrong in doing so, God alone knows—it is those that have this ability whom for the present I call dialecticians.

SOCRATES. But now tell me what we ought to call them if we take instruction from Lysias and yourself. Or is what I have been describing precisely that art of oratory thanks to which Thrasymachus and the rest of them have not only made themselves masterly orators, but can do the same for anyone else who cares to bring offerings to these princes amongst men?

PHAEDRUS. Doubtless they behave like princes, but assuredly they do not possess the kind of knowledge to which you refer. No, I think you are right in calling the procedure that you have described dialectical; but we still seem to be in the dark about rhetoric.

SOCRATES. What? Can there really be anything of value that admits of scientific acquisition despite the lack of that procedure? If so, you and I should certainly not disdain it, but should explain what this residuum of rhetoric actually consists in.

PHAEDRUS. Well, Socrates, of course there is plenty of matter in the rhetorical manuals.

SOCRATES. Thank you for the reminder. The first point, I suppose, is that a speech must being with a Preamble. You are referring, are you not, to such niceties of the art?

E   PHAEDRUS. Yes.

SOCRATES. And next comes Exposition accompanied by Direct Evidence; thirdly Indirect Evidence, fourthly Probabilities; besides which there are the Proof and Supplementary Proof mentioned by the Byzantine master of rhetorical artifice.

PHAEDRUS. You mean the worthy Theodorus?

267A   SOCRATES. Of course; and we are to have a Refutation and Supplementary Refutation both for prosecution and defence. And can we leave the admirable Evenus of Paros out of the picture, the inventor of Covert Allusion and Indirect Compliment and (according to some accounts) of the Indirect Censure in mnemonic verse? A real master, that. But we won't disturb the rest of Tisias and Gorgias, who realised that probability deserves more respect than truth, who could make trifles seem important and

B   important points trifles by the force of their language, who dressed up novelties as antiques and vice versa, and found out how to argue concisely or at interminable length about anything and everything. This last accomplishment provoked Prodicus once to mirth when he heard me mention it: he remarked that he and he alone had discovered what sort of speeches the art demands: to wit, neither long ones nor short, but of fitting length.

PHAEDRUS. Masterly, Prodicus!

SOCRATES. Are we forgetting Hippias? I think Prodicus's view would be supported by the man of Elis.

PHAEDRUS. No doubt.

C   SOCRATES. And then Polus: what are we to say of his *Muses' Treasury of Phrases* with its Reduplications and Maxims and Similes, and of words *à la* Licymnius which that master made him a present of as a contribution to his fine writing?

PHAEDRUS. But didn't Protagoras in point of fact produce some such works, Socrates?

SOCRATES. Yes, my young friend: there is his *Correct Diction*, and many other excellent works. But to pass now to the application of pathetic language to the poor and aged, the master in that style seems to me to be the mighty

D   man of Chalcedon, who was also expert at rousing a crowd to anger and then soothing them down again with his spells, to quote his own saying; while at casting aspersions and dissipating them, whatever their source, he was unbeatable.

But to resume: on the way to conclude a speech there seems to be general agreement, though some call it Recapitulation and others by some other name.

PHAEDRUS. You mean the practice of reminding the audience towards the end of a speech of its main points?

SOCRATES. Yes. And now if you have anything further to add about the art of rhetoric—

PHAEDRUS. Only a few unimportant points.

SOCRATES. If they are unimportant, we may pass them over. But let us look at what we have got in a clearer light, to see what power the art possesses, and when.   268A

PHAEDRUS. A very substantial power, Socrates, at all events in large assemblies.

SOCRATES. Yes indeed. But have a look at it, my good sir, and see whether you discern some holes in the fabric, as I do.

PHAEDRUS. Do show them me.

SOCRATES. Well, look here: Suppose someone went up to your friend Eryximachus, or his father Acumenus, and said 'I know how to apply such treatment to a patient's body as will induce warmth or coolness, as I choose: B
I can make him vomit, if I see fit, or go to stool, and so on and so forth. And on the strength of this knowledge I claim to be a competent physician, and to make a competent physician of anyone to whom I communicate this knowledge.' What do you imagine they would have to say to that?

PHAEDRUS. They would ask him, of course, whether he also knew which patients ought to be given the various treatments, and when, and for how long.

SOCRATES. Then what if he said 'Oh, no: but I expect my pupils to manage   C
what you refer to by themselves'?

PHAEDRUS. I expect they would say 'That man is mad: he thinks he has made himself a doctor by picking up something out of a book, or coming across some common drug or other, without any real knowledge of medicine.'

SOCRATES. Now suppose someone went up to Sophocles or Euripides and said he knew how to compose lengthy dramatic speeches about a trifling matter, and quite short ones about a matter of moment; that he could write pathetic passages when he chose, or again passages of intimidation and menace, and   D
so forth; and that he considered that by teaching these accomplishments he could turn a pupil into a tragic poet.

PHAEDRUS. I imagine that they too would laugh at anyone who supposed that you could make a tragedy otherwise than by so arranging such passages as to exhibit a proper relation to one another and to the whole of which they are parts.

SOCRATES. Still I don't think they would abuse him rudely, but rather treat him as a musician would treat a man who fancied himself to be a master of harmony simply because he knew how to produce the highest possible note and the lowest possible on his strings. The musician would not be so rude as   E
to say 'You miserable fellow, you're off your head': but rather, in the gentler language befitting his profession 'My good sir, it is true that one who proposes to become a master of harmony must know the things you speak of: but it is perfectly possible for one who has got as far as yourself to have

not the slightest real knowledge of harmony. You are acquainted with what has to be learnt before studying harmony: but of harmony itself you know nothing.'

PHAEDRUS. Perfectly true.

269A SOCRATES. Similarly then Sophocles would tell the man who sought to show off to himself and Euripides that what he knew was not tragic composition but its antecedents; and Acumenus would make the same distinction between medicine and the antecedents of medicine.

PHAEDRUS. I entirely agree.

SOCRATES. And if 'mellifluous' Adrastus, or shall we say Pericles, were to hear of those admirable artifices that we were referring to just now—the Brachylogies and Imageries and all the rest of them, which we enumerated and deemed it necessary to examine in a clear light—are we to suppose that they would address those who practise and teach this sort of thing, under

B the name of the art of rhetoric, with the severity you and I displayed, and in rude, coarse language? Or would they, in their ampler wisdom, actually reproach us and say 'Phaedrus and Socrates, you ought not to get angry, but to make allowances for such people; it is because they are ignorant of dialectic that they are incapable of properly defining rhetoric, and that in turn leads them to imagine that by possessing themselves of the requisite

C antecedent learning they have discovered the art itself. And so they teach these antecedents to their pupils, and believe that that constitutes a complete instruction in rhetoric; they don't bother about employing the various artifices in such a way that they will be effective, or about organising a work as a whole: that is for the pupils to see to for themselves when they come to make speeches.'

PHAEDRUS. Well yes, Socrates: I dare say that does more or less describe what the teachers and writers in question regard as the art of rhetoric; personally I

D think what you say is true. But now by what means and from what source can one attain the art of the true rhetorician, the real master of persuasion?

SOCRATES. If you mean how can one become a finished performer, then probably—indeed I might say undoubtedly—it is the same as with anything else: if you have an innate capacity for rhetoric, you will become a famous rhetorician, provided you also acquire knowledge and practice; but if you lack any of these three you will be correspondingly unfinished. As regards the art itself (as distinct from the artist) I fancy that the line of approach adopted by Lysias and Thrasymachus is not the one I have in view.

PHAEDRUS. Then what is?

E SOCRATES. I am inclined to think, my good friend, that it was not surprising that Pericles became the most finished exponent of rhetoric there has ever been.

PHAEDRUS. Why so?

270A SOCRATES. All the great arts need supplementing by a study of Nature: your artist must cultivate garrulity and high-flown speculation; from that source alone can come the mental elevation and thoroughly finished execution of which you are thinking; and that is what Pericles acquired to supplement his inborn capacity. He came across the right sort of man, I fancy, in Anaxagoras, and by enriching himself with high speculation and coming to recognise the nature of wisdom and folly—on which topics of course Anaxagoras was always discoursing—he drew from that source and applied to the art of rhetoric what was suitable thereto.

PHAEDRUS. How do you mean?

SOCRATES. Rhetoric is in the same case as medicine, don't you think?   B

PHAEDRUS. How so?

SOCRATES. In both cases there is a nature that we have to determine, the nature of body in the one, and of soul in the other, if we mean to be scientific and not content with mere empirical routine when we apply medicine and diet to induce health and strength, or words and rules of conduct to implant such convictions and virtues as we desire.

PHAEDRUS. You are probably right, Socrates.

SOCRATES. Then do you think it possible to understand the nature of the soul   C
satisfactorily without taking it as a whole?

PHAEDRUS. If we are to believe Hippocrates the Asclepiad, we can't under-stand even the body without such a procedure.

SOCRATES. No, my friend, and he is right. But we must not just rely on Hippocrates: we must examine the assertion and see whether it accords with the truth.

PHAEDRUS. Yes.

SOCRATES. Then what is it that Hippocrates and the truth have to say on this   D
matter of nature? I suggest that the way to reflect about the nature of anything is as follows: first, to decide whether the object in respect of which we desire to have scientific knowledge, and to be able to impart it to others, is simple or complex; secondly, if it is simple, to inquire what natural capacity it has of acting upon another thing, and through what means; or by what other thing, and through what means, it can be acted upon; or, if it is complex, to enumerate its parts and observe in respect of each what we observe in the case of the simple object, to wit what its natural capacity, active or passive, consists in.

PHAEDRUS. Perhaps so, Socrates.

SOCRATES. Well, at all events, to pursue an inquiry without doing so would be   E
like a blind man's progress. Surely we mustn't make out that any sort of scientific inquirer resembles a blind or deaf person. No, it is plain that if we are to address people scientifically, we shall show them precisely what is the real and true nature of that object on which our discourse is brought to bear. And that object, I take it, is the soul.

PHAEDRUS. To be sure.

SOCRATES. Hence the speaker's whole effort is concentrated on that, for it is   271A
there that he is attempting to implant conviction. Isn't that so?

PHAEDRUS. Yes.

SOCRATES. Then it is plain that Thrasymachus, or anyone else who seriously proffers a scientific rhetoric, will, in the first place, describe the soul very precisely, and let us see whether it is single and uniform in nature or, analogously to the body, complex; for to do that is, we maintain, to show a thing's nature.

PHAEDRUS. Yes, undoubtedly.

SOCRATES. And secondly he will describe what natural capacity it has to act upon what, and through what means, or by what it can be acted upon.

PHAEDRUS. Quite so.

B   SOCRATES. Thirdly, he will classify the types of discourse and the types of soul, and the various ways in which souls are affected, explaining the reasons in each case, suggesting the type of speech appropriate to each type of soul, and showing what kind of speech can be relied on to create belief in one soul and disbelief in another, and why.

PHAEDRUS. I certainly think that would be an excellent procedure.

SOCRATES. Yes: in fact I can assure you, my friend, that no other scientific method of treating either our present subject or any other will ever be found, whether in the models of the schools or in speeches actually delivered. But the present-day authors of manuals of rhetoric, of whom you have heard, are cunning folk who know all about the soul but keep their knowledge out of sight. So don't let us admit their claim to write scientifically until they compose their speeches and writings in the way we have indicated.

PHAEDRUS. And what way is that?

SOCRATES. To give the actual words would be troublesome; but I am quite ready to say how one ought to compose if he means to be as scientific as possible.

PHAEDRUS. Then please do.

D   SOCRATES. Since the function of oratory is in fact to influence men's souls, the intending orator must know what types of soul there are. Now these are of a determinate number, and their variety results in a variety of individuals. To the types of soul thus discriminated there corresponds a determinate number of types of discourse. Hence a certain type of hearer will be easy to persuade by a certain type of speech to take such-and-such action for such-and-such reason, while another type will be hard to persuade. All this the orator must fully understand; and next he must watch it actually occurring,

E   exemplified in men's conduct, and must cultivate a keenness of perception in following it, if he is going to get any advantage out of the previous instruction that he was given in the school. And when he is competent to say what type of man is susceptible to what kind of discourse; when, further,

272A   he can, on catching sight of so-and-so, tell himself 'That is the man, that character now actually before me is the one I heard about in school, and in order to persuade him of so-and-so I have to apply *these* arguments in *this* fashion'; and when, on top of all this, he has further grasped the right occasions for speaking and for keeping quiet, and has come to recognise the right and the wrong time for the Brachylogy, the Pathetic Passage, the Exacerbation and all the rest of his accomplishments, then and not till then has he well and truly achieved the art. But if in his speaking or teaching or

B   writing he fails in any of these requirements, he may tell you that he has the art of speech, but one mustn't believe all one is told.

And now maybe our author will say 'Well, what of it, Phaedrus and Socrates? Do you agree with me, or should we accept some other account of the art of speech?'

PHAEDRUS. Surely we can't accept any other, Socrates; still it does seem a considerable business.

SOCRATES. You are right, and that makes it necessary thoroughly to overhaul all our arguments, and see whether there is some easier and shorter way of arriving at the art; we don't want to waste effort in going off on a long rough road, when we might take a short smooth one. But if you can help us at all through what you have heard from Lysias or anyone else, do try to recall it.   C

PHAEDRUS. As far as trying goes, I might; but I can suggest nothing on the spur of the moment.

SOCRATES. Then would you like me to tell you something I have heard from those concerned with these matters?

PHAEDRUS. Why, yes.

SOCRATES. Anyhow, Phaedrus, we are told that even the devil's advocate ought to be heard.

PHAEDRUS. Then you can put his case.   D

SOCRATES. Well, they tell us that there is no need to make such a solemn business of it, or fetch such a long compass on an uphill road. As we remarked at the beginning of this discussion, there is, they maintain, absolutely no need for the budding orator to concern himself with the truth about what is just or good conduct, nor indeed about who are just and good men whether by nature or education. In the lawcourts nobody cares a rap for the truth about these matters, but only about what is plausible. And that is the same as what is probable, and is what must occupy the attention of the would-be master of the art of speech. Even actual facts ought sometimes not to be stated, if they don't tally with probability; they should be replaced by what is probable, whether in prosecution or defence; whatever you say, you simply must pursue this probability they talk of, and can say good-bye to the truth for ever. Stick to that all through your speech, and you are   273A
equipped with the art complete.   E

PHAEDRUS. Your account, Socrates, precisely reproduces what is said by those who claim to be experts in the art of speech. I remember that we did touch briefly on this sort of contention a while ago; and the professionals regard it as a highly important point.

SOCRATES. Very well then, take Tisias himself; you have thumbed him carefully, so let Tisias tell us this: does he maintain that the probable is anything other than that which commends itself to the multitude?   B

PHAEDRUS. How could it be anything else?

SOCRATES. Then in consequence, it would seem, of that profound scientific discovery he laid down that if a weak but brave man is arrested for assaulting a strong but cowardly one, whom he has robbed of his cloak or some other garment, neither of them ought to state the true facts; the coward should say that the brave man didn't assault him single-handed, and the brave man should contend that there were only the two of them, and then have

C   recourse to the famous plea 'How could a little fellow like me have attacked a big fellow like him?' Upon which the big fellow will not avow his own poltroonery but will try to invent some fresh lie which will probably supply his opponent with a means of refuting him. And similar 'scientific' rules are given for other cases of the kind. Isn't that so, Phaedrus?

PHAEDRUS. To be sure.

SOCRATES. Bless my soul! It appears that he made a brilliant discovery of a buried art, your Tisias, or whoever it really was and whatever he is pleased to be called after. But, my friend, shall we or shall we not say to him—

D   PHAEDRUS. Say what?

SOCRATES. This: 'In point of fact, Tisias, we have for some time before you came on the scene been saying that the multitude get their notion of probability as the result of a likeness to truth; and we explained just now that these likenesses can always be best discovered by one who knows the truth. Therefore if you have anything else to say about the art of speech, we should be glad to hear it; but if not we shall adhere to the point we made just now, namely that unless the aspirant to oratory can on the one hand list the

E   various natures amongst his prospective audiences, and on the other divide things into their kinds and embrace each individual thing under a single form, he will never attain such success as is within the grasp of mankind. Yet he will assuredly never acquire such competence without considerable diligence, which the wise man should exert not for the sake of speaking to and dealing with his fellow-men, but that he may be able to speak what is pleasing to the gods, and in all his dealings to do their pleasure to the best of his ability. For you see, Tisias, what we are told by those wiser than

274A   ourselves is true, that a man of sense ought never to study the gratification of his fellow-slaves, save as a minor consideration, but that of his most excellent masters. So don't be surprised that we have to make a long detour: it is because the goal is glorious, though not the goal you think of.' Not but what those lesser objects also, if you would have them, can best be attained (so our argument assures us) as a consequence of the greater.

PHAEDRUS. Your project seems to be excellent, Socrates, if only one could carry it out.

B   SOCRATES. Well, when a man sets his hand to something good, it is good that he should take what comes to him.

PHAEDRUS. Yes, of course.

SOCRATES. Then we may feel that we have said enough about the art of speech, both the true art and the false?

PHAEDRUS. Certainly.

SOCRATES. But there remains the question of propriety and impropriety in writing, that is to say the conditions which make it proper or improper. Isn't that so?

PHAEDRUS. Yes.

SOCRATES. Now do you know how we may best please God, in practice and in theory, in this matter of words?

PHAEDRUS. No indeed. Do you?

SOCRATES. I can tell you the tradition that has come down from our   C
forefathers, but they alone know the truth of it. However, if we could
discover that for ourselves, should we still be concerned with the fancies of
mankind?

PHAEDRUS. What a ridiculous question! But tell me the tradition you speak of.

SOCRATES. Very well. The story is that in the region of Naucratis in Egypt
there dwelt one of the old gods of the country, the god to whom the bird
called Ibis is sacred, his own name being Theuth. He it was that invented   D
number and calculation, geometry and astronomy, not to speak of draughts
and dice, and above all writing. Now the king of the whole country at that
time was Thamus, who dwelt in the great city of Upper Egypt which the
Greeks call Egyptian Thebes, while Thamus they call Ammon. To him
came Theuth, and revealed his arts, saying that they ought to be passed on
to the Egyptians in general. Thamus asked what was the use of them all: and
when Theuth explained, he condemned what he thought the bad points   E
and praised what he thought the good. On each art, we are told, Thamus
had plenty of views both for and against; it would take too long to give them
in detail, but when it came to writing Theuth said 'Here, O king, is a
branch of learning that will make the people of Egypt wiser and improve
their memories: my discovery provides a recipe for memory and wisdom'.
But the king answered and said 'O man full of arts, to one is it given to
create the things of art, and to another to judge what measure of harm and
of profit they have for those that shall employ them. And so it is that you, by   275A
reason of your tender regard for the writing that is your offspring, have
declared the very opposite of its true effect. If men learn this, it will implant
forgetfulness in their souls: they will cease to exercise memory because they
rely on that which is written, calling things to remembrance no longer
from within themselves, but by means of external marks; what you have
discovered is a recipe not for memory, but for reminder. And it is no true
wisdom that you offer your disciples, but only its semblance; for by telling
them of many things without teaching them you will make them seem to   B
know much, while for the most part they know nothing; and as men filled,
not with wisdom, but with the conceit of wisdom, they will be a burden to
their fellows.'

PHAEDRUS. It is easy for you Socrates, to make up tales from Egypt or
anywhere else you fancy.

SOCRATES. Oh, but the authorities of the temple of Zeus at Dodona, my
friend, said that the first prophetic utterances came from an oak-tree. In
fact the people of those days, lacking the wisdom of you young people, were
content in their simplicity to listen to trees or rocks, provided these told the   C
truth. For you apparently it makes a difference who the speaker is, and what
country he comes from: you don't merely ask whether what he says is true or
false.

PHAEDRUS. I deserve your rebuke, and I agree that the man of Thebes is right
in what he said about writing.

SOCRATES. Then anyone who leaves behind him a written manual, and likewise anyone who takes it over from him, on the supposition that such writing will provide something reliable and permanent, must be exceedingly simple-minded; he must really be ignorant of Ammon's utterance, if

D   he imagines that written words can do anything more than remind one who knows that which the writing is concerned with.

PHAEDRUS. Very true.

SOCRATES. You know, Phaedrus, that's the strange thing about writing, which makes it truly analogous to painting. The painter's products stand before us as though they were alive: but if you question them, they maintain a most majestic silence. It is the same with written words: they seem to talk to you as though they were intelligent, but if you ask them anything about what they say, from a desire to be instructed, they go on telling you just the same

E   thing for ever. And once a thing is put in writing, the composition, whatever it may be, drifts all over the place, getting into the hands not only of those who understand it, but equally of those who have no business with it; it doesn't know how to address the right people, and not address the wrong. And when it is ill-treated and unfairly abused it always needs its parent to come to its help, being unable to defend or help itself.

276A   PHAEDRUS. Once again you are perfectly right.

SOCRATES. But now tell me, is there another sort of discourse, that is brother to the written speech, but of unquestioned legitimacy? Can we see how it originates, and how much better and more effective it is than the other?

PHAEDRUS. What sort of discourse have you now in mind, and what is its origin?

SOCRATES. The sort that goes together with knowledge, and is written in the soul of the learner: that can defend itself, and knows to whom it should speak and to whom it should say nothing.

PHAEDRUS. You mean no dead discourse, but the living speech, the original of which the written discourse may fairly be called a kind of image.

B   SOCRATES. Precisely. And now tell me this: if a sensible farmer had some seeds to look after and wanted them to bear fruit, would he with serious intent plant them during the summer in a garden of Adonis, and enjoy watching it producing fine fruit within eight days? If he did so at all, wouldn't it be in a holiday spirit, just by way of pastime? For serious purposes wouldn't he behave like a scientific farmer, sow his seeds in suitable soil, and be well content if they came to maturity within eight months?

C   PHAEDRUS. I think we may distinguish as you say, Socrates, between what the farmer would do seriously and what he would do in a different spirit.

SOCRATES. And are we to maintain that he who has knowledge of what is just, honourable and good has less sense than the farmer in dealing with his seeds?

PHAEDRUS. Of course not.

SOCRATES. Then it won't be with serious intent that he 'writes them in water' or that black fluid we call ink, using his pen to sow words that can't either speak in their own defence or present the truth adequately.

PHAEDRUS. It certainly isn't likely.

SOCRATES. No, it is not. He will sow his seed in literary gardens, I take it, and D
write when he does write by way of pastime, collecting a store of refreshment both for his own memory, against the day 'when age oblivious comes',
and for all such as tread in his footsteps; and he will take pleasure in
watching the tender plants grow up. And when other men resort to other
pastimes, regaling themselves with drinking-parties and such like, he will
doubtless prefer to indulge in the recreation I refer to.

PHAEDRUS. And what an excellent one it is, Socrates! How far superior to the E
other sort is the recreation that a man finds in words, when he discourses
about justice and the other topics you speak of.

SOCRATES. Yes indeed, dear Phaedrus. But far more excellent, I think, is the
serious treatment of them, which employs the art of dialectic. The
dialectician selects a soul of the right type, and in it he plants and sows his
words founded on knowledge, words which can defend both themselves 277A
and him who planted them, words which instead of remaining barren
contain a seed whence new words grow up in new characters; whereby the
seed is vouchsafed immortality, and its possessor the fullest measure of
blessedness that man can attain unto.

PHAEDRUS. Yes, that is a far more excellent way.

SOCRATES. Then now that that has been settled, Phaedrus, we can proceed to
the other point.

PHAEDRUS. What is that?

SOCRATES. The point that we wanted to look into before we arrived at our
present conclusion. Our intention was to examine the reproach levelled
against Lysias on the score of speech-writing, and therewith the general B
question of speech-writing and what does and does not make it an art. Now
I think we have pretty well cleared up the question of art.

PHAEDRUS. Yes, we did think so, but please remind me how we did it.

SOCRATES. The conditions to be fulfilled are these: first, you must know the
truth about the subject that you speak or write about: that is to say, you must
be able to isolate it in definition, and having so defined it you must next
understand how to divide it into kinds, until you reach the limit of division;
secondly, you must have a corresponding discernment of the nature of the C
soul, discover the type of speech appropriate to each nature, and order and
arrange your discourse accordingly, addressing a variegated soul in a
variegated style that ranges over the whole gamut of tones, and a simple soul
in a simple style. All this must be done if you are to become competent,
within human limits, as a scientific practitioner of speech, whether you
propose to expound or to persuade. Such is the clear purport of all our
foregoing discussion.

PHAEDRUS. Yes, that was undoubtedly how we came to see the matter.

SOCRATES. And now to revert to our other question, whether the delivery and D
composition of speeches is honourable or base, and in what circumstances
they may properly become a matter of reproach, our earlier conclusions
have, I think, shown—

PHAEDRUS. Which conclusions?

SOCRATES. They have shown that any work, in the past or in the future, whether by Lysias or anyone else, whether composed in a private capacity or in the role of a public man who by proposing a law becomes the author of a political composition, is a matter of reproach to its author (whether or no the reproach is actually voiced) if he regards it as containing important truth of permanent validity. For ignorance of what is a waking vision and what is a mere dream-image of justice and injustice, good and evil, cannot truly be acquitted of involving reproach, even if the mass of men extol it.

PHAEDRUS. No indeed.

SOCRATES. On the other hand, if a man believes that a written discourse on any subject is bound to contain much that is fanciful: that nothing that has ever been written whether in verse or prose merits much serious attention — and for that matter nothing that has ever been spoken in the declamatory fashion which aims at mere persuasion without any questioning or exposition: that in reality such compositions are, at the best, a means of reminding those who know the truth: that lucidity and completeness and serious importance belong only to those lessons on justice and honour and goodness that are expounded and set forth for the sake of instruction, and are veritably written in the soul of the listener: and that such discourses as these ought to be accounted a man's own legitimate children — a title to be applied primarily to such as originate within the man himself, and secondarily to such of their sons and brothers as have grown up aright in the souls of other men: the man, I say, who believes this, and disdains all manner of discourse other than this, is, I would venture to affirm, the man whose example you and I would pray that we might follow.

PHAEDRUS. My own wishes and prayers are most certainly to that effect.

SOCRATES. Then we may regard our literary pastime as having reached a satisfactory conclusion. Do you now go and tell Lysias that we two went down to the stream where is the holy place of the Nymphs, and there listened to words which charged us to deliver a message, first to Lysias and all other composers of discourses, secondly to Homer and all others who have written poetry whether to be read or sung, and thirdly to Solon and all such as are authors of political compositions under the name of laws: to wit, that if any of them has done his work with a knowledge of the truth, can defend his statements when challenged, and can demonstrate the inferiority of his writings out of his own mouth, he ought not to be designated by a name drawn from those writings, but by one that indicates his serious pursuit.

PHAEDRUS. Then what names would you assign him?

SOCRATES. To call him wise, Phaedrus, would, I think, be going too far: the epithet is proper only to a god; a name that would fit him better, and have more seemliness, would be 'lover of wisdom', or something similar.

PHAEDRUS. Yes, that would be quite in keeping.

SOCRATES. On the other hand, one who has nothing to show of more value than the literary works on whose phrases he spends hours, twisting them this way and that, pasting them together and pulling them apart, will rightly, I suggest, be called a poet or speech-writer or law-writer.

PHAEDRUS. Of course.

SOCRATES. Then that is what you must tell your friend.

PHAEDRUS. But what about yourself? What are you going to do? You too have a friend who should not be passed over.

SOCRATES. Who is that?

PHAEDRUS. The fair Isocrates. What will be your message to him, Socrates, and what shall we call him?

SOCRATES. Isocrates is still young, Phaedrus, but I don't mind telling you the future I prophesy for him.   279A

PHAEDRUS. Oh, what is that?

SOCRATES. It seems to me that his natural powers give him a superiority over anything that Lysias has achieved in literature, and also that in point of character he is of a nobler composition; hence it would not surprise me if with advancing years he made all his literary predecessors look like very small fry; that is, supposing him to persist in the actual type of writing in which he engages at present; still more so, if he should become dissatisfied with such work, and a sublimer impulse lead him to do greater things. For that mind of his, Phaedrus, contains an innate tincture of philosophy.

Well then, there's the report I convey from the gods of this place to   B
Isocrates my beloved, and there's yours for your beloved Lysias.

PHAEDRUS. So be it. But let us be going, now that it has become less oppressively hot.

SOCRATES. Oughtn't we first to offer a prayer to the divinities here?

PHAEDRUS. To be sure.

SOCRATES. Dear Pan, and all ye other gods that dwell in this place, grant that I may become fair within, and that such outward things as I have may not war   C
against the spirit within me. May I count him rich who is wise; and as for gold, may I possess so much of it as only a temperate man might bear and carry with him.

Is there anything more we can ask for, Phaedrus? The prayer contents me.

PHAEDRUS. Make it a prayer for me too, since friends have all things in common.

SOCRATES. Let us be going.

Rhetorica ad Alexandrum

The *Rhetorica ad Alexandrum* has come down to us as a work of Aristotle, but it is probably basically pre-Aristotelian. The prevailing view is that it was written by Anaximenes of Lampsacus (ca. 380–320 B.C.), another of Alexander the Great's tutors. The dedicatory preface from "Aristotle to Alexander" (which we have omitted in our selection) is almost certainly a later addition to lend authority to what is essentially a technical handbook. Our excerpt, which opens the treatise proper, reviews the qualities of the different kinds of speeches and outlines their basic techniques.

Rhetorica ad Alexandrum

Public speeches are of three kinds, parliamentary, ceremonial and forensic. 1421b7
Of these there are seven species, exhortation, dissuasion, eulogy, vituperation,
accusation, defence, and investigation—either by itself or in relation to
another species. This list enumerates the species to which public speeches
belong; and we shall employ them in parliamentary debates, in arguing legal
cases about contracts, and in private intercourse. We may be able to discuss
them most readily if we take the species seriatim and enumerate their qualities,
their uses and their arrangement.

First let us discuss exhortation and dissuasion, as these are among the forms
most employed in private conversation and in public deliberation.

Speaking generally, exhortation is an attempt to urge people to some line of
speech or action, and dissuasion is an attempt to hinder people from some line
of speech or action. These being their definitions, one delivering an exhortation must prove that the courses to which he exhorts are just, lawful, expedient,
honourable, pleasant and easily practicable; or failing this, in case the courses
he is urging are disagreeable, he must show that they are feasible, and also that
their adoption is unavoidable. One dissuading must apply hindrance by the
opposite means: he must show that the action proposed is not just, not lawful,
not expedient, not honourable, not pleasant and not practicable; or failing this,
that it is laborious and not necessary. All courses of action admit of both these
descriptions, so that no one having one or other of these sets of fundamental
qualities available need be at a loss for something to say.

These, then, are the lines of argument at which those exhorting or dissuading ought to aim. I will try to define the nature of each, and to show from what
sources we can obtain a good supply of them for our speeches.

What is just is the unwritten custom of the whole or the greatest part of
mankind, distinguishing honourable actions from base ones. The former are to
honour one's parents, do good to one's friends and repay favours to one's
benefactors; for these and similar rules are not enjoined on men by written laws   1422a
but are observed by unwritten custom and universal practice. These then are
the just things.

Law is the common agreement of the state enjoining in writing how men are
to act in various matters.

What is expedient is the preservation of existing good things, or the
acquisition of goods that we do not possess, or the rejection of existing evils, or
the prevention of harmful things expected to occur. Things expedient for
individuals you will classify under body, mind and external possessions.
Expedient for the body are strength, beauty, health; for the mind, courage,
wisdom, justice; expedient external possessions are friends, wealth, property;
and their opposites are inexpedient. Expedient for a state are such things as

Reprinted by permission of the publishers and The Loeb Classical Library from *Rhetorica ad
Alexandrum* (1421b7–1427b37), in *Aristotle: Problems*, vol. 2, trans. H. Rackham, Cambridge, Mass.:
Harvard University Press, 1981.

concord, military strength, property and a plentiful revenue, good and numerous allies. And briefly, we consider all things that resemble these expedient, and things opposite to these inexpedient.

Honourable things are those from which some distinction or some distinguished honour will accrue to the agents, pleasant things are those that cause delight, easy ones those accomplished with very little time and labour and expense, practicable all those that are able to be done, necessary those the performance of which does not rest with ourselves but which are as they are in consequence, as it were, of divine or human compulsion.

Such is the nature of the just, the lawful, the expedient, the honourable, the pleasant, the easy, the practicable and the necessary. We shall find plenty to say about them by using these conceptions in themselves as stated above, and also their analogies and their opposites and the previous judgements of them made by the gods or by men of repute or by judges or by our opponents.

The nature of justice we have, then, already explained. The argument from analogy to the just is as follows: 'As we deem it just to obey our parents, in the same way it behoves our sons to copy the conduct of their fathers,' and 'As it is just to do good in return to those who do us good, so it is just not to do harm to those who do us no evil.' This is the way in which we must take the analogous to the just; and we must illustrate the actual example given from its opposites: 'As it is just to punish those who do us harm, so it is also proper to do good in return to those who do us good.' The judgement of men of repute as to what is just you will take thus: 'We are not alone in hating and doing harm to our enemies, but Athens and Sparta also judge it to be just to punish one's enemies.' This is how you will pursue the topic of the just, taking it in several forms.

The nature of legality we have previously defined; but when it serves our purpose we must bring in the person of the legislator and the terms of the law, and next the argument from analogy to the written law. This may be as follows: 'As the lawgiver has punished thieves with the severest penalties, so also deceivers ought to be severely punished, because they are thieves who steal our minds'; and 'Even as the lawgiver has made the next of kin the heirs of those who die childless, so in the present case I ought to have the disposal of the freedman's estate, because as those who gave him his freedom are dead and gone, it is just that I myself being their next of kin should have control of their freedman.' This is how the topic of analogy to the legal is taken. That of its opposite is taken as follows: 'If the law prohibits the distribution of public property, it is clear that the lawgiver judged all persons who take a share in it to be guilty of an offence.' 'If the laws enjoin that those who direct the affairs of the community honourably and justly are to be honoured, it is clear that they deem those who destroy public property deserving of punishment.' This is the way in which what is legal is illustrated from its opposites. It is illustrated from previous judgements thus: 'Not only do I myself assert that this was the intention of the lawgiver in enacting this law, but also on a former occasion when Lysitheides put forward considerations very similar to those now advanced by me the court voted in favour of this interpretation of the law.' This is how we shall pursue the topic of legality, exhibiting it in several forms.

The nature of expediency has been defined in what came before; and we must include in our speeches with the topics previously mentioned any argument from expediency also that may be available, and pursue the same method as that which we followed in dealing with legality and justice, displaying the expedient also in many forms. The argument from analogy to the expedient may be as follows: 'As it is expedient in war to post the bravest men in the front line, so it is profitable in the constitution of states for the wisest and most just to rank above the multitude; and 'As it is expedient for people in health to be on their guard against contracting disease, so also it is expedient for states enjoying a period of concord to take precautions against the rise of faction.' This is the mode of treatment which you will pursue in multiplying cases of analogy to the expedient. You will demonstrate the expedient from cases of the opposite thus: 'If it is profitable to honour virtuous citizens, it would be expedient to punish vicious ones'; 'If you think it inexpedient for us to go to war with Thebes single-handed, it would be expedient for us to make an alliance with Sparta before going to war with Thebes.' This is how you will demonstrate the expedient from cases of the opposite. The proper way to take the opinion of judges of repute is as follows: 'When Sparta had defeated Athens in war she decided that it would be expedient for herself not to enslave the city; and again when Athens in cooperation with Thebes had it in her power to destroy Sparta, she decided that it would be expedient for her to let it survive.'

1423a

You will have plenty to say on the topics of justice, legality and expediency by pursuing them in this manner. Develop those of honour, facility, pleasure, practicability and necessity in a similar way. These rules will give us plenty to say on these topics.

Next let us determine the number and nature of the subjects about which and the considerations on which we deliberate in council-chambers and in parliaments. If we clearly understand the various classes of these, the business in hand at each debate will itself supply us with arguments specially adapted to it, while we shall readily be able to produce general ideas applicable to the particular matter in hand if we have been familiar with them long before. For these reasons, therefore, we must classify the matters that universally form the subject of our deliberations in common.

To speak summarily therefore, the subjects about which we shall make public speeches are seven in number: our deliberations and speeches in council and in parliament must necessarily deal with either religious ritual, or legislation, or the form of the constitution, or alliances and treaties with other states, or war, or peace, or finance. These, then, being the subjects of our deliberations in council and of our speeches in parliament, let us examine each of them, and consider the ways in which we can deal with them when making a speech.

In speaking about rites of religion, three lines can be taken: either we shall say that we ought to maintain the established ritual as it is, or that we ought to alter it to a more splendid form, or alter it to a more modest form. When we are saying that the established ritual ought to be maintained, we shall draw arguments from considerations of right by saying that in all countries it is deemed wrong to depart from the ancestral customs, that all the oracles enjoin on mankind the performance of their sacrifices in the ancestral manner, and that it is the religious observances of the original founders of cities and builders of the gods' temples that it behoves us most to conserve. Arguing from expediency, we shall say that the performance of the sacrifices in the ancestral manner will be advantageous either for individual citizens or for the community on the ground of economy, and that it will profit the citizens in respect of courage because if they are escorted in religious processions by heavy infantry, cavalry and light-armed troops the pride that they will take in this will make them more courageous. We can urge it on the ground of honour if it has resulted in the festivals being celebrated with so much splendour; on the ground of pleasure if a certain elaboration has been introduced into the sacrifices of the gods merely as a spectacle; on the ground of practicability if there has been neither deficiency nor extravagance in the celebrations. These are the lines we must pursue when we are advocating the established order, basing our considerations on the arguments already stated or arguments similar to them, and on such explanation of our case as is feasible.

When we are advocating the alteration of the sacrificial rites in the direction of greater splendour, we shall find plausible arguments for changing the ancestral institutions in saying (1) that to add to what exists already is not to destroy but to amplify the established order; (2) that in all probability even the gods show more benevolence towards those who pay them more honour; (3) that even our forefathers used not to conduct the sacrifices always on the same lines, but regulated their religious observances both private and public with an eye to the occasions and to the prosperity of their circumstances; (4) that this is the manner in which we administer both our states and our private households in all the rest of our affairs as well; (5) and also specify any benefit or distinction or pleasure that will accrue to the state if these recommendations are carried out, developing the subject in the manner explained in the former cases. When, on the other hand, we are advocating a reduction to a more modest form, we must first (1) direct our remarks to the condition of the times and show how the public are less prosperous now than they were previously; then argue (2) that probably it is not the cost of the sacrifices but the piety of those who offer them that give pleasure to the gods; (3) that people who do a thing that is beyond their capacity are judged by both gods and men to be guilty of great folly; (4) that questions of public expenditure turn not only on the human factor but also on the good or bad state of finance. These, then, and similar lines of argument will be available to support our proposals with regard to sacrifices. Let us now define what is the best form of sacrifice, in order that we may know how to frame proposals and pass laws for its regulation. The best of all sacrificial ceremonies is one organized in a manner that is pious towards the gods, moderate in expense, of military benefit, and brilliant as a spectacle. It will show piety to the gods if the ancestral ritual is preserved; it will be moderate in expense if not all the offerings carried in procession are used up; brilliant as a spectacle if lavish use is made of gold and things of that sort which are not used up in the celebration; of military advantage if cavalry and infantry in full array march in the procession.

These considerations will provide us with the finest ways of organizing the ceremonies of religion; and what has been said before will inform us of the lines that may be followed in public speeches about the various forms of religious celebration.

Let us next in a similar manner discuss the subject of law and the constitution of the state. Laws may be briefly described as common agreements of a state, defining and prescribing in writing various rules of conduct.

In democracies legislation should make the general run of minor offices elected by lot (for that prevents party faction) but the most important offices elected by the vote of the community; under this system the people having sovereign power to bestow the honours on whom they choose will not be jealous of those who obtain them, while the men of distinction will the more cultivate nobility of character, knowing that it will be advantageous for them to stand in good repute with their fellow-citizens. This is how the election of officials should be regulated by law in a a democracy. A detailed discussion of the rest of the administration would be a laborious task; but to speak summarily, precautions must be taken to make the laws deter the multitude from plotting against the owners of landed estates and engender in the wealthy an ambition to spend money on the public services. This the law might effect if some offices were reserved for the propertied classes, as a return for what they spent on public objects, and if among the poorer people the laws paid more respect to the tillers of the soil and the sailor class than to the city rabble, in order that the wealthy may be willing to undertake public services and the multitude may devote itself to industry and not to cadging. In addition to this there should be strict laws laid down prohibiting the distribution of public lands and the confiscation of property on the decease of the owners, and severe penalties should be imposed on those who transgress these enactments. A public burial-ground in a fine situation outside the city should be assigned to those who fall in war, and their sons should receive public maintenance till they come of age. Such should be the nature of the legal system enacted in a democracy.

In the case of oligarchies, the laws should assign the offices on an equal footing to all those sharing in citizenship. Election to most of the offices should be by lot, but for the most important it should be by vote, under oath, with a secret ballot and very strict regulations. The penalties enacted for those attempting to insult any of the citizens should in an oligarchy be very heavy, as the multitude resents insolent treatment more than it is annoyed by exclusion from office. Also differences between the citizens should be settled as quickly as possible and not allowed to drag on; and the mob should not be brought together from the country to the city, because such gatherings lead to the masses making common cause and overthrowing the oligarchies.

And, speaking generally, the laws in a democracy should hinder the many from plotting designs upon the property of the wealthy, and in an oligarchy they should deter those who have a share in the government from treating the weaker men with insolence and toadying to their fellow-citizens. These considerations will inform you of the objects at which the laws and framework of the constitution of the state should aim.

One who wishes to advocate a law has to prove that it will be equal for the citizens, consistent with the other laws, and advantageous for the state, best of all as promoting concord, or failing that, as contributing to the noble qualities

b

of the citizens or to the public revenues or to the good repute of the commonwealth or the power of the state or something else of the kind. In speaking against a proposal the points to consider are, first, is the law not impartial? next, will it be really at variance with the other laws and not in agreement with them? and in addition, instead of promoting any of the objects stated, will it on the contrary be detrimental to them?

This will supply us with plenty of material for making proposals and speeches about laws and the constitution of the commonwealth.

We will proceed to the consideration of alliances and covenants with other states. Covenants must necessarily be framed in accordance with regulations and common agreements; and it is necessary to secure allies on occasions when people by themselves are weak or when a war is expected, or to make an alliance with one nation because it is thought that this will deter another nation from war. These and a number of additional similar reasons are the grounds for making allies; and when one wishes to support the formation of an alliance it is necessary to show that the situation is of this nature, and to prove if possible that the contracting nation is reliable in character, and has done the state some service previously, and is very powerful and a near neighbour, or failing this, you must collect together whichever of these advantages do exist. When you are opposing the alliance you can show first that it is not necessary to make it now, secondly that the proposed allies are not really reliable, thirdly that they have treated us badly before, or if not, that they are remote in locality and not really able to come to our assistance on the suitable occasions. From these and similar considerations we shall be well supplied with arguments to use in opposing and in advocating alliances.

Again, let us in the same manner pick out the most important considerations on the question of peace and war. The following are the arguments for making war on somebody: that we have been wronged in the past, and now that opportunity offers ought to punish the wrongdoers, or, that we are being wronged now, and ought to go to war in our own defence — or in defence of our kinsmen or of our benefactors; or, that our allies are being wronged and we ought to go to their help; or, that it is to the advantage of the state in respect of glory or wealth or power or the like. When we are exhorting people to go to war we should bring together as many of these arguments as possible, and afterwards show that most of the factors on which success in war depends are on the side of those whom we are addressing. Success is always due either to the favour of the gods which we call good fortune, or to man-power and efficiency, or financial resources, or wise generalship, or to having good allies, or to natural advantages of locality. When exhorting people to war we shall select and put forward those among these and similar topics that are most relevant to the situation, belittling the resources of the adversaries and magnifying and amplifying our own.

If, on the other hand, we are trying to prevent a war that is impending, we must first employ arguments to prove either that no grievance exists at all or that the grievances are small and negligible; next we must prove that it is not expedient to go to war, by enumerating the misfortunes that befall mankind in war, and in addition we must show that the factors conducive to victory in war (which are those that were enumerated just above) are more to be found on the

1425a

side of the enemy. These are the considerations to be employed to avert a war that is impending. When we are trying to stop a war that has already begun, if those whom we are advising are getting the upper hand, the first thing to say is that sensible people should not wait till they have a fall but should make peace while they have the upper hand, and next that it is the nature of war to ruin many even of those who are successful in it, whereas it is the nature of peace to save the vanquished while allowing the victors to enjoy the prizes for which they went to war; and we must point out how many and how incalculable are the changes of fortune that occur in war. Such are the considerations to be employed in exhorting to peace those who are gaining the upper hand in a war. Those who have encountered a reverse we must urge to make peace on the ground of what has actually happened to them, and on the ground that they ought to learn from their misfortunes not to be exasperated with their wrongful aggressors, and because of the dangers that have already resulted from not making peace, and because it would be better to sacrifice a portion of their possessions to the stronger power than to be vanquished in war and lose their lives as well as their property. And briefly, we have to realize that it is the way of all mankind to bring their wars with one another to an end either when they think that their adversaries' claims are just, or when they quarrel with their allies or grow tired of the war or afraid of the enemy, or when internal faction breaks out among them.

Consequently if you collect those among all of these and similar points that are most closely related to the facts, you will not be at a loss for appropriate matter for a speech about war and peace.

It still remains for us to discuss finance. The first thing to be considered is whether any part of the national property has been neglected, and is neither producing revenue in or set apart for the service of religion. I refer, for example, to neglect of some public places the sale or lease of which to private citizens might bring revenue to the state; for that is a very common source of income. If nothing of this sort is available, it is necessary to have a system of taxation based on property qualifications, or for the poor to be under the duty of rendering bodily service in emergencies while the rich furnish money and the craftsmen arms. To put it briefly, when introducing financial proposals one must say that they are fair to the citizens, permanent and productive, and that the plans of the opposition have the opposite qualities.

What has been said has shown us the subjects that we shall employ in parliamentary speeches, and the portions of those subjects that we shall use in composing speeches of exhortation and of dissuasion. Next let us put forward for our consideration the eulogistic and vituperative species of oratory.

The eulogistic species of oratory consists, to put it briefly, in the amplification of creditable purposes and actions and speeches and the attribution of qualities that do not exist, while the vituperative species is the opposite, the minimization of creditable qualities and the amplification of discreditable ones. Praiseworthy things are those that are just, lawful, expedient, noble, pleasant and easy to accomplish (the exact nature of these qualities and where to find materials for enlarging on them has been stated in an earlier passage. When eulogizing one must show in one's speech that one of these things

b

1426a

belongs to the person in question or to his actions, as directly effected by him or produced through his agency or incidentally resulting from his action or done as a means to it or involving it as an indispensable condition of its performance; and similarly in vituperating one must show that the qualities opposite to these belong to the person vituperated. Instances of incidental result are bodily health resulting from devotion to athletics, loss of health as a result of a neglect of exercise, increased intellectual ability resulting from the pursuit of philosophy, destitution resulting from neglect of one's affairs. Examples of things done as a means are when men endure many toils and dangers for the sake of receiving a wreath of honour from their compatriots, or neglect everyone else for the sake of gratifying the persons they are in love with. Examples of indispensable conditions are a supply of sailors as indispensable for a naval victory and the act of drinking as indispensable for intoxication. By pursuing such topics in the same manner as those discussed before you will have a good supply of matter for eulogy and vituperation.

To put it briefly, you will be able to amplify and minimize all such topics by pursuing the following method. First you must show, as I lately explained, that the actions of the person in question have produced many bad, or good, results. This is one method of amplification. A second method is to introduce a previous judgement—a favourable one if you are praising, an unfavourable one if you are blaming—and then set your own statement beside it and compare them with one another, enlarging on the strongest points of your own case and the weakest ones of the other and so making your own case appear a strong one. A third way is to set in comparison with the thing you are saying the smallest of the things that fall into the same class, for thus your case will appear magnified, just as men of medium height appear taller when standing by the side of men shorter than themselves. Also the following way of amplifying will be available in all cases. Supposing a given thing has been judged a great good, if you mention something that is its opposite, it will appear a great evil; and similarly supposing something is considered a great evil, if you mention its opposite, it will appear a great good. Another possible way of magnifying good or bad actions is if you prove that the agent acted intentionally, arguing that he had long premeditated doing the acts, that he repeatedly set about doing them, that he went on doing them a long time, that no one else had attempted them before, that he did them in conjunction with persons whom no one else had acted with or in succession to persons whom no one else had followed, that he was acting willingly, that he was acting deliberately, that we should all be happy, or unfortunate, if we all acted like him. One must also argue one's case by employing comparison, and amplify it by building up one point on another, as follows: 'It is probable that anybody who looks after his friends, also honours his own parents; and anybody who honours his parents will also wish to benefit his own country.' And in brief, if you prove a man responsible for many things, whether good or bad, they will bulk large in appearance. You must also consider whether the matter bulks larger when divided up into parts or when stated as a whole, and state it in whichever way it makes a bigger show. By pursuing these methods in amplifications you will be able to make them most numerous and most effective.

To minimize either good points or bad ones by your speeches you will pursue the opposite method to that which we have described in the case of magnifying—best of all, if you prove the person not to be responsible at all, or failing that, only responsible for the fewest and smallest things possible.

These rules instruct us how we are to amplify or minimize whatever matters we are bringing forward for eulogy or vituperation. The materials for amplification are useful in the other species of oratory as well, but it is in eulogy and vituperation that they are most efficacious. The above remarks will make us adequately equipped in regard to them.

Let us next in a similar manner define the elements composing and the proper mode of employing the species of oratory used in accusation and defence—the oratory connected with forensic practice. To put it briefly, the oratory of accusation is the recital of errors and offences, and that of defence the refutation of errors and offences of which a man is accused or suspected. These being the functions of each of these species, the line to take in accusing is to say, in a case where your accusation refers to wickedness, that the actions of your adversaries are actually dishonest and illegal and detrimental to the mass of the citizens, and when it refers to folly, that they are detrimental to the agent himself, disgraceful, unpleasant and impracticable. These and similar accusations are the line of attack against persons guilty of wickedness or folly. But accusers must also be careful to notice what are the kinds of offences for which there are punishments fixed by law and which are the offences in regard to which the penalties are decided by the jury. In cases where the law has determined the penalty, the accuser must direct his attention solely to proving that the act has been committed. When the jury assess, he must amplify the offences and the errors of his opponents, and if possible prove that the defendant committed the offence of his own free will, and not from a merely casual intention, but with a very great amount of preparation; or if it is not possible to prove this, but you think the other side will try to prove that the accused made a mistake in some way, or that although intending to act honourably in the matter he failed by bad luck, you must dissipate compassion by telling your audience that men have no business to act first and afterwards say they have made a mistake, but that they ought to look before they leap; and next, that even if the defendant really did make a mistake or have bad luck, it is more proper for him to be punished for his failures and mistakes than a person who has committed neither; moreover, the lawgiver did not let off people who make mistakes but made them liable to justice, or else everybody would be making mistakes. Also say that if they listen to a man who puts up a defence of that sort, they will have many people doing wrong on purpose, as if they bring it off they will be able to do whatever they like, and if they fail they will escape being punished by saying that it was an accident. This is the sort of argument which accusers must employ to dissipate compassion; and, as has been said before, they must employ amplification to show that their opponents' actions have been attended by many bad consequences.

These, then, are the division composing the species of oratory used in accusation.

The defensive species comprises three methods. A defendant must either

1427a

prove that he did none of the things he is charged with; or if he is forced to admit them, he must try to show that what he did was lawful and just and noble and to the public advantage; or if he cannot prove this, he must attempt to gain forgiveness by representing his acts as an error or misfortune, and by showing that only small mischief has resulted from them. You must distinguish between injustice, error, and misfortune: define injustice as the deliberate commission of evil, and say that for offences of that sort the severest penalties should be inflicted; declare that a harmful action done unwittingly is an error; and class a failure to carry out some honourable intention, if it is not due to oneself but to other people or to luck, as misfortune. Also say that unjust conduct is peculiar to wicked people, but that error and misfortune in one's actions is not peculiar to yourself alone but is common to all mankind, including the members of the jury. You must claim to receive compassion for being forced to plead guilty to a charge of that sort, making out that error and

b   misfortune are shared by your hearers. A defendant must have in view all the offences for which the laws have fixed the punishments and for which the jury assesses the penalties; and in a case where the law fixes the punishments he should show that he did not commit the act at all or that his conduct was lawful and right, whereas when the jury has been made the assessor of the penalty, he should not in the same way deny having committed the act, but try to show that he did his adversary little damage and that that was involuntary.

These and similar arguments will supply us with plenty of material in accusations and defences. It still remains for us to discuss the species of oratory employed in investigation.

Investigation may be summarily defined as the exhibition of certain intentions or actions or words as inconsistent with one another or with the rest of someone's conduct. The investigator must try to find some point in which either the speech that he is investigating is self-contradictory or the actions or the intentions of the person under investigation run counter to one another. This is the procedure—to consider whether perhaps in the past after having first been a friend of somebody he afterwards became his enemy and then became the same man's friend again; or committed some other inconsistent action indicating depravity; or is likely in the future, should opportunities befall him, to act in a manner contrary to his previous conduct. Similarly observe also whether something that he says when speaking now is contrary to what he has said before; and likewise also whether he has ever adopted a policy contrary to his previous professions, or would do so if opportunities offered. And on similar lines you should also take the features in the career of the person under investigation inconsistent with his other habits of conduct that are estimable. By thus pursuing the investigational species of oratory there is no method of investigation that you will leave out.

All the species of oratory have now been distinguished. They are to be employed both separately, when suitable, and jointly, with a combination of their qualities—for though they have very considerable differences, yet in their practical application they overlap. In fact the same is true of them as of the various species of human beings; these also are partly alike and partly different

1427b37 in their appearance and in their perceptions.

Aristotle

Aristotle (384–322 B.C.) opens the *Rhetoric* by likening that art to dialectic (not Plato's philosophic dialectic, which seeks the truth, but the dialectic of conversational argument and discussion). Since the purpose of rhetoric is to find the appropriate means of persuasion on any subject and for any occasion (1.1.14 and 2.1), it must essentially treat proofs which lead to persuasion. Proof *(pistis)* is a very broad term that includes the sense of credibility of an argument as well as the conviction created in the listener. This sort of proof is not the absolute demonstration *(apodeixis)* of scientific reasoning that Aristotle develops in his Organon and that is based on necessary and absolutely true premises, because human beings are normally persuaded by conclusions based on the appearances and probabilities that make up the contexts of everyday life.

The relationship of the logical, scientific demonstrations of syllogistic reasoning to the rhetorical demonstrations of enthymeme and example are discussed in our first selection from the *Prior Analytics*. The rhetorical syllogism or enthymeme is related to the scientific syllogism, and the rhetorical use of examples to the inductive process. According to Aristotle, the reasoning employed by both dialectic and rhetoric is based on probabilities and generally accepted truths. He calls such reasoning "topical;' that is, it involves the mastery of predetermined mental places *(topoi)*, providing the practitioner with a ready method of choosing arguments, of thinking effectively on his feet. The second and third selections here are from the *Topica* and introduce the reader to the parallel process of dialectical reasoning.

The first selection from the *Rhetoric* opens the treatise and gives Aristotle's overview of the subject, and basic distinctions. Here he observes that there are three main sources of proof in any speech where conviction and persuasion are created: in the speaker's *ēthos* or character, in the audience's *pathos* or emotional reaction, and in the *logos* or intellectual content (1.2.3–6). The opening of Book 2, which follows, develops Aristotle's general theory of ethical and pathetic proofs. Our next four selections from the *Rhetoric* focus on the third source where Aristotle's principle interest and his principle contribution to rhetorical theory lie, the *logos* or content of speeches. They treat essential considerations of proofs and *topoi*, the places to find proofs.

Our final selection begins Aristotle's important discussion of style *(lexis)* in Book 3, where, as in the *Poetics*, the importance of metaphor is emphasized.

Prior Analytics

Induction, Example, Probability, Enthymeme

68b8   It is evident, then, how the terms are conditioned as regards conversions and as representing degrees of preferability and the reverse. We must now observe that not only dialectical and demonstrative syllogisms are effected by means of the figures already described, [1] but also rhetorical syllogisms and in general every kind of mental conviction, whatever form it may take. For all our beliefs are formed either by means of syllogism or from induction.

Induction, or inductive reasoning, consists in establishing a relation between one extreme term and the middle term by means of the other extreme; [2] e.g., if B is the middle term of A and C, in proving by means of C that A applies to B; for this is how we effect inductions. E.g., let A stand for 'long-lived,' B for 'that which has no bile' and C for the long-lived individuals such as man and horse and mule. Then A applies to the whole of C [for every bileless animal is long-lived]. But B, 'not having bile,' also applies to all C. Then if C is convertible with B, i.e., if the middle term is not wider in extension, A must apply to B. For it has been shown above that if any two predicates apply to the same subject and the extreme is convertible with one of them, then the other predicate will also apply to the one which is convertible. We must, however, understand by C the sum of all the particular instances; for it is by taking all of these into account that induction proceeds.

This kind of syllogism is concerned with the first or immediate premiss. Where there is a middle term, the syllogism proceeds by means of the middle; where there is not, it proceeds by induction. There is a sense in which induction is opposed to syllogism, for the latter shows by the middle term that the major extreme applies to the third, while the former shows by means of the third that the major extreme applies to the middle. Thus by nature the syllogism by means of the middle is prior and more knowable; but syllogism by induction is more apparent to us.

We have an Example when the major extreme is shown to be applicable to the

Reprinted by permission of the publishers and The Loeb Classical Library from Aristotle, *Prior Analytics* (68b8–69a19, 70a3–70a28), vol. 1, trans. Hugh Tredennick, Cambridge, Mass.: Harvard University Press, 1967.

1. Figures. The *Prior Analytics* systematically treats the laws of inference and develops Aristotle's system of syllogistic reasoning. Figures are the various kinds of syllogism.

2. Term. A syllogism has three terms or parts, one extreme in the major premise, one in the minor, and the middle term in both, making the conclusion possible. Aristotle is clearly less comfortable with and less confident in the power of induction. He even thinks of the inductive process in the context of syllogistic deduction. The problem for him is that, although the conclusions that result from inductions are easier to perceive, they lack the absolute conclusiveness of the results of syllogistic reasoning. Inductions are in a sense always incomplete. We in the twentieth century can easily see the basis for Aristotle's position in our vastly developing knowledge of the sciences, where the ongoing acquisition of new data and the finding and recognition of new particulars regularly require the alteration and even discarding of previous results of inductive observation, the outmoded scientific "laws" of the past.

middle term by means of a term similar to the third.[3] It must be known both that the middle applies to the third term and that the first applies to the term similar to the third. *E.g.*, let A be 'bad,' B 'to make war on neighbours,' C 'Athens against Thebes' and D 'Thebes against Phocis.' Then if we require to prove that war against Thebes is bad, we must be satisfied that war against neighbours is bad. Evidence of this can be drawn from similar examples, *e.g.*, that war by Thebes against Phocis is bad. Then since war against neighbours is bad, and war against Thebes is against neighbours, it is evident that war against Thebes is bad. Now it is evident that B applies to C and D (for they are both examples of making war on neighbours), and A to D (since the war against Phocis did Thebes no good); but that A applies to B will be proved by means of D. The same method will obtain supposing that our conviction that the middle term is related to the extreme is drawn from more than one similar term.

Thus it is evident that an example represents the relation, not of part to whole or of whole to part, but of one part to another, where both are subordinate to the same general term, and one of them is known. It differs from induction in that the latter, as we saw, shows from an examination of all the individual cases that the (major) extreme applies to the middle, and does not connect the conclusion with the (minor) extreme; whereas the example does connect it and does not use all the individual cases for its proof. 69a19

A probability is not the same as a sign. The former is a generally accepted 70a3 premiss; for that which people know to happen or not to happen, or to be or not to be, usually in a particular way, is a probability: *e.g.*, that the envious are malevolent or that those who are loved are affectionate. A sign, however, means a demonstrative premiss which is necessary or generally accepted. That which coexists with something else, or before or after whose happening something else has happened, is a sign of that something's having happened or being.

An enthymeme is a syllogism from probabilities or signs; and a sign can be taken in three ways — in just as many ways as there are of taking the middle term in the several figures: either as in the first figure or as in the second or as in the third.[4] *E.g.*, the proof that a woman is pregnant because she has milk is by the first figure; for the middle term is 'having milk.' A stands for 'pregnant,' B for 'having milk,' and C for 'woman.' The proof that the wise are good because Pittacus was good is by the third figure. A stands for 'good,' B for 'the wise,' and C for Pittacus. Then it is true to predicate both A and B of C; only we do not state the latter, because we know it, whereas we formally assume the former. The proof that a woman is pregnant because she is sallow is intended to be by the middle figure; for since sallowness is a characteristic of women in pregnancy, and is associated with this

3. Example. The point of the illustrations here is that particular examples are related to each other horizontally by recognizable similarity. Thus (using Aristotle's designations), being satisfied that *B* is the general truth that includes *C*, our recognition of a basic similarity between *C* and *D* will allow us to draw the same conclusion (*A*) for *D* as we did for *C*.

4. Enthymeme (literally "a thing held in the mind"). The "several figures" of the examples that follow are based on the three figures or kinds of syllogism Aristotle develops.

particular woman, they suppose that she is proved to pregnant. A stands for 'sallowness,' B for 'being pregnant' and C for 'woman.'

If only one premiss is stated, we get only a sign; but if the other premiss is assumed as well, we get a syllogism, *e.g.*, that Pittacus is high-minded, because those who love honour are high-minded, and Pittacus loves honour; or again that 70a28 the wise are good, because Pittacus is good and also wise.

Topica

Kinds of Reasoning

The purpose of the present treatise is to discover a method by which we shall 100a18 be able to reason from generally accepted opinions about any problem set before us and shall ourselves, when sustaining an argument, avoid saying anything self-contradictory. First, then, we must say what reasoning is and what different kinds of it there are, in order that dialectical reasoning may be apprehended; for it is the search for this that we are undertaking in the treatise which lies before us.

Reasoning is a discussion in which, certain things having been laid down, something other than these things necessarily results through them. Reasoning is *demonstration* when it proceeds from premises which are true and primary or of such a kind that we have derived our original knowledge of them through premises which are primary and true. Reasoning is *dialectical* which reasons from generally accepted opinions. Things are true and primary which command belief through themselves and not through anything else; for regarding the first principles of science it is unnecessary to ask any further question as to 'why,' but each principle should of itself command belief. Generally accepted opinions, on the other hand, are those which commend themselves to all or to the majority or to the wise — that is, to all of the wise or to the majority or to the most famous and distinguished of them. Reasoning is *contentious* if it is based on opinions which appear to be generally accepted but are not really so, or if it merely appears to be based on opinions which are, or appear to be, generally accepted. For not every opinion which appears to be generally accepted is actually so accepted. For in none of the so-called generally accepted opinions is the illusory appearance entirely manifest, as happens in the case of the principles of contentious arguments; for usually the nature of untruth in these is immediately obvious to those who have even a small power of comprehension. Therefore, of the above-mentioned contentious reasonings the former should actually be called reasoning, but the other should be called, not reasoning, but contentious reasoning, because it appears to reason but does not really do so.

Furthermore, besides all the above-mentioned reasonings, there are false reasonings based on premises peculiar to certain sciences, as happens in geometry and the sciences kindred to it. For this kind seems to differ from the reasonings already mentioned; for the man who constructs a false figure reasons neither from true and primary premises nor from generally accepted opinions; for he does not fall within the definition, since he does not take as his premises either universally accepted opinions or those which commend themselves to the majority or to the wise — that is to all of the wise or to the majority or to the most distinguished of them, — but his process of reasoning is

Reprinted by permission of the publishers and The Loeb Classical Library from Aristotle, *Topica* (100a18–102b26, 108b34–109a33, 114b25–115a24), vol. 2, trans. E. S. Forster, Cambridge, Mass.: Harvard University Press, 1966.

based on assumptions which are peculiar to the science but not true; for he reasons falsely either by describing the semicircles improperly or by drawing lines as they should not be drawn.

Let the above then be a description in outline of the different kinds of reasoning. In general, as regards all those already mentioned and to be mentioned hereafter, let this much distinction suffice for us, since we do not propose to give the exact definition of any of them but merely wish to describe them in outline, considering it quite enough, in accordance with the method which we have set before us, to be able to recognize each of them in some way or other.

After the above remarks the next point is to explain for how many and for what purposes this treatise is useful. They are three in number, mental training, conversations and the philosophic sciences. That it is useful for mental training is obvious on the face of it; for, if we have a method, we shall be able more easily to argue about the subject proposed. It is useful for conversations, because, having enumerated the opinions of the majority, we shall be dealing with people on the basis of their own opinions, not of those of others, changing the course of any argument which they appear to us to be using wrongly. For the philosophic sciences it is useful, because, if we are able to raise difficulties on both sides, we shall more easily discern both truth and falsehood on every point. Further, it is useful in connexion with the ultimate bases of each science; for it is impossible to discuss them at all on the basis of the principles peculiar to the science in question, since the principles are primary in relation to everything else, and it is necessary to deal with them through the generally accepted opinions on each point. This process belongs peculiarly, or most appropriately to dialectic; for, being of the nature of an investigation, it lies along the path to the principles of all methods of inquiry.

We shall possess the method completely when we are in a position similar to that in which we are with regard to rhetoric and medicine and other such faculties; that is to say, when we carry out our purpose with every available means. For neither will the rhetorician seek to persuade nor the physician to heal by every expedient; but if he omits none of the available means, we shall say that he possesses the science in an adequate degree.

We must, then, first consider on what bases our method rests; for if we could grasp to how many and to what kind of objects our arguments are directed and on what bases they rest, and how we are to be well provided with these, we should sufficiently attain the end which is set before us. Now the bases of arguments are equal in number and identical with the subjects of reasonings. For arguments arise from 'propositions,' while the subjects of reasonings are 'problems.' Now every proposition and every problem indicates either a genus or a peculiarity or an accident; for the differentia also, being generic in character, should be ranged with the genus. But since part of the peculiarity indicates the essence and part does not do so, let the peculiarity be divided into the two above-mentioned parts and let that which indicates the essence be called a 'definition,' and let the remaining part be termed a 'property' in accordance with the nomenclature usually assigned in these cases. It is clear therefore, from what has been said, that, as a result of the division just made, there are four alternatives in all, either property or definition or genus or accident. But let no one suppose that we mean that each of these stated by itself is a proposition or a problem, but only that problems and propositions are made up of these. The problem and the proposition differ in the way in which they are stated. If we say, "Is not 'pedestrian biped animal' a definition of man?" or "Is not 'animal' the genus of man?" a proposition is formed. But if we say, "Is 'pedestrain biped animal' a definition of man, or not?" a problem is formed. Similary too with the other cases. It naturally follows, therefore, that the problems and the propositions are equal in number; for you will be able to make a problem out of any proposition by altering the way in which it is stated.

We must next say what definition, property, genus and accident are. A *definition* is a phrase indicating the essence of something. The definition is asserted either as a phrase used in place of a term, or as a phrase used in place of a phrase; for it is possible to define some things also which are indicated by a phrase. But it is obvious that everyone who makes an assertion by means of a term in any way whatever, does not assert the definition of the thing, because every definition is a phrase of a certain kind. However, such a statement as "That which is seemly is beautiful" must also be put down as being 'definitory,' and likewise the question "Are sensation and knowledge the same thing or different?" For when we are dealing with definitions, we spend most of our time discussing whether things are the same or different. In a word, let us call 'definitory' everything which comes under the same kind of inquiry as do definitions; and it is self-evident that all the above-mentioned instances are of this kind. For when we can argue that things are the same or that they are different, we shall by the same method have an abundance of arguments for dealing with definitions also; for when we have shown that a thing is not the same as another we shall have destroyed the definition. The converse of what we have just said does not, however, hold good; for it is not enough for the construction of a definition to show that one thing is the same as another; but, in order to destroy a definition, it is enough to show that it is not the same.

A *property* is something which does not show the essence of a thing but belongs to it alone and is predicated convertibly of it. For example, it is a property of man to be capable of learning grammar; for if a certain being is a man, he is capable of learning grammar, and if he is capable of learning grammar, he is a man. For no one calls anything a property which can possibly belong to something else; for example, he does not say that sleep is a property of man, even though at one moment it might happen to belong to him only. If, therefore, any such thing were to be called a property, it will be so called not absolutely but as at a certain time or in a certain relation; for 'to be on the right-hand side' is a property at a certain time, and 'biped' is actually assigned as a property in a certain relation, for example, as a property of man in relation to a horse or a dog. That nothing which can possibly belong to something other than a certain thing is a convertible predicate of that thing is obvious; for it does not necessarily follow that if anything is sleeping it is a man.

A *genus* is that which is predicated in the category of essence of several things which differ in kind. Predicates in the category of essence may be described as such things as are fittingly contained in the reply of one who has been asked "What is the object before you?" For example, in the case of man, if someone is asked what the object before him is, it is fitting for him to say "An animal." The question whether one thing is in the same genus as another thing or in a different one, is also a 'generic' question; for such a question also falls under the same kind of inquiry as the genus. For having argued that 'animal' is the genus of man and likewise also of ox, we shall have argued that they are in the same genus; but if we show that it is the genus of the one but not of the other, we shall have argued that they are not in the same genus.

An *accident* is that which is none of these things—neither definition, nor property, nor genus—but still belongs to the thing. Also it is something which can belong and not belong to any one particular thing; for example, 'a sitting position' can belong or not belong to some one particular thing. This is likewise true of 'whiteness'; for there is nothing to prevent the same thing being at one time white and at another not white. The second of these definitions of accident is the better; for when the first is enunciated, it is necessary, if one is to understand it, to know beforehand what is meant by 'definition' and 'genus' and 'property,' whereas the second suffices of itself to enable us to know what is meant without anything more. We may place also in the category of accident comparisons of things with one another, when they are described in terms derived in any way from accident; for example, the questions "Is the honourable or the expedient preferable?" and "Is the life of virtue or the life of enjoyment more pleasant?" and any other question which happens to be expressed in a similar kind of way; for in all such cases the question is to which of the two does the predicate more properly belong as an accident. It is self-evident that nothing prevents the accident from being temporarily or relatively a property; for example, the position of sitting, though it is an accident, will at the time be a property, when a man is the only person seated, while, if he is not the only person seated, it will be a property in relation to any persons who are not seated. Thus nothing prevents the accident from becoming both a relative

102b26   and a temporary property, but it will never be a property absolutely.

Two Major *Topoi:* Universals-Particulars and Greater-Lesser

108b34   Some problems are universal, other particular. Examples of universal problems are "Every pleasure is good," and "No pleasure is good": examples of particular problems are "Some pleasure is good," and "Some pleasure is not good." Universally constructive and destructive methods are common to both kinds of problem; for when we have shown that some predicate belongs in all instances, we shall also have shown that it belongs in some particular instance, and, similarly, if we show that it does not belong in any instance, we shall also have shown that it does not belong in every instance. First, then, we must speak of universally destructive methods, because such methods are common both to universal and to particular problems and because people bring forward theses asserting the presence of a predicate rather than its absence, while those who are arguing against them seek to demolish them. It is very difficult to convert an appropriate appellation which is derived from an 'accident'; 'for only in the case of accidents can something be predicated conditionally and not universally.[1] For conversion must necessarily be based on the definition and the property and the genus. For example, if "to be a biped pedestrian animal is an attribute of A," it will be true to say by conversion that "A is a biped pedestrian animal." So too if the appellation is derived from genus; for, if "to be an animal is an attribute of A," then "A is an animal." The same thing occurs in the case of a property; if "to be receptive of grammar is an attribute of B," then "B will be receptive of grammar." For it is impossible for any of these attributes to belong or not belong in part only; but they must belong or not belong absolutely. In the case of accidents, however, there is nothing to prevent an attribute belonging in part only (*e.g.*, whiteness or justice), and so it is not enough to show that whiteness or justice is an attribute of a man in order to show that he is white or just; for it is possible to argue that he is only partly white or just. In the case of accidents, therefore, conversion is not necessarily possible.

We must also define the errors which occur in problems, which are of two kinds, being due either to misrepresentation or to violation of the established use of language. Those who employ misrepresentation and assert that a thing has some attribute which it has not, commit error; while those who call things by names which do not belong to them (*e.g.*, calling a plane-tree a man) violate the established nomenclature.   109a33

Again, you must take the case of like things and see if the same is true of   114b25
them; for example, if one form of knowledge deals with several subjects, so also does one form of opinion, and if to have sight is to see, then also to have hearing is to hear, and so with the other examples both of things which are like and of things that are generally considered to be like. This commonplace is useful for both purposes; for if something is true of one of the like things, it is also true of the others, but if it is not true of one of them, it is not true of the others either. You must also see whether conditions are alike in the case of a single thing and a number of things; for there is sometimes a discrepancy. For example, if to 'know' a thing is to 'think of' a thing, then to 'know many things' is to 'think of many things.' But this is not so; for it is possible to know many things and not to be thinking of them. If, therefore, the second statement is not true, then the first, which dealt with a single thing, namely, 'to know a thing' is 'to think of a thing,' is not true either.

Moreover you must derive material from the greater and the less degrees. There are four commonplaces connected with the greater and the less degrees. One is to see whether the greater degree follows the greater degree; for

---

1. Predicates and accidents. Predicates or categories are what can be said or asserted about any subject. (Aristotle's *On Interpretation* discusses how to put subjects and predicates together.) There are ten of them, treated in the *Categories*: substance/essence, quality, quantity, relation, place, time, situation, state, action/activity, and suffering/passivity. From these Aristotle develops the four predicables (definition, property, genus, and accident) described in the previous selection (*Topica* 1.4–5).

example, if pleasure is good, and greater pleasure is a greater good, and if to commit injustice is an evil, whether to commit a greater injustice is also a greater evil. This commonplace is useful for both purposes; for, if the increase of the accident follows the increase of the subject, as described above, it is obvious that it is really an accident of the subject, but if it does not follow it, it is not an accident of it. This result must be obtained by induction. Here is another commonplace; when one predicate is applied to two subjects, then, if it does not belong to the one to which there is the greater likelihood of its belonging, it does not belong either to the one to which it is less likely to belong; and if it belongs to that to which it is less likely to belong, it belongs also to that to which it is more likely to belong. Again, if two predicates are applied to one subject, then, if the one which is more generally regarded as belonging to the one subject does not belong, neither does that which is less generally so regarded; or, if the predicate which is less generally regarded as belonging does belong, then so also does that which is more generally so regarded. Further, when two predicates are applied to two subjects, if the predicate which is more generally regarded as belonging to one of the subjects does not belong, neither does the other predicate belong to the other subject; or, if the predicate which is less generally regarded as belonging to the one subject does belong, then the other predicate also belongs to the other subject.

Furthermore, you can derive material from the fact that a predicate belongs, or is generally regarded as belonging, in a like degree, in three ways, namely, those described in the last three commonplaces already mentioned in connexion with the greater degree. For, if one predicate belongs, or is generally regarded as belonging, to two subjects in a like degree, then, if it does not belong to the one, it does not belong to the other either, and, if it belongs to the one, it belongs to the other also. Or, if two predicates belong in a like degree to the same subject, if the one does not belong, neither does the other, whereas, if the one does belong, so also does the other. The same thing also happens if two predicates belong in a like degree to two subjects; for if the one predicate does not belong to the one subject, neither does the other predicate belong to the other subject, while, if the one predicate belongs to the one subject, then the
115a24   other predicate also belongs to the other subject.

Rhetoric

Definition and Kinds of Rhetoric

Rhetoric is a counterpart of Dialectic; for both have to do with matters that 1354a1
are in a manner within the cognizance of all men and not confined to any
special science. Hence all men in a manner have a share of both; for all, up to a
certain point, endeavour to criticize or uphold an argument, to defend
themselves or to accuse. Now, the majority of people do this either at random
or with a familiarity arising from habit. But since both these ways are possible,
it is clear that matters can be reduced to a system, for it is possible to examine
the reason why some attain their end by familiarity and others by chance; and
such an examination all would at once admit to be the function of an art.

Now, previous compilers of "Arts" of Rhetoric have provided us with only a
small portion of this art, for proofs are the only things in it that come within
the province of art; everything else is merely an accessory. And yet they say
nothing about enthymemes which are the body of proof, but chiefly devote
their attention to matters outside the subject; for the arousing of prejudice,
compassion, anger, and similar emotions has no connexion with the matter in
hand, but is directed only to the dicast.[1] The result would be that, if all trials
were now carried on as they are in some States, especially those that are well
administered, there would be nothing left for the rhetorician to say. For all
men either think that all the laws ought so to prescribe, or in fact carry out the
principle and forbid speaking outside the subject, as in the court of Areopagus,
and in this they are right. For it is wrong to warp the dicast's feelings, to arouse
him to anger, jealousy, or compassion, which would be like making the rule
crooked which one intended to use. Further, it is evident that the only business
of the litigant is to prove that the fact in question is or is not so, that it has
happened or not; whether it is important or unimportant, just or unjust, in all
cases in which the legislator has not laid down a ruling, is a matter for the
dicast himself to decide; it is not the business of the litigants to instruct him.

First of all, therefore, it is proper that laws, properly enacted, should
themselves define the issue of all cases as far as possible, and leave as little as
possible to the discretion of the judges; in the first place, because it is easier to
find one or a few men of good sense, capable of framing laws and pronouncing
judgements, than a large number; secondly, legislation is the result of long
consideration, whereas judgements are delivered on the spur of the moment,
so that it is difficult for the judges properly to decide questions of justice or
expediency. But what is most important of all is that the judgement of the
legislator does not apply to a particular case, but is universal and applies to the

Reprinted by permission of the publishers and The Loeb Classical Library from Aristotle, *The "Art" of
Rhetoric* (1354a1–1360b13, 1377b12–1378a29, 1362a15–1365b28, 1367b28–1367b36, 1368a10–
1369b32, 1375a22–1375a25, 1391b7–1403b5, 1403b6–1404a19, 1404b1–1405b34), vol. 22, trans. John
Henry Freese, Cambridge, Mass.: Harvard University Press, 1975.

1. Dicast. In Athens the dicasts tried and passed judgment on all kinds of cases and questions at law.
They were appointed by lot from the body of free citizens over thirty years of age.

future, whereas the member of the public assembly and the dicast have to decide present and definite issues, and in their case love, hate, or personal interest is often involved, so that they are no longer capable of discerning the truth adequately, their judgement being obscured by their own pleasure or pain.

All other cases, as we have just said, should be left to the authority of the judge as seldom as possible, except where it is a question of a thing having happened or not, of its going to happen or not, of being or not being so; this must be left to the discretion of the judges, for it is impossible for the legislator to foresee such questions. If this is so, it is obvious that all those who definitely lay down, for instance, what should be the contents of the exordium or the narrative, or of the other parts of the discourse, are bringing under the rules of art what is outside the subject; for the only thing to which their attention is devoted is how to put the judge into a certain frame of mind. They give no account of the artificial proofs, which make a man a master of rhetorical argument.[2]

Hence, although the method of deliberative and forensic Rhetoric is the same, and although the pursuit of the former is nobler and more worthy of a statesman than that of the latter, which is limited to transactions between private citizens, they say nothing about the former, but without exception endeavour to bring forensic speaking under the rules of art. The reason of this is that in public speaking it is less worth while to talk of what is outside the subject, and that deliberative oratory lends itself to trickery less than forensic, because it is of more general interest. For in the assembly the judges decide upon their own affairs, so that the only thing necessary is to prove the truth of the statement of one who recommends a measure, but in the law courts this is not sufficient; there it is useful to win over the hearers, for the decision concerns other interests than those of the judges, who, having only themselves to consider and listening merely for their own pleasure, surrender to the pleaders but do not give a real decision. That is why, as I have said before, in many places the law prohibits speaking outside the subject in the law courts, whereas in the assembly the judges themselves take adequate precautions against this.

It is obvious, therefore, that a system arranged according to the rules of art is only concerned with proofs; that proof is a sort of demonstration, since we are most strongly convinced when we suppose anything to have been demonstrated; that rhetorical demonstration is an enthymeme, which, generally speaking, is the strongest of rhetorical proofs; and lastly, that the enthymeme is a kind of syllogism. Now, as it is the function of Dialectic as a whole, or of one of its parts, to consider every kind of syllogism in a similar manner, it is clear that he who is most capable of examining the matter and forms of a syllogism will be in the highest degree a master of rhetorical argument, if to this he adds a knowledge of the subjects with which enthymemes deal and the differences

---

2. Artificial proofs are those that are subject to and come under the art of rhetoric. Inartificial proofs (the testimony elicited from witnesses, evidence of signs, etc.) cannot be controlled by the art of the rhetor. See the discussion that follows in 1.2.

between them and logical syllogisms. For, in fact, the true and that which resembles it come under the purview of the same faculty, and at the same time men have a sufficient natural capacity for the truth and indeed in most cases attain to it; wherefore one who divines well in regard to the truth will also be able to divine well in regard to probabilities.

It is clear, then, that all other rhetoricians bring under the rules of art what is outside the subject, and have rather inclined to the forensic branch of oratory. Nevertheless, Rhetoric is useful, because the true and the just are naturally superior to their opposites, so that, if decisions are improperly made, they must owe their defeat to their own advocates; which is reprehensible. Further, in dealing with certain persons, even if we possessed the most accurate scientific knowledge, we should not find it easy to persuade them by the employment of such knowledge. For scientific discourse is concerned with instruction, but in the case of such persons instruction is impossible; our proofs and arguments must rest on generally accepted principles, as we said in the *Topics*, when speaking of converse with the multitude. Further, the orator should be able to prove opposites, as in logical arguments; not that we should do both (for one ought not to persuade people to do what is wrong), but that the real state of the case may not escape us, and that we ourselves may be able to counteract false arguments, if another makes an unfair use of them. Rhetoric and Dialectic alone of all the arts prove opposites; for both are equally concerned with them. However, it is not the same with the subject matter, but, generally speaking, that which is true and better is naturally always easier to prove and more likely to persuade. Besides, it would be absurd if it were considered disgraceful not to be able to defend oneself with the help of the body, but not disgraceful as far as speech is concerned, whose use is more characteristic of man than that of the body. If it is argued that one who makes an unfair use of such faculty of speech may do a great deal of harm, this objection applies equally to all good things except virtue, and above all to those things which are most useful, such as strength, health, wealth, general-ship; for as these, rightly used, may be of the greatest benefit, so, wrongly used, they may do an equal amount of harm.

It is thus evident that Rhetoric does not deal with any one definite class of subjects, but, like Dialectic, [is of general application]; also, that it is useful; and further, that its function is not so much to persuade, as to find out in each case the existing means of persuasion. The same holds good in respect to all the other arts. For instance, it is not the function of medicine to restore a patient to health, but only to promote this end as far as possible; for even those whose recovery is impossible may be properly treated. It is further evident that it belongs to Rhetoric to discover the real and apparent means of persuasion, just as it belong to Dialectic to discover the real and apparent syllogism. For what makes the sophist is not the faculty but the moral purpose. But there is a difference: in Rhetoric, one who acts in accordance with sound argument, and one who acts in accordance with moral purpose, are both called rhetoricians; but in Dialectic it is the moral purpose that makes the sophist, the dialectician being one whose arguments rest, not on moral purpose but on the faculty.

Let us now endeavour to treat of the method itself, to see how and by what means we shall be able to attain our objects. And so let us as it were start again, and having defined Rhetoric anew, pass on to the remainder of the subject.

Rhetoric then may be defined as the faculty of discovering the possible means of persuasion in reference to any subject whatever. This is the function of no other of the arts, each of which is able to instruct and persuade in its own special subject; thus, medicine deals with health and sickness, geometry with the properties of magnitudes, arithmetic with number, and similarly with all the other arts and sciences. But Rhetoric, so to say, appears to be able to discover the means of persuasion in reference to any given subject. That is why we say that as an art its rules are not applied to any particular definite class of things.

As for proofs, some are inartificial, others artificial. By the former I understand all those which have not been furnished by ourselves but were already in existence, such as witnesses, tortures, contracts, and the like; by the latter, all that can be constructed by system and by our own efforts. Thus we have only to make use of the former, whereas we must invent the latter.

Now the proofs furnished by the speech are of three kinds. The first depends upon the moral character of the speaker, the second upon putting the hearer into a certain frame of mind, the third upon the speech itself, in so far as it proves or seems to prove.

The orator persuades by moral character when his speech is delivered in such a manner as to render him worthy of confidence; for we feel confidence in a greater degree and more readily in persons of worth in regard to everything in general, but where there is no certainty and there is room for doubt, our confidence is absolute. But this confidence must be due to the speech itself, not to any preconceived idea of the speaker's character;[3] for it is not the case, as some writers of rhetorical treatises lay down in their "Art," that the worth of the orator in no way contributes to his powers of persuasion; on the contrary, moral character, so to say, constitutes the most effective means of proof. The orator persuades by means of his hearers, when they are roused to emotion by his speech; for the judgements we deliver are not the same when we are influenced by joy or sorrow, love or hate; and it is to this alone that, as we have said, the present-day writers of treatises endeavour to devote their attention. (We will discuss these matters in detail when we come to speak of the emotions.) Lastly, persuasion is produced by the speech itself, when we establish the true or apparently true from the means of persuasion applicable to each individual subject.

Now, since proofs are effected by these means, it is evident that, to be able to grasp them, a man must be capable of logical reasoning, of studying characters and the virtues, and thirdly the emotions—the nature and character of each,

3. This point is incalculably important. The speech itself creates the audience's confidence in the speaker, and hence *ēthos* is itself a kind of proof that predisposes the audience to listen favorably to whatever the speaker has to say. See the discussion in Kennedy, *Persuasion*, 91.

its origin, and the manner in which it is produced. Thus it appears that Rhetoric is as it were an offshoot of Dialectic and of the science of Ethics, which may be reasonably called Politics. That is why Rhetoric assumes the character of Politics, and those who claim to possess it, partly from ignorance, partly from boastfulness, and partly from other human weaknesses, do the same. For, as we said at the outset, Rhetoric is a sort of division or likeness of Dialectic, since neither of them is a science that deals with the nature of any definite subject, but they are merely faculties of furnishing arguments. We have now said nearly enough about the faculties of these arts and their mutual relations.

But for purposes of demonstration, real or apparent, just as Dialectic possesses two modes of argument, induction and the syllogism, real or apparent, the same is the case in Rhetoric; for the example is induction, and the enthymeme a syllogism, and the apparent enthymeme an apparent syllogism. Accordingly I call an enthymeme a rhetorical syllogism, and an example rhetorical induction. Now all orators produce belief by employing as proofs either examples or enthymemes and nothing else; so that if, generally speaking, it is necessary to prove any fact whatever either by syllogism or by induction—and that this is so is clear from the *Analytics*—each of the two former must be identical with each of the two latter. The difference between example and enthymeme is evident from the *Topics*, where, in discussing syllogism and induction, it has previously been said that the proof from a number of particular cases that such is the rule, is called in Dialectic induction, in Rhetoric example; but when, certain things being posited, something different results by reason of them, alongside of them, from their being true, either universally or in most cases, such a conclusion in Dialectic is called a syllogism, in Rhetoric an enthymeme.

It is evident that Rhetoric enjoys both these advantages—for what has been said in the *Methodica*[4] holds good also in this case—for rhetorical speeches are sometimes characterized by examples and sometimes by enthymemes, and orators themselves may be similarly distinguished by their fondness for one or the other. Now arguments that depend on examples are not less calculated to persuade, but those which depend upon enthymemes meet with greater approval. Their origin and the way in which each should be used will be discussed later; for the moment let us define more clearly these proofs themselves.

Now, that which is persuasive is persuasive in reference to some one, and is persuasive and convincing either at once and in and by itself, or because it appears to be proved by propositions that are convincing; further, no art has the particular in view, medicine for instance what is good for Socrates or Callias, but what is good for this or that class of persons (for this is a matter that comes within the province of an art, whereas the particular is infinite and cannot be the subject of a true science); similarly, therefore, Rhetoric will not consider what seems probable in each individual case, for instance to Socrates or

4. A lost treatise.

Hippias, but that which seems probable to this or that class of persons.[5] It is the same with Dialectic, which does not draw conclusions from any random premises—for even madmen have some fancies—but it takes its material from subjects which demand reasoned discussion, as Rhetoric does from those which are common subjects of deliberation.

The function of Rhetoric, then, is to deal with things about which we deliberate, but for which we have no systematic rules; and in the presence of such hearers as are unable to take a general view of many stages, or to follow a lengthy chain of argument. But we only deliberate about things which seem to admit of issuing in two ways; as for those things which cannot in the past, present, or future be otherwise, no one deliberates about them, if he supposes that they are such; for nothing would be gained by it. Now, it is possible to draw conclusions and inferences partly from what has been previously demonstrated syllogistically, partly from what has not, which however needs demonstration, because it is not probable. The first of these methods is necessarily difficult to follow owing to its length, for the judge is supposed to be a simple person; the second will obtain little credence, because it does not depend upon what is either admitted or probable. The necessary result then is that the enthymeme and the example are concerned with things which may, generally speaking, be other than they are, the example being a kind of induction and the enthymeme a kind of syllogism, and deduced from few premises, often from fewer than the regular syllogism; for if any one of these is well known, there is no need to mention it, for the hearer can add it himself. For instance, to prove that Dorieus was the victor in a contest at which the prize was a crown, it is enough to say that he won a victory at the Olympic games; there is no need to add that the prize at the Olympic games is a crown, for everybody knows it.

But since few of the propositions of the rhetorical syllogism are necessary, for most of the things which we judge and examine can be other than they are, human actions, which are the subject of our deliberation and examination, being all of such a character and, generally speaking, none of them necessary; since, further, facts which only generally happen or are merely possible can only be demonstrated by other facts of the same kind, and necessary facts by necessary propositions (and that this is so is clear from the *Analytics*), it is evident that the materials from which enthymemes are derived will be sometimes necessary, but for the most part only generally true; and these materials being probabilities and signs, it follows that these two elements must correspond to these two kinds of propositions, each to each. For that which is probable is that which generally happens, not however unreservedly, as some define it, but that which is concerned with things that may be other than they are, being so related to that in regard to which it is probable as the universal to the particular. As to signs, some are related as the particular to the universal,

---

5. An indication of Aristotelian reality. Thus, according to Aristotle's thinking, a particular murderer's guilt will depend, in part at least, on how well the particulars of his case relate to the probable patterns for murderers generally. For example, if it is thought that murderers generally leave the scenes of their crimes, and a certain person accused of murder did not leave the scene, then (all other things being equal) that person is probably not the murderer.

others as the universal to the particular. Necessary signs are called *tekmēria*; those which are not necessary have no distinguishing name. I call those necessary signs from which a logical syllogism can be constructed, wherefore such a sign is called *tekmērion*; for when people think that their arguments are irrefutable, they think that they are bringing forward a *tekmērion*, something as it were proved and concluded; for in the old language *tekmar* and *peras* have the same meaning (limit, conclusion).

Among signs, some are related as the particular to the universal; for instance, if one were to say that all wise men are just, because Socrates was both wise and just. Now this is a sign, but even though the particular statement is true, it can be refuted, because it cannot be reduced to syllogistic form. But if one were to say that it is a sign that a man is ill, because he has a fever, or that a woman has had a child because she has milk, this is a necessary sign. This alone among signs is a *tekmērion*; for only in this case, if the fact is true, is the argument irrefutable. Other signs are related as the universal to the particular, for instance, if one were to say that it is a sign that this man has a fever, because he breathes hard; but even if the fact be true, this argument also can be refuted, for it is possible for a man to breathe hard without having a fever. We have now explained the meaning of probable, sign, and necessary sign, and the difference between them; in the *Analytics* we have defined them more clearly and stated why some of them can be converted into logical syllogisms, while others cannot.

We have said that example is a kind of induction and with what kind of material it deals by way of induction. It is neither the relation of part to whole, nor of whole to part, nor of one whole to another whole, but of part to part, of like to like, when both come under the same genus, but one of them is better known that the other. For example, to prove that Dionysius is aiming at a tyranny, because he asks for a bodyguard, one might say that Pisistratus before him and Theagenes of Megara did the same, and when they obtained what they asked for made themselves tyrants. All the other tyrants known may serve as an example of Dionysius, whose reason, however, for asking for a bodyguard we do not yet know. All these examples are contained under the same universal proposition, that one who is aiming at a tyranny asks for a bodyguard.

We have now stated the materials of proofs which are thought to be demonstrative. But a very great difference between enthymemes has escaped the notice of nearly every one, although it also exists in the dialectical method of syllogisms. For some of them belong to Rhetoric, some syllogisms only to Dialectic, and others to other arts and faculties, some already existing and others not yet established. Hence it is that this escapes the notice of the speakers, and the more they specialize in a subject, the more they transgress the limits of Rhetoric and Dialectic. But this will be clearer if stated at greater length.

I mean by dialectical and rhetorical syllogisms those which are concerned with what we call "topics," which may be applied alike to Law, Physics, Politics, and many other sciences that differ in kind, such as the topic of the more or less, which will furnish syllogisms and enthymemes equally well for Law, Physics, or any other science whatever, although these subjects differ in kind. Specific topics on the other hand are derived from propositions which are peculiar to each species or genus of things; there are, for example, propositions about Physics which can furnish neither enthymemes nor syllogisms about Ethics, and there are propositions concerned with Ethics which will be useless for furnishing conclusions about Physics; and the same holds good in all cases. The first kind of topics will not make a man practically wise about any particular class of things, because they do not deal with any particular subject matter; but as to the specific topics, the happier a man is in his choice of propositions, the more he will unconsciously produce a science quite different from Dialectic and Rhetoric. For if once he hits upon first principles, it will no longer be Dialectic or Rhetoric, but that science whose principles he has arrived at. Most enthymemes are constructed from these specific topics, which are called particular and special, fewer from those that are common or universal. As then we have done in the *Topics*, so here we must distinguish the specific and universal topics, from which enthymemes may be constructed. By specific topics I mean the propositions peculiar to each class of things, by universal those common to all alike. Let us then first speak of the specific topics, but before doing so let us ascertain the different kinds of Rhetoric, so that, having determined their number, we may separately ascertain their elements and propositions.

The kinds of Rhetoric are three in number, corresponding to the three kinds of hearers. For every speech is composed of three parts: the speaker, the subject of which he treats, and the person to whom it is addressed, I mean the hearer, to whom the end or object of the speech refers. Now the hearer must necessarily be either a mere spectator or a judge, and a judge either of things past or of things to come. For instance, a member of the general assembly is a judge of things to come; the dicast, of things past; the mere spectator, of the ability of the speaker. Therefore there are necessarily three kinds of rhetorical speeches, deliberative, forensic, and epideictic.

The deliberative kind is either hortatory or dissuasive; for both those who give advice in private and those who speak in the assembly invariably either exhort or dissuade. The forensic kind is either accusatory or defensive; for litigants must necessarily either accuse or defend. The epideictic kind has for its subject praise or blame.

Further, to each of these a special time is appropriate: to the deliberative the future, for the speaker, whether he exhorts or dissuades, always advises about things to come; to the forensic the past, for it is always in reference to things done that one party accuses and the other defends; to the epideictic most appropriately the present, for it is the existing condition of things that all those who praises or blame have in view. It is not uncommon, however, for epideictic speakers to avail themselves of other times, of the past by way of recalling it, or of the future by way of anticipating it.

Each of the three kinds has a different special end, and as there are three kinds of Rhetoric, so there are three special ends.[6] The end of the deliberative

6. End *(telos)* is the purpose of anything, the last of Aristotle's four causes: efficient, formal, material, and final.

speaker is the expedient or harmful; for he who exhorts recommends a course of action as better, and he who dissuades advises against it as worse; all other considerations, such as justice and injustice, honour and disgrace, are included as accessory in reference to this. The end of the forensic speaker is the just or the unjust; in this case also all other considerations are included as accessory. The end of those who praise or blame is the honourable and disgraceful; and they also refer all other considerations to these. A sign that what I have stated is the end which each has in view is the fact that sometimes the speakers will not dispute about the other points. For example, a man on trial does not always deny that an act has been committed or damage inflicted by him, but he will never admit that the act is unjust; for otherwise a trial would be unnecessary. Similarly, the deliberative orator, although he often sacrifices everything else, will never admit that he is recommending what is inexpedient or is dissuading from what is useful; but often he is quite indifferent about showing that the enslavement of neighbouring peoples, even if they have done no harm, is not an act of injustice. Similarly, those who praise or blame do not consider whether a man has done what is expedient or harmful, but frequently make it a matter for praise that, disregarding his own interest, he performed some deed of honour. For example, they praise Achilles because he went to the aid of his comrade Patroclus, knowing that he was fated to die, although he might have lived. To him such a death was more honourable, although life was more expedient.

From what has been said it is evident that the orator must first have in readiness the propositions on these three subjects. Now, necessary signs, probabilities, and signs are the propositions of the rhetorician; for the syllogism universally consists of propositions, and the enthymeme is a syllogism composed of the propositions above mentioned. Again, since what is impossible can neither have been done nor will be done, but only what is possible, and since what has not taken place nor will take place can neither have been done nor will be done, it is necessary for each of the three kinds of orators to have in readiness propositions dealing with the possible and the impossible, and as to whether anything has taken place or will take place, or not. Further, since all, whether they praise or blame, exhort or dissuade, accused or defend, not only endeavour to prove what we have stated, but also that the same things, whether good or bad, honourable or disgraceful, just or unjust, are great or small, either in themselves or when compared with each other, it is clear that it will be necessary for the orator to be ready with propositions dealing with greatness and smallness and the greater and the less, both universally and in particular; for instance, which is the greater or less good, or act of injustice or justice; and similarly with regard to all other subjects. We have now stated the topics concerning which the orator must provide himself with propositions; after this, we must distinguish between each of them individually, that is, what the three kinds of Rhetoric, deliberative, epideictic, and forensic, are concerned with.

We must first ascertain about what kind of good or bad things the deliberative orator advises, since he cannot do so about everything, but only about things which may possibly happen or not. Everything which of necessity either is or will be, or which cannot possibly be or come to pass, is outside the scope of deliberation. Indeed, even in the case of things that are possible advice is not universally appropriate; for they include certain advantages, natural and accidental, about which it is not worth while to offer advice. But it is clear that advice is limited to those subjects about which we take counsel; and such are all those which can naturally be referred to ourselves and the first cause of whose origination is in our own power; for our examination is limited to finding out whether such things are possible or impossible for us to perform.

However, there is no need at present to endeavour to enumerate with scrupulous exactness or to classify those subjects which men are wont to discuss, or to define them as far as possible with strict accuracy, since this is not the function of the rhetorical art but of one that is more intelligent and exact, and further, more than its legitimate subjects of inquiry have already been assigned to it. For what we have said before is true: that Rhetoric is composed of analytical science and of that branch of political science which is concerned with Ethics, and that it resembles partly Dialectic and partly sophistical arguments. But in proportion as anyone endeavours to make of Dialectic or Rhetoric, not what they are, faculties, but sciences, to that extent he will, without knowing it, destroy their real nature, in thus altering their character, by crossing over into the domain of sciences, whose subjects are certain definite things, not merely words. Nevertheless, even at present we may mention such matters as it is worth while to analyse, while still leaving much for political science to investigate.

Now, we may say that the most important subjects about which all men deliberate and deliberative orators harangue, are five in number, to wit: ways and means, war and peace, the defence of the country, imports and exports, legislation.

Accordingly, the orator who is going to give advice on ways and means should be acquainted with the nature and extent of the State resources, so that if any is omitted it may be added, and if any is insufficient, it may be increased. Further, he should know all the expenses of the State, that if any is superfluous, it may be removed, or, if too great, may be curtailed. For men become wealthier, not only by adding to what they already possess, but also by cutting down expenses. Of these things it is not only possible to acquire a general view from individual experience, but in view of advising concerning them it is further necessary to be well informed about what has been discovered among others.

In regard to war and peace, the orator should be acquainted with the power of the State, how great it is already and how great it may possibly become; of what kind it is already and what additions may possibly be made to it; further, what wars it has waged and its conduct of them. These things he should be acquainted with, not only as far as his own State is concerned, but also in reference to neighbouring States, and particularly those with whom there is a likelihood of war, so that towards the stronger a pacific attitude may be maintained, and in regard to the weaker, the decision as to making war on them may be left to his own State. Again, he should know whether their forces are like or unlike his own, for herein also advantage or disadvantage may lie. With reference to these matters he must also have examined the results, not only of the wars carried on by his own State, but also of those carried on by others; for similar results naturally arise from similar causes.

Again, in regard to the defence of the country, he should not be ignorant how it is carried on; he should know both the strength of the guard, its character, and the positions of the guard-houses (which is impossible for one who is unacquainted with the country), so that if any guard is insufficient it may be increased, or if any is superfluous it may be disbanded, and greater attention devoted to suitable positions.

Again, in regard to food, he should know what amount of expenditure is sufficient to support the State; what kind of food is produced at home or can be imported; and what exports and imports are necessary, in order that contracts and agreements may be made with those who can furnish them; for it is necessary to keep the citizens free from reproach in their relations with two classes of people—those who are stronger and those who are useful for commercial purposes.

With a view to the safety of the State, it is necessary that the orator should be able to judge of all these questions, but an understanding of legislation is of special importance, for it is on the laws that the safety of the State is based. Wherefore he must know how many forms of government there are; what is expedient for each; and the natural causes of its downfall, whether they are peculiar to the particular form of government or opposed to it. By being ruined by causes peculiar to itself, I mean that, with the exception of the perfect form of government, all the rest are ruined by being relaxed or strained to excess. Thus democracy, not only when relaxed, but also when strained to excess, becomes weaker and will end in an oligarchy; similarly, not only does an aquiline or snub nose reach the mean, when one of these defects is relaxed, but when it becomes aquiline or snub to excess, it is altered to such an extent that even the likeness of a nose is lost. Moreover, with reference to acts of legislation, it is useful not only to understand what form of government is expedient by judging in the light of the past, but also to become acquainted with those in existence in other nations, and to learn what kinds of government are suitable to what kinds of people. It is clear, therefore, that for legislation books of travel are useful, since they help us to understand the laws of other nations, and for political debates historical works. All these things, however, belong to Politics and not to Rhetoric.

Such, then, are the most important questions upon which the would-be deliberative orator must be well informed. Now let us again state the sources whence we must derive our arguments for exhortation or discussion on these and other questions.

Men, individually and in common, nearly all have some aim, in the attainment of which they choose or avoid certain things. This aim, briefly stated, is happiness and its component parts. Therefore, for the sake of illustration, let us ascertain what happiness, generally speaking, is, and what its parts consist in; for all who exhort or dissuade discuss happiness and the

things which conduce or are detrimental to it. For one should do the things which procure happiness or one of its parts, or increase instead of diminishing
1360b13 it, and avoid doing those things which destroy or hinder it or bring about what is contrary to it.

Ethical and Pathetic Proofs

1377b12   Such then are the materials which we must employ in exhorting and dissuading, praising and blaming, accusing and defending, and such are the opinions and propositions that are useful to produce conviction in these circumstances; for they are the subject and source of enthymemes, which are specially suitable to each class (so to say) of speeches. But since the object of Rhetoric is judgement—for judgements are pronounced in deliberative rhetoric and judicial proceedings are a judgement—it is not only necessary to consider how to make the speech itself demonstrative and convincing, but also that the speaker should show himself to be of a certain character and should know how to put the judge into a certain frame of mind. For it makes a great difference with regard to producing conviction—especially in demonstrative, and, next to this, in forensic oratory—that the speaker should show himself to be possessed of certain qualities and that his hearers should think that he is disposed in a certain way towards them; and further, that they themselves should be disposed in a certain way towards him. In deliberative oratory, it is more useful that the orator should appear to be of a certain character, in forensic, that the hearer should be disposed in a certain way; for opinions vary, according as men love or hate, are wrathful or mild, and things appear either altogether different, or different in degree; for when a man is favourably disposed towards one on whom he is passing judgement, he either thinks that the accused has committed no wrong at all or that his offence is trifling; but if he hates him, the reverse is the case. And if a man desires anything and has good hopes of getting it, if what is to come is pleasant, he thinks that it is sure to come to pass and will be good; but if a man is unemotional or not hopeful it is quite the reverse.

For the orator to produce conviction three qualities are necessary; for, independently of demonstrations, the things which induce belief are three in number. These qualities are good sense, virtue, and goodwill; for speakers are wrong both in what they say and in the advice they give, because they lack either all three or one of them. For either through want of sense they form incorrect opinions, or, if their opinions are correct, through viciousness they do not say what they think, or, if they are sensible and good, they lack goodwill; wherefore it may happen that they do not give the best advice, although they know what it is. These qualities are all that are necessary, so that the speaker who appears to possess all three will necessarily convince his hearers. The means whereby he may appear sensible and good must be inferred from the classification of the virtues; for to make himself appear such he would employ the same means as he would in the case of others. We must now speak of goodwill and friendship in our discussion of the emotions.

The emotions are all those affections which cause men to change their opinion in regard to their judgements, and are accompanied by pleasure and pain; such are anger, pity, fear, and all similar emotions and their contraries. And each of them must be divided under three heads; for instance, in regard to anger, the disposition of mind which makes men angry, the persons with whom they are usually angry, and the occasions which give rise to anger. For if we knew one or even two of these heads, but not all three, it would be impossible to arouse that emotion. The same applies to the rest. Just as, then, we have given a list of propositions in what we have previously said, we will do the same here and divide the emotions in the same manner. 1378a29

Deliberative *Topoi*

It is evident, then, what things, likely to happen or already existing, the 1362a15 orator should aim at, when exhorting, and what when dissuading; for they are opposites. But since the aim before the deliberative orator is that which is expedient, and men deliberate, not about the end, but about the means to the end, which are the things which are expedient in regard to our actions; and since, further, the expedient is good, we must first grasp the elementary notions of good and expedient in general

Let us assume good to be whatever is desirable for its own sake, or for the sake of which we choose something else, that which is the aim of all things, or of all things that possess sensation or reason; or would be, if they could acquire the latter. Whatever reason might assign to each and whatever reason does assign to each in individual cases, that is good for each; and that whose presence makes a man fit and also independent; and independence in general; and that which produces or preserves such things, or on which such things follow, or all that is likely to prevent or destroy their opposites.

Now things follow in two ways—simultaneously or subsequently; for instance, knowledge is subsequent to learning, but life is simultaneous with health. Things which produce act in three ways; thus, healthiness produces health; and so does food; and exercise as a rule. This being laid down, it necessarily follows that the acquisition of good things and the loss of evil things are both good; for it follows simultaneously on the latter that we are rid of that which is bad, and subsequently on the former that we obtain possession of that which is good. The same applies to the acquisition of a greater in place of a less good, and a less in place of a greater evil; for in proportion as the greater exceeds the less, there is an acquisition of the one and a loss of the other. The virtues also must be a good thing; for those who possess them are in a sound condition, and they are also productive of good things and practical. However, we must speak separately concerning each—what it is, and of what kind. Pleasure also must be a good; for all living creatures naturally desire it. Hence it follows that both agreeable and beautiful things must be good; for the former produce pleasure, while among beautiful things some are pleasant and others are desirable in themselves.

To enumerate them one by one, the following things must necessarily be good. Happiness, since it is desirable in itself and self-sufficient, and to obtain it we choose a number of things. Justice, courage, self-control, magnanimity, magnificence, and all other similar states of mind, for they are virtues of the soul. Health, beauty, and the like, for they are virtues of the body and produce many advantages; for instance, health is productive of pleasure and of life, wherefore it is thought to be best of all, because it is the cause of two things which the majority of men prize most highly. Wealth, since it is the excellence of acquisition and productive of many things. A friend and friendship, since a friend is desirable in himself and produces many advantages. Honour and good repute, since they are agreeable and produce many advantages, and are generally accompanied by the possession of those things for which men are honoured. Eloquence and capacity for action; for all such faculties are productive of many advantages. Further, natural cleverness, good memory, readiness to learn, quick-wittedness, and all similar qualities; for these faculties are productive of advantages. The same applies to all the sciences, arts, and even life, for even though no other good should result from it, it is desirable in itself. Lastly, justice, since it is expedient in general for the common weal.

These are nearly all the things generally recognized as good; in the case of doubtful goods, the arguments in their favour are drawn from the following. That is good the opposite of which is evil, or the opposite of which is advantageous to our enemies; for instance, if it is specially advantageous to our enemies that we should be cowards, it is clear that courage is specially advantageous to the citizens. And, speaking generally, the opposite of what our enemies desire or of that in which they rejoice, appears to be advantageous; wherefore it was well said: "Of a truth Priam would exult." This is not always the case, but only as a general rule, for there is nothing to prevent one and the same thing being sometimes advantageous to two opposite parties; hence it is said that misfortune brings men together, when a common danger threatens them.

That which is not in excess is good, whereas that which is greater than it should be, is bad. And that which has cost much labour and expense, for it at once is seen to be an apparent good, and such a thing is regarded as an end, and an end of many efforts; now, an end is a good. Wherefore it was said: "And they would [leave Argive Helen for Priam and the Trojans] to boast of," and "It is disgraceful to tarry long," and the proverb, "[to break] the pitcher at the door."

And that which many aim at and which is seen to be competed for by many; for that which all aim at was recognized as a good, and the majority may almost stand for "all." And that which is the object of praise, for no one praises that which is not good. And that which is praised by enemies; for if even those who are injured by it acknowledge its goodness, this amounts to a universal recognition of it; for it is because of its goodness being evident that they acknowledge it, just as those whom their enemies praise are worthless. Wherefore the Corinthians imagined themselves insulted by Simonides, when the wrote, "Ilium does not blame the Corinthians." And that which one of the practically wise or good, man or woman, has chosen before others, as

Athena chose Odysseus, Theseus Helen, the goddesses Alexander (Paris), and Homer Achilles.

And, generally speaking, all that is deliberately chosen is good. Now, men deliberately choose to do the things just mentioned, and those which are harmful to their enemies, and advantageous to their friends, and things which are possible. The last are of two kinds: things which might happen, and things which easily happen; by the latter are meant things that happen without labour or in a short time, for difficulty is defined by labour or length of time. And anything that happens as men wish is good; and what they wish is either what is not evil at all or is less an evil than a good, which will be the case for instance, whenever the penalty attached to it is unnoticed or light. And things that are peculiar to them, or which no one else possesses, or which are out of the common; for thus the honour is greater. And things which are appropriate to them; such are all things befitting them in respect of birth and power. And things which they think they lack, however unimportant; for none the less they deliberately choose to acquire them. And things which are easy of accomplishment, for being easy they are possible; such things are those in which all, or most men, or those who are equals or inferiors have been successful. And things whereby they will gratify friends or incur the hatred of enemies. And all things that those whom they admire deliberately choose to do. And those things in regard to which they are clever naturally or by experience; for they hope to be more easily successful in them. And things which no worthless man would approve, for that makes them the more commendable. And things which they happen to desire, for such things seem not only agreeable, but also better. Lastly, and above all, each man thinks those things good which are the object of his special desire, as victory of the man who desires victory, honour of the ambitious man, money of the avaricious, and so in other instances. These then are the materials from which we must draw our arguments in reference to good and the expedient.

But since men often agree that both of two things are useful, but dispute which is the more so, we must next speak of the greater good and the more expedient. Let one thing, then, be said to exceed another, when it is as great and something more—and to be exceeded when it is contained in the other. "Greater" and "more" always imply a relation with less; "great" and "small," "much" and "little" with the general size of things; the "great" is that which exceeds, and that which falls short of it is "small"; and similarly "much" and "little." Since, besides, we call good that which is desirable for its own sake and not for anything else, and that which all things aim at and which they would choose if they possessed reason and practical wisdom; and that which is productive or protective of good, or on which such things follow; and since that for the sake of which anything is done is the end, and the end is that for the sake of which everything else is done, and that is good for each man which relatively to him presents all these conditions, it necessarily follows that a larger number of good things is a greater good than one or a smaller number, if the one or the smaller number is reckoned as one of them; for it exceeds them and that which is contained is exceeded.

And if that which is greatest in one class surpass that which is greatest in another class, the first class will surpass the second; and whenever one class surpasses another, the greatest of that class will surpass the greatest of the other. For instance, if the biggest man is greater than the biggest woman, men in general will be bigger than women; and if men in general are bigger than women, the biggest man will be bigger than the biggest woman; for the superiority of classes and of the greatest things contained in them are proportionate. And when this follows on that, but not that on this [then "that" is the greater good]; for the enjoyment of that which follows is contained in that of the other. Now, things follow simultaneously, or successively, or potentially; thus, life follows simultaneously on health, but not health on life; knowledge follows subsequently on learning [but not learning on knowledge]; and simple theft potentially on sacrilege, for one who commits sacrilege will also steal. And things which exceed the same thing by a greater amount [than something else] are greater, for they must also exceed the greater. And things which produce a greater good are greater; for this we agreed was the meaning of productive of greater. And similarly, that which is produced by a greater cause; for if that which produces health is more desirable than that which produces pleasure and a greater good, then health is a greater good than pleasure. And that which is more desirable in itself is superior to that which is not; for example, strength is a greater good than the wholesome, which is not desirable for its own sake, while strength is; and this we agreed was the meaning of a good. And the end is a greater good than the means; for the latter is desirable for the sake of something else, the former for its own sake; for instance, exercise is only a means for the acquirement of a good constitution. And that which has less need of one or several other things in addition is a greater good, for it is more independent (and "having less need" means needing fewer or easier additions). And when one thing does not exist or cannot be brought into existence without the aid of another, but that other can, then that which needs no aid is more independent, and accordingly is seen to be a greater good.

And if one thing is a first principle, and another not; if one thing is a cause and another not, for the same reason; for without cause or first principle nothing can exist or come into existence. And if there are two first principles or two causes, that which results from the greater is greater; and conversely, when there are two first principles or two causes, that which is the first cause or principle of the greater is greater. It is clear then, from what has been said, that a thing may be greater in two ways; for if it is a first principle but another is not, it will appear to be greater, and if it is not a first principle [but an end], while another is; for the end is greater and not a first principle. Thus, Leodamas, when accusing Callistratus, declared that the man who had given the advice was more guilty than the one who carried it out; for if he had not suggested it, it could not have been carried out. And conversely, when accusing Chabrias, he declared that the man who had carried out the advice was more guilty than the one who had given it; for it could not have been carried out, had there not been someone to do so, and the reason why people devised plots was that others might carry them out.

And that which is scarcer is a greater good than that which is abundant, as gold than iron, although it is less useful, but the possession of it is more valuable, since it is more difficult of acquisition. From another point of view, that which is abundant is to be preferred to that which is scarce, because the use of it is greater, for "often" exceeds "seldom"; whence the saying: "Water is best." And, speaking generally, that which is more difficult is preferable to that which is easier of attainment, for it is scarcer; but from another point of view that which is easier is preferable to that which is more difficult; for its nature is as we wish.[7] And that, the contrary or the deprivation of which is greater, is the greater good. And virtue is greater than non-virtue, and vice than non-vice; for virtues and vices are ends, the others not. And those things whose works are nobler or more disgraceful are themselves greater; and the works of those things, the vices and virtues of which are greater, will also be greater, since between causes and first principles compared with results there is the same relation as between results compared with causes and first principles. Things, superiority in which is more desirable or nobler, are to be preferred; for instance, sharpness of sight is preferable to keenness of smell; for sight is better than smell. And loving one's friends more than money is nobler, whence it follows that love of friends is nobler than love of money. And, on the other hand, the better and nobler things are, the better and nobler will be their superiority; and similarly, those things, the desire for which is nobler and better, are themselves nobler and better, for greater longings are directed towards greater objects. For the same reason, the better and nobler the object, the better and nobler are the desires.

And when the sciences are nobler and more dignified, the nobler and more dignified are their subjects; for as is the science, so is the truth which is its object, and each science prescribes that which properly belongs to it; and, by analogy, the nobler and more dignified the objects of a science, the nobler and more dignified is the science itself, for the same reasons. And that which men of practical wisdom, either all, or more, or the best of them, would judge, or have judged, to be a greater good, must necessarily be such, either absolutely or in so far as they have judged as men of practical wisdom. The same may be said in regard to everything else; for the nature, quantity, and quality of things are such as would be defined by science and practical wisdom. But our statement only applies to goods; for we defined that as good which everything, if possessed of practical wisdom, would choose; hence it is evident that that is a greater good to which practical wisdom assigns the superiority. So also are those things which better men possess, either absolutely, or in so far as they are better; for instance courage is better than strength. And what the better man would choose, either absolutely or in so far as he is better;[8] thus, it is better to suffer wrong than to commit it, for that is what the juster man would choose. And that which is more agreeable rather than that which is less so; for all things pursue pleasure and desire it for its own sake; and it is by these conditions that

---

7. In this section we can see Aristotle thinking topically.
8. This is what Socrates argues (to Polus) in Plato's *Gorgias*.

the good and the end have been defined. And that is more agreeable which is less subject to pain and is agreeable for a longer time. And that which is nobler than that which is less noble; for the noble is that which is either agreeable or desirable in itself. And all things which we have a greater desire to be instrumental in procuring for ourselves or for our friends are greater goods, and those as to which our desire is least are greater evils. And things that last longer are preferable to those that are of shorter duration, and those that are safer to those that are less so;[9] for time increases the use of the first and the wish that of the second; for whenever we wish, we can make greater use of things that are safe.

And things in all cases follow the relations between co-ordinates and similar inflexions; for instance, if "courageously" is nobler than and preferable to "temperately," then "courage" is preferable to "temperance," and it is better to be "courageous" than "temperate." And that which is chosen by all is better than that which is not; and that which the majority choose than that which the minority choose; for, as we have said, the good is that which all desire, and consequently a good is greater, the more it is desired. The same applies to goods which are recognized as greater by opponents or enemies, by judges, or by those whom they select; for in the one case it would be, so to say, the verdict of all mankind, in the other that of those who are acknowledged authorities and experts. And sometimes a good is greater in which all participate, for it is a disgrace not to participate in it; sometimes when none or only a few participate in it, for it is scarcer. And things which are more praiseworthy, since they are nobler. And in the same way things which are more highly honoured, for honour is a sort of measure of worth; and conversely those things are greater evils, the punishment for which is greater. And those things which are greater than what is acknowledged, or appears, to be great, are greater. And the same whole when divided into parts appears greater, for there appears to be superiority in a greater number of things. Whence the poet says that Meleager was persuaded to rise up and fight by the recital of: "All the ills that befall those whose city is taken; the people perish, and fire utterly destroys the city, and strangers carry off the children."

Combination and building up, as employed by Epicharmus, produce the same effect as division, and for the same reason; for combination is an exhibition of great superiority and appears to be the origin and cause of great things. And since that which is harder to obtain and scarcer is greater, it follows that special occasions, ages, places, times, and powers, produce great effects; for if a man does things beyond his powers, beyond his age, and beyond what his equals could do, if they are done in such a manner, in such a place, and at such a time, they will possess importance in actions that are noble, good, or just, or the opposite. Hence the epigram on the Olympian victor: "Formerly, with a rough basket on my shoulders, I used to carry fish from Argos to Tegea." And Iphicrates lauded himself, saying, "Look what I started from!" And that which is natural is a greater good than that which is acquired, because it is harder. Whence the poet says: "Self-taught am I." And that which

9. This summary illustrates the relativity of values so crucial to deliberative and forensic rhetoric.

is the greatest part of that which is great is more to be desired; as Pericles said in his Funeral Oration, that the removal of the youth from the city was like the year being robbed of its spring. And those things which are available in greater need, as in old age and illness, are greater goods. And of two things that which is nearer the end proposed is preferable. And that which is useful for the individual is preferable to that which is useful absolutely; that which is possible to that which is impossible; for it is the possible that is useful to us, not the impossible. And those things which are at the end of life; for things near the end are more like ends.

And real things are preferable to those that have reference to public opinion, the latter being defined as those which a man would not choose if they were likely to remain unnoticed by others. It would seem then that it is better to receive than to confer a benefit; for one would choose the former even if it should pass unnoticed, whereas one would not choose to confer a benefit, if it were likely to remain unknown. Those things also are to be preferred, which men would rather possess in reality than in appearance, because they are nearer the truth; wherefore it is commonly said that justice is a thing of little importance, because people prefer to appear just than to be just; and this is not the case, for instance, in regard to health. The same may be said of things that serve several ends; for instance, those that assist us to live, to live well, to enjoy life, and to do noble actions; wherefore health and wealth seem to be the greatest goods, for they include all these advantages. And that which is more free from pain and accompanied by pleasure is a greater good; for there is more than one good, since pleasure and freedom from pain combined are both goods. And of two goods the greater is that which, added to one and the same, makes the whole greater. And those things, the presence of which does not escape notice, are preferable to those which pass unnoticed, because they appear more real; whence being wealthy would appear to be a greater good than the appearance of it. And that which is held most dear, sometimes alone, sometimes accompanied by other things, is a greater good. Wherefore he who puts out the eye of a one-eyed man and he who puts out one eye of another who has two, does not do equal injury; for in the former case, a man has been deprived of that which he held most dear.

These are nearly all the topics from which arguments may be drawn in persuading and dissuading; but the most important and effective of all the means of persuasion and good counsel is to know all the forms of government and to distinguish the manners and customs, institutions, and interests of each; for all men are guided by considerations of expediency, and that which preserves the State is expedient. Further, the declaration of the authority is authoritative, and the different kinds of authority are distinguished according to forms of government; in fact, there are as many authorities as there are forms of government.   1365b28

Epideictic and Forensic Topoi

Now praise is language that sets forth greatness of virtue; hence it is 1367b28 necessary to show that a man's actions are virtuous. But encomium deals with

achievements—all attendant circumstances, such as noble birth and education, merely conduce to persuasion; for it is probable that virtuous parents will
have virtuous offspring and that a man will turn out as he has been brought up.
Hence we pronounce an encomium upon those who have achieved something. Achievements, in fact, are signs of moral habit; for we should praise
even a man who had not achieved anything, if we felt confident that he was
likely to do so. Blessing and felicitation are identical with each other, but are
not the same as praise and encomium, which, as virtue is contained in
1367b36 happiness, are contained in felicitation.

1368a10   We must also employ many of the means of amplification; for instance, if a
man has done anything alone, or first, or with a few, or has been chiefly
responsible for it; all these circumstances render an action noble. Similarly,
topics derived from times and seasons, that is to say, if our expectation is
surpassed. Also, if a man has often been successful in the same thing; for this is
of importance and would appear to be due to the man himself, and not to be
the result of chance. And if it is for his sake that distinctions which are an
encouragement or honour have been invented and established; and if he was
the first on whom an encomium was pronounced, as Hippolochus, or to whom
a statue was set up in the market-place, as to Harmodius and Aristogiton. And
similarly in opposite cases. If he does not furnish you with enough material in
himself, you must compare him with others, as Isocrates used to do, because
of his inexperience of forensic speaking. And you must compare him with
illustrious personages, for it affords ground for amplification and is noble, if he
can be proved better than men of worth. Amplification is with good reason
ranked as one of the forms of praise, since it consists in superiority, and
superiority is one of the things that are noble. That is why, if you cannot
compare him with illustrious personages, you must compare him with
ordinary persons, since superiority is thought to indicate virtue. Speaking
generally, of the topics common to all rhetorical arguments, amplification is
most suitable for epideictic speakers, whose subject is actions which are not
disputed, so that all that remains to be done is to attribute beauty and
importance to them. Examples are most suitable for deliberative speakers, for
it is by examination of the past that we divine and judge the future.
Enthymemes are most suitable for forensic speakers, because the past, by
reason of its obscurity, above all lends itself to the investigation of causes and to
demonstrative proof. Such are nearly all the materials of praise or blame, the
things which those who praise or blame should keep in view, and the sources of
encomia and invective; for when these are known their contraries are obvious,
since blame is derived from the contrary things.
    We have next to speak of the number and quality of the propositions of
which those syllogisms are constructed which have for their object accusation
and defence. Three things have to be considered; first, the nature and the
number of the motives which lead men to act unjustly; secondly, what is the
state of mind of those who so act; thirdly, the character and dispositions of

those who are exposed to injustice. We will discuss these questions in order, after we have first defined acting unjustly.

Let injustice, then, be defined as voluntarily causing injury contrary to the law. Now, the law is particular or general. By particular, I mean the written law in accordance with which a state is administered; by general, the unwritten regulations which appear to be universally recognized. Men act voluntarily when they know what they do, and do not act under compulsion. What is done voluntarily is not always done with premeditation; but what is done with premeditation is always known to the agent, for no one is ignorant of what he does with a purpose. The motives which lead men to do injury and commit wrong actions are depravity and incontinence. For if men have one or more vices, it is in that which makes him vicious that he shows himself unjust; for example, the illiberal in regard to money, the licentious in regard to bodily pleasures, the effeminate in regard to what makes for ease, the coward in regard to dangers, for fright makes him desert his comrades in peril; the ambitious in his desire for honour, the irascible owing to anger, one who is eager to conquer in his desire for victory, the rancorous in his desire for vengeance; the foolish man from having mistaken ideas of right and wrong, the shameless from his contempt for the opinion of others. Similarly, each of the rest of mankind is unjust in regard to his special weakness.

This will be perfectly clear, partly from what has already been said about the virtues, and partly from what will be said about the emotions. It remains to state the motives and character of those who do wrong and of those who suffer from it. First, then, let us decide what those who set about doing wrong long for or avoid; for it is evident that the accuser must examine the number and nature of the motives which are to be found in his opponent; the defendant, which of them are not to be found in him. Now, all human actions are either the result of man's efforts or not. Of the latter some are due to chance, others to necessity. Of those due to necessity, some are to be attributed to compulsion, others to nature, so that the things which men do not do of themselves are all the result of chance, nature, or compulsion. As for those which they do of themselves and of which they are the cause, some are the result of habit, others of longing, and of the latter some are due to rational, others to irrational longing. Now wish is a [rational] longing for good, for no one wishes for anything unless he thinks it is good; irrational longings are anger and desire. Thus all the actions of men must necessarily be referred to seven causes: chance, nature, compulsion, habit, reason, anger, and desire.

But it is superfluous to establish further distinctions of men's acts based upon age, moral habits, or anything else. For if the young happen to be irascible, or passionately desire anything, it is not because of their youth that they act accordingly, but because of anger and desire. Nor is it because of wealth or poverty; but the poor happen to desire wealth because of their lack of it, and the rich desire unnecessary pleasures because they are able to procure them. Yet in their case too it will not be wealth or poverty, but desire, that will be the mainspring of their action. Similarly, the just and the unjust, and all the others who are said to act in accordance with their moral habits, will act from the same causes, either from reason or emotion, but some from good characters and emotions, and others from the opposite. Not but that it does happen that such and such moral habits are followed by such and such consequences; for it may be that from the outset the fact of being temperate produces in the temperate man good opinions and desires in the matter of pleasant things, in the intemperate man the contrary. Therefore we must leave these distinctions on one side, but we must examine what are the usual consequences of certain conditions. For, if a man is fair or dark, tall or short, there is no rule that any such consequences should follow, but if he is young or old, just or unjust, it does make a difference. In a word, it will be necessary to take account of all the circumstances that make men's characters different; for instance, if a man fancies himself rich or poor, fortunate or unfortunate, it will make a difference. We will, however, discuss this later; let us now speak of what remains to be said here.

Things which are the result of chance are all those of which the cause is indefinite, those which happen without any end in view, and that neither always, nor generally, nor regularly. The definition of chance will make this clear. Things which are the result of nature are all those of which the cause is in themselves and regular; for they turn out always, or generally, in the same way. As for those which happen contrary to nature there is no need to investigate minutely whether their occurrence is due to a certain force of nature or some other cause (it would seem, however, that such cases also are due to chance). Those things are the result of compulsion which are done by the agents themselves in opposition to their desire or calculation. Things are the result of habit, when they are done because they have often been done. Things are the result of calculation which are done because, of the goods already mentioned, they appear to be expedient either as an end or means to an end, provided they are done by reason of their being expedient; for even the intemperate do certain things that are expedient, for the sake, not of expediency, but of pleasure. Passion and anger are the causes of acts of revenge. But there is a difference between revenge and punishment; the latter is inflicted in the interest of the sufferer, the former in the interest of him who inflicts it, that he may obtain satisfaction. We will define anger when we come to speak of the emotions. Desire is the cause of things being done that are apparently pleasant. The things which are familiar and to which we have become accustomed are among pleasant things; for men do with pleasure many things which are not naturally pleasant, when they have become accustomed to them.

In short, all things that men do of themselves either are, or seem, good or pleasant; and since men do voluntarily what they do of themselves, and involuntarily what they do not, it follows that all that men do voluntarily will be either that which is or seems good, or that which is or seems pleasant. For I reckon among good things the removal of that which is evil or seems evil, or the exchange of a greater evil for a less, because these two things are in a way desirable; in like manner, I reckon among pleasant things the removal of that which is or appears painful, and the exchange of a greater pain for a less. We must therefore make ourselves acquainted with the number and quality of expedient and pleasant things. We have already spoken of the expedient when discussing deliberative rhetoric; let us now speak of the pleasant. And we must regard our definitions as sufficient in each case, provided they are neither 1369b32 obscure nor too precise.

Forensic Inartificial Proofs

Following on what we have just spoken of, we have now briefly to run over what 1375a22 are called the inartificial proofs, for these properly belong to forensic oratory. These proofs are five in number: laws, witnesses, contracts, torture, oaths.   1375a25

Artificial Proofs

Now the employment of persuasive speeches is directed towards a judge- 1391b7 ment; for when a thing is known and judged, there is no longer any need of argument. And there is judgement, whether a speaker addresses himself to a single individual and makes use of his speech to exhort or dissuade, as those do who give advice or try to persuade, for this single individual is equally a judge, since, speaking generally, he who has to be persuaded is a judge; if the speaker is arguing against an opponent or against some theory, it is just the same, for it is necessary to make use of speech to destroy the opposing arguments, against which he speaks as if they were the actual opponent; and similarly in epideictic speeches, for the speech is put together with reference to the spectator as if he were a judge. Generally speaking, however, only he who decides questions at issue in civil controversies is a judge in the proper sense of the word, for in judicial cases the point at issue is the state of the case, in deliberative the subjects of deliberation. We have already spoken of the characters of forms of government in treating of deliberative rhetoric, so that it has been determined how and by what means we must make our speeches conform to those characters.

Now, since each kind of Rhetoric, as was said, has its own special end, and in regard to all of them we have gathered popular opinions and premises whence men derive their proofs in deliberative, epideictic, and judicial speeches, and, further, we have determined the special rules according to which it is possible to make our speeches ethical, it only remains to discuss the topics common to the three kinds of rhetoric. For all orators are obliged, in their speeches, also to make use of the topic of the possible and impossible, and to endeavour to show, some of them that a thing will happen, others that it has happened. Further, the topic of magnitude is common to all kinds of Rhetoric, for all men employ extenuation or amplification whether deliberating, praising or blaming, accusing or defending. When these topics have been determined, we will endeavour to say what we can in general about enthymemes and examples, in order that, when we have added what remains, we may carry out what we proposed at the outset. Now, of the commonplaces amplification is most appropriate to epideictic rhetoric, as has been stated; the past to forensic, since things past are the subject of judgement; and the possible and future to deliberative.

Let us first speak of the possible and the impossible. If of two contrary things it is possible that one should exist or come into existence, then it would seem that the other is equally possible; for instance, if a man can be cured, he can also be ill; for the potentiality of contraries, *qua* contraries, is the same. Similarly, if of two like things the one is possible, so also is the other. And if the harder of two things is possible, so also is the easier. And if it is possible for a thing to be made excellent or beautiful, it is possible for it to be made in general; for it is harder for a beautiful house to be made than a mere house. Again, if the beginning is possible, so also is the end; for no impossible thing comes, or begins to come, into existence; for instance, that the diameter of a square should be commensurable with the side of a square is neither possible nor could be possible. And when the end is possible, so also is the beginning; for all things arise from a beginning. And if that which is subsequent in being or generation can come into being, so then can that which is antecedent; for instance, if a man can come into being, so can a child, for the child is antecedent; and similarly, if a child can come into being, so can a man, for the child is a beginning. And things which we love or desire naturally are possible; for as a rule no one loves the impossible or desires it. And those things which form the subject of sciences or arts can also exist and come into existence. And so with all those things, the productive principles of which reside in those things which we can control by force or persuasion, when they depend upon those whose superiors, masters, or friends we are. And if the parts are possible, so also is the whole; and if the whole is possible, so also are the parts, speaking generally; for instance, if the front, toe-cap, and upper leather, can be made, then shoes can be made, and if shoes, then the above parts. And if the whole genus is among things possible to be made, so is the species, and if the species, so the genus; for example, if a vessel can be built, so can a trireme, if a trireme can, so can a vessel. If of two naturally corresponding things one is possible, so also is the other; for instance, if the double is possible, so is the half, if the half, so the double. If a thing can be made without art or preparation, much the more can it be made with the help of art and carefulness. Whence it was said by Agathon: "And moreover we have to do some things by art, while others fall to our lot by compulsion or chance." And if a thing is possible for those who are inferior, or weaker, or less intelligent, it will be still more so for those whose qualities are the opposite; as Isocrates said, it would be very strange if he were unable by himself to find out what Euthynus had learnt [with the help of others]. As for the impossible, it is clear that there is a supply of arguments to be derived from the opposite of what has been said about the possible.

The question whether a thing has or has not happened must be considered from the following points of view. In the first place, if that which is naturally less likely has happened, then that which is more likely will most probably have happened. If that which usually happens afterwards has happened, then that which precedes must also have happened; for instance, if a man has forgotten a thing, he must once have learnt it. If a man was able and wished to do a thing, he has done it; for all men do a thing, when they are able and resolve to do it, for nothing hinders them. Further, if a man wished to do it and there was no external obstacle; if he was able to do it and was in a sate of anger; if he was able and desired to do it; for men as a rule, whenever they can, do those things which they long for, the vicious owing to want of self-control, the virtuous because they desire what is good. And if anything was on the point of being done, it most probably was done; for it is likely that one who was on the point of doing something has carried it out. And if all the natural antecedents or causes of a thing have happened; for instance, if it has lightened, it has also thundered; and if a man has already attempted a crime, he has also committed it. And if all the natural consequences or motives of actions have happened, then the antecedent or the cause has happened; for instance, if it has thundered, it has also lightened, and if a man has committed a crime he has also attempted it. Of all these things some are so related necessarily, others only as a general rule. To establish that a thing has not happened, it is evident that our argument must be derived from the opposite of what has been said.

In regard to the future, it is clear that one can argue in the same way; for if we are able and wish to do a thing, it will be done; and so too will those things which desire, anger, and reasoning urge us to do, if we have the power. For this reason also, if a man has an eager desire, or intention, of doing a thing, it will probably be done; since, as a rule, things that are about to happen are more likely to happen than those which are not. And if all the natural antecedents have happened; for instance, if the sky is cloudy, it will probably rain. And if one thing has been done with a view to another, it is probable that the latter will also be done; for instance, if a foundation has been laid, a house will probably be built.

What we have previously said clearly shows the nature of the greatness and smallness of things, of the greater and less, and of things great and small generally. For, when treating of deliberative rhetoric, we spoke of greatness of goods, and of the greater and less generally. Therefore, since in each branch of Rhetoric the end set before it is a good, such as the expedient, the noble, or the just, it is evident that all must take the materials of amplification from these. To make any further inquiry as to magnitude and superiority absolutely would be waste of words; for the particular has more authority than the general for practical purposes. Let this suffice for the possible and impossible; for the question whether a thing has happened, or will happen, or not; and for the greatness or smallness of things.

It remains to speak of the proofs common to all branches of Rhetoric, since the particular proofs have been discussed. These common proofs are of two kinds, example and enthymeme (for the maxim is part of an enthymeme). Let us then first speak of the example; for the example resembles induction, and induction is a beginning.

There are two kinds of examples; namely, one which consists in relating things that have happened before, and another in inventing them oneself. The latter are subdivided into comparisons or fables, such as those of Aesop and the Libyan. It would be an instance of the historical kind of example, if one were to say that it is necessary to make preparations against the Great King and not to allow him to subdue Egypt; for Darius did not cross over to Greece until he had obtained possession of Egypt; but as soon as he had done so, he did. Again, Xerxes did not attack us until he had obtained possession of that country, but when he had, he crossed over; consequently, if the present Great King shall do the same, he will cross over, wherefore it must not be allowed. Comparison is illustrated by the sayings of Socrates; for instance, if one were to say that magistrates should not be chosen by lot, for this would be the same as choosing as representative athletes not those competent to contend, but those on whom the lot falls; or as choosing any of the sailors as the man who should take the helm, as if it were right that the choice should be decided by lot, not by a man's knowledge.

A fable, to give an example, is that of Stesichorus concerning Phalaris, or that of Aesop on behalf of the demagogue. For Stesichorus, when the people of Himera had chosen Phalaris dictator and were on the point of giving him a body guard, after many arguments related a fable to them: "A horse was in sole occupation of a meadow. A stag having come and done much damage to the pasture, the horse, wishing to avenge himself on the stag, asked a man whether he could help him to punish the stag. The man consented, on condition that the horse submitted to the bit and allowed him to mount him javelins in hand. The horse agreed to the terms and the man mounted him, but instead of obtaining vengeance on the stag, the horse from that time became the man's slave. So then," said he, "do you take care lest, in your desire to avenge yourselves on the enemy, you be treated like the horse. You already have the bit, since you have chosen a dictator; if you give him a body-guard and allow him to mount you, you will at once be the slaves of Phalaris." Aesop, when defending at Samos a demagogue who was being tried for his life, related the following anecdote. "A fox, while crossing a river, was driven into a ravine. Being unable to get out, she was for a long time in sore distress, and a number of dog-fleas clung to her skin. A hedgehog, wandering about, saw her and, moved with compassion, asked her if he should remove the fleas. The fox refused and when the hedgehog asked the reason, she answered: 'They are already full of me and draw little blood; but if you take them away, others will come that are hungry and will drain what remains to me.' You in like manner, O Samians, will suffer no more harm from this man, for he is wealthy; but if you put him to death, others will come who are poor, who will steal and squander your public funds." Fables are suitable for public speaking, and they have this advantage that, while it is difficult to find similar things that have really happened in the past, it is easier to invent fables; for they must be invented, like comparisons, if a man is capable of seizing the analogy; and this is easy if one studies philosophy. Thus, while the lessons conveyed by fables are easier to provide, those derived from facts are more useful for deliberative oratory, because as a rule the future resembles the past.

If we have no enthymemes, we must employ examples as demonstrative proofs, for conviction is produced by these; but if we have them, examples must be used as evidence and as a kind of epilogue to the enthymemes. For if they stand first, they resemble induction, and induction is not suitable to rhetorical speeches except in very few cases; if they stand last they resemble evidence, and a witness is in every case likely to induce belief. Wherefore also it is necessary to quote a number of examples if they are put first, but one alone is sufficient if they are put last; for even a single trustworthy witness is of use. We have thus stated how many kinds of examples there are, and how and when they should be made use of.

In regard to the use of maxims, it will most readily be evident on what subjects, and on what occasions, and by whom it is appropriate that maxims should be employed in speeches, after a maxim has been defined. Now, a maxim is a statement, not however concerning particulars, as, for instance, what sort of a man Iphicrates was, but general; it does not even deal with all general things, as for instance that the straight is the opposite of the crooked, but with the objects of human actions, and with what should be chosen or avoided with reference to them. And as the enthymeme is, we may say, the syllogism dealing with such things, maxims are the premises or conclusions of enthymemes without the syllogism. For example: "No man who is sensible ought to have his children taught to be excessively clever." is a maxim; but when the why and the wherefore are added, the whole makes an enthymeme; for instance, "for, not to speak of the charge of idleness brought against them, they earn jealous hostility from the citizens." Another example: "There is no man who is happy in everything" or "There is no man who is really free." The latter is a maxim, but taken with the next verse it is an enthymeme: "for he is the slave of either wealth or fortune." Now, if a maxim is what we have stated, it follows that maxims are of four kinds; for they are either accompanied by an epilogue or not. Now all those that state anything that is contrary to the general opinion or is a matter of dispute, need demonstrative proof; but those that do not, need no epilogue, either because they are already known, as, for instance, "Health is a most excellent thing for a man, at least in our opinion," for this is generally agreed; or because, no sooner are they uttered than they are clear to those who consider them, for instance, "He is no lover who does not love always." As for the maxims that are accompanied by an epilogue, some form part of an enthymeme, as "No one who is sensible," etc., while others are enthymematic, but are not part of an enthymeme; and these are most highly esteemed. Such are those maxims in which the reason of what is said is apparent: for instance, "Being a mortal, do not nourish immortal wrath;" to say that one should not always nourish immortal wrath is a maxim, but the addition "being a mortal" states the reason. It is the same with "A mortal should have mortal, not immortal thoughts."

It is evident, therefore, from what has been said, how many kinds of maxims there are, and to what it is appropriate to apply them in each case. For in the case of matters of dispute or what is contrary to the general opinion, the epilogue is necessary; but either the epilogue may be put first and the conclusion used as a maxim, as, for example, if one were to say, "As for me, since one ought neither to be the object of jealousy nor to be idle, I say that children ought not to be educated"; or put the maxim first and append the epilogue. In all cases where the statements made, although not paradoxical, are obscure, the reason should be added as concisely as possible. In such cases

Laconic apophthegms and riddling sayings are suitable; as, for instance, to say what Stesichorus said to the Locrians, that they ought not to be insolent, lest their cicadas should be forced to chirp from the ground. The use of maxims is suitable for one who is advanced in years, and in regard to things in which one has experience; since the use of maxims before such an age is unseemly, as also is story-telling; and to speak about things of which one has no experience shows foolishness and lack of education. A sufficient proof of this is that rustics especially are fond of coining maxims and ready to make display of them.

To express in general terms what is not general is especially suitable in complain or exaggeration, and then either at the beginning or after the demonstration. One should even make use of common and frequently quoted maxims, if they are useful; for because they are common, they seem to be true, since all as it were acknowledge them as such; for instance, one who is exhorting his soldiers to brave danger before having sacrificed may say, "The best of omens is to defend one's country," and if they are inferior in numbers, "The chances of war are the same for both," and if advising them to destroy the children of the enemy even though they are innocent of wrong, "Foolish is he who, having slain the father, suffers the children to live."

Further, some proverbs are also maxims; for example, "An Attic neighbour." Maxims should also be used even when contrary to the most popular sayings, such as "Know thyself" and "Nothing in excess," either when one's character is thereby likely to appear better, or if they are expressed in the language of passion. It would be an instance of the latter if a man in a rage were to say, "It is not true that a man should know himself; at any rate, such a man as this, if he had known himself, would never have claimed the chief command." And one's character would appear better, if one were to say that it is not right, as men say, to love as if one were bound to hate, but rather to hate as if one were bound to love. The moral purpose also should be made clear by the language, or else one should add the reason; for example, either by saying "that it is right to love, not as men say, but as if one were going to love for ever, for the other kind of love would imply treachery"; or thus, "The maxim does not please me, for the true friend should love as if he were going to love for ever. Nor do I approve the maxim 'Nothing in excess,' for one cannot hate the wicked too much."

Further, maxims are of great assistance to speakers, first, because of the vulgarity of the hearers, who are pleased if an orator, speaking generally, hits upon the opinions which they specially hold. What I mean will be clear from the following, and also how one should hunt for maxims. The maxim, as we have said, is a statement of the general; accordingly, the hearers are pleased to hear stated in general terms the opinion which they have already specially formed. For instance, a man who happened to have bad neighbours or children would welcome any one's statement that nothing is more troublesome than neighbours or more stupid than to beget children. Wherefore the speaker should endeavour to guess how his hearers formed their preconceived opinions and what they are, and then express himself in general terms in regard to them. This is one of the advantages of the use of maxims, but another is greater; for it makes speeches ethical. Speeches have this character, in which the moral purpose is clear. And this is the effect of all maxims, because he who employs them in a general manner declares his moral preferences; if then the maxims are good, they show the speaker also to be a man of good character. Let this suffice for what we had to say concerning maxims, their nature, how many kinds of them there are, the way they should be used, and what their advantages are.

Let us now speak of enthymemes in general and the manner of looking for them, and next of their topics; for each of these things is different in kind. We have already said that the enthymeme is a kind of syllogism, what makes it so, and in what it differs from the dialectic syllogisms; for the conclusion must neither be drawn from too far back nor should it include all the steps of the argument. In the first case its length causes obscurity, in the second, it is simply a waste of words, because it states much that is obvious. It is this that makes the ignorant more persuasive than the educated in the presence of crowds; as the poets say, "the ignorant are more skilled at speaking before a mob." For the educated use commonplaces and generalities, whereas the ignorant speak of what they know and of what more nearly concerns the audience. Wherefore one must not argue from all possible opinions, but only from such as are definite and admitted, for instance, either by the judges themselves or by those of whose judgement they approve. Further, it should be clear that this is the opinion of all or most of the hearers; and again, conclusions should not be drawn from necessary premises alone, but also from those which are only true as a rule.

First of all, then, it must be understood that, in regard to the subject of our speech or reasoning, whether it be political or of any other kind, it is necessary to be also acquainted with the elements of the question, either entirely or in part; for if you know none of these things, you will have nothing from which to draw a conclusion. I should like to know, for instance, how we are to give advice to the Athenians as to making war or not, if we do not know in what their strength consists, whether it is naval, military, or both, how great it is, their sources of revenue, their friends and enemies, and further, what wars they have already waged, with what success, and all similar things? Again, how could we praise them, if we did not know of the naval engagement at Salamis or the battle of Marathon, or what they did for the Heraclidae, and other similar things? for men always base their praise upon what really are, or are thought to be, glorious deeds. Similarly, they base their censure upon actions that are contrary to these, examining whether those censured have really, or seem to have, committed them; for example, that the Athenians subjugated the Greeks, and reduced to slavery the Aeginetans and Potidaeans who had fought with distinction on their side against the barbarians, and all such acts, and whatever other similar offences may have been committed by them. Similarly, in accusation and defence, speakers argue from an examination of the circumstances of the case. It makes no difference in doing this, whether it is a question of Athenians or Lacedaemonians, of a man or a god. For, when advising Achilles, praising or censuring, accusing or defending him, we must grasp all that really belongs, or appears to belong to him, in order that we may praise or censure in accordance with this, if there is anything noble or disgraceful; defend or accuse, if there is anything just or unjust; advise, if there is anything expedient or harmful. And similarly in regard to any subject whatever. For instance, in regard to justice, whether it is good or not, we must consider the question in the light of what is inherent in justice or the good.

Therefore, since it is evident that all men follow this procedure in demonstration, whether they reason strictly or loosely—since they do not derive their arguments from all things indiscriminately, but from what is inherent in each particular subject, and reason makes it clear that it is impossible to prove anything in any other way—it is evidently necessary, as has been stated in the *Topics*, to have first on each subject a selection of premises about probabilities and what is most suitable. [10] As for those to be used in sudden emergencies, the same method of inquiry must be adopted; we must look, not at what is indefinite but at what is inherent in the subject treated of in the speech, marking off as many facts as possible, particularly those intimately connected with the subject; for the more facts one has, the easier it is to demonstrate, and the more closely connected they are with the subject, the more suitable are they and less common. By common I mean, for instance, praising Achilles because he is a man, or one of the demigods, or because he went on the expedition against Troy; for this is applicable to many others as well, so that such praise is no more suited to Achilles than to Diomedes. By particular I mean what belongs to Achilles, but to no one else; for instance, to have slain Hector, the bravest of the Trojans, and Cycnus, who prevented all the Greeks from disembarking, being invulnerable; to have gone to the war when very young, and without having taken the oath; and all such things.

One method of selection then, and this the first, is the topical. Let us now speak of the elements of enthymemes (by element and topic of enthymeme I mean the same thing). But let us first make some necessary remarks. There are two kinds of enthymemes, the one demonstrative, which proves that a thing is or is not, and the other refutative, the two differing like refutation and syllogism in Dialectic. The demonstrative enthymeme draws conclusions from admitted premises, the refutative draws conclusions disputed by the adversary. We know nearly all the general heads of each of the special topics that are useful or necessary; for the propositions relating to each have been selected, so that we have in like manner already established all the topics from which enthymemes may be derived on the subject of good or bad, fair or foul, just or unjust, characters, emotions, and habits. Let us now endeavour to find topics about enthymemes in general in another way, noting in passing those which are refutative and those which are demonstrative, and those of apparent enthymemes, which are not really enthymemes, since they are not syllogisms. After this has been made clear, we will settle the question of solutions and objections, and whence they must be derived to refute enthymemes.

---

10. Here (2.22.10–11) Aristotle expresses his rationale for *topoi*, based on probability and propriety or suitability.

One topic of demonstrative enthymemes is derived from opposites; for it is necessary to consider whether one opposite is predicable of the other, as a means of destroying an argument, if it is not, as a means of constructing one, if it is; for instance, self-control is good, for lack of self-control is harmful; or as in the *Messeniacus*, "If the war is responsible for the present evils, one must repair them with the aid of peace." And, "For if it is unfair to be angry with those who have done wrong unintentionally, it is not fitting to feel beholden to one who is forced to do us good." Or, "If men are in the habit of gaining credit for false statements, you must also admit the contrary, that men often disbelieve what is true."

Another topic is derived from similar inflexions, for in like manner the derivatives must either be predicable of the subject or not; for instance, that the just is not entirely good, for in that case good would be predicable of anything that happens justly; but to be justly put to death is not desirable.

Another topic is derived from relative terms. For if to have done rightly or justly may be predicated of one, then to have suffered similarly may be predicated of the other; there is the same relation between having ordered and having carried out, as Diomedon the tax-gatherer said about the taxes, "If selling is not disgraceful for you, neither is buying disgraceful for us." And if rightly or justly can be predicated of the sufferer, it can equally be predicated of the one who inflicts suffering; if of the latter, then also of the former. However, in this there is room for a fallacy. For if a man has suffered justly, he has suffered justly, but perhaps not at your hands. Wherefore one must consider separately whether the sufferer deserves to suffer, and whether he who inflicts suffering is the right person to do so, and then make use of the argument either way; for sometimes there is a difference in such a case, and nothing prevents [its being argued], as in the *Alcmaeon* of Theodectes: "And did no one of mortals loathe thy mother?" Alcmaeon replied: "We must make a division before we examine the matter." And when Alphesiboea asked "How?", he rejoined, "Their decision was that she should die, but that it was not for me to kill her." Another example may be found in the trial of Demosthenes and those who slew Nicanor. For since it was decided that they had justly slain him, it was thought that he had been justly put to death. Again, in the case of the man who was murdered at Thebes, when the defendants demanded that the judges should decide whether the murdered man deserved to die, since a man who deserved it could be put to death without injustice.

Another topic is derived from the more and less. For instance, if not even the gods know everything, hardly can men; for this amounts to saying that if a predicate, which is more probably affirmable of one thing, does not belong to it, it is clear that it does not belong to another of which it is less probably affirmable. And to say that a man who beats his father also beats his neighbours, is an instance of the rule that, if the less exists, the more also exists. Either of these arguments may be used, according as it is necessary to prove either that a predicate is affirmable or that it is not. Further, if there is no question of greater or less; whence it was said, "Thy father deserves to be pitied for having lost his children; is not Oeneus then equally to be pitied for having lost an illustrious offspring?" Others instances are: if Theseus did no wrong, neither did Alexander (Paris); if the sons of Tyndareus did no wrong, neither did Alexander; and if Hector did no wrong in slaying Patroclus, neither did Alexander in slaying Achilles; if no other professional men are contemptible, then neither are philosophers; if generals are not despised because they are frequently defeated, neither are the sophists; or, if it behoves a private citizen to take care of your reputation, it is your duty to take care of that of Greece.

Another topic is derived from the consideration of time. Thus Iphicrates, in his speech against Harmodius, says: "If, before accomplishing anything, I had demanded the statue from you in the event of my success, you would have granted it; will you then refuse it, now that I have succeeded? Do not therefore make a promise when you expect something, and break it when you have received it." Again, to persuade the Thebans to allow Philip to pass through their territory into Attica, they were told that "if he had made this request before helping them against the Phocians, they would have promised; it would be absurd, therefore, if they refused to let him through now, because he had thrown away his opportunity and had trusted them."

Another topic consists in turning upon the opponent what has been said against ourselves; and this is an excellent method. For instance, in the *Teucer* . . . and Iphicrates employed it against Aristophon, when he asked him whether he would have betrayed the fleet for a bribe; when Aristophon said no, "Then," retorted Iphicrates, "if you, Aristophon, would not have betrayed it, would I, Iphicrates, have done so?" But the opponent must be a man who seems the more likely to have committed a crime; otherwise, it would appear ridiculous, if anyone were to make use of such an argument in reference to such an opponent, for instance, as Aristides; it should only be used to discredit the accuser. For in general the accuser aspires to be better than the defendant; accordingly, it must always be shown that this is not the case. And generally, it is ridiculous for a man to reproach others for what he does or would do himself, or to encourage others to do what he does not or would not do himself.

Another topic is derived from definition. For instance, that the *daimonion* is nothing else than a god or the work of a god; but he who thinks it to be the work of a god necessarily thinks that gods exist. When Iphicrates desired to prove that the best man is the noblest, he declared that there was nothing noble attaching to Harmodius and Aristogiton, before they did something noble; and, "I myself am more akin to them than you; at any rate, my deeds are more akin to theirs than yours." And as it is said in the *Alexander* that it would be generally admitted that men of disorderly passions are not satisfied with the enjoyment of one woman's person alone. Also, the reason why Socrates refused to visit Archelaus, declaring that it was disgraceful not to be in a position to return a favour as well as an injury. In all these cases, it is by definition and the knowledge of what the thing is in itself that conclusions are drawn upon the subject in question.

Another topic is derived from the different significations of a word, as explained in the *Topics*, where the correct use of these terms has been discussed.

Another, from division. For example, "There are always three motives for wrongdoing; two are excluded from consideration as impossible; as for the third, not even the accusers assert it."

Another, from induction.[11] For instance, from the case of the woman of Peparethus, it is argued that in matters of parentage women always discern the truth; similarly, at Athens, when Mantias the orator was litigating with his son, the mother declared the truth; and again, at Thebes, when Ismenias and Stilbon were disputing about a child, Dodonis declared that Ismenias was its father, Thettaliscus being accordingly recognized as the son of Ismenias. There is another instance in the "law" of Theodectes: "If we do not entrust our own horses to those who have neglected the horses of others, or our ships to those who have upset the ships of others; then, if this is so in all cases, we must not entrust our own safety to those who have failed to preserve the safety of others." Similarly, in order to prove that men of talent are everywhere honoured, Alcidamas said: "The Parians honoured Archilochus, in spite of his evil-speaking; the Chians Homer, although he had rendered no public services; the Mytilenaeans Sappho, although she was a woman; the Lacedaemonians, by no means a people fond of learning, elected Chilon one of their senators; the Italiotes honoured Pythagoras, and the Lampsacenes buried Anaxagoras, although he was a foreigner, and still hold him in honour. . . . The Athenians were happy as long as they lived under the laws of Solon, and the Lacedaemonians under those of Lycurgus; and at Thebes, as soon as those who had the conduct of affairs became philosophers, the city flourished."

Another topic is that from a previous judgement in regard to the same or a similar or contrary matter, if possible when the judgement was unanimous or the same at all times; if not, when it was at least that of the majority, or of the wise, either all or most, or of the good; or of the judges themselves or of those whose judgement they accept, or of those whose judgement it is not possible to contradict, for instance, those in authority, or of those whose judgement it is unseemly to contradict, for instance, the gods, a father, or instructors; as Autocles said in his attack on Mixidemides, "If the awful godesses were content to stand their trial before the Areopagus, should not Mixidemides?" Or Sappho, "Death is an evil; the gods have so decided, for otherwise they would die." Or as Aristippus, when in his opinion Plato had expressed himself too presumptuously, said, "Our friend at any rate never spoke like that," referring to Socrates. Hegesippus, after having first consulted the oracle at Olympia, asked the god at Delphi whether his opinion was the same as his father's, meaning that it would be disgraceful to contradict him. Helen was a virtuous woman, wrote Isocrates, because Theseus so judged; the same applies to Alexander (Paris), whom the goddesses chose before others. Evagoras was virtuous, as Isocrates says, for at any rate Conon in his misfortune, passing over everyone else, sought his assistance.

11. This *topos* involves the accumulation of examples.

Another topic is that from enumerating the parts, as in the *Topics:* What kind of movement is the soul? for it must be this or that. There is an instance of this in the *Socrates* of Theodectes: "What holy place has he profaned? Which of the gods recognized by the city has he neglected to honour?"

Again, since in most human affairs the same thing is accompanied by some bad or good result, another topic consists in employing the consequence to exhort or dissuade, accuse or defend, praise or blame. For instance, education is attended by the evil of being envied, and by the good of being wise; therefore we should not be educated, for we should avoid being envied; nay rather, we *should* be educated, for we should be wise. This topic is identical with the "Art" of Callippus, when you have also included the topic of the possible and the others which have been mentioned.

Another topic may be employed when it is necessary to exhort or dissuade in regard to two opposites, and one has to employ the method previously stated in the case of both. But there is this difference, that in the former case things of any kind whatever are opposed, in the latter opposite. For instance, a priestess refused to allow her son to speak in public; "For if," said she, "you say what is just, men will hate you; if you say what is unjust the gods will." On the other hand, "you *should* speak in public; for if you say what is just, the gods will love you, if you say what is unjust, men will." This is the same as the proverb, "To buy the swamp with the salt"; and retorting a dilemma on its proposer takes place when, two things being opposite, good and evil follow on each, the good and evil being opposite like the things themselves.

Again, since men do not praise the same things in public and in secret, but in public chiefly praise what is just and beautiful, and in secret rather wish for what is expedient, another topic consists in endeavouring to infer its opposite from one or other of these statements. This topic is the most weighty of those that deal with paradox.

Another topic is derived from analogy in things. For instance, Iphicrates, when they tried to force his son to perform public services because he was tall, although under the legal age, said: "If you consider tall boys men, you must vote that short men are boys." Similarly, Theodectes in his "law," says: "Since you bestow the rights of citizenship upon mercenaries such as Strabax and Charidemus on account of their merits, will you not banish those of them who have wrought such irreparable misfortunes?"

Another topic consists in concluding the identity of antecedents from the identity of results. Thus Xenophanes said: "There is as much impiety in asserting that the gods are born as in saying that they die; for either way the result is that at some time or other they did not exist." And, generally speaking, one may always regard as identical the results produced by one or other of any two things: "You are about to decide, not about Isocrates alone, but about education generally, whether it is right to study philosophy." And, "to give earth and water is slavery," and "to be included in the common peace implies obeying orders." Of two alternatives, you should take that which is useful.

Another topic is derived from the fact that the same men do not always choose the same thing before and after, but the contrary. The following enthymeme is an example: "If, when in exile, we fought to return to our country [it would be monstrous] if, now that we have returned, we were to return to exile to avoid fighting"! This amounts to saying that at one time they preferred to hold their ground at the price of fighting; at another, not to fight at the price of not remaining.

Another topic consists in maintaining that the cause of something which is or has been is something which would generally, or possibly might, be the cause of it; for example, if one were to make a present of something to another, in order to cause him pain by depriving him of it. Whence it has been said: "It is not from benevolence that the deity bestows great blessings upon many, but in order that they may suffer more striking calamities." And these verses from the *Meleager* of Antiphon: "Not in order to slay the monster, but that they may be witnesses to Greece of the valour of Meleager." And the following remark from the *Ajax* of Theodectes, that Diomedes chose Odysseus before all others, not to do him honour, but that his companion might be his inferior; for this may have been the reason.

Another topic common to forensic and deliberative rhetoric consists in examining what is hortatory and dissuasive, and the reasons which make men act or not. Now, these are the reasons which, if they exist, determine us to act, if not, not; for instance, if a thing is possible, easy, or useful to ourselves or our friends, or injurious and prejudicial to our enemies, or if the penalty is less than the profit. From these grounds we exhort, and dissuade from their contraries. It is on the same grounds that we accuse and defend; for what dissuades serves for defence, what persuades, for accusation. This topic comprises the whole "Art" of Pamphilus and Callippus.

Another topic is derived from things which are thought to happen but are incredible, because it would never have been thought so, if they had not happened or almost happened. And further, these things are even more likely to be true; for we only believe in that which is, or that which is probable: if then a thing is incredible and not probable, it will be true; for it is not because it is probable and credible that we think it true. Thus, Androcles of Pitthus, speaking against the law, being shouted at when he said "the laws need a law to correct them," went on, "fishes need salt, although it is neither probable nor credible that they should, being brought up in brine; similarly, pressed olives need oil, although it is incredible that what produces oil should itself need oil."

Another topic, appropriate to refutation, consists in examining contradictories, whether in dates, actions, or words, first, separately in the case of the adversary, for instance, "he says that the loves you, and yet he conspired with the Thirty;" next, separately in your own case, "he says that I am litigious, but he cannot prove that I have ever brought an action against anyone"; lastly, separately in the case of your adversary and yourself together: "he has never yet lent anything, but I have ransomed many of you."

Another topic, when men or things have been attacked by slander, in reality or in appearance, consists in stating the reason for the false opinion for there must be a reason for the supposition of guilt. For example, a woman embraced her son in a manner that suggested she had illicit relations with him, but when the reason was explained, the slander was quashed. Again, in the *Ajax* of Theodectes, Odysseus explains to Ajax why, although really more courageous than Ajax, he is not considered to be so.

Another topic is derived from the cause. If the cause exists, the effect exists; if the cause does not exist, the effect does not exist; for the effect exists with the cause, and without cause there is nothing. For example, Leodamas, when defending himself against the accusation of Thrasybulus that his name had been posted in the Acropolis but that he had erased it in the time of the Thirty, declared that it was impossible, for Thirty would have had more confidence in him if his hatred against the people had been graven on the stone.

Another topic consists in examining whether there was or is another better course than that which is advised, or is being, or has been, carried out. For it is evident that, if this has not been done, a person has not committed a certain action; because no one, purposely or knowingly, chooses what is bad. However, this argument may be false; for often it is not until later that it becomes clear what was the better course, which previously was uncertain.

Another topic, when something contrary to what has already been done is on the point of being done, consists in examining them together. For instance, when the people of Elea asked Xenophanes if they ought to sacrifice and sing dirges to Leucothea, or not, he advised them that, if they believed her to be a goddess they ought not to sing dirges, but if they believed her to be a mortal, they ought not to sacrifice to her.

Another topic consists in making use of errors committed, for purposes of accusation or defence. For instance, in the *Medea* of Carcinus, some accuse Medea of having killed her children, — at any rate, they had disappeared; for she had made the mistake of sending them out of the way. Medea herself pleads that she would have slain, not her children, but her husband Jason; for it would have been a mistake on her part not to have done this, if she had done the other. This topic and kind of enthymeme is the subject of the whole of the first "Art" of Theodorus.

Another topic is derived from the meaning of a name. For instance, Sophocles says, "Certainly thou art iron, like thy name." This topic is also commonly employed in praising the gods. Conon used to call Thrasybulus "the man bold in counsel," and Herodicus said of Thrasymachus, "Thou art ever bold in fight," and of Polus, "Thou art ever Polus (colt) by name and colt by nature," and of Draco the legislator that his laws were not those of a man, but of a dragon, so severe were they. Hecuba in Euripides speaks thus of Aphro-dite: "And rightly does the name of the goddess begin like the word aphro-syne (folly);" and Chaeremon of Pentheus, "Pentheus named after his unhappy future." Enthymemes that serve to refute are more popular than those that serve to demonstrate, because the former is a conclusion of opposites in a small compass, and things in juxtaposition are always clearer to the audience. But of all syllogisms, whether refutative or demonstrative, those are specially applauded, the result of which the hearers foresee as soon as they are begun, and not because they are superficial (for as they listen they congratulate themselves on anticipating the conclusion); and also those which the hearers are only so little behind that they understand what they mean as soon as they are delivered.

But as it is possible that some syllogisms may be real, and others not real but only apparent, there must also be real and apparent enthymemes, since the enthymeme is a kind of syllogism.

Now, of the topics of apparent enthymemes one is that of diction, which is of two kinds. The first, as in Dialectic, consists in ending with a conclusion syllogistically expressed, although there has been no syllogistic process, "therefore it is neither this nor that," "so it must be this or that"; and similarly in rhetorical arguments a concise and antithetical statement is supposed to be an enthymeme; for such a style appears to contain a real enthymeme. This fallacy appears to be the result of the form of expression. For the purpose of using the diction to create an impression of syllogistic reasoning it is useful to state the heads of several syllogisms: "He saved some, avenged others, and freed the Greeks"; for each of these propositions has been proved by others, but their union appears to furnish a fresh conclusion.

The second kind of fallacy of diction is homonymy. For instance, if one were to say that the mouse is an important animal, since from it is derived the most honoured of all religious festivals, namely, the mysteries; of if, in praising the dog, one were to include the dog in heaven (Sirius), or Pan, because Pindar said, "O blessed one, whom the Olympians call dog of the Great Mother, taking every form," or were to say that the dog is an honourable animal, since to be without a dog is most dishonourable. And to say that Hermes is the most sociable of the gods, because he alone is called common; and that words are most excellent, since good men are considered worthy, not of riches but of consideration; for λόγου ἄξιος has a double meaning.

Another fallacy consists in combining what is divided or dividing what is combined. For since a thing which is not the same as another often appears to be the same, one may adopt the more convenient alternative. Such was the argument of Euthydemus, to prove, for example, that a man knows that there is a trireme in the Piraeus, because he knows the existence of two things, the Piraeus and the trireme; or that, when one knows the letters, one also knows the word made of them, for word and letters are the same thing. Further, since twice so much is unwholesome, one may argue that neither is the original amount wholesome; for it would be absurd that two halves separately should be good, but bad combined. In this way the argument may be used for refutation, in another way for demonstration, if one were to say, one good thing cannot make two bad things. But the whole topic is fallacious. Again, one may quote what Polycrates said of Thrasybulus, that he deposed thirty tyrants, for here he combines them; or the example of the fallacy of division in the *Orestes* of Theodectes: "It is just that a woman who has killed her husband" should be put to death, and that the son should avenge the father; and this in fact is what has been done. But if they are combined, perhaps the act ceases to be just. The same might also be classed as an example of the fallacy of omission; for the name of the one who should put the woman to death is not mentioned.

Another topic is that of constructing or destroying by exaggeration, which takes place when the speaker, without having proved that any crime has actually been committed, exaggerates the supposed fact; for it makes it appear either that the accused is not guilty, when he himself exaggerates it, or that he is guilty, when it is the accuser who is in a rage. Therefore there is no enthymeme; for the hearer falsely concludes that the accused is guilty or not, although neither has been proved.

Another fallacy is that of the sign, for this argument also is illogical. For instance, if one were to say that those who love one another are useful to States, since the love of Harmodius and Aristogiton overthrew the tyrant Hipparchus; or that Dionysius is a thief, because he is a rascal; for here again the argument is inconclusive; not every rascal is a thief although every thief is a rascal.

Another fallacy is derived from accident; for instance, when Polycrates says of the mice, that they rendered great service by gnawing the bowstrings. Or if one were to say that nothing is more honourable than to be invited to a dinner, for because he was not invited Achilles was wroth with the Achaeans at Tenedos; whereas he was really wroth because he had been treated with disrespect, but this was an accident due to his not having been invited.

Another fallacy is that of the Consequence. For instance, in the *Alexander* (Paris) it is said that Paris was high-minded, because he despised the companionship of the common herd and dwelt on Ida by himself; for because the high-minded are of this character, Paris also might be thought high-minded. Or, since a man pays attention to dress and roams about at night, he is a libertine, because libertines are of this character. Similarly, the poor sing and dance in the temples, exiles can live where they please; and since these things belong to those who are apparently happy, those to whom they belong may also be thought happy. But there is a difference in conditions; wherefore this topic also falls under the head of omission.

Another fallacy consists of taking what is not the cause for the cause, as when a thing has happened at the same time as, or after, another; for it is believed that what happens after is produced by the other, especially by politicians. Thus, Demades declared that the policy of Demosthenes was the cause of all the evils that happened, since it was followed by the war.

Another fallacy is the omission of when and how. For instance, Alexander (Paris) had a right to carry off Helen, for the choice of a husband had been given her by her father. But (this was a fallacy), for it was not, as might be thought, for all time, but only for the first time; for the father's authority only lasts till then. Or, if one should say that it is wanton outrage to beat a free man; for this is not always the case, but only when the assailant gives the first blow.

Further, as in sophistical disputations, an apparent syllogism arises as the result of considering a thing first absolutely, and then not absolutely, but only in a particular case. For instance, in Dialectic, it is argued that that which is not *is*, for that which is not *is* that which is not; also, that the unknown can be known, for it can be known of the unknown that it is unknown. Similarly, in Rhetoric, an apparent enthymeme may arise from that which is not absolutely probable but only in particular cases. But this is not to be understood absolutely, as Agathon says: "One might perhaps say that this very thing is probable, that many things happen to men that are not probable;" for that which is contrary to probability nevertheless does happen, so that that which is contrary to probability is probable. If this is so, that which is improbable will be probable. But not absolutely; but as, in the case of sophistical disputations, the argument becomes fallacious when the circumstances, reference, and manner are not added, so here it will become so owing to the probability being not probable absolutely but only in particular cases. The "Art" of Corax is composed of this topic. For if a man is not likely to be guilty of what he is accused of, for instance if, being weak, he is accused of assault and battery, his defence will be that the crime is not probable; but if he is likely to be guilty, for instance, if he is strong, it may be argued again that the crime is not probable, for the very reason that it was bound to appear so. It is the same in all other cases; for a man must either be likely to have committed a crime or not. Here, both the alternatives appear equally probable, but the one is really so, the other not probable absolutely, but only in the conditions mentioned. And this is what "making the worse appear the better argument" means. Wherefore men were justly disgusted with the promise of Protagoras; for it is a lie, not a real but an apparent probability, not found in any art except Rhetoric and Sophistic. So much for real or apparent enthymemes.

Next to what has been said we must speak of refutation. An argument may be refuted either by a counter syllogism or by bringing an objection. It is clear that the same topics may furnish countersyllogisms; for syllogisms are derived from probable materials and many probabilities are contrary to one another. An objection is brought, as shown in the *Topics*, in four ways: it may be derived either from itself, or from what is similar, or from what is contrary, or from what has been decided. In the first case, if for instance the enthymeme was intended to prove that love is good, two objections might be made; either the general statement that all want is bad, or in particular that Caunian love would not have become proverbial, unless some forms of love had been bad. An objection from what is contrary is brought if, for instance, the enthymeme is that the good man does good to all his friends; it may be objected: But the bad man does not do harm [to all his friends]. An objection from what is similar is brought, if the enthymeme is that those who have been injured always hate, by arguing that those who have been benefited do not always love. The fourth kind of objection is derived from the former decisions of well-known men. For instance, if the enthymeme is that one should make allowance for those who are drunk, for their offence is the result of ignorance, it may be objected that Pittacus then is unworthy of commendation, otherwise he would not have laid down severer punishment for a man who commits an offence when drunk.

Now the material of enthymemes is derived from four sources—probabilities, examples, necessary signs, and signs. Conclusions are drawn from probabilities, when based upon things which most commonly occur or seem to occur; from examples, when they are the result of induction from one or more similar cases, and when one assumes the general and then concludes the particular by an example; from necessary signs, when based upon that which is necessary and ever exists; from signs, when their material is the general or the particular, whether true or not. Now, the probable being not what occurs invariably but only for the most part, it is evident that enthymemes of this character can always be refuted by bringing an objection. But the objection is often only apparent, not real; for he who brings the objection endeavours to show, not that the argument is not probable, but that it is not necessary. Wherefore, by the employment of this fallacy, the defendant always has an advantage over the accuser. For since the latter always bases his proof upon probabilities, and it is not the same thing to show that an argument is not probable as to show that it is not necessary, and that which is only true for the most part is always liable to objection (otherwise it would not be probable, but constant and necessary), —then the judge thinks, if the refutation is made in this manner, either that the argument is not probable, or that it is not for him to decide, being deceived by the fallacy, as we have just indicated. For his judgement must not rest upon necessary arguments alone, but also upon probabilities; for this is what is meant by deciding according to the best of one's judgement. It is therefore not enough to refute an argument by showing that it is not necessary; if must also be shown that it is not probable. This will be attained if the objection itself is specially based upon what happens generally. This may take place in two ways, from consideration either of the time or of the facts. The strongest objections are those in which both are combined; for a thing is more probable, the greater the number of similar cases.

Signs and enthymemes based upon signs, even if true, may be refuted in the manner previously stated; for it is clear from the *Analytics* that no sign can furnish a logical conclusion. As for enthymemes derived from examples, they may be refuted in the same manner as probabilities. For if we have a single fact that contradicts the opponent's example, the argument is refuted as not being necessary, even though examples, more in number and of more common occurrence, are otherwise; but if the majority and greater frequency of examples is on the side of the opponent, we must contend either that the present example is not similar to those cited by him, or that the thing did not take place in the same way, or that there is some difference. But necessary signs and the enthymemes derived from them cannot be refuted on the ground of not furnishing a logical conclusion, as is clear from the *Analytics*; the only thing that remains is to prove that the thing alleged is non-existent. But if it is evident that it is true and that it is a necessary sign, the argument at once becomes irrefutable; for, by means of demonstration, everything at once becomes clear.

Amplification and depreciation are not elements of enthymeme (for I regard element and topic as identical), since element (or topic) is a head under which several enthymemes are included, but they are enthymemes which serve to show that a thing is great or small, just as others serve to show that it is good or bad, just or unjust, or anything else. All these are the materials of syllogisms and enthymemes; so that if none of these is a topic of enthymeme, neither is amplification or depreciation. Nor are enthymemes by which arguments are refuted of a different kind from those by which they are established; for it is clear that demonstration or bringing an objection is the means of refutation. By the first the contrary of the adversary's conclusion is demonstrated; for instance, if he has shown that a thing has happened, his opponent shows that it has not; if he has shown that a thing has not happened, he shows that it has. This, therefore, will not be the difference between them; for both employ the same arguments; they bring forward enthymemes to show that the thing is or that it is not. And the objection is not an enthymeme, but, as I said in the *Topics*, it is stating an opinion which is intended to make it clear that the adversary's syllogism is not logical, or that he has assumed some false premise. Now, since there are three things in regard to speech, to which special attention should be devoted, let what has been said suffice for examples, maxims, enthymemes, and what concerns the intelligence generally; for the sources of a supply of arguments and the means of refuting them. It only remains to speak of style and arrangement.   1403b5

Style

There are three things which require special attention in regard to speech: 1403b6 first, the sources of proofs; secondly, style; and thirdly, the arrangement of the parts of the speech. We have already spoken of proofs and stated that they are three in number, what is their nature, and why there are only three; for in all cases persuasion is the result either of the judges themselves being affected in a certain manner, or because they consider the speakers to be of a certain character, or because something has been demonstrated. We have also stated the sources from which enthymemes should be derived — some of them being special, the others general commonplaces.

We have therefore next to speak of style; for it is not sufficient to know what one ought to say, but one must also know how to say it, and this largely contributes to making the speech appear of a certain character. In the first place, following the natural order, we investigated that which first presented itself — what gives things themselves their persuasiveness; in the second place, their arrangement by style; and in the third place, delivery, which is of the greatest importance, but has not yet been treated of by any one. In fact, it only made its appearance late in tragedy and rhapsody, for at first the poets themselves acted their tragedies. It is clear, therefore, that there is something of the sort in rhetoric as well as in poetry, and it has been dealt with by Glaucon of Teos among others. Now delivery is a matter of voice, as to the mode in which it should be used for each particular emotion; when it should be loud, when low, when intermediate; and how the tones, that is, shrill, deep, and intermediate, should be used; and what rhythms are adapted to each subject. For there are three qualities that are considered, —volume, harmony, rhythm. Those who use these properly nearly always carry off the prizes in dramatic contests, and as at the present day actors have greater influence on the stage than the poets, it is the same in political contests, owning to the corruptness of our forms of government. But no treatise has yet been composed on delivery, since the matter of style itself only lately came into notice; and rightly considered it is thought vulgar. But since the whole business of Rhetoric is to influence opinion, we must pay attention to it, not as being right, but necessary; for, as a matter of right, one should aim at nothing more in a speech than how to avoid exciting pain or pleasure. For justice should consist in fighting the case with the facts alone, so that everything else that is beside demonstration is superfluous; nevertheless, as we have just said, it is of great importance owing to the corruption of the hearer. However, in every system of instruction there is some slight necessity to pay attention to style; for it does make a difference, for the purpose of making a thing clear, to speak in this or that manner; still, the difference is not so very great, but all these things are mere outward show for pleasing the hearer; wherefore no one teaches geometry in this way.

Now, when delivery comes into fashion, it will have the same effect as acting. Some writers have attempted to say a few words about it, as Thrasymachus, in his *Eleoi*; and in fact, a gift for acting is a natural talent and depends less upon art, but in regard to style it is artificial. Wherefore people who excel in this in their turn obtain prizes, just as orators who excel in delivery; 1404a19 for written speeches owe their effect not so much to the sense as to the style.

1404b1   Let this suffice for the consideration of these points. In regard to style, one of its chief merits may be defined as perspicuity. This is shown by the fact that the speech, if it does not make the meaning clear, will not perform its proper function; neither must it be mean, nor above the dignity of the subject, but appropriate to it; for the poetic style may be is not mean, but it is not appropriate to prose. Of nouns and verbs it is the proper ones that make style perspicuous; all the others which have been spoken of in the *Poetics* elevate and make it ornate; for departure from the ordinary makes it appear more dignified. In this respect men feel the same in regard to style as in regard to foreigners and fellow-citizens. Wherefore we should give our language a "foreign air"; for men admire what is remote, and that which excites admiration is pleasant. In poetry many things conduce to this and there it is appropriate; for the subjects and persons spoken of are more out of the common. But in prose such methods are appropriate in much fewer instances, for the subject is less elevated; and even in poetry, if fine language were used by a slave or a very young man, or about quite unimportant matters, it would be hardly becoming; for even here due proportion consists in contraction and amplification as the subject requires. Wherefore those who practises this artifice must conceal it and avoid the appearance of speaking artificially instead of naturally; for that which is natural persuades, but the artificial does not. For men become suspicious of one whom they think to be laying a trap for them, as they are of mixed wines. Such was the case with the voice of Theodorus as contrasted with that of the rest of the actors; for his seemed to be the voice of the speaker, that of the others the voice of some one else. Art is cleverly concealed when the speaker chooses his words from ordinary language and puts them together like Euripides, who was the first to show the way.

Nouns and verbs being the components of speech, and nouns being of the different kinds which have been considered in the *Poetics*, of these we should use strange, compound, or coined words only rarely and in few places. We will state later in what places they should be used; the reason for this has already been mentioned, namely, that it involves too great a departure from suitable language. Proper and appropriate words and metaphors are alone to be employed in the style of prose; this is shown by the fact that no one employs anything but these. For all use metaphors in conversation, as well as proper and appropriate words; wherefore it is clear that, if a speaker manages well, there will be something "foreign" about his speech, while possibly the art may not be detected, and his meaning will be clear. And this, as we have said, is the chief merit of rhetorical language. (In regard to nouns, homonyms are most useful to the sophist, for it is by their aid that he employs captious arguments, and synonyms to the poet. Instances of words that are both proper and synonymous are "going" and "walking": for these two words are proper and have the same meaning.)

It has already been stated, as we have said, in the *Poetics*, what each of these things is, how many kinds of metaphor there are, and that it is most important both in poetry and in prose. But the orator must devote the greater attention to them in prose, since the latter has fewer resources than verse. It is metaphor above all that gives perspicuity, pleasure, and a foreign air, and it cannot be learnt from anyone else; but we must make use of metaphors and epithets that are appropriate. This will be secured by observing due proportion; otherwise there will be a lack of propriety, because it is when placed in juxtaposition that contraries are most evident. We must consider, as a red cloak suits a young man, what suits an old one; for the same garment is not suitable for both. And if we wish to ornament our subject, we must derive our metaphor from the better species under the same genus; if to depreciate it, from the worse. Thus, to say (for you have two opposites belonging to the same genus) that the man who begs prays, or that the man who prays begs (for both are forms of asking) is an instance of doing this; as, when Iphicrates called Callias a mendicant priest instead of a torch-bearer, Callias replied that Iphicrates himself could not be initiated, otherwise he would not have called him mendicant priest but torch-bearer; both titles indeed have to do with a divinity, but the one is honourable, the other dishonourable. And some call actors flatterers of Dionysus, whereas they call themselves "artists." Both these names are metaphors, but the one is a term of abuse, the other the contrary. Similarly, pirates now call themselves purveyors; and so it is allowable to say that the man who has committed a crime has "made a mistake," that the man who has "made a mistake" is "guilty of crime," and that one who has committed a theft has either "taken" or "ravaged." The saying in the *Telephus* of Euripides, "Ruling over the oar and having landed in Mysia," is inappropriate, because the word "ruling" exceeds the dignity of the subject, and so the artifice can be seen. Forms of words also are faulty, if they do not express an agreeable sound; for instance, Dionysius the Brazen in his elegiacs speaks of poetry as "the scream of Calliope;" both are sounds, but the metaphor is bad, because the sounds have no meaning.

Further, metaphors must not be far-fetched, but we must give names to things that have none by deriving the metaphor from what is akin and of the same kind, so that, as soon as it is uttered, it is clearly seen to be akin, as in the famous enigma, "I saw a man who glued bronze with fire upon another." There was no name for what took place, but as in both cases there is a kind of application, he called the application of the cupping-glass "gluing." And, generally speaking, clever enigmas furnish good metaphors; for metaphor is a kind of enigma, so that it is clear that the transference is clever. Metaphors should also be derived from things that are beautiful, the beauty of a word consisting, as Licymnius says, in its sound or sense, and its ugliness in the same. There is a third condition, which refutes the sophistical argument; for it is not the case, as Bryson said, that no one ever uses foul language, if the meaning is the same whether this or that word is used; this is false; for one word is more proper than another, more of a likeness, and better suited to putting the matter before the eyes. Further, this word or that does not signify a thing under the same conditions; thus for this reason also it must be admitted that one word is fairer or fouler than the other. Both, indeed, signify what is fair or foul, but not *qua* fair or foul; or if they do, it is in a greater or less degree. Metaphors therefore should be derived from what is beautiful either in sound, or in signification, or to sight, or to some other sense. For it does make a difference, for instance, whether one says "rosy-fingered morn," rather than "purple-fingered," or, what is still worse, "red fingered."

As for epithets, they may be applied from what is vile or disgraceful, for instance, "the matricide," or form what is more honourable, for instance, "the avenger of his father." When the winner in a mule-race offered Simonides a small sum, he refused to write an ode, as if he thought it beneath him to write on half-asses; but when he gave him a sufficient amount, he wrote, "Hail, daughters of storm-footed steeds!" and yet they were also the daughters of asses. Further, the use of diminutives amounts to the same. It is the diminutive which makes the good and the bad appear less, as Aristophanes in the *Babylonians* jestingly uses "goldlet, cloaklet, afrontlet, diseaselet" instead of "gold, cloak, affront, disease."

But one must be careful to observe the due mean in their use as well as in that of 1405b34 epithets.

3

Greco-Roman Rhetoric

By the second century B.C., the Roman republic had come to dominate the Mediterranean world. Greece and much of Asia Minor were conquered in this century, and hordes of Greek slaves were introduced into Roman life as stewards, businessmen, educators, and tutors. The superior intellectual and artistic achievements of Hellenistic culture had a tremendous impact on Roman civilization. Included in this influence was rhetorical theory and practice.

Public speaking was already vital to Roman life. The people ruled through their magistrates and the Senate. Leaders were elected in popular assemblies, which also debated issues and passed legislation. Both prosecutors and defendants (or their representatives) exercised their forensic skills in a well-developed legal system.

The Roman educational system quickly incorporated Hellenistic methods of rhetorical instruction, which reflected a long tradition from Gorgias, Isocrates, and Aristotle down through Hermagoras. After local training from a tutor or teacher, upper- and middle-class Roman youths frequently pursued advanced education in rhetoric at one of the prominent Hellenistic centers of learning: Athens, Rhodes, or Pergamum.

The earliest Latin works on rhetorical theory date from the first decades of the first century B.C. and reflect the development of Greek technical manuals. The *Rhetorica ad Herennium* and Cicero's early *De Inventione* are Latin continuations of the kind of manuals represented by the *Rhetorica ad Alexandrum*, with the addition of the latest organizing principles from Hermagoras. Cicero's subsequent works on rhetorical theory reflect most of the rhetorical developments in ancient Greece and Rome. In the works by Cicero's Epicurean contemporary Philodemus, we also see the continuing debate on the basic philosophical questions regarding rhetoric's status and functions.

From the end of the first century A.D., Quintilian's magnificent *Institutio Oratoria* provides an even more comprehensive survey of the entire history of rhetorical theory and instruction, starting with Corax and Tisias and concluding with Quintilian's own practice — now in a different, imperial setting where many of the former applications for rhetoric no longer existed. Quintilian's contemporary, Tacitus, laments the demise of the turbulent Republican days that preceded the politically stable but rhetorically stifling empire.

Rhetorica ad Herennium

The earliest complete rhetorical text extant in Latin, the *Rhetorica ad Herennium* is a first-century B.C. handbook reflecting Hellenistic rhetoric. Although its author is unknown, from the close relationship of its first two books on invention to Cicero's early *De Inventione*, it was thought to have been by Cicero until the Renaissance. No matter who the actual author, the work's combination of comprehensive scope and simple clarity has contributed to its enormous influence on the history of writing in the West. In the first selection that follows, the whole subject of rhetoric is reviewed. The next two selections illustrate the thoroughly "topical" and by this time prescriptively formulaic approach to finding the right things to say in the introductions and conclusions of speeches. The final selection is the oldest extant treatment of delivery. Its equally prescriptive directions give us an interesting view of ancient public speaking.

Rhetorica ad Herennium

Overview of Rhetoric

My private affairs keep me so busy that I can hardly find enough leisure to devote to study, and the little that is vouchsafed to me I have usually preferred to spend on philosophy. Yet your desire, Gaius Herennius, has spurred me to compose a work on the Theory of Public Speaking, lest you should suppose that in a matter which concerns you I either lacked the will or shirked the labour. And I have undertaken this project the more gladly because I knew that you had good grounds in wishing to learn rhetoric, for it is true that copiousness and facility in expression bear abundant fruit, if controlled by proper knowledge and a strict discipline of the mind.

That is why I have omitted to treat those topics which, for the sake of futile self-assertion, Greek writers have adopted. For they, from fear of appearing to know too little, have gone in quest of notions irrelevant to the art, in order that the art might seem more difficult to understand. I, on the other hand, have treated those topics which seemed pertinent to the theory of public speaking. I have not been moved by hope of gain or desire for glory, as the rest have been, in undertaking to write, but have done so in order that, by my painstaking work, I may gratify your wish. To avoid prolixity, I shall now begin my discussion of the subject, as soon as I have given you this one injunction: Theory without continuous practice in speaking is of little avail; from this you may understand that the precepts of theory here offered ought to be applied in practice.

The task of the public speaker is to discuss capably those matters which law and custom have fixed for the uses of citizenship, and to secure as far as possible the agreement of his hearers. There are three kinds of causes which the speaker must treat: Epideictic, Deliberative, and Judicial. The epideictic kind is devoted to the praise or censure of some particular person. The deliberative consists in the discussion of policy and embraces persuasion and dissuasion. The judicial is based on legal controversy, and comprises criminal prosecution or civil suit, and defence.

Now I shall explain what faculties the speaker should possess, and then show the proper means of treating these causes.

The speaker, then, should possess the faculties of Invention, Arrangement, Style, Memory, and Delivery. Invention is the devising of matter, true or plausible, that would make the case convincing. Arrangement is the ordering and distribution of the matter, making clear the place to which each thing is to be assigned. Style is the adaptation of suitable words and sentences to the matter devised. Memory is the firm retention in the mind of the matter, words, and arrangement. Delivery is the graceful regulation of voice, countenance, and gesture.

All these faculties we can acquire by three means: Theory, Imitation, and

Reprinted by permission of the publishers and The Loeb Classical Library from *Rhetorica ad Herennium* (1.1–2, 1.4–7, 2.30–31, 3.11–15), trans. Harry Caplan, Cambridge, Mass.: Harvard University Press, 1981.

Practice. By theory is meant a set of rules that provide a definite method and system of speaking. Imitation stimulates us to attain, in accordance with a studied method, the effectiveness of certain models in speaking. Practice is assiduous exercise and experience in speaking.

Since, then, I have shown what causes the speaker should treat and what kinds of competence he should possess, it seems that I now need to indicate how the speech can be adapted to the theory of the speaker's function.

Introductions

1.4   In view of these considerations, it will be in point to apply the theory of Introductions to the kind of cause. There are two kinds of Introduction: the Direct Opening, in Greek called the *Prooimion*, and the Subtle Approach, called the *Ephodos*. The Direct Opening straightway prepares the hearer to attend to our speech. Its purpose is to enable us to have hearers who are attentive, receptive, and well-disposed. If our cause is of the doubtful kind, we shall build the Direct Opening upon goodwill, so that the discreditable part of the cause cannot be prejudicial to us. If our cause is of the petty kind, we shall make our hearers attentive. If our cause is of the discreditable kind, unless we have hit upon a means of capturing goodwill by attacking our adversaries, we must use the Subtle Approach, which I shall discuss later. And finally, if our cause is of the honourable kind, it will be correct either to use the Direct Opening or not to use it. If we wish to use it, we must show why the cause is honourable, or else briefly announce what matters we are going to discuss. But if we do not wish to use the Direct Opening, we must begin our speech with a law, a written document, or some argument supporting our cause.

Since, then, we wish to have our hearer receptive, well-disposed, and attentive, I shall disclose how each state can be brought about. We can have receptive hearers if we briefly summarise the cause and make them attentive; for the receptive hearer is one who is willing to listen attentively. We shall have attentive hearers by promising to discuss important, new, and unusual matters, or such as appertain to the commonwealth, or to the hearers themselves, or to the worship of the immortal gods; by bidding them listen attentively; and by enumerating the points we are going to discuss. We can by four methods make our hearers well-disposed: by discussing our own person, the person of our adversaries, that of our hearers, and the facts themselves.

5   From the discussion of our own person we shall secure good will by praising our services without arrogance and revealing also our past conduct toward the republic, or toward our parents, friends, or the audience, and by making some reference to . . . provided that all such references are pertinent to the matter in question; likewise by setting forth our disabilities, need, loneliness, and misfortune, and pleading for our hearers' aid, and at the same time showing that we have been unwilling to place our hope in anyone else.

From the discussion of the person of our adversaries we shall secure goodwill by bringing them into hatred, unpopularity, or contempt. We shall force hatred upon them by adducing some base, high-handed, treacherous, cruel, impudent, malicious, or shameful act of theirs. We shall make our adversaries unpopular by setting forth their violent behaviour, their dominance, factiousness, wealth, lack of self-restraint, high birth, clients, hospitality, club allegiance, or marriage alliances, and by making clear that they rely more upon these supports than upon the truth. We shall bring our adversaries into contempt by presenting their idleness, cowardice, sloth, and luxurious habits.

From the discussion of the person of our hearers goodwill is secured if we set forth the courage, wisdom, humanity, and nobility of past judgements they have rendered, and if we reveal what esteem they enjoy and with what interest their decision is awaited.

From the discussion of the facts themselves we shall render the hearer well-disposed by extolling our own cause with praise and by contemptuously disparaging that of our adversaries.

Now I must explain the Subtle Approach. There are three occasions on which   6
we cannot use the Direct Opening, and these we must consider carefully: (1) when our cause is discreditable, that is, when the subject itself alienates the hearer from us; (2) when the hearer has apparently been won over by the previous speakers of the opposition; (3) or when the hearer has become wearied by listening to the previous speakers.

If the cause has a discreditable character, we can make our Introduction with the following points: that the agent, not the action, ought to be considered; that we ourselves are displeased with the acts which our opponents say have been committed, and that these are unworthy, yes, heinous. Next, when we have for a time enlarged upon this idea, we shall show that nothing of the kind has been committed by us. Or we shall set forth the judgement rendered by others in an analogous cause, whether that cause be of equal, or less, or greater importance; then we shall gradually approach our own cause and establish the analogy. The same result is achieved if we deny an intention to discuss our opponents or some extraneous matter and yet, by subtly inserting the words, do so.

If the hearers have been convinced, if our opponent's speech has gained their credence—and this will not be hard for us to know, since we are well aware of the means by which belief is ordinarily effected—if, then, we think belief has been effected, we shall make our Subtle Approach to the cause by the following means: the point which our adversaries have regarded as their strongest support we shall promise to discuss first; we shall begin with a statement made by the opponent, and particularly with that which he has made last; and we shall use Indecision, along with an exclamation of astonishment: "What had I best say?" or "To what point shall I first reply?"

If the hearers have been fatigued by listening, we shall open with something that may provoke laughter—a fable, a plausible fiction, a caricature, an ironical inversion of the meaning of a word, an ambiguity, innuendo, banter, a naïvety, an exaggeration, a recapitulation, a pun, an unexpected turn, a comparison, a novel tale, a historical anecdote, a verse, or a challenge or a smile of approbation directed at some one. Or we shall promise to speak otherwise than as we have prepared, and not to talk as others usually do; we shall briefly explain what the other speakers do and what we intend to do.

7   Between the Subtle Approach and the Direct Opening there is the following difference. The Direct Opening should be such that by the straightforward methods I have prescribed we immediately make the hearer well-disposed or attentive or receptive; whereas the Subtle Approach should be such that we effect all these results covertly, through dissimulation, and so can arrive at the same vantage-point in the task of speaking. But though this three-fold advantage — that the hearers constantly show themselves attentive, receptive, and well-disposed to us — is to be secured throughout the discourse, it must in the main be won by the Introduction to the cause.

Now, for fear that we may at some time use a faulty Introduction, I shall show what faults must be avoided. In the Introduction of a cause we must make sure that our style is temperate and that the words are in current use, so that the discourse seems unprepared. An Introduction is faulty if it can be applied as well to a number of causes; that is called a banal Introduction. Again, an Introduction which the adversary can use no less well is faulty, and that is called a common Introduction. That Introduction, again, is faulty which the opponent can turn to his own use against you. And again that is faulty which has been composed in too laboured a style, or is too long; and that which does not appear to have grown out of the cause itself in such a way as the have an intimate connection with the Statement of Facts; and, finally, that which fails to make the hearer well-disposed or receptive or attentive.

Conclusions

2.30   Conclusions, among the Greeks called *epilogoi*, are tripartite, consisting of the Summing Up, Amplification, and Appeal to Pity. We can in four places use a Conclusion: in the Direct Opening, after the Statement of Facts, after the strongest argument, and in the Conclusion of the speech.

The Summing Up gathers together and recalls the points we have made — briefly, that the speech may not be repeated in entirety, but that the memory of it may be refreshed; and we shall reproduce all the points in the order in which they have been presented, so that the hearer, if he has committed them to memory, is brought back to what he remembers. Again, we must take care that the Summary should not be carried back to the Introduction or the Statement of Facts. Otherwise the speech will appear to have been fabricated and devised with elaborate pains so as to demonstrate the speaker's skill, advertise his wit, and display his memory. Therefore the Summary must take its beginning from the Division. Then we must in order and briefly set forth the points treated in the Proof and Refutation.

Amplification is the principle of using Commonplaces to stir the hearers. To amplify an accusation it will be most advantageous to draw commonplaces from ten formulae.

(1) The first commonplace is taken from authority, when we call to mind of what great concern the matter under discussion has been to the immortal gods, or to our ancestors, or kings, states, barbarous nations, sages, the Senate; and again, especially how sanction has been provided in these matters by laws.

(2) The second commonplace is used when we consider who are affected by

these acts on which our charge rests; whether all men, which is a most shocking thing; or our superiors, such as are those from whom the commonplace of authority is taken; or our peers, those in the same situation as we with respect to qualities of character, physical attributes, and external circumstances; or our inferiors, whom in all these respects we excel.

(3) By means of the third commonplace we ask what would happen if the same indulgence should be granted to all culprits, and show what perils and disadvantages would ensue from indifference to this crime.

(4) By means of the fourth commonplace we show that if we indulge this man, many others will be the more emboldened to commit crimes — something which the anticipation of a judicial sentence has hitherto checked.

(5) By the fifth commonplace we show that if once judgement is pronounced otherwise than as we urge, there will be nothing which can remedy the harm or correct the jurors' error. Here it will be in point for us to make a comparison with other mistakes, so as to show that other mistakes can either be moderated by time or corrected designedly, but that so far as the present mistake is concerned, nothing will serve either to alleviate or to amend it.

(6) By means of the sixth commonplace we show that the act was done with premeditation, and declare that for an intentional crime there is no excuse, although a rightful plea of mercy is provided for an unpremeditated act.

(7) By means of the seventh commonplace we show that it is a foul crime, cruel, sacrilegious, and tyrannical; such a crime as the outraging of women, or one of those crimes that incite wars and life-and-death struggles with enemies of the state.

(8) By means of the eighth commonplace we show that it is not a common but a unique crime, base, nefarious, and unheard-of, and therefore must be the more promptly and drastically avenged.

(9) The ninth commonplace consists of a comparison of wrongs, as when we shall say it is a more heinous crime to debauch a free-born person that to steal a sacred object, because the one is done from unbridled licentiousness and the other from need.

(10) By the tenth commonplace we shall examine sharply, incriminatingly, and precisely, everything that took place in the actual execution of the deed and all the circumstances that usually attend such an act, so that by the enumeration of the attendant circumstances the crime may seem to be taking place and the action to unfold before our eyes.

We shall stir Pity in our hearers by recalling the vicissitudes of fortune; by 31 comparing the prosperity we once enjoyed with our present adversity; by enumerating and explaining the results that will follow for us if we lose the case; by entreating those whose pity we seek to win, and by submitting ourselves to their mercy; by revealing what will befall our parents, children, and other kinsmen through our disgrace, and at the same time showing that we grieve not because of our own straits but because of their anxiety and misery; by disclosing the kindness, humanity, and sympathy we have dispensed to others; by showing that we have ever, or for a long time, been in adverse circumstances; by deploring our fate or bad fortune; by showing that our heart will be brave and patient of adversities. The Appeal to Pity must be brief, for nothing dries more quickly than a tear.

Delivery

3.11   Many have said that the faculty of greatest use to the speaker and the most
valuable for persuasion is Delivery. For my part, I should not readily say that any
one of the five faculties is the most important; that an exceptionally great
usefulness resides in the delivery I should boldly affirm. For skilful invention,
elegant style, the artistic arrangement of the parts comprising the case, and the
careful memory of all these will be of no more value without delivery, than
delivery alone and independent of these. Therefore, because no one has written
carefully on this subject—all have thought it scarcely possible for voice, mien,
and gesture to be lucidly described, as appertaining to our sense-experience—
and because the mastery of delivery is a very important requisite for speaking, the
whole subject, as I believe, deserves serious consideration.

Delivery, then, includes Voice Quality and Physical Movement. Voice Quality
has a certain character of its own, acquired by method and application. It has
three aspects: Volume, Stability, and Flexibility. Vocal volume is primarily the
gift of nature; cultivation augments it somewhat, but chiefly conserves it.
Stability is primarily gained by cultivation; declamatory exercise augments it
somewhat, but chiefly conserves it. Vocal flexibility—the ability in speaking to
vary the intonations of the voice at pleasure—is primarily achieved by declamatory exercise. Thus with regard to vocal volume, and in a degree also to stability,
since one is the gift of nature and the other is acquired by cultivation, it is pointless
to give any other advice than that the method of cultivating the voice should be
12   sought from those skilled in this art. It seems, however, that I must discuss
stability in the degree that it is conserved by a system of declamation, and also
vocal flexibility (this is especially necessary to the speaker), because it too is
acquired by the discipline of declamation.

We can, then, in speaking conserve stability mainly by using for the Introduction a voice as calm and composed as possible. For the windpipe is injured if filled
with a violent outburst of sound before it has been soothed by soft intonations.
And it is appropriate to use rather long pauses—the voice is refreshed by
respiration and the windpipe is rested by silence. We should also relax from
continual use of the full voice and pass to the tone of conversation; for, as the
result of changes, no one kind of tone is spent, and we are complete in the entire
range. Again, we ought to avoid piercing exclamations, for a shock that wounds
the windpipe is produced by shouting which is excessively sharp and shrill, and
the brilliance of the voice is altogether used up by the outburst. Again, at the end
of the speech it is proper to deliver long periods in one unbroken breath, for then
the throat becomes warm, the windpipe is filled, and the voice, which has been
used in a variety of tones, is restored to a kind of uniform and constant tone. How
often must we be duly thankful to nature, as here! Indeed what we declare to be
beneficial for conserving the voice applies also to agreeableness of delivery, and,
as a result, what benefits our voice likewise finds favour in the hearer's taste. A
useful thing for stability is a calm tone in the Introduction. What is more
disagreeable than the full voice in the Introduction to a discourse? Pauses
strengthen the voice. They also render the thoughts more clear-cut by separating

them, and leave the hearer time to think. Relaxation from a continuous full tone conserves the voice, and the variety gives extreme pleasure to the hearer too, since now the conversational tone holds the attention and now the full voice rouses it. Sharp exclamation injures the voice and likewise jars the hearer, for it has about it something ignoble, suited rather to feminine outcry than to manly dignity in speaking. At the end of the speech a sustained flow is beneficial to the voice. And does not this, too, most vigorously stir the hearer at the Conclusion of the entire discourse? Since, then, the same means serve the stability of the voice and agreeableness of delivery, my present discussion will have dealt with both at once, offering as it does the observations that have seemed appropriate on stability, and the related observations on agreeableness. The rest I shall set forth somewhat later, in its proper place.

Now the flexibility of the voice, since it depends entirely on rhetorical rules, 13 deserves our more careful consideration. The aspects of Flexibility are Conversational Tone, Tone of Debate, and Tone of Amplification. The Tone of Conversation is relaxed, and is closest to daily speech. The Tone of Debate is energetic, and is suited to both proof and refutation. The Tone of Amplification either rouses the hearer to wrath or moves him to pity.

Conversational tone comprises four kinds: the Dignified, the Explicative, the Narrative, and the Facetious. The Dignified, or Serious, Tone of Conversation is marked by some degree of impressiveness and by vocal restraint. The Explicative in a calm voice explains how something could or could not have been brought to pass. The Narrative sets forth events that have occurred or might have occurred. The Facetious can on the basis of some circumstance elicit a laugh which is modest and refined.

In the Tone of Debate are distinguishable the Sustained and the Broken. The Sustained is full-voiced and accelerated delivery. The Broken Tone of Debate is punctuated repeatedly with short, intermittent pauses, and is vociferated sharply.

The Tone of Amplification includes the Hortatory and the Pathetic. The Hortatory, by amplifying some fault, incites the hearer to indignation. The Pathetic, by amplifying misfortunes, wins the hearer over to pity.

Since, then, vocal flexibility is divided into three tones, and these in turn subdivide into eight others, it appears that we must explain what delivery is appropriate to each of these eight subdivisions.

(1) For the Dignified Conversational Tone it will be proper to sue the full throat 14 but the calmest and most subdued voice possible, yet not in such a fashion that we pass from the practice of the orator to that of the tragedian. (2) For the Explicative Conversational Tone one ought to use a rather thin-toned voice, and frequent pauses and intermissions, so that we seem by means of the delivery itself to implant and engrave in the hearer's mind the points we are making in our explanation. (3) For the Narrative Conversational Tone varied intonations are necessary, so that we seem to recount everything just as it took place. Our delivery will be somewhat rapid when we narrate what we wish to show was done vigorously, and it will be slower when we narrate something else done in leisurely fashion. Then, corresponding to the content of the words, we shall modify the delivery in all the kinds of tone, now to sharpness, now to kindness, or now to

sadness, and now to gaiety. If in the Statement of Facts there occur any declarations, demands, replies, or exclamations of astonishment concerning the facts we are narrating, we shall give careful attention to expressing with the voice the feelings and thoughts of each personage. (4) For the Facetious Conversational Tone, with a gentle quiver in the voice, and a slight suggestion of a smile, but without any trace of immoderate laughter, one ought to shift one's utterance smoothly from the Serious Conversational tone to the tone of gentlemanly jest.

Since the Tone of Debate is to be expressed either through the Sustained or the Broken, when the (5) Sustained Tone of Debate is required, one ought moderately to increase the vocal volume, and, in maintaining an uninterrupted flow of words, also to bring the voice into harmony with them, to inflect the tone accordingly, and to deliver the words rapidly in a full voice, so that the voice production can follow the fluent energy of the speech. (6) For the Broken Tone of Debate we must with deepest chest tones produce the clearest possible exclamations, and I advise giving as much time to each pause as to each exclamation.

For (7) the Hortatory Tone of Amplification we shall use a very thin-toned voice, moderate loudness, an even flow of sound, frequent modulations, and the utmost speed. (8) For the Pathetic Tone of Amplification we shall use a restrained voice, deep tone, frequent intermissions, long pauses, and marked changes.

15   On Voice Quality enough has been said. Now it seems best to discuss Physical Movement.

Physical movement consists in a certain control of gesture and mien which renders what is delivered more plausible. Accordingly the facial expression should show modesty and animation, and the gestures should not be conspicuous for either elegance or grossness, lest we give the impression that we are either actors or day labourers. It seems, then, that the rules regulating bodily movement ought to correspond to the several divisions of tone comprising voice. To illustrate: (1) For the Dignified Conversational Tone, the speaker must stay in position when he speaks, lightly moving his right hand, his countenance expressing an emotion corresponding to the sentiments of the subject—gaiety or sadness or an emotion intermediate. (2) For the Explicative Conversational Tone, we shall incline the body forward a little from the shoulders, since it is natural to bring the face as close as possible to our hearers when we wish to prove a point and arouse them vigorously. (3) For the Narrative Conversational Tone, the same physical movement as I have just set forth for the Dignified will be appropriate. (4) For the Facetious Conversational Tone, we should by our countenance express a certain gaiety, without changing gestures.

(5) For the sustained Tone of Debate, we shall use a quick gesture of the arm, a mobile countenance, and a keen glance. (6) For the Broken Tone of Debate, one must extend the arm very quickly, walk up and down, occasionally stamp the right foot, and adopt a keen and fixed look.

(7) For the Hortatory Tone of Amplification, it will be appropriate to use a somewhat slower and more deliberate gesticulation, but otherwise to follow the procedure for the Sustained Tone of Debate. (8) For the Pathetic Tone of Amplification, one ought to slap one's thigh and beat one's head, and sometimes to use a calm and uniform gesticulation and a sad and disturbed expression.

I am not unaware how great a task I have undertaken in trying to express physical movements in words and portray vocal intonations in writing. True, I was not confident that it was possible to treat these matters adequately in writing. Yet neither did I suppose that, if such a treatment were impossible, it would follow that what I have done here would be useless, for it has been my purpose merely to suggest what ought to be done. The rest I shall leave to practice. This, nevertheless, one must remember: good delivery ensures that what the orator is saying seems to come from his heart.

Cicero

Cicero (106–43 B.C.) was the greatest Roman orator. Furthermore, he made important contributions to rhetorical theory, not only in setting forth his own ideas but also in developing the concepts and assessing the contributions of others.

Our first four selections come from the *Brutus*, a conversational dialogue in which Titus Pomponius Atticus (the friend who edited and published Cicero's letters to him) and Marcus Junius Brutus (the best-known Brutus, for whom the work is titled) are imagined joining Cicero himself in an important critical discussion of the history of oratory with a special focus on the Attic and Asiatic styles. The subjects of our selections are: the Greeks, Gorgias and Isocrates; the two greatest Roman orators of the generation before Cicero, Lucius Licinius Crassus (140–91 B.C., who tutored Cicero) and Marcus Antonius (143–87 B.C., the grandfather of the famous Mark Antony); and the greatest contemporary speaker other than Cicero, Quintus Hortensius Hortalus (114–50 B.C.).

Next come two selections from Cicero's early *De Inventione*. This work contains the first extant discussion of the systematic organization of *topoi* into issues (*staseis*, or in Latin *status* or *constitutiones*), which had been developed by Hermagoras (second century B.C.). In our first excerpt from the *De Inventione*, Cicero attempts to refine and correct Hermagoras' concept of the underlying bases or grounds of argument. The second selection from that work follows one important issue through its subdivisions. In later works Cicero compresses the issues from four to three and slightly redefines them, but the continuing popularity and enormous influence of the *De Inventione* in Western culture make it a primary source for an understanding of the issues.

Following the *De Inventione* are three brief selections from the *De Partitione Oratoria* or *Partitiones Oratoriae*. Here Cicero describes an important theory of arrangement, which he attributes to the Middle Academy, outlines the organization of an epideictic speech, and explains how arrangement can have an important effect on the audience. In this simplistic dialogue, Cicero's son is imagined as a pupil asking his expert father appropriately leading questions.

Our final four selections come from Book 3 of *De Oratore*, which develops one of the best-known discussions of style in Latin. Our passages treat the essentials of style, the purposes of stylistic embellishment, prose rhythm, and the three basic styles. This conversational dialogue is modeled, according to Cicero, after the dialogues of Aristotle. The same Antonius and Crassus (the mouthpiece for Cicero in *De Oratore*) talk about all aspects of rhetoric with a number of younger orators. Included among them is Quintus Lutatius Catulus (died 87 B.C.), who is repeatedly addressed in Book 3. (Catulus delivered the first funeral oration for a woman—his mother.)

Brutus

Early Orators

"But when it was recognized what power lay in speech carefully prepared and   30
elaborated as a work of art, then suddenly a whole host of teachers of oratory arose:
Gorgias of Leontini, Thrasymachus of Calchedon, Protagoras of Abdera, Prodicus of Ceos, Hippias of Elis, all of whom enjoyed great honour in their day.
They and many others of the same time professed, not without arrogance to be
sure, to teach how by the force of eloquence the worse (as they called it) could be   31
made the better cause. Opposed to them was Socrates, who with characteristic
adroitness of argumentation made it a practice to refute their doctrines. Out of the
wealth of his discourses there emerged a group of men of great learning, and to
them is attributed the first discovery of the philosophy which deals with good and
evil, with human life and society, as distinguished from the philosophy of nature,
which belonged to an earlier time. But, since this field of knowledge is alien to
our present purpose, I relegate philosophers to another time and return to orators,
from whom I have digressed.

"In the old age of those whom I have just mentioned Isocrates came forward,   32
whose house became a veritable training-school or studio of eloquence open to all
Greece. He was a great orator and an ideal teacher, but he shrank from the broad
daylight of the forum, and within the walls of his school brought to fullness a
renown such as no one after him has in my judgement attained. He wrote much of
surpassing excellence and taught others. He was in other respects superior to his
predecessors, and particularly he was the first to recognize that even in prose,
while strict verse should be avoided, a certain rhythm and measure should be   33
observed. Before him there was nothing structure-like, so to speak, in the joining
of words, and no rhythmical rounding out of the sentence, or, if it did occur, it
was not apparent that it was deliberately intended. That may perhaps be a matter
of praise, but in any case it came about then at times from natural feeling and
chance, rather than by rule or design. For it is true that by some natural instinct   34
the expression of a thought may fall into a periodic form and conclusion, and
when it is thus gathered up in fitting words it ends often with a rhythmical
cadence. The reason is that the ear itself judges what is complete, what is
deficient, and the breath by natural compulsion fixes a limit to the length of the
phrase. If the breath labours, not to say fails utterly, the effect is painful.

Crassus

"Equal in rank with him[1] some placed Lucius Crassus, others assigned to   143
Crassus a higher place. But in one thing the judgement of all was in agreement,
that no one who could employ the services of either of these as advocate required

Reprinted by permission of the publishers and The Loeb Classical Library from Cicero, *Brutus* (30–
34, 143–149, 184–186, 193–198, 284–291, 325–327), vol. 5, trans. G. L. Hendrickson, Cambridge,
Mass.: Harvard University Press, 1971.

1. Marcus Antonius, who has just been discussed.

the help of any other man's talent. For my part, though I assign to Antonius all that I have pointed out above, yet I hold that nothing could have been more perfect than Crassus. He possessed great dignity, and combined with dignity a pleasantry and wit, not smart nor vulgar, but suited to the orator; his Latinity was careful and well chosen, but without affected preciseness; in presentation and argument his lucidity was admirable; in handling questions whether of the civil 144 law or of natural equity and justice he was fertile in argument and in analogies. As Antonius possessed incredible skill in creating a presumption of probability, in allaying or in provoking a suspicion, so in interpretation, in definition, in unfolding the implications of equity no one could surpass the resourcefulness of Crassus. I could illustrate this by other examples, but I will take especially the 145 case of Manius Curius before the centumvirs. Crassus there spoke so well against the written word in behalf of general considerations of equity and justice that Quintus Scaevola, with all his acuteness and readiness in technical law (the interpretation of which was the question at issue in that case), was completely overwhelmed by the wealth of arguments and precedents adduced by his opponent. The handling of the case by these two pleaders of like age and like consular rank, each upholding the law from opposite points of view, was such that Crassus was allowed to be the ablest jurist in the ranks of orators, Scaevola the best orator in the ranks of jurists.

"As for Scaevola, he was at once very shrewd in getting at the true significance and applicability of principles of civil law or natural equity, and remarkably adept 146 at finding the precise words suited to the thing in question with greatest brevity. Therefore let him stand for us, in respect of interpretation, elucidation, and general exposition, as an orator worthy of our highest admiration; in this I have never seen his equal. In amplification, in embellishment, in refutation, he was rather the critic to be feared than the orator to be admired. But let us come back to Crassus."

147   Here Brutus remarked: "Though I thought that I knew Scaevola adequately from what I used to hear from Gaius Rutilius, whom I met often at the house of my friend Scaevola, yet I did not know that his reputation as a speaker was so great. It is a pleasure to learn that we have had in our public life a man so accomplished 148 and of such distinguished ability."

"Do not question, Brutus, that our state has never produced more distinguished talent than these two men. As a moment ago I called one the ablest speaker of jurisconsults, the other the ablest jurisconsult of speakers, so their differences in other respects were such that you could hardly choose which one you would rather be like. Crassus was most frugal of the elegant; Scaevola most elegant of the frugal; Crassus along with kindliness and affability had a certain severity; 149 Scaevola with much severity was not without kindliness and affability. You could go on in this way no end, but I fear that I should seem to have invented all this for the sake of saying it in a certain way; still the fact was so. All virtue, Brutus, according to your school of the Old Academy, consists in the mean, and thus both these men made it a guiding principle to follow a middle course; but it fell out so that while each one possessed a part of the other's characteristic merit, both had their own undivided."

Evaluation of Orators

"Why," said Atticus, "should you be concerned for general approbation if only 184
you can win the assent of Brutus here?"

"You are quite right, Atticus," I replied. "This discussion about the reasons for
esteeming an orator good or bad I much prefer should win the approval of you and
of Brutus, but as for my oratory I should wish it rather to win the approval of the
public. The truth is that the orator who is approved by the multitude must
inevitably be approved by the expert. What is right or wrong in a man's speaking I
shall be able to judge, provided I have the ability and knowledge to judge; but
what sort of an orator a man is can only be recognized from what his oratory
effects. Now there are three things in my opinion which the orator should effect: 185
instruct his listener, give him pleasure, stir his emotions. By what virtues in the
orator each one of these is effected, or from what faults the orator fails to attain the
desired effect, or in trying even slips and falls, a master of the art will be able to
judge. But whether or not the orator succeeds in conveying to his listeners the
emotions which he wishes to convey, can only be judged by the assent of the
multitude and the approbation of the people. For that reason, as to the question
whether an orator is good or bad, there has never been disagreement between
experts and the common people. Can you suppose that, in the lifetime and 186
activity of those whom I have named above, the ranking of orators in the
judgement of the people and of experts was not the same? If you had put to any
man of the common people this question: 'Who is the greatest orator in our
commonwealth?' he might have hesitated as between Antonius or Crassus, or one
might have named Antonius, another Crassus. Would no one have expressed a
preference to them for Philippus, with all his charm and dignity and wit, whom I,
deliberately weighing such qualities in the scale of theory, have placed next to
them? Certainly not; for this is the very mark of supreme oratory, that the supreme
orator is recognized by the people.

There is however this difference, that the crowd sometimes gives its approval to 193
an orator who does not deserve it, but it approves without comparison. When it is
pleased by a mediocre or even bad speaker it is content with him; it does not
apprehend that there is something better; it approves what is offered, whatever its
quality; for even a mediocre orator will hold its attention, if only he amounts to
anything at all, since there is nothing that has so potent an effect upon human
emotions as well-ordered and embellished speech.

"Thus, for example, what common man listening to Quintus Scaevola in 194
behalf of Marcus Coponius, the case to which I referred before, would have
expected, or indeed would have thought it possible, to hear anything more
finished or more nicely expressed or in any respect better? It was Scaevola's object 195
to prove that Manius Curius (who had been named as heir in the event that an
expected posthumous son should die before said son had reached his majority)
could not become heir, because in fact no posthumous son was born. How full
and precise he was on testamentary law, on ancient formulas, on the manner in
which the will should have been drawn if Curius were to be recognized as heir

196   even if no son were born; what a snare was set for plain people if the exact wording
      of the will were ignored, and if intentions were to be determined by guess-work,
      and if the written words of simple-minded people were to be perverted by the
197   interpretation of clever lawyers. How much he had to say about the authority of his
      father, who had always upheld the doctrine of strict interpretation, and in general
      how much concerning observance of the civil law as handed down! In saying all
      this with mastery and knowledge, and again with his characteristic brevity and
      compactness, not without ornament and with perfect finish, what man of the
      people would have expected or thought that anything better could be said?

      "Crassus, however, in rebuttal began with a story of a boy's caprice, who while
      walking along the shore found a thole-pin, and from that chance became
      infatuated with the idea of building himself a boat to it. He urged that Scaevola in
      like manner, seizing upon no more than a thole-pin of fact and captious reason,
      had upon it made out a case of inheritance imposing enough to come before the
      centumviral court. From this beginning, and following it up with other sugges-
      tions of like character, he captivated the ears of all present and diverted their
      minds from earnest consideration of the case to a mood of pleasantry—one of the
      three things which I have said it was the function of the orator to effect.
      Thereupon he urged that the will, the real intention of the testator, was this: that
      in the event of no son of his surviving to the age of legal competence—no matter
      whether such a son was never born, or should die before that time—Curius was to
      be his heir; that most people wrote their wills in this way and that it was valid
      procedure and always had been valid. With these and many similar arguments he
198   won credence—which is another of the three functions of the orator. He then
      passed over to general right and equity; defended observance of the manifest will
      and intention of the testator; pointed out what snares lay in words, not only in wills
      but elsewhere, if obvious intentions were ignored; what tyrannical power Scaevola
      was arrogating to himself if no one hereafter should venture to make a will unless
      in accordance with his idea. Setting forth all this, at once with earnestness and
      abundant illustration, and with great variety of clever and amusing allusion, he
      provoked such admiration and won such assent that no opposition seemed
      possible. This was an example of that function of the orator which in my division
      was third, but in significance first and greatest. Now that judge of ours, from the
      ranks of the plain people, who had admired the one speaker when heard by
      himself, on hearing the other would abandon his first estimate as absurd. But the
      trained critic on the other hand, listening to Scaevola, would have recognized at
      once that his oratory lacked something of richness and resourcefulness. If
      however when the case was over you had asked both of our judges which of the two
      orators was superior, you would find beyond a doubt that the judgement of the
      expert was never at variance with the judgement of the masses.

True Attic Style

284   Here Brutus interposed; "Our good friend Calvus liked to think of himself as
      Attic. That was the reason for that meagreness of style which he cultivated
      deliberately."

"Yes, I know," I replied; "so he said; but he was in error and caused others to err with him. If one holds that those who do not rant, nor speak pedantically nor with affectation, are Attic, he will be quite right in admiring no one who is not Attic. Tasteless bombast and preciosity he will abominate as a form of madness; sanity and wholesomeness of style he will look upon as a decent and almost religious obligation in an orator. This should be the common judgement of all orators. But 285 if meagreness and dryness and general poverty are put down as Attic, with of course the proviso that it must have finish and urbanity and precision, that is good so far as it goes. But because there are in the category of Attic other qualities better than these, one must beware not to overlook the gradations and dissimilarities, the force and variety of Attic orators. 'My aim is,' you say, 'to imitate Attic models.' Which, pray? for they are not all of one type. Who, for example, are more unlike than Demosthenes and Lysias? Than either of them and Hyperides, than all of these and Aeschines? Whom then are you going to imitate? If one only, do you mean that all the others did not speak pure Attic? If all, how can you imitate them when they are so unlike each other? And here I venture to put this question: did Demetrius of Phaleron speak pure Attic? To me at least his orations exhale the very fragrance of Athens. But, you say, he is more florid (if I may use the term) than Hyperides or Lysias. That was, I presume, his natural bent or perhaps his deliberate choice.

"Take another example: there were two orators of the same time wholly unlike 286 each other yet both thoroughly Attic, Charisius and Demochares. Of these the former was the author of many speeches which he wrote for others, in which he appears to have made Lysias his model; the latter, Demochares, nephew of Demosthenes, wrote some speeches and was author of a history of Athens in his own time, written in a style rather oratorical than historical. (It was Charisius whom Hegesias strove to be like, and he regarded himself so thoroughly Attic that he considered the native Attic writers almost uncouth rustics in comparison with 287 himself. But where will you find anything so broken, so minced, anything so puerile as that balance and antithesis which he cultivated?) 'Our aim is to be Attic.' Good. 'Are these two then Attic orators?' Surely; who can deny it? 'These are the men we imitate.' But how, when they are so unlike one another and unlike still others unnamed? 'Thucydides,' you say, 'we strive to imitate.' Very good, if you are thinking of writing history, but not if you contemplate pleading cases. Thucydides was a herald of deeds, faithful and even grand, but our forensic speech with its wrangling, its atmosphere of the court-room, he never used. As for the speeches which he introduced (and they are numerous) I have always praised them; but imitate them?—I could not if I wished, nor should I wish to, I imagine, if I could. To illustrate: it is as if a man were found of Falernian wine, but did not want it so new as last year's, nor again so old as to search out a cask from the vintages of Opimius or Anicius. 'But those brands are acknowledged to be the best!' Yes I know, but too old a wine has not the mellowness which we want, and in fact it is scarcely longer fit to drink. If that then is one's feeling, need he go to the 288 other extreme and hold, if he wants a potable wine, that it must be drawn from the fresh vat? Certainly not; he would look for a wine of moderate age. In like manner I hold that those friends of yours do well to shun this new oratory still in a state of ferment, like must from the basin of the wine-press, and conversely that they ought not to strive for the manner of Thucydides, —splendid doubtless, but, like the vintage of Anicius, too old. Thucydides himself if he had lived at a somewhat later time would have been mellower and less harsh.

289   " 'Should we then make Demosthenes our model?' There, by heavens, you have it! and what better I ask, do we seek, what better can we wish for? But we do not it is true succeed in our effort; these fellows however, our self-styled Atticists, quite obviously it would seem do succeed in what they have set themselves. They don't even see, not only that history records it, but it must have been so, that when Demosthenes was to speak all Greece flocked to hear him. But when these Atticists of ours speak they are deserted not only by the curious crowd, which is humiliating enough, but even by the friends and supporters of their client. So then if to speak in a pinched and meagre way is Attic, why let them enjoy their title of Atticists. But let them come to the place of assembly, let them speak before a

290   praetor standing to give his opinion without a jury. The benches call for a louder and fuller voice. This is what I wish for my orator-when it is reported that he is going to speak let every place on the benches be taken, the judges' tribunal full, the clerks busy and obliging in assigning or giving up places, a listening crowd thronging about, the presiding judge erect and attentive; when the speaker rises the whole throng will give a sign for silence, then expressions of assent, frequent applause; laughter when he wills it, or if he wills, tears; so that a mere passer-by observing from a distance, though quite ignorant of the case in question, will recognize that he is succeeding and that a Roscius is on the stage. If this is what happens be assured that he is speaking like an Attic orator, that he is faring as we

291   read of Pericles, of Hyperides, of Aeschines, of Demosthenes most of all. But if they prefer rather a style of speaking that is acute and judicious, while at the same time pure, sound, and matter-of-fact, which does not make use of any bolder oratorical embellishment, and if moreover they will have it that this style is peculiarly and properly Attic, they are quite right in their approbation. For in an art so comprehensive and so varied there is a place even for such small refinements of workmanship. Our conclusion then will be, not that all who speak in an Attic style speak well, but that all who speak well deserve the title of Attic. But now let us come back to Hortensius. "

Hortensius and Asiatic Style

325   "If we raise the question, why in his youth Hortensius enjoyed a more brilliant reputation than in his age, we shall find two good reasons: first, because his oratorical style was the Asiatic, a manner condoned in youth, but less suited to age. Of the Asiatic style there are two types, the one sententious and studied, less characterized by weight of thought than by the charm of balance and symmetry. Such was Timaeus the historian; in oratory Hierocles of Alabanda in my boyhood, and even more so his brother Menecles, both of whose speeches are masterpieces in this Asiatic style. The other type is not so notable for wealth of sententious phrase, as for swiftness and impetuosity—a general trait of Asia at the present time—combining with this rapid flow of speech a choice of words refined

and ornate. This is the manner of which Aeschylus of Cnidus and my contemporary Aeschines of Miletus were representatives. Their oratory had a rush and movement which provoked admiration, but it lacked elaborate symmetry of   326 phrase and sentence. Both of these styles, as I have said, are better suited to youth; in older men they lack weight and dignity. Thus Hortensius, skilled in both manners, won great applause as a young man, for he made a cult of those gracefully pointed phrases in the manner of Menecles and used them often; but as with the Greek, so with him, they were often merely graceful and of pleasant sound, not necessary nor always useful; and again his language could be swift and vibrant without loss of careful finish. This sort of thing was not looked upon with favour by older men, —how often have I seen Philippus listening to him with a derisive smile, sometimes even with anger and impatience! —but all the younger generation was filled with admiration, and the people were carried away by it. In   327 the judgement of the public the young Hortensius was pre-eminent and easily held the first place; for though his type of eloquence lacked weight and authority, still it seemed suited to his youth, and at any rate, because some beauty of natural endowment perfected by assiduous practice shone forth in him, and because his words were put compactly into artistic periods, he provoked great and universal admiration. But when official honours and the authority demanded of age called for something more substantial, he remained the same when the same style no longer became him. When for some time he had relaxed that practice and application which had formerly been unremitting, though his earlier habit of neatly balanced phrase and thought remained, it was now no longer dressed out with the same richness of language as formerly. For this reason perhaps, Brutus, he pleased you less than he would have if you had heard him while still burning with his earlier fire and at the height of his power."

De Inventione

Issues

1.10   Every subject which contains in itself a controversy to be resolved by speech
and debate involves a question about a fact, or about a definition, or about the
nature of an act, or about legal processes. This question, then, from which the
whole case arises, is called *constitutio* or the "issue." The "issue" is the first
conflict of pleas which arises from the defence or answer to our accusation, in this
way: "You did it"; "I did not do it," or "I was justified in doing it." When the
dispute is about a fact, the issue is said to be conjectural *(coniecturalis)*, because
the plea is supported by conjectures or inferences. When the issue is about a
definition, it is called the definitional issue, because the force of the term must
be defined in words. When, however, the nature of the act is examined, the
issue is said to be qualitative, because the controversy concerns the value of the
act and its class or quality. But when the case depends on the circumstance that
it appears that the right person does not bring the suit, or that he brings it
against the wrong person, or before the wrong tribunal, or at a wrong time,
under the wrong statute, or the wrong charge, or with a wrong penalty, the
issue is called translative because the action seems to require a transfer to
another court or alteration in the form of pleading. There will always be one of
these issues applicable to every kind of case; for where none applies, there can
be no controversy. Therefore it is not fitting to regard it as a case at all.

11   As to the dispute about a fact, this can be assigned to any time. For the
question can be "What has been done?" *e.g.*, "Did Ulysses kill Ajax?" and
"What is being done?," *e.g.*, "Are the Fregellans friendly to the Roman
people?," and what is going to occur, *e.g.* "If we leave Carthage untouched,
will any harm come to the Roman state?"

The controversy about a definition arises when there is agreement as to the fact
and the question is by what word that which has been done is to be described.
In this case there must be a dispute about the definition, because there is no
agreement about the essential point, not because the fact is not certain, but
because the deed appears differently to different people, and for that reason
different people describe it in different terms. Therefore in cases of this kind the
matter must be defined in words and briefly described. For example, if a sacred
article is purloined from a private house, is the act to be adjudged theft or
sacrilege? For when this question is asked, it will be necessary to define both
theft and sacrilege, and to show by one's own description that the act in dispute
should be called by a different name from that used by the opponents.

12   There is a controversy about the nature or character of an act when there is
both agreement as to what has been done and certainty as to how the act should
be defined, but there is a question nevertheless about how important it is or of

Reprinted by permission of the publishers and The Loeb Classical Library from Cicero, *De
Inventione* (1.10–16, 2.71.5–103.8), vol. 2, trans. H. M. Hubbell, Cambridge, Mass.: Harvard
University Press, 1960.

what kind, or in general about its quality, *e.g.* was it just or unjust, profitable or unprofitable? It includes all such cases in which there is a question about the quality of an act without any controversy about definition. Hermagoras divided this genus into four species: deliberative, epideictic, equitable, and legal. I think I ought to criticize this error of his—no inconsiderable error as I think—but briefly lest if we pass it by in silence we be thought to have failed to follow him without good reason, or if we linger on the point too long, we seem to have hindered and delayed the presentation of the rules to be laid down in the rest of the book.

If deliberative and epideictic are genera of argument they cannot rightly be thought to be species of any one genus of argument. For the same thing can be genus in relation to one thing and species in relation to another, but cannot be both genus and species in relation to the same thing. Moreover the deliberative and epideictic are genera of arguments. For either there is no classification of arguments or there are only forensic arguments, or there are three genera, forensic, epideictic, and deliberative. To say that there is no classification of arguments when he says that there are many and gives rules for them, is madness. How can there be only one genus—the forensic—when deliberative and epideictic are not similar to each other and are far different from the forensic kind and each has its own end to which it may be referred? It follows, therefore, that there are, in all, three genera of arguments. Deliberative and epideictic cannot rightly be regarded as species of any kind of argument. He was wrong, then, in saying that they are species of the qualitative issue.

Wherefore if they cannot rightly be regarded as species of a genus of argument, there will be much less justification for regarding them as sub-heads of a species of argument. But the "issue" is nothing but a sub-head of argument. For the argument is not subsumed under the issue but the issue is subsumed under the argument. But epideictic and deliberative cannot rightly be regarded as species of a genus of argument, because they are themselves the genera of argument; there will be much less justification for regarding them as sub-heads of this species which is here described. In the second place, if the issue, either entire or any part of it, is an answer to an accusation, then that which is not an answer to an accusation cannot be either an issue or a sub-head of an issue. But if what is not an answer to an accusation is neither an issue or a sub-head of an issue, deliberative and epideictic speeches are not an issue or a sub-head of an issue. If, then, the issue, either entire or any part of it, is the answer to an accusation, deliberative and epideictic speeches cannot be either an issue or a sub-head of an issue. But he himself is of the opinion that the issue is the answer to an accusation. He ought, therefore, to be of the opinion that epideictic and deliberative speeches are not the issue or a sub-head of the issue. And he will be pressed by the same argument whether he defines issue as the first assertion of his cause by the accuser or the first plea of the defendant. For all the same difficulties will attend him.

Furthermore a conjectural argument cannot at one and the same time and from the same point of view and under the same system of classification be both conjectural and definitive, nor can a definitive argument be at one and the same time and from the same point of view and under the same system of

13

14

classification both definitive and translative. And, to put it generally, no issue or sub-head of an issue can have its own scope and also include the scope of another issue, because each one is studied directly by itself and in its own nature, and if another is added, the number of issues is doubled but the scope of any one issue is not increased. But a deliberative argument generally includes at one and the same time and from the same point of view and under the same system of classification an issue, or *constitutio*, the conjectural, qualitative, definitional, or translative, either any one of these or at times more than one. Therefore it is not itself an issue or a sub-head of an issue. The same thing is wont to occur in the demonstrative (or epideictic) speech. These then, as we said before, are to be regarded as the genera of oratory and not as sub-heads under any issue.

Therefore this issue, which we call the qualitative issue, seems to us to have two subdivisions, equitable and legal. The equitable is that in which there is a question about the nature of justice and right or the reasonableness of reward or punishment. The legal is that in which we examine what the law is according to the custom of the community and according to justice: at Rome the jurisconsults are thought to be in charge of the study of this subject. The equitable is itself divided into two parts, the absolute and the assumptive. The absolute is that which contains in itself the question of right and wrong done. The assumptive is that which of itself provides no basis for a counter plea, but seeks some defence from extraneous circumstances. It has four division, *concessio* (confession and avoidance), *remotio criminis* (shifting the charge), *relatio criminis* (retort of the accusation), and *comparatio* (comparison). Confession and avoidance is used when the accused does not defend the deed but asks for pardon. This is divided into two parts: *purgatio* and *deprecatio*. It is *purgatio* when the deed is acknowledged but *intent* is denied; it has three parts, ignorance, accident, necessity. *Deprecatio* is used when the defendant acknowledges that he has given offence and has done so intentionally, and still asks to be forgiven; this can very rarely occur. It is shifting of the charge when the defendant tries to shift to another the charge brought against himself by transferring to another either the act or the intent or the power to perform the act. This can be done in two ways: either the cause or the act itself is attributed to another. The cause is attributed when the deed is said to have been done because of the power and authority of another; the deed is transferred when it is alleged that another should have done it or could have done it. The retort of the charge is used when the defendant claims that the deed was done lawfully because some one had first illegally provoked him. Comparison is used when it is argued that some other action was lawful and advantageous, and then it is pleaded that the misdemeanour which is charged was committed in order to make possible this advantageous act.

In the fourth issue which we call the translative there is a controversy when the question arises as to who ought to bring the action or against whom, or in what manner or before what court or under what law or at what time, and in general when there is some argument about changing or invalidating the form of procedure. Hermagoras is thought to be the inventor of this issue, not that orators did not use it before his day — many did use it frequently — but because earlier writers of text-books did not notice it nor include it with the issues.

Since his invention of the term many have found fault with it, not misled by ignorance, I think, for the case is perfectly plain, so much as they have been kept from adopting it by a spirit of envy and a desire to disparage a rival.

The Assumptive Equitable Issue

Now let us consider the assumptive branch of the equitable issue. The issue 2.71.5 is said to be assumptive when the act taken by itself cannot be approved, but is defended by some argument from extraneous circumstances. There are four subdivisions: *comparatio* (comparison), *relatio criminis* (retort of the accusation), *remotio criminis* (shifting the charge), *concessio* (confession and avoidance).

Comparatio (comparison) is the case where some act which cannot be 72 approved by itself, is defended by reference to the end for which it was done. It is of this sort: A certain commander, being surrounded by the enemy and unable to escape in any way, made an agreement with them to surrender the arms and baggage, and withdraw with his men. The agreement was carried out. He lost the arms and baggage but saved the soldiers from a hopeless situation. He is accused of lese-majesty. Here an issue of definition confronts 73 us, but let us examine only the topic that we are discussing. The charge is: "It was not right to abandon the arms and baggage." The answer is: "It was right." The question is: "Was it right?" The reason is: "I did it because otherwise all the soldiers would have perished." The denial is either concerned with fact: "They would not have perished," or another concerned with fact: "That was not the reason why you did it," (from which the point for decision becomes, "Would they have perished?" or "Was that the reason why he did it?") or this one involving comparison which we want for our present discussion: "But surely it was better to lose the soldiers than to surrender the arms and baggage to the enemy." From this arises the point for the judge's decision: "Granted that all the soldiers were going to perish unless they had come to this agreement, was it better to lose the soldiers or to come to these terms?"

One should treat this kind of case by topics peculiar to itself and also adapt 74 the principles and rules which apply in the other issues. And in particular by making inferences one should attack the comparison which the accused will make with the act of which he is accused. This will be done, if it is denied that the result would have followed which the counsel for the defence say would have followed if the act now before the court for judgement had not been performed; or if it is shown to have been done in a different fashion or for a reason other than that alleged by the defendant. Arguments in support of this statement of the defence and likewise arguments used by the opponents to demolish it will be derived from the conjectural issue. Furthermore, if the defendant is brought to trial for a definite crime, as in this case—for he is accused of lese-majesty—one should employ definition and the rules for its use. And it frequently happens in this kind of case that one must use both inference and definition; and if any other issue applies it will be permissible to transfer its rules to the case in hand in a similar way. For the chief task of the prosecutor is to attack by all possible means the act because of which the defendant thinks that some concession should be made to him. This is easy if he proceeds to invalidate it by using as many issues as possible.

75   But comparison itself separated from the other kinds of dispute will be considered on its own merits, if the act which is compared is shown not to have been honourable or advantageous or necessary, or not advantageous or honourable or necessary to such a degree. In the second place the prosecutor should separate the crime which he charges from the act which the counsel for the defence brings in for comparison. He will accomplish this if he shows that it is not usual or right for events to move in this way and that there is no reason why *this* should be done for *that*, as for example that for the safety of the soldiers the instruments provided for their safety should be surrendered to the enemy. Then he should compare the harm with the advantage and in general contrast the crime with the act which is praised by the counsel for the defence, or is shown to have been necessary to do, and by belittling this act should magnify the enormity of the wrong. This can be done, if it is shown that the action which the defendant avoided is more honourable, more advantageous or more
76   necessary than that which he performed. But the essence and nature of honour, advantage and necessity will be investigated in connexion with the rules for deliberative speeches. Then it will be necessary to expound this whole question of comparison as if it were a deliberative case and to discuss it in the light of the rules for deliberative speeches. Take, for instance, this problem which we stated above: "Granted that all the soldiers were going to perish unless they had come to this agreement, was it better to let the soldiers perish or to come to this agreement?" This should be treated along the lines of a deliberative speech, just as if the matter were to come up for an inquiry about policy. In the places where the prosecutor has brought in other forms of the issue, the counsel for the defence likewise will work up his defence on the basis of these issues; but all the other topics which pertain exclusively to comparison he will discuss so as to turn them against the prosecutor.
77   The common topics will be: of the prosecutor, to inveigh against a man who when he confesses to a deed that is base or disadvantageous or both, yet seeks some defence, and to bring out the inexpediency or the baseness of the deed with great indignation; of the counsel for the defence, that no deed should be judged inexpedient or base, or for that matter advantageous or honourable unless it is known with what intent, at what time and for what reason it was done. This topic is so general in its application that if well handled it will have great persuasive force in such a case. And a second common topic is that in which the magnitude of the service performed is demonstrated and enlarged upon by reference to the
78   advantage or honour or necessity of the deed; and a third, in which by a vivid verbal picture the event is brought before the eyes of the audience, so that they will think that they too would have done the same if they had been confronted with the same situation and the same cause for action at the same time.

A retort of the charge occurs when the defendant admits the act of which he is accused but shows that he was justified in doing it because he was influenced by an offence committed by the other party. The following is an example: Horatius after killing the Curiatii and losing his two brothers returned home in triumph. He noticed his sister not distressed by the death of her brothers, but repeatedly calling on the name of Curiatius, her betrothed, with groans and tears. Filled with rage he killed the girl. He is brought to trial. The charge is: "You killed your sister without warrant." The answer is: "I was justified in killing her." The question is: "Was he justified in killing her?" The defendant's reason is: "For she was distressed at the death of our enemies; she was unmoved by the fall of her brothers; she was grieved that I and the Roman people were victorious." The prosecutor's answer is: "Nevertheless she ought not to have been killed by her brother uncondemned." From this the point for decision arises: "Granted that Horatia was unmoved by the death of her brothers, and was distressed at the death of our enemies and did not rejoice over the victory of her brother and the Roman people, ought she to have been killed by her brother without condemnation?"

79

In this kind of case it will be proper first to take from the other issues what assistance they may offer, as was directed in connexion with "comparison," then, if there shall be opportunity one may use some issue to defend the person to whom the guilt is transferred; then one may show that the offence which the defendant imputes to the other party is less serious than that with which he himself is charged. Next one may use the forms of *translatio* (transfer) and show by whom and through whom and how and at what time it was proper that action should be brought and the case adjudged and decided; and at the same time one may point out that punishment should not be inflicted before judgement is given. Then one should also point to the laws and courts of justice by which the crime which the defendant avenged on his own authority, could have been punished in accordance with custom and judicial process. Then the prosecutor should deny that it is right to listen to the charge which the defendant brings against the other party, which he himself, the very man who brings it, was unwilling to submit to a court of law, and then claim that an act which has not been passed upon by a court should be regarded as not done. After that he should call attention to the shamelessness of those who now accuse before a jury one whom they themselves have condemned without a jury, and are now trying an offence which they have already punished with their own hands. After that he should argue that the judicial process will be disturbed, and that the judges will go beyond their authority if they pass judgement at the same time on the defendant and the person whom the defendant accuses; then he should point out what disastrous results will follow if it is established that men may avenge crimes with crimes and injuries with injuries; and if the prosecutor had been willing to do the same there would have been no need of this trial either; and if everyone should act in the same way there would be no trials at all. After that it will be pointed out that even if she had been condemned whom the defendant blames for his offence, he himself could not have inflicted the punishment on her; therefore it is intolerable that he who could not with is own hand have exacted the penalty from her even if she had been condemned, should have inflicted punishment on one who has not even been brought to trial. Then he will demand that the defendant produce the law under which he acted. Then, just as we suggested in the case of comparison that the prosecutor should disparage as much as possible the deed

80

81

82

which is cited by way of comparison, so in this case he should compare the fault of the person to whom the blame is transferred with the crime of him who says that he was justified in committing it; afterward it should be pointed out that the one act is not of such a nature that because of it the other should have been done. Finally, as in case of comparison, the point for decision is taken up and dilated upon in accordance with the rules for a deliberative speech.

83   The counsel for the defence will answer the arguments which will be brought in from other issues by using the topics which have already been set forth; he will support his attempt to lay the blame on some one else, first, by magnifying the culpability and audacity of the person on whom he lays the blame, and by placing the scene vividly before the eyes of the jury with an intense display of indignation, if opportunity presents, coupled with vehement complaint; secondly, by proving that he punished the offence more lightly than the offender deserved, and by comparing the punishment which he inflicted with the crime that she had committed. In the next place he should attack by contrary reasoning the arguments which have been presented by the prosecutor in such a way that they can be refuted and turned to the advantage of the

84   opposing side; the last three are of this kind. But the force of the severest attack of the prosecutors, by which they point out that the whole judicial process will be thrown into confusion if privilege is given of punishing offences without convicting the criminal, will be lessened, in the first place if it is demonstrated that the offence was of such a nature that it would seem intolerable not only to a good man, but to any sort of free man at all; in the second place that it was so manifest that it could not be questioned even by the offender; then that it was of such a nature that he who punished it was in duty bound to punish it; that it was not so right or so honourable for the offence to be brought before a court as to

85   have it avenged in the manner in which it was and by the person by whom it was; then that the case was so clear that there was no point in having a court pass upon it. And here it must be made plain by arguments and similar means that there are many offences so foul and undisputed that it is not only unnecessary but even inexpedient to wait for the trial to take place.

The prosecutor will use the common topic against the man who when he cannot deny the crime with which he is charged, nevertheless raises some hope for himself by disturbing the due course of the law. This is the place for showing the advantages of orderly trials and for complaining about the fate of one who was punished without being convicted, and for denouncing the audacity and

86   cruelty of him who inflicted the punishment. The defendant will speak against the audacity of the criminal on whom he took revenge, and lament his own lot, saying that a deed should be judged not by the name attached to it, but in the light of the intent of the person who performed it, and of the cause and of the time; showing what ill results will follow from someone's wrongdoing or crime unless such wanton and manifest audacity were avenged by him whose reputation, parents, children or something which must and ought to be dear to all men, is affected by such conduct.

Remotio criminis (shifting of the charge) occurs when the accusation for the offence which is alleged by the prosecutor is shifted to another person or thing. It is done in two ways: sometimes the responsibility is shifted and sometimes the

act itself. Let us take the following as an example of the shifting of the   87
responsibility: The Rhodians appointed certain men as ambassadors to Athens.
The treasury board did not give them the money for travelling expenses which
should have been given. The ambassadors did not set out. They are accused.
The charge is: "They should have set out." The answer is: "They should not."
The question is: "Should they?" The defendant's reason is: "The money for
expenses which is regularly paid from the public funds, was not paid by the
treasurer." The refutation is: "Nevertheless you should have performed the task
assigned to you by the state." The point for the judge's decision is: "Granted
that the money which was due the ambassadors from the public funds was not
paid to them, should they nonetheless have discharged their duties?"

In this kind of case, as in the other, the first requisite is to see if any help can
be got from the issue of fact or from any other issue. In the second place many
arguments used in comparison and in retort of the charge can be adapted to
this case also.

The prosecutor will first defend, if he can the person who the defendant says   88
was responsible for the act. If he cannot do this, he will say that this court is not
concerned with the fault of that other person, but only with the fault of the man
whom he is accusing. Then he will say that each man should think of his own
duty; that if one official has done wrong, that is no reason why the other should;
finally, if the treasurer has been delinquent he ought to be accused separately,
as the ambassador is, and that the accusation of the treasurer should not be
joined with the defence of the ambassador.

The defendant, after treating the other points which arise from other issues,
will argue as follows about the actual shifting of the charge: first, he will show by   89
whose fault the event happened; then since it happened through another's fault,
he will show that it was not possible or obligatory for him to do what the
prosecutor says he should have done. What was possible will be examined with
reference to the principles of advantage, in which an element of necessity is
involved; what was obligatory, with reference to honour. Both these topics will be
treated more precisely under deliberative oratory. In the next place counsel will
assert that the defendant did everything in his power; it was due to another's fault
that less was done than was proper. Then, in pointing out the other's fault, it   90
will be necessary to show what good will and devotion the defendant exhibited,
and to support this statement by evidence like the following: his diligence in
other offices, his previous acts and words; and that it was advantageous to him
to do it, and disadvantageous not to, and that doing it was more consistent with
his past life than to fail to do it through the fault of another. But if the blame is
shifted not to a definite person but to some circumstance, as, for instance, in
this same case, if the treasurer had died, and for that reason the ambassadors
did not receive the money, then as there is no opportunity to accuse another or
to avoid responsibility, it will be proper to use all the other arguments without
change, and to take such arguments as may fit from the topics of *concessio*
(confession and avoidance) which we must discuss presently.

Both sides will have available about the same common topics as in the   91
divisions of "assumptive" issue already discussed. But the following will most
assuredly be used: the prosecutor will arouse indignation at the deed; the

defendant will claim that he ought not to be punished since the fault is in another and not in himself.

The act itself is shifted when the defendant denies that the act imputed to him concerned him or his duty, and says that if there was any criminality in the act, it should not be attributed to him. This kind of case is illustrated as follows: In ratifying the treaty which was made once upon a time with Samnites, a youth of noble birth held the sacrifical pig as ordered by his general. The treaty, however, was disavowed by the Senate and the commander was surrendered to the Samnites, whereupon some one in the Senate said that the youth also, who held the pig, ought to be surrendered. The charge is: "He ought to be surrendered." The answer is: "He ought not." The question is: "Ought he to be surrendered?" The defendant's reason is: "It was not my duty nor was it in my power, since I was so young and a private soldier, and there was a commander with supreme power and authority to see that an honourable treaty was made." The prosecutor's reply is: "But since you had a part in a most infamous treaty sanctioned by solemn religious rites, you ought to be surrendered." The point for decision is: "Granted that he who had no authority took part in making the treaty and in performing the holy rites, should he be surrendered to the enemy or not?" This kind of case differs from the former in that in the former the defendant grants that he ought to have done what he prosecutor says ought to have been done, but attributes to some thing or person the cause which interfered with his desires, without pleas of confession and avoidance. For these pleas have a greater influence as will be recognized presently. But in this case he must not accuse the other party nor transfer the blame to another but prove that this act did not and does not bear any relation to himself, his powers or his duty. And in this case there is this new point, that even the prosecutor often makes his accusation by shifting the responsibility as in the case of one who accuses a man who while praetor called the people to arms for a campaign, when there were consuls in office. For just as in the former instance the defendant denied any connexion between the act and his duty or powers, so in this case the prosecutor by denying that the act is connected with the duty or power of the accused man, supports his accusation by this very line of reasoning. In this case both sides ought to use all the principles of honour and advantage, historical parallels, evidence and reasoning from analogy to inquire what is each one's duty, right and power, and whether such right, duty or power has, or has not been given to the man on trial.

Common topics ought to be suggested by the circumstances of the case, if it affords grounds for denunciation or complaint.

Concessio (confession and avoidance) is the plea in which the defendant does not as a matter of fact approve of the deed itself, but asks that it be pardoned. It has two forms, *purgatio* and *deprecatio*. *Purgatio* is the plea by which the intent of the accused is defended but not his act. It has three forms, ignorance, accident, necessity.

It is a plea of ignorance when the accused claims that he was not aware of something. For instance, a certain people had a law that prohibited the sacrifice of a bull-calf to Diana. Some sailors tossed on the deep by a terrible storm vowed that if they could gain the harbour which was in sight, they would sacrifice a bull-calf to the divinity whose temple stood there. It so happened that in that port there was a shrine of that Diana to whom it was unlawful to sacrifice a bull-calf. Ignorant of the law they landed and sacrificed a bull-calf. They are brought to trial. The charge is: "You sacrificed a bull-calf to the divinity to whom it was unlawful." The answer consists in confession and avoidance. The reason is: "I did not know that it was unlawful." The prosecutor's reply is: "Nevertheless, since you have done what was unlawful, you deserve punishment." The point for the judge's decision is: "Granted that he did what he ought not, and did not know that he ought not, does he deserve punishment?"

Chance will be brought into the plea of avoidance when it is shown that the   96
defendant's intention was thwarted by some act of Fortune, as in the following case: The Lacedaemonians had a law that visited capital punishment on a contractor who did not furnish the animals for a certain sacrifice. When the day for the sacrifice was at hand, the man who had taken the contract began to drive the animals from the country to the city. Then suddenly a great storm came up, and the river Eurotas which flows by Lacedaemon became so high and rapid that the victims could not by any possibility be driven across at that point. The   97
contractor to show his intent placed all the animals on the bank so as to be seen by those across the river. Although every one knew that his efforts had been thwarted by the sudden rise of the river, nevertheless some citizens put him on trial for his life. The charge is: "The animals which you were bound to furnish for the sacrifice were not at hand." The answer is confession and avoidance. The reason is: "The river rose suddenly and for that reason they could not be driven across." The prosecutor's reply is: "Nevertheless since the provisions of the law were not carried out, you deserve punishment." The point for the judge's decision is: "Granted that the contractor acted contrary to law in this case in which his efforts were thwarted by the sudden rise of the river, does he deserve punishment?"

Necessity is brought in when the accused is defended as having done what he   98
did because of some force beyond his control, as follows: There is a law at Rhodes that if any ship with a ram is caught in the harbour it is confiscated. There was a violent storm at sea, and the force of the wind compelled the sailors against their will to put into the harbour of Rhodes. The treasurer claims the ship as public property, the master of the vessel denies that it ought to be confiscated. The charge is: "A ship with a ram has been caught in the harbour." The answer is confession and avoidance. The reason is: "We were driven into the harbour by force and necessity." The prosecutor's reply is: "Nevertheless the ship ought to be confiscated according to law." The point for the judge's decision is: "Granted that the law confiscates a ship with a ram caught in the harbour, and that this ship was driven into port by the force of the storm against the desire of the crew, should it be confiscated?"

We have placed the examples of these three varieties together because similar   99
rules for argument are given for them. For in all of these, first the prosecutor should, if the facts of the case provide any opportunity, introduce the argument from conjecture, so as to prove by some inference that the act which, it will be asserted, was performed involuntarily, was really done intentionally. Then he should introduce a definition of necessity or chance or ignorance and accompany the definition by examples in which ignorance or accident or necessity

seem to have played a part, and separate the defendant's story from these, that is to show the dissimilarity between the cases, because the matter was such that it could not be unknown, fortuitous or necessary. After that he should show that it could have been avoided, or by the use of reason could have been foreseen if he had done thus and so, or could have been guarded against if he had not done thus and so. Furthermore he may show by definitions that this should not be called ignorance or chance or necessity, but laziness, carelessness or folly. And if in any case yielding to necessity seems to involve an act of baseness he should weave in common topics and prove in rebuttal that it was better to endure any fate, even death, rather than yield to such a necessity. And then by use of the topics described under legal issue, he should inquire into the nature of law and equity and as if it were a case under the "absolute" section of the issue of equity consider this point by itself without reference to other things. At this point, if opportunity offers, he should cite examples of those who have not been pardoned though offering a similar excuse, and argue that they were by comparison more worthy of pardon, and adopt the arguments of a deliberative speech, that it is base and inexpedient to condone the act which has been committed by the opponent; saying that this is a serious case and that great harm will ensue if this act is overlooked by those who have the power to punish it.

The defendant, on the other hand, will be able to turn all these arguments about and use them for a different conclusion; in particular, however, he will spend some time in defending his good intentions and in magnifying the circumstances which thwarted his purpose; saying that it was impossible to do more than he did, that in all things one should regard the intent and that he cannot be convicted because he is free of guilt, and that under his name the weakness common to all men may be condemned; finally, that nothing is more shocking than that he who is free of guilt should not be free of punishment.

Now for the common topics: the prosecutor will attack the plea of confession and avoidance and point out what a chance is offered for transgression if it is once established that the thing to be inquired into is not the act but the excuse for the act. The defendant may lament the misfortune which has befallen one not because of his fault but from *force majeure*, enlarge on the power of fortune and the infirmity of mankind, and beg the jury to consider his intent and not the result. With all of which there should be combined a lament over his own tribulations and a denunciation of the cruelty of his opponents.

No one should be surprised if he sees in these or in other examples a dispute over the letter of the law also. We shall have to speak separately about this question because certain kinds of cases are considered straightforwardly on their own merits, while others involve some other form of dispute. Therefore when all forms have been studied, it will not be hard to transfer to each case anything in this form, too, which shall be appropriate; as in all these examples of confession and avoidance there is involved a dispute about the letter of the law, which goes by the name of the letter and the intent. But because we were speaking of confession and avoidance we gave the rules for that; in another place we shall discuss the letter and the intent.

De Partitione Oratoria

Method of Arranging Arguments

CICERO JUNIOR. What is the next step then?   9

CICERO SENIOR. Having found your arguments, to put them together; and in an unlimited inquiry the order of arrangement is almost the same as that in the arrangement of topics which I have explained; but in a limited inquiry we must also employ the means designed to excite the emotions.

CICERO JUNIOR. How then do you explain these?

CICERO SENIOR. I have a set of instructions adapted both for producing conviction and for exciting emotion. As a conviction is a firmly established opinion, while emotion is the excitement of the mind to either pleasure or annoyance or fear or desire—for there are all these kinds of emotion and each kind has several divisions—, I adapt the whole method of arrangement to the purpose of the inquiry; for the purpose of the statement is to convince, and that of the case is both to convince and to excite emotion. Consequently when I have dealt with the case, which contains the statement, I shall have spoken of them both.

CICERO JUNIOR. What have you to say then about the case?   10

CICERO SENIOR. I say that it varies according to the class of the audience. For a member of the audience is either merely a hearer or an arbitrator, *i.e.* an estimater of fact and opinion; consequently it must aim either at giving pleasure to the hearer or at causing him to make some decision. But he makes a decision either about things that are past, as a judge does, or about things in the future, as the senate does; so there are these three divisions, dealing with judgement, with deliberation and with embellishment, the latter has obtained its special name from the fact that it is particularly employed in panegyrics.

CICERO JUNIOR. What objects will the speaker put before him in the three   11
kinds of style you mention?

CICERO SENIOR. In embellishment, he will aim at giving pleasure; in judgement, at arousing either severity or clemency in the judge; in persuasion, at inspiring either hope or alarm in a member of a deliberative body.

CICERO JUNIOR. Why then do you set out the classes of cases at this point?

CICERO SENIOR. So that I may adjust my scheme of arrangement to the purpose of each.

CICERO JUNIOR. How so pray?   12

CICERO SENIOR. Because in speeches the purpose of which is to give pleasure there are various methods of arrangement. For we either keep to chronological order or to arrangement in classes; or we ascend from smaller matters to larger, or glide down from larger ones to smaller; or we group these with

Reprinted by permission of the publishers and The Loeb Classical Library from Cicero, *De Partitione Oratoria* (9–15, 45–47, 74–75, 90–94), vol. 4, trans. H. Rackham, Cambridge, Mass.: Harvard University Press, 1982.

complete irregularity, intertwining small matters with great ones, simple with complicated, obscure with clear, cheerful with gloomy, incredible with probable—all of these methods falling under the head of embellishment.

13   CICERO JUNIOR. Well, what do you aim at in the case of deliberation?

CICERO SENIOR. Opening passages either brief or often absent altogether—for members of a deliberative body are prepared to listen for their own sake. Nor indeed in many cases is much narration needed; for narrative deals with matters past or present, but persuasion deals with the future. Consequently the whole of the speech must be applied to convincing and arousing emotion.

14   CICERO JUNIOR. Well, what is the system of arrangement in judicial cases?

CICERO SENIOR. It is not the same for the prosecutor as for the defendant, because the prosecutor follows the order of the facts and after arranging his series of arguments ready in his hand like a spear, states them vehemently, draws his conclusions freely, supports them with documents and decrees and the evidence of witnesses, and dwells upon them in detail with greater precision, employing the principles of perorating that are effective in arousing feeling, both in the rest of his speech when he diverges a little from his line of discourse, and with greater vehemence in the concluding peroration. For his object is to make the judge angry.

15   CICERO JUNIOR. What must the defendant do on the other side?

CICERO SENIOR. His entire procedure must be widely different. His opening remarks must be chosen for the purpose of securing goodwill; narrations must either be cut down if they are tiresome, or dropped altogether if they are entirely wearisome; corroborations put forward to carry conviction must either be done away with as a separate item, or thrown into the background, or covered up with digressions; while peroration passages must be devoted to securing compassion.

CICERO JUNIOR. Shall we always be able to keep to the plan of arrangement that we desire?

CICERO SENIOR. Certainly not; the prudent and cautious speaker is controlled by the reception given by his audience—what it rejects has to be modified.

45   CICERO JUNIOR. Now that I know where to find means of obtaining credence, I next want to be told how each successive topic is to be handled in speaking.

CICERO SENIOR. I take it that what you desire to hear about is ratiocination, which is the process of developing the argument. [This process, derived from the topics that have been set forth, requires completing and clarifying in detail.]

CICERO JUNIOR. Clearly that is exactly what I require.

46   CICERO SENIOR. Well then, ratiocination as I said just now, is the process of developing the argument; but this process is achieved when you have assumed either indubitable or probable premises from which to draw a conclusion that appears in itself either doubtful or less probable. And there are two kinds of ratiocination, one of which aims directly at convincing and

the other devotes itself to exciting feeling. It proceeds directly, when it has put forward a proposition to prove, and has chosen the arguments to support its case, and after establishing these has returned to the proposition and drawn the conclusion; but the other form of ratiocination proceeds in the opposite way, backward: it first assumes the premises that it wants and establishes these, and then after exciting emotion throws in at the end what ought to have been premised at the start. Ratiocination also permits the 47 following variety of methods, a not unpleasing divergence, when we put a question to ourselves or cross-examine ourselves or make an appeal or express a desire—forms of expression which with a great many others serve to decorate our sentences. But we shall be able to avoid monotony by not always starting from the point we are making, and if we do not prove all our points by advancing arguments, and sometimes lay down quite shortly statements that will be sufficiently obvious, and do not always hold it necessary formally to draw the conclusion that will follow from them, if it is obvious.

Epideictic Arrangement

But as things good or evil occupy three classes, external goods, goods of the 74 body and goods of the mind, the class to take first is that of external goods, which are headed by the man's family: this must be praised briefly and with moderation, or, if it is disgraceful, omitted, or if of low station, either passed over or so treated as to increase the glory of the person you are praising; next, if the facts permit, you must speak of his fortune and estate; and then of his personal endowments, among which it is easiest to praise a handsome appearance, as providing a very great indication of virtue. Next one must come to the man's achievements, as to which 75 there are three possible methods of arrangement: either one must keep their chronological order, or speak of the most recent first, or classify a number of different actions under the virtues to which they belong.

Pathetic Arrangement

And because it is necessary to adapt one's discourse to conform not only with 90 the truth but also with the opinions of one's hearers, the first point that we must grasp is that mankind falls into two classes, one uninstructed and uncultivated, which always prefers utility to moral value, and other humane and cultivated, which places true worth above all other things. Consequently the latter class of people give the first place to distinction, honour, glory, good faith, justice and all the forms of virtue, while the former class put the profits and emoluments of gain first. And also pleasure, which is the greatest enemy of virtue and adulterates the true essence of the good by deceptive imitations, and which is most eagerly pursued by all the most uncivilized people, who place it in front of not only things of moral value but also necessaries, it will quite often have to receive your praise in advisory speeches, when you are giving counsel to persons of that class.

And it must be noticed how much more energetically people fly from what is 91 evil than they pursue what is good. Neither indeed do they seek after what is honourable so much as they try to avoid what is disgraceful. Who would seek to gain honour and glory and praise and any distinction so keenly as he flees from ignominy and discredit and contumely and disgrace? The pain that these inflict gives weighty evidence that the human race was designed by nature for what is honourable, although it has been corrupted by bad education and erroneous opinions. Consequently, in exhorting and advising, although our aim will be to

92   teach by what method it is possible for us to attain the good and avoid the evil, nevertheless in addressing well educated people we shall speak most of glory and honour, and shall give our chief attention to the kinds of virtue that are exercised in protecting and increasing the common advantage of mankind. Whereas if we are speaking in the presence of the unlearned and ignorant, it is profits and rewards, pleasures and modes of avoiding pain that must be put forward; and references to contumely and disgrace must also be added, for there is nobody so boorish that he is not deeply sensitive to contumely and disgrace, even though he

93   be less influenced by actual considerations of honour. Consequently what has been said will supply information as to considerations of utility, while practicablity, with which are also usually included the questions of facility and of expediency, is chiefly to be looked at in the light of the causes productive of the various objects in view. Causes are of several kinds, some producing a result intrinsically and others contributing to its production. Let us call the former

94   efficient causes, and class the latter as indispensable accessory causes. An efficient cause is either absolute and complete in itself or auxiliary and associated in producing an effect; a force of the latter kind varies and is sometimes more and sometimes less effective, with the further consequence that the term 'cause' often denotes only the most powerful cause. There are other causes which are called efficient either as being initiatory or as ultimate. When the question is raised what is the best thing to do, the motive causing acceptance of the solution is either expediency or hope of effective success.

De Oratore

Essentials of Style

"I had to make these prefatory observations, in order that, in case the 3.37
considerations I put forward should not all be adapted to the taste of all of you and
to the kind of oratory that you severally favour, you may understand that the kind I
am describing is the one that I most approve of myself.

"Well then, it is the business of an orator both to argue the points that Antonius
has enumerated and also to express them in a particular style. Now what better
style of expression can there be—I will consider delivery later—than that our
language should be correct, lucid, ornate and suitably appropriate to the
particular matter under consideration? Now as to the two first-mentioned quali-   38
ties, I do not suppose that I shall be expected to give an account of purity and
lucidity of language, as it is not our task to teach oratory to a person who does not
know the language, nor to hope that one who cannot speak correct Latin should
speak ornately, nor yet that one who does not say something that we can
understand can possibly say something that we shall admire. Let us therefore
leave these qualities, which are easy to learn and indispensable; for one of them is
conveyed by books and by elementary education, and the other is employed for
the purpose of making an individual's statements understood, which obviously
while indispensable is at the same time the merest minimum. But all correct   39
choice of diction, although it is formed by knowledge of literature, is nevertheless
increased by reading the orators and poets; for the old masters, who did not yet
possess the ability to embellish their utterances, almost all of them had an
eminently clear style, and those who have made themselves familiar with their
language, will be unable to speak anything but good Latin, even if they want to.
All the same they must not employ words that are no longer in customary use,
except occasionally and sparingly, for the sake of decoration, as I will explain; but
one who has diligently steeped himself in the old writings while employing words
in current usage will be able to employ the choicest among them.

Embellishment

"Well then, the embellishment of oratory is achieved in the first place by 3.96
general style and by a sort of inherent colour and flavour; for that it shall be
weighty and pleasing and scholarly and gentlemanly and attractive and polished,
and shall possess the requisite amount of feeling and pathos, is not a matter of
particular divisions of the framework, but these qualities must be visible in the
whole structure. But further, in order to embellish it with flowers of language and
gems of thought, it is not necessary for this ornamentation to be spread evenly
over the entire speech, but it must be so distributed that there may be brilliant
jewels placed at various points as a sort of decoration. Consequently it is necessary   97

Reprinted by permission of the publishers and The Loeb Classical Library from Cicero, *De Oratore*
3.37–39, 3.96–97, 3.173–186, 3.190–191, 3.199–201), vol. 4, trans. H. Rackham, Cambridge, Mass.:
Harvard University Press, 1982.

to choose the style of oratory best calculated to hold the attention of the audience, and not merely to give them pleasure but also to do so without giving them too much of it—for I do not imagine that you look to me at this point for the warning to avoid an impoverished and uncultivated style, and expressions that are vulgar or out of date; your talents and also your ages demand from me something more important.

Prose Rhythm

3.173   "After attention to this matter comes also the consideration of the rhythm and shape of the words, a point which I am afraid Catulus here may consider childish; for the old Greek masters held the view that in this prose style it is proper for us to use something almost amounting to versification, that is, certain definite rhythms. For they thought that in speeches the close of the period ought to come not when we are tired out but where we may take breath, and to be marked not by the punctuation of the copying clerks but by the arrangement of the words and of the thought; and it is said that Isocrates first introduced the practice of tightening up the irregular style of oratory which belonged to the early days, so his pupil Naucrates writes, by means of an element of rhythm, designed to give pleasure to

174   the ear. For two contrivances to give pleasure were devised by the musicians, who in the old days were also the poets, verse and melody, with the intention of overcoming satiety in the hearer by delighting the ear with the rhythm of the words and the mode of the notes. These two things therefore, I mean the modulation of the voice and the arrangement of words in periods, they thought proper to transfer from poetry to rhetoric, so far as was compatible with the severe character of oratory.

175   "In this matter an extremely important point is, that although it is a fault in oratory if the connexion of the words produces verse, nevertheless we at the same time desire the word-order to resemble verse in having a rhythmical cadence, and to fit in neatly and be rounded off; nor among the many marks of an orator is there one that more distinguishes him from an inexperienced and ignorant speaker, than that the tiro pours out disorderly stuff as fast as he can with no arrangement, and ends a sentence not from artistic considerations but when his breath gives out, whereas the orator links words and meaning together in such a manner as to

176   unfold his thought in a rhythm that is at once bound and free. For after enclosing it in the bonds of form and balance, he loosens and releases it by altering the order, so that the words are neither tied together by a definite metrical law nor left so free as to wander uncontrolled.

"How then pray shall we enter on so great an undertaking with confidence in our ability to attain this capacity of rhythmical utterance? The difficulty of the thing is not as great as its importance; for there is nothing so delicate or flexible, or

177   that follows so easily wherever one leads it, as speech. Speech is the material used alike for making verses and irregular rhythms. Also it is the material for prose of various styles and many kinds; for the vocabulary of conversation is the same as that of formal oratory, and we do not choose one class of words for daily use and another for full-dress public occasions, but we pick them up from common life as

they lie at our disposal, and then shape them and mould them at our discretion, like the softest wax. Consequently at one moment we use a dignified style, at another a plain one, and at another we keep a middle course between the two; thus the style of our oratory follows the line of thought we take, and changes and turns to suit all the requirements of pleasing the ear and influencing the mind of the 178 audience. But in oratory as in most matters nature has contrived with incredible skill that the things possessing most utility also have the greatest amount of dignity, and indeed frequently of beauty also. We observe that for the safety and security of the universe this whole ordered world of nature is so constituted that the sky is a round vault, with the earth at its centre, held stationary by its own force and stress; and the sun travels round it, approaching towards the constellation of mid-winter and then gradually rising towards the opposite direction; while the moon receives the sun's light as it advances and retires; and five stars accomplish the same courses with different motion and on a different route. This 179 system is so powerful that a slight modification of it would make it impossible for it to hold together, and it is so beautiful that no lovelier vision is even imaginable. Now carry your mind to the form and figure of human beings or even of the other living creatures: you will discover that the body has no part added to its structure that is superfluous, and that its whole shape has the perfection of a work of art and not of accident. Take trees: in these the trunk, the branches and lastly the leaves are all without exception designed so as to keep and to preserve their own nature, yet nowhere is there any part that is not beautiful. Let us leave nature and 180 contemplate the arts: in a ship, what is so indispensable as the sides, the hold, the bow, the stern, the yards, the sails and the masts? yet they all have such a graceful appearance that they appear to have been invented not only for the purpose of safety but also for the sake of giving pleasure. In temples and colonnades the pillars are to support the structure, yet they are as dignified in appearance as they are useful. Yonder pediment of the Capitol and those of the other temples are the product not of beauty but of actual necessity; for it was in calculating how to make the rain-water fall off the two sides of the roof that the dignified design of the gables resulted as a by-product of the needs of the structure—with the consequence that even if one were erecting a citadel in heaven, where no rain could fall, it would be thought certain to be entirely lacking in dignity without a pediment.

"The same is the case in regard to all the divisions of a speech—virtually 181 unavoidable practical requirements produce charm of style as a result. It was failure or scantiness of breath that originated periodic structure and pauses between words, but now that this has once been discovered, it is so attractive, that even if a person were endowed with breath that never failed, we should still not wish him to deliver an unbroken flow of words; for our ears are only gratified by a style of delivery which is not merely endurable but also easy for the human lungs. 182 Consequently though the longest group of words is that which can be reeled off in one breath, this is the standard given by nature; the standard of art is different. For among the variety of metres, a frequent use of the iambus and the tribrach[1] is

1. A tribrach is a foot of three successive short syllables.

interdicted to the orator by Aristotle, the master of your school, Catulus. Nevertheless they invade our Roman oratory and conversational style automatically; yet these rhythms have a very marked beat, and the foot is too short. Consequently Aristotle asks us to employ primarily the heroic metre, in which it is quite legitimate to carry on for the space of two feet or a little more, provided we do not fall into downright verse or something resembling verse: "Both of the

183 maids are tall, and they . . ." These three feet suit the beginning of a period well enough. But the same authority specially approves of the paean, of which there are two varieties, beginning either with a long syllable followed by three short ones, like the phrases 'stóp doing it,' 'gét on to it,' 'préss down on it,' or else with three consecutive shorts with a long carrying on at the end, examples of which are 'beaten them áll,' 'clatter of hoóves'; and the philosopher mentioned approves of using the former kind of paean at the beginning and the later kind at the end. But as a matter of fact this latter paean is almost the same—not in number of syllables but in length as it affects the ear, which is a sharper and more reliable test—as the cretic, which consists of long, short, long: for instance: "Whére can Í gó for hélp? Whát's the néxt? Whére awáy . . ." The was the rhythm used by Fannius at the beginning of a speech: 'Noble lords, if the threats hurled by this . . .' Aristotle considers this foot more suitable for ends of clauses, which he desires to end as a rule with a long syllable.

184   " 'These points however do not call for such close attention and care as is practised by the poets; for them it is a requirement of actual necessity and of the metrical forms themselves that the words shall be so framed in the line that there may not be less or more by even a single breath than the length required. Prose is less fettered, and its designation as 'free style' is quite a correct one, only this does not mean that it is free to go loose or to roam about, but that it is not in chains and supplies its own control. For I agree with the opinion of Theophrastus, that at all events polished and systematic prose must have a rhythm, though not rigid, yet

185 fairly loose. In fact, as he divines, not only have the metres used for the verse now in vogue with us blossomed out later into a more drawn-out metre, the anapaest, from which has flowed the looser and more sumptuous dithyramb, whose members and feet, as the same writer says, occur widely in all opulent prose; but also, if all sounds and utterances contain an element of rhythm possessing certain beats and capable of being measured by its regular intervals, it will be proper to reckon this kind of rhythm as a merit in prose, provided that it is not used in an unbroken succession. For if a continuous flow of verbiage unrelieved by intervals must be considered rough and unpolished, what other reason is there to reject it except that nature herself modulates the voice to gratify the ear of mankind? and

186 this cannot be achieved unless the voice contains an element of rhythm. But in a continuous flow there is no rhythm; rhythm is the product of a dividing up, that is of a beat marking equal and also frequently varying intervals,—the rhythm that we can notice in falling drops of water, because they are separated by intervals, but cannot detect in a fast flowing river. But if this continuous series of words in prose is much neater and more pleasing if it is divided up by joints and limbs than if it is carried right on without a break, the limbs in question will need management; and if they are shorter at the end, this makes a break in the periodic

structure of the words— for 'period' is the Greek name for these turning-points of speech. Consequently the later clauses must either be equal to the preceding ones, and the last ones to the first, or they must be longer, which is even better and more pleasing.

"Well, then," said Crassus, "we must make our style conform to this law of 3.190 rhythm both by practice in speaking and by using the pen, which is a good tool for giving style and polish both to other forms of composition and particularly to oratory. All the same, this is not so laborious a job as it looks, nor is it necessary to regulate these matters by the strictest rule of the metricians or musicians; all that we have to achieve is that the language shall not be diffuse and rambling, stopping short of the mark or wandering on too far, and that the parts of the structure shall be distinct and the periods finished. And at the same time it is not necessary to use long sentences and periods all the time; on the contrary, the discourse should frequently be divided up into smaller members, although these themselves should possess a rhythmical unity of structure. Nor need you worry about the paeans or   191 the dactyls we were talking about: they will turn up in prose of their own accord— yes, they will fall in and report themselves as present without being summoned. Only let your habitual practice in writing and speaking be to make the thoughts end up with the words, and the combination of the words themselves spring from good long free metres, specially the dactylic or the first paean or the cretic,[2] though with a close of various forms and clearly marked, for similarity is particularly noticed at the close; and if the first and last feet of the sentences are regulated on this principle, the metrical shapes of the parts in between can pass unnoticed, only provided that the actual period is not shorter than the ear expected or longer than the strength and the breath can last out.

Three Styles

"I have practically concluded, to the best of my ability, my account of the few 3.199 factors that I deemed most important for the decoration of oratory, having discussed the value of particular words, combination of words, and rhythm and shape of sentence. But if you also want to hear about general character and tone of diction, there is the full and yet rounded style of oratory, the plain style that is not devoid of vigour and force, and the style which combines elements of either class and whose merit is to steer a middle course. These three styles should exhibit a certain charm of colouring, not as a surface varnish but as permeating their   200 arterial system. Then finally our orator must be shaped in regard to both his words and his thoughts in the same way as persons whose business is the handling of weapons are trained in style, so that just as people who practise fencing or boxing think that they must give consideration not only to avoiding or striking blows but also to grace of movement, similarly he may aim on the one hand at neatness of

---

2. The first paean is described above (183), a long syllable followed by three short ones. The cretic foot has three syllables, a long followed by a short and a long.

structure and grace in his employment of words and on the other hand at impressiveness in expressing his thoughts.

"Now there is an almost incalculable supply both of figures of speech and of figures of thought, a thing of which I know you are perfectly well aware; but there is this difference between the figurative character of language and of thought, that the figure suggested by the words disappears if one alters the words, but that of the
201   thoughts remains whatever words one chooses to employ. And even if as a matter of fact you do attend to this, still I think you ought to be warned not to imagine that there is anything else essential to the orator, at all events anything outstanding and remarkable, except to be careful in his vocabulary to keep to the three rules stated already, to use metaphorical words frequently, new coinages occasionally, and words that are actually archaic rarely. Then again, in the general structure of the language, after we have mastered smoothness of arrangement and the principle of rhythm that I spoke of, we then must vary and intersperse all our discourse with brilliant touches both of thought and of language.

Philodemus

A talented epigrammatist, Philodemus (ca. 110–35 B.C.) came to Roman Italy as a popularizer of Epicurean philosophy. None of his undistinguished prose writings were known until the excavations of Herculaneum. In the ruins of a magnificent villa probably belonging to his student and wealthy patron, L. Calpurnius Piso, were found a number of charred papyri. Among these are fragments of a seven-book work, *On Rhetoric*, containing a contentious and ill-tempered argument for Philodemus' own peculiar variation of the Epicurean view of rhetoric.

As reconstructed, the text of *On Rhetoric* is interesting but frequently confusing. Books 1 and 2 discuss the nature of art and whether rhetoric is an art. According to Philodemus, only the epideictic branch of rhetoric involves art. This branch he calls *sophistikē*, while lumping both the deliberative and forensic branches under the term *rhetorikē*. His third category is *politikē* or political science. Neither *rhetorikē* nor *politikē* involves art. Book 3 is apparently totally lost, and we have only the remains in Book 4 of a detailed critique of traditional rhetorical instruction. Book 5 goes on to attack the traditional claims of forensic and deliberative rhetoric.

Our first selection comes from Book 6, where Philodemus attacks the various philosophical schools that favored instruction in rhetoric. The second, from Book 7, continues that attack, while focusing on the utility of rhetoric and its relationship to political activity.

On Rhetoric

Selections from Book 6

Now let us take up the story about Aristotle, that he taught rhetoric in the afternoon, saying, " 'Tis a shame to be silent and allow Isocrates to speak." He showed his opinion clearly enough by writing treatises on the art of rhetoric, and by making politics a branch of philosophy.

He alleged many reasons for engaging in politics; first, that one who has no knowledge of what is done in governments finds them unfriendly to him; secondly, that a good government will be favorable to the growth of philosophy; thirdly, that he was disgusted with most of the contemporary statesmen and their continual rivalry for office. One banished to a country where the people admire rhetoric but lack the most necessary education (i.e. philosophy) if he had some experience in rhetoric might lead them in a short time to the realms of philosophy. But we object that to practice rhetoric is toilsome to body and soul, and we would not endure it. [Rhetoric] is most unsuitable for one who aims at quiet happiness, and compels one to meddle more or less with affairs, and provides no more right opinion or acquaintance with nature than one's ordinary style of speaking, and draws the attention of young men from philosophy the true horn of Amalthea and directs it to the sophistical rhyton. . . . If he knew that he could not attain the highest position or become a philosopher because of various hindering circumstances, he might propose to teach grammar, music or tactics. For we can find no reason why anyone with the least spark of nobility in his nature should become a sophist, as one *could* find reason for pursuing practical rhetoric; for the claim that the former leads to the latter is ridiculous. Consequently Aristotle's practice and his remark were not philosophic. Why is it more disgraceful to be silent and permit Isocrates to speak than to live in a city and allow Manes to dig, or to stay on land and allow the Phoenician trader to be tossed by the waves, or to pass one's life in safety as a private citizen and allow Themistocles to enjoy the perils of a general? He ought to have refused to rival Isocrates, in order that he might not seem to be acting from envy. Either he judged it disgraceful by the standards of the multitude, or by natural standards. If by the latter why did he not consider it naturally disgraceful to speak on the public platform like a hired rhetor, rather than to speak like the divine philosophers. Why did he abandon his exhortation of the young, and attempt the road to ruin which was followed by Isocrates' pupils and by other sophists? Why did he prefer to make collections of laws, constitutions, etc., in short to be a polymath and teach all manner of subjects? In this he was less noble than the rhetors, in that the rhetors try to provide power, and offer rhetorical hypotheses not merely for the calm of the soul but also for the health of the body. In short he became a more dangerous and deadly foe of Epicurus than those who openly engaged in politics. If he was searching for truth, why did he choose Isocratean rhetoric rather than political rhetoric which he considered different from that of Isocrates? If it was the political branch that he was practicing, it was ridiculous for him to say that it was a disgrace to

Reprinted by permission of the publishers and The Connecticut Academy of Arts and Sciences from Philodemus, *The Rhetorica of Philodemus* (selections from books 6 and 7), trans. Harry M. Hubbell, *Transactions of the Connecticut Academy of Arts and Sciences* 23 (Sept. 1920): 329–32, 351–59.

allow Isocrates to speak, if he did not intend to speak like him. I do not mention the fact that none of his pupils could succeed in either art, because Isocrates had forestalled him; and Isocrates after teaching rhetoric devoted himself to the quieter and as he said, more wonderful study—philosophy. He had strange reasons too for urging them to a study of politics. First that if they acquired experience and undertook a political career immediately, because of their occupation in it they would appear lacking in a proper philosophical training. But if they had no experience they could not be statesmen unless they studied a very long time, and if they waited for the state to become orderly they were neglecting the means of making it orderly (viz. philosophical politics).

Not even a woman would be so foolish as to choose the worse when the better is present. He urged Philip not to aspire to be king of Persia.

There is no use for one who rules badly what is near him, and can rule well what he is not permitted to rule. Of the reasons why he urges that one who has the ability to govern should go into politics, the first applies to himself rather than to one who takes no thought for the community. For if he thought that one who took no interest in current events would have no friend, as a matter of fact he had none, or could not keep a friend any length of time. Philosophy does not prevent a man's advance; it did not prevent Aristotle. If prevented from obtaining anything, philosophy is not brought into contempt, because it needs no help from any man.

His second reason was dissatisfaction with political conditions. But the golden age is past and sudden improvements are impossible.

Selections from Book 7

What is more violent than saying that rhetoric promises nothing except the power of speaking. It is plainly false that the power of speaking cannot include any of the other qualities which it professes to include. . . . rhetoric is better designed for the transaction of private than of public business.

Power of speech can be considered from different standpoints. When he mentions Themistocles and Pericles he means statesmen like Phocion; if he named Isocrates and Matris he makes a partial error. For Themistocles and Pericles have always been considered consummate rhetors. If Matris and his school are called rhetors, as he said, he ought not to apply this term to the political rhetors but to the other class, just as we would confine the term rhetors to Demosthenes and Callistratus and others of their class, who are said to have possessed political power, of whom we spoke in another section.

Now changing our subject we shall show that the so-called sophists seem to us to have more power in political rhetoric than the theorists in politics. Now we have already treated in a previous section the idea that sophistic or panegyric or whatever it may be called, by means of which some exercise the power of speech in assembly and forum, may easily be called rhetoric. That statement "He is a good rhetor" simply means that he is experienced and skilled in speaking. For as we say "good rhetor" we say "good artist" meaning "skillful"; "good rhetor" might also mean "morally good." . . .

. . . of those who were statesmen and had acquired this faculty, and of those who do not have it but succeed by dint of experience, of these many are better in character, many are very good, some have private virtues; some who have studied philosophy are justly considered more attractive than these.

In examining political matters he is not accurate, as we have shown in the passages referring to his statements. And when he considers rhetoric and the rhetor equivalent to politics and the statesman, he is inaccurate.

We shall inquire whether rhetoric is politics, and if there is a faculty which produces rhetors and statesmen; and again whether politics is exactly equivalent to rhetoric; and we shall make a careful inquiry as to whether the art of rhetoric is also the art of politics. We meet these questions as follows: sophistical rhetoric does not include a study of politics, and it is not political science; the rhetorical schools do not produce the political faculty or statesmen prepared for practical speaking and success in ecclesia and other public gatherings; and rhetoric *qua* rhetoric is not politics, and the rhetor is not a statesman and public speaker; and by no means do we agree with the statement made by some that rhetoric is politics; and we deny that the rhetor is always a statesman, not even in the narrower sense of the word among the ancients by which every one who spoke before the people was called a rhetor. Each of these topics we shall try to explain more fully.

Now it is made clear by Epicurus in many passages in his book Περὶ ῥητορικῆς[1] written with reference to those who are able to persuade, and by Metrodorus in the first book Περὶ ποιημάτων[2] that by rhetor the masters of the Epicurean school understand a person possessing technical training who has political experience, and is able to discover what is of advantage to states. But we are content with the passage quoted just above against Nausiphanes, in which to a certain extent the word is used in accordance with accepted usage. For he divided the term rhetoric, and made it refer to panegyric, and to the faculty, "by which from experience and investigation of political events one could perceive well what is advantageous to the multitude." . . . the phrase "as such" is added, and besides the phrase "there is not need of much argument." . . . We shall prove that if by rhetor he considered one who has political experience, if he adds the sophist's art to his equipment, it is plain from mere examination that rhetoric possesses something over and above politics, and the rhetor something over and above the statesman — namely effectiveness of speech; he certainly possesses experience in politics.

According to Greek usage one does not call Demosthenes and Callistratus and the like statesmen more than rhetors, and in that they are called rhetors they are called statesmen; but those who deliver epideictic orations and speeches more charming than theirs are not called rhetors in the same sense that these are called rhetors, of if they are so called it is because one speaks after a common form of concept. Consequently why is it not possible to call all rhetoric politics, in so far as it is rheotric, and to call the rhetor a statesman? Why not call a rhetor *qua* rhetor a δημηγόρος.[3] For the phrase "in short he is a δημηγόρος" means in so far as he is called δημηγόρος, and not differently from the rhetor, in as much as the δημηγόρος is also called rhetor. Therefore Metrodorus says that Callistratus and Demosthenes, in so far as they possessed rhetoric were δημηγόροι; but in the first book Περὶ ποιημάτων he appears to disagree saying, "There is no faculty and science of persuading the multitude."

1. *Peri rhētorikēs*, or *On the Art of Rhetoric.*
2. *Peri poiēmatōn*, or *On Poetic Compositions.*
3. *Dēmēgoros*, a popular orator or demagogue.

The art of politics then is understood to be experimental knowledge of constitutions and laws, and a knack which enables one to accept the guidance of states. Rhetoric is considered to include along with this the equipment and faculty for speaking. Now whoever has this experience, but lacks effectiveness in speaking, evidently possesses the political faculty and is a statesman, but he cannot be a rhetor, because though they possess experience in government and much greater knowledge of constitutions and laws and revenues and other things which pertain to the management of states, than the rhetors have, and actually do govern their countries, many who possess this experience do not possess the rhetorical faculty or such equipment as do those who are properly called rhetors; many in fact have no rhetorical ability at all.

The rhetors on the other hand would not seem to anyone to lack rhetoric, which is the proper possession of a rhetor. For none of those called by common consent powerful and noble rhetors can be found without political experience and faculty. But it is not one of the attributes of sophistical rhetoric *qua* rhetoric to be the art of politics, nor is the sophistical rhetor, *qua* rhetor, a statesman; nor is the statesman *qua* statesman, a rhetor, as is evident from what Epicurus says in his Περὶ ῥητορικῆς and Metrodorus in the first book Περὶ ποιημάτων, and Hermarchus in an epistle to Theophides.

Now if every art has its own peculiar field, we shall not expect navigation to produce geometricians and grammarians, nor is the knowledge of these sciences an attribute of a sailor. Why should we any more expect that statesmen or men prudent, courageous and highminded should be produced by this rhetoric *qua* rhetoric, and that such qualities are peculiar to rhetoric? For as we certainly would not say that the majority of people possess these qualities in so far as they possess the rhetorical faculty, but that they are good geometricians and grammarians, brave and just, and philosophers in a greater rather than in a less degree than those who possess the rhetorical faculty; and that many who have the advantages of rhetoric plainly lack the abovementioned sciences; in similar fashion, since many who not only have not acquired the rhetorical faculty, but have not studied at all with the sophists, nor have acquired a technical knowledge through practical study with a rhetor, still speak powerfully in public, and to use the term in its common meaning are artists and possess technical ability [whereas many from the schools can not speak successfully]. . . . Many of those trained in sophistic after the fashion of Isocrates have no political capacity or experience, and are unable to speak in public. If they ever attempt it the audience die a-laughing; since this is true, as geometry and grammar have no need of rhetoric, and it cannot produce these sciences, so the art of politics is not the property of the rhetorical sophist, and they do not produce statesmen.

Some one will say, "If because some are able without study of rhetoric to speak ably, we separate statesmanship from rhetoric on the ground that it is not peculiar to rhetoric, take away too the panegyric style of rhetoric which the rhetoricians practice both in writing and in the spoken word. . . . For many could imitate this, though they have not studied with the sophists, but merely because they are talented; and without having the technical treatises composed in the schools, would imitate the work of some sophist."

"Charm really helps in public speaking. Some who have acquired a rhythmical style from these schools have become considerably more pleasing in public assemblies."

The same is probably true of studies in poetry and philosophy. Some would certainly be harmed by rhetoric; certainly many sacrifice their natural gifts and character, and what they learn in the schools is not persuasive or successful with their audience.

Such is our discussion of the subjects mentioned. If anyone reproaches us with poverty, we shall be content with what we have, and shall not take up rhetoric to make money.

But when they say, as Anaximenes does, that people would not pay the rhetoricians for instruction unless they acquired completely the power to speak in public they speak stupidly. For by this line of reasoning one could prove that soothsaying and . . . are arts, and have greater right to be called arts than philosophy because the professors of these arts receive larger pay than the philosopher. It is senseless to compare faculties in this way, nor does the fact that some pay money to rhetors prove that statesmen are produced by rhetoric. One must not think that we have mentioned this proof merely for the sake of talking, but that it is true, and that those are mistaken who pay money to sophists. Epicurus says, "Whenever they listen to their displays and panegyric speeches, and are beguiled because the speech is not about a contract nor public policy as it is in assembly and court (for in these they pay close attention to the speaker, because they have something at stake in the assembly, and they are bound by an oath if they are sitting on the jury, whereas in the case of sophistical displays they care nothing for the oath, for they have not sworn to judge fairly nor do they care whether what is said is advantageous to the state or not, for it is not a question of war and peace, such as they have to vote on at times; and if the speech deals with war or peace or some other subject discussed in assemblies, it does not deal with a timely or pressing question, consequently they listen to displays without any feeling of anxiety) whenever they listen to such a speech they give no heed whether it is advantageous or disadvantageous, or even true or false, but are beguiled by the sound and the periods, parisoses and antitheses and homoioteleuta, and think that if they could talk like that they would succeed in assembly and court, failing to recognize that they would not endure anyone who spoke like that in assembly or court. That is why they spend money on sophists. Then immediately they recognize that they have lost their money, for they get no result but hard feeling and worry; hard feeling because they have been trained in rhetoric, and if their speech is successful they are thought to mislead the jury; but if they fail they think they have paid the sophist in vain; they are anxious about these very points, and still more how they will seem to come off with the speech, or about not misleading the jury by appearances. They have these troubles, and besides they have to attend carefully to conjunctions and cases, not abiding by their own rules but by those of others. For these and other reasons some study with the rhetoricians; in some of these they are deceived more than in others as we have stated above.

The rhetors among the sophists behave no better, not even when they say that one can prove that their art produces statesmen from the fact that some of their pupils are able to plead causes and conduct themselves properly before the assembly, in the same way that one could prove that the art of grammar produces people able to read and write from the fact that those who have attended the school can do this. Their argument works against them rather than for them, since everybody who studies the art of grammar learns to read and write, and no one learns without studying. But many who study rhetoric cannot speak in public, in fact this is true of the majority, and many who have not studied can speak—they outnumber those who have studied. Therefore we must agree that those who have studied and are statesmen, are such not by virtue of acquiring the faculty which the sophist professes to impart, but from other reasons. Such would be remarkable natural ability for acquiring the rhetorical faculty, and ardor in practicing in politics when once they have shown themselves desirous of rhetorical instruction, and have filled themselves with political speeches which involve a considerable degree of imitation, and, last of all, a spirit of meddling, which is the source of most political experience. There are many other causes, consequently their statement is unsound. And so, although there is such a connection between these studies, nevertheless rhetors skilled in swaying the passions are not produced by these studies any more than by such studies as grammar and philosophy. It thus appears vain to claim that these studies produce the political faculty; just because some statesmen come from these schools one cannot claim that rhetoric produces them. So much for that.

When they ask, who is a statesman if we cannot call the rhetors statesmen, it is easy to answer, laymen, but they are not the only ones or the majority, but the rhetors are the statesmen, however these are not the panegyrical rhetors, but those who engage in real contests; also many are statesmen who are not rhetors but possess the political faculty. But it is foolish and senseless to inquire what this faculty is, to say that it is the faculty which produces statesmen, and then to add that rhetoric is the art of politics, and produces statesmen.

When they argue as follows: "It is the task of the statesman to govern the state, to advise, to have experience in embassies, constitutions, decrees, etc., and the rhetor understands all this," grant that this can be proven, and let us allow for the sake of argument that rhetors *qua* rhetors possess knowledge and ability in these matters, yet it must be objected that some statesmen who are not rhetors possess all these qualifications. If by rhetors they mean those trained in the schools, we shall simply laugh at them; if they mean the practical rhetors, they will not find us opposing them. For they claim for themselves nothing ridiculous.

When they say that it is ridiculous to separate the political faculty from perfect rhetoric, for it is included in the concept of rhetoric, just as those skilled in the art of medicine possess a knowledge of what is healthful and harmful, they are exceedingly amusing. For how can that which is not acknowledged to include politics be granted to include politics by preconception? But the announced claims of rhetoric do not include this; only a confusion of thought includes this with rhetoric without proving that it belongs to rhetoric. There is no need of further argument in reply to the claim that states have been managed by rhetors. For even if we grant that it has been done by the political rhetors, *qua* statesmen, we shall not grant that it has been done by the rhetoricians, and if by them, not *qua* rhetoricians. It is the same way with the claim that it is the rhetors, not the philosophers, who have busied themselves with political affairs. They may use this argument against others, we grant that philosophy does not produce statesmen. Some babblers they produce who use the same words that the statesmen use, but not for that shall we grant that it produces the political faculty. If we worked on this principle we should soon be granting every thing which they profess to write about.

Now that we have finished this chapter, it remains for us to discuss the question whether the rhetor because of his rhetoric would become a *good* statesman. As for the rhetor produced by the schools, how could we say that *qua* rhetor he could become a good statesman, seeing that *qua* rhetor he is not a statesman at all? In regard to the political rhetor we think the case stands thus: the phrase "good statesman" means either a capable and experienced statesman, or one morally good. According to the former interpretation, *qua* rhetor, we say that he is a good statesman, just as we call the artistic flautist, *qua* flautist, an artistic flautist, and so a good flautist. According to the second interpretation we no longer say that the rhetor *qua* rhetor would be a good statesman. In the first place he is estimated according to his experience in what is advantageous to the state, and in speaking, just as the physician is estimated according to his knowledge of what is healthful and unhealthful. If he possesses this, no matter what his character is, there is nothing to prevent his being a rhetor. The same must be understood of one who is not a rhetor but a statesman. There would be objection if he had to be good, *qua* rhetor. For the expression *qua* rhetor means that in this he is a rhetor, and from the same condition and no other can a rhetor arise; but it is plain to all that many are capable rhetors, but bad morally. "*Qua*" is of this nature; if it is added it cannot be removed. Since this is so, we do not consider the political faculty by itself useful either to those who possess it or to the states, but that it is often the cause of irreparable dissensions in the sense that what gives the impulse is the cause. If it is accompanied by uprightness of character it often contributes great blessing to states, and sometimes greater good to its possessors than to private citizens, but oftentimes greater woe, as is proven by their lives. And if anyone says that the good statesman ought to have many virtues, and that states are saved not by rhetors *qua* statesmen, but by good statesmen, he will be right. It would be well if the statesman studied philosophy in order that he might be more actively good, and for this reason we say that philosophy if it were associated generally with the political state of mind and in individual cases made suggestions applicable to political management, would produce a wonderful improvement. He would be a good rhetor and statesman who possessed kindness, uprightness and temperance in his private life, education, wisdom which is the outgrowth of his natural ability, and combined with all these, astuteness.

Quintilian

Marcus Fabius Quintilianus (A.D. ca. 30–100) became wealthy as a practitioner and especially as a renowned teacher of oratory in imperial Rome. His *Institutio Oratoria* is the most comprehensive study of rhetoric that has come down to us from antiquity. Quintilian's humane good sense and engaging personality (which are nicely illustrated in our first selection, the preface) pervade the *Institutio* and enhance its value as an exceptional insight into classical rhetoric.

In our second selection, from Book 2, Quintilian considers basic questions about the nature and art of rhetoric. The third selection outlines the three kinds of oratory. The excerpt that follows (from Book 7) discusses in detail the arrangements of one kind of proof and of the process of definition. The fifth selection here is a famous discussion of the importance of reading in the training of an orator. Quintilian's complete treatment of memory follows. Coming at the end of the main period of classical rhetoric (from Gorgias down to imperial Roman times), it reflects an important accumulation of wisdom on the subject. In our seventh and final selection, Quintilian details his arguments for the Isocratean position that the orator must be a good man.

Institutio Oratoria

Book 1

Preface

Having at length, after twenty years devoted to the training of the young, obtained leisure for study, I was asked by certain of my friends to write something on the art of speaking. For a long time I resisted their entreaties, since I was well aware that some of the most distinguished Greek and Roman writers had bequeathed to posterity a number of works dealing with this

2 subject, to the composition of which they had devoted the utmost care. This seemed to me to be an admirable excuse for my refusal, but served merely to increase their enthusiasm. They urged that previous writers on the subject had expressed different and at times contradictory opinions, between which it was very difficult to choose. They thought therefore that they were justified in imposing on me the task, if not of discovering original views, at least of passing

3 definite judgment on those expressed by my predecessors. I was moved to comply not so much because I felt confidence that I was equal to the task, as because I had a certain compunction about refusing. The subject proved more extensive than I had first imagined; but finally I volunteered to shoulder a task which was on a far larger scale than that which I was originally asked to undertake. I wished on the one hand to oblige my very good friends beyond their requests, and on the other to avoid the beaten track and the necessity of

4 treading where others had gone before. For almost all others who have written on the art of oratory have started with the assumption that their readers were perfect in all other branches of education and that their own task was merely to put the finishing touches to their rhetorical training; this is due to the fact that they either despised the preliminary stages of education or thought that they were not their concern, since the duties of the different branches of education are distinct one from another, or else, and this is nearer the truth, because they had no hope of making a remunerative display of their talent in dealing with subjects, which, although necessary, are far from being showy: just as in

5 architecture it is the superstructure and not the foundations which attracts the eye. I on the other hand hold that the art of oratory includes all that is essential for the training of an orator, and that it is impossible to reach the summit in any subject unless we have first passed through all the elementary stages. I shall not therefore refuse to stoop to the consideration of those minor details, neglect of which may result in there being no opportunity for more important things, and propose to mould the studies of my orator from infancy, on the

6 assumption that his whole education has been entrusted to my charge. This work I dedicate to you, Marcellus Victorius. You have been the truest of

Reprinted by permission of the publishers and The Loeb Classical Library from Quintilian, *Institutio Oratoria* (1.preface, 2.14.5–6, 2.15.33–34, 2.17.1–9, 2.17.25–36, 3.7.1–6, 3.8.1–3, 3.8.6, 3.9.1–2, 7.2.27–34, 7.3.19–35, 10.1.16–36, 11.2.1–51, 12.1.1–13, 12.1.23–32), vols. 1, 3, 4, trans. H. E. Butler, Cambridge, Mass.: Harvard University Press, 1976.

friends to me and you have shown a passionate enthusiasm for literature. But good as these reasons are, they are not the only reasons that lead me to regard you as especially worthy of such a pledge of our mutual affection. There is also the consideration that this book should prove of service in the education of your son Geta, who, young though he is, already shows clear promise of real talent. It has been my design to lead my reader from the very cradle of speech through all the stages of education which can be of any service to our budding orator till we have reached the very summit of the art. I have been all the more 7 desirous of so doing because two books on the art of rhetoric are at present circulating under my name, although never published by me or composed for such a purpose. One is a two days' lecture which was taken down by the boys who were my audience. The other consists of such notes as my good pupils succeeded in taking down from a course of lectures on a somewhat more extensive scale: I appreciate their kindness, but they showed an excess of enthusiasm and a certain lack of discretion in doing my utterances the honour of publication. Consequently in the present work although some passages 8 remain the same, you will find many alterations and still more additions, while the whole theme will be treated with greater system and with as great perfection as lies within my power.

My aim, then, is the education of the perfect orator. The first essential for 9 such an one is that he should be a good man, and consequently we demand of him not merely the possession of exceptional gifts of speech, but of all the excellences of character as well. For I will not admit that the principles of 10 upright and honourable living should, as some have held, be regarded as the peculiar concern of philosophy. The man who can really play his part as a citizen and is capable of meeting the demands both of public and private business, the man who can guide a state by his counsels, give it a firm basis by his legislation and purge its vices by his decisions as a judge, is assuredly no other than the orator of our quest. Wherefore, although I admit I shall make 11 use of certain of the principles laid down in philosophical textbooks, I would insist that such principles have a just claim to form part of the subject-matter of this work and do actually belong to the art of oratory. I shall frequently be 12 compelled to speak of such virtues as courage, justice, self-control; in fact scarcely a case comes up in which some one of these virtues is not involved; every one of them requires illustration and consequently makes a demand on the imagination and eloquence of the pleader. I ask you then, can there be any doubt that, wherever imaginative power and amplitude of diction are re-quired, the orator has a specially important part to play? These two branches of 13 knowledge were, as Cicero has clearly shown, so closely united, not merely in theory but in practice, that the same men were regarded as uniting the qualifications of orator and philosopher. Subsequently this single branch of study split up into its component parts, and thanks to the indolence of its professors was regarded as consisting of several distinct subjects. As soon as speaking became a means of livelihood and the practice of making an evil use of the blessings of eloquence came into vogue, those who had a reputation for eloquence ceased to study moral philosophy, and ethics, thus abandoned by 14 the orators, became the prey of weaker intellects. As a consequence certain persons, disdaining the toil of learning to speak well, returned to the task of forming character and establishing rules of life and kept to themselves what is, if we *must* make a division, the better part of philosophy, but presumptuously laid claim to the sole possession of the title of philosopher, a distinction which neither the greatest generals nor the most famous statesmen and administrators have ever dared to claim for themselves. For they preferred the performance to

15   the promise of great deeds. I am ready to admit that many of the old philosophers inculcated the most excellent principles and practised what they preached. But in our own day the name of philosopher has too often been the mask for the worst vices. For their attempt has not been to win the name of philosopher by virtue and the earnest search for wisdom; instead they have sought to disguise the depravity of their characters by the assumption of a stern and austere mien accompanied by the wearing of a garb differing from that of

16   their fellow men. Now as a matter of fact we all of us frequently handle those themes which philosophy claims for its own. Who, short of being an utter villain, does not speak of justice, equity and virtue? Who (and even common country-folk are no exception) does not make some inquiry into the causes of natural phenomena? As for the special uses and distinctions of words, they should be a subject of study common to all who give any thought to the

17   meaning of language. But it is surely the orator who will have the greatest mastery of all such departments of knowledge and the greatest power to express it in words. And if ever he had reached perfection, there would be no need to go to the schools of philosophy for the precepts of virtue. As things stand, it is occasionally necessary to have recourse to those authors who have, as I said above, usurped the better part of the art of oratory after its desertion by the orators and to demand back what is ours by right, not with a view to appropriating their discoveries, but to show them that they have appropriated

18   what in truth belonged to others. Let our ideal orator then be such as to have a genuine title to the name of philosopher: it is not sufficient that he should be blameless in point of character (for I cannot agree with those who hold this opinion): he must also be a thorough master of the science and the art of

19   speaking, to an extent that perhaps no orator has yet attained. Still we must none the less follow the ideal, as was done by not a few of the ancients, who, though they refused to admit that the perfect sage had yet been found, none the

20   less handed down precepts of wisdom for the use of posterity. Perfect eloquence is assuredly a reality, which is not beyond the reach of human intellect. Even if we fail to reach it, those whose aspirations are highest, will attain to greater heights than those who abandon themselves to premature despair of ever reaching the goal and halt at the very foot of the ascent.

21   I have therefore all the juster claim to indulgence, if I refuse to pass by those minor details which are none the less essential to my task. My first book will be concerned with the education preliminary to the duties of the teacher of rhetoric. My second will deal with the rudiments of the schools of rhetoric and

22   with problems connected with the essence of rhetoric itself. The next five will be concerned with Invention, in which I include Arrangement. The four

following will be assigned to Eloquence, under which head I include Memory and Delivery. Finally there will be one book in which our complete orator will be delineated; as far as my feeble powers permit, I shall discuss his character, the rules which should guide him in undertaking, studying and pleading cases, the style of his eloquence, the time at which he should cease to plead cases and the studies to which he should devote himself after such cessation. In the course of these discussions I shall deal in its proper place with the method of teaching by which students will acquire not merely a knowledge of those things to which the name of art is restricted by certain theorists, and will not only come to understand the laws of rhetoric, but will acquire that which will increase their powers of speech and nourish their eloquence. For as a rule the result of the dry textbooks on the art of rhetoric is that by straining after excessive subtlety they impair and cripple all the nobler elements of style, exhaust the lifeblood of the imagination and leave but the bare bones, which, while it is right and necessary that they should exist and be bound each to each by their respective ligaments, require a covering of flesh as well. I shall therefore avoid the precedent set by the majority and shall not restrict myself to this narrow conception of my theme, but shall include in my twelve books a brief demonstration of everything which may seem likely to contribute to the education of an orator. For if I were to attempt to say all that might be said on each subject, the book would never be finished.

    There is however one point which I must emphasise before I begin, which is this. Without natural gifts technical rules are useless. Consequently the student who is devoid of talent will derive no more profit from this work than barren soil from a treatise on agriculture. There are, it is true, other natural aids, such as the possession of a good voice and robust lungs, sound health, powers of endurance and grace, and if these are possessed only to a moderate extent, they may be improved by methodical training. In some cases, however, these gifts are lacking to such an extent that their absence is fatal to all such advantages as talent and study can confer, while, similarly, they are of no profit in themselves unless cultivated by skilful teaching, persistent study and continuous and extensive practice in writing, reading and speaking.

23

24

25

26

27

General Considerations

    To resume, then, rhetoric (for I shall now use the name without fear of captious criticism) is in my opinion best treated under the three following heads, the art, the artist and the work. The art is that which we should acquire by study, and is the art of speaking well. The artist is he who has acquired the art, that is to say, he is the orator whose task it is to speak well. The work is the achievement of the artist, namely good speaking. Each of these three *general* divisions is in its turn divided into *species*. Of the two latter divisions I shall speak in their proper place. For the present I shall proceed to a discussion of the first.

2.14.5

    The first question which confronts us is "What is rhetoric?" Many definitions have been given; but the problem is really twofold. For the dispute turns

2.15.1

either on the quality of the thing itself or on the meaning of the words in which it s defined. The first and chief disagreement on the subject is found in the fact that some think that even bad men may be called orators, while others, of

2   whom I am one, restrict the name of orator and the art itself to those who are good. Of those who divorce eloquence from that yet fairer and more desirable title to renown, a virtuous life, some call rhetoric merely a power, some a science, but not a virtue, some a practice, some an art, though they will not allow the art to have anything in common with science or virtue, while some

3   again call it a perversion of art or κακοτεχνѕα. These persons have as a rule held that the task of oratory lies in persuasion or speaking in a persuasive manner: for this is within the power of a bad man no less than a good. Hence we get the common definition of rhetoric as the power of persuading. What I call a power, many call a capacity, and some a faculty. In order therefore that

4   there may be no misunderstanding I will say that by power I mean δύναμις. This view is derived from Isocrates, if needed the treatise on rhetoric which circulates under his name is really from his hand. He, although far from agreeing with those whose aim is to disparage the duties of an orator, somewhat rashly defined rhetoric as πειθους δημιουργός, the "worker of persuasion": for I cannot bring myself to use the peculiar derivative which Ennius applies to Marcus Cethegus in the phrase *suadae medulla*, the

5   "marrow of persuasion." Again Gorgias, in the dialogue of Plato that takes its title from his name, says practically the same thing, but Plato intends it to be taken as the opinion of Gorgias, not as his own. Cicero in more than one

6   passage defined the duty of an orator as "speaking in a persuasive manner." In his *Rhetorica* too,[1] a work which it is clear gave him no satisfaction, he makes the end to be persuasion. But many other things have the power of persuasion, such as money, influence, the authority and rank of the speaker, or even some sight unsupported by language, when for instance the place of words is supplied by the memory of some individual's great deeds, by his lamentable appearance or the beauty of his person.

2.15.33   For my part, I have undertaken the task of moulding the ideal orator, and as my first desire is that he should be a good man, I will return to those who have sounder opinions on the subject. Some however identify rhetoric with politics, Cicero calls it a *department of the science of politics* (and science of politics and philosophy are identical terms), while others again call it a *branch of*

34   *philosophy*, among them Isocrates. The definition which bests suits its real character is that which makes rhetoric the *science of speaking well*. For this definition includes all the virtues of oratory and the character of the orator as well, since no man can speak well who is not good himself.

2.17.1   However, if I were to indulge my own inclinations in expatiating on this subject, I should go on for ever. Let us therefore pass to the next question and

2   consider whether rhetoric is an art. No one of those who have laid down rules

1. Referring to Cicero's *De Inventione*; see for example 1.5.6.

for oratory has ever doubted that it is an art. It is clear even from the titles of their books that their theme is the art of rhetoric, while Cicero defines rhetoric as *artistic eloquence*. And it is not merely the orators who have claimed this distinction for their studies with a view to giving them an additional title to respect, but the Stoic and Peripatetic philosophers for the most part agree with them. Indeed I will confess that I had doubts as to whether I should discuss this portion of my inquiry, for there is no one, I will not say so unlearned, but so devoid of ordinary sense, as to hold that building, weaving or moulding vessels from clay are arts, and at the same time to consider that rhetoric, which, as I have already said, is the noblest and most sublime of tasks, has reached such a lofty eminence without the assistance of art. For my own part I think that those who have argued against this view did not realise what they were saying, but merely desired to exercise their wits by the selection of a difficult theme, like Polycrates, when he praised Busiris and Clytemnestra; I may add that he is credited with a not dissimilar performance, namely the composition of a speech which was delivered against Socrates.

Some would have it that rhetoric is a natural gift though they admit that it can be developed by practice. So Antonius in the *de Oratore* of Cicero styles it a *knack derived from experience*, but denies that it is an art: this statement is however not intended to be accepted by us as the actual truth, but is inserted to make Antonius speak in character, since he was in the habit of concealing his art. Still Lysias is said to have maintained this same view, which is defended on the ground that uneducated persons, barbarians and slaves, when speaking on their own behalf, say something that resembles an *exordium*, state the facts of the case, prove, refute and plead for mercy just as an orator does in his peroration. To this is added the quibble that nothing that is based on art can have existed before the art in question, whereas men have always from time immemorial spoken in their own defence or in denunciation of others: the teaching of rhetoric as an art was, they say, a later invention dating from about the time of Tisias and Corax: oratory therefore existed before art and consequently cannot be an art. For my part I am not concerned with the date when oratory began to be taught. Even in Homer we find Phoenix as an instructor not only of conduct but of speaking, while a number of orators are mentioned, the various styles are represented by the speeches of three of the chiefs and the young men are set to contend among themselves in contests of eloquence: moreover law-suits and pleaders are represented in the engravings on the shield of Achilles. It is sufficient to call attention to the fact that everything which art has brought to perfection originated in nature. Otherwise we might deny the title of art to medicine, which was discovered from the observation of sickness and health, and according to some is entirely based upon experiment: wounds were bound up long before medicine developed into an art, and fevers were reduced by rest and abstention from food, long before the reason for such treatment was known, simply because the state of the patient's health left no choice.

So too the doctor seeks to heal the sick; but if the violence of the disease or   2.17.25

the refusal of the patient to obey his regimen or any other circumstance prevent his achieving his purpose, he will not have fallen short of the ideals of his art, provided he has done everything according to reason. So too the orator's purpose is fulfilled if he has spoken well. For the art of rhetoric, as I

26   shall show later, is realised in action, not in the result obtained. From this it follows that there is no truth in yet another argument which contends that arts know when they have attained their end, whereas rhetoric does not. For every speaker is aware when he is speaking well. These critics also charge rhetoric with doing what no art does, namely making use of vices to serve its ends,

27   since it speaks the thing that is not and excites the passions. But there is no disgrace in doing either of these things, as long as the motive be good: consequently there is nothing vicious in such action. Even a philosopher is at times permitted to tell a lie, while the orator must needs excite the passions, if

28   that be the only way by which he can lead the judge to do justice. For judges are not always enlightened and often have to be tricked to prevent them falling into error. Give me philosophers as judges, pack senates and assemblies with philosophers, and you will destroy the power of hatred, influence, prejudice and false witness; consequently there will be very little scope for eloquence

29   whose value will lie almost entirely in its power to charm. But if, as is the case, our hearers are fickle of mind, and truth is exposed to a host of perils, we must call in art to aid us in the fight and employ such means as will help our case. He who has been driven from the right road cannot be brought back to it save by a fresh détour.

30   The point, however, that gives rise to the greatest number of these captious accusations against rhetoric, is found in the allegation that orators speak indifferently on either side of a case. From which they draw the following arguments: no art is self-contradictory, but rhetoric does contradict itself; no art tries to demolish what itself has built, but this does happen in the operations of rhetoric; or again: — rhetoric teaches either what ought to be said or what ought not to be said; consequently it is not an art because it teaches what ought not to be said, or because, while it teaches what ought to be said, it

31   also teaches precisely the opposite. Now it is obvious that all such charges are brought against that type of rhetoric with which neither good men nor virtue herself will have anything to do; since if a case be based on injustice, rhetoric has no place therein and consequently it can scarcely happen even under the most exceptional circumstances that an orator, that is to say, a good man, will

32   speak indifferently on either side. Still it is in the nature of things conceivable that just causes may lead two wise men to take different sides, since it is held that wise men may fight among themselves, provided that they do so at the bidding of reason. I will therefore reply to their criticisms in such a way that it will be clear that these arguments have no force even against those who

33   concede the name of orator to persons of bad character. For rhetoric is not self-contradictory. The conflict is between case and case, not between rhetoric and itself. And even if persons who have learned the same thing fight one another, that does not prove that what they have learned is not an art. Were that so, there could be no art of arms, since gladiators trained under the same master are

often matched against each other; nor would the pilot's art exist, because in   34
sea-fights pilots may be found on different sides; nor yet could there be an art of
generalship, since general is pitted against general. In the same way rhetoric
does not undo its own work. For the orator does not refute his own arguments,
nor does rhetoric even do so, because those who regard persuasion as its end, or
the two good men whom chance has matched against one another seek merely
for probabilities: and the fact that one thing is more credible than another, does
not involve contradiction between the two. There is no absolute antagonism   35
between the probable and the more probable, just as there is none between that
which is white and that which is whiter, or between that which is sweet and
that which is sweeter. Nor does rhetoric ever teach that which ought not to be
said, or that which is contrary to what ought to be said, but solely what ought
to be said in each individual case. But though the orator will as a rule maintain   36
what is true, this will not always be the case: there are occasions when the
public interest demands that he should defend what is untrue.

The Three Kinds of Oratory

I will begin with the class of *causes* which are concerned with praise and   3.7.1
blame. This class appears to have been entirely divorced by Aristotle, and
following him by Theophrastus, from the practical side of oratory (which they
call πραγματική) and to have been reserved solely for the delectation of
audiences, which indeed is shown to be its peculiar function by its name,   2
which implies display. Roman usage on the other hand has given it a place in
the practical tasks of life. For funeral orations are often imposed as a duty on
persons holding public office, or entrusted to magistrates by decree of the
senate. Again the award of praise or blame to a witness may carry weight in the
courts, while it is also a recognised practice to produce persons to praise the
character of the accused. Further the published speeches of Cicero directed
against his rivals in the election to the consulship, and against Lucius Piso,
Clodius and Curio, are full of denunciation, and were notwithstanding
delivered in the senate as formal expressions of opinion in the course of debate.   3
I do not deny that some compositions of this kind are composed solely with a
view to display, as, for instance, panegyrics of gods and heroes of the past, a
consideration which provides the solution of a question which I discussed a
little while back, and proves that those are wrong who hold that an orator will
never speak on a subject unless it involves some problem. But what problem is   4
involved by the praise of Jupiter Capitolinus, a stock theme of the sacred
Capitoline contest, which is undoubtedly treated in regular rhetorical form?
However, just as panegyric applied to practical matters requires proof, so too
a certain semblance of proof is at times required by speeches composed
entirely for display. For instance, a speaker who tells how Romulus was the son   5
of Mars and reared by the she-wolf, will offer as proofs of his divine origin the
facts that when thrown into a running stream he escaped drowning, that all his
achievements were such as to make it credible that he was the offspring of the
god of battles, and that his contemporaries unquestionably believed that he

6   was translated to heaven. Some arguments will even wear a certain semblance
         of defence: for example, if if the orator is speaking in praise of Hercules, he will
         find excuses for his hero having changed raiment with the Queen of Lydia and
         submitted to the tasks which legend tells us she imposed upon him. The
         proper function however of panegyric is to amplify and embellish its themes.

3.8.1   I am surprised that *deliberative* oratory also has been restricted by some
         authorities to questions of expediency. If it should be necessary to assign one
         single aim to deliberative I should prefer Cicero's view that this kind of oratory
         is primarily concerned with what is honourable. I do not doubt that those who
         maintain the opinion first mentioned adopt the lofty view that nothing can be
2   expedient which is not good. That opinion is perfectly sound so long as we are
         fortunate enough to have wise and good men for counsellors. But as we most
         often express our views before an ignorant audience, and more especially
         before popular assemblies, of which the majority is usually uneducated, we
         must distinguish between what is honourable and what is expedient and
3   conform our utterances to suit ordinary understandings. For there are many
         who do not admit that what they really believe to be the honourable course is
         sufficiently advantageous, and are misled by the prospect of advantage into
         approving courses of the dishonourable nature of which there can be no
         question: witness the Numantine treaty[2] and the surrender of the Caudine
         Forks.

3.8.6   The *deliberative* department of oratory (also called the *advisory* depart-
         ment), while it deliberates about the future, also enquires about the past, while
         it functions are twofold and consist in advising and dissuading.
           Deliberative oratory does not always require an *exordium*, such as is
         necessary in forensic speeches, since he who asks an orator for his opinion is
         naturally well disposed to him. But the commencement, whatever be its
         nature, must have some resemblance to an *exordium*. For we must not begin
         abruptly or just at the point where the fancy takes us, since in every subject
         there is something which naturally comes first.

3.9.1   I now come to the forensic kind of oratory, which presents the utmost
         variety, but whose duties are no more than two, the bringing and rebutting of
         charges. Most authorities divide the forensic speech into five parts: the
         exordium, the *statement of facts*, the *proof*, the *refutation*, and the *peroration*.
         To these some have added the *partition into heads*, *proposition* and *digression*,
2   the two first of which form part of the *proof*. For it is obviously necessary to
         propound what you are going to *prove* as well as to conclude. Why then, if
         proposition is a part of a speech, should not *conclusion* be also? *Partition* on the

---

2. These allude to the defeats of two Roman armies, one by the Numantians in 137 B.C. and the
other at the hands of the Samnite general, Gavius Pontius, in 321 B.C.. In both cases, humiliating peace
treaties, sparing the defeated Roman soldiers, were first negotiated and then repudiated by the Senate.

other hand is merely one aspect of *arrangement*, and *arrangement* is a part of rhetoric itself, and is equally distributed through every theme of oratory and their whole body, just as are *invention* and *style*.

Arrangements of Conjectural Proof and Definition

Conjecture is, in the first place, based on what is past, under which I include 7.2.27 persons, causes and intent. For in dealing with a case we first ask what the accused intended to do, next what he was in a position to do, and lastly what he actually did. Consequently the first point on which we must fix our attention is 28 the character of the accused. It is the business of the accuser to make any charge that he may bring against the accused not merely discreditable, but as consistent as possible with the crime for which he is arraigned. For example, if he calls a man accused of murder a debauchee or an adulterer, the discredit attaching to such charges will no doubt tell against the accused, but will, on the other hand, do less to prove the case than if he shows him to be bold, insolent, cruel or reckless. On the other hand, counsel for the defence must, as 29 far as possible, aim at denying, excusing or extenuating such charges, or, if that be impossible, show that they are not relevant to the case. For there are many charges which not only have no mutual resemblance, but may even at times contradict each other, as for instance if a man accused of theft is called prodigal or careless. For it is not likely that one and the same man should at once despise money and covet it. If such means of defence are not available, we 30 must take refuge with the plea that the charges made are not relevant to the case, that because a man has committed certain sins, it does not follow that he has committed all, and that the accusers ventured to make such false charges merely because they hoped by injuring and insulting the accused to be able to overwhelm him with the unpopularity thus created. There are also other 31 topics which arise from and against the statement of the case by the prosecution. The defence may begin by drawing arguments from the person involved, and will at times urge on general grounds that it is incredible that a father has been killed by his son or that a commander has betrayed his country to the enemy. The answer to such arguments is easy, for we may urge that bad men are capable of every crime, as is shown by every-day occurrences, or that the atrocious nature of a crime is but a poor argument against its having been 32 committed. At times we may base our arguments on the special circumstances of the person involved. This may be done in various ways: rank, for example, may be pleaded in defence of the accused, or at times, on the other hand, may be employed to prove his guilt on the ground that he trusted to his rank to secure impunity. Similarly poverty, humble rank, wealth may be used as arguments for or against the accused according to the talent of the advocate. 33 Upright character, however, and the blamelessness of his past life are always of the utmost assistance to the accused. If no charge is made against his character, counsel for the defence will lay great stress on this fact, while the accuser will attempt to restrict the judge to the sole consideration of the actual issue which the court has to decide, and will say that there must always be a

34   first step in crime and that a first offence is not to be regarded as the occasion for celebrating a feast in honour of the defendant's character. So much for the methods of reply which will be employed by the prosecution. But he will also in his opening speech endeavour to dispose the judges to believe that it is not so much that he is unable, as that he is unwilling to bring any charge against the character of the accused. Consequently it is better to abstain from casting any slur on the past life of the accused than to attack him with slight or frivolous charges which are manifestly false, since such a proceeding discredits the rest of our argument. Further, the advocate who brings no charges against the accused may be believed to have omitted all reference to past offences on the ground that such reference was not necessary, while the advocate who heaps up baseless charges thereby admits that his only argument is to be found in the past life of the accused, and that he has deliberately preferred to risk defeat on this point rather than say nothing at all about it.

7.3.19   The order to be followed in definition is invariable. We first ask *what* a thing is, and then, whether it is *this*. And there is generally more difficulty in the establishment than in the application of a definition. In determining what a thing is, there are two things which require to be done: we must establish our
20   own definition and destroy that of our opponent. Consequently in the schools, where we ourselves imagine our opponent's reply, we have to introduce two definitions, which should suit the respective sides of the case as well as it is in our power to make them. But in the courts we must give careful consideration to the question whether our definition may not be superfluous and irrelevant or ambiguous or inconsistent or even of no less service to our opponents than to ourselves, since it will be the fault of the pleader if any of these errors occur.
21   On the other hand, we shall ensure the right definition, if we first make up our minds what it is precisely that we desire to effect: for, this done, we shall be able to suit our words to serve our purpose. To make my meaning clearer, I will follow my usual practice and quote a familiar example. "A man who has stolen
22   private money from a temple is accused of sacrilege." There is no doubt about his guilt; the question is whether the name given by the law applies to the charge. It is therefore debated whether the act constitutes sacrilege. The accuser employs this term on the ground that the money was stolen from a temple: the accused denies that the act is sacrilege, on the ground that the money stolen was private property, but admits that it is theft. The prosecutor will therefore give the following definitions, "It is sacrilege to steal anything from a sacred place." The accused will reply with another definition, "It is
23   sacrilege to steal something sacred." Each impugns the other's definition. A definition may be overthrown on two grounds: it may be false or it may be too narrow. There is indeed a possible third ground, namely irrelevance, but this is
24   a fault which no one save a fool will commit. [It is a false definition if you say, "A horse is a rational animal," for though the horse is an animal, it is irrational. Again, a thing which is common to something else cannot be a property of the thing defined.] In the case under discussion, then, the accused alleges that the definition given by the accuser is false, whereas the accuser

cannot do the same by his opponent's definition, since to steal a sacred object is undoubtedly sacrilege. He therefore alleges that the definition is too narrow and requires the addition of the words "or from a sacred place." But the most effective method of establishing and refuting definitions is derived from the examination of properties and differences, and sometimes even from considerations of etymology, while all these considerations will, like others, find further support in equity and occasionally in conjecture. Etymology is rarely of assistance, but the following will provide an example of its use. "For what else is a 'tumult' but a disturbance of such violence as to give rise to abnormal alarm? And the name itself is derived from this fact." Great ingenuity may be exercised with regard to properties and differences, as for instance in the question whether a person assigned to his creditor for debt, who is condemned by the law to remain in a state of servitude until he has paid his debt, is actually a slave. One party will advance the following definition, "A slave is one who is legally in a state of servitude." The other will produce the definition, "A slave is one who is in a state of servitude on the same terms as a slave (or, to use the older phrase, 'who serves as a slave')." This definition, though it differs considerably from the other, will be quite useless unless it is supported by properties and differences. For the opponent will say that the person in question is actually serving as a slave or is legally in a state of servitude. We must therefore look for properties and differences, to which in passing I devoted a brief discussion in my fifth book. A slave when manumitted becomes a freedman: a man who is assigned for debt becomes a free man on the restoration of his liberty. A slave cannot acquire his freedom without the consent of his master: a man assigned for debt can acquire it by paying his debt without the consent of his master being necessary. A slave is outside the law; a man assigned for debt is under the law. Turning to properties, we may note the following which are possessed by none save the free, the three names (praenomen, nomen and cognomen) and membership of a tribe, all of which are possessed by the man assigned for debt.

By settling what a thing is we have come near to determining its identity, for our purpose is to produce a definition that is applicable to our case. Now the most important element in a definition is provided by quality, as, for example, in the question whether love be a form of madness. To this point in our procedure belong those proofs which according to Cicero are peculiar to definition, that is, proofs drawn from antecedents, consequents, adjuncts, contraries, causes, effects and similarities, with the nature of which I have already dealt. I will, however, quote a passage from the *pro Caccina* in which Cicero includes brief proofs drawn from origins, causes, effects, antecedents and consequents: "Why then did they fly? Because they were afraid. What were they afraid of? Obviously of violence. Can you then deny the beginning, when you have admitted the end?" But he also argued from similarity: "Shall not that which is called violence in war be called violence in peace as well?" Arguments may also be drawn from contraries, as for instance in the question whether a love-potion can be a poison, in view of the fact that a poison is not a love-potion.

25

26

27

28

29

30

31   In order that my young students (and I call them mine, because the young student is always dear to me) may form a clearer conception of this second kind of definition, I will once more quote a fictitious controversial theme. "Some young men who were in the habit of making merry together decided to dine on the sea-shore. One of their party failed to put in an appearance, and they raised a tomb to him and inscribed his name thereon. His father on his return from overseas chanced to land at this point of the shore, read the name and hung

32   himself. It is alleged that the youths were the cause of his death." The definition produced by the accuser will run as follows: "The man whose act leads to another's death is the cause of his death." The definition given by the accused will be, "He who wittingly commits an act which must necessarily lead to another's death, is the cause of his death." Without any formal definition it would be sufficient for the accuser to argue as follows: "You were the cause of his death, for it was your act that led to his death: but for your act

33   he would still be alive." To which the accused might answer, "It does not necessarily follow that the man whose act leads to another's death should be condemned forthwith. Were this so, the accuser, witnesses and judges in a capital case would all be liable to condemnation. Nor is the cause of death always a guilty cause. Take for instance the case of a man who persuades another to go on a journey or sends for his friend from overseas, with the result that the latter perishes in a shipwreck, or again the case of a man who invites

36   another to dine, with the result that the guest dies of indigestion. Nor is the act of the young men to be regarded as the sole cause of death. The credulity of the old man and his inability to bear the shock of grief were contributory causes. Finally, had he been wiser or made of sterner stuff, he would still be alive. Moreover the young men acted without the least thought of doing harm, and the father might have suspected from the position of the tomb and the traces of haste in its construction that it was not a genuine tomb. What ground then is there for condemning them, for everything else that constitutes homicide is lacking save only the contributory act?"

35   Sometimes we have a settled definition on which both parties are agreed, as in the following example from Cicero: "Majesty resides in the dignity of the Roman power and the Roman people." The question however, is, whether that majesty has been impaired, as for example in the case of Cornelius. But even although the case may seem to turn on definition, the point for decision is one of quality, since there is no doubt about the definition, and must be assigned to the *qualitative basis*. It is a mere accident that I have come to mention quality at this moment, but in point of fact quality is the matter that comes next in order for discussion.

Reading

10.1.16   But the advantages conferred by reading and listening are not identical. The speaker stimulates us by the animation of his delivery, and kindles the imagination, not by presenting us with an elaborate picture, but by bringing us into actual touch with the things themselves. Then all is life and movement, and we receive the new-born offspring of his imagination with enthusiastic approval. We are moved not merely by the actual issue of the trial, but by all that the orator himself has at stake. Moreover his voice, the grace of his gestures, the adaptation of his delivery (which is of supreme importance in oratory), and, in a word, all his excellences in combination, have their educative effect. In reading, on the other hand, the critical faculty is a surer guide, inasmuch as the listener's judgment is often swept away by his preference for a particular speaker, or by the applause of an enthusiastic audience. For we are ashamed to disagree with them, and an unconscious modesty prevents us from ranking our own opinion above theirs, though all the time the taste of the majority is vicious, and the *claque* may praise even what does not really deserve approval. On the other hand, it will sometimes also happen that an audience whose taste is bad will fail to award the praise which is due to the most admirable utterances. Reading, however, is free, and does not hurry past us with the speed of oral delivery; we can re-read a passage again and again if we are in doubt about it or wish to fix it in the memory. We must return to what we have read and reconsider it with care, while, just as we do not swallow our food till we have chewed it and reduced it almost to a state of liquefaction to assist the process of digestion, so what we read must not be committed to memory for subsequent imitation while it is still in a crude state, but must be softened and, if I may use the phrase, reduced to a pulp by frequent re-perusal.

For a long time also we should read none save the best authors and such as are least likely to betray our trust in them, while our reading must be almost as thorough as if we were actually transcribing what we read. Nor must we study it merely in parts, but must read through the whole work from cover to cover and then read it afresh, a precept which applies more especially to speeches, whose merits are often deliberately disguised. For the orator frequently prepares his audience for what is to come, dissembles and sets a trap for them and makes remarks at the opening of his speech which will not have their full force till the conclusion. Consequently what he says will often seem comparatively ineffective where it actually occurs, since we do not realise his motive and it will be necessary to re-read the speech after we have acquainted ourselves with all that it contains. Above all, it is most desirable that we should familiarise ourselves with the facts of the case with which the speech deals, and it will be well also, wherever possible, to read the speeches delivered on both sides, such as those of Aeschines and Demosthenes in the case of Ctesiphon, of Servius Sulpicius and Messala for and against Aufidia, of Pollio and Cassius in the case of Asprenas, and many others. And even if such speeches seem unequal in point of merit, we shall still do well to study them carefully with a view to understanding the problems raised by the cases with which they deal: for example, we should compare the speeches delivered by Tubero against Ligarius and by Hortensius in defence of Verres with those of Cicero for the opposite side, while it will also be useful to know how different orators pleaded the same case. For example, Calidius spoke on the subject of Circero's house, Brutus wrote a declamation in defence of Milo, which Cornelius Celsus wrongly believes to have been actually delivered in court,

17

18

19

20

21

22

23

and Pollio and Messalla defended the same clients, while in my boyhood remarkable speeches delivered by Domitius Afer, Crispus Passienus and Decimus Laelius in defence of Volusenus were in circulation.

24   The reader must not, however, jump to the conclusion that all that was uttered by the best authors is necessarily perfect. At times they lapse and stagger beneath the weight of their task, indulge their bent or relax their efforts. Sometimes, again, they give the impression of weariness: for example, Cicero

25   thinks that Demosthenes sometimes nods, and Horace says the same of Homer himself. For despite their greatness they are still but mortal men, and it will sometimes happen that their reader assumes that anything which he finds in them may be taken as a canon of style, with the result that he imitates their defects (and it is always easier to do this than to imitate their excellences) and

26   thinks himself a perfect replica if he succeeds in copying the blemishes of great men. But modesty and circumspection are required in pronouncing judgment on such great men, since there is always the risk of falling into the common fault of condemning what one does not understand. And, if it is necessary to err on one side or the other, I should prefer that the reader should approve of everything than that he should disapprove of much.

27   Theophrastus says that the reading of poets is of great service to the orator, and has rightly been followed in this view by many. For the poets will give us inspiration as regards the matter, sublimity of language, the power to excite every kind of emotion, and the appropriate treatment of character, while minds that have become jaded owing to the daily wear and tear of the courts will find refreshment in such agreeable study. Consequently Cicero recom-

28   mends the relaxation provided by the reading of poetry. We should, however, remember that the orator must not follow the poets in everything, more especially in their freedom of language and their license in the use of figures. Poetry has been compared to the oratory of display, and further, aims solely at giving pleasure, which it seeks to secure by inventing what is not merely

29   untrue, but sometimes even incredible. Further, we must bear in mind that it can be defended on the ground that it is tied by certain metrical necessities and consequently cannot always use straightforward and literal language, but is driven from the direct road to take refuge in certain by-ways of expression; and compelled not merely to change certain words, but to lengthen, contract, transpose or divide them, whereas the orator stands armed in the forefront of

30   the battle, fights for a high stake and devotes all his effort to winning the victory. And yet I would not have his weapons defaced by mould and rust, but would have them shine with a splendour that shall strike terror to the heart of the foe, like the flashing steel that dazzles heart and eye at once, not like the gleam of gold or silver, which has no warlike efficacy and is even a positive peril to its wearer.

31   History, also, may provide the orator with a nutriment which we may compare to some rich and pleasant juice. But when we read it, we must remember that many of the excellences of the historian require to be shunned by the orator. For history has a certain affinity to poetry and may be regarded as a kind of prose poem, while it is written for the purpose of narrative, not of

proof, and designed form beginning to end not for immediate effect or the instant necessities of forensic strife, but to record events for the benefit of posterity and to win glory for its author. Consequently, to avoid monotony of narrative, it employs unusual words and indulges in a freer use of figures. Therefore, as I have already said, the famous brevity of Sallust, than which nothing can be more pleasing to the leisured ear of the scholar, is a style to be avoided by the orator in view of the fact that his words are addressed to a judge who has his mind occupied by a number of thoughts and is also frequently uneducated, while, on the other hand, the milky fullness of Livy is hardly of a kind to instruct a listener who looks not for beauty of exposition, but for truth and credibility. We must also remember that Cicero thinks that not even Thucydides or Xenophon will be of much service to an orator, although he regards the style of the former as a veritable call to arms and considers that the latter was the mouthpiece of the Muses. It is, however, occasionally permissible to borrow the graces of history to embellish our digressions, provided always that we remember that in those portions of our speech which deal with the actual question at issue we require not the swelling thews of the athlete, but the wiry sinews of the soldier, and that the cloak of many colours which Demetrius of Phalerum was said to wear is but little suited to the dust and heat of the forum. There is, it is true, another advantage which we may derive from the historians, which, however, despite its great importance, has no bearing on our present topic; I refer to the advantage derived from the knowledge of historical facts and precedents, with which it is most desirable that our orator should be acquainted; for such knowledge will save him from having to acquire all his evidence from his client and will enable him to draw much that is germane to his case from the careful study of antiquity. And such arguments will be all the more effective, since they alone will be above suspicion of prejudice or partiality. 32 33 34

The fact that there is so much for which we must have recourse to the study of the philosophers is the fault of orators who have abandoned to them the fullest portion of their own task. The Stoics more especially discourse and argue with great keenness on what is just, honourable, expedient and the reverse, as well as on the problems of theology, while the Socratics give the future orator a first-rate preparation for forensic debates and the examination of witnesses. But we must use the same critical caution in studying the philosophers that we require in reading history or poetry; that is to say, we must bear in mind that, even when we are dealing with the same subjects, there is a wide difference between forensic disputes and philosophical discussions, between the law-courts and the lecture-room, between the precepts of theory and the perils of the bar. 35 36

Memory

Some regard memory as being no more than one of nature's gifts; and this view is no doubt true to a great extent; but, like everything else, memory may be improved by cultivation. And all the labour of which I have so far spoken 11.2.1

will be in vain unless all the other departments be co-ordinated by the animating principle of memory. For our whole education depends upon memory, and we shall receive instruction all in vain if all we hear slips from us, while it is the power of memory alone that brings before us all the store of precedents, laws, rulings, sayings and facts which the orator must possess in abundance and which he must always hold ready for immediate use. Indeed it

2 is not without good reason that memory has been called the treasure-house of eloquence. But pleaders need not only to be able to retain a number of facts in their minds, but also to be quick to take them in; it is not enough to learn what you have written by dint of repeated reading; it is just as necessary to follow the order both of matter and words when you have merely thought out what you are going to say, while you must also remember what has been said by your opponents, and must not be content merely with refuting their arguments in the order in which they were advanced, but must be in a position to deal with

3 each in its appropriate place. Nay, even extempore eloquence, in my opinion, depends on no mental activity so much as memory. For while we are saying one thing, we must be considering something else that we are going to say: consequently, since the mind is always looking ahead, it is continually in search of something which is more remote: on the other hand, whatever it discovers, it deposits by some mysterious process in the safe-keeping of

4 memory, which acts as a transmitting agent and hands on to the delivery what it has received from the imagination. I do not conceive, however, that I need dwell upon the question of the precise function of memory, although many hold the view that certain impressions are made upon the mind, analogous to those which a signet-ring makes on wax. Nor, again, shall I be so credulous, in view of the fact that the retentiveness or slowness of the memory depends upon

5 our physical condition, as to venture to allot a special art to memory. My inclination is rather to marvel at its powers of reproducing and presenting a number of remote facts after so long an interval, and, what is more, of so doing not merely when we seek for such facts, but even at times of its own accord, and

6 not only in our waking moments, but even when we are sunk in sleep. And my wonder is increased by the fact that even beasts, which seem to be devoid of reason, yet remember and recognise things, and will return to their old home, however far they have been taken from it. Again, is it not an extraordinary inconsistency that we forget recent and remember distant events, that we

7 cannot recall what happened yesterday and yet retain a vivid impression of the acts of our childhood? And what, again, shall we say of the fact that the things we search for frequently refuse to present themselves and then occur to us by chance, or that memory does not always remain with us, but will even sometimes return to us after it has been lost? But we should never have realised the fullness of its power nor its supernatural capacities, but for the fact that it is

8 memory which has brought oratory to its present position of glory. For it provides the orator not merely with the order of his thoughts, but even of his words, nor is its power limited to stringing merely a few words together; its capacity for endurance is inexhaustible, and even in the longest pleadings the

9 patience of the audience flags long before the memory of the speaker. This fact

may even be advanced as an argument that there must be some art of memory and that the natural gift can be helped by reason, since training enables us to do things which we cannot do before we have had any training or practice. On the other hand, I find that Plato asserts that the use of written characters is a hindrance to memory, on the ground, that is, that once we have committed a thing to writing, we cease to guard it in our memory and lose it out of sheer carelessness. And there can be no doubt that concentration of mind is of the utmost importance in this connexion; it is, in fact, like the eyesight, which turns to, and not away from, the objects which it contemplates. Thus it results that after writing for several days with a view to acquiring by heart what we have written, we find that our mental effort has of itself imprinted it on our memory.   10

The first person to discover an art of memory is said to have been   11
Simonides, of whom the following well-known story is told. He had written an ode of the kind usually composed in honour of victorious athletes, to celebrate the achievement of one who had gained the crown for boxing. Part of the sum for which he had contracted was refused him on the ground that, following the common practice of poets, he had introduced a digression in praise of Castor and Pollux, and he was told that, in view of what he had done, he had best ask for the rest of the sum due from those whose deeds he had extolled. And according to the story they paid their debt. For when a great banquet was given   12
in honour of the boxer's success, Simonides was summoned forth from the feast, to which he had been invited, by a message to the effect that two youths who had ridden to the door urgently desired his presence. He found no trace of them, but what followed proved to him that the gods had shown their   13
gratitude. For he had scarcely crossed the threshold on his way out, when the banqueting hall fell in upon the heads of the guests and wrought such havoc among them that the relatives of the dead who came to seek the bodies for burial were unable to distinguish not merely the faces but even the limbs of the dead. Then it is said, Simonides, who remembered the order in which the guests had been sitting, succeeded in restoring to each man his own dead.   14
There is, however, great disagreement among our authorities as to whether this ode was written in honour of Glaucus of Carystus, Leocrates, Agatharcus or Scopas, and whether the house was at Pharsalus, as Simonides himself seems to indicate in a certain passage, and as is recorded by Apollodorus, Eratosthenes, Euphorion and Eurypylus of Larissa, or at Crannon, as is stated by Apollas Callimachus, who is followed by Cicero, to whom the wide circula-   15
tion of this story is due. It is agreed that Scopas, a Thessalian noble, perished at this banquet, and it is also said that his sister's son perished with him, while it is thought that a number of descendants of an elder Scopas met their death at the same time. For my own part, however, I regard the portion of the story   16
which concerns Castor and Pollux as being purely fictitious, since the poet himself has nowhere mentioned the occurrence; and he would scarcely have kept silence on an affair which was so much to his credit.

This achievement of Simonides appears to have given rise to the observation   17
that it is an assistance to the memory if localities are sharply impressed upon the mind, a view the truth of which everyone may realise by practical

18   experiment. For when we return to a place after considerable absence, we not merely recognise the place itself, but remember things that we did there, and recall the persons whom we met and even the unuttered thoughts which passed through our minds when we were there before. Thus, as in most cases, art originates in experiment. Some place is chosen of the largest possible extent and characterised by the utmost possible variety, such as a spacious house divided into a number of rooms. Everything of note therein is carefully committed to the memory, in order that the thought may be enabled to run through all the details without let or hindrance. And undoubtedly the first task is to secure that there shall be no delay in finding any single detail, since an idea which is to lead by association to some other idea requires to be fixed in

19   the mind with more than ordinary certitude. The next step is to distinguish something which has been written down or merely thought of by some particular symbol which will serve to jog the memory; this symbol may have reference to the subject as a whole, it may, for example, be drawn from navigation, warfare, etc., or it may, on the other hand, be found in some particular word. (For even in cases of forgetfulness one single word will serve to restore the memory.) However, let us suppose that the symbol is drawn from navigation, as, for instance, an anchor, or from warfare, as, for example, some

20   weapon. These symbols are then arranged as follows. The first thought is placed, as it were, in the forecourt; the second, let us say, in the living-room; the remainder are placed in due order all round the *impluvium* and entrusted not merely to bedrooms and parlours, but even to the care of statues and the like. This done, as soon as the memory of the facts requires to be revived, all these places are visited in turn and the various deposits are demanded from their custodians, as the sight of each recalls the respective details. Consequently, however large the number of these which it is required to remember, all are linked one to the other like dancers hand in hand, and there can be no mistake since they join what precedes to what follows, no trouble being

21   required except the preliminary labour of committing the various points to memory. What I have spoken of as being done in a house, can equally well be done in connexion with public buildings, a long journey, the ramparts of a city, or even pictures. Or we may even imagine such places to ourselves. We require, therefore, places, real or imaginary, and images or symbols, which we must, of course, invent for ourselves. By images I mean the words by which we distinguish the things which we have to learn by heart: in fact, as Cicero says,

22   we use "places like wax tablets and symbols in lieu of letters." It will be best to give his words *verbatim:* "We must for this purpose employ a number of remarkable places, clearly envisaged and separated by short intervals: the images which we use must be active, sharply-cut and distinctive, such as may occur to the mind and strike it with rapidity." This makes me wonder all the more, how Metrodorus should have found three hundred and sixty different localities in the twelve signs of the Zodiac through which the sun passes. It was doubtless due to the vanity and boastfulness of a man who was inclined to vaunt his memory as being the result of art rather than of natural gifts.

23   I am far from denying that those devices may be useful for certain purposes,

as, for example, if we have to reproduce a number of names in the order in which we heard them. For those who use such aids place the things which have to be remembered in localities which they have previously fixed in the memory; they put a table, for instance, in the forecourt, a platform in the hall and so on with the rest, and then, when they retrace their steps, they find the objects where they had placed them. Such a practice may perhaps have been of use to those who, after an auction, have succeeded in stating what object they had sold to each buyer, their statements being checked by the books of the money-takers; a feat which it is alleged was performed by Hortensius. It will, however, be of less service in learning the various parts of a set speech. For thoughts do not call up the same images as material things, and a symbol requires to be specially invented for them, although even here a particular place may serve to remind us, as, for example, of some conversation that may have been held there. But how can such a method grasp a whole series of connected words? I pass by the fact that there are certain things which it is impossible to represent by symbols, as, for example, conjunctions. We may, it is true, like shorthand writers, have definite symbols for everything, and may select an infinite number of places to recall all the words contained in the five books of the second pleading against Verres, and we may even remember them all as if they were deposits placed in safe-keeping. But will not the flow of our speech inevitably be impeded by the double task imposed upon our memory? For how can our words be expected to flow in connected speech, if we have to look back at separate symbols for each individual word? Therefore the experts mentioned by Cicero as having trained their memory by methods of this kind, namely Charmadas, and Metrodorus of Scepsis, to whom I have just referred, may keep their systems for their own use. My precepts on the subject shall be of a simpler kind.

    If a speech of some length has to be committed to memory, it will be well to learn it piecemeal, since there is nothing so bad for the memory as being overburdened. But the sections into which we divide it for this purpose should not be very short: otherwise they will be too many in number, and will break up and distract the memory. I am not, however, prepared to recommend any definite length; it will depend on the natural limits of the passage concerned, unless, indeed, it be so long as itself to require subdivision. But some limits must be fixed to enable us, by dint of frequent and continuous practice, to connect the words in their proper order, which is a task of no small difficulty, and subsequently to unite the various sections into a whole when we go over them in order. If certain portions prove especially difficult to remember, it will be found advantageous to indicate them by certain marks, the remembrance of which will refresh and stimulate the memory. For there can be but few whose memory is so barren that they will fail to recognise the symbols with which they have marked different passages. But if anyone is slow to recognise his own signs, he should employ the following additional remedy, which, though drawn from the mnemonic system discussed above, is not without its uses: he will adapt his symbols to the nature of the thoughts which tend to slip from his memory, using an anchor, as I suggested above, if he has to speak of a ship, or a

24

25

26

27

28

29

30   spear, if he has to speak of a battle. For symbols are highly efficacious, and one
idea suggests another: for example, if we change a ring from one finger to
another or tie a thread round it, it will serve to remind us of our reason for so
doing. Specially effective are those devices which lead the memory from one
thing to another similar thing which we have got to remember; for example, in
the case of names, if we desire to remember the name Fabius, we should think
of the famous Cunctator, whom we are certain not to forget, or of some friend

31   bearing the same name. This is specially easy with names such as Asper,
Ursus, Naso, or Crispus, since in these cases we can fix their origin in our
memory. Origin again may assist us to a better remembrance of derivative
names, such as Cicero, Verrius, or Aurelius. However, I will say no more on
this point.

32   There is one thing which will be of assistance to everyone, namely, to learn a
passage by heart from the same tablets on which he has committed it to
writing. For he will have certain tracks to guide him in his pursuit of memory,
and the mind's eye will be fixed not merely on the pages on which the words
were written, but on individual lines, and at times he will speak as though he
were reading aloud. Further, if the writing should be interrupted by some
erasure, addition or alteration, there are certain symbols available, the sight of

33   which will prevent us from wandering from the track. This device bears some
resemblance to the mnemonic system which I mentioned above, but if my
experience is worth anything, is at once more expeditious and more effective.
The question has been raised as to whether we should learn by heart in silence;
it would be best to do so, save for the fact that under such circumstances the
mind is apt to become indolent, with the result that other thoughts break in.
For this reason the mind should be kept alert by the sound of the voice, so that
the memory may derive assistance from the double effort of speaking and

34   listening. But our voice should be subdued, rising scarcely above a murmur.
On the other hand, if we attempt to learn by heart from another reading aloud,
we shall find that there is both loss and gain; on the one hand, the process of
learning will be slower, because the perception of the eye is quicker than that
of the ear, while, on the other hand, when we have heard a passage once or
twice, we shall be in a position to test our memory and match it against the
voice of the reader. It is, indeed, important for other reasons to test ourselves
thus from time to time, since continuous reading has this drawback, that it
passes over the passages which we find hard to remember at the same speed as

35   those which we find less difficulty in retaining. By testing ourselves to see
whether we remember a passage, we develop greater concentration without
waste of time over the repetition of passages which we already know by heart.
Thus, only those passages which tend to slip from the memory are repeated
with a view to fixing them in the mind by frequent rehearsal, although as a rule
the mere fact that they once slipped our memory makes us ultimately
remember them with special accuracy. Both learning by heart and writing
have this feature in common: namely, that good health, sound digestion, and
freedom from other preoccupations of mind contribute largely to the success

36   of both. But for the purpose of getting a real grasp of what we have written

under the various heads, division and artistic structure will be found of great value, while, with the exception of practice, which is the most powerful aid of all, they are practically the only means of ensuring an accurate remembrance of what we have merely thought out. For correct division will be an absolute safeguard against error in the order of our speech, since there are certain points not merely in the distribution of the various questions in our speech, but also in their development (provided we speak as we ought), which naturally come first, second, and third, and so on, while the connexion will be so perfect that nothing can be omitted or inserted without the fact of the omission or insertion being obvious. We are told that Scaevola, after a game of draughts in which he made the first move and was defeated, went over the whole game again in his mind on his way into the country, and on recalling the move which had cost him the game, returned to tell the man with whom he had been playing, and the latter acknowledged that he was right. Is order, then, I ask you, to be accounted of less importance in a speech, in which it depends entirely on ourselves, whereas in a game our opponent has an equal share in its development? Again, if our structure be what it should, the artistic sequence will serve to guide the memory. For just as it is easier to learn verse than prose, so it is easier to learn prose when it is artistically constructed than when it has no such organisation. If these points receive attention, it will be possible to repeat *verbatim* even such passages as gave the impression of being delivered extempore. My own memory is of a very ordinary kind, but I found that I could do this with success on occasions when the interruption of a declamation by persons who had a claim to such a courtesy forced me to repeat part of what I had said. There are persons still living, who were then present to witness if I lie.

37

38

39

However, if anyone asks me what is the one supreme method of memory, I shall reply, practice and industry. The most important thing is to learn much by heart and to think much, and, if possible, to do this daily, since there is nothing that is more increased by practice or impaired by neglect than memory. Therefore boys should, as I have already urged, learn as much as possible by heart at the earliest stage, while all who, whatever their age, desire to cultivate the power of memory, should endeavour to swallow the initial tedium of reading and re-reading what they have written or read, a process which we may compare to chewing the cud. This task will be rendered less tiresome if we begin by confining ourselves to learning only a little at a time, in amounts not sufficient to create disgust: we may then proceed to increase the amount by a line a day, an addition which will not sensibly increase the labour of learning, until at last the amount we can attack will know no limits. We should begin with poetry and then go on to oratory, while finally we may attempt passages still freer in rhythm and less akin to ordinary speech, such, for example, as passages from legal writers. For passages intended as an exercise should be somewhat difficult in character if they are to make it easy to achieve the end for which the exercise is designed; just as athletes train the muscles of their hands by carrying weights of lead, although in the actual contests their hands will be empty and free. Further, I must not omit the fact,

40

41

42

43   the truth of which our daily practice will teach us, that in the case of the slower type of mind the memory of recent events is far from being exact. It is a curious fact, of which the reason is not obvious, that the interval of a single night will greatly increase the strength of the memory, whether this be due to the fact that it has rested from the labour, the fatigue of which constituted the obstacle to success, or whether it be that the power of recollection, which is the most important element of memory, undergoes a process of ripening and maturing during the time which intervenes. Whatever the cause, things which could not be recalled on the spot are easily co-ordinated the next day, and time itself, which is generally accounted one of the causes of forgetfulness, actually serves

44   to strengthen the memory. On the other hand, the abnormally rapid memory fails as a rule to last and takes its leave as though, its immediate task accomplished, it had no further duties to perform. And indeed there is nothing surprising in the fact that things which have been implanted in the memory for some time should have a greater tendency to stay there.

The difference between the powers of one mind and another, to which I have just referred, gives rise to the question whether those who are intending to speak should learn their speeches *verbatim* or whether it is sufficient to get a good grasp of the essence and the order of what they have got to say. To this

45   problem no answer is possible that will be of universal application. Give me a reliable memory and plenty of time, and I should prefer not to permit a single syllable to escape me: otherwise writing would be superfluous. It is specially important to train the young to such precision, and the memory should be continually practised to this end, that we may never learn to become indulgent to its failure. For this reason I regard it as a mistake to permit the student to be prompted or to consult his manuscript, since such practices merely encourage carelessness, and no one will ever realise that he has not got his theme by heart,

46   if he has no fear of forgetting it. It is this which causes interruptions in the flow of speech and makes the orator's language halting and jerky, while he seems as though he were learning what he says by heart and loses all the grace that a well-written speech can give, simply by the fact that he makes it obvious that he has written it. On the other hand, a good memory will give us credit for quickness of wit as well, by creating the impression that our words have not been prepared in the seclusion of the study, but are due to the inspiration of the

47   moment, an impression which is of the utmost assistance both to the orator and to his cause. For the judge admires those words more and fears them less which he does not suspect of having been specially prepared beforehand to outwit him. Further, we must make it one of our chief aims in pleading to deliver passages which have been constructed with the utmost care, in such manner as to make it appear that they are but casually strung together, and to suggest that we are thinking out and hesitating over words which we have, as a matter of fact, carefully prepared in advance.

48   It should now be clear to all what is the best course to adopt for the cultivation of memory. If, however, our memory be naturally somewhat dull or time presses, it will be useless to tie ourselves down rigidly to every word, since if we forget any one of them, the result may be awkward hesitation or

even a tongue-tied silence. It is, therefore, far safer to secure a good grasp of the facts themselves and to leave ourselves free to speak as we will. For the loss of even a single word that we have chosen is always a matter for regret, and it is hard to supply a substitute when we are searching for the word that we had written. But even this is no remedy for a weak memory, except for those who have acquired the art of speaking extempore. But if both memory and this gift be lacking, I should advise the would-be orator to abandon the toil of pleading altogether and, if he has any literary capacity, to betake himself by preference to writing. But such a misfortune will be of but rare occurrence. 49

For the rest there are many historical examples of the power to which memory may be developed by natural aptitude and application. Themistocles is said to have spoken excellently in Persian after a year's study; Mithridates is recorded to have known twenty-two languages, that being the number of the different nations included in his empire; Crassus, surnamed the Rich, when commanding in Asia had such a complete mastery of five different Greek dialects, that he would give judgement in the dialect employed by the plaintiff in putting forward his suit; Cyrus is believed to have known the name of every soldier in his army, while Theodectes is actualy said to have been able to repeat any number of verses after only a single hearing. I remember that it used to be alleged that there were persons still living who could do the same, though I never had the good fortune to be present at such a performance. Still, we shall do well to have faith in such miracles, if only that he who believes may also hope to achieve the like. 50

51

The Ideal Orator

The orator then, whom I am concerned to form, shall be the orator as defined by Marcus Cato, "a good man, skilled in speaking." But above all he must possess the quality which Cato places first and which is in the very nature of things the greatest and most important, that is, he must be a good man. This is essential not merely on account of the fact that, if the powers of eloquence serve only to lend arms to crime, there can be nothing more pernicious than eloquence to public and private welfare alike, while I myself, who have laboured to the best of my ability to contribute something of value to oratory, shall have rendered the worst of services to mankind, if I forge these weapons not for a soldier, but for a robber. But why speak of myself? Nature herself will have proved not a mother, but a stepmother with regard to what we deem her greatest gift to man, the gift that distinguishes us from other living things, if she devised the power of speech to be the accomplice of crime, the foe to innocency and the enemy of truth. For it had been better for men to be born dumb and devoid of reason than to turn the gifts of providence to their mutual destruction. But this conviction of mine goes further. For I do not merely assert that the ideal orator should be a good man, but I affirm that no man can be an orator unless he is a good man. For it is impossible to regard those men as gifted with intelligence who on being offered the choice between the two paths of virtue and of vice choose the latter, nor can we allow them prudence, when by 12.1.1

2

3

4   the unforeseen issue of their own actions they render themselves liable not merely to the heaviest penalties of the laws, but to the inevitable torment of an evil conscience. But if the view that a bad man is necessarily a fool is not merely held by philosophers, but is the universal belief of ordinary men, the fool will most assuredly never become an orator. To this must be added the fact that the mind will not find leisure even for the study of the noblest of tasks, unless it first be free from vice. The reasons for this are, first, that vileness and virtue cannot jointly inhabit in the selfsame heart and that it is as impossible for one and the

5   same mind to harbour good and evil thoughts as it is for one man to be at once both good and evil: and secondly, that if the intelligence is to be concentrated on such a vast subject as eloquence it must be free from all other distractions, among which must be included even those preoccupations which are free from blame. For it is only when it is free and self-possessed, with nothing to

6   divert it or lure it elsewhere, that it will fix its attention solely on that goal, the attainment of which is the object of its preparations. If on the other hand inordinate care for the development of our estates, excess of anxiety over household affairs, passionate devotion to hunting or the sacrifice of whole days to the shows of the theatre, rob our studies of much of the time that is their due (for every moment that is given to other things involves a loss of time for study), what, think you, will be the results of desire, avarice, and envy, which waken

7   such violent thoughts within our souls that they disturb our very slumbers and our dreams? There is nothing so preoccupied, so distracted, so rent and torn by so many and such varied passions as an evil mind. For when it cherishes some dark design, it is tormented with hope, care and anguish of spirit, and even when it has accomplished its criminal purpose, it is racked by anxiety, remorse and the fear of all manner of punishments. Amid such passions as these what room is there for literature or any virtuous pursuit? You might as well look for

8   fruit in land that is choked with thorns and brambles. Well then, I ask you, is not simplicity of life essential if we are to be able to endure the toil entailed by study? What can we hope to get from lust or luxury? Is not the desire to win praise one of the strongest stimulants to a passion for literature? But does that mean that we are to suppose that praise is an object of concern to bad men? Surely every one of my readers must by now have realised that oratory is in the main concerned with the treatment of what is just and honourable? Can a bad

9   and unjust man speak on such themes as the dignity of the subject demands? Nay, even if we exclude the most important aspects of the question now before us, and make the impossible concession that the best and worst of men may have the same talent, industry and learning, we are still confronted by the question as to which of the two is entitled to be called the better orator. The answer is surely clear enough: it will be he who is the better man. Conse-

10   quently, the bad man and the perfect orator can never be identical. For nothing is perfect, if there exists something else that is better. However, as I do not wish to appear to adopt the practice dear to the Socratics of framing answers to my own questions, let me assume the existence of a man so obstinately blind to the truth as to venture to maintain that a bad man equipped with the same talents, industry and learning will be not a whit inferior to the good man as an orator;

and let me show that he too is mad. There is one point at any rate which no one will question, namely, that the aim of every speech is to convince the judge that the case which it puts forward is true and honourable. Well then, which will do this best, the good man or the bad? The good man will without doubt more often say what is true and honourable. But even supposing that his duty should, as I shall show may sometimes happen, lead him to make statements which are false, his words are still certain to carry greater weight with his audience. On the other hand bad men, in their contempt for public opinion and their ignorance of what is right, sometimes drop their mask unawares, and are impudent in the statement of their case and shameless in their assertions. Further, in their attempt to achieve the impossible they display an unseemly persistency and unavailing energy. For in lawsuits no less than in the ordinary paths of life, they cherish depraved expectations. But it often happens that even when they tell the truth they fail to win belief, and the mere fact that such a man is its advocate is regarded as an indication of the badness of the case.

However, let us fly in the face of nature and assume that a bad man has been discovered who is endowed with the highest eloquence. I shall none the less deny that he is an orator. For I should not allow that every man who has shown himself ready with his hands was necessarily a brave man, because true courage cannot be conceived of without the accompaniment of virtue. Surely the advocate who is called to defend the accused requires to be a man of honour, honour which greed cannot corrupt, influence seduce, or fear dismay. Shall we then dignify the traitor, the deserter, the turncoat with the sacred name of orator? But if the quality which is usually termed goodness is to be found even in quite ordinary advocates, why should not the orator, who has not yet existed, but may still be born, be no less perfect in character than in excellence of speech? It is no hack-advocate, no hireling pleader, nor yet, to use no harsher term, a serviceable attorney of the class generally known as *causidici*, that I am seeking to form, but rather a man who to extraordinary natural gifts has added a thorough mastery of all the fairest branches of knowledge, a man sent by heaven to be the blessing of mankind, one to whom all history can find no parallel, uniquely perfect in every detail and utterly noble alike in thought and speech. How small a portion of all these abilities will be required for the defence of the innocent, the repression of crime or the support of truth against falsehood in suits involving questions of money? It is true that our supreme orator will bear his part in such tasks, but his powers will be displayed with brighter splendour in greater matters than these, when he is called upon to direct the counsels of the senate and guide the people from the paths of error to better things. Was not this the man conceived by Virgil and described as quelling a riot when torches and stones have begun to fly:

"Then, if before their eyes some statesman grave
Stand forth, with virtue and high service crowned,
Straight are they dumb and stand intent to hear."

11

12

13

12.1.23

24

25

26

27

Here then we have one who is before all else a good man, and it is only after this
that the poet adds that he is skilled in speaking: "His words their minds control,

28   their passions soothe." Again, will not this same man, whom we are striving to
form, if in time of war he be called upon to inspire his soldiers with courage for
the fray, draw for his eloquence on the innermost precepts of philosophy? For
how can men who stand upon the verge of battle banish all the crowding fears
of hardship, pain and death from their minds, unless those fears be replaced by

29   the sense of the duty that they owe their country, by courage and the lively
image of a soldier's honour? And assuredly the man who will best inspire such
feelings in others is he who has first inspired them in himself. For however we
strive to conceal it, insincerity will always betray itself, and there was never in

30   any man so great eloquence as would not begin to stumble and hesitate so soon
as his words ran counter to his inmost thoughts. Now a bad man cannot help
speaking things other than he feels. On the other hand, the good will never be
at a loss for honourable words or fail to find matter full of virtue for utterance,
since among his virtues practical wisdom will be one. And even though his
imagination lacks artifice to lend it charm, its own nature will be ornament

31   enough, for if honour dictate the words, we shall find eloquence there as well.
Therefore, let those that are young, or rather let all of us, whatever our age,
since it is never too late to resolve to follow what is right, strive with all our
hearts and devote all our efforts to the pursuit of virtue and eloquence; and
perchance it may be granted to us to attain to the perfection that we seek. For
since nature does not forbid the attainment of either, why should not someone

32   succeed in attaining both together? And why should not each of us hope to be
that happy man? But if our powers are inadequate to such achievement, we
shall still be the better for the double effort in proportion to the distance which
we have advanced toward either goal. At any rate let us banish from our hearts
the delusion that eloquence, the fairest of all things, can be combined with
vice. The power of speaking is even to be accounted an evil when it is found in
evil men; for it makes its possessors yet worse than they were before.

Tacitus

Cornelius Tacitus (A.D. ca. 56–115) was a distinguished orator who had a reasonably important public career in the imperial government. He is now known for his historical, biographical, and geographical writings, which were discovered in the Renaissance. The *Dialogue on Orators* is a perceptive review of the changes in rhetorical practice, expertise, and education from the end of the Roman Republic in the first century B.C. down to Tacitus' own day at the end of the first century A.D.

Four actual personages are imagined (in the manner of Cicero's dialogues) discussing these changes: the orators Julius Secundus (mentioned by Quintilian) and Marcus Aper; the military officer Vipstanus Messalla; and the tragic dramatist Curiatus Maternus. We have excerpted from the last half of the *Dialogue*. Here Messalla and Maternus characterize the changes from earlier to contemporary oratory in the context of a social decline that is an ironic result of the changing political climate, from turbulent Republican days to the stable but stifling rule of the Empire. Our selection treats the theoretical background of rhetorical education as well as practical rhetorical experience and training.

Dialogue on Orators

24   "There is no mistaking, is there," said Maternus, when Aper had finished speaking, "our friend's passionate impetuosity? With what a flow of words, with what a rush of eloquence, did he champion the age in which we live! With what readiness and versatility did he make war upon the ancients! What natural ability and inspiration, and more than that, what learning and skill did he display, borrowing from their own armoury the very weapons which he was afterwards to turn against themselves! All the same, Messalla, he must not be allowed to make you break your promise. It is not a defence of antiquity that we need, and in spite of the compliments Aper has just been paying us, there is no one among us whom we would set alongside of those who have been the object of his attack. He does not think there is, any more than we do. No; adopting an old method and one much in vogue with Roman philosophers, what he did was to take on himself the role of an opponent. Well then, do you set before us, not a eulogy of the ancients (their renown is their best eulogy), but the reasons why we have fallen so far short of their eloquence, and that though chronology has proved to demonstration that from the death of Cicero to the present time is an interval of only one hundred and twenty years."

25   Thereupon Messalla spoke as follows: "I shall keep to the lines you have laid down, Maternus; Aper's argument does not need any lengthy refutation. He began by raising an objection which hinges, as it seems to me, on a mere name. Aper thinks it incorrect to apply the term 'ancients' to persons who are known to have lived only one hundred years ago. Now I am not going to fight about a word; he may call them 'ancients' or 'ancestors,' or anything else he likes, so long as it is admitted that the eloquence of those days stood higher than ours. No more have I any objection to another part of his argument: I agree that not only at different but at the same epochs more types of eloquence than one have made their appearance. But just as in Attic oratory the palm is awarded to Demosthenes, while next in order comes Aeschines, Hyperides, Lysias, and Lycurgus, and yet this era of eloquence is by universal consent considered as a whole the best; so at Rome it was Cicero who outdistanced the other speakers of his own day, while Calvus and Asinius and Caesar and Caelius and Brutus are rightly classed both above their predecessors and above those who came after them. In the face of this generic agreement it is unimportant that there are special points of difference. Calvus is more concise, Asinius more vigorous, Caesar more stately, Caelius more pungent, Brutus more dignified, Cicero more impassioned, fuller, and more forceful; yet they all exhibit the same healthfulness of style, to such an extent that if you take up all their speeches at the same time you will find that, in spite of diversity of talent, there is a certain family likeness in taste and aspiration. As to their mutual recriminations—and there do occur in their correspondence some passages that reveal the bad blood there was between them—that is to be charged against them

Reprinted by permission of the publishers and The Loeb Classical Library from Tacitus, *Dialogue on Orators* (24–42), trans. W. Peterson, rev. M. Winterbottom, Cambridge, Mass.: Harvard University Press, 1980.

not as orators, but as human beings. With Calvus and Asinius—yes, and with Cicero himself—it was quite usual, I take it, to harbour feelings of jealousy and spite; they were liable to all the failings that mark our poor human nature. To my thinking Brutus is the only one of them who showed no rancour and no ill-will: in straightforward and ingenuous fashion he spoke out what was in his mind. Was it likely that Brutus would have any ill-will for Cicero? Why, he does not seem to me to have felt any for Julius Caesar himself. As to Servius Galba and Gaius Laelius, and any of the other 'ancients,' speaking comparatively, whom Aper so persistently disparaged, their case does not call for any defence; I am free to admit that their style of eloquence had the defects that are incidental to infancy and immaturity.

"If, however, one had to choose a style without taking that supreme and perfect   26 form of eloquence into account, I should certainly prefer the fiery spirit of Gaius Gracchus or the mellowness of Lucius Crassus to the coxcombry of a Maecenas or the jingle-jangle of a Gallio; for it is undoubtedly better to clothe what you have to say even in rough homespun than to parade it in the gay-coloured garb of a courtesan. There is a fashion much in vogue with quite a number of counsel nowadays that ill befits an orator, and is indeed scarce worthy even of a man. They make it their aim, by wantonness of language, by shallow-pated conceits, and by irregular arrangement, to produce the rhythms of stage-dancing; and whereas they ought to be ashamed even to have such a thing said by others, many of them actually boast that their speeches can be sung and danced to, as though that were something creditable, distinguished, and clever. This is the origin of the epigram, so shameful and so wrong-headed but yet so common, which says that at Rome 'orators speak voluptuously and actors dance eloquently.' With reference to Cassius Severus, who is the only one our friend Aper ventured to name, I should not care to deny that, if he is compared with those who came after him, he may be called a real orator, through a considerable portion of his compositions contains more of the choleric element than of good red blood. Cassius was the first to treat lightly the arrangement of his material, and to disregard propriety and restraint of utterance. He is unskilful in the use of the weapons of his choice, and so keen is he to hit that he quite frequently loses his balance. So, instead of being a warrior, he is simply a brawler. As already stated, however, compared with those who came after him, he is far ahead of them in all-round learning, in the charm of his wit, and in sheer strength and pith. Aper could not prevail on himself to name any of those successors of Cassius, and to bring them into the firing-line. My expectation, on the other hand, was that after censuring Asinius and Caelius and Calvus, he would bring along another squad, and would name a greater or at least an equal number from whom we might pit one against Cicero, another against Caesar, and so, champion against champion, throughout the list. Instead of this he has restricted himself to a criticism of certain stated orators among the 'ancients,' without venturing to commend any of their successors, except in the most general terms. He was afraid, I fancy, of giving offence to many by specifying only a few. Why, almost all our professional rhetoricians plume themselves on their pet conviction that each of them is to be ranked as superior to Cicero, though distinctly inferior to Gabinianus.

"I shall not hesitate, on the other hand, to name individuals in order to show, by the citation of instances, the successive stages in the decline and fall of eloquence."

27   Thereupon Maternus exclaimed: "Spare us that, and rather make good your promise. We do not want you to lead up to the conclusion that the ancients excelled us in eloquence. I regard that as an established fact. What we are asking for is the reasons of the decline. You said a little while ago that this forms a frequent subject of consideration with you: that was when you were in a distinctly milder frame of mind, and not so greatly incensed against contemporary eloquence—in fact, before Aper gave you a shock by his attack on your ancestors."

"My good friend Aper's discourse did not shock me," Messalla replied, "and no more must you be shocked by anything that may chance to grate upon your ears. You know that it is the rule in talks of this kind to speak out one's inmost convictions without prejudice to friendly feeling."

"Go on," said Maternus, "and in dealing with the men of olden times see that you avail yourself of all the old-fashioned outspokenness which we have fallen away from even more than we have from eloquence."

28   "My dear Maternus," Messalla continued, "the reasons you ask for are not far to seek. You know them yourself, and our good friends Secundus and Aper know them too, though you want me to take the role of the person who holds forth on views that are common to all of us. Everybody is aware that it is not for lack of votaries that eloquence and the other arts as well have fallen from their former high estate, but because of the laziness of our young men, the carelessness of parents, the ignorance of teachers, and the decay of the old-fashioned virtue. It was at Rome that this backsliding first began, but afterwards it permeated Italy and now it is making its way abroad. You know provincial conditions, however, better than I do; I am going to speak of the capital and of our home-grown Roman vices, which catch on to us as soon as we are born, and increase with each successive stage of our development. But first I must say a word or two about the rigorous system which our forefathers followed in the matter of the upbringing and training of their children.

"In the good old days, every man's son, born in wedlock, was brought up not in the chamber of some hireling nurse, but in his mother's lap, and at her knee. And that mother could have no higher praise than that she managed the house and gave herself to her children. Again, some elderly relative would be selected in order that to her, as a person who had been tried and never found wanting, might be entrusted the care of all the youthful scions of the same house; in the presence of such an one no base word could be uttered without grave offence, and no wrong deed done. Religiously and with the utmost delicacy she regulated not only the serious tasks of her youthful charges, but their recreations also and their games. It was in this spirit, we are told, that Cornelia, the mother of the Gracchi, directed their upbringing, Aurelia that of Caesar, Atia of Augustus: thus it was that these mothers trained their princely children. The object of this rigorous system was that the natural disposition of every child, while still sound at the core and untainted, not warped as yet by any vicious tendencies, might at once lay hold with heart and soul on virtuous accomplishments, and whether its bent was towards the army, or the law, or the pursuit of eloquence, might make that its sole aim and its all-absorbing interest.

"Nowadays, on the other hand, our children are handed over at their birth to   29 some silly little Greek serving-maid, with a male slave, who may be anyone, to help her—quite frequently the most worthless member of the whole establishment, incompetent for any serious service. It is from the foolish tittle-tattle of such persons that the children receive their earliest impressions, while their minds are still green and unformed; and there is not a soul in the whole house who cares a jot what he says or does in the presence of his baby master. Yes, and the parents themselves make no effort to train their little ones in goodness and self-control; they grow up in an atmosphere of laxity and pertness, in which they come gradually to lose all sense of shame, and all respect both for themselves and for other people. Again, there are the peculiar and characteristic vices of this metropolis of ours, taken on, as it seems to me, almost in the mother's womb—the passion for play actors, and the mania for gladiatorial shows and horse-racing; and when the mind is engrossed in such occupations, what room is left over for higher pursuits? How few are to be found whose home-talk runs to any other subjects than these? What else do we overhear our younger men talking about whenever we enter their lecture-halls? And the teachers are just as bad. With them, too, such topics supply material for gossip with their classes more frequently than any others; for it is not by the strict administration of discipline, or by giving proof of their ability to teach that they get pupils together, but by pushing themselves into notice at morning calls and by the tricks of toadyism.

"I pass by the first rudiments of education, though even these are taken too   30 lightly: it is in the reading of authors, and in gaining a knowledge of the past, and in making acquaintance with things and persons and occasions that too little solid work is done. Recourse is had instead to the so-called rhetoricians. As I mean to speak in the immediate sequel of the period at which this vocation first made its way to Rome, and of the small esteem in which it was held by our ancestors, I must advert to the system which we are told was followed by those orators whose unremitting industry and daily preparation and continuous practice in every department of study are referred to in their own published works. You are of course familiar with Cicero's 'Brutus,' in the concluding portion of which treatise—the first part contains a review of the speakers of former days—he gives an account of his own first beginnings, his gradual progress, and what I may call his evolution as an orator. He tells us how he studied civil law with Q. Mucius, and thoroughly absorbed philosophy in all its departments as a pupil of Philo the Academic and Diodotus the Stoic; and not being satisfied with the teachers who had been accessible to him at Rome, he went to Greece, and travelled also through Asia Minor, in order to acquire a comprehensive training in every variety of knowledge. Hence it comes that in Cicero's works one may detect the fact that he was not lacking in a knowledge of mathematics, of music, or linguistics—in short, of any department of the higher learning. Yes, Cicero was quite at home in the subtleties of dialectic, in the practical lessons of ethical philosophy, in the changes and origins of natural phenomena. Yes, my good friends, that is the fact: it is only from a wealth of learning, and a multitude of accomplishments, and a knowledge that is universal that his marvellous eloquence wells forth like a mighty stream. The orator's function and activity is not, as is the case with other pursuits, hemmed in all round within narrow boundaries. He only deserves the name who has the ability to speak on any and every topic with grace and distinction of style, in a manner fitted to win conviction, appropriately to the dignity of his subject-matter, suitably to the case in hand, and with resulting gratification to his audience.

31   "This was fully understood by the men of former days. They were well aware that, in order to attain the end in view, the practice of declamation in the schools of rhetoric was not the essential matter—the training merely of tongue and voice in imaginary debates which had no point of contact with real life. No, for them the one thing needful was to stock the mind with those accomplishments which deal with good and evil, virtue and vice, justice and injustice. It is this that forms the subject-matter of oratory. Speaking broadly, in judicial oratory our argument turns upon fair dealing, in the oratory of debate upon advantage, in eulogies upon moral character, though these topics quite frequently overlap. Now it is impossible for any speaker to treat them with fullness, and variety, and elegance, unless he has made a study of human nature, of the meaning of goodness and the wickedness of vice, and unless he has learnt to appreciate the significance of what ranks neither on the side of virtue nor on that of vice. This is the source from which other qualifications also are derived. The man who knows what anger is will be better able either to work on or to mollify the resentment of a judge, just as he who understands compassion, and the emotions by which it is aroused, will find it easier to move him to pity. If your orator has made himself familiar with these branches by study and practice, whether he has to address himself to a hostile or a prejudiced or a grudging audience, whether his hearers are ill-humoured or apprehensive, he will feel their pulse, and will handle them in every case as their character requires, and will give the right tone to what he has to say, keeping the various implements of his craft lying ready to hand for any and every purpose. There are some with whom a concise, succinct style carries most conviction, one that makes the several lines of proof yield a rapid conclusion: with such it will be an advantage to have paid attention to dialectic. Others are more taken with a smooth and steady flow of speech, drawn from the fountain-head of universal experience: in order to make an impression upon these we shall borrow from the Peripatetics their stock arguments, suited and ready in advance for either side of any discussion. Combativeness will be the contribution of the Academics, sublimity that of Plato, and charm that of Xenophon; nay, there will be nothing amiss in a speaker taking over even some of the excellent aphorisms of Epicurus and Metrodorus, and applying them as the case may demand. It is not a professional philosopher that we are delineating, nor a hanger-on of the Stoics, but the man who, while he ought to drink deeply at certain springs of knowledge, should also wet his lips at them all. That is the reason why the orators of former days made a point of acquiring a knowledge of civil law, while they received a tincture also of literature, music, and mathematics. In the cases that come one's way, what is essential in most instances, indeed almost invariably, is legal

knowledge, but there are often others in which you are expected to be well versed also in the subjects just mentioned.

"Do not let anyone argue in reply that it is enough for us to be coached in some   32
straightforward and clearly defined issue in order to meet the case immediately before us. To begin with, the use we make of what belongs to ourselves is quite different from our use of what we take on loan: there is obviously a wide gulf between owning what we give out and borrowing it from others. In the next place, breadth of culture is an ornament that tells of itself even when one is not making a point of it: it comes prominently into view where you would least expect it. This fact is fully appreciated not only by the learned and scholarly portion of the audience, but also by the rank and file. They cheer the speaker from the start, protesting that he has been properly trained, that he has gone through all the points of good oratory, and that he is, in short, an orator in the true sense of the word: and such an one cannot be, as I maintain, and never was any other than he who enters the lists of debate with all the equipment of a man of learning, like a warrior taking the field in full armour. Our clever speakers of today, however, lose sight of this ideal to such an extent that one can detect in their pleadings the shameful and discreditable blemishes even of our everyday speech. They know nothing of statute-law, they have no hold of the decrees of the senate, they go out of their way to show contempt for the law of the constitution, and as for the pursuit of philosophy and the sages' saws they regard them with downright dismay. Eloquence is by them degraded, like a discrowned queen, to a few commonplaces and cramped conceits. She who in days of yore reigned in the hearts of men as the mistress of all the arts, encircled by a brilliant retinue, is now curtailed and mutilated, shorn of all her state, all her distinction, I had almost said all her freedom, and is learnt like any vulgar handicraft.

"This then I take to be the first and foremost reason why we have degenerated to such an extent from the eloquence of the orators of old. If you want witnesses, what weightier evidence can I produce than Demosthenes among the Greeks, who is said to have been one of Plato's most enthusiastic students? Our own Cicero tells us too — I think in so many words — that anything he accomplished as an orator he owed not to the workshops of the rhetoricians, but to the spacious precincts of the Academy. There are other reasons, important and weighty, which ought in all fairness to be unfolded by you, since I have now done my part and have us usual run up against quite a number of people who will be sure to say, if my words chance to reach their ears, that it is only in order to cry up my own pet vanities that I have been extolling a knowledge of law and philosophy as indispensable to the orator."

"Nay," said Maternus, "it seems to me that you have failed so far to fulfil the task   33
you undertook. You have only made a beginning of it, and you have traced out for us what I take to be nothing more than the bare outline of the subject. You have spoken, it is true, of the accomplishments which formed as a rule the equipment of the orators of bygone days, and you have set forth our indolence and ignorance in strong contrast to their enthusiastic and fruitful application. But I am looking for what is to come next. You have taught me the extent of their knowledge and our

abysmal ignorance: what I want also to know about is the methods of training by which it was customary for their young men, when about to enter on professional life, to strengthen and develop their intellectual powers. For the true basis of eloquence is not theoretical knowledge only, but in a far greater degree natural capacity and practical exercise. To this view I am sure you will not demur, and our friends here, to judge by their looks, seem to indicate concurrence."

Both Aper and Secundus expressed agreement with this statement, whereupon Messalla made what may be called a fresh start. "Since I have given," he said, "what seems to be a sufficient account of the first beginnings and the germs of ancient oratory, by setting forth the branches on which the orators of former days were wont to base their training and instruction, I shall now proceed to take up their practical exercises. And yet theory itself involves practice, and it is impossible for anyone to grasp so many diverse and abstruse subjects, unless his theoretical knowledge is re-enforced by practice, his practice by natural ability, and his ability by experience of public speaking. The inference is that there is a certain identity between the method of assimilating what you express and that of expressing what you have assimilated. But if anyone thinks this a dark saying, and wants to separate theory from practice, he must at least admit that the man whose mind is fully furnished with such theoretical knowledge will come better prepared to the practical exercises which are commonly regarded as the distinctive training of the orator.

34 "Well then, in the good old days the young man who was destined for the oratory of the bar, after receiving the rudiments of a sound training at home, and storing his mind with liberal culture, was taken by his father, or his relations, and placed under the care of some orator who held a leading position at Rome. The youth had to get the habit of following his patron about, of escorting him in public, of supporting him at all his appearances as a speaker, whether in the law courts or on the platform, hearing also his word-combats at first hand, standing by him in his duellings, and learning, as it were, to fight in the fighting-line. It was a method that secured at once for the young students a considerable amount of experience, great self-possession, and a goodly store of sound judgement: for they carried on their studies in the light of open day, and amid the very shock of battle, under conditions in which any stupid or ill-advised statement brings prompt retribution in the shape of the judge's disapproval, taunting criticism from your opponent — yes, and from your own supporters expressions of dissatisfaction. So it was a genuine and unadulterated eloquence that they were initiated in from the very first; and though they attached themselves to a single speaker, yet they got to know all the contemporary members of the bar in a great variety of both civil and criminal cases. Moreover a public meeting gave them the opportunity of noting marked divergences of taste, so that they could easily detect what commended itself in the case of each individual speaker, and what on the other hand failed to please. In this way they could command, firstly, a teacher, and him the best and choicest of his kind, one who could show forth the true features of eloquence, and not a weak imitation; secondly, opponents and antagonists, who fought with swords, not with wooden foils; and thirdly, an audience always numerous and always different, composed of friendly and unfriendly critics, who would not let

any points escape them, whether good or bad. For the oratorical renown that is great and lasting is built up, as you know, quite as much among the opposition benches as on those of one's own side; indeed, its growth in that quarter is sturdier, and takes root more firmly. Yes, under such instructors the young man who is the subject of this discourse, the pupil of real orators, the listener in the forum, the close attendant on the law-courts, trained to his work in the school of other people's efforts, who got to know his law by hearing it cited every day, who became familiar with the faces on the bench, who made the practice of public meetings a subject of constant contemplation, and who had many opportunities of studying the vagaries of the popular taste—such a youth, whether he undertook to appear as prosecutor or for the defence, was competent right away to deal with any kind of case, alone and unaided. Lucius Crassus was only eighteen when he impeached Gaius Carbo, Caesar twenty when he undertook the prosecution of Dolabella, Asinius Pollio twenty-one when he attacked Gaius Cato, and Calvus not much older when he prosecuted Vatinius. The speeches they delivered on those occasions are read to this day with admiration.

"But nowadays our boys are escorted to the schools of the so-called 'professors of   35
rhetoric'—persons who came on the scene just before the time of Cicero but failed to find favour with our forefathers, as is obvious from the fact that the censors Crassus and Domitius ordered them to shut down what Cicero calls their 'school of shamelessness.' They are escorted, as I was saying, to these schools, of which it would be hard to say what is most prejudicial to their intellectual growth, the place itself, or their fellow-scholars, or the studies they pursue. They place has nothing about it that commands respect—no one enters it who is not as ignorant as the rest; there is no profit in the society of the scholars, since they are all either boys or young men who are equally devoid of any feeling of responsibility whether they take the floor or provide an audience; and the exercises in which they engage largely defeat their own objects. You are of course aware that there are two kinds of subject-matter handled by these professors, the deliberative and the disputations.[1] Now while, as regards the former, it is entrusted to mere boys, as being obviously of less importance and not making such demands on the judgement, the more mature scholars are asked to deal with the latter—but, good heavens! what poor quality is shown in their themes, and how unnaturally they are made up! Then in addition to the subject-matter that is so remote from real life, there is the bombastic style in which it is presented. And so it comes that themes like these: 'the reward of the king-killer,' or 'the outraged maid's alternatives,' or 'a remedy for the plague,' or 'the incestuous mother,' and all the other topics that are treated every day in the school, but seldom or never in actual practice, are set forth in magniloquent phraseology; but when the speaker comes before a real tribunal . . .

[Maternus is now speaking.] ". . . . to have regard to the subject in hand. With   36
him it was an impossibility to give forth any utterance that was trivial or commonplace. Great oratory is like a flame: it needs fuel to feed it, movement to fan it, and it brightens as it burns.

1. The reference here is to two kinds of rhetorical exercises: *suasoriae*, deliberative speeches of advice, usually based on real historical situations, and *controversiae*, forensic speeches in hypothetical legal cases.

"At Rome too the eloquence of our forefathers owed its development to the same conditions. For although the orators of today have also succeeded in obtaining all the influence that it would be proper to allow them under settled, peaceable, and prosperous political conditions, yet their predecessors in those days of unrest and unrestraint thought they could accomplish more when, in the general ferment and without the strong hand of a single ruler, a speaker's political wisdom was measured by his power of carrying conviction to the unstable populace. This was the source of the constant succession of measures put forward by champions of the people's rights, of the harangues of state officials who almost spent the night on the hustings, of the impeachments of powerful criminals and hereditary feuds between whole families, of schisms among the aristocracy and never-ending struggles between the senate and the commons. All this tore the commonwealth in pieces, but it provided a sphere for the oratory of those days and heaped on it what one saw were vast rewards. The more influence a man could wield by his powers of speech, the more readily did he attain to high office, the further did he, when in office, outstrip his colleagues in the race for precedence, the more did he gain favour with the great, authority with the senate, and name and fame with the common people. These were the men who had whole nations of foreigners under their protection, several at a time; the men to whom state officials presented their humble duty on the eve of their departure to take up the government of a province, and to whom they paid their respects on their return; the men who, without any effort on their own part, seemed to have praetorships and consulates at their beck and call; the men who even when out of office were in power, seeing that by their advice and authority they could bend both the senate and the people to their will. With them, moreover, it was a conviction that without eloquence it was impossible for anyone either to attain to a position of distinction and prominence in the community, or to maintain it: and no wonder they cherished this conviction, when they were called on to appear in public even when they would rather not, when it was not enough to move a brief resolution in the senate, unless one made good one's opinion in an able speech, when persons who had in some way or other incurred odium, or else were definitely charged with some offence, had to put in an appearance in person, when, moreover, evidence in criminal trials had to be given not indirectly or by affidavit, but personally and by word of mouth. So it was that eloquence not only led to great rewards, but was also a sheer necessity; and just as it was considered great and glorious to have the reputation of being a good speaker, so, on the other hand, it was accounted discreditable to be inarticulate and incapable of utterance.

37   "Thus it was a sense of shame quite as much as material reward that gave them an incentive. They wanted to be ranked with patrons rather than poor dependents; they could not bear to let inherited connections pass into the hands of strangers; and they had to avoid the reputation for apathy and incompetence that would either keep them from obtaining office or make their official careers a failure. I wonder if you have seen the ancient records which are still extant in the libraries of collectors, and which are even now being compiled by Mucianus: they have already been arranged and edited in eleven volumes, I think, of Proceedings and five of Letters. They make it clear that Gnaeus Pompeius and Marcus Crassus

rose to power not only as warriors and men of might, but also by their talent for oratory; that the Lentuli and the Metelli and the Luculli and the Curios and all the great company of our nobles devoted great care and attention to these pursuits; and that in their day no one attained to great influence without some gift of eloquence.

"There was a further advantage in the high rank of the persons who were brought to trial and the importance of the interests involved, factors which are also in a great degree conducive to eloquence. For it makes a good deal of difference whether you are briefed to speak about a case of theft, or a rule of procedure, and the provisional order of a magistrate, or about electioneering practices, the robbery of a province, and the murder of fellow-citizens. It is better, of course, that such horrors should not occur at all, and we must regard that as the most enviable political condition in which we are not liable to anything of the kind. Yet when these things did happen, they furnished the orators of the day with ample material. Hand in hand with the importance of the theme goes the growing ability to cope with it, and it is a sheer impossibility for anyone to produce a great and glorious oration unless he has found a theme to correspond. It is not, I take it, the speeches which he composed in the action he brought against his guardians that give Demosthenes his name and fame, nor does Cicero rest his claims to greatness as an orator on his defence of Publius Quintius or Licinius Archias. No, it was a Catiline, a Milo, a Verres, an Antonius that made his reputation for him. I do not mean that it was worth the country's while to produce bad citizens, just in order that our orators might have an ample supply of material; but let us bear in mind the point at issue, as I keep urging you to do, realising that our discourse is dealing with an art which comes to the front more readily in times of trouble and unrest. We all know that the blessings of peace bring more profit and greater happiness than the horrors of war; yet war produces a larger number of good fighters than peace. It is the same with eloquence. The oftener it takes its stand in the lists, the more numerous the strokes it gives and receives, the more powerful the opponents and the more keenly contested the issues it deliberately selects, in like proportion does eloquence carry its head higher and more erect before the eyes of men, deriving ever greater lustre from the very hazards it encounters. For men are naturally prone, while courting security for themselves, to admire whatever has an element of risk.

"I pass on to the organisation and procedure of the old law-courts. It may 38 nowadays have become more practical, but all the same the forum as it then was provided a better training-ground for oratory. There was no obligation on any speaker to complete his pleading within an hour or two at the most; adjournments were always in order; as regards a time-limit, each man was a law to himself; and no attempt was made to define either how many days the case was to take or how many counsel were to be employed in it. It was Gnaeus Pompeius who, in his third consulship, first introduced limitations in regard to these matters. He may be said to have curbed eloquence with bit and bridle, without however cancelling the provision that everything should be done in court, according to law, and before a praetor. The best proof you can have of the greater importance of the cases dealt with by the praetors in former days is the fact that actions before the centumviral court, which are now considered to outrank all others, used to be so much overshadowed by the prestige of other tribunals that there is not a single speech, delivered before that court, that is read today, either by Cicero, or by Caesar, or by Brutus, or by Caelius, or by Calvus, or in fact by any orator of rank. The only exceptions are the speeches of Asinius Pollio entitled 'For Urbinia's Heirs,' and yet these are just the ones which he delivered well on in the middle of the reign of Augustus, when in consequence of the long period of peace, and the unbroken spell of inactivity on the part of the commons and of peaceableness on the part of the senate, by reason also of the working of the great imperial system, a hush had fallen upon eloquence, as indeed it had upon the world at large.

39   "My next point will perhaps strike you as trivial and ridiculous, but I shall make it, even if only to excite your ridicule. Take those gowns into which we squeeze ourselves when we chat with the court, a costume that shackles movement, do we ever reflect how largely responsible they are for the orator's loss of dignity? Or think of the recitation-halls and record-offices in which pretty well most cases are nowadays despatched, have they not also greatly contributed to the emasculation of eloquence? Why, just as with blood-horses it takes a roomy track to show their mettle, so orators need a spacious field in which to expatiate without let or hindrance, if their eloquence is not to lose all its strength and pith. Moreover, painstaking preparation and the anxious effort for stylistic finish are found after all to do more harm than good. The judge often asks when you are going to come to the point, and you are bound to make a start as soon as he puts the question. Just as often he imposes silence in the middle of proofs or evidence. All the time the speaker has only two or three for an audience, and the hearing goes forward in what is a scene of desolation. But your public speaker can't get along without 'hear, hear,' and the clapping of hands. He must have what I may call his stage. This the orators of former times could command day after day, when the forum was packed by an audience at the same time numerous and distinguished, when persons who had to face the hazard of a public trial could depend on being supported by shoals of clients and fellow-tribesmen, and by deputations also from the country towns; half Italy, in fact, was there to back them. These were the days when the people of Rome felt that in quite a number of cases they had a personal stake in the verdict. We know on good authority that both the impeachment and the defence of a Cornelius, a Scaurus, a Milo, a Bestia, a Vatinius brought the whole community together *en masse*: so that it would have been impossible for even the most frigid of speakers not to be enkindled and set on fire by the mere clash of partisan enthusiasm. That is why the quality of the published orations that have come down to us is so high that it is by these more than by any others that the speakers who appeared on either side actually take rank.

40   "Think again of the incessant public meetings, of the privilege so freely accorded of inveighing against persons of position and influence — yes, and of the glory you gained by being at daggers drawn with them, in the days when so many clever speakers could not let even a Scipio alone, or a Sulla, or a Pompeius, and when, taking a leaf out of the book of stage-players, they made public meetings also the opportunity of launching characteristically spiteful tirades against the

leading men of the state: how all this must have inflamed the able debater and added fuel to the fire of his eloquence!

"The art which is the subject of our discourse is not a quiet and peaceable art, or one that finds satisfaction in moral worth and good behaviour: no, really great and famous oratory is a foster-child of licence, which foolish men called liberty, an associate of sedition, a goad for the unbridled populace. It owes no allegiance to any. Devoid of discipline, it is insulting, off-hand, and overbearing. It is a plant that does not grow under a well-regulated constitution. Does history contain a single instance of any orator at Sparta, or in Crete, two states whose political system and legislation were more stringent than any other on record? It is equally true to say that in Macedonia and in Persia eloquence was unknown, as indeed it was in all states that were content to live under a settled government. Rhodes has had some orators, Athens a great many: in both communities all power was in the hands of the populace — that is to say, the untutored democracy, in fact the mob. Likewise at Rome, so long as the constitution was unsettled, so long as the country kept wearing itself out with factions and dissensions and disagreements, so long as there was no peace in the forum, no harmony in the senate, no restraint in the courts of law, no respect for authority, no sense of propriety on the part of the officers of state, the growth of eloquence was doubtless sturdier, just as untilled soil produces certain vegetation in greater luxuriance. But the benefit derived from the eloquence of the Gracchi did not make up for what the country suffered from their laws, and too dearly did Cicero pay by the death he died for his renown in oratory.

"In the same way what little our orators have left them of the old forensic   41 activities goes to show that our civil condition is still far from being ideally perfect. Does anyone ever call us lawyers to his aid unless he is either a criminal or in distress? Does any country town ever ask for our protection except under pressure either from an aggressive neighbour or from internal strife? Are we ever retained for a province except where robbery and oppression have been at work? Yet surely it were better to have no grievances than to need to seek redress. If a community could be found in which nobody ever did anything wrong, orators would be just as superfluous among saints as are doctors among those that need no physician. For just as the healing art is very little in demand and makes very little progress in countries where people enjoy good health and strong constitutions, so oratory has less prestige and smaller consideration where people are well behaved and ready to obey their rulers. What is the use of long arguments in the senate, when good citizens agree so quickly? What is the use of one harangue after another on public platforms, when it is not the ignorant multitude that decides a political issue, but a monarch who is the incarnation of wisdom? What is the use of taking a prosecution on one's own shoulders when misdeeds are so few and so trivial, or of making oneself unpopular by a defence of inordinate length, when the defendant can count on a gracious judge meeting him halfway? Believe me, my friends, you who have all the eloquence that the times require: if you had lived in bygone days, or if the orators who rouse our admiration had lived today — if some deity, I say, had suddenly made you change places in your lives and epochs, you would have attained to their brilliant reputation for eloquence just as surely as they would show your restraint and self-control. As things are, since it is impossible for anybody to to enjoy at one and the same time great renown and great repose, let everyone make the most of the blessings his own times afford without disparaging any other age."

42 When Maternus had finished speaking, "There were some points," Messalla said, "to which I should like to take exception, and others which, I think, might call for fuller treatment. But the hour grows late."

"Some other time," Maternus replied, "we shall take the matter up again, whenever you please. We can then discuss again anything in my argument that may have struck you as needing further elucidation."

With that he rose from his seat and put his arms round Aper, saying, "We shall both denounce you—I to the poets and Messalla to the lovers of antiquity."

"And I," said Aper, "shall denounce both of you to the teachers of rhetoric and the professors."

They beamed on each other, and we went our ways.

4

Educational Rhetoric

H andbooks of preliminary exercises, *progymnasmata*, were used by rhetoricians
to teach young students the basic techniques of composition. The four extant
progymnasmata belong to the Christian era, but their roots are in the methods
of training in rhetoric developed by the sophists of the fifth century B.C. Cicero tell us
(*Brutus* 46–47) that Protagoras and Gorgias used exercises to teach rhetorical technique. The Romans adopted the method from the Greek rhetoricians. Quintilian (2.4)
describes twelve exercises that are very similar to those of the Greek *progymnasmata*.

Rhetorical exercises were useful not only for training future public men in the art of
speaking persuasively, but also for teaching the fundamentals of literary composition.
In much of the Greek and Roman literature of the Christian era one finds structural
units that resemble the rhetorical exercises set forth in the *progymnasmata*. But such
generic composition is also true of literature composed during the reign of the emperor
Augustus. According to George Kennedy:

Latin literature shows signs of progymnasmatic compositional blocks as early as the Augustan age.
The *Heroides* of Ovid are versified *prosopopoeiae*, and the *Metamorphoses* is in a sense a stringing
together of myths, *prosopopoeiae*, narratives, comparisons, and *ekphraseis*. Among Greek writers
of the First Century, Dio Chrysostom probably best exemplifies the adaptation of progymnasmata
to extended composition, but the *Parallel Lives* of Plutarch contain the most famous examples of
synkriseis.[1]

A Greek novel of the late second century A.D. opens with an *ekphrasis*. It is a
description of a "painted picture of a tale of love." This is also a description of the plot of
the novel itself, for the author says that he offers his tale as a "literary pendant to that
painted picture." The novel is, of course, Longus' *Daphnis and Chloe*, one of the most
widely admired works of fiction from late antiquity. Recent critical interest in the
ancient novel calls for an awareness of such *progymnasmatic* techniques on the part of
the modern student.

In antiquity, a boy began his training under a grammarian, who taught him how to
read and write. Under the grammarian he also studied literature, beginning with
Homer. And he may have been given some of the fundamentals of simple exposition.
When he went on to the rhetorician, he studied the techniques of persuasion. All this
was merely preliminary to the major activity of the schools of rhetoric, which was the

---

1. *Greek Rhetoric*, 56.

giving of declamations on judicial themes. For example, the opening scene of Petronius' *Satyricon* gives a vivid contemporary picture, albeit cynical, of such declamational activity.

In this section we present, first, the prefaces to the *Progymnasmata* of Theon and Nicolaus. In their prefaces, the only *progymnasmatic* prefaces extant, these writers discuss the educational objectives of preliminary exercises. Finally, we give the complete *Progymnasmata* of Aphthonius, since it not only became the most authoritative of these handbooks in the Byzantine east, but also, and more important, it came to be widely used in the schools of the European west. Rudolph Agricola translated it into Latin in the fifteenth century.

The *Progymnasmata* of Aphthonius contains fourteen exercises, beginning with simple exercises: *muthos* (fable) and *diēgēma* (narrative). The exercises become more and more complex, and the work ends with the *nomou eisphora* (introduction of a law). Through his working out of such exercises, the student learned simple methods of argumentation useful for deliberative and epideictic contests. He also acquired some compositional skill in the arrangement of topics, and he learned something about style.

Theon

Aelius Theon was a sophist who lived at Alexandria in Egypt in the first century A. D. Theon's treatise is the earliest of the four extant *progymnasmata*, and it was very popular in late antiquity. Only the *Progymnasmata* of Theon and Nicolaus (see the following selection) have prefaces extant. We present Theon's preface here for the first time in English.

While giving us a contemporary's justification of these early exercises, Theon also lets us see which authors from the classical age of Greece were still being read in the schools of his day. In the first part of his preface, Theon sets forth his educational program, rhetorical training by means of the study of ancient authors (liberal arts), and he defends his choice of exercises. All *progymnasmata*, he says, are training for future historians and poets as well as for future orators. In the second part, he amplifies what he has said earlier by giving more examples from Greek literature of the classical period. Finally, some attention is given to the composition of sentences and to style. Included in the advice on correcting the work of pupils is the very humane reminder that not every pupil has been endowed with the same natural ability, and so compensation should be made for this. Theon also mentions that each kind of speech has a delivery appropriate to it alone.

Progymnasmata

Preface

1.

The ancestors of our speakers, particularly those of good repute, thought it improper to attain in any way to the art of speaking without having first in a certain manner engaged in philosophy and having been filled full of her great mind as a result. But now the majority of speakers are so lacking in understanding of such literature that they rush to give a speech without any preparation at all in that knowledge that is called general, and the crudest thing of all is that they hurl themselves into forensic and deliberative speeches without proper training, indeed learning content "on the job" after the manner of the proverb "The potter's craft is in the pot." Let others, however, write about the other things that the future speaker must learn. But now I shall attempt to transmit those things that it is necessary to know and to be reasonably trained in before one makes a speech. Although there are some others who have written about these things too, my own expectation is that it will be no small thing for those who undertake to make speeches to comprehend. For not only have we invented some things new to the traditional exercises, but also we have attempted to define each thing so as to be able to say, when asked what each of them is, that, for example, a fable [*muthos*]is a false story that resembles truth. Furthermore, we have made clear their difference from one another. We have also transmitted materials for each of the speeches, and we have shown besides how someone most carefully might use them.

And so it is quite evident that these exercises are altogether beneficial to those who take up the art of rhetoric. For he who has recited a narration [*diēgēsis*] and a fable well and with versatility will also compose a history well and that which by itself in the speeches is called a narrative [*diēgēma*] (for history is none other than a "system" of narration.) He who has the ability to refute [*anaskeuasai*] or confirm [*kataskeuasai*] these things is perhaps little inferior to those who make speeches. For all the things that we create in the forensic speeches are here also: first, *proemium* and narrative; next, we attempt to reply to each of the things that have been said in the narrative or in the fable and to find a refutation [*elenchos*] for each; we further consider how we shall arrange well each of the proofs [*epicheirēmata*]; and we both strengthen and also take apart other things concerning which it would be too lengthy to speak at present.

Furthermore, training through the *chreia* not only produces a certain power of speech but also a good and useful character since we are being trained in the aphorisms of wise men. Both the so-called *koinos topos*[1] and description [*ekphrasis*] have benefit that is

A translation from the Greek by Patricia P. Matsen, 1987.

1. By *topos* Theon means an exercise in amplification, and only here does he use the attributive *koinos* with *topos*. When he deals with this exercise later, he gives this definition: "*Topos* is a composition amplificatory of an acknowledged act, either a sinful action or a brave deed; for *topos* is twofold: one kind is against those who have acted wickedly, for example, against a tyrant, a traitor, a murderer, a spendthrift; the other kind is on behalf of those who have accomplished some good and useful thing, for example, on behalf of a tyrannicide, a prince, a lawgiver. . . . And it differs from encomia and invectives, because those are spoken about definite persons and with demonstration" (*peri topou*). In his *Progymnasmata* Hermogenes explains the attributive *koinos*: "And it is called 'common' *topos* because it

254

conspicuous since the ancients have used them everywhere, all the historians making use of description to the fullest extent and the rhetoricians, *topos*. Moreover, *prosōpopoeia* is not only training for history but also for public speaking, conversation, and poetry. Even in daily life, even in our associations with each other, it is very useful, and it is most serviceable for the speeches of our written works. For this reason we praise Homer first because he has bestowed appropriate speeches on each of the persons as they are introduced, but we find fault with Euripides because Hecuba lectures out of season.

Furthermore, the exercise of comparison [*sunkrisis*] is useful even in the forensic speeches when we are comparing wrongs with wrongs or kindnesses with kindnesses and, likewise, even in encomia when we are comparing or contrasting good deeds, but in deliberative speeches the benefit is altogether evident. For the speeches of those who deliberate are about the choice of one of two things.

But concerning thesis, what could one say? For it is no different than hypothesis, except that it is not indicative of limited persons, place, time, manner, and cause; for example, a thesis is *If it is appropriate for besieged persons to send an army abroad*, and a hypothesis is *If it is appropriate for Athenians besieged by Peloponnesians to send an army to Sicily*. Likewise, both opposition [*katēgoria*] and defense [*apologia*] of laws are not the least part of the hypothesis. The finest, at any rate, of the Demosthenic speeches are those in which there is a dispute about a law or a decree, and I mention the "On the Crown," the "Against Androtion," the "Against Timocrates," the "For Leptines," and the "Against Aristocrates;" for there was little difference, except that Aristocrates wrote not a law [*nomos*] but a decree [*psēphisma*]. Nor am I myself ignorant of the encomium, that it is a form of hypothesis. For the forms of hypothesis are three: encomiastic (the very one that Aristotle and his followers used to call epideictic), forensic, deliberative; but since we are often accustomed to assign even the younger pupils to write encomia, for this reason I placed it among my *progymnasmata*, and at the same time I deferred the lesson simpler.

Further, reading out loud, as one of our elders said—I think it was Apollonius of Rhodes—is the "Nurse of Diction." For if we receive very fine imprints on our soul from fine exempla, we shall also imitate them; and who would not receive gladly the recitation, taking readily things that have been laboriously produced by others? Moreover, just as those who desire to paint have no profit from observing the works of Apelles, Protogenes, and Antiphilus unless they themselves attempt to paint, so also for those who intend to be orators neither the words of our elders, nor the multitude of their

is applied against every temple robber and on behalf of every prince" (*peri koinou topou*). Aphthonius' definition is similar to that of Hermogenes. Indeed, this exercise is similar to one used by the early sophists. In the *Brutus* Cicero writes: "Protagoras prepared written discussions of important matters, now called commonplaces [*loci communes*]. Gorgias did the same, composing eulogies and invectives against particular things, because he regarded it as especially the function of the orator to be able to increase merit by praising and to diminish it again by invective. Antiphon of Rhamnus had similar compositions written out" (46–47, as quoted in Kerferd 31). Moreover, the *progymnasmatic topos* is not Aristotle's "topic." Nor is it the "commonplace" of contemporary handbooks on rhetoric; for example, R. A. Lanham defines commonplace as "a general argument, observation, or description a speaker could memorize for use on any number of possible occasions" (110). Lanham's definition seems to be a combination of *thesis*, *gnōmē*, and *ekphrasis*!

thoughts, nor purity of diction, nor composition at harmony with itself, nor urbane recitation, nor absolutely any of the beauty in the art of rhetoric is useful unless each one himself exercise himself in writings each and every day.

But paraphrase is not without use, as has been said or thought by some; for to speak well, they say, prevails once, but twice is not possible. But these people have very much missed the truth. Indeed, since thought is not moved by one matter in one way so as for the image that joins it to move forward in like manner but in more ways (indeed at one time when we are giving opinions, at another when we are asking questions, at another when we are inquiring, at another when we are praying, at another when we are in any other manner bringing out that which was thought), nothing prevents our bringing out in all ways equally well that which was imagined. But proof of this is with both the poets and the historians, and generally all the ancients have manifestly made the best use of paraphrase, not only remodeling their own things but also those of one another. Paraphrasing Homer, when he says,

> For such is the mind of men who dwell on earth
> As the father of men and gods may bring for a day,

> [*Odyssey* 18.136–37]

Archilochus says,

> Glaucus, son of Leptines, such a spirit for mortal
> Men is born as Zeus brings for a day.

And again, Homer has spoken of a city's capture in this manner,

> They kill the men, and fire levels the city,
> But others lead away the children and deep-
> belted women.

> [*Iliad* 9.593–94]

And Demosthenes, thus: "Now when we were on our way to Delphi, it was of necessity to see all these things, houses razed to the ground, walls taken away, a land men in the prime of life, but a few women and little children and pitiable old men." [19.361] And Aeschines, thus: "But look away in your thoughts to their misfortunes and imagine that you see the city being taken, destruction of walls, burning of houses, temples being pillaged, women and children being led into slavery, old men, old women, too late unlearning their freedom."[3.157]

Furthermore, Thucydides says, "The living have jealousy toward the adversary, but that which does not impede is honored with unopposed good will" [2.45]. And Theopompus: "For I know that with ill will many examine the living, but for the dead they relax their jealousy with the length of years." And Demosthenes, thus: "For who of all men does not know that some envy, more or less, subsists for all the living, but not even one of their enemies hates those who are dead?" [18.330]

And, of course, Philistus in his *History of Sicily* transferred from Thucydides' *History* the whole Athenian war. And Demosthenes into his "Against Meidias" transferred the content of Lysias' and Lycurgus' speeches on hubris and that of Isaeus from his speeches against Diocles for hubris. And you might find also in Isocrates' "Panegyricus" the things said in Lysias' "Epitaphius" and "Olympicus."

Furthermore, Demosthenes himself often paraphrases himself, not only transferring things said elsewhere by himself in other speeches, but also he has often manifestly said the same things countless times in one speech, yet he escapes the notice of his hearers because of the variety of his expression. In the "Against Meidia," he says, "For who of us does not know that for wrongdoers not to be punished is the cause of the coming into being of many such things [Meidias hit Demosthenes in the face at the Great Dionysia while Demosthenes was wearing the sacred robe of a *choregus*] and that the only cause of no one's committing violence in the future is for the one whoever is caught to pay a penalty which is suitable?" [21.526] And in his "Against Aristocrates" — but the same thing is also in his "Against Androtion" — "For if anything had ever been done not according to the laws and you had imitated this, you would not justly get off for this reason, but, conversely, much more be convicted and condemned, you would not have written these things, so, if you are punished, another will not write" [23.653; 22.595]. And in the "Philippics" he has kept on mentioning the same subjects up and down; and in the "For Leptines" he has said no few times that the prosperous ought not to be deprived of their gifts. And in the "On the Crown," the statement that it was not just to make an accusation at the completion of those things that had been done, but to cross-examine singly the acts of administration, has been diffused over all the speech; and who does not know his hackneyed statements concerning the release of captives in his speech "Concerning the Dishonest Embassy"?

Furthermore, the idea of elaboration [*to tēs exergasias eidos*] is helpful in many other places, but especially in second speeches, and counterstatement [*antirrhēsis*] is helpful in replies by the defendant.

And we shall arrange the exercises themselves in this way. First, from the *chreia*,[2] for this is brief and easy to remember; then, from the fable and the narration, except for the refutation [*anaskeuē*] and confirmation [*kataskeuē*] of these, for it is reasonable somehow that these be later than the others. Indeed, all are agreed that the speaker's task is to demonstrate the points in dispute and to amplify the points that have been proven. Therefore, by reason of its nature and use the demonstrative argument precedes and the amplificatory follows, for it is necessary first to bring convincing proof that someone is a traitor and then to cause the listeners to be provoked at the great wrong done, his treason. Even as we said that by nature demonstration precedes amplification, surely it does not follow to keep the exercise thus also, but altogether the opposite, for the easiest things precede the more difficult, and it is easier to amplify the visible than to demonstrate the unseen. Wherefore, taking our own ability to try our hand and to refute or to confirm as our starting point, we ourselves shall begin from the *topos*; next, from description; and then, from *prosōpopoeia*; then, we shall practice with encomia; then, with comparisons; for these are things that are granted by common consent and are open to no contradiction. But after these, we shall practice with exercises that are the subject of dispute. And of them there is first the refutation of *chreiai*; then, of Aesopian fables and of historical and mythical narrations; next, that of theses; and then, that of laws.

Furthermore, from the beginning, we shall employ reading out loud, recitation, and

2. Theon says that his first exercise will be the *chreia*, but in the Greek manuscripts the *chreia* follows the fable and the narrative. Apparently someone, probably in the sixth century, edited Theon's *Progymnasmata* in order to make the arrangement of his exercises conform to those of Hermogenes, Aphthonius, and Nicolaus. See Hock and O'Neil, 65–66.

paraphrase; but elaboration and, much more, counterstatement, when we have achieved some skill.

2.

Concerning the training of the young, including also the use of progymnasmata in ancient authors. First of all, it is necessary that the teacher know well and recount examples of each exercise from collections of ancient writings and assign them to his pupils to learn by heart. For example, of *chreia*, what kind is that in the first book of Plato's *Republic*: "Once a man approached Sophocles, the poet. 'Sophocles,' he said, 'how are you in relation to matters of Aphrodite? Are you yet able to be with women?' 'Hush, sir!' said he, 'On the contrary, most gladly have I got free of them, just as a slave who has run away from a raving mad, savage master' " [329C]. And of fable, what kind is the one in Herodotus concerning the flute player; and concerning the horse in Philistus, those in his first and second books, respectively; and in the twentieth book of Theopompus' *Philippica*, the one about war and hubris, which Philip narrates to the plenipotentiaries of the Chalcidians; and the one about the dog and the sheep in the second book of Xenophon's *Memorabilia*.

The finest examples of narration in the fabulous mode would be Plato's in the second book of the *Republic* concerning the ring of Gyges, and in the *Symposium* concerning the origin of Eros, and concerning matters in the House of Hades in the *Phaedo* and in the tenth book of the *Republic*; and in Theopompus, in the eighth book of the *Philippica*, that of Silenus. But of narration in the factual mode, the finest examples would be that concerning Cylon in Herodotus and Thucydides; that concerning Amphilochus, the son of Amphiaraus, in the [second] book of Thucydides; and those concerning Cleobis and Biton from the first book of Herodotus. But Ephorus in his seventh book and Philistus in his first book have also the one concerning the arrival of Daedalus at the court of Cocalus, the king of the Sicanians. And you would find in Demosthenes' "Concerning the Dishonest Embassy" a plain [*ischnon*] and polished [*glaphuron*] narrative concerning the Olympic Festival that was held by Philip after the capture of Olynthus.

And we have also in the ancient writers refutations and confirmations of *chreiai*, *gnōmai*, assertions [*apophaseis*], and such. And, of course, one might fit into this form all those things said by Ephorus in the eleventh book of his *Histories* regarding the assertions concerning the Nile set down by older writers.

Concerning these narratives in the fabulous mode that the Greeks relate: in the second book of Herodotus [we find] how the Egyptians attempted to sacrifice to Zeus their visitor Heracles, but he slaughtered many myriads of them; and in the first book of Ephorus, the one concerning the fifty daughters of Thespius—all being virgins—with whom they say Heracles had sexual intercourse at the same time; and concerning Aristodemus, how he met his end by being struck by lightning.

And it is possible to take some of the factual narrations also from Herodotus, such as matters from the fourth book concerning the whole earth's being separated into three parts: one part named Europe, another Libya, and the third Asia; also from Thucydides, from the first book, matters concerning the slaying of Hipparchus by Harmodius and Aristogeiton and their party.

But we can take even more things from other works of history: from Ephorus, in the first book, matters concerning the division of the Peloponnesus at the time of the return of the Heraclidae; and from Theopompus, from the twenty-fifth book of the *Philippica*, that the Hellenic oath is falsely reported, which the Athenians say the Greeks swore before the battle of Plataea in respect of the foreigners, and the covenant of the Athenians in respect of the king. And yet also all do not at the same time sing the praises of the battle that had taken place at Marathon, and "In how many other respects," he [Theopompus] says, "does the city of the Athenians make false pretensions and mislead the Greeks."

Similarly, it is also possible to discover in the ancient writers the so-called *topos*, just as the Demosthenic statement in the "On the Crown": "For among the Greeks, not some but all, there was found to be so great a crop of traitors, of bribe takers, and of men hostile to the gods," and so forth [18.245]; furthermore, that of Lycurgus against the adulterer in the "Against Lycophron"; and that of Hyperides against the courtesans in the "Against Aristagora." In similar fashion we shall set forth all the rest in the section concerning *topoi*.

Many descriptions have been composed by the writers of old, as, for instance, in Thucydides, the plague in the second book, and in the third, the circumvallation of the Plataeans, and elsewhere, a sea battle and an action of cavalry; and in Plato, in the *Timaeus*, descriptions of Sais; also in Herodotus, in the second book, the seven walls in Ecbatana. But we have also in the ninth book of the *Philippica* of Theopompus, Tempe in Thessaly, which is between two large mountains, Ossa and Olympus, and in the middle there flows through them the Pencius, into which flow together all the rivers in Thessaly. And in Philistus, in the eighth book, are descriptions of the preparation of Dionysius the tyrant against the Carthaginians and of the manufacture of weapons, ships, and engines of war, and in the eleventh book, descriptions of his being carried out for burial and the ornamentation of his funeral pyre.

But what could be a finer example of *prosōpopoeia* than the poetry of Homer, the dialogues of Plato and the other Socratics, and the plays of Menander?

Moreover, from Isocrates we have encomia, and from Plato, Thucydides, Hyperides, and Lysias, funeral orations [*epitaphioi*], and from Theopompus, the encomium of Philip and the encomium of Alexander, also the *Agesilaus* of Xenophon.

There are comparisons in the ancient writers, especially in Demosthenes, in the "For Leptines," when he wishes to choose Conon before Themistocles, and you could find also in Xenophon, in the *Symposium*, Socrates testifying to Callias that love for the soul is far better than love for the body.

For training in theses, it is possible to take examples from both Aristotle and Theophrastus, for ascribed to them are many books of theses. And, actually, some final headings have been composed by the orators; indeed, entire speeches could be considered to be more or less characteristic of a thesis, as both the "Concerning the Wedding Presents," which is ascribed to Lysias, and the "Concerning the Abortion," for in the one it is asked whether the bride ought to have secure possession of the presents given her by the bridegroom, and in the other it is asked whether the embryo is a human being and whether women are free from liability for their abortions. Although they say that Lysias is not the author of these speeches, it is not a thankless task for pupils to read them too for the sake of training. But it is also possible to find in every speech a final heading: for example, in Demosthenes' "Against the Ejectment of Onetor," *If confes-*

sions upon torture are true, and in Aeschines' "Against Timarchus," *If rumors are true*, and so forth.

Moreover, we shall also have in abundance refutation of laws in many places in most of the orators, but most completely in Demosthenes in the "Against Timocrates," the "Against Aristocrates," and the "For Leptines," and confirmations both in others and in Lysias in the "For Diocles," in defense of the law against the orators. For, although the ancients have not made use of all the subjects that have been transmitted by us by reason of their not having composed their speeches for training but for contests, nevertheless they do indicate at least the whole disposition of such speeches.

Furthermore, that the ancients were not neglectful of paraphrase either is clear from that which has been said a littler earlier.

And many subjects have been more elaborated in some than in others. At any rate, the matter of the Cylonian Pollution has been more elaborated by Thucydides than by Herodotus and Euphron; and Demosthenes has surpassed Hyperides in elaborating the political upheaval that had befallen the Athenians, "When in the evening someone came and reported that Elateia had been captured" [18.284]. But, when one is looking out for that which has been better elaborated, it is also possible to compare to each other both histories and whole speeches, comparing, for example, the speeches of Demosthenes to those of Hyperides and Theopompus' *Hellenic Histories* to those of Xenophon.

And it is possible to discover counterstatement certainly in the speeches in which the one accuses and the other makes a defense in reply to those accusations; for example, in the "Against Ctesiphon" of Aeschines, and in Demosthenes' "On the Crown," and, further, in the "Concerning the Dishonest Embassy" of both. And you would find it also in histories: in Thucydides, in the first book, in the defense of the Corinthians against the Corcyrians, and in the third book, those of Diodotus and Cleon. And in Plato it is possible to see both elaboration and counterstatement. For example, in the *Phaedrus*, after having spoken on the same question as Lysias, he [Socrates] replies in turn to both his and Lysias' speeches; and in the *Republic*, having joined with Thrasymachus in speaking to the starting points concerning justice made by Glaucon and Adeimantus and company, immediately after this he [Socrates] replies to the whole assertion.

Now I have set these things forth, not supposing that all are useful to all beginners, but in order that we may know that training in exercises is altogether a necessity not only for those who are likely to speak in public but also if someone wishes to pursue the craft [*dunamis*] of poets or writers of history or any other discourse. For these things are, as it were, the foundations of every "idea" of discourse, and however one brings them before the soul of the young, it is necessary that things thereafter turn out in the same way. Therefore, in addition to what has been said, it is necessary that the teacher himself produce for himself in a very fine manner some refutations and confirmations and assign them to his pupils to recite, in order that they, when impressed, may be able to imitate after the manner of their training. And when also they themselves become able to write, one must dictate to them the arrangement of the headings and of the proofs [*epicheirēmata*], and one must point out also the occasion for digression and for amplification and all the rest, and one must make clear also the character [*ēthos*] of the problem.

But one must show concern also for the composition of sentences by teaching all the means of avoiding bad composition, especially the style [*lexis*] that possesses meter and rhythm, as the majority of the compositions of the orator Hegesias and the so-called Asian orators;[3] and some of those of Epicurus, such as also he writes perhaps to Idomeneus: "ō panta tama kinēmata terpna nomisas ek neou"; and of those published as his (but we do not as yet now find them among his works): "lege dē moi Poluain, estin ha prin men megalē chara genētai."[4] Now such things are both completely blameable and have the badness of their composition in full view, but it is worthy of excuse whenever someone falls into those meters that indeed have a resemblance to prose, such as is the iambic, on which account also all the prose writers unwittingly fall into this class. Ephorus, at any rate, in his "Concerning Diction," in the course of his discussion forbidding the use of rhythmical speech, has immediately at the beginning spoken a verse, saying: "palin de peri tēs enrhuthmou diexeimi."[5]

It is no less necessary to aim at dignity [*euprepeia*] also, so as not openly to lay bare shameful things but to gloss them over, as Aeschines, when attacking Demosthenes for an unmentionable vice, says that he does not cleanse his body nor even the place from which he sends forth his voice.

But, in addition to these things, the style [*hermēneia*] must be both clear [*saphēs*] and distinct [*enargēs*]; for it is necessary not only to recite but also to introduce the word [*logos*] to the thought [*dianoia*] of the audience, so as for Homer's statement to come into being: "Easily I shall speak a word and put it in mind" [*Odyssey* 2.146].

Furthermore, correction is not taking away from the beginning all mistakes, but a few, very much in plain view, in order that the pupil may not be reduced to despondency and become disheartened for exercises thereafter, and at the same time, let the one who corrects indicate why the mistake has occurred and how it is possible to make it better. But it is far more helpful to assign the young to write on some of those problems that have already been elaborated by the ancients, for example, *topos* or narration or description or encomium or thesis or some other of such things, and after this to make them read the works of those men in order that, if they should have written in like manner, they may be persuaded, but if not, at least they should have the ancients themselves as correctors.

Moreover, since we do not all have natural ability for all things (and some are wanting in emotions [*pathē*], but concerning characteristics [*ēthē*] are more successful, others contrariwise, others deficient in both, but produce arguments [*enthumēmata*] better), one must attempt to increase the natural advantages and to fill up the deficiencies with amplifications, in order that we may be able to speak well not only in respect of the great

---

3. Noted for his bad taste, Hegesias of Magnesia (early third century B.C.) was the founder of "Asianism," the florid style of rhetoric.

4. Apparently Theon considers the rhythm of Epicurus' prose a lyrical one. The line "ō panta tama kinēmata terpna nomisas ek neou" breaks down into these feet: spondee, tribrach, ionic a maiore, trochee, anapest, cretic. The line "lege dē moi Poluain, estin ha prin men megalē chara genētai" breaks down into these feet: ionic a minore, anapest, dactyl, trochee, anapest, iambus, bacchius. (In the second quotation, Spengel's text has been corrected by the translator to conform to Usener's in the Teubner edition of Epicurus. Theon is the only source for these fragments of Epicurus.)

5. It is possible to analyze this line as an irrational iambic trimeter. Theon is the only source for this fragment of Ephorus. For a good brief discussion of ancient prose rhythm, see the *Oxford Classical Dictionary*, 2d ed., s.v. "prose rhythm."

problems, as Aeschines, and the small ones, as Lysias, but also that we may have preparation for both, as Demosthenes.

And, finally, one must attempt also to learn thoroughly the appropriate delivery [*hupokrisis*] for each kind [*idea*] of discourse.

Nicolaus

Nicolaus, a sophist who taught rhetoric in Constantinople in the fifth century A.D., probably drew on Theon (see previous selection) when he wrote his own *Progymnasmata*, the latest of these treatises. All of Nicolaus' works were lost in antiquity and today only his *Progymnasmata* is known. This lay hidden in anonymous scholia to Aphthonius and in a manuscript in the British Museum until the nineteenth century when it was recovered by the scholars E. Finckh and H. Graeven. Only the *Progymnasmata* of Nicolaus and Theon have prefaces extant. We present Nicolaus' preface here for the first time in English.

Nicolaus' preface is brief and entirely theoretical, consisting of successive definitions and divisions borrowed from previous authorities. His purpose here is to state how the individual exercises relate to the various parts of rhetoric, and as such, the preface is an important statement of pedagogic theory. In fact, Nicolaus' preface beautifully encapsulates the main points of classical rhetoric.

Progymnasmata

Preface

A *progymnasma* is in general a practice of moderate matters toward a strengthening of greater ones, and a rhetorical *progymnasma* is an introductory study through composi- tions of the parts and types of rhetoric, a useful preliminary training. The determining factor lies in the idea "a useful preliminary training in the parts and types of rhetoric," since by means of the *progymnasmata* we practice with each of the parts or types singly, not with all parts or types of rhetoric at once. For since the highest types of rhetoric are three—I am speaking of forensic, deliberative, and panegyric—it is necessary to know that neither to all these types nor to them as wholes does each of the *progymnasmata* furnish its proper use, but to some of all and to parts of them as wholes. For some *progymnasmata* produce things useful to forensic, such as refutation, confirmation, the *koinos topos*, and so forth; others to deliberative, just as the fable and the *gnōmē*; and others to panegyric, as the encomium and the invective. But not to them as wholes, for otherwise it would suffice for those who learn these things, I mean the *progymnasmata*, to be set free from rhetorical matters and from industry concerning the divisions of each type. Not to them as wholes therefore, just as we said, are the *progymnasmata* useful, but to parts of them as wholes. And the types of rhetoric are three, since indeed also the hearers, who characterize the affected persons, have come together either to make a judgment or to deliberate or to celebrate. Everything in accusation and defense is a distinguishing feature [*idion*] of the forensic type, and the purpose [*telos*] is the just thing; of the deliberative type the distinguishing feature is exhortation and dissuasion, and the purpose is the expedient; of the panegyric type the distinguishing feature is the encomiastic and the censorious, and the purpose is the beautiful. But so much for this.

And again, there being five parts of the political speech, namely *proemia*, narrations, antitheses, rebuttals, epilogues, to these also do the *progymnasmata* supply their own service. For some teach the use of the *proemia*; others teach the use of the narrations; others teach the use of the contests in the antitheses and rebuttals; and there are some also for the epilogues. We shall speak about these later, dealing with them severally, for the present speaking only so far by way of preface what will be of use also generally: that a *proemium* is a discourse preparing and favorably disposing the listener toward the subject matter of the speech, and its task [*ergon*] and purpose (for some thought [them] the same thing) are to produce attention, docility, and good will; and a narration is an exposition of matters in the hypothesis favorably inclined toward the speaker, or an exposition of a matter having happened or as having happened, and its task and purpose are to make for the hearer a transmission and explanation of the matter; and an antithesis is the objection issuing from the opponent, dissolving the means of persuasion in us and transferring the hearer into a more reasonable act of thinking; and a rebuttal is that which removes the harm resulting from the objection and draws the hearer back into the original means of persuasion and persuades him to go into an approval of the question that is being put forth. Further, an epilogue is a discourse that leads itself back upon demonstrations that have been said beforehand, encompassing a collecting of matters,

A translation from the Greek by Patricia P. Matsen, 1987.

characters, and emotions, and its task consists also of this, says Plato, "at last to remind the listeners of the things that have been said" [*Phaedrus* 267D]. But this [is enough] concerning the definition in question.

Furthermore, we may as well also present the definition of the art of rhetoric itself. Rhetoric is accordingly, as Diodorus says, "a power [*dunamis*]of invention and expression with order of the possible means of persuasion in every discourse."[1] A power, moreover, is a matter in a central position, which it is possible to use both well and badly, such as wealth, strength, a knife, for someone might use these things both well and for the contrary. And accordingly he called the art of rhetoric "power" for this reason, since indeed one might use it both for things not beautiful and not such, and [a power] of "invention and expression," since this is the task of the speaker: to invent the things that are necessary in every proposed problem, and to handle them well, and to express them in the best way; but the purpose is not by any means to persuade—for this is also the opinion of the Stagirite[2]—but to speak persuasively, omitting none of the things that are possible to have been said. Thus also Socrates in the *Gorgias* calls [rhetoric] "persuasion's demiurge" [453A]. Moreover, rhetoric is named either from speaking flowingly [*rhudēn*] or from advocating the law, for the Dorians call the law *rhētra*. So much, however, concerning rhetoric for the present.

1. Diodorus is unknown.
2. Aristotle.

Aphthonius

Aphthonius of Antioch (A.D. ca. 350–400) was a student of Libanius, the influential orator and sophist of the fourth century A.D. We present here his entire *Progymnasmata*.[1] It is historically the most important of these handbooks.[2] It is also the most valuable to us because it is the only one to provide complete examples of the exercises themselves.

There are fourteen exercises: fable, narrative, chreia, gnōmē, refutation, confirmation, koinos topos, encomium, invective, comparison, ēthopoeia, ekphrasis, thesis, introduction of a law. Thus Aphthonius' handbook is similar to that attributed to Hermogenes, except there is no exercise for invective and there are no model exercises in the Hermogenic treatise. On the other hand, these works differ from that of Theon; for in Theon's treatise, *gnōmē* is regarded as a variant of *chreia*, refutation and confirmation are not separate exercises but are methods employed in other exercises, and *ēthopoeia* is called *prosōpopoeia*.

In Aphthonius' *Progymnasmata*, each exercise has the same general format. First, Aphthonius gives a definition (*horos*) of the exercise; next, he subdivides the exercise into its subordinate forms (*diaeresis*); then, he gives a complete example of the exercise, that is to say, a model fable, narrative, and so on. In his introductory remarks, Aphthonius sometimes talks about etymology and characters of style. He does not try, however, to relate an exercise to a particular part of the oration or to any general theory of rhetoric as a whole as do later rhetoricians. Thus, this is a very simple handbook that would appeal to young students.

---

1. Ray Nadeau's translation was, as he termed it, "the first English version of the Greek text upon which the many Latin editions and, ultimately and indirectly, Rainolde's adaptation were founded" (264). The translation which we present here is a revision of the Nadeau translation. Only a few minor changes have been made in Nadeau's translation of Aphthonius' model exercises. On the other hand, each of Aphthonius' introductory sections on the definition and division of a particular exercise has been newly translated.

2. "The simplicity of the discussion, the clarity of the divisions, and the inclusion of examples, as is expressly noted in later prolegomena to the treatise, won for Aphthonius the authoritative place he had in Byzantine times. An extensive body of commentary . . . was built up over the next millenium, and the treatise was translated into Latin by Rudolph Agricola in the late Fifteenth century, making it available for wide use in the schools of Western Europe" (Kennedy, *Greek Rhetoric*, 60). See also Clark.

Progymnasmata

1. Definition of Fable [*muthos*]

The fable came from poets, but it has become common as a means of advice also by public speakers. But fable is a false statement giving the semblance of truth. And, changing its names, it is called after its creators, Sybaritic, Cilician, and Cyprian,[1] but the name Aesopian generally prevails because Aesop composed fables best of all.

The divisions of fable are rational, ethical, and mixed: rational is that in which a human being is imagined doing something; ethical is that which represents faithfully the character of animals; but mixed is from both, irrational and rational.

If you place in front the moral for the sake of which the fable has been assigned, you will call it a *promuthion*, but an *epimuthion* if you add it last.

A Fable: That of the Ants and Tree Crickets Urging on Youths to Work

It was the middle of the summer and the tree crickets were chirping away in tuneful song, but it was the lot of the ants to work and gather in the harvest so that they might thence be able to supply themselves during the winter. When winter came, the ants subsisted on these stores; their lot was one of enjoyment brought to fulfillment, but joy ended in want for the tree crickets.

So it is that youthful folly that has not been prone to work fares ill in its old age.

2. Definition of Narrative [*diēgēma*]

Narrative is the exposition of an action that has happened or as though it had happened. But it differs from narration [*diēgēsis*] as does a poem [*poiēma*] from an entire poetical work [*poiēsis*], for the entire *Iliad* is a poetical work, but "The Making of the Arms of Achilles" is a poem.

The divisions of narrative are: dramatic, or fictitious; historical, based on ancient report; and political, which orators use in their contests.

Narrative has six constant attributes: the person who acted, the action done, at what time, in what place, in what manner, for what cause.

The virtues of narrative are four: clarity [*saphēneia*], brevity [*suntomia*], persuasiveness [*pithanotēs*], and purity of language [*hellēnismos*].

A Narrative: That Concerning a Rose

Let anyone marveling at the beauty of the rose consider the misfortune of Aphrodite. For the goddess was in love with Adonis but Ares, in turn, was in love with her; in other words, the goddess had the same regard for Adonis that Ares had for Aphrodite. God loved goddess and goddess was pursuing mortal; the longing was the same, even though

Reprinted by permission of the publishers and the original translator from "The *Progymnasmata* of Aphthonius," trans. Ray Nadeau, *Speech Monographs* 19 (Nov. 1952): 264–85, rev. Patricia P. Matsen, 1987.

1. Foreign sources for fables are occasionally mentioned by Greek writers; for example, Aristophanes mentions Sybaris (*Wasps* 1259), but no examples of these kinds of fables are extant.

the species was different. The jealous Ares, however, wanted to do away with Adonis in the belief that the death of Adonis would bring about a release of his love. Consequently, Ares attacked his rival but the goddess, learning of his action, was hurrying to the rescue. As she stumbled into the rosebush because of her haste, she fell among the thorns and the flat of her foot was pierced. Flowing from the wound, the blood changed the color of the rose to its familiar appearance and the rose, though white in its origin, came to be as it now appears.

3. Definition of Chreia

Chreia is a brief reminiscence referring to some person in a well-aimed manner, and being useful [*chreiōdēs*], it is called *chreia*.

The divisions of *chreia* are verbal, active, and mixed. Verbal is that which makes the utility clear by means of reporting a saying; for example, Plato said that the twigs of virtue are produced by sweat and toil. Active is that which points out an action; for example, Pythagoras, when asked how long might the life of human beings be, made a brief appearance and then disappeared, thus making his appearance a measure of life. And mixed is that from both, a saying and an action; for example, Diogenes, when he had seen a lad misbehaving, struck the slave attendant and said, "Why, indeed, do you teach such things?"

Now this is the division of the *chreia*, and you should work it out by means of the following headings: encomiastic, paraphrastic, statement of the cause, from the contrary, by comparison, by example, with testimony of ancients, with a brief epilogue.

A Verbal Chreia:
Isocrates Said That the Root of Education Is Bitter, but Sweet Are Its Fruits

Encomiastic. It is fitting that Isocrates should be admired for his art, which gained for him an illustrious reputation. Just what it was, he demonstrated by practice and he made the art famous; he was not made famous by it. It would take too long a time to go into all the ways in which he benefited humanity, whether he was phrasing laws for rulers on the one hand or advising individuals on the other, but we may examine his wise remark on education.

Paraphrastic. The lover of learning, he says, is beset with difficulties at the beginning, but these eventually end as advantages. That is what he so wisely said, and we shall wonder at it as follows.

Statement of the cause. The lovers of learning search out the leaders in education, to approach whom is fearful and to desert whom is folly. Fear waits upon the boys, both in the present and in the future. After the teachers come the slave attendants, fearful to look at and dreadful when angered. Further, the fear is as swift as the misdeed and, after fear, comes the punishment. Indeed, they punish the faults of the boys, but they consider the good qualities only fit and proper. The fathers are even more harsh than the slave attendants in choosing the streets, enjoining the boys to go straight along them and being suspicious of the marketplace. If there has been need of punishment, however, they do not understand the true nature of it, but the youth approaching manhood is invested with good character through these trials.

From the contrary. If anyone, on the other hand, should flee from the teachers out of fear of these things, or if he should run away from his parents, or if he should turn away from the slave attendants, he has completely deprived himself of their teaching and he has lost an education along with the fear. All these considerations influenced the saying of Isocrates that the root of learning is bitter.

Comparison. For just as those who work the earth throw the seeds down on the earth with toil, but with a greater pleasure they gather together the produce, in the same manner those seeking after an education with toil have received the subsequent renown.

Example. Let me call to mind the life of Demosthenes; in one respect, it was more beset with hardships than that of any other rhetor, but from another point of view, his life came to be more glorious than any other. For he was so preeminent in his zeal that the adornment was often taken from his head,[2] since the best adornment stems from virtue. Moreover, he devoted to his labors those energies that others squander on pleasures.

Testimony of ancients. Consequently, there is reason to marvel at Hesiod's saying that the road to virtue is hard, but easy it is to traverse the heights, thus contriving the same thought as Isocrates. For that which Hesiod terms a road, Isocrates calls a root; in different terms, both are conveying the same idea.

Epilogue. In regard to these things, there is reason for those looking back on Isocrates to marvel at him for having expressed himself so beautifully on the subject of education.

4. Definition of Gnōmē

Gnōmē is a statement in summary form with declarations, urging on to something, or averting it.
The divisions of *gnōmē* are protreptic, *apotreptic*, declarative, simple, compound, persuasive, true, hyperbolic.

Protreptic: "One should treat a guest kindly when he is present, but one should let him be on his way whenever he wishes." [*Odyssey* 15.74]
Apotreptic: "It is not meet for a man who is counseling to sleep all the night long." [*Iliad* 2.24]
Declarative: "There is obviously need of money and, without it, none of the things lacking can be brought into being." [author unknown]
Simple: "The one best omen is to fight for the fatherland." [*Iliad* 12.243]
Compound: "It is not a good thing to have many kings: let there be only one." [*Iliad* 2.204]
Persuasive: "Each man is of such a character as that of those in whose company he takes pleasure." [Euripides fragment]
True: "It is not possible to find in anyone a life free of pain." [Euripides fragment]
Hyperbolic: "The earth nourishes nothing weaker than man." [*Odyssey* 18.130]

Now this is the division of the *gnōmē*, and you should work it out by means of the

2. Perhaps Aphthonius means that the admirers of Demosthenes used to pull out locks of his hair for keepsakes.

headings for the *chreia*: encomiastic, paraphrastic, statement of the cause, from the contrary, by comparison, by example, with testimony of ancients, with a brief epilogue. But the *chreia* differs from the *gnōmē* in that the *chreia* is sometimes also active, but the *gnōmē* is always verbal, and in that the *chreia* must be attributed to a person, but the *gnōmē* goes out impersonally.

A Protreptic Gnōmē: "To Flee Poverty, O Cyrnus,
One Must Fall Down from Rocky Heights into the Depths of the Sea"

Encomiastic. In fashioning advice in preference to fables, Theognis did not permit poetic composition to be disparaged. For, seeing that the poets considered fable telling important, he, while leaving fables alone, brought together in his verse instructions on how one ought to live, thus both maintaining the loveliness of verse and, in addition, bringing in the advantage of his instruction. And one might praise Theognis for many things, but especially for those wise statements that he made concerning poverty. And what does he say?

Paraphrastic. Let the one who lives with poverty be content to fall down, as it is better to depart from life before acquiring the sun as a witness to his disgrace. And these are the wise statements that he made but how beautifully is easy to see.

Statement of the cause. Indeed, the one who lives with poverty, at the beginning when he is among boys, does not practice virtue, and when he appears before men, he will do every most troublesome thing, for when he serves as an ambassador, he will forsake his fatherland for money, and when he speaks in the assembly, he will address money, and when assigned to sit as a juror, he will take bribes for his votes.

From the contrary. Not such, however, are those who are free of poverty, for while they are boys, they practice the finest things, and when they appear before men, they do all things openly, supplying, on the one hand, a chorus for the festivals, and on the other, Comparison

And just as those who are held down by a terrible bond have their bond as a hindrance against action, in the same manner also have those who live with poverty received their lack of means as an impediment to free speech.

Examples. Consider the fact that Irus, the same who was an Ithacan, did not share the same security as the other citizens, but he so much identified himself with want that the name of poverty was changed. For having been originally given the name of Arnaeus, he came to be called Irus, a new name derived from his acting as a servant. But why is there need to speak of Irus? Indeed, when Odysseus, the leader of the Ithacans, pretended poverty upon returning to his native land, he shared the vicissitudes of poverty in being thrust from his own home and being subjected to abuse from the maidservants. Such is poverty, and so far as consists with opinion, it is hard to bear.

Testimony of ancients. Wherefore, indeed, I must admire Euripides for saying that it is an evil to be in want and that it is impossible for poverty to give rise to nobility of soul.

Epilogue. And so, how is it possible to give Theognis the admiration that is his due for saying such wise things concerning poverty?

5. Definition of Refutation [*anaskeuē*]

Refutation is an overthrowing of any matter at hand. But one must demolish neither those things clearly manifest nor those utterly impossible, but those that hold an intermediate position.

It is necessary for those engaged in refutation to state first the false assertion of the opposition; next, to add the exposition of the matter; and, then, to use these headings: first, unclear and improbable; after this, impossible, illogical, and unsuitable; and, finally, to add inexpedient.

Moreover, this preliminary exercise encompasses within itself all the power of the art.

A Refutation: That Matters Concerning Daphne Are Improbable

From the false assertion of the opposition. To inveigh against the poets is indeed absurd, for they rise up personally to contradict themselves by making such fabrications in former times in regard to the gods. Now, how is it not unreasonable that these individuals, on the one hand, have shown no regard at all for the gods, but that we, on the other, have respect for the poets? Indeed, I have long grieved at all the gods being trampled in the mire, especially Apollo, whom they made the leader of their very own art, for the following are the mythic tales that they invented about Apollo's Daphne.

Exposition. Daphne, they say, came forth from earth and Ladon, and excelling all in beauty, she won the Pythian as her lover. Moreover, being in love, he pursued; yet, pursuing, he could not catch her, but the earth, welcoming a daughter, put forth a blossom having the same name as the maiden. Thereupon, he crowned himself with her in her changed form, and the plant becomes a crown offered at the Pythian tripod because of his love for the mortal maiden, and the flower becomes a token of his art. Such were the things that they fabricated; it remains to make a test of these as follows.

From the unclear. Daphne came forth from Ladon and earth with what proof of her birth? For, whereas she was human, did they possess another nature beside this one? Further, how did Ladon have intercourse with the earth? By flooding it with his waters? Each and every one of the rivers, then, are to be called husbands of earth, for all overflow it. Moreover, if a human being has been born of a river, it follows that it is possible for a river to be born of man, for descendants give evidence of their begetters. Indeed, what name do they give to a marriage of river and earth? A hymeneal is for conscious beings, but the earth did not spring forth from conscious beings. Accordingly, one must either classify Daphne among the streams, or one must establish Ladon among men.

From the impossible. But let it be so; let it be conceded to the poets that Daphne was born of earth and Ladon. Once born, by whom was the child brought up? Even if you concede her birth, her childhood turns out to be impossible. For where did the child have a place to dwell? With the parent, I suppose? And what human being endures living in a river? The father would forget that he was drowning the child in the flowing currents rather than rearing her in the waters. Or, you say, the child spent her time under the earth beside her mother? Then, she passed unnoticed, and in this way, she had no one to observe her. But love would not come into being for one whose beauty was concealed.

From the unsuitable. And, if you wish, let us also concede the above to the poets. How was a god in the throes of love, and how through desire did he falsify his nature? Love is the most vexatious thing in the world, and to attribute the worst evils to the gods is blasphemy, for if the gods do indeed suffer all diseases, in what respect are they still superior to human beings? If they undergo the very worst thing, love, in what respect do they differ from most men, when they too are suffering the most grievous burden? But their nature neither knows the emotion, nor does the Pythian seem to have been a suitor.

From the illogical. Furthermore, how did the Pythian in his pursuit of the maiden come off second best to a mortal? Men are superior to women—and do women get a greater share, then, of the gods? How is it that that which is inferior to mortal men still overcame gods? Further, how did the mother react when her daughter was reluctant? Did she reckon marriage among things of no value? How, then, did she herself become a mother? Or, among good things? Why, then, did she deprive the child of its privileges? Therefore, either she did not become a mother, or having become one, she is to be considered an unworthy one.

From the inexpedient. Further, why did the earth act contrary to her familiar deeds? She distressed the Pythian by rescuing her daughter—and was she trying to win him over again by returning her? There was no need to please, if she wished to vex. Moreover, why was the god crowned with laurel at the tripods? The flower became a symbol of pleasure, but the prophetic power is offered as a sign of virtue. How, therefore, did the Pythian reconcile things that were not disposed by nature to be brought together? How was the cause on a mortal plane but the effect on an immortal one?

Let there be an end to this consideration of the poets, lest I seem to be crying out against them.

6. Definition of Confirmation [*kataskeuē*]

Confirmation is showing proof for any matter at hand. But one must confirm neither those things clearly manifest nor those utterly impossible, but those that hold an intermediate position. And it is necessary for those engaged in confirmation to treat it in a manner that is exactly the opposite of refutation. First, one must speak of the good reputation of the proponent; then, in turn, to make the exposition and to make use of the opposite headings: the clear instead of the unclear, the probable for the improbable, the possible in place of the impossible, the logical instead of the illogical, the suitable for the unsuitable, and the expedient in place of the inexpedient.

This exercise encompasses all the power of the art.

A Confirmation: That Matters concerning Daphne Are Probable

From the good reputation of the proponents. He who speaks against the poets seems to me to be speaking against the Muses themselves, for if the poets pass on those things that they relate with the approval of the Muses, how would not he who was seeking to condemn these saying of the poets be contradicting the Muses themselves? As for me, I respect the judgment of the poets above all, especially that of the man who stated truly that Daphne was the beloved of the Pythian. Take, for example, the statement that some refuse to believe: "Daphne," he says, "came forth from earth and Ladon."

Exposition from the clear. Why, in heaven's name, is this unbelievable? Do not all things have earth and water as a source? Does not the seed of life come before the elements? Further, if everything that is born comes from earth and water, Daphne affirms the common stock of all things in her having come forth from earth and Ladon. But though sprung from the common source of all, she excelled the others in beauty — and very reasonably so. For that which is yielded first from the earth comes forth together with the beauty of its origin. For there are many bodily generations in which beauty is observed, but the first to appear is the most highly developed of all. Reasonably then, as the first one born of earth, Daphne excelled the others in beauty.

From the probable. Since Daphne excelled in beauty, the Pythian fell in love with the maiden — and very reasonably. For if anything beautiful lives on earth, it all came forth from gods. Furthermore, if beauty is an exceptionally fortunate attribute of the good things on earth, beauty could have a god as an admirer in the eyes of those to whom beauty is a gift of the gods. For all the gods are fond of those things that they present as gifts.

From the possible. And the god in love undertook to correct his condition. For the virtues have these characteristics: they have to be won through effort, and apart from tribulations, it is not possible to win a virtue. Wherefore, he labored in love, and though loving, he did not win his objective, for it is impossible to attain the end of a virtue. Consequently, they are not detracting from the nature of the gods when they say the Pythian was in love, but they are declaring that the nature of the virtue is responsible; that is, the object of pursuit leaves its mark on the pursuer.

From the logical. And the mother took unto herself the fleeing maid. For all mortal things have been of such a nature; they hasten on to that from which they sprang. On this account, Daphne returns to the earth from which she came forth.

From the suitable. And having received the maid, the earth yielded up a plant. For both activities belong to earth, since men are constantly falling to her and trees are being brought forth from her.

From the expedient. And the plant, having made its appearance, became instrumental in honor to Apollo. For the gods do not leave plants outside of their concern, but they crown themselves with growing things. For the first fruits of earth are dedicated to gods and become a symbol of prophetic power. This, too, I believe is fitting. For they call the maiden Sophrona, and oracular powers proceed from moderation. By those in whose eyes the maid knew no pleasure, she is dedicated to virtues. For it could not be possible for one who was morbidly affected to foretell the future.

For these reasons I admire the poets, and because of this, I esteem measure. [In Greek the word *metron* (measure) means both poetic meter and moderation.]

7. Definition of Koinos Topos

Koinos topos is a composition amplifactory of inherent evils. It is so called because it is applied in common to all those who participate in the same matter, for example, argument against a traitor applied in common to all those who shared in the deed.

Because the *koinos topos* does not have a *proemium*, it is like a second speech and an epilogue, but we make up a pattern for *proemia* for the purpose of training the young. After these, you will place headings: first, from the contrary; then, you will make the exposition not as though explaining, for it is understood, but as if spurring on the listener. After this, you will make the comparison, attaching greater blame to the accused through contrast; then, a heading, so-called intention [*gnōmē*], attacking the motive of the doer; then, a digression [*parekbasis*], shrewdly castigating his past life; next, rejection of pity; and lastly, the final headings of the preliminary exercise: legality, justice, expediency, practicability, honor, result.

A *Koinos Topos:* Against a Despot

Proemium A. Inasmuch as laws are established among us and courts of justice are part of our political structure, that man who breaks the laws must pay a penalty to law. For, if it were likely that he would become more moderate by winning acquittal in the present case, perhaps one would have let him off from the trial. But since by escaping now he will be more violent, wherein is it right that leniency in the present should bring about a beginning of despotic rule?

Proemium B. Indeed, all others who have judging allotted to them acquire no harm at all from the acquittal of those brought to trial. But acquittal of a despot will inflict harm upon the judges, for judging is no longer allowed when a despot has gained control.

From the contrary. It seems to me that you will grasp more precisely the meaning of the present case if you examine the judgments of our ancestors, for our forefathers, as if with good intent toward us, planned a state free of domination—and with every good reason. Since at different times different fortunes befall mankind and alter the judgment of men, they balanced the vagaries of fortune against the uniformity of laws and thus devised norms of conduct from which they worked out one standard of judgment for all. So it was that law came into being for the bodies of citizens as the rectifier of evils caused by misfortunes.

Exposition. With no thought for any of these matters, that man has conceived a very evil purpose, that of altering the constitution of the state. This is what he would say to himself: "Why are these things so, O Gods? Though I have been shown to be above the crowd, shall I suffer myself to have equality with the rest in every single case? And am I allowing my fortune to acquire wealth in vain, if I shall be providing the same things for the many? Shall poor men assemble to form judgment on me? And is that which seems best to the many to become a law for me? What escape, then, shall there be from these things? I will seize the citadel and I will put the law aside to perish wretchedly; thus I will be the law to the many, not they to me." These are the ideas that he broached to himself without bringing them to fulfillment, for the good will of the gods intervened. Now may these things for which we still owe thanks to the gods not preserve this man from danger today.

Comparison. A murderer is dreadful but the despot is worse. For the former commits his foul deeds against a single person of no consequence; the latter changes all the fortunes of the state. Accordingly, the crime of a manslayer is less serious than that of a despot by as much as the offense of a moment falls short of the murder of all.

Intention. It is the practice for all other men, even if they commit the most heinous crimes, at least to distinguish the intention from the deed; only the despot does not have the temerity to say that his act was involuntary. For if he were unwilling to undertake the course of tyranny, perhaps one would have excused him on the basis of intention. But since he did so deliberately, how is it just to absolve from responsibility a man who had, prior to the acts, become involved by intention?

Digression. Indeed, all other people who come before us in judgment are on trial only for the present circumstances, and because of their past life, they are often freed. Only the present defendant is judged on both lives. For he did not conduct his past life with moderation and his present is more damaging than the past, so that he has to give satisfaction both for those offenses that he earlier committed and for those that he committed in later times.

Rejection of pity. Who, then, will win his release by appeals for mercy? His children, I suppose? But when they wail, then you may consider the laws to have been established. Surely, it is more just by far to cast a vote for them than for the children of this man. For through the children of this man the despotism would have been confirmed, but through the laws you have yourselves won the right to pass judgment. And so, you are more just in casting your vote in accordance with these laws through which you have been established as judges.

Legality. And if it is lawful to honor those freeing the fatherland, it follows that those reducing it to slavery are to be punished.

Justice. And it is just that a penalty should be fixed among us equal to the harm that this man has done.

Expediency. Further, the despot will pay what is due by falling, for he will be causing the laws to have prevailed.

Practicability. Moreover, it is easy to accomplish punishment of the present offender. For, whereas this man needed armed guards to set up his despotism, we in our turn will not need allies to put an end to the despot. But the vote of judges will suffice to destroy the entire power of despotism.

8. Definition of Encomium

Encomium is a composition expository of inherent excellences. It has been so called from the singing in villages [*en kōmais*] in days of old; furthermore, they used to call alleys *kōmai*. And it differs from a hymn [*humnos*] and a complimentary address [*epainos*] in that the hymn is of gods but the encomium is of mortals, and the complimentary address is produced in a short time but the encomium is brought forth according to rules of art.

The proper subjects of encomia are persons, things, times, places, animals, and also plants; persons like Thucydides or Demosthenes, things like justice or moderation, times like spring or summer, places like harbors or gardens, animals like a horse or an ox, and plants like an olive or a vine. And you may make an encomium in common and individually; in common, as all Athenians, separately, as one Athenian.

Now this is the division of the encomium, and you should work it out by means of the following headings: you will make a *proemium* suitable to the subject at hand; then, you will put the class [*genos*], which you will divide into nation, city, ancestors, and parents; next, upbringing, which you will divide into habits, art, and laws; then, you will compose the greatest heading of the encomia, the deeds, which you will divide into those relating to soul, body, and fortune — soul as courage or wisdom, body as beauty or swiftness or strength, and fortune as power, wealth, and friends — in addition to these, the comparison, attaching greater excellence to that which is being praised through contrast; then, an epilogue more akin to a prayer.

An Encomium of Thucydides

To honor the inventors of useful things for their very fine contributions is just, and just it is that the light coming forth from those men be turned with good reason upon those who displayed it. Accordingly, I shall laud Thucydides by choosing to honor him with the history of the man himself. Moreover, it is a good thing that honor be given to all benefactors, but especially to Thucydides above others, because he invented the finest of all things. For it is neither possible to find anything superior to history in these circumstances, nor is it possible to find one more skillful in history than Thucydides.

Accordingly, Thucydides came from a land that gave him both life and a profession. For he was not born from an indifferent quarter but from whence history came, and by gaining Athens as his mother of life, he had kings for ancestors, and the stronger part of his good fortune proceeded from his earlier ancestry. By gaining both force of ancestry and democratic government, the advantage from one supplied a check upon the other, preventing his being rich unjustly through political equality and concealing public poverty through the affluence of his descent.

Having come upon the scene with such advantages, he was reared under a civil polity and laws that are by nature better than others. Knowing how to live both under arms and under law, he determined to be in one and the same person both a philosopher and a general, neither depriving history of military experience nor placing battles in the class of intellectual virtue. Further, by combining things that were naturally separate, he made a single career in things for which he had no single set of rules.

As he arrived at manhood, he kept seeking an opportunity for the display of those qualities in which he had been well disciplined. And fortune soon produced the war, and he made the actions of all the Greeks his personal concern. He became the custodian of the things that the war brought to pass, for he did not allow time to erase the deeds separately accomplished. Among these, the capture of Plataea is famous, the ravages of Attica were made known, the Athenian circumnavigation of the Peloponnesus was described, and Naupactus was a witness to sea battles. By collecting these things in writing, Thucydides did not allow them to escape notice. Lesbos was won, and the fact is proclaimed to this day; a battle was fought against the Ambraciotes, and time has not obscured the event; the unjust decree of the Lacedaemonians is not unknown. Sphacteria and Pylos, the great achievement of the Athenians, has not escaped unseen. Where the Corcyraeans speak in the assembly at Athens, the Corinthians present answers to them. The Aeginetans go to Lacedaemon with accusations. Archidamus is discreet before the assembly, but Sthenelaides is urging them on to war. And to these examples, add Pericles, holding a Spartan embassy in no esteem and not allowing the Athenians to make trouble when they were suffering. Once and for all, these things are preserved for all time by Thucydides' book.

Does anyone really compare Herodotus with him? But Herodotus narrates for pleasure, whereas this man utters all things for the sake of truth. To the extent that entertainment is less worthy than a regard for the truth, to that degree does Herodotus fall short of the virtues of Thucydides.

There would be many other points to mention about Thucydides, if the great number of his praises did not prevent the enumeration of all of them.

An Encomium of Wisdom

It is a fortunate thing to acquire wisdom, but to praise it according to its worth is impossible; so much of happiness stems from it, that it is established as a common possession of gods.

For one god pursues one bent; another god, another. Hera presides over weddings; Ares, along with Athena, over wars. Hephaestus forges beside a fire, and Poseidon guides the seafarers. One god labors at one thing, another at another, but all have a share in wisdom and Zeus in particular more than all the rest. For he is recognized as wiser than all to the degree that he is more powerful than the gods. And wisdom inspires trust in the sovereignty of Zeus; indeed, the gods acquired it as an innate quality and it proceeded to the earth, where the children of the gods brought it into this life. Therefore, it remains for us to marvel at the poets, also, because they made children of gods out of Palamades, Nestor, and any other man among those of earlier times who is acclaimed in song as being very wise without standing forth among gods by nature. Otherwise, they would have been established as gods themselves, and they would proclaim their share of the virtue by their community of birth. But since they had acquired the virtue of the gods, they were recognized as children of gods, and they appear to be among gods whose possession of wisdom came forth as a token of their origin.

Furthermore, wisdom holds sway over critical times on both sides. For some qualities are popular only in time of peace, while others are admired only in time of war, but wisdom alone understands how to be master of either situation, as if they were one and the same. For she engages in war as though entirely ignorant of peace; conversely, she partakes of peace in such a way as to seem altogether unaware of battles. And over whatever field she presides, it is considered to be within her province alone, for she makes laws in time of peace and makes use of every variety of tranquility, but in wars she points the way to victories. Wisdom, available to effect victory in arms, does not permit another quality to be successful in the assemblies, but she knows how to rule over both alike, those at war and those at peace.

Wisdom alone interprets the will of the gods, for she alone knows the future like a god. She opens up the land to farmers and allots the sea to sailors. Without wisdom it is not possible to reap the fruits of the earth, nor in turn, is it possible to embark upon a ship without someone to pilot it wisely. Thus it is that whatever the sea lavishes and whatever the land produces for mankind, these things have been brought into being as a discovery of wisdom. She did not leave in obscurity the secrets that heaven keeps to itself, for wisdom alone discovered for man the measure of the sun's circuit and the course of each of the stars. Even now, the wise man is not ignorant of the state of the earth and only wisdom discloses how we shall be in our final state. She captured Troy; a clever strategem accomplished that which a very long time was unable to capture. She put an end to the entire power of the Persians by lighting upon a unique plan. The eye of Cyclops was put out, after Odysseus had planned a clever device. In short, if anything is superior, it has resulted from wisdom.

Is there anyone, indeed, who will compare bravery to her? But what power is able to accomplish is the gift of wisdom, and if you take away prudence from bravery, it is left accused of defect.

There would be many other points to mention about wisdom, but it is not practicable to discuss them in detail.

9. Definition of Invective [*psogos*]

Invective is a composition expository of inherent evils. It differs, however, from the *koinos topos* in that the *koinos topos* calls for punishment, whereas the invective has only charges. And it is divided by the very same headings as the encomium; further, the invective has the same number of subjects as the encomium: persons, things, times, places, animals, and also plants. And you may make an invective in common and individually. When you are making your proemium, you will compose the *genos*, which you will divide in the same way as for the encomium, and you will place the upbringing and the deeds and the comparison and the epilogue just as in the encomia.

Invective of Philip

It is not fitting either to abandon virtue without commendation or to pass over baseness without censure, because advantage accrues both when good is praised and evil is criticized. It is indeed fitting that each and every one of those disposed to evil should be criticized, and this is especially true of Philip to the degree by which he surpassed all the wicked.

For he came forth from a people that is the worst of the barbarians, seeking to move from place to place because of cowardice. For the people of Argos first thrust them forth; then, wandering aimlessly, they fled to the country that they now have. They effected this settlement through a double misfortune, in that they gave way before the stronger and cast out the weaker; through cowardice and greed, they could not agree on a settled abode. And being the scion of such a people, he came from a city even more undistinguished, for Macedonians are the worst of the barbarians, and Pella is the meanest city of the land of the Macedonians, one whose men do not fare well even when sold into slavery abroad. Coming from such a land, he had the most uncouth forefathers in the county, for this man's ancestor was another Philip who was not accepted as ruler of the land because of his birth. Then came Amyntas, his father, who needed the help of others for a kingdom; for the Athenians restored him, when he was driven out.

And distinguished by such a background, he lived as a hostage with the Thebans and, though staying in the midst of Greece, he did not change his way of life as a result of the association but added a barbarian incontinence to Greek customs. And although all qualities are different for Greeks and barbarians, this one man was on both sides producing an equal wickedness in unlike peoples.

First, he enslaved his own kin, thus showing his distrust of those from whom he was descended. Then, attacking his neighbors, he destroyed them. He carried off the Paeonians; he attacked the Illyrians; he invaded and seized the land of the Triballi, laying hold of as much of the possessions of the tribes as had the misfortune to be close by. He captured in battle the bodies of the barbarians but not their minds along with their bodies, for those who became slaves because of arms were dreaming of revolt, and they were free in thought who were slaves in fact. And after overwhelming the neighbors of these barbarians, he kept marching in his advance against the Greeks. First, he subdued those cities of the Greeks that were in Thrace, capturing Amphipolis and subjugating Pydna, taking Potidaea along with them, and not considering Pherae as apart from Pagasae, nor Magnesia as apart from Pherae, but all the cities of Thessaly were taken and they bore enslavement as a sign of their common relationship.

But it is also fitting to tell about the death of this man, for as he subjected everything to himself as he advanced and through treachery enslaved those who made treaties with him, the gods, in anger because of the broken treaties, brought about a death appropriate for him. For they did not destroy him in battle, nor did they make heroism a witness to his death, but they put an end to him amid nothing but worldly pleasures, thus making pleasure a shroud worthy of the evil deeds of Philip, so that both in life and in death he might have witnesses to his incontinence.

Indeed, who will compare Echetus[3] to this man? At least Echetus, though cutting off bits of extremities, left the rest of the body; the latter destroyed whole bodies with all their parts. Philip is more terrible than Echetus to the same degree that a destruction of a whole is more painful than the destruction of a part.

Throughout his life, Philip never knew when to stop, but we must stop further discussion about him.

10. Definition of Comparison [*sunkrisis*]

Comparison is a composition made comparative by the process of placing side by side with the subject that which is greater or equal to it. And it is necessary for those making a comparison either to place fine things beside good things or worthless things beside worthless things or small things beside the greater. And in general the comparison is a double encomium or an invective combined with an encomium. Moreover, each element of a comparison has become absolutely forceful [*deinos*] but especially that which places small things beside the greater.

There are as many proper subjects for a comparison as there are for both invective and encomium: persons, things, times, places, animals, and also plants.

But those engaging in comparing must not place a whole beside a whole, for this is flat and not impressive, but a heading beside a heading, for this is indeed impressive. Since dividing is a mode of encomium, not of comparison, there is no comparison in it, because indeed the entire exercise is a comparison.

3. Echetus, a king of unknown habitat, was proverbial for his cruelty; see *Odyssey* 18.83–87 and 21.308.

A Comparison of Achilles and Hector

Seeking to compare virtue with virtue, I am going to measure the son of Peleus by the standard of Hector, for the virtues are to be honored in themselves. Compared, they become even more worthy of imitation.

Accordingly, both were born of not one land, but each alike sprang from one that is famous. One was of Phthia, whence came the name of Greece itself. The other was of Troy, whose builders were the first of the gods. To the degree that having been born in similar lands is not an inferiority in regard to commendation, by that degree Hector is not excelled by Achilles. And being born, the one as well as the other, of a praiseworthy land, both belonged to families of equal stature. For each was descended from Zeus. Achilles was the son of Peleus, Peleus of Aeacus, and Aeacus of Zeus; Hector, likewise, came from Priam and Laomedon, Laomedon from Dardanus, and Dardanus was a son of Zeus. And having been born with Zeus as a progenitor, they had forefathers nearly alike. For the ancestors of Achilles were Aeacus and Peleus, of whom the former freed the Greeks from want and the latter was allotted marriage with a goddess as a prize for his prowess in overcoming the Lapithes. On Hector's side, Dardanus was a forefather who formerly lived with the gods, and his father, Priam, was in command of a city whose walls were built by gods. To the degree that there was similarity in living with the gods and association with superior beings, by that degree is Hector about equal to Achilles.

And descended from such ancestors, both were brought up for courage. The one was reared by Chiron, while Priam was the tutor of the other by contributing lessons in virtue through his natural relationship. Just as an education in virtue is equal in both instances, so to them both does it bring equal fame.

When both arrived at manhood, they gained similar stature out of a single struggle, for in the first place, Hector led the Trojans and he was the protector of Troy as long as he survived. He remained in alliance with gods during that time, and when he fell, he left Troy lying vulnerable. Achilles, on the other hand, was the leader of Greece in arms; by terrifying all, he was prevailing against the Trojans, and he had the help of Athena in the contest, but when he fell, he deprived the Achaeans of gaining the upper hand. Overcome through Athena, the former [Hector] was destroyed; the latter [Achilles] fell, struck down at the hands of Apollo. And both, having sprung from gods, were taken off by gods; whence they drew their beginning, they also derived the end of their lives. To the degree that there was similarity in life and in death, by that degree is Hector on a par with Achilles.

It would be possible to say many other things on the virtue of both, except that both have nearly equal renown for their deeds.

11. Definition of Ethopoeia

Ethopoeia is an imitation of the character [*ēthos*] of a proposed person. And its forms are three: *eidōlopoeia*, *prosōpopoeia*, *ēthopoeia*. Ethopoeia, which has a known person, is invented as to character only, whence ethopoeia takes its name, for example, what words a Heracles might say when an Eurystheus is giving him commands. Here, Heracles is known, but we invent his character when speaking. Eidolopoeia has a known person, but one dead and having ceased from speaking [*eidōlon*], as Eupolis invented in *Demes* and Aristeides in his "On the Four," whence eidolopoeia takes its name. It is *prosōpopoeia* whenever all things are invented, both character and person [*prosōpon*], just as when Menander created Elenchus, for the elenchus is a thing and not a person at all, whence *prosōpopoeia* takes its name, for a person is invented along with his character.

Further, ethopoeia has these divisions: the pathetical, the ethical, and the mixed. The pathetical are those that show emotion in relation to everything, such as what words a Hecuba might speak when Troy is fallen. The ethical are those that introduce character only, such as what words a landsman might say when he has seen the sea for the first time. And the mixed are those that have both together, such as what words an Achilles might speak to a Patroclus who lies dead as he makes his decision to fight, for the decision is his character, and a fallen comrade is his emotion [*pathos*].

Moreover, you will work out your ethopoeia with a style that is clear, concise, fresh, unconstrained, free from every complication and figure, and in place of headings, you will divide it by the three periods of time: present, past, and future.

A Pathetical Ethopoeia: What Words Niobe Might Say While Her Children Lie Dead

Childless now, who seemed blest with many children before, what kind of fortune am I exchanging for others? And the great number has become a want and I have become the mother of not a single child, I who appeared to be the foremost of many in this regard, so that it was better to have lacked the power to give birth than to give birth for tears! Those robbed [of children] are more unfortunate than those not giving birth, for through the rivalry [with Leto] I have come to a grievous loss.

But woe is me! I am bearing a misfortune akin to that of the one breeding me; I descended from Tantalus, who once lived with the gods but he was then banished from the society of gods. And descended from Tantalus, I confirm the relationship by these misfortunes. I was associated with Leto; I fare badly because of her, and I have brought that association to the destruction of children; connection with a goddess brings me to misfortune. Before I entered into the rivalry with Leto, I was a happier mother, but having become well known, I am at a loss for offspring, which I had in abundance before the rivalry. And now weeping for each child falls to my lot and also bewailing the loss of what was a great source of pride.

Whither may I turn? To what things shall I cling? What kind of tomb will be of use to me in the face of the destruction of all the fallen children? The honors have ended in misfortunes. But why do I mourn for these things, since it is allowed to ask heaven that another nature be given in exchange? I have seen an only escape from the misfortunes, namely, to withdraw toward that state that is insensible of anything. But I am more fearful lest, appearing in that form, I should continue weeping.

12. Definition of Ekphrasis

Ekphrasis is a descriptive composition bringing the thing set forth distinctly to view.

One must describe persons, things, times, places, animals, and also plants; persons, just as Homer describes [Eurybates in the *Odyssey*]: "He was round in the shoulders, bronzed, with thick, curling hair"; things, like battles on land and sea, just as the historian describes them; times, like spring and summer, in recounting as many kinds of flowers as come forth from them; places, as the same Thucydides speaks of Chimerium, the port of the Thesprotians, in telling exactly what shape it has. And it is necessary for those who describe persons to go from the first elements to the last, that is to say, from head to foot; in describing things, from those earlier than these and those things now in these and whatever is wont to spring from these things; in describing times and places, from those surrounding and those within them.

The divisions of *ekphrasis* are the simple and the compound. Further, the simple are such as those recounting land or sea battles; the compound are such as those taking up things and times at the same time, just as Thucydides describes the night battle in Sicily. For, in connection with the battle, he traced how it was conducted, and in connection with the night, he traced how it was.

Moreover, it is necessary for those who describe to produce the representation in a relaxed [*aneimenos*] style, but ornamented with a variety of figures, and, in short, to represent faithfully the things being described.

A Description of the Acropolis at Alexandria

The citadels were set up, of course, for the common security of the cities, for they were the highest points of cities. But citadels are not fortified with more structures than cities are fortified with. And a central area of Athens held the citadel of the Athenians, while the hilltop that Alexander caused to be built up in his own city he named for whom it was erected. For he placed it on the highest point of the city, and it is more accurate to call it an acropolis than that on which the Athenians used to take counsel. For it has such [characteristics] as this speech recounts.

Any high point, proceeding to a summit, projects far above the land, and it is called an acropolis for a twofold reason by those for whom it is raised to a high point [*akra*] and for whom it has been arranged over a high point of a city [*polis*]. Approaches to this particular [acropolis] are not alike; here, there is a path, and there, it has become a place of entry, and the approaches quickly change their names, being called according to the character that they have. For here it is possible to approach on foot, and passage exists for both those entering publicly and by carriage. There, when it is impracticable to proceed by carriage, flights of steps have been raised up successively. For a flight of steps tends always toward the larger, as if leading from a lesser one, and it goes even higher, not ending until reaching the hundredth step. For an effect giving the impression of perfect proportion is the goal of numbering. A forecourt, enclosed by latticed gates of moderate height, then receives the staircases. And there also, four very large columns rise up, providing many ways into one entrance area. Then upon these columns rests a certain structure, exposing columns of ordinary height that are not of only one color, but vying with one another [in color], they are added to the structure as ornament. Moreover, the ceiling for this building comes to a circle and around this circle has been affixed the greatest of all written records.

To one entering the acropolis itself, one area is divided into four equal sides; the plan of the arrangement is like that of a hollow rectangle with an open court surrounded by a colonnade in the center. And [other] colonnades succeed this open court; these are distinguished by matched columns, and as for their size, it is that beyond which it is impossible to find a greater one. Each colonnade comes to an end against another transverse colonnade, and a double column is the division in reference to each colonnade, since it marks, on the one hand, the ending of one and, on the other, the beginning anew of another. Within the colonnades, enclosures were built, some having become repositories for the books available to the diligent for study, thus spurring on an entire city to a mastery of learning; others were established long ago to honor the gods. For colonnades, there is a roof adorned with gold, and the capitals of columns are worked in bronze overlaid with gold. Nor is there only one adornment of the open court, for another is different—it has the battles of Perseus. And one of the columns rising above the others in height occupies the center position, thereby attracting attention to the place. Anyone going along does not yet know where he is proceeding, unless he uses the column as a sign of the ways. And being visible all round, it so makes the acropolis on land and on sea. The beginnings of things encircle the top of the pillar; before arriving at the middle of the open court, however, a divided structure has been erected for gates, and these gates were long ago named after the gods. Moreover, two obelisks of stone rise up and also a fountain considered better than that of the Pisistratidae.

And the marvel took form, having an unbelievable number of builders. One individual not being sufficient for the task, so to speak, successive creators of the entire acropolis were seen to the number of twelve.

To one coming down from the acropolis, there is here a level place resembling a footrace course, and that became the name for the place. And there is another place of the same length but not going along on a level course.

Indeed, the beauty [of the acropolis] is beyond the power of words, and if anything has been neglected, it happened as a result of awe. And as for those things that it was not possible to describe, they were omitted.

13. Definition of Thesis

Thesis is a logical examination of any matter under consideration.

The forms of thesis are political and theoretical. The political are those that admit of an action that holds a city together; for example, whether one should marry, whether one should sail, whether one should build fortifications, for when they take place, all these things hold a city together. The theoretical are those that are considered by the mind alone; for example, whether heaven is spherical, whether there are many worlds. Moreover, men do not have access to these things for testing, but they are observed by the mind alone.

A thesis differs from a hypothesis in that the hypothesis has attendant circumstances, but the thesis is without attendant circumstances. Attendant circumstances are person, action, cause, and the rest; for example, the question, *Should one fortify?*, is a thesis, an examination without a person, but the statement, *The Lacedaemonians are planning to fortify Sparta because the Persians are invading*, is a hypothesis, for it has a person *Lacedaemonians considering*, and as action *Sparta being fortified*, and as cause *Persians invading*.

Moreover, for the first time among the preliminary exercises, the thesis admits antithesis and the solution [*lusis*] concerning a question.

Further, the thesis is divided, first, by the so-called approach [*ephodos*], which you will speak instead of *proemia*; next, you will use the final headings: legality, justice, expediency, practicability.

A Thesis: Should One Marry?

Let the one seeking to measure the entire question in a few words hold marriage in high esteem. For it came from heaven or, rather, it filled heaven with the gods and a father was set up for them, whence originates the title of father. And having sired gods, marriage produced the natural powers to preserve them. Then, coming down to earth, it endowed all the other things with reproductive power. And bringing under its control those things that did not know how to be lasting, marriage cleverly devised the maintaining of them through their successors. First of all, it stirs men to bravery; it is through these [brave men], since marriage knows how to produce children and wives over whom war is fought, that marriage adds bravery to its gifts. Further, it provides righteous men along with the brave; it is through these [righteous men], since men who are anxious about the things in which posterity takes pride do those things justly, that marriage produces righteous men at the same time as brave men. Nay more, it makes men wise whom it inspires to provide for the dearest ones. And by way of paradox, marriage knows how to supply self-control, and moderation is mingled with the pursuit of pleasures; it is through these [temperate men], since it adds convention to the pleasures, that marriage supplies the pleasures of moderation in support of the convention; and that which by itself is brought as an accusation against itself is admired [when joined] with marriage. If, therefore, marriage produces gods and, after them, each of their descendants in succession, if it provides brave and just men at the same time, and if it furnishes wise and temperate men, how ought one not to esteem marriage as much as possible?

Antithesis. "Yes," he says, "but marriage is a cause of misfortunes."

Solution. You seem to me to be making a charge against fortune, not against marriage. For fortune, not marriage, produces things that men who fare badly encounter, whereas the things that marriage contributes to humankind are not at all those contributed by a desire of gain from fortune. Therefore, it is better to marvel at marriage for the fine things it encompasses, rather than to criticize it for the evil things fortune brings forth. But if we do, indeed, assign the worst of man's misfortunes to marriage, why should one rather refrain from marriage? There are those difficulties that you ascribe to business; these things would not by any means exert an influence toward an escape from business, would they? And let me examine one by one the activities to [each of] which is attributed what you are perhaps charging. Thunderbolts afflict those farming, and hailstorms harass them. Yet a thunderbolt does not spoil the soil for husbandmen, nor do they flee the soil, but they continue tilling it, even if something coming down from the heavens causes damage. On the other hand, seafarers are unfortunate, and attacking storms buffet their ships. Yet they do not thereafter abandon sailing on account of those things that they have suffered in turn, but they attribute the misfortune to chance and they wait for the passage provided by the sea. Furthermore, struggles and battles destroy the lives of the combatants; still, they do not avoid battles because by fighting they will fall; instead, because those fighting are admired, they have become reconciled to death and they join in concealing the attendant drawback because of the associated benefit. For one should not flee from whatever good things there are because of bad attributes, but because of the good things one should endure the worst.

Surely then, it is unreasonable that on one side farmers, sailors, and as many as are serving in the army besides, should endure the difficulties arrayed against them for the sake of the praises associated with these activities, but that on the other side we should look down upon marriage because it brings with it a degree of vexation.

Antithesis. "Yes," he says, "but it introduced widowhood for wives and orphanhood for children."

Solution. These are the evils of death, and nature is cognizant of the misfortune; you seem to me to be critical of marriage on the ground that it does not make men gods and to censure marriage because it has not included mortal things for gods. Tell me, then, why do you criticize marriage for the things that death brings about? Why do you ascribe to weddings things such as those which nature [alone] understands? Grant that he who was born to die will die. Further, if men die because they have lived life's span and in dying bereave one dwelling in the same house and make an orphan of him, why will you say that marriage has finished off those things brought about by nature alone? I, on the contrary, hold that marriage corrects orphanhood and widowhood. To one a father is dead and thus a child is an orphan; but marriage brings in another father for the orphans, and this misfortune does not stem from marriage but is veiled completely by marriage, and marriage becomes the occasion of the disappearance of orphanhood, not the beginning of it. And so nature brought widowhood with death, but marriage effected a change with wedding songs. For marriage, as though standing guard over her gift, presents to a man in wedlock the one for whom death has accomplished a bereavement. For those things that it introduced from the first, it restores again when taken away; thus, marriage knows how to take away widowhood, not how to inflict it. Nay more, a father is deprived of children through death, but through the marriage he has a share of others. And he becomes a father for the second time who does not assent to being one but once. Why, therefore, do you pervert the fine things of marriage into a fault of marriage? Further, you seem to me not to be seeking to dishonor the wedding song but to be commending it. For by the very things you force us to enumerate as pleasures of the wedding songs, you have become an admirer, not an accuser of marriage, and you force us to be amazed at betrayers of marriage, and you make the accusations against marriage a list of good features.

Antithesis. "Yes," he says, "but marriage is wearisome."

Solution. And what is set up to halt drudgery like marriage? Whatever is some, through wedding songs it is taken away. Further, there is pleasure generally in coming together with a wife in intercourse. How pleasant it is for a man to go with a wife to the marriage bed! With how great pleasure is a child anticipated! And expected, does he appear! And having appeared, will he call a father! He is then started along his training with care and [soon] he is working with a father and addressing the people in the Assembly and taking care of a father; he becomes everything that it is necessary to be.

Epilogue. It is impossible to cover in a speech the favors that marriage knows how to bestow. A mighty thing is marriage, both for producing gods and for granting to mortals for whom it devises a means of continuing life, that they seem to be gods. And it guides those needing strict rules, it urges a consideration of self-control, and it seeks after pleasures, as many as are obviously not worthy of blame. Wherefore, it is established among all that marriage should be reckoned of the greatest worth.

14. Definition: Introduction of a Law [*nomou eisphora*]

Moreover, some have conceded that the introduction of the law is an exercise [*gumnasma*]. Indeed, it is almost a complete hypothesis, yet it does not preserve all the characteristics of the hypothesis; for it brings into it a person, yet not one known to all. Whence it is more than a thesis, but less than a hypothesis. By the means that it generally admits the appearance of a person, it goes beyond the thesis; by the same means by which it does not keep the attendant circumstances clear, it falls short of a hypothesis. Further, an introduction of a law is a double exercise: an advocacy and an opposition of an established law. And a law is "an invention and gift of gods, a resolution of wise men, and a corrective of the errors in regard to both" [Demosthenes?]. Further, this is the division of the introduction of the law. And you will work it out by means of headings by which you also work out the deliberation on matter of fact or action: constitutionality, justice, expediency, practicability. And you will put *proemia*, and you will pace the counterargument after the *proemia*; then, you will use the aforementioned headings, whence also in this respect it [introduction of a law] differs from a thesis.

An Opposition of a Law That Requires That the Adulterer Be Put to Death on the Spot

I shall neither entirely approve of the law, nor shall I criticize the thing decreed in every detail. In the ways in which it operates against the crimes of adulterers, I shall approve of the law as passed; in the same ways, it does not face a vote of judges and, therefore, I censure the system. If one avoids courts of justice because of having decided on the corruption of those judging, he is convicted of having a low attitude toward the judges. But if you consider that the courts are just, and in what way they are just, how is it right to approve of the judges but to remove the law from those judging? Further, of all the other regulations that vie with the established laws, some contradict certain laws in the city-states, some are in agreement with others — only the present law has come forth as contrary to all. You seem to me to examine the law by far more fairly, if you decide it like all the things customarily ruled on by you: the generals, the priesthoods, the laws in general. I am little short of saying that of all things that are done best in battle, each undergoes the scrutiny of judges. And he is a general whom the one giving judgment has approved; he is a priest whom the judge has confirmed; a law is valid that has been closely examined before others; and exploits in battle do not warrant awards unless they have first been certified. Then, how is it not unreasonable that all face the examiners but that only the law under consideration escapes a vote of the judges?

Antithesis A. "Yes," he says, "but great are the wrongs of adulterers."

Rebuttal. But why are not those of murderers greater? Do we hold that the traitors are of less account than others? And are not temple robbers worse than those who betray? But still the man caught in these crimes faces those judging, and neither does a traitor suffer punishment without the judge's casting his vote; neither does it fall to the lot of a murderer to die without the prosecutor's proving the act, nor does it befall those stealing the things of the Higher Powers to suffer until it is within the power of those judging to study these matters. Then, is it not unseemly that the greater crimes face a decision before those judging, and that no one of these seem to exist if a judge has not cast his vote? And that only an adulterer is to suffer without inquiry, being inferior to the others in that he lacks judging more than the others?

Antithesis B. "And what will be the difference in executing an adulterer or in handing him over to the judges, if from both he will sustain the same death?"

Rebuttal. There is as much distinction as exists between a despot and a law, and there is as much difference as there is between popular government and absolute rule. For it is characteristic of a despot to kill whom he wishes; of a law, to execute one justly convicted. And the commons present for approval those things that they are considering in assembly, but an absolute rule uses force and does not consult; the things that commons and laws administer together, absolute rule does entirely without regard for opposition in accordance with ruling alone and a preference for arbitrary decision. How, then, is there no difference in killing the adulterer or in handing him over to those judging? And yet, in addition, the one who kills an adulterer on his own behalf makes himself master of the one who has committed the crime, but the one who turns him over to a judge makes the court of justice master of the culprit. It is better, I presume, that the one judging, rather than the accuser, become the master. And, indeed, the one killing an adulterer on his own behalf is suspected of taking away the good name of another, but the one who has presented an adulterer for judgment has only seemed motivated by just reasons.

Antithesis. "Yes," he says, "but the one falling on the spot suffers a more terrible retribution, for some advantage will accrue in the time until judgment."

Rebuttal. On the other hand, he will indeed have the same punishment if he is brought to trial, for he will endure a more troublesome life along with these things: waiting to suffer is more grievous than to have suffered, and the putting off of retribution seems an addition to a penalty. One expecting to die will die many times, and he will have a suspense worse than the execution, whereas the adulterer falling on the spot is not keenly aware of his falling. The swiftness of the vengeance takes away its sting. A death that occurs before it is expected is unaccompanied by pain, but one that is many times anticipated after it has once fallen due measures the vengeances by the expectations. Consider further by placing arguments side by side. The one killing an adulterer on his own behalf gains not a single witness, but one handing him over to the judges gains many observers of the punishment—and more painful than retribution is a situation surrounded by many observers. And, besides, it will be useful to adulterers to fall secretly, for they will leave the feeling among many that they died because of enmity. But when the incident is scrutinized before the judges, the one dying will suffer an undisputed penalty; thus it is that to attack an adulterer secretly by oneself will be different from handing him over to judges.

The adulterer attains a wicked and complete extreme of premeditated wrongs; it follows that he should first be convicted, then executed, and that he should be judged rather than suffer punishment before judgment, because a publicly executed adulterer will make the parentage of the children better known. For no one will be uncertain to whom the child belongs by birth as a descendant of departed adulterers. The wrong is in the regular order of nature and a regular vote should be undertaken, inasmuch as I fear that, if an adulterer escapes notice as to the circumstances under which he was destroyed, he may leave behind many others of his ilk. For others will strive to emulate one for whose death they do not know the reasons, and the punishment will become, not the end, but the beginning of crime.

5

The Rhetoric of Style

S tyle was necessarily an integral component of classical oratory, because without an arresting style, the speaker would lose the attention of his audience. Since style was so central to rhetoric, it early became included in the five-part canon of invention, arrangement, style, memory, and delivery.

The discovery that vellum or parchment sheets could be folded and bound into books made it infinitely easier to scan a text than it had been when long sheets of rolled papyrus were used. There was consequently more interest in the written applications of rhetoric—a process George A. Kennedy describes as *letteraturizzazione*. The new ease of reading and studying books made it possible to analyze style more closely than before, and new qualities of style were recognized, which soon found their way into rhetorical handbooks.

Another result of increased literacy was a growing awareness that written style might differ from oratorical style. The four ancient authorities excerpted here show some indication of this. Dionysius, for example, says that Antiphon, Aeschylus, and Thucydides used an austere word arrangement with "grand and dignified rhythms" that are "noble, splendid, and free." Dionysius points out that the austere structure is not composed in complete sentences, has little concern for transitions, and sounds "unpolished, grand, plain-spoken, unembellished, with archaism and the patina of age as its beauty" (22).

Dionysius contrasts this style with the smooth arrangement of words characterized by the works of Euripides and Isocrates. Here the clauses are carefully constructed into complete sentences, using smooth and euphonious words. This style, says Dionysius, is like finely woven cloth; it is achieved by "exactly fitting joints which leave the intervals between the words imperceptible" (23).

What Dionysius prefers, however, is a style falling somewhere between these two extremes of rough and smooth. He cites the practitioners of this mixed structure as Homer, Demosthenes, Plato, and Sophocles. (Archaeological evidence indicates that Dionysius' recommendations accurately mirror ancient literary tastes. Of the thousands of manuscripts unearthed at Oxyrhynchus in Egypt covering ten centuries, the two most popular authors were Homer and Demosthenes; Plato and Sophocles were among the top twelve.)

In the conclusion of *On the Arrangement of Words* Dionysius also offers an interesting insight on the writing methods of "the sophists Isocrates and Plato." Isocrates was known to have spent at least ten years polishing one of his discourses, and Plato "never gave up combing and curling his dialogues, refashioning them in all kinds of ways" (25).

Since these writers paid so much attention to style, Dionysius seems to feel a good orator should do no less.

Writing perhaps a hundred years after Dionysius, Demetrius analyzes style and concludes that there are actually four kinds, rather than three. To Demetrius, good style is either plain, elevated, elegant, or forceful. Like Cicero, Demetrius points out the negative aspects of the corresponding faulty styles. For example, plain style should not be dull or arid, and forceful style must not be allowed to become unpleasant or frigid through crudity, fragmentation, or overlong sentences.

Demetrius differs with Dionysius on the question of spontaneity. He warns against excess "attention to niceties of smoothness and harmony" (5.300) because he thinks it detracts from force and vigor. Demetrius also recognizes the need to use veiled language — for instance, when addressing rulers — but feels that even when euphemisms must be employed, the style can still be forceful. He cites several interesting examples of indirect styles: Aristippean maxims, Xenophontic precepts, and Socratic questions.

Both Dionysius and Demetrius gave advice primarily for spoken rhetoric. Their works abound with references to the sound of words, the danger of the speaker running out of breath, the figures orators employ, and so on. Longinus, on the other hand, addresses himself primarily to writers. This is obvious even from the title of his work: *On Great Writing, or On the Sublime*. In it, Longinus immediately confronts the question of whether great writers are born or made. From this, he goes on to identify the "five sources most productive of great writing (8.1–2).

At first, it would seem that we have simply moved from Dionysius' three structures to Demetrius' four styles to Longinus' five sources. But *On the Sublime* does not just classify styles in a new and different way. It is the first extant organized effort to discover what makes writing good and to explain the part played by inspiration or greatness of thought. Because Longinus' attempts were so successful, he is considered one of the innovators of literary criticism.

Like Longinus, Hermogenes examines rhetoric with a view towards what makes it good. He approaches his analyses not with the intention of identifying particular kinds of style but with the more difficult goal of considering "each type in itself, to show, for example, what Solemnity is and how it is produced, or what Asperity is or Simplicity, and likewise in respect to the other types" (215). Both in his goals and his title, *Peri ideōn*, some scholars have perceived echoes of Plato's *ideai* or forms. Whether or not Hermogenes was applying Plato's concept of ideal forms to qualities of style, his treatise marks another theoretical leap in ancient approaches to the subject.

In identifying seven basic excellences of style, Hermogenes greatly increases the number of aspects under discussion. Furthermore, as Kennedy points out, some of Hermogenes' types are subdivided. Thus he ends up explaining twenty different concepts of style.

We chose to present the following four excerpts in the order in which they appear because it seemed most logical to proceed from the few to the many, from the simple to the complex, and from those works based on oratory to those based on written composition.

Dionysius of Halicarnassus

Dionysius (ca. 60–8 B.C.) was born in Halicarnassus in Asia Minor, but he moved to Rome when he was thirty. There he taught rhetoric and wrote a multivolume history called *Roman Antiquities*. The fact that about half of this work is composed of speeches shows that Dionysius was indeed a "rhetorical historian who tried to make his account of history dramatic and effective"[1]; that is, he practiced what he preached.

Dionysius wrote only in Greek, since he wanted to restore the classical standard of rhetoric known as Atticism. To this end, he wrote several essays on literary history and criticism, such as *On the Ancient Orators*. *On the Arrangement of Words* or *De compositione verborum* is both a milestone in literary criticism and a rhetorical handbook that deals with the importance of word order or arrangement. In it, Dionysius gives more practical advice than that offered by Longinus, and more extensive than that offered by Demetrius.

The version we present here is a recent translation (1972) of three excerpts from *On the Arrangement of Words*. Bracketed notes in the text by the translator, D. A. Russell, summarize the passages that have been omitted.

1. Thompson, 304.

On the Arrangement of Words

Introduction: The Value and Difficulty of the Subject

1   'And this, my dear child, is *my* present to you', as Helen says in Homer when she entertains Telemachus. This is your first birthday since you came to man's estate; and to me it is the happiest of days, and one that I delight to honour. It is no 'work of my hands' that I send you, as Helen said when she gave the boy the robe nor is it only 'against the season of marriage' or a gift to give joy to a bride. It is the product and child of my studies and my brain, a possession and a thing of service against all the needs in life that involve speech. If I have any right understanding in the matter, nothing can be more necessary than my present undertaking, both to all students of practical oratory, of whatever age and disposition, and especially to you young beginners, my dear Metilius Rufus, son of my excellent and much respected friend.

The study of any kind of speech involves, one may say, two kinds of exercise, one concerning thought and the other concerning words. The former touches more on that department of rhetoric which deals with content, the latter on that which deals with language. Aspirants to eloquence necessarily pursue these two branches equally, but the knowledge which leads to content and good judgement regarding content is slow of acquisition and difficult for the young; indeed it cannot be expected of the beardless youth, because it belongs rather to the mature understanding, disciplined by later life, nurtured by long research into words and facts and by long experience of misfortune, both one's own and others'. Linguistic taste, on the other hand, blossoms in the young. Every youth's mind is excited by the charms of language and acquires irrational, almost inspirational, impulses in this direction. The first instruction and training needs therefore to be careful and intelligent, if the beginner is to be saved from uttering 'what words soever come to a blundering tongue' and putting phrases together at random, and made both to select a pure and noble vocabulary and to deploy it by an arrangement which combines dignity with charm. It is on this subject, therefore, the first the young student should pursue, that I now 'send you a song for love', a treatise on the arrangement of words. This is a topic which few of the older writers of textbooks on rhetoric or logic thought of discussing, and no one, I am sure, has yet discussed it adequately or worked it out in detail. If I have leisure, I will write you another book on word-selection, so that you may have a complete treatment of the department of rhetoric relating to language. Expect it this time next year, if the gods keep me safe and healthy — if indeed it is my destiny to enjoy these blessings. For the present, pray accept this work, which the promptings of providence put into my head to write.

Here, then, are the headings under which my discussion falls:

What is the nature of arrangement? Wherein lies its power? What are its aims

Dionysius of Halicarnassus, *On the Arrangement of Words* (1–4, 6–13, 20–26, with omissions), trans. D. A. Russell, in *Ancient Literary Criticism*, ed. D. A. Russell and M. Winterbottom, Oxford: Oxford University Press, 1972. Reprinted by permission of Oxford University Press.

and how does it achieve them? What are the characteristics of each variety of it, and which (in my view) is the best?

What is that poetic quality, smooth on the tongue and sweet to the ear, which prose acquires as a result of arrangement? What, too, is the force in a poetical manner that imitates unaffected speech and achieves great success in the imitation?

By what practices can that quality and that force be attained?

These, in broad outline, are the questions I wish to discuss. Now I begin.

Arrangement (*sunthesis*) is, as its name implies, a placing (*thesis*) of the parts of   2
speech — what some call the elements of language — beside one another. The-odectes, Aristotle, and the philosophers of those days took the number of these parts of speech to be three: nouns, verbs, and conjunctions. Their successors, especially the leaders of the Stoic sect, made it up to four, separating 'articles' from 'conjunctions'. Subsequent writers distinguished 'appellatives' from 'substantive nouns' and so made five, while a sixth element was added by the distinction made by some between nouns and pronouns. The number has been multiplied: adverbs are distinguished from verbs, prepositions from articles, participles from appellatives, and so on. It would be a long story.

Now it is the combination and juxtaposition of these primary parts of speech — three or four or however many there are — which produces what are called cola; the connection of these in turn completes the period; and periods make up the entire discourse. The function of arrangement is thus to place words properly in relation to each other, to give cola their appropriate connection, and to articulate the discourse properly in periods. It is the second main subject in order under the general head of language — word-selection comes first and has a natural priority — but the charm, conviction, and force which arrangement imparts are of considerably greater importance. Word-selection is a complex and extensive subject, much discussed by philosophers and orators; arrangement comes second, and has had nothing like so much discussion. Nevertheless, it should not be regarded as paradoxical that it possesses force and power enough to put all the works of the other into the shade. We must remember what happens in other spheres. In arts which require materials of different kinds and make a combined product of them — building, carpentry, embroidery, and the like — the capacities of arrangement come second in order to those of selection, but they have greater importance. It is not absurd that the same should be true of speech; however, there is no harm in offering evidence for this, so as not to appear to take disputable propositions for granted.

Every expression by which a thought is signified is either metrical or unmetri-   3
cal. Either kind, if given beautiful rhythmical form (*harmonia*), is able to beautify either metre or prose. Thrown out ignorantly and randomly, either kind ruins even the value of the thought it expresses.

Many poets, many historians, philosophers and orators, have chosen with care and taste beautiful words appropriate to their needs, but have wasted their efforts by giving them a careless and tasteless rhythmical form. Others, taking vulgar and contemptible words but arranging them with charm and distinction, have invested their writing with great elegance. The relation of arrangement to selection seems in a sense analogous to that of words to thought. Just as there is no profit in a good idea unless one gives it the setting of fine words, so it is no use finding pure and elegant expressions unless one gives them the appropriate setting of rhythmical form.

In order not to give the impression of putting forward statements without demonstration, I will try to show by a practical example why I am convinced that arrangement is a higher and more significant study than selection. I shall offer a preliminary taste both of poetry and of prose. Let us take Homer as our poet, and Herodotus as our prose-writer. They offer material enough for forming an opinion about the rest.

Odysseus, in Homer, is lodging with the swineherd. He is about to have breakfast, according to the old custom, around dawn. Telemachus appears, returning from his visit to the Peloponnese. It is a scene of ordinary life, beautifully expressed. The lines themselves will show where the excellence of the style lies:

> Meanwhile, in the hut, Odysseus and the swineherd made breakfast;
> it was dawn, and they lit the fire.
> They had sent out the herdsmen with the pigs to pasture.
> Now on Telemachus the noisy dogs fawned, they did not bark
> at his approach. Odysseus noticed the dogs whining,
> and there was a sound of footsteps.
> He spoke at once to Eumaeus, who was just by.
> 'Eumaeus, some friend must be coming
> or someone well-known; the dogs are not barking,
> they are whining, and I hear the sound of footsteps.'
> He had not finished speaking, when his own son stood at the door.
> Up leapt the swineherd, surprised; the bowl,
> in which he was mixing the bright wine, fell from his hands.
> He ran to meet his master.
> He kissed him on the head, on both his eyes,
> on both his hands. His tears fell warm and fast.   [16.1–16]

I am sure it would be universally acknowledged that this passage attracts and charms the ear and is not inferior to the most agreeable piece of poetry. But where does its persuasiveness lie? What makes the piece what it is? Is it the selection of words or the arrangement? No one, I am convinced, could attribute it to the former: the whole context is made up of the most commonplace and undis-tinguished words, which any farmer or seaman or artisan—anyone who took no trouble to speak well—might have found ready to hand. Without the metre, they will seem poor and unattractive; there are no fine metaphors, no hypallages, no catachreses, no trope of any kind—and not even any obscure archaic words or foreign or newly-coined terms. What alternative have we, then, but to attribute the beauty of the piece to the arrangement? Homer, as everybody of course knows, contains countless such examples. This one suffices for the present occasion, since all we want is a reminder. . . .

[Dionysius then gives a prose example, Herodotus 1. 8–10—the story of Gyges and Candaules. He follows this with some poetical examples intended to show

how a change of order will produce different rhythms and effects. We omit this, as it is almost impossible to translate adequately and because it adds little that is new to the argument.]

"Arrangement" In Prose: A Novel Subject

To make it easier to see how prose can be affected, like verse, by a change of arrangement, though the words remain the same, I will take the beginning of Herodotus' history, because many people know it well, changing only the dialect: 4

Croesus was a Lydian by race, the son of Alyattes, and the ruler of tribes west of the Halys, which flows from the south between Syria and Paphlagonia and debouches in the north in the sea called the Euxine.   [1.6]

Change the rhythmical form, and the shape of the sentence will no longer be sinuous and suitable to history, but in the direct manner of the law-court:

Croesus was the son of Alyattes, by race a Lydian, and ruler of the west of the Halys tribes: the Halys flowing from the south, between Syria and Paphlagonia, into the sea called the Euxine debouches in the north.

This style may be thought not very different from that of this passage of Thucydides:

Epidamnus is a city on the right as you enter the Ionian gulf; neighbouring it are the Taulantioi, barbarians, an Illyrian tribe.   [1.24]

Next I am going to change the same passage round and give it another shape. Thus:

Of Alyattes, the son was Croesus, by race a Lydian, and west of Halys ruler of the tribes; the Halys from the south flowing between Syria and Paphlagonia towards the north debouches in the so-called Euxine Sea.

This is Hegesianic arrangement, cheap, vulgar, effeminate. Hegesias is high priest of all this nonsense:

> After a good feast a good we celebrate again;
> From Magnesia I come, the great, a man of Sipylus;
> Not a small drop into the Thebans' water spat Dionysus; sweet it is, but makes men mad.

Let this suffice for examples. I think I have now made my point clear, that arrangement has a greater effect than word-selection. It would be fair to make a comparison with Homer's Athena, who made Odysseus look different on different occasions, now small and wrinkled and ugly "like a poor beggar or an old man," now, after another touch from the same wand,

taller and stronger to see; and from his head
made thick locks tumble, like the hyacinth flower.

Similarly arrangement, taking the same words, makes thoughts seem at one
moment ugly, low, and beggarly, and at another lofty, rich, and beautiful. Skilful
arrangement of words is, indeed, what most distinguishes poet from poet and
orator from orator. The ancients, almost all of them, took great pains about this.
This is why their poems and lyrics and prose are so beautiful. Of their successors,
only a few took trouble; and in the end the subject fell into total neglect, and
nobody thought it necessary or indeed contributory in any way to the beauty of
writing. They therefore left behind them writings which no one can bear to read
to the end. I am referring to Phylarchus, Douris, Polybius, Psaon, Demetrius of
Callatis, Hieronymus, Antigonus, Heraclides, Hegesianax, and innumerable
others. If I mentioned all their names, 'the day would be too short'. And why be
surprised at these, when professors of philosophy and writers of logic textbooks
are so miserably inefficient at the arrangement of words that one is really ashamed
to mention it? No need to go further for a sufficient instance than Chrysippus the
Stoic. No one has given a better or more exact treatment of logic—nor written a
book, a famous and distinguished book anyway, in a worse style. Yet some of these
philosophers claim to take this subject seriously, as a necessary part of linguistic
study, and have written handbooks on the combination of parts of speech; but
they all strayed far from the truth and did not even dream of what it really is that
makes arrangement agreeable and beautiful. When I resolved on putting this
book together, I investigated previous researches, and especially those of the Stoic
philosophers, knowing that they had devoted considerable thought to linguistic
questions—one must give them their due. But I found no work by any author of
any note, small or great, bearing on the subject I proposed; the two treatises of
Chrysippus 'On the combination (*suntaxis*) of the parts of speech' are concerned
not with rhetoric but with logic, as those who have read them know. They deal
with the 'combination' of propositions, true and false, possible and impossible,
admissible, variable, ambiguous, and so forth; they have no practical value for
oratory, at least as far as elegance and beauty, the aims of word-arrangement, are
concerned. I therefore abandoned this study, and began to inquire independently
to see whether I could discover some natural starting-point, the best kind of first
principle, it is generally believed, for any subject or inquiry. I had got hold of
some observations and thought that things were going well, when I realized that
the road was not leading me in the direction in which I started and in which I had
to travel. I therefore desisted. But perhaps I had better touch on the inquiry I thus
abandoned, and say why I did so, lest anyone should think that it is ignorance and
not deliberate intention that leads me to pass it over. . . .
[This false trail is the logical-syntactical determination of order: e.g. nouns before
verbs because substance is logically prior to accident; adverbs after verbs. Dionysius shows that this principle does not stand up to test—sometimes a beautiful
arrangement obeys these rules, but often it does not. He dismisses it, and comes
to his main positive thesis.]

6   The science of arrangement has three functions: (i) to see what combinations

produce a total character which is beautiful and agreeable; (ii) to know what configuration of each of the elements to be combined will improve the joint effect; (iii) to recognize and execute in an appropriate fashion any necessary modification of the original elements—subtraction, addition, or alteration. Let me explain these three functions more clearly by means of the analogy of constructive arts which everyone understands—building, ship-construction, and the like. When a builder has provided himself with the material from which he is going to construct the house—stones, timber, tiles, and so on—he proceeds to put the house together. He first considers three problems: he sees what sorts of stone, timber, and brick must be fitted together, how each of them should be placed and on which side, and finally how to trim and shape anything which does not fit with ease, so as to make it do so. The shipbuilder does the same. Similarly, the good arranger of the parts of speech. First, he considers what verb, noun, or other part of speech is appropriately combined with what other, and how the combination can be made good or better (not every arrangement affects the ear in the same way). Secondly, he decides what forms of noun, verb, or other word will be more agreeable, or more appropriate to the subject. For example: in nouns which will give the better over-all impression, singulars or plurals, nominatives or oblique cases? If some masculines can be turned into feminines, or feminines into masculines, or these genders into neuters, which is the best form? And so on. Similarly with verbs. Are active or passive forms better? In what moods—'verbal cases' some call them—should verbs be expressed in order to acquire the best position? What tense differences should they indicate? And so on, with the other natural modifications of verbs. (The same precautions should be taken with the other parts of speech also, but I do not want to go into detail.) Thirdly, he decides whether any selected verb or noun needs alteration of form to secure better sound or setting. This question is a rich one in poetry, but there is less to it in prose, though it does occur where opportunity allows. . . .

[Examples follow: *toutonī*, the emphatic and deictic form, for *touton* ('this'); *katidōn* 'seeing' for the uncompounded *idōn*; and various other examples of changed or modified words.]

Cola

One branch of the science of arrangement is thus that which deals with the primary parts and elements of speech. There is also, as I said at the beginning, the theory of 'cola', which needs longer and more elaborate treatment. This is what I shall now attempt to expound in my own way.   7

Cola must be fitted together so as to appear germane and suited to one another. They must be shaped in the best possible way. They must, finally, be prepared beforehand where necessary by reduction, enlargement, or any modification of which they are susceptible. Experience teaches all this, for it often happens that a given colon, if placed before or after some other one, proves harmonious and dignified, whereas in any other company it is unpleasing and without dignity. An example will make this clearer. In the speech of the Plataeans in Thucydides there is a very prettily composed and emotionally charged passage which reads thus:

You, Lacedaemonians, our only hope, we fear you may not be firm.

Now suppose one were to break up this combination and re-organize the cola thus:

You, Lacedaemonians, we fear you may not be firm, our only hope.

Does the charm or the emotion remain the same if the cola are arranged like this? Of course not! . . .
[A further example—Demosthenes 18. 119—follows; the points made are hardly translatable.]

8   If this is the theory of the combination of cola, what about that of their conformation? Not all thoughts admit the same kind of expression. We say some things as statements, some as questions, some as wishes or instructions, some in doubt, some as hypothetical, and so on; and we endeavour to form our words in a manner consequent on these differences. So there are many conformations (*schēmatismoi*) of speech, as there are of thought. They cannot be embraced under a few headings—indeed they may well be infinite in number. They require long discussion and profound investigation. Consequently, the same colon will have a different effect if it has a different conformation. I will illustrate this by an example. If Demosthenes had said 'When I had spoken, I made the proposal; and when I had made it, I went on the embassy; and when I went, I convinced the Thebans', would it have been as effective as it is in its existing form? 'I did not speak and then make no proposal; nor propose and then go on no embassy; nor go and then not convince the Thebans.' To explain all the forms of which cola are capable would take a very long time. The above suffices as an introduction.

9   On the other hand, it does not take long to show that some cola admit modifications—such as the addition of elements not necessary for the sense, or subtractions which make the meaning incomplete, and which poets and prose writers adopt solely for the sake of rhythmical form, to lend charm and beauty. Who would not agree that the following passage of Demosthenes is pleonastic in virtue of an unnecessary addition made for the sake of the rhythmical form? 'A man who schemes and intrigues to entrap me is at war with me, even if so far he isn't throwing spears or shooting arrows.' Here 'shooting arrows' is added not out of necessity but to make the concluding colon, otherwise harsher and more disagreeable to the ear than it should be, pleasanter by the addition. Again, take Plato's period from his Funeral Speech: who would not admit that unnecessary redundancies of diction have contributed to it? 'For deeds well done, in words skilfully spoken, come remembrance and honour for the doers from the hearers.' Here 'from the hearers' has no essential function; its purpose is to make the final colon equal in length and impact to the preceding one. Again, consider the famous tricolon in Aeschines: 'You call him against yourself, you call him against the laws, you call him against democracy.' Is not this of the same type? Aeschines has divided into three cola what could have been put in one: 'You call him against yourself and the laws and democracy.' The words 'you call' are repeated not out of necessity but to make the rhythmical form (*harmonia*) more agreeable.
    So much for additions to cola. What about curtailments? These occur when

some essential point is going to cause pain and annoyance to the listener, while its removal makes the rhythm more pleasing. A metrical example may be taken from Sophocles:

> I close my eyes, I open them, I rise,
> More guarding than I'm guarded.

Here the second line consists of two incomplete cola: the complete sense would be

> more guarding others myself than guarded by others.

This however would have been contrary to the rules of metre and would not have had the present charm. Now for a prose instance: 'That to deprive everyone of immunity in the course of accusing some is an unjust man's part—this I will pass over.' Here each of the first two cola has been curtailed. The full expression would have been: 'That, to deprive everyone of immunity, even those who have a rightful claim, in the course of accusing some people as being unsuitable recipients of it, is an unjust man's part—this I will pass over.' But Demosthenes decided not to make more ado about the exactness of meaning of the cola than about the rhythm.

I should like to take the same principle as being true of what are called periods. Here too, prior and secondary periods must be arranged in their proper order, whenever periodic writing is in place—which is not always; and indeed, the question of when and to what extent periods should be used and when not, is also a topic in the science of arrangement.

Having settled these points, I come next to the question of the proper aims of   10 the student of good word-arrangement, and the principles on which these aims may be attained. In the most general terms, there seem to be two objects which composers, whether of verse or of prose, ought to have as their aim: pleasure and beauty. The ear seeks both of these, resembling in this respect the eye, which, in contemplating sculpture, painting, carving, or any other work of men's hands, finds satisfaction and has no further longings as soon as it discovers pleasure and beauty in them. Let no one think it a paradox that I make two separate aims, and separate pleasure from beauty—nor think it odd for me to regard a style as pleasurably but not beautifully organized, or vice versa. The real world produces such results, and there is nothing novel in my claim. The style of Thucydides, for instance, or that of Antiphon of Rhamnus, is arranged as beautifully as any—no one could find fault with them on this score—but not very pleasurably. On the other hand, the styles of Ctesias, the historian from Cnidos, and of the Socratic Xenophon, are pleasurably composed but not as beautifully as one might have wished. (I am speaking in broad terms, not absolutely, for Thucydides and Antiphon certainly contain examples of pleasurable arrangement, and Xenophon and Ctesias of beautiful.) Herodotus' arrangement possesses both qualities: it is both pleasurable and beautiful.

The four most important elements which make a style pleasurable and   11 beautiful are: melody, rhythm, variety, and the accompanying virtue of appropriateness. Under 'pleasurableness' I class: freshness, charm, euphony, sweetness, persuasiveness, and the like. Under 'beauty' I class: magnificence, weight, solemnity, dignity, the patina of age, and so on. These seem to me to be the most important elements—the main headings, as it were. These, and perhaps no others, are the aims that all serious writers of verse or lyric or what is called 'pedestrian' speech set before themselves. Many good writers have excelled in one or both of these manners. It is not possible for me to give examples of them all here—it would waste the whole book. Moreover, if I am in duty bound to discuss some one of them, and evidence is to be required, another occasion will be more suitable—namely, when I come to outline the types (*charactēres*) of rhythmic arrangements (*harmoniai*). For the moment, the above suffices. I return now to the distinction I made of pleasurable and beautiful arrangements, so that my argument may proceed, as they say, according to plan.

I said then that the ear is pleased by tunes, by rhythms, and finally by variations, and in each case by what is appropriate. Experience shall testify to the truth of my words; no one can find fault with a witness who agrees with our common feelings. Who indeed has not found himself affected and charmed by one style and unaffected by another, or soothed by one rhythm and exasperated by another? I sometime think, in a crowded theatre, packed with a miscellaneous and uneducated crowd, that I can see how we all have a natural affinity with melody and rhythm, because I notice a popular lyre-player howled down by the mob for striking a wrong note and ruining the piece, or an *aulos*-player of supreme skill at his instrument suffering the same fate for blowing an unresonant note or not closing his mouth and so producing a false note or being what is called out of tune. And yet if one asked a layman to take the instrument and perform one of the actions which he was blaming the musician for doing badly, he couldn't do it. Why? Because this is a matter of knowledge, which we do not all share, whereas the other is a feeling which nature imparts to all. I have noticed the same thing with regard to rhythms. Everyone becomes angry and uncomfortable when a step or movement or gesture is made with incorrect timing and the rhythm thereby obscured. It might be thought that, while melody and rhythm give pleasure and we are all bewitched by them, variations and propriety do not possess that degree of charm and grace and do not have the same effect on all ears. But this would be wrong; correctness in this field does charm us all, as incorrectness causes us distress. For proof of this, I draw attention to the fact that instrumental and vocal music and dancing, if successful in achieving charm at every point but lacking timely variation or erring in propriety, produce in the end a heavy, sated feeling or a disagreeable sense of the inappropriateness to the subject.

All this is no irrelevant comparison. The science of oratory is a sort of music which differs quantitatively not qualitatively from the vocal and instrumental kind; words too have their melody and rhythm, their variation and propriety, so that in oratory too the ear is delighted by melody, seduced by rhythm, gratified by variety, and everywhere seeks what properly belongs. It is simply a difference of degree. . . .

[The following passage, on accent, is valuable for what it tells us of the nature of the Greek accent but very technical and of little interest for criticism.]

12   Not all elements of speech affect the ear in the same way, any more than all visible objects affect the sense of vision similarly or all tasted things the sense of

taste, or in general all stimuli their appropriate sense. Some sounds give a sweet effect, some a bitter, some a rough, some a smooth, and so on. This is due to the nature of the letters of which speech consists, which have many and various potentialities, and to the multifarious combinations of syllables. Since the elements of speech have this important capacity, but their nature cannot be changed, the only resource remaining is to obscure the untoward effects of some of them by mixing, blending, and juxtaposing. Rough must be mixed with smooth, soft with hard, euphonious with cacophonous, short with long, sounds easily articulated with those that are more difficult, and so on. All these elements must be combined as occasion demands. We must avoid a succession of many short words — this fragments the auditory impression — or of too many long ones. Words of similar accentuation or quantity should not be juxtaposed. With nouns and adjectives, frequent changes of case are desirable; if one case continues too long, it seriously offends the ear. The monotony produced by the juxtaposition of many nouns or verbs or other parts of speech must be broken up; we have to be on our guard against satiety. Nor should we stay always with the same figure, but make frequent changes, nor keep on introducing the same tropes, but vary them; nor begin or end with the same words again and again beyond all proper occasion.

I should not like to be thought to imply that the devices I recommend will always produce pleasure, or their opposites annoyance. I am not such a fool. I know that pleasure results on occasion both from repetition and from the avoidance of repetition. All I say is that we should always look for the proper occasion, because this is the best criterion of pleasure and its opposite. Now no rhetorician or philosopher has so far laid down a definite technique for 'occasion'; even Gorgias of Leontini, the first to attempt the subject, wrote nothing worth reading about it. Nor indeed is it the kind of thing to fall into the framework of a technique; 'occasion' is something to be tracked down not by knowledge but by opinion. This opinion is better acquired by those who have exercised themselves often and on many subjects, and it only rarely and accidentally as it were falls to the lot of those who do not bother with exercise.

I must now proceed to other points. A writer who aims at making a pleasing impression on the ear by his word-arrangement must observe certain principles. First, he must *either* combine together words which are harmonious, rhythmical, and euphonious, and which lend sweetness or softness or, more generally, comfort to the senses, *or* link words without these characteristics to others which do have power to charm, so that the grace of the latter puts the disagreeable quality of the former into the shade. Wise generals do something of the kind with armies — they let the strong conceal the weak, so that the whole force becomes serviceable. Secondly, sameness must be broken by timely variety; in all things variety is sweet. Finally — and most important — he must give his subject the type of structure (*harmonia*) appropriate to it.

There is no need, in my opinion, to feel shy of any noun or verb in common use, unless it is something which it would be shameful to mention. My view is that no part of speech signifying any object or action is too low or dirty or otherwise disagreeable to find some appropriate place in our writing. Trust your word-arrangement, I would advise, and come out with your words bravely and confidently. You have plenty of models: Homer, in whom the most commonplace words can be found, Demosthenes, Herodotus, and so on; I shall mention them all later, and make the appropriate comments on each.

These few observations—many more might be made—must suffice as general indications on the pleasant kind of word-arrangement.

13   To proceed, then. If I were asked how, and on what principles, a *beautiful* structure might be produced, I should give the same answers as for the pleasant kind. The same factors go to the making of both—noble melody, dignified rhythm, splendid modulation (*metabolē*, 'variation'), propriety in all these respects. As there is a pleasant kind of diction, so there is a noble one; as there is a smooth rhythm, so there is a grand one; modulation confers both charm and tension; propriety, finally, has no characteristics at all if it does not possess a good share of the beautiful. All these considerations make me say that the beautiful in structure of language must be sought by the same means as the pleasing. . . . [Dionysius now proceeds to discuss the four main factors in turn. 'Melody' depends largely on the natural qualities of sounds and syllables. This discussion, and that of rhythm and 'modulation' or 'variety', are detailed, depending largely on untranslatable features of Greek onomatopoeic words and the like, and often unconvincing. Of interest in the history of linguistic theory, this section is of little critical significance. We resume at the point where Dionysius passes to *propriety* in this field.]

Propriety

20   It remains to consider propriety. Propriety is a necessary concomitant to all the rest. Any work which is lacking herein, lacks, if not its whole effect, at least the most important part of it. This is not the occasion for a discussion of the entire subject, which is a profound study needing lengthy exposition. I shall content myself with discussing what I can of this topic—not indeed the whole or the major part—so far as it concerns the field here under consideration.

It would be generally agreed that 'propriety' consists in what suits the persons or actions to be handled. Just as word-selection can be proper or improper to a subject, so surely can word-arrangement. Ordinary life gives evidence of this: when we are angry or pleased, sorrowful or afraid, or in any other troubled or emotional state, we employ a different word-arrangement from when we think that there is nothing to perturb or grieve us. It would be an interminable task to enumerate all the species of propriety, but I will make one point which is both the most readily made and the most general in application. When people report events of which they have been eye-witnesses, even though their state of mind does not change, they do not use the same word-arrangement for everything, but imitate what they are reporting even in the way they put words together; this is a natural instinct, not the result of effort. Observing this, the good poet or orator should imitate whatever he is speaking about not only in his selection of words but in his arrangement of them. Homer does this, superb genius that he is, despite the fact that he possesses only one metre and few rhythms; he is none the less always innovating and using his ingenuity within this field, so that we see the things happening as much as we hear them described. I will give a few instances out of the large number possible.

The Stone of Sisyphus

In his story to the Phaeacians, Odysseus, after relating his own wanderings and his descent to Hades, comes to the visions of the horrors there. In this context, he relates the sufferings of Sisyphus, for whom, they say, the gods of the underworld ordained an end to labour when he succeeded in rolling a stone over a certain hill—this being, however, impossible, because the stone always fell back again whenever it got to the top. It is worth while noticing how he depicts this imitatively with the help of the actual arrangement of the words:

> kai mēn Sīsuphon eiseidon krater' alge' ekhonta,
> lāan bastazonta pelōrion amphoterēsin.
> ētoi ho men skēriptomenos khersin te posin te
> lāan anō ōtheske potī lophon.

> And I saw Sisyphus too in great distress,
> lifting a huge stone in his two hands;
> and straining with his hands and feet
> he pushed the stone up, up the hill.   [11.593–96]

Here it is the arrangement which makes all the happenings clear—the weight of the stone, the laborious shifting of it from the ground, Sisyphus straining with his limbs and climbing the hill, the rock pushed up with difficulty. That is undeniable. But just how is each of these effects achieved? Not automatically or accidentally. First: in the two lines in which he is rolling the rock uphill, all the words except two are monosyllables or disyllables. Second: in each of the two lines, the long syllables are half as many again as the short. Again: the joints between the words are set wide apart and there are perceptible intervals, resulting from the clash of vowels or the combination of semivowels and consonants. Moreover, the rhythms of which the whole composition is made are dactyls and spondees, the grandest of all and those with the broadest spread. What then is the effect of these various factors? The monosyllables and disyllables, leaving as they do numerous intervals between one word and the next, reproduce the slowness of the work; the long syllables with their rests and impediments reproduce its resistance, heaviness, and difficulty; the gaps between words and the juxtaposition of harsh sounds reproduce the interruption and hesitations of the action, and the immensity of the labour; finally, the rhythms, with their impression of drawn-out length, represent the stretching limbs and straining apart of Sisyphus, and the resistance of the stone. That this is the work not of nature improvising but of art endeavouring to imitate events is shown by the ensuing lines. Homer does not use the same style for the return of the stone from the top and its rolling downhill; he speeds up and concentrates the arrangement of the words. Beginning in the old manner,

> all' hote melloi
> akron huperbaleein . . .

> but when it was just
> about to pass the top,   [11.596–97]

he then adds

> tot' epistrepsaske krataiis;
> autis epeita pedonde kulindeto lāas anaidēs,
>
> then momentum took control,
> and down to the bottom rattled the unmanageable boulder.   [11.597–98]

Does not the word-arrangement roll downhill with the weight of the rock—or rather, the speed of the narrative overtake the momentum of the stone? I believe it does. Once again—why? The answer is worth noticing. The line which represents the downward movement of the rock contains no monosyllabic, and only two disyllabic, words. This, in the first place, accelerates rather than extends the intervals. Further, of the seventeen syllables in the line, ten are short and only seven long and those not perfect ones: the expression is therefore inevitably contracted and compressed under the influence of the shortness of the syllables. Again, no word has any appreciable separation from the next: no vowel is in juxtaposition with another vowel, no semivowel or consonant with semivowel— and these are the features which roughen or break up word-structure. There is no perceptible interval, you see, if the words are not separated. Instead, they slide into one another to form a single movement; in a manner of speaking they all become a single word through the exact fitting of the joins. Most wonderful of all, no long rhythm—spondee or bacchius[1]—such as naturally falls into a heroic metre, is to be found in the line except at the end. The others are all dactyls—and even they have their irrational syllables so much accelerated that some hardly differ from trochees. There is nothing to hinder a composition made up of such elements from running smoothly and easily and flowingly.

Many similar examples could be cited from Homer. I content myself with these, to leave myself room for my remaining topics. The above remarks do, I believe, comprise the most important and essential points to be kept in mind by those who wish to produce pleasing or beautiful word-arrangement, either in poetry or in prose. What I could not set down—minor and more recondite matters, too numerous to be easily embraced in one work—I will communicate in the course of our daily exercises, when I will also adduce the evidence of many good poets, historians, and orators. For the moment, I confine myself to essentials of my promised plan which have so far been omitted. I shall consider what different types of word-arrangement there are, and what is the general character of each. I shall state what writers are supreme in each kind, and offer specimens. This done, I shall elucidate a problem commonly discussed—namely, what it is that makes prose seem like poetry though it remains prose in form, and what makes poetical expression resemble prose while it preserves the dignity of poetry: most good writers of prose or poetry have these qualities. I must try, therefore, to say what I think about this problem too.

---

1. In Greek poetry, a spondee is a metrical foot consisting of two long syllables; a bacchius is two spondees with a short syllable in the middle of them.

But I begin with the first point.

The Types of Word-Arrangement

I certainly think that there *are* many specific differences in word-arrangement.   21
They are not easily seen in a general view or enumerated with exactness. Indeed, every individual has his own particular quality of word-arrangement, as he has his particular quality of looks. Painting is not a bad analogy. People who paint pictures all use the same paints, but the mixtures they produce are quite different from one another. Similarly, in language, whether in poetry or not, we all use the same words, but we do not put them together in the same way.

The *generic* differences, however, number, in my opinion, only three. Call them what you please, when you have been told their characteristics and differences. I know no literal terms for them, and so treat them as having no proper names and call them instead by metaphorical ones: the dry or austere, the smooth, the well-tempered—though how this last comes into being I know not, 'my mind is divided to utter the truth': is it by deficiency in both extremes or by their combination? It is hard to make a safe guess here; perhaps therefore it is better to say that there are many intermediate terms formed by the relaxation or intensification of the extremes. In music, the middle note is equidistant from the top and the bottom, but in literature the middle style is not equidistant from the two extremes: it is distinguishable only roughly, as with crowds, heaps, and the like. This, however, is not the moment for this question: I must keep my promise, and discuss the particular kinds—not indeed saying all I could (that would be a long story) but making the most salient points.

Austere Arrangement

The characteristics of the austere type of structure are the following. It requires that   22
words should be securely positioned and given safe standing, so that each word can be seen all round, while the various parts keep a respectable distance from each other and are separated by perceptible intervals. It is no disadvantage either if the joints are frequently rough and awkward, like building stones laid together not properly squared or smoothed but unworked and improvised. It is often, moreover, given greater length by the use of big words that cover a lot of space, while contraction into a few syllables is thoroughly alien to it except under dire necessity.

So much for the aims and preferences of this manner in regard to words. They apply likewise to cola, where it also affects grand and dignified rhythms, and dislikes equalized or similar cola, or any that are slaves to inexorable rules, wanting only the noble, splendid, and free. It prefers the appearance of nature to that of art, the expression of emotion to that of character. As to periods, it has generally no desire to construct such as complete the sense within their own compass; if this should accidentally happen, it seeks to demonstrate its artlessness and simplicity by employing no additions unhelpful to the sense merely to complete the period, by making no attempt to secure striking or smooth clausulae, no calculations to ensure that the period is the right length for the speaker's breath, and indeed no endeavour of any such kind. This type of structure has further characteristics of its own: it is flexible in the use of cases, varied in figures, has few conjunctions and no articles, often despises connection, is unpolished, grand, plain-spoken, unembellished, with archaism and the patina of age as its beauty. This type has had many devotees in poetry, history and oratory. Specially distinguished are Antimachus of Colophon and Empedocles the scientist in epic, Pindar in lyric, Aeschylus in tragedy, Thucydides in history, Antiphon in oratory.

Smooth Arrangement

23   The smooth type of arrangement, which I placed second, has the following characteristics. It does not seek 'all-round visibility' for every individual word, or a broad secure base for them all, or long intervals between them. Any effect of slowness or stability is alien. The aim is words in motion, words bearing down on one another, carried along on the stability afforded by their support of one another, like a perpetually flowing stream. This style likes the individual parts to merge into one another, to be woven together so as to appear as far as possible like one continuous utterance. This is achieved by exactly fitting joints which leave the intervals between the words imperceptible. It is like cloth finely woven together or pictures in which the light merges into the shade. All the words are expected to be euphonious, smooth, soft, virginal; it hates rough, recalcitrant syllables, and has a cautious attitude towards anything at all bold or risky.

Not satisfied with suitable joins and smooth connections between words, this manner aims also at a close interweaving of cola, the whole building up to a period. It limits the length of the colon — not too short, not unduly long — and of the period, which should be such that an adult man's breath can control it. It cannot tolerate non-periodic writing, a period not divided into cola, or a colon out of proportion. It employs rhythms that are not very long but medium or quite short. The ends of its periods must be rhythmical and precisely based. Connections between periods here are formed on the opposite principle from those between words: this type of writing merges words but distinguishes periods and tries to make *them* visible all round, as it were. Its favourite figures are not the more archaic or such as produce an impression of solemnity or weight or tension, but the luxurious and blandishing kind, full of deceptive and theatrical qualities. To put it more generally, this manner has in all important respects the opposite characteristics to the former; no more need be said.

It remains to enumerate its distinguished practitioners. Of epic writers, the finest exponent of this manner is, I think, Hesiod; of lyric poets Sappho, and then Anacreon and Simonides; among the tragic poets there is only Euripides; strictly speaking there is no historian, though Ephorus and Theopompus are nearer than most. Among orators, we have Isocrates. . . .
[Examples again follow; the first is Sappho's ode to Aphrodite — the only extant complete poem of Sappho.]

The Mixed Structure

24   The third kind of structure, midway between the two just mentioned, I call the

mixed kind, for want of a proper and better name. It has no special form, but is a reasonable combination of the other two, a sort of selection of the best features of each. To my way of thinking, it deserves the first prize, because it is a mean—and excellence is a mean in life and actions too, according to Aristotle and his school—though it is to be seen, as I said above, in broad outline, not in detail, and has many specific differences. Its users do not all make the same thing out of it, but some stress some features and some others, intensifying or underplaying the same elements in different ways; its successful practitioners, despite differences of approach, have all profited. Towering above them all, "the source of all the rivers, seas, and springs" [*Iliad* 21.196–97], is, we must say, Homer. Every passage in him that one touches is exquisitely elaborated in both the austere and smooth manners. The others who have practised the same 'mean' are very much his inferiors, though well worth study in their own right. Stesichorus and Alcaeus are the lyric poets, Sophocles the tragedian, Herodotus the historian, Demosthenes the orator. Among the philosophers, in my estimation, are to be seen Democritus, Plato, and Aristotle; it is impossible to find any who have combined styles more successfully than these.

Importance of the Subject

At this point I suspect an attack from persons who have had no general education   25
but practise the day-to-day part of rhetoric without method or system. They must be answered. We must not be thought to let the case go by default.

Now this is what they will say. 'Was Demosthenes such a poor drudge that whenever he wrote a speech he had to have measures and rhythms to apply, like a modeller, and tried to fit his cola to these patterns, turning his words up and down, and watching his quantities and pauses, his cases and conjugations, fussing about all the tiny modifications of which the parts of speech are capable? A man of that ability would be a fool to devote himself to trivial pedantry of that sort.' This kind of scoff and jeer is not hard to repulse. First, it would not be odd if a man whose reputation for eloquence transcended all his predecessors, and who was composing eternal works and submitting himself to the authority of all-testing time, should want to avoid adopting any word or fact rashly, and should pay great attention both to the arrangement of his thoughts and to beauty of expression—especially as his contemporaries were publishing works more like fine carving and engraving than writing. I mean the sophists Isocrates and Plato. Isocrates, to take the minimum estimate, spent ten years writing the *Panegyricus*, and Plato, in the course of his eighty years, never gave up combing and curling his dialogues, refashioning them in all kinds of ways. Every scholar knows the anecdotes of his industry, especially the story of the tablet found after his death containing the opening sentence of the *Republic*, with the words arranged in various ways: 'I went down yesterday to the Piraeus with Glaucon the son of Ariston.' What was odd then in Demosthenes' also taking thought for euphony, harmony, and the avoidance of random and unconsidered placings of word or thought? It seems to me much more appropriate for an orator composing public speeches as a permanent memorial of his ability to take care of the smallest detail, than for painters and engravers, displaying the skill and industry of their hands on perishable material, to expend their craftsmanship on veins and down and bloom and similar minutiae. These seem to me reasonable arguments; one might add that it was only to be expected that, as a young beginner, Demosthenes should have been careful in everything, so far as human endeavour could go, but that when long exercise had given mastery and shaped forms and models in his mind of everything he practised, he became able to produce his results with ease and as a matter of habit. The same sort of thing happens in other arts whose end is activity or creation of some kind. For example, skilled players of the lyre or harp or *aulos*, when they hear an unfamiliar tune, finger it out on their instruments with the speed of thought, with no trouble at all; but while they are still learning, it takes much time and trouble for them to grasp the force of the various notes. At that stage, their hands were not in the habit of performing what they were bidden. It was later, when long practice had established a habit as strong as nature, that they succeeded in their efforts. There is no need for other examples. One fact, that we all know, is enough to explode all the nonsense. When we learn our letters, we first learn their names, then their shapes and functions, then syllables and what happens to them, only then words and their accidents—lengthenings and shortenings, accents, and so on. Then, when we have acquired knowledge of these things, we begin to write and read, at first slowly and syllable by syllable; it takes a long time to form firm models in our minds, but when that has happened we do it easily, and run through any book presented to us accurately and speedily. We must suppose that word-arrangement and facility with cola develop in the same way in expert performers. It is no wonder if the inexpert and ignorant are surprised and incredulous if anyone achieves perfect control through his skill.

26   So much for the scoffers at technical advice. I come next to some remarks on lyrical and metrical arrangement having a close resemblance to prose. The first cause of this type (as of the unmetrical equivalent) is the way in which the *words* are made to fit, the second is the combination of the *cola*, the third the balance of the *periods*. Success in this department requires multifarious variety in the handling and joining of words and the construction of cola with divisions at the right intervals, not complete at the ends of lines but dividing the metre; the cola in fact must be unequal and heterogeneous, often contracted into shorter *commata*, while the periods, at least juxtaposed ones, must not be equal in length or similar in form; irregularity in rhythm and metre gives the closest approximation to prose. Composers of epic, iambic, and other homogeneous metres cannot divide their verses up by variety of metrical or rhythmical form, but have to keep always to the same pattern; lyric poets on the other hand are allowed to combine many metres or rhythms in one period. Single-metre composers, therefore, when they break up their lines by dividing them by cola in a variety of ways, disintegrate and destroy the exactness of the metre, and when they compose periods of varying length and form cause us to forget it altogether. The lyric poets on the other hand, with their polymetric strophes, effect heterogeneous and unequal divisions of unequal and heterogeneous cola; these two features prevent us from getting a grip of any consistent rhythm, and this produces poetry with a great similarity to

prose. Even if metaphorical, foreign, rare, and otherwise poetic words remain in the poem, there is still this resemblance.

I should not wish anyone to think me unaware that what is called 'prosiness' is generally supposed to be a fault, or convict me of ignorance because I regard a fault as a virtue in poetry or prose. I ask my critic to hear how I think good work can be distinguished from bad in this field also. As I understand it, one kind of prose writing is private—garrulous and trivial—and the other public, containing a large element of elaboration and art. When I find a poem resembling the garrulous and trivial type of prose, I put it down as ridiculous; if it resembles the elaborate and artistic, I think it deserves our attention and imitation. Now if these two types of prose had different names, the two types of poets which resemble them would have different names also. But in fact, the good and the worthless are both called prose, and it is therefore quite right to call poetry good if it resembles good prose and bad if it resembles bad, and not be disturbed by the identity of name. A similarity of name applied to two different things will not prevent us from seeing the nature of both.

Demetrius

The identity of the author of *On Style* is unknown. In the Middle Ages, the handbook was thought to have been written about 270 B.C. by Demetrius of Phalerum, an Athenian philosopher and statesman. More recently, however, some experts have come to believe that *On Style* could not have been written before the middle of the first century A.D.[1] It seems possible, therefore, that the Demetrius in question may have been the scholar from Tarsus who was described by Plutarch around 83 A.D. This Demetrius traveled to Britain on behalf of the emperor Domitian and may have served as a scribe and teacher in the household of Domitian's governor of Britain, Agricola. This would explain why Demetrius included a section on letter writing (the first in antiquity) in the handbook, as well as his rather professorial tone and his focus on written rather than on spoken oratory.

The handbook treats style both theoretically and practically. Unlike previous critics, Demetrius proposes four rather than two or three kinds of style. The three that are reflected in Cicero's *De Oratore* 3.3 are really two basic extremes with a third, moderated variation directly in between. Demetrius explicitly reflects the traditional two extremes, the "plain" and "grand" styles (36), but he rejects the notion that his other two, the "elegant" and the "forceful" are intermediates between them (37). Perhaps his introduction of the forceful kind of style is an attempt to account for the power of Demosthenic oratory. However, Demetrius also offers some original insights about how style should suit its subject matter.

We have omitted the first section of *On Style*, which deals with types of sentences and clauses, except for a brief explanation of hypotaxis (which Demetrius calls the compacted style) and of parataxis (which he terms the disjointed style.) The excerpts that follow include Demetrius' introduction of the four simple types of style and his advice on letter writing, which he believes requires the plain style. The next chapter, on the forceful style,[2] is the conclusion of Demetrius' handbook.

---

1. W. Rhys Roberts offers a detailed examination of the authorship question in his introduction to *On Style*, 257–93. Grube, however, presents convincing evidence in favor of the earlier date, 39–56.
2. In the translation that follows, the forceful style is called forcible.

On Style

The origin of the period is as follows. There are two kinds of style. The first is   1.12
termed the "compacted" style, namely, that which consists of periods. It is found in
the rhetorical discourses of Isocrates, Gorgias, and Alcidamas, in which the periods
succeed one another with no less regularity than the hexameters in the poetry of
Homer. The second style bears the name of "disjointed," inasmuch as the
members into which it is divided are not closely united. Hecataeus is an example;
and so for the most part is Herodotus, and the older writers in general. Here is an
instance: "Hecataeus of Miletus thus relates. I write these things as they seem to
me to be true. For the tales told by the Greeks are, as it appears to me, many and
absurd." Here the members seem thrown upon one another in a heap without the
binding or propping, and without the mutual support, which we find in periods.

The members in a periodic style may, in fact, be compared to the stones which   13
support and hold together a vaulted dome. The members of the disconnected style
resemble stones which are simply thrown about near one another and not built
into a structure.

So there is something trim and neat in the older method of writing. It resembles   14
ancient statues, the art of which was thought to consist in their succinctness and
spareness. The style of the writers who followed is like the works of the sculptor
Pheidias, since it already exhibits in some degree the union of grandeur with finish.

My own personal view is that discourse should neither, like that of Giorgias,   15
consist wholly of a string of periods, nor be wholly disconnected like the ancient
writings, but should rather combine the two methods. It will then be elaborate
and simple at the same time, and draw charm from both sources, being neither
too untutored nor too artificial. Public speakers who employ accumulated
periods are as giddy-pated as tipsy men, and their hearers are sickened by the lack
of true persuasiveness; sometimes, indeed, they loudly declaim the endings of the
periods which they foresee and forestall.

The simple types of style are four in number: the "plain," the "elevated," the   2.36
"elegant," the "forcible." In addition there are the various combinations of these
types. Not every style, however, can be combined with every other. The elegant is
found united with the plain and the elevated, and the forcible with both alike.
The elevated alone cannot be combined with the plain, but the pair stand, as it
were, in irreconcilable opposition and contrast. For this reason some writers
maintain that there are no other types of style besides these two, to which the
other two are intermediate only. The elegant style is, thus, regarded as akin to the
plain, and the forcible as akin to the elevated, as though the first contained
something slight and dainty, and the second something massive and grand.

Such a view is absurd. We can see for ourselves that, with the exception of the   37
two opposites just mentioned, any style may be combined with any other. In the
poetry of Homer, for example, as well as in the prose of Plato, Xenophon,

Reprinted by permission of the publishers and The Loeb Classical Library from Demetrius, *On Style*
(1.12–15, 2.36–37, 4.223–239, 5.240–304), trans. W. Rhys Roberts, Cambridge, Mass.: Harvard
University Press, 1973.

Herodotus, and many other writers, great elevation is joined to great vigour and charm. The number of types of style is, therefore, that already indicated. The mode of expression appropriate to each will be found to be of the following kind.

4.223   We will next treat of the epistolary style, since it too should be plain. Artemon, the editor of Aristotle's *Letters*, says that a letter ought to be written in the same manner as a dialogue, a letter being regarded by him as one of the two sides of a dialogue.

224   There is perhaps some truth in what he says, but not the whole truth. The letter should be a little more studied than the dialogue, since the latter reproduces an extemporary utterance, while the former is committed to writing and is (in a way) sent as a gift.

225   Who (one may ask) would, in conversation with a friend, so express himself as does Aristotle when writing to Antipater on the subject of the aged exile? "If he is doomed to wander to the uttermost parts of the earth, an exile hopeless of recall, it is clear that we cannot blame men (like him) who wish to return home—to Hades." A man who conversed in that fashion would seem not to be talking but to be making an oratorical display.

226   Frequent breaks in a sentence such as . . . are not appropriate in letters. Such breaks cause obscurity in writing, and the gift of imitating conversation is less appropriate to writing than to a speech in debate. Consider the opening of the *Euthydemus*: "Who was it, Socrates, with whom you were conversing yesterday in the Lyceum? Quite a large crowd was surrounding your party." And a little farther on Plato adds: "Nay, he seems to me to be some stranger, the man with whom you were conversing. Who was he, pray?" All such imitative style better suits an actor; it does not suit written letters.

227   The letter, like the dialogue, should abound in glimpses of character. It may be said that everybody reveals his own soul in his letters. In every other form of composition it is possible to discern the writer's character, but in none so clearly as in the epistolary.

228   The length of a letter, no less than its style, must be kept within due bounds. Those that are too long, and further are rather stilted in expression, are not in sober truth letters but treatises with the heading "My dear So-and-So." This is true of many of Plato's, and of that of Thucydides.

229   There should be a certain degree of freedom in the structure of a letter. It is absurd to build up periods, as if you were writing not a letter but a speech for the law courts. And such laboured letter-writing is not merely absurd; it does not even obey the laws of friendship, which demand that we should "call a spade a spade," as the proverb has it.

230   We must also remember that there are epistolary topics, as well as an epistolary style. Aristotle, who is thought to have been exceptionally successful in attaining the epistolary manner, says: "I have not written to you on this subject, since it was not fitted for a letter."

231   If anybody should write of logical subtleties or questions of natural history in a letter, he writes indeed, but not a letter. A letter is designed to be the heart's good wishes in brief; it is the exposition of a simple subject in simple terms.

Ornament, however, it may have in the shape of friendly bits of kindly advice,   232
mixed with a good few proverbs. This last is the only philosophy admissible in it—
the proverb being the wisdom of a people, the wisdom of the world. But the man
who utters sententious maxims and exhortations seems to be no longer talking
familiarly in a letter but to be speaking *ex cathedra*.

Aristotle, however, sometimes uses actual proofs, but in the way appropriate to   233
a letter. For instance, wishing to show that large towns and small have an equal
claim to be well treated, he says: "The gods are as great in one as in the other; and
since the Graces are gods, they will be held as great a treasure by you in one as in
the other." The point he wishes to prove is fitted for a letter, and so is the proof
itself.

Since occasionally we write to States or royal personages, such letters must be   234
composed in a slightly heightened tone. It is right to have regard to the person to
whom the letter is addressed. The heightening should not, however, be carried so
far that we have a treatise in place of a letter, as is the case with those of Aristotle to
Alexander and with that of Plato to Dion's friends.

In general it may be remarked that, from the point of view of expression, the   235
letter should be a compound of these two styles, the graceful and the plain. —So
much with regard to letter-writing and the plain style.

Side by side with the plain style is found a defective counterpart, the so-called   236
"arid" style. This, again, has three sources, the first of which is the thought, as
when someone says of Xerxes that "he was coming down to the coast with all his
following." He has quite belittled the event by saying "with all his following" in
place of "with the whole of Asia."

In diction aridity is found when a writer narrates a great event in terms as trivial   237
as those applied by the Gadarene to the battle of Salamis. And someone said of the
despot Phalaris that "Phalaris was in a way a nuisance to the people of Acragas."
So momentous a sea-fight and so cruel a despot ought not to have been described
by such words as "in a way" and "nuisance," but in impressive terms appropriate
to the subject.

Aridity may also be due to composition. This is so when the detached clauses   238
are many, as in the *Aphorisms*: "Life is short, art long, opportunity fleeting,
experience deceptive." It is so, again, when, in dealing with an important matter,
the member is broken and not completed. Someone, for example, when accusing
Aristeides for not being present at the battle of Salamis, said, "Why, Demeter
came unbidden and fought on our side; but Aristeides, no." Here the abrupt
ending is inappropriate and ill-timed. Abrupt endings of this kind should be
reserved for other occasions.

Often the thought is in itself frigid, and what we now term "affected," while the   239
composition is abrupt and tries to disguise the licence of the thought. Someone
says of a man who embraced his wife when dead: "he does not embrace the
creature again." The meaning even a blind man can see, as the saying goes; but
the words are so huddled together as to hide to some extent the licence of the
thing, and to produce what is now called by the name of "tasteless aridity," being
made up of two vices, bad taste in the thought and aridity in the way the words are
put together.

5.240   We now come to the quality of force. It is clear, from what has already been said, that force also, like the styles previously described, may have three sources. Some things are forcible in themselves, so that those who speak about them seem to be forcible, even if they are not forcible speakers. Theopompus, for instance, in a certain passage speaks about the flute-girls in the Peiraeus, the stews, and the sailors who pipe and sing and dance; and through using all these vigorous words he seems to be forcible, although he has spoken feebly.

241   In respect of composition this type of style requires, first of all, phrases in place of members. Length paralyses intensity, while much meaning conveyed in a brief form is the more forcible. An example is the message of the Lacedaemonians to Phillip: "Dionysius at Corinth." If they had expanded the thought at full length, saying "Dionysius has been deposed from his sovereignty and is now a beggarly schoolmaster at Corinth," the result would have been a bit of narrative rather than a taunt.

242   The Lacedaemonians had a natural turn for brevity of speech under all circumstances. Brevity is, indeed, more forcible and peremptory, while prolixity is suited for begging and praying.

243   For this reason symbolic expressions are forcible, as resembling brief utterances. We are left to infer the chief of the meaning from a short statement, as though it were a sort of riddle. Thus the saying "your cicalas shall chirp from the ground" is more forcible in this figurative form than if the sentence had simply run "your trees shall be hewed down."

244   In this style the periods should be brought to a definite point at the end. The periodic form is forcible, while looseness of structure is more naive and betokens an innocent nature. This is true of all old-fashioned style, the ancients being distinguished by naiveté.

245   It follows that, in the forcible style, we must avoid old-fashioned traits both of character and of rhythm, and regard the forcible style at present in vogue as our special goal. Now, for the members, cadences of the following kind, "I have agreed to advocate my clients' case to the best of my ability," keep closest to the rhythm I have mentioned.

246   But violence, too, may in composition produce force. Yes, in many passages words hard to pronounce are forcible, just as uneven roads are forcible. Demosthenes' words are a case in point: "(he has deprived) you of the bestowal—you of the prerogative."

247   We should avoid antitheses and exact symmetry of words in the period, since in place of force they render the style laboured and often frigid. Theopompus, for example, when inveighing against the intimates of Philip, enfeebled his invective by the following antithesis: "men-slayers in nature, they were men-harlots in life." The hearer, having his attention fixed on this over-done, or rather ill-done, art completely forgets to be angry.

248   We shall often find ourselves constrained by the very nature of the subject matter to construct sentences which are rounded, indeed, but forcible too, as in the following passage of Demosthenes: "If any of the former parties had been convicted, you would not have made this proposal; so if you are convicted now, no other will make the proposal in future." This particular arrangement obviously

grew naturally out of the subject and the order of words evoked by it. Not even by violent perversion could a writer easily have framed the sentence otherwise. There are many topics in handling which we are swept along by the subject itself, just as though we were running down a slope.

It also conduces to force to place the most striking expression at the end. If this   249 be surrounded and enveloped, its point is blunted. Let the following sentence of Antisthenes serve as an example: "for almost a shock of pain will be caused by a man starting up out of brushwood." If a writer were to change the order thus, "for a man starting up out of brushwood will almost cause a shock of pain," he will be saying the same thing but will no longer be believed to be saying the same.

Excessive antithesis, already condemned in the case of Theopompus, is out of   250 place also in that well-known passage in which Demosthenes says: "You were initiating, I was initiated; you taught, I attended classes; you took minor parts in the theatre, I was a spectator; you were driven off the boards, I hissed." The elaborate parallelism of clauses produces the impression of false artifice; of trifling, rather than of honest indignation.

An uninterrupted series of periods, although inappropriate in other styles, is   251 favourable to force. Its crowded succession will convey the impression of line recited after line—forcible lines like the choliambic.

These massed periods should, however, be short (of two members, say), since peri-   252 ods formed of many members will bring with them ornament rather than force.

Conciseness is so favourable to this style that a sudden lapse into silence is often   253 yet more forcible, as when Demosthenes says: "I could on my part . . . . . . but I do not desire to say anything offensive; only, my opponent accuses at a great advantage." The orator's reserve is here more effective than any possible retort could have been.

And (strange though it may seem) even obscurity often produces force, since   254 what is distantly hinted is more forcible, while what is plainly stated is held cheap.

Occasionally cacophony produces vigour, especially if the subject requires   255 harshness of sound, as in Homer's line:

> Then shuddered the Trojans, beholding the writhing serpent.

It would have been possible to construct the line more euphoniously, without violating the metre, thus:

> Then shuddered the Trojans, the writhing serpent beholding.

But there would then have seemed to be nothing terrific whether in the speaker or in the serpent itself.

On this model we may venture other similar experiments, such as the order   256 πάντα ἔγραψεν ἄν for πάντα ἄν ἔγρυψεν, or παρεγένετο οὐχί for οὐ παρεγένετο.

In this style we shall, also, sometimes end with the conjunction δέ or τέ,   257 notwithstanding the instructions we have received to avoid terminations of the kind. Such endings are often useful, as in the words "He did not applaud him, though he deserved it: he insulted him, on the contrary (ἠτίμασε δέ)"; or as in "Schoenus too, Scolus too." In Homer elevation is the result of ending thus with conjunctions.

258   Force of style will also mark a sentence of this kind: "He turned upside down, in his folly and his impiety too, things sacred and things holy too." In general, smoothness and a pleasant cadence are characteristic of the elegant, not of the forcible style. Indeed, these two styles seem to be direct opposites.

259   In many passages the air of vigour is due to a dash of fun. This is so in comedies; and all the Cynic manner is of this character. Crates' words are an instance: "There lieth a dim land under a lurid smoke-pall smothered."

260   So with a saying of Diogenes at Olympia, when (at the conclusion of the race between the men in armour) he ran up and proceeded to proclaim himself victor at the Olympic games over all mankind "as a perfect gentleman." This exclamation excites mingled laughter and applause, and there is a light touch of mordant wit about it too.

261   So also with his words to the handsome youth, when wrestling with whom Diogenes unawares assumed an unseemly position. The lad was frightened and started back. "Never fear, my dear boy," he exclaimed, "I am not your match in *that* way." There is wit in the ready reply and point in the hidden meaning. And it may be said in general that every variety of Cynic speech reminds you of a dog that is ready to bite even while he fawns.

262   Orators will always employ, as they always have employed, this weapon of sarcasm. Witness Lysias and his remark to an old woman's lover that "it was easier to count her teeth than her fingers." He has represented the grandam in a most repulsive and a most ridiculous light. So, too, Homer with his already quoted words, "Noman will I eat last."

263   We shall next show how force can be secured by rhetorical figures. It can be secured by figures conveying the speaker's thought. Take, for instance, that which is called "praetermission," as in "I pass over Olynthus, Methone, Apollonia, and two-and-thirty towns in the direction of Thrace." In these words the orator has said everything he wished, while professing to have passed everything over in his desire to proceed to weightier matters.

264   The figure "aposiopesis"[1] already mentioned, which partakes of the same character, will also make expression more forcible.

265   Another figure of thought—the so-called "prosopopoeia"—may be employed to produce energy of style, as in the words: "Imagine that your ancestors, or Hellas, or your native land, assuming a woman's form, should address such and such reproaches to you."

266   Plato uses the figure in his Funeral Oration: "Children, that you are sprung from noble sires, etc." He does not speak in his own person, but in that of their ancestors. The personification makes the passage much more vehement and forcible, or rather makes it quite dramatic.

267   The forms and figures of thought will, therefore, be employed in the way described; the instances cited may suffice to serve as a sample. As for the figures of language, the more ingeniously they are chosen, the more forcible can discourse be made. Take the figure "redoubling," as for example: "Thebes, Thebes, our

1. *Aposiopesis*, discussed by Demetrius in section 253, means to abruptly break off speaking.

neighbour-state, has been torn from the heart of Greece." The repetition of the proper name has a powerful effect.

The same thing is true of the figure "anaphora," as in the words: "against 268 yourself you summon him; against the laws you summon him; against the democracy you summon him." Here the figure in question is threefold. It is, as has been already said, an "epanaphora," because of the repetition of the same word at the commencement of each clause; an "asyndeton," because of the absence of conjunctions; and a "homoeoteleuton," because of the recurring termination "you summon him." And force is the cumulative result of the three figures. Were we to write "against yourself and the laws and the democracy you summon him," the force would vanish together with the figures.

It should be observed that, above all figures, abruptness causes force; as "he 269 walks through the market-place, puffing out his cheeks, raising his eyebrows, keeping step with Pythocles." If the words be tied together by conjunctions, they will be tamer.

The figure called "climax" may also be employed. It is exemplified in the 270 following sentence of Demosthenes: "I did not speak thus, and then fail to move a resolution; I did not move a resolution, and then fail to act as an envoy; I did not act as an envoy, and then fail to convince the Thebans." This sentence seems to climb ever higher and higher. If it were rewritten thus, "having expressed my views and moved a resolution, I acted as an envoy and convinced the Thebans," it would be a mere recital of events, with nothing forcible about it.

In a word, the figures of speech help the speaker in delivery and in debate; 271 lending especially the effect of abruptness — in other words, of energy. — With regard to both kinds of figures what has been said must suffice.

In the forcible style the same kinds of diction may always be employed as in the 272 elevated style, but not with the same end in view. By the use of metaphor force can be gained, as in the words: "Python was blustering and rushing upon you in full flood."

So, too, by the use of similes, as in Demosthenes' expression: "this decree 273 caused the danger which then threatened the city to pass by even as a cloud."

But detailed comparisons do not suit the forcible style owing to their length; as 274 "like as a gallant hound, ignorant of danger, charges a boar recklessly." There is an air of beauty and finish about this sentence. But the aim of the forcible style is to be sharp and short like the exchange of blows.

Compound words also lend vigour, as is seen in those which usage often forms 275 so forcibly, as "earthward-hurled," "slant-shelving," and the like. Many similar examples may be found in the orators.

We should endeavour to use picturesque words. For example, we may say of a 276 man who has acted violently and unscrupulously, that "he has elbowed his way through"; of one who has used violence openly and recklessly, that "he has hewed his way through, he has swept aside obstacles"; of one who has had recourse to guile and evasion, that "he has wormed his way" or "slipped through," — or whatever expression is equally appropriate to the subject.

A discreet use of elaborate language produces not only dignity but vigour of 277 style. For instance: "It is not, Aeschines, that you ought to speak without holding out your palm, but that you ought to be an ambassador without holding out your palm."

278   And similarly: "Nay, he was appropriating Euboea . . . . . ." The object of the rise in tone is not to make the style dignified, but to make it forcible. This occurs when in mid-height of our exaltation we are denouncing some opponent. So, in these two passages, Aeschines and Philip are respectively denounced.

279   In speaking it is sometimes forcible to address questions to the audience without disclosing one's own view. For instance: "Nay, he was appropriating Euboea and establishing a fortress to command Attica; and in so doing was he wronging us and violating the peace, or was he not?" The orator forces his hearer into a sort of corner, so that he seems to be brought to task and to have no answer. If the positive statement "he was wronging us and violating the peace" were substituted, the effect would be that of precise information rather than of cross-examination.

280   The figure called "epimone," which is a mode of expression going beyond the bare statement of fact, will contribute very greatly to force of style. An example of it may be quoted from Demosthenes: "Men of Athens, a terrible disease has fallen upon Hellas." Thus abbreviated, the sentence would not have been terrible.

281   Some trace of vigour may perhaps be found even in what is called "euphemism," that kind of language which makes inauspicious things appear auspicious and impious acts appear pious. An speaker once urged that the golden Statues of Victory should be melted down, so that the proceeds might be used to prosecute the war. But he did not say outright, "Let us cut up the Victories for the war." Such a proposal would have seemed impious and like an insult to the goddesses. He put it in the more euphemistic form: "We will seek the co-operation of the Victories for the war." This expression seems to suggest not the cutting up of the Victories, but the conversion of them into allies.

282   The sayings of Demades, also, though thought to have a peculiar, even eccentric turn, possess a certain force, which they owe to innuendo, to the employment of an allegorical element, and (lastly) to hyperbole.

283   This is an example: "Alexander is not dead, men of Athens; or the whole world would have scented the corpse." The use of "scented" in place of "perceived" is allegorical and hyperbolical alike; and the idea of the whole world perceiving it suggests the might of Alexander. Further, the words convey a thrilling effect, which is the joint result of the three causes. And every such sensation is forcible, since it inspires fear.

284   Of the same kind are the words: "It was not I that wrote this resolution, but the war wrote it with Alexander's spear"; and these: "The might of Macedon, after losing Alexander, resembles the Cyclops with his blinded eye."

285   And elsewhere: "A State, no longer the sea-warrior of the days of our ancestors, but a lean and slippered crone supping her posset." Here the expression "crone" is used figuratively for a weak and declining State, whose impotence it indicates in an exaggerated way. The words "supping her posset" imply ironically that the city was at that time occupied with feasts and banquets and was squandering the war-funds.

286   Enough has been said with respect to the Demadean vigour, which indeed has dangers of its own and is not easily copied. There is in its nature something

poetical, if allegory, hyperbole, and innuendo are poetical. But it is poetry with a dash of burlesque in it.

Next comes the so-called "covert allusion." This the orators of our day employ   287
to a ridiculous extent, coupling it with low, and (so to say) suggestive, innuendo. The true "covert allusion" depends on two conditions, good taste and circumspection.

Good taste is shown in the *Phaedo*, where Plato desires to reproach Aristippus   288
and Cleombrotus because they were feasting at Aegina when Socrates was lying for many days imprisoned at Athens, and did not cross to visit their friend and master, although they were less than twenty-five miles from Athens. He has not said all this in express terms (for that would have been an open reproach), but with fitting tact as follows. Phaedo is asked who were with Socrates. He enumerates the men one by one. Next he is asked whether Aristippus too and Cleombrotus were present. "No," he answers; "they were in Aegina." Everything that precedes owes its point to the words "they were in Aegina." The passage seems far more effective because its effect is produced by the fact itself and not by an explicit statement. So, although he might no doubt have openly reproached Aristippus and his companions without incurring any risk, Plato has done so indirectly.

But in addressing a despot, or any other ungovernable person, we may often be   289
driven to use veiled language if we wish to censure him. Demetrius of Phalerum dealt in this way with the Macedonian Craterus who was seated aloft on a golden couch, wearing a purple mantle and receiving the Greek embassies with haughty pride. Making use of a covert phrase, he said tauntingly: "We ourselves once welcomed these men as ambassadors together with yon Craterus." By the use of the demonstrative *yon* all the pride of Craterus is indicated and rebuked covertly.

Under the same heading comes the reply of Plato to Dionysius who had broken a   290
promise and then denied having ever made it: "I, Plato, have made you no promise; but as to *you*—well, heaven knows!" Dionysius is thus convicted of falsehood, while the form of the words is at once dignified and circumspect.

Words are often used with an equivocal meaning. If anyone wishes to practise   291
this art and to deal in censures which seem unintentional hits, he has an example ready to his hand in the passage of Aeschines about Telauges. Almost the entire account of Telauges will leave one puzzled as to whether it is meant as admiration or as mockery. This ambiguous way of speaking, although not irony, yet has a suggestion of irony.

Figures may be employed in yet another way, as for instance in this case:—   292
Since great lords and ladies dislike to hear their own faults mentioned, we shall therefore, when counselling them to refrain from faults, not speak in direct terms; we shall, rather, blame some other persons who have acted in the same manner. For example, in addressing the tyrant Dionysius, we shall inveigh against the tyrant Phalaris and the cruelty of Phalaris. Or we shall praise individuals who have acted in the opposite way to Dionysius, saying of Gelo or Hiero (for example) that they were like fathers and educators of Sicily. The hearer is admonished without feeling himself censured; he emulates Gelo, the subject of these praises, and covets praise for himself.

One has often to exercise such caution in dealing with our sovereign lords.   293

Because he had only one eye, Philip would grow angry if anyone named the Cyclops in his presence or used the word "eye" at all. Hermeias, the ruler of Atarneus, though for the most part of a gentle nature as it is said, became restive (because he was a eunuch) when hearing anybody speak of a "surgeon's knife," of "amputation," or of "excision." I have mentioned these facts out of a desire to bring into clear relief the true character of great potentates, and to show that it specially calls for that wary form of language which bears the name of "covert allusion."

294   It must be observed, however, that great and powerful democracies no less than despots often require these ceremonious forms of language. An instance in point is the Athenian republic, which in the hour of its ascendancy over Greece harboured such flatterers as Cleon and Cleophon. Flattery no doubt is shameful, while adverse criticism is dangerous. It is best to pursue the middle course, that of the covert hint.

295   At times we shall compliment the very man who has failings not on his failings but on his proved avoidance of them. We shall remind an irascible person that yesterday he was praised for the indulgence he showed to So-and-So's errors, and that he is a pattern to the citizens among whom he moves. Every man gladly takes himself as a model and is eager to add praise to praise, or rather to win one uniform record of praise.

296   In fine, it is with language as with a lump of wax, out of which one man will mould a dog, another an ox, another a horse. One will deal with his subject in the way of exposition and asseveration, saying (for example) that "men leave property to their children, but they do not therewith leave the knowledge which will rightly use the legacy": a way of putting it which is called "Aristippean." Another will (as Xenophon commonly does) express the same thought in the way of precept, as "men ought to leave not only money to their children, but also the knowledge which will use the money rightly."

297   What is specifically called the "Socratic" manner—one which seems to have excited the emulation of Aeschines and Plato in no common degree—would recast the foregoing proposition in an interrogative form, somewhat as follows. "My dear lad, how much property has your father left you? Is it considerable and not easily assessed? It is considerable, Socrates. Well now, has he also left you the knowledge which will use it rightly?" In this way Socrates insensibly drives the lad into a corner; he reminds him that he is ignorant; he urges him to get instruction. And all this naturally and in perfect taste, and with an entire absence of what is proverbially known as "Gothic bluntness."

298   Such dialogues met with great success in the days of their first invention, or rather they took society by storm through their verisimilitude, their vividness, their nobly didactic character. —With regard to moulded speech and the employment of figures, this treatment must suffice.

299   Smoothness of composition (such as is employed particularly by the followers of Isocrates, who avoid the concurrence of vowels) is not altogether suited to forcible language. In many cases greater force will result from an actual clashing, as "when the Phocian war broke out originally, owing not to me, as I was not then engaged in public life." If you were to change the words and fit them together

thus: "when through no fault of mine the conflict began in the Phocian War, since I was not then engaged in public life," you would rob them of a good part of their force, since in many passages the very clang of clashing vowels may be held to make a sentence more forcible.

The fact is that words which are actually unpremeditated, and are as it were a   300
spontaneous growth, will give an impression of vigour, especially when we are manifesting our anger or our sense of injustice. Whereas anxious attention to niceties of smoothness and harmony does not betoken anger so much as elegant trifling and a desire to exhibit one's powers.

It has already been said that the "figure" of abruptness has a forcible effect. The   301
same may now be said of abrupt composition on a larger scale. Hipponax is a case in point. In his desire to assail his enemies, he shattered his verse, and caused it to limp instead of walking erect. By destroying the rhythm, he made the measure suitable for energetic invective, since correct and melodious rhythm would be fitter for eulogy than for satire. — Thus much with regard to the collision of vowels.

Side by side with the forcible style there is found, as might be expected, a   302
corresponding faulty style, called "the unpleasant." It occurs in the subject matter when a speaker mentions publicly things which are disgusting and defile the lips. The man, for instance, who accused Timandra of having lived a wanton life, bespattered the court with a description of her slop-basin, her pennies, her mat, and many similar tokens of her ill-fame.

Composition has an unpleasant sound, if it seems disjointed, as (for example)   303
"this and that being thus, death." So, too, when the members are in no way linked to one another, but resemble fragmentary pieces. And long, continuous periods which run the speaker out of breath cause not only satiety but actual aversion.

Often objects which are themselves pleasant enough lose their attractiveness   304
owing to the words applied to them. Cleitarchus, for instances, when describing the wasp, an insect like a bee, says: "It lays waste the hill-country, and dashes into the hollow oaks." This might have served for a description of some wild ox, or of the Erymanthian boar, rather than of a species of bee. The result is that the passage is both unpleasant and frigid. And in a way these two defects lie close together.

Longinus

On Great Writing, or On the Sublime was first attributed to Cassius Longinus, a famous rhetorician of the third century A.D. Because of the treatise's discussion of government and literature in the last chapter, however, some scholars have concluded that it must date back to the first century A.D.[1] *On the Sublime* may indeed have been composed by an early critic named Longinus, but since he is not mentioned by any other classical writer, nothing is known of him except from this one manuscript. When the treatise was rediscovered in the sixteenth century, however, it quickly became both popular and influential. Known as *Longinus On the Sublime*, it was used and praised by writers such as Pope, Milton, and Gibbon.

On the Sublime is an ambitious work of criticism that attempts to explain why certain works are excellent. In his analysis, "Longinus" discovers five sources of excellence or sublimity. Like Demetrius' idea of the forceful style, Longinus' concept of the sublime has to do with power, impact, and intensity.

In this selection, we have omitted Longinus' explanation of the last three sources of the sublime: figures of thought and speech, noble diction, and dignity in word arrangement. The excerpt below contains the preface to *On the Sublime* and what is extant from the first half of the treatise (chapters 1–15). Here Longinus discusses the characteristics of sublimity and explains its most important source: greatness of thought.

1. Russell and Winterbottom outline the evidence for first-century authorship, 461.

On the Sublime

When you and I, my dear Postumius Terentianus, studied Caecilius' mono-   1
graph on Great Writing together, we felt, as you know, that it was not worthy of its
subject, failed to make the most of its opportunities, and gave little help to the
reader, which surely an author should aim to do above all else. Two things are
required from every specialized treatise: it should clarify its subject and, in the
second place, but actually more important, it should tell us how and by what
methods we can attain it and make it ours. Now Caecilius does try to show what
great writing is — as if we did not know it! — and gives a great many examples, but
he somehow fails to tell us how we can strengthen our natural talents and to some
extent acquire greatness. This he omits as if it were superfluous. However, we
should perhaps not blame the man for what he does not say but rather praise him
for his intention and his earnestness.

Since you requested that I too should produce some commentary on great
writing as a favor to you, let us see whether our study has led to anything which
may be useful to public speakers. You, as befits a man of your talents, will help me
with frank criticism of the points I am about to make, for indeed it was well said
that what we have in common with the gods is kindly service and truthfulness.

In writing to a scholar like yourself, my dear friend, there is no need for me to
begin by establishing at length that great passages have a high distinction of
thought and expression to which great writers owe their supremacy and their
lasting renown. Great writing does not persuade; it takes the reader out of himself.
The startling and amazing is more powerful than the charming and persuasive, if
it is indeed true that to be convinced is usually within our control whereas
amazement is the result of an irresistible force beyond the control of any
audience. We become aware of a writer's inventive skill, the structure and
arrangement of his subject matter, not from one or two passages, but as these
qualities slowly emerge from the texture of the whole work. But greatness appears
suddenly; like a thunderbolt it carries all before it and reveals the writer's full
power in a flash. These reflections and others of the same kind, my dear
Terentianus, you could yourself supply out of your own experience.

The first problem we have to face is whether greatness and depth in literature is   2
a matter of art. Some people maintain that to bring such things under technical
rules is merely to deceive oneself. "Great writers are born, not made," says one
author, "and there is only one kind of art: to be born with talent." The products of
nature are thought to be enfeebled and debased when reduced to dry bones by
systematic precepts. But I say that this will be proved otherwise if one considers
that natural talent, though generally a law unto itself in passionate and distinguished passages, is not usually random or altogether devoid of method. Nature
supplies the first main underlying elements in all cases, but study enables one to
define the right moment and appropriate measure on each occasion, and also
provides steady training and practice.

Reprinted with permission of Hackett Publishing Co., Inc. from Longinus, *On Great Writing (On the Sublime)* (1–15), trans. with introduction by G. M. A. Grube. Published by Bobbs-Merrill, Library of Liberal Arts, 1957.

Great qualities are too precarious when left to themselves, unsteadied and unballasted by knowledge, abandoned to mere impulse and untutored daring; they need the bridle as well as the spur. Demosthenes shows that this is true in everyday life when he says that while the greatest blessing is good fortune, the second, no less important, is good counsel, and that the absence of the second utterly destroys the first. We might apply this to literature, with talent in the place of fortune and art in that of counsel. The clinching proof is that only by means of art can we perceive the fact that certain literary effects are due to sheer inborn talent. If, as I said, those who object to literary criticism would ponder these things, they would, I think, no longer consider the investigation of our subject extravagant or useless.

.   .   .   .

3
. . . the hearth's tall flames be quenched.
And, should I see a single householder,
I'll weave a coronal of torrential fire,
Burn down the roof, consume it all to ashes.
No noble utterance have I spoken yet.

These expressions are not tragic but theatrical: I mean the coronals, the spewing up to heaven, the image of Boreas playing the flute, and all the rest. The result is not forcefulness but turgidity of language and confusion of images. Examined in a clear light, the passage sinks from being awe-inspiring to triviality. If incongruous turgidity is unforgivable in tragedy, a naturally dignified genre which even admits some bombast, it can hardly be suitable in a discourse which deals with facts.

So people laugh at the expressions used by Gorgias of Leontini, such as his "Xerxes, the Zeus of the Persians" and "the vultures, living graves"; also at some phrases of Callisthenes which are not elevated but up in the air. They laugh even more at Cleitarchus, a superficial writer who, in the words of Sophocles, "puffs on a small flute without any stops." Amphicrates, Hegesias, and Matris do the same thing; they often believe themselves inspired, but theirs is no Bacchic frenzy; they are triflers.

Turgidity seems to be one of the most difficult faults to avoid, for those who aim at greatness try to escape the charge of feeble aridity and are somehow led into turgidity, believing it "a noble error to fail in great things." As in the body, so in writing, hollow and artificial swellings are bad and somehow turn into their opposite, as, they say, nothing is drier than dropsy.

While turgidity attempts to reach beyond greatness, puerility is its direct opposite, altogether a lowly, petty, and ignoble fault. What is puerility? Clearly, it is an artificial notion overelaborated into frigidity. Writers slip into this kind of thing through a desire to be unusual, elaborate, and, above all, pleasing. They run aground on tawdriness and affectation.

In emotional passages we find a third kind of error which borders on puerility. Theodorus used to call it *parenthyrsos* or false enthusiasm. It is a display of passion, hollow and untimely, where none is needed, or immoderate where moderation is required. For writers are frequently carried away by artificial emotions of their own making which have no relation to their subject matter. Like drunkards, they are beside themselves, but their audience is not, and their passion naturally appears unseemly to those who are not moved at all. However, we shall deal with emotion elsewhere.

The other of the faults we mentioned—namely, frigidity—abounds in Tim-   4 aeus, in other respects an able writer and not without occasional greatness. Though learned and ingenious, he is, however, most critical of errors in others while unaware of his own; he is so eager always to discover strange conceits that he frequently lapses into extreme childishness. One or two things I will quote, though Caecilius has already seized upon most of them. Praising Alexander the Great, Timaeus says: "He conquered all Asia in less time than Isocrates took to write his *Panegyric* on war with Persia." This comparison of the Macedonian with the Sophist is astonishing; evidently, O Timaeus, the Spartans were far behind Isocrates in valor, since they took thirty years to conquer Messene while he marshaled his *Panegyric* in only ten! And how does he elaborate his description of the Athenians captured in Sicily? "Because of their impiety toward Hermes and the mutilation of his images, they were punished largely at the hands of one man who was a descendant of the outraged god on his father's side, Hermocrates the son of Hermon." I am surprised, my dear Terentianus, that he does not say of the tyrant Dionysius: "Because of his impiety toward Zeus and Heracles, he was deposed by Dion and Heraclides."

Why speak of Timaeus when literary giants like Xenophon and Plato, brought up in Socrates' school as they were, forget themselves in feeble displays of wit? The former writes of the young Spartans in his *Constitution of the Lacedaemonians*: "They were less likely to speak than stone statues, bronze images were more likely to glance aside, you would think them more modest than the very pupils of their eyes." To speak of "modest pupils" is more like Amphicrates than Xenophon, as if, by Heracles, one could believe that the glances of all these men were modest, whereas impudence, as the saying goes, is betrayed especially by the eyes, and the poet says of a bold man: "Wine-bibber, with the eyes of a dog."

And then Timaeus, as if he had come upon something worth stealing, does not leave this frigid phrase to Xenophon. He is talking of Agathocles who abducted his cousin and kidnaped her in the middle of her wedding: "Who would do this whose eyes had modest, not immodest pupils!"

But then the otherwise divine Plato refers to writing tablets by saying: "They shall write down these records and keep cypress-wood memorials of them in their temples." And elsewhere he says: "As for the walls, Megillus, I should agree with Sparta to let the city walls sleep in the ground and not to rouse them." The expression used by Herodotus is not much better when he says that beautiful women are "a pain to the eyes." He has, it is true, some excuse in that the speakers are barbarians and they are drunk, but even through the mouths of such characters one should not disgrace oneself before posterity by such petty expressions.

All such frivolities in discourse are due to the same cause, namely, a desire for   5 novel conceits, the chief mania of our time. Good things and bad come from much the same sources. Beauties of style, great ability, and also the wish to please contribute to effective writing, yet these very things are the elements and sources of failure as well as of success. The same is true of variety, hyperbole, and the use of the poetic plural. We shall show later the risks involved in their use. At the moment we must note the problem and suggest ways of avoiding the pitfalls which beset those who attempt great writing.

6   We can do so, my friend, if we first gain some dear knowledge and critical judgment of what is truly great. This is not easy to attain, for literary judgment is the last outgrowth of long experience. Nevertheless, to speak in precepts, it is perhaps not impossible to acquire discernment in some such way as this.

7   One should realize, my friend, that, as in everyday life, nothing is noble which it is noble to despise. Wealth, honors, reputation, absolute power, and all things which are accompanied by much external and theatrical pomp—these no sensible man would count as blessings, since to despise them is in itself no mean blessing. Rather than those who possess these things, men admire those great souls who could possess them but in fact disdain them. And so it is with distinguished passages in poetry or prose; we must beware of the mere outward semblance of greatness, which is overlaid with many carelessly fashioned ornaments but on closer scrutiny proves to be hollow conceit. This it is nobler to despise than to admire.

Our soul is naturally uplifted by the truly great; we receive it as a joyous offering; we are filled with delight and pride as if we had ourselves created what we heard.

Any piece of writing which is heard repeatedly by a man of intelligence and experience yet fails to stir his soul to noble thoughts and does not leave impressed upon his mind reflections which reach beyond what was said, and which on further observation is seen to fade and be forgotten—that is not truly great writing, as it is only remembered while it is before us. The truly great can be pondered again and again; it is difficult, indeed impossible to withstand, for the memory of it is strong and hard to efface.

Consider truly great and beautiful writing to be that which satisfies all men at all times; for whenever men of different occupations, lives, interests, generations, and tongues all have one and the same opinion on the same subject, then the agreed verdict of such various elements acquires an authority so strong that the object of its admiration is beyond dispute.

8   There are, we might say, five sources most productive of great writing. All five presuppose the power of expression without which there is no good writing at all. First and most important is vigor of mental conception, which we defined in our work on Xenophon. Second is strong and inspired emotion. Both of these are for the most part innate dispositions. The others are benefited also by artistic training. They are: the adequate fashioning of figures (both of speech and of thought), nobility of diction which in turn includes the choice of words and the use of figurative and artistic language; lastly, and including all the others, dignified and distinguished word-arrangement.

Let us now investigate what is included under each heading; but first we must preface our discussion by pointing out that Caecilius omitted some things. For example, he neglects emotion. If he did so because he believed greatness and passion to be one and the same thing, so that they coincide and naturally correspond, he is mistaken. There are lowly emotions which do not go with great writing: pity, grief and fear; there are also great passages devoid of passion. Among innumerable examples we have the lines of the poet on the Aloadae:[1]

> On top of high Olympus then they strove
> To pile Mount Ossa, then again on Ossa
> Mightly Pelion with its quivering forests,
> Thus making them a stairway up to Heaven

and the even mightier words that follow:

> And this had they accomplished. . . .

The encomia, ceremonial, and display speeches of our orators are full of weighty and great passages, but they are mostly devoid of passion. Hence we find that passionate speakers rarely write encomia, while those who do write them are the least passionate.

On the other hand, if Caecilius thought that passion was not worth mentioning because it does not contribute to great writing, he was altogether deceived. For I would make bold to say that nothing contributes to greatness as much as noble passion in the right place; it breathes the frenzied spirit of its inspiration upon the words and makes them, as it were, prophetic.

However that may be, our first source of greatness—I mean natural high-mindedness—is the most important. It is inborn rather than acquired, but we must nevertheless educate the mind to greatness as far as possible and impregnate it, as it were, with a noble exaltation. How? you will ask. I have written elsewhere that great writing is the echo of a noble mind. Hence the thought alone can move one to admiration even without being uttered, because of its inherent nobility. For example, the silence of Ajax in the Nekuia[2] is superb, greater than any speech he could make.

We should, then, first establish the source of this greatness, and that a true writer's mind can be neither humble nor ignoble. Men whose thoughts and concerns are mean and petty throughout life cannot produce anything admirable or worthy of lasting fame. The authors of great works are endowed with dignity of mind, and literary excellence belongs to those of high spirit.

As Alexander replied to Parmenio who said: "I would have been satisfied . . ."

. . . .

. . . the distance from earth to heaven." One might take this to be the measure of Homer as well as of Strife. Quite unlike this is Hesiod's description of Gloom, if indeed the *Shield* too is a work of his:

> Snot from her nostrils flows. . . .   [267]

The image is not awesome but loathsome. How, on the other hand, does Homer magnify the divine?

---

1. The Aloadae were giants who tried to attack the gods and who were destroyed by Zeus. (*Odyssey* 11.315–317.)
2. "Nekuia" is the traditional title of Book 11 of the *Odyssey*, in which Odysseus visits the underworld.

> Far as a man can see from a high rock
> Over the wine-dark ocean's wide expanse,
> The thundering steeds of gods leap at one bound!   [*Iliad* 5.770–72]

He measures their leaps in cosmic dimensions. Would not this extravagance of grandeur make one exclaim that if the divine steeds were to leap twice in succession they would find no place to land within the universe? The imagery of the Battle of the Gods too is superlative:

> The heavens trumpeted, and high Olympus . . .   [*Iliad* 21.388]

> In terror Hades, Lord of all the dead,
> Leapt screaming from his throne, for fear Poseidon,
> The god of earthquake, cleave the earth apart
> And bare his dark abode to gods and men,
> That awesome hell, loathed even by the gods   [*Iliad* 22.61–65]

You see, my friend, how the whole earth is torn apart from its depths, the underworld itself is laid bare, and all things in heaven and hell, mortal and immortal, share the perils of this war and this battle. These things are terrifying; yet from another point of view they are, unless understood allegorically, altogether impious and transgress the boundaries of good taste.

Homer's stories of wounds, factions, revenge, tears, chains, and confused passions among the gods make the men of the Trojan War as far as possible into gods and the gods into men. Our lives of misfortune find a haven from ills in death. As for the Homeric gods, it is their miseries rather than their divine nature which are made immortal.

Far superior to the Battle of the Gods are those passages which represent the divine as truly pure and mighty, as in the lines on Poseidon which many critics have discussed:

> Great forests, mountains, the summits of Ida,
> The Trojan city and the Achaean fleet
> Trembled as great Poseidon strode the earth.

> Over the waves he drove, and all the beasts
> In the deep ocean, joyful, knew their lord
> And the waves gladly parted; on they flew.   [*Iliad* 13.passim]

In this manner also the lawgiver of the Jews, no ordinary man, after he had made a worthy place for divine power in his work, expressed that power clearly when he wrote at the beginning of his Laws: "And God said." What? "Let there be light, and there was light; let there be land, and there was land" [Gen. 1:3–7].

I trust I shall not weary you, my friend, if I compare with this one more passage from our poet, this time about humans, so that we may realize how he is wont to rise to heroic greatness. The words are spoken by Ajax who is helpless because fog and paralyzing darkness have spread over the Greeks in battle:

> Ward off this gloomy darkness, father Zeus,
> Restore the light, grant that our eyes may see,
> And in the light destroy us, if you must.   [*Iliad* 17.645–47]

How well this describes the feelings of Ajax! He does not pray for life, for that prayer were unworthy of the hero, but no display of bravery is possible in the disabling darkness and he is angry because he cannot fight. So he prays for immediate light in order that, even if Zeus is against him, he may meet a death worthy of his virtue. Here Homer blows upon the fires of battle like a directing wind, and his own feelings can be described as:

> Mad, as Ares is mad when hurling his spear,
> As is deadly fire raging on the hills
> Or in the forest deep; and from his lips
> Foam started. . . .   [*Iliad* 15.605–7]

Throughout the *Odyssey* (and there are many reasons why we must examine it also) Homer shows that storytelling is characteristic of genius in the decline of old age. There are many other indications that he composed the *Odyssey* after the *Iliad*, besides the fact that it contains many episodes of the Trojan War, remnants from the *Iliad*, and tributes of lamentation and pity which imply knowledge of deeds done long ago. The *Odyssey* may well be considered as a sequel to the *Iliad*.

> There lie Ajax the warrior, Achilles,
> Patroclus, like to the gods in council,
> And my own son beloved. . . .   [*Odyssey* 3.109–11]

This, I think, is also the reason why the whole *Iliad*, written at the height of the poet's inspiration, is full of dramatic action, while the *Odyssey* is mostly narrative, which is characteristic of old age. One might compare the Homer of the *Odyssey* to the setting sun: the grandeur remains but not the intensity. The tension is not as great as in those famous lays of the *Iliad*, the great passages are not sustained without weakening, there is no such continuous outpouring of passion and suffering, no such versatility or realism or condensation of imaginative truth. It is like an ocean that has withdrawn into itself, into the solitude of its own boundaries. Greatness ebbs and flows, as the poet wanders into the mythical and the incredible. In saying this I do not forget the storm scenes of the *Odyssey*, the adventure with the Cyclops, and other things. When I speak of old age, it is the old age of Homer still, but in it all the stories are more important than the action.

The object of this digression is, as I said, to show that genius past its prime easily turns at times to nonsense, such as the stories of the wineskin, Circe's turning men into a herd of swine (weeping piglets, as Zoïlus called them), the doves nurturing Zeus like a nestling, the ten days without food after shipwreck, and the unconvincing slaughter of the suitors. What else can we call these stories, in truth, but the dreaming of a Zeus? Another reason for discussing the *Odyssey* is that you may realize that the declining passion of great writers of prose and poetry is apt to relax into character stories, such as the sketches of life in the house of Odysseus. Such descriptions of ordinary life are more like a comedy of manners.

Let us consider now whether we can point to any other factor which can make 10 writing great. There are, in every situation, a number of features which combine to make up the texture of events. To select the most vital of these and to relate them to one another to form a unified whole is an essential cause of great writing. One writer charms the reader by the selection of such details, another by the manner in which he presses them into close relationship.

Sappho, for example, selects on each occasion the emotions which accompany the frenzy of love. She takes these from among the constituent elements of the situation in actual life. How does she excel? In her skillful choice of the most important and intense details and in relating them to one another:

> Peer of gods he seemeth to me, the blissful
> Man who sits and gazes at thee before him,
> Close beside thee sits, and in silence hears thee
> Silvery speaking,
>
> Laughing Love's low laughter. Oh this, this only
> Stirs the troubled heart in my breast to tremble,
> For should I but see thee a little moment,
> Straight is my voice hushed;
>
> Yea, my tongue is broken, and through and through me
> 'Neath the flesh, impalpable fire runs tingling;
> Nothing see mine eyes, and a noise of roaring
> Waves in my ears sounds;
>
> Sweat runs down in rivers, a tremor seizes
> All my limbs and paler than grass in autumn,
> Caught by pains of menacing death, I falter,
> Lost in the love trance. [3]

Do you not marvel how she seeks to make her mind, body, ears, tongue, eyes, and complexion, as if they were scattered elements strange to her, join together in the same moment of experience? In contradictory phrases she describes herself as hot and cold at once, rational and irrational, at the same time terrified and almost dead, in order to appear afflicted not by one passion but by a swarm of passions. Lovers do have all those feelings, but it is, as I said, her selection of the most vital details and her working them into one whole which produce the outstanding quality of the poem.

In the same way, as I believe, Homer picks out what is hardest to endure when describing a storm. The author of the *Arimaspeia*, on the other hand, thinks this awe-inspiring:

> It is a marvel to us, to our minds,
> That men should dwell at sea, so far from land.
> Unfortunate creatures, many ills are theirs,
> Their eyes fixed on the sky, their minds on the deep.
> Often to heaven they raise up their hands
> In a sad prayer from their heaving hearts. [4]

Everyone can plainly see that there is here more froth than terror. How does Homer do it? Here is an example among many:

3. Grube is quoting J. A. Symond's translation (1883). Longinus is our only source for this famous ode.
4. Herodotus attributes this to Aristeas of Proconnesus; the work is not extant.

He rushed upon them, as a wave storm-driven,
Boisterous beneath black clouds, on a swift ship
Will burst, and all is hidden in the foam;
Meanwhile the wind tears thundering at the mast.
And all hands tremble, pale and sore afraid,
As they are carried close from under death.   [*Iliad* 15.624–28]

Aratus tried to adapt the same idea:

Thin planks keep death away.   [*Phainomena* 287]

He has made his description trivial and smooth instead of terrifying. Indeed, he has circumscribed the danger in the words "planks keep death away," for in fact they do keep it away! Homer does not limit the danger to one moment; instead, he draws a picture of men avoiding destruction many times, at every wave; he forces and compels into unnatural union prepositions which are not easily joined together when he says "*from under* death." He has tortured his line into conformity with the impending disaster, and by the compactness of his language he brilliantly represents the calamity and almost stamps upon the words the very shape of the peril: "they are carried from under death." The same is true of Archilochus' description of a shipwreck and of Demosthenes' description of news of defeat reaching Athens in the passage which begins: "It was evening . . ." [*On the Crown* 169].[5]

These writers have sifted out the most significant details on the basis of merit, so to speak, and joined them harmoniously without inserting between them anything irrelevant, frivolous, or artificial; such additions spoil the total effect just as the imperfect adjustment of massive stones that are fitted together into a wall spoils the whole structure if chinks and fissures are left between them.

The quality called amplification is akin to those we have already discussed. It occurs wherever circumstances of the case admit many pauses and fresh starts from time to time and fine, well-rounded passages succeed one another, increasing the effect at every step. Amplification consists of the development of commonplaces, emotional intensification, emphasis on facts, stylistic elaborations, the rearrangement of subject matter, or emotional appeals. There are innumerable kinds of amplification, but the speaker should realize that not one of them is completely effective when divorced from greatness, except perhaps in appeals to pity or attempts to disparage. 11

All other kinds of amplification, if divorced from greatness, are like a body without a soul and become slack and hollow. And since the selection of vital details and their arrangement into a unified whole, which we discussed above, also constitute a kind of elaboration, we should, for the sake of clarity, explain where the difference lies, and also that between amplification and greatness.

I am not satisfied with the definition of amplification given in the textbooks. 12
They say that amplification is a manner of expression which enhances the subject. This might equally well be a definition of greatness or of passion or of

5. This refers to the capture of Elatea.

figurative language, for all these enhance the subject in some way, but they differ from one another. Greatness implies distinction, amplification implies quantity; the former can exist in a single thought, the latter always involves length and a certain abundance. In general terms, amplification means expatiating upon the various aspects and topics involved in a situation; it strengthens and elaborates a description by dwelling upon it. It differs in this way from proof becaue the latter demonstrates a point . . .

. . . .

. . . opulently, like a sea, it often spreads into wide open grandeur. The orator, being more passionate, has, as might be expected, much fire and flaming spirit. The other, secure in his dignity and proud magnificence, while not frigid, is not as compact

In much the same way, my dear Terentianus, Cicero and Demosthenes differ in their great passages—in so far as a Greek like myself can be allowed to judge. Demosthenes' greatness is usually more abrupt; he is always forceful, rapid, powerful, and intense; he may be compared to the lightning or the thunderbolt which burns and ravages. Cicero, to me, is like an enveloping conflagration which spreads all around and crowds upon us, a vast steady fire which flares up in this direction or that and is fed intermittently. You Romans would be better judges of this, but the tense greatness of Demosthenes is more suited to moments of intense and violent passion when the audience must be altogether swept off its feet. The right time for the Ciceronian copiousness is when the audience must be overwhelmed by a flood of words; it is appropriate when elaborating a common-place, in perorations for the most part, in digressions, descriptions, and display speeches, in works of history and natural science as well as on many other occasions.

13   You have read the *Republic* and you know that Plato's writing (to return to him) flows in a smooth and copious stream, yet achieves greatness. You remember his manner:

> The inexperienced in wisdom and virtue, ever occupied with feasting and such, are carried downward, and there, as is fitting, they wander their whole life long, neither ever looking upward to the truth above them nor rising toward it, nor tasting pure and lasting pleasures. Like cattle, always looking downward with their heads bent toward the ground and the banquet tables, they feed, fatten, and fornicate. In order to increase their possessions they kick and butt with horns and hoofs of steel and kill each other, insatiable as they are.
> [*Republic* 9.586 a–b]

Plato shows us, if we are willing to listen, that there is another road to greatness besides those already mentioned. What is this road? It is the emulation and imitation of the great prose writers and poets of the past. This, my dear friend, is an aim we should never abandon. Many a man derives inspiration from another spirit in the same way as the Pythian priestess at Delphi, when she approaches the tripod at the place where there is a cleft in the ground, is said to inhale a divine vapor; thus at once she becomes impregnated with divine power and, suddenly inspired, she utters oracles. So from the genius of the ancients exhalations flow, as from the sacred clefts, into the minds of those who emulate them, and even those little inclined to inspiration become possessed by the greatness of others.

Was it only Herodotus who was very Homeric? There were Stesichorus and Alcaeus before him, and then Plato, more than any other writer, draws many channels from that great Homeric river into his own work. We might have had to prove this, if Ammonius and his school had not classified and recorded his debts in detail.[6] This is not stealing; it is like modeling oneself upon beautiful characters, images, or works of art. Plato would not, I think, have reached the same heights in his philosophical expositions, nor so frequently have ventured upon poetic matter or style, if he had not, like a young antagonist breaking a lance with an established champion, eagerly contended with Homer for the first place, overambitiously perhaps, but certainly not without profit. In the words of Hesiod, this kind of strife is a blessing to men [*Works and Days* 11–24]. And in truth this is a beautiful and worthy contest, in which even defeat by one's predecessors is not without glory.

And it is right for us, too, whenever we are laboring over a piece of writing   14
which requires greatness in thought or expression, to imagine how Homer might perchance have said it, how Plato, or Demosthenes, or in history Thucydides, would have made it great. For as we emulate them, these eminent personages are present in our minds and raise us to a higher level of imaginative power. The more so if we add the thought: "How would these words of mine strike Homer or Demosthenes? What would they think of them?" It is indeed a trial to submit our work to such a jury and to such an audience, and to imagine, if only in play, that we have to give an account of our literary stewardship to these giants as our judges and witnesses.

An even greater incentive is to ask the question: how will posterity receive what I write? For if a man is actually afraid to utter anything that looks beyond his own life and time, then his mind's conceptions are destined to be imperfect and blind; they will miscarry, nor ever grow into the perfection which deserves later fame.

Besides this, my young friend, a most effective way of attaining weight, dignity,   15
and realism is provided by the imagination. Some call it image-making. In the general sense, any thought present in the mind and producing speech is called imagination, but in its now prevailing sense the word applies when ecstasy or passion makes you appear to see what you are describing and enables you to make your audience see it. You will be aware that imagination has a different aim in oratory than in poetry. The poet seeks to enthrall, the orator aims at vividness. Both, however, attempt to excite their audience.

> Mother, I beg you, do not set on me
> The snaky Furies with their bleeding eyes.
> Closer and closer they are rushing at me . . .   [Euripides *Orestes* 255–57]

and:

> Alas! She slays me. Whither shall I flee?   [Euripides *Iphigenia in Tauris* 291]

---

6. Ammonius was most likely a student of Aristarchus in the second century B.C.

Here the poet himself sees the Furies, and very nearly compels his audience to see what he has imagined. Euripides spares no pains in wringing tragic effects from the two passions of madness and love and he is probably more successful in this than in anything else, though he is bold enough in other kinds of imaginative effort. He had little natural genius, yet he forced such talent as he had to rise to tragedy very often, and in all his great passages, like Homer's wounded lion,

> He lashes with his tail his ribs and flank
> And goads himself to battle . . .   [*Iliad* 20.170–71]

For example, when Helios hands the reins to Phaethon, he says:

> "Invade not on your course the Libyan sky;
> It has no moisture, and its burning heat
> Will scorch your chariot wheels. . . ."

Then he goes on:

> "Hold on your course toward the Pleiades."
> The youth, when he thus ended, snatched the reins;
> He lashed the winged team, the bridle loosed.
> They flew into the valleys of the sky.
> Astride the Sirian star the father followed
> Wisely advising: "Drive this way. Here turn
> Your chariot. . . ."   [Euripides *Phaethon*, a lost play]

Would you not think that the poet's mind itself travels along in the chariot and shares the perils of that winged team's flight? If it had not followed them on their heavenly journey, he could not have thus depicted it. The words of his Cassandra are of the same kind: "Nay, horse-loving Trojans . . ." [Euripides *Alexander*, a lost play].

Aeschylus is daring in his flights of heroic imagination. He says of the Seven against Thebes:

> The seven captains, leaders of the host,
> Slaughtered a bull over a black-rimmed shield;
> Steeping their hands in the bull's flowing gore
> They swore by Ares, Enyo, bloody Panic . . .   [*Seven against Thebes* 42–46]

swearing an oath of mutual loyalty unto death, pitilessly. But at times Aeschylus' conceptions are harsh, left in the rough, as it were, uncarded. Even Euripides, when he tries to compete with him, runs this risk. Aeschylus, in describing the Epiphany of Dionysus [in a play that is not lost], paradoxically says that the palace of Lycurgus is inspired:

> The halls possessed, the roof in Bacchic frenzy,

whereas Euripides expresses the same thought by a different and more pleasing phrase:

> Then the whole mountain joined in Bacchic frenzy.   [*Bacchae* 726]

Sophocles displays supreme imaginative power when describing Oedipus preparing his own burial amidst divine portents, or Achilles appearing above his tomb before the departing Greeks, though I doubt if anyone has represented this last scene more vividly than Simonides. However, we cannot quote all such passages.

Poetic imagination, as already mentioned, admits the more fabulous and incredible, whereas the best feature of the orator's images is actuality and probability. When this rule is broken, when a prose image is poetical and fabulous and altogether impossible, the result is weird and precarious, as when our clever orators see Furies, as tragic poets do, and the noble fellows cannot realize the simple fact that when Orestes says

> Unhand me, you who midst my band of Furies,
> Gripping me fast to hurl me down to Hell . . .   [*Orestes* 264–65]

he sees the Furies because he is mad! What then is the function of oratorical imagination? Perhaps to contribute vigor and passion also in other ways, but, above all, when mingled with practical argumentation, to master the hearer rather than persuade him, as in this passage of Demosthenes:

If at this moment loud shouting were heard outside the courthouse and we were told that the gates of the prison are open and the prisoners escaping, no man, young or old, is so indifferent that he would not give all the help he can. And if someone then came to tell us that this is the man who let them out, he would be killed at once, before he had a chance to speak . . .   [*Against Timocrates* 208]

Hyperides does the same. He had been brought to trial because of his proposal, after the defeat of Athens, to free the slaves. He said: "It was not I, the speaker, who framed this bill, but the battle of Chaeroneia" [Plutarch *Moralia* 848d–850b]. In the midst of practical arguments he uses his imagination, and thus goes beyond persuasion. In all such cases the more dynamic phrase catches our ear; our attention is drawn away from the argument's proof and we are startled by an imaginative picture which conceals the actual argument by its own brilliance. This is natural enough; when two things are joined into one, the stronger diverts to itself the power of the weaker.

This will be enough about greatness derived from ideas and due to nobility of mind, emulation, or imagination.

Hermogenes

Hermogenes of Tarsus (A.D. ca. 161–?), according to Philostratus' account, did not live up to his early promise as a public speaker. In fact, so promising a speaker was the young Hermogenes that the emperor Marcus Aurelius, when he was touring the East in A.D. 176, came to hear him speak. After that, Hermogenes' powers of oratory seem to have failed, and he became a rhetorician.

Of the four treatises attributed to Hermogenes, two are certainly genuine: *On Staseis* (*Peri tōn staseōn*) and *On Types of Style* (*Peri ideōn*). *On Types of Style* is the most important of his works. "It had great influence throughout the Byzantine period and significant use in the Renaissance, when it was translated into Latin and influenced composition in major Western European literature."[1]

On Types of Style deals with seven qualities of style which are found blended perfectly together in Demosthenes: clarity (*saphēneia*), grandeur (*megethos*), beauty (*kallos*), rapidity (*gorgotēs*), character (*ēthos*), sincerity (*alētheia*), and force (*deinotēs*). These "types" (*ideai*) are rather like the virtues of style (*aretai lexeōs*) of Dionysius of Halicarnassus and Theophrastus, but Hermogenes' system is much the more complicated.

We present here only the first four chapters of *On Types of Style*. The first chapter is a labyrinthine introduction in which Hermogenes lays down the basic points to be covered in the work as a whole. In chapters 2–4, Hermogenes shows how *saphēneia* or clarity is produced through two other qualities, *katharotēs* or purity and *eukrineia* or distinctness.[2]

The parenthetical citations in the following translation refer to the orations of Demosthenes. The translator has used brackets to explain technical terms and to expand on Hermogenes' comments.

---

1. Kennedy, *Greek Rhetoric*, 96. See also Patterson.
2. For a summary and an evaluation of the entire work, see Kennedy, *Greek Rhetoric*, 96–101.

On Types of Style

1. Introduction

I think that the types (*ideai*) of style are perhaps the most necessary subject for the orator to understand, both what their characteristics are and how they are produced. This knowledge would be indispensable to anyone who wanted to be able to evaluate the style of others, either of the older writers or of those who have lived more recently, with reference to what is excellent and accurate, and what is not. And if someone wished to be the craftsman of fine and noble speeches himself, speeches such as the ancients produced, an acquaintance with this theory is also indispensable, unless he is going to stray far from what is accurate. Indeed imitation and emulation of the ancients that depend upon mere experience and some irrational knack cannot, I think, produce what is correct, even if a person has a lot of natural ability. Natural abilities, without some training, dashing off without guidance at random, could in fact go particularly badly. But with a knowledge and understanding of this topic, when anyone wishes to emulate the ancients he would not fail even if he has only moderate ability. Of course he will be most successful if he also has natural talents, in which case he would produce a much better speech. But if we do not have natural abilities, we must try to achieve what can be learned and taught, since that is in our control. Those with less natural ability could quickly overtake those who are naturally talented, by means of practice and correct training.

Since, therefore, the study of the types is so important and so necessary to those who want to be good speakers and good critics (and even more so to those who want to do both), you should not be amazed if we should discover that this is a difficult topic and not such as to require simple handling. Nothing good can be produced easily, and I should be surprised if there were anything better for men, since we are logical animals, than fine and noble *logoi* and every kind of them.

Before I proceed to the actual instruction concerning each of these topics, I shall make one preliminary point. Our discussion will not be concerned with the style peculiar to Plato or Demosthenes or any other writer, although that will be discussed later. For now, we propose to consider each type in itself, to show, for example, what Solemnity is and how it is produced, or what Asperity is or Simplicity, and likewise in respect to the other types. But since we need this study in order to appreciate individual authors, if we choose the author who uses a style that is especially varied and that really combines all the types, in discussing his style we shall have discussed them all. For if we demonstrate the individual features of such an author and the general character of his work, what its constituents are, and what sort of thing it is and why, we shall have given an accurate account of every type of style and we shall have demonstrated how they can be combined and how, as a result of these combinations, the style can be poetical or unpoetical, panegyrical, deliberative, forensic, or, in general, of any particular kind.

Now, the man who, more than anyone else, practiced this kind of oratory and was continuously diversifying his style is, in my opinion, Demosthenes. Therefore if we

From Hermogenes' *On Types of Style* (1.1–4) trans. Cecil W. Wooten. © 1987. The University of North Carolina Press. Reprinted by permission.

discuss him and what is found in his work, we shall in effect have discussed all the types of style. No one should criticize my approach or my choice of Demosthenes until he has studied everything that I am going to say. I think that if one will pay close attention to what follows, he will find me worthy of admiration, especially for my clarity of arrangement, rather than criticism.

This is the main point in reference to Demosthenes: he had so mastered political oratory that he was always combining styles everywhere. When he gave a deliberative speech, for example, he did not separate it rigorously from a judicial speech or a panegyrical speech, but mixed the characteristics of all three in the same speech, regardless of what kind of oratory he was practicing. Anyone who studies his style carefully will easily recognize this. But it seems to me to be very difficult to discover exactly what elements he uses to create such a style, elements which, in combination with one another, produce panegyric and other kinds of oratory. It is no less difficult, indeed, for one who has discovered them to explain them clearly. Nor is there anyone, as far as I know, who has yet dealt with this topic with precision and clarity. have undertaken it have discussed it in a confused and hesitating way, and their accounts are totally muddled. Moreover, even those who have seemed to make valid observations about the orator, because they have studied his works in detail, at least to the best of their ability, say little or nothing about the general characteristics of his work. In other words they do not discuss types of style such as Solemnity or Simplicity. Consequently, although they might tell us something about Demosthenes and the individual aspects of his work that they discuss, they tell us nothing about style in general or the types of style, whether in meter, in poetry, or in prose.

Now, although it is difficult to perceive these types and to explain them clearly and to avoid the faults of our predecessors, nevertheless we must attempt to do so in the manner that we proposed earlier. If we can demonstrate accurately and specifically, in reference to the individual elements and basic principles of composition that make up the style of Demosthenes, how many there are and how they are produced and in what way they are combined to generate this effect or that, we shall have discussed all the various styles in general. As Demosthenes himself says, "This is a bold promise, and it will soon be put to the test, and whosoever wishes will be my judge" (4.15).

These are the elements that make up the style of Demosthenes taken as a whole: Clarity, Grandeur, Beauty, Rapidity, Character, Sincerity, and Force. I say "taken as a whole" because these are interwoven and interpenetrate one another, for that is the nature of Demosthenes' style. Of these types some exist separately and by themselves, others have subordinate types under them through which they are produced, and others share certain elements in common with other types. In general, to repeat what I have just said, some of the types are classes of other more general types, some share common elements with other types, although they are quite distinct from all the others, and some exist on their own quite independently of the others. Exactly what I mean by all this will become clearer as we proceed to discuss each type individually.

But first we must state the elements that are common to all speeches and without which no speech could exist, since once we have understood these we shall follow more easily when we discuss the subordinate types, mentioned earlier, out of which other types are produced.

Every speech has a thought or thoughts, an approach to the thought, and a style that is appropriate to these. Likewise, style has its own peculiar properties: figures [of speech], clauses (*kōla*), word order, cadences, and rhythm. Rhythm is produced by word order and pauses, since to arrange words in a certain way and to pause at certain times gives the speech a certain rhythm.

Since what I have said may not be clear, I shall clarify it with an example. Suppose you want to create Sweetness. The thoughts that are characteristic of Sweetness are those that are related to mythology and similar topics, which we shall discuss later in the section on Sweetness. The approaches [or modes of treating the subject matter] involve dealing with the topic as the principal theme and in a narrative fashion rather than treating it allusively or in some other indirect way. The style is that which depends much on adjectives and is subtle; if poetical, it must avoid elevation and natural diffuseness. All diction characteristic of Purity will also be appropriate. Figures of speech are permitted, but only those that involve straightforward grammar and no interruptions. The clauses should be short, a little longer than *kommata* or even equal to *kommata*. The arrangement of the words, because of the nature of the diction, should be relaxed but should not, on the other hand, be totally disjointed, since some of the pleasure derived from Sweetness is achieved through rhythm. The basic metrical unit employed should be dactylic (¯ ˘ ˘) or anapaestic (˘ ˘ ¯). (Anyone who discusses rhythm and word order should also treat syllables and letters, since rhythm is created from these, along with cadences, as will become clear later in our discussion. The cadences appropriate to Sweetness are rather stately.) Rhythm results from word order and cadence, although it is separate from them, just as the shape of a house or of a ship is created when stones or pieces of wood are put together in a certain way with certain restrictions placed on the construction, although the shape of the house or of the ship is quite different from the manner of putting the building materials together and the limitations on that.

All kinds of style, consequently, can be classified under the following headings, which denote those factors through which a particular style is produced: thought, approach, diction, figures, clauses, word order, cadence, and rhythm. I am sure that in spite of what has already been said there is need for some further clarification about these matters, but I do not agree with those who think that they can be clarified by means of examples. Of course I agree that examples should eventually be adduced, but I do not think that everything would be clear in this discussion if we brought forth some examples now. On the contrary, if we here produced examples of each of the factors mentioned above, the discussion would become very lengthy, and greater confusion might arise because of that. Moreover, it was not my object to discuss Sweetness at the moment, since we shall discuss that later in detail, but only to show through what factors each kind of style is produced in its pure state. Having been instructed concerning these things, we will be able, I hope, to follow the rest of the discussion more easily. To that I now return.

Thus every type of style is created out of the elements discussed above. But it is very difficult, nearly impossible in fact, to find among any of the ancients a style that is throughout composed of elements such as thought, approach, diction, etc., characteristic of only one kind of style; it is by the predominance of features belonging to one type that each acquires his particular quality. I exclude Demosthenes. Unlike others, he does not favor features that are characteristic of one particular type, although there is one subtype that he does use more often than the others. That is Abundance. (In the discussion of Grandeur and Abundance I shall discuss in detail why that is the case.) But as I was saying, he shows a preference only for a style that is a fraction or subclass of one type. Otherwise he uses each type when and where it should be used. He can scale down excessively elevated and brilliant thoughts by certain approaches or figures or by some other means. Similarly, he can raise up and give vigor to thoughts that are trivial and of little importance. And in a similar way, by mixing each of the other types with features that are not appropriate or peculiar to it, he diversifies his style and thus makes everything fit together and creates a unity in which all the various types are interwoven. Thus from all the beauties of style, this one, the Demosthenic, the most beautiful, has been created.

Therefore, as I said before, strictly speaking, it is not possible to find accurately in any of the ancient orators a single style, because it is clearly a mistake to use only one and not to vary one's style. But each has a predominance of characteristics that are typical of one style or another, and that is what produces his own peculiar style. By "having a predominance of" I do not mean that he uses a great number of those elements that create a particular type, such as approach, figures, word order, cadence, etc., although that may be so, but that he uses those elements that are most characteristic of each type. This is really what creates a particular type, and "having a predominance of" means "uses those elements that are most effective in creating each type." Sometimes, if someone uses, even excessively, some of the factors that produce a particular style but does not employ those that are most characteristic of that style, he will fail to produce the effect at which he was aiming. We shall turn now to the effect that is produced by the various elements that make up the different styles.

First of all, and the most important, is the thought. Second comes the diction. Third in importance are figures of speech and fourth are figures of thought, which are the same as the approach. Figures of thought, however, hold the most important position in the type Force, where they are the most important of all the elements that produce that style, as will be shown later. We shall put word order and cadence last, although they are often more important than their ranking here would indicate, especially in poetry. For one of these factors without the other contributes little or nothing to the style of the speech, but together, especially in combination with rhythm, they can have a tremendous impact. Musicians, in fact, would probably argue that they are more important than the thought itself. They will say that rhythm in and of itself, even without any meaningful speech, is more effective than style. And suitable rhythms, they say, can please the soul more than any panegyrical speech, or cause it more pain than any rhetorical appeal to pity, or stir up our spirits more than any vehement and violent speech. They may provoke us about all these points, but we shall not quarrel with them. Put rhythm first or last in importance or in the middle, as you wish. I shall be content to show what rhythms are appropriate to each type of style and to what extent rhythm can be applied to prose without turning it into song. If rhythm is as important in prose style as it is in music, let it be put first in importance. If not, it will be put in the order of importance that seems suitable to me. My feeling is that rhythm does sometimes contribute a great deal to the production of one style rather than another, but not so much as the musicians say.

We have summarized briefly everything that has been said previously, and now we shall come to a discussion of the types themselves. We have already discussed (a) what the elements are that create the types of style, (b) what the effect of these is, (c) from what elements the style of Demosthenes is composed, and (d) why we think that it is necessary to choose this orator as our example. I also made the following point: it is not possible to find any of the types of style, such as Solemnity, used continuously and elaborated in isolation from the other types in any of the ancient orators—unless one calls an individual manner of speaking a "type" and speaks, for example, of the "Demosthenic" or "Platonic" type. Moreover, since it is not possible to understand or appreciate a mixture, in reference to style or anything else, and it is certainly not possible to create a mixture until we recognize the various elements out of which the mixture was (to understand gray, for example, we must first understand black and white), we must ignore the style of individual writers such as Plato, Demosthenes, and Xenophon and proceed to examine separately the most basic elements of style itself. One who starts from this point can then easily go on to appreciate and describe individual authors, detecting their careful combinations, whether he wants to study and emulate one of the ancients or someone more recent.

Let us thus proceed to our subject and discuss the types from which the style of Demosthenes is composed. By separating out the various subtypes from which these are created and by observing how they are woven together, we shall be able to define each of them accurately. The types that are blended together in the style of Demosthenes are these: Clarity, Grandeur, Beauty, Rapidity, Character, Sincerity, and Force. We shall discuss all of these, but first we shall explain Clarity and the subtypes that create it. You should not be surprised to find that some types share certain characteristics with others. A certain thought or subject matter, for example, or a certain type of diction might be characteristic of several types. The use of simple clauses with the noun in the nominative case (*to tēs orthotētos schēma*), for example, such as in the sentence "There is a certain Sannio, the man who trains tragic choruses" (21.58), is characteristic both of Clarity and Simplicity. Such a sentence is both clear and simple. This is true of other features of style as well. Likewise Asperity and Florescence have thoughts that are common to both of them. Reproaches, for example, are usually delivered in the rough style that we have called Asperity. But if they are delivered [not in short, choppy clauses, but] in longer clauses with some amplification, they create Florescence, [which is a milder form of criticism]. Similarly Florescence shares certain characteristics with Brilliance. Each type is different from the others although it might share similar features with them, just as men are different from the other animals but in being mortal they are similar to them, and we are different from the gods in that we are mortal but we are similar to them in that we are reasonable creatures. Likewise some of the types have characteristics that are common to other types.

But this is enough about preliminary matters. Now we must proceed to the discussion of Clarity, the opposite of which is obscurity (*asapheia*), and we have put it first since every speech needs to be clear. The elements out of which Clarity is produced are Purity and Distinctness.

2. Clarity (*Saphēneia*)

As I said, Purity and Distinctness create Clarity. Purity is produced by all the factors discussed above: thought, approach, diction, etc. Distinctness, on the other hand, is mainly a question of approach, although some of the other factors discussed above might also contribute to it.

First of all we must discuss Purity, the opposite of which in some ways, but not all, is Abundance, which we shall treat in the discussion of Grandeur and Dignity.

3. Purity (*Katharotēs*)

The thoughts that are characteristic of Purity are common, everyday thoughts that occur to everyone. They are clear, even without any explanation, and familiar to most people and are not at all recondite or abstruse. Examples are the sentence given earlier, "There is a certain Sannio, the man who trains tragic choruses" (21.58), or "The Thirty Tyrants are said to have borrowed money from the Spartans to be used against those who were in the Peiraeus" (20.11). We should look at these thoughts by themselves, and not at the reasons for their use, because if we do that, we shall suspect that they have other qualities and are not really "pure," although they are in fact perfectly pure if they are considered on their own. Pure thoughts are thus very often used to introduce a topic, such as when Demosthenes begins two speeches with the sentences "Spoudias and I have wives who are sisters" (41.1) or "Men of Athens, I am a sharer of this loan" (56.1). In general there are many examples of these kinds of thoughts in Demosthenes' private speeches and quite a few even in the public speeches.

There is really only one approach that is appropriate to this type. A speech is especially pure and clear when someone narrates a simple fact and begins with the fact itself and does not add anything that is extraneous to the topic. The speaker will not amplify his theme, for example, by discussing the genus of which what he is narrating is only a species, or by discussing the whole of which it is only a part. He will not treat what is indefinite about his topic or what is unclear, or bring in the judgment of judges, or talk about the quality of the act that he is narrating or compare it with other events, or anything like that. All those approaches are characteristic of Abundance, which is the opposite of Purity. One can also create Abundance by discussing aspects of an action that are related to it, [but not really necessary to understanding what took place,] such as place, time, actor, manner, or cause. But a speech that is pure must completely overlook these aspects of an action in its approach, or at least it must not relate them until the bare facts of the situation have been set forth. Even someone who discusses these [basically extraneous] matters, or some of them, can make his speech appear to be pure by employing other aspects of style that create Purity, such as figures and diction, and this is a sort of approach that is characteristic of Purity. Such a speaker will give the impression of speaking "purely," but that will not really be the case. And in fact he will be amplifying the topic.

It is easy to see this approach in the works of Demosthenes. When he says, for example, "Having been insulted, gentlemen of Athens, and having suffered such things at the hands of Conon here" and so on (54.1), he has put everything in a pure way for the sake of the introduction of the subject, and the examples cited earlier illustrate the same technique. He has started with the bare facts of the case, and these passages consequently have an appearance of Purity and ordinary common speech. In each case what is said next amplifies the topic, although it is not really noticeable since the introduction has been straightforward. Thus it is clear from these examples that sometimes speeches can appear to be pure when they are not so in fact.

It is characteristic of the approach that is most typical of Purity to use narration and not to introduce the facts of the case in any other way. For narration is an approach, not a figure, as some think. You could use many figures in your narration, nominative cases and oblique cases, subdivisions and divisions. Generally, in fact, a narration is created out of many figures, and things that are figures themselves are not usually created out of other figures. Narration must thus be considered an approach. In any case, whether it is an approach or a figure, one must realize that narration is useful in creating Purity. These, then, are the topics and approaches that are characteristic of this type of style.

The diction that is appropriate to Purity is everyday language that everyone uses, not that which is abstruse or harsh-sounding. When Homer says, for example, "He climbed the rough track" (*Odyssey* 14.1), the word "track" sounds unusual here as does the phrase in Demosthenes, "ate it right up [the man's nose]" (25.62). In fact there are other examples of this in Demosthenes: "hamstrung" (3.31), "having sold himself" (19.13), and "mutilating and mugging and ravaging Greece" (9.22). These expressions and expressions like them are vivid and give the style a certain Grandeur, but they are not pure. That is why with many of these expressions there is a need for clarification. When Demosthenes says "hamstrung," for example, he then explains what he means by adding "since you have been stripped of your money and your allies," and this makes the thought clearer. (The style of Isocrates, by the way, is generally very pure.)

The figure that is most characteristic of Purity is the use of a straightforward construction with the noun in the nominative case (*orthotes*), as Demosthenes does when he says, "For I, gentlemen of Athens, fell out with a worthless and quarrelsome man" (24.6). As I was saying before, it is necessary to consider this statement on its own and to see whether it is pure, regardless of what is said after it. For what is said next does not allow the style to remain pure. That is the case also with the examples mentioned earlier about Sannio and the wives who were sisters. I can prove that the use of straightforward sentences with the subject in the nominative case is most characteristic of Purity. If you use the oblique cases, even though you are narrating facts, you always amplify the speech. The oblique cases, since their use involves subordinate clauses, introduce other, unnecessary thoughts. And just as the use of simple clauses with the subject in the nominative case is the opposite of complex sentences where the subject of an action is often in an oblique case, so Abundance, taken as a whole, is the opposite of Purity, taken as a whole.

What I mean will be clear from the following example. If you say "Candaules was" and "Croesus was," using a straightforward sentence with the subject in the nominative case, you make the sentence pure and clear. If you use subordination and say "When Croesus was" or "Since Candaules was," the style is no longer pure and clear. There is at the outset some confusion, since it is necessary that some other thought follow, and the lengthy expression produces a certain lack of Clarity. If Heredotus, for example (1.7), had said, "Since Croesus was a Lydian by birth, and since he was the son of Alyattes, and since he ruled those nations on this side of the Halys River," the point that he really wanted to make would have been kept in suspense; [and this does not make for Clarity]. And it would be even less clear if the subordination at the beginning of the sentence were prolonged. But Herodotus uses short clauses that are marked off from one another by brief pauses: "Croesus was a Lydian by birth, and he was the son of Alyattes, and he ruled those nations." In general, therefore, any means of expression that does not amplify the thought makes the style pure.

Let me take another example. In the speech *Against Meidias* (13) Demosthenes says, "For when I came forward and volunteered to serve as chorus master, [when the assembly at which the archon assigned the flute-players was meeting . . . and when there were arguments and disputes, since the tribe of Pandionis for two years had not appointed one, you, gentlemen of Athens, welcomed my offer]." This sentence is amplified, both in thought and by figures, [by reason of the many thoughts that are expressed in it and because Demosthenes here uses three levels of subordination]. If, however, you wanted to retain the details of the incident, which is characteristic of Abundance, but to narrate them in a way that is characteristic of Purity, you would say: "For two years the tribe of Pandionis had not appointed a chorus master. The assembly was meeting. The archon was assigning the flute-players. There were arguments and disputes. I came forward and offered my services." And if someone should express all his thoughts in such a way he would make his speech clearer, although it would have no Grandeur or power so far as the diction and its features are concerned.

You should not be surprised if we have mentioned Abundance as if you knew what it was in spite of the fact that we have not really discussed it. In a stylistic discussion of this sort that is the only way to proceed; [We would have had to use comparisons and contrasts] even if we had begun our discussion with another style other than Clarity. For almost all the types of style can best be described by looking at them in relation to other types. Sometimes this can best be done by contrast, as here, when we said that those means of expression are pure that are the opposite of those that create Abundance. Sometimes the point can be made more clearly by means of comparison. This was our approach at the beginning of the present discussion when we stated that Clarity is produced by Distinctness and Purity, although we had not yet defined clearly what these were. But [just as we eventually explained Purity, and shall soon explain Distinctness,] so eventually we shall also discuss Abundance. Now we must return to our discussion. [First, though, I want to make a final point about expression.] Unnatural word order or twisted and contorted sentences are also detrimental to Purity, and these, like Abundance, must also be avoided to be clear.

We now turn to a discussion of the kinds of clauses that are most characteristic of Purity. It is clear from what has already been said that these should be short, like *kommata*, and that they should express complete thoughts in themselves. Long clauses and periodic sentences are inappropriate in a pure style.

The structure of a pure sentence must first of all be straightforward and consist of only one clause, and there should be little concern about avoiding hiatus. The avoidance of hiatus is more typical of an elaborate style than of one that is straightforward and pure. The rhythm should be rather prosaic and conversational and should use metrical configurations such as iambs ($\smile\ -$) and trochees ($-\ \smile$) [into which conversation naturally falls], as Demosthenes does in the following sentence (24.6): *egō găr, ō Athēnaioi, prosekrousă anthrōpōi ponērōi*. It is not necessary to demand precision here, nor is it possible. It is enough for the feet at the beginning of the sentence to consist of iambs and trochees and for the rest of the sentence to contain more iambs and trochees than dactyls ($-\ \smile\ \smile$), anapests ($\smile\ \smile\ -$), and other less conversational meters. Indeed it is appropriate that other meters be mixed with the iambs and the trochees so that the style does not become completely metrical. In other words the sentence should have some natural rhythm but it should not be regularly metrical like poetry. Prose rhythm, which is created by word order and cadence, should be metrical to some extent but not overly so. The meter that is appropriate will be determined by the kind of style that is being used. Here, for example, as we have said, iambs and trochees are most suitable for Purity. However, to give an example of what I was saying before, in the line *hoûtos* | *ástrăt-* | *ēi-* | *ás hě-* | *ălō* | *kaì kě]* | *chrētaí* | *symphŏ-* | *rāi* (21.58) there is a brief interruption of the regular metrical pattern in the word *astrateias* since the last syllable is long where one would expect a short syllable. In fact, if you wanted to excuse this, you could call it a pure trochaic tetrameter catalectic, which normally consists of four pairs of trochees, although a spondee (⁻ ⁻) can be substituted for a trochee. But I have said enough about the word order that is appropriate to Purity.

And it should be clear from what I have already said that the cadences should be similar to the metrical configurations produced by the order of the words. In other words, if iambs and trochees have predominated in the rest of the sentence, the final cadence should also be iambic or trochaic so that the overall rhythm of the sentence, which is produced by word order and cadences, will be primarily iambic or trochaic. That means that the prose will be metrical in nature but not strictly metrical like poetry. [So the cadences used in Purity should be iambic or trochaic.]

All these factors—the word order, insofar as it falls into regular metrical patterns; the cadences; and the rhythm of the entire sentence, which results from word order and cadence—are difficult to grasp and have consequently been explained by us in great detail. They do not, however, contribute very much to Purity of style, although they do contribute something. This is the case with most, if not all, types of style as well, as I said earlier when I mentioned musicians and argued that metrical considerations are less important in producing a particular style than other factors. It is really the subject matter, and the diction, and the approaches, and the types of clauses and figures used, that create one style or another, although rhythmical considerations do have some effect. In some of the types, in fact, rhythm is very important, especially in Beauty and any sort of well-wrought style, as will be very clear when we discuss Beauty. Such considerations are obviously also extremely important in poetry, but that does not concern us here and it is quite evident to everyone. Therefore let this discussion concerning Purity come to a close.

4. Distinctness (*Eukrineia*)

Distinctness possesses some characteristics that naturally produce Clarity, but in general it is the ally of Purity in attaining the aim of that type of style. The goal of Purity is to make the speech clear, and Distinctness sets the speech back on the right course and makes it clear what the speaker is doing if there is any unavoidable obscurity in it, as often happens in public speaking. Distinctness is primarily concerned with the approach of the speech. It is the function of Distinctness to determine what aspects of the case the judges should consider first and what they should consider second and to make that clear to them. When Demosthenes, for example, says in the speech *On the False Embassy* (4), outlining how he will handle the argument, "What should be included in the account that an ambassador makes to the city of his embassy? He should discuss first of all what reports he made, and secondly what advice he gave, and thirdly what instructions you gave to him," he brings considerable Clarity to his presentation, especially since in the speech he does not intend to deal with the facts of the case in chronological order but very forcefully deals with later events first (although we cannot consider here why that is a forceful approach). To treat events out of their normal chronological sequence often makes a speech clearer and also more forceful. That is what Demosthenes does in the speech *Against Aristocrates* (8). But he forewarns the audience that he will take that approach: "First of all I must explain why you hold the Chersonese safely." Then he explains that it [the reason] is the quarrel among the Thracians. For what he wanted to demonstrate would have been unclear if he had attacked Charidemus first on the grounds that he was furthering the power of Cersobleptes and then said, "Why then do you hold the Chersonese safely?" But as it is, he has established at the very outset, in the proemium to the speech, before discussing Charidemus and Cersobleptes, that he is concerned about how the Athenians can safely hold the Cherosonese and will not through deception be stripped of it again. And having made it clear at the outset that it is important for the Athenians to encourage dissension among the Thracians if they want to maintain their holdings in the Chersonese, he has made the speech distinct and clear. Whether this approach is also forceful is another question.

As I was saying, the approach is primarily responsible for making a speech distinct, although other factors also can create the same effect. Thoughts, for example, that give appropriate background material make the speech distinct, such as the following that one finds in Demosthenes (18.17): "It is necessary, men of Athens, and fitting as well, to remind you what the situation was like in those times so that you might consider how it relates, in all its details, to the present crisis." Thoughts that delineate clearly what is going to be said and in what order also create Distinctness, as Demosthenes does in the following passage (23.18): "I have undertaken to demonstrate to you three things, first that the decree is illegal, second that it is not in the city's best interests, and third that Charidemus is not worthy to obtain what you have proposed, and it is perhaps just that you choose what point I will argue first." Then he says, "If you want to consider the illegality of the decree first, I will discuss that now." I have often asserted that what I have said should not be criticized if the example that I have given involves something in addition to Distinctness. The passage cited above is clever and forceful as well as being distinct, but this is not the place to discuss that.

Moreover, "completions" (*symplēroseis*), thoughts and approaches that signal that one train of thought is being brought to a close and that another is being introduced, also make the speech distinct, especially when the speaker makes clear the nature of the new thought, as Demosthenes does in the following passage (18.136): "One of this hothead's political acts was such as I have described. Let me remind you of another." Then he begins this section of the speech, "When Philip sent Pytho of Byzantium," etc. He uses the same approach when he says (20.41), "It is necessary to consider not only how Leucon may not be treated unjustly, but also whether any other has done you a service," etc. There are many examples of this, but these illustrate what thoughts are characteristic of Distinctness.

In addition to the approaches already discussed it is also characteristic of Distinctness to follow in the speech the natural order of events and arguments, putting first things first and second things second, as Isocrates does so often. This is not particularly forceful and is not characteristic of Demosthenes. That is why he uses techniques that make his approach clear, as we showed a little earlier, although sometimes it is more forceful to adhere to the natural order of things. But we will discuss that more precisely in our treatment of the approach that is characteristic of Force.

Moreover, if one follows the natural order of topics, to put the counterproposition (*antithesis*) before its refutation (*lysis*) creates Distinctness. Isocrates almost always does this, although Demosthenes is inconsistent in this respect. The latter arranges his material in such a way that it will be most beneficial to his own point of view, sometimes putting the counterproposition first and sometimes last and sometimes in the middle. At times, in other words, he refutes the arguments of his opponent before he offers his own proposals. At other times he introduces his own proposal first, and sometimes he puts his own proposal in the middle of the refutation of the arguments of his opponent. We will discuss more precisely how proposals should be introduced in the section on the approach that is most characteristic of Force. These, however, are the approaches that make for Distinctness. And the style that creates Distinctness is the same as that which is characteristic of Purity.

The figures that are characteristic of Distinctness include, first of all, definition by means of enumerating the components that make up a group (*to kat' athroisin hōrismenon*), such as "Here he said two things, this and that." Thus the hearer does not expect more than two things and foresees what is going to be said second. And so, by accumulating various entities that make up a group, the speaker makes it clear beforehand what he will say. Similarly, dividing a whole into its parts (*merismos*) and enumerating its characteristics (*aparithmēsis*) create Distinctness. The introduction of new thoughts generally amplifies and expands a speech, but if the speaker shows to his audience at the outset of his argument what new thought will follow he has made his whole approach clear from the beginning. If he says, "I will treat this first," he notifies the audience that he will say something else second. Demosthenes does this at the beginning of the speech *On the Chersonese* when he says, "On the one hand (*men*), public speakers ought," and this causes the audience to expect that he will answer the anticipatory conjunction. These are some of the approaches that are characteristic of Distinctness.

A speech also becomes distinct whenever the speaker asks himself a question and then replies after a brief pause. Demosthenes often does this by saying something like "Why do I say this?" or "How then is this true?" or "Why is this so?" He uses many such devices in the speech *Against Aristocrates*, since he is examining an illegal procedure, a topic that demands a great deal of Clarity. Repetitions (*epanalēpseis*) also are especially useful when the orator wants to create Distinctness and Clarity. When you introduce a thought in such a way that another thought will logically follow, but then are forced to deal with other matters before coming to the thought that has already been promised, you must repeat what you have said earlier, so that your organization will not seem to be confused and unclear. Demosthenes often does this. In the *Second Olynthiac*, for example, he says: "I do not choose to discuss Philip's strength and by such arguments to urge you to do what is necessary. Why?" (3). Then he gives his reasons. Although he then says many things that support his basic point of view, he does not introduce immediately the thought that seems to follow naturally from what had been said before, namely "But there are other matters that I will discuss" (4). This procedure could have made the speech unclear. Therefore he repeats, in effect, what he had said earlier, "I will pass over these topics" (4), before introducing the matters that he will discuss. That has made the speech distinct and clear. In the speech *On the False Embassy*, moreover, he says: "Why then do I say this? My first and most important reason, gentlemen of Athens, is so that none of you should be amazed when you hear me relating certain episodes" (25). Then after interjecting many details and completing his argument on this point, he repeats what he had said earlier so that the argument will be clear: "This was the first and most important reason for narrating these facts. And what was the second, which is no less important than the first?" (27). There are, in fact, many examples of this technique in Demosthenes. But this is enough discussion of the figures that create Distinctness. The clauses, the arrangement of the words, the cadences, and the rhythms that produce Distinctness are the same as those that are characteristic of Purity.

Let this discussion suffice concerning Clarity. One must realize (I feel quite sure of this) that a speech will not be clear if it does not exemplify the characteristics that produce Purity or Distinctness, or at least some of them. The opposite of Distinctness is confusion, which happens whenever a speaker deals with a topic verbosely and at great length but does not employ those techniques that create Distinctness. That is a defect. But lack of Clarity in and of itself is not always a fault, since indirect expressions (*emphaseis*), such as "And there were those supporting the proposal for some reason — but I will pass over that" (18.21), and "figured problems" do not narrate facts clearly, although we cannot say that they have been introduced in a faulty way or make a speech defective. But that brings up the question of Grandeur, which we shall treat in the next section. Clarity needs a certain amount of Grandeur and majesty (*onkos*), since insignificance and vulgarity are not far away from extreme Clarity, and Grandeur is the counter to that.

6

The Rhetoric of Later Antiquity

When the Roman republic was replaced by an empire under Augustus Caesar, the uses of rhetoric began to change. Even though the emperors kept up appearances by continuing the Senate, political decisions were no longer in the hands of the people. Consequently, effective oratory was not needed to influence legislation. Furthermore, the need for rhetoric in the judicial arena was greatly reduced by the efficient Roman legal system.

With two out of the three traditional types of rhetoric thus diminished, it was only natural that interest in the third type heightened. In other words, to an orator epideictic rhetoric provided opportunities that were no longer offered by the judicial and deliberative forums. For all practical purposes, rhetoric was thus reduced to the art of declamation.

It has been suggested that these changes caused the first- and second-century movement known as the second sophistic. During this time, traveling sophists delivered orations to large crowds who paid to hear their speeches. But these orators were more than public entertainers. Somewhat like today's televangelists, they "encouraged belief in inherited values of religion and morality in the most polished and elegant form, and they contributed significantly to the stability of a society whose major goal was preservation of the status quo in the face of barbarian attack and new religious movements."[1]

Throughout the second sophistic, epideictic rhetoric developed many different methods of praising many different categories of people, places, and things. In order to catalog and describe these genres, Menander Rhetor wrote his third-century handbooks, *Peri epideiktikōn*. The selection we have reprinted is unusual because it departs from the strict conventions that usually governed traditional epideictic oratory. In *The Talk*, Menander gives advice to would-be sophists on how to deliver an informal speech. However, an informal talk does not mean impromptu, much less unsophisticated. Menander tells the speaker to do research in order to discover facts and good examples of the deeds done by the person being praised. Furthermore, Menander's advice on how to add "sweetness" to the talk suggests that his theories of style are in the Hermogenic tradition.

Another effect of the imperial Roman government was the increasing change in focus of rhetoric from the spoken towards the written. A good example of this tendency is the career of Tacitus. George A. Kennedy points out that Tacitus was not only one of the

---

1. Kennedy, *Classical Rhetoric*, 38.

leading Roman orators but also a discerning theoretician on contemporary issues in rhetoric (as we can see from his *Dialogue on Orators*). Yet Tacitus abandoned the field of oratory and turned to writing histories.

By the time the Roman empire came under Christian influence in the fourth century, church leaders had discovered that rhetoric could be effectively used by Christians. Although Christian rhetoric is usually associated primarily with sermons, the fathers of the church also recognized the value of written forms of rhetoric. In fact the nineteenth-century collection of the writings of the Greek and Latin fathers edited by J. P. Migne takes up almost four hundred large folio volumes.

We present excerpts from both a Greek father of the church (Basil) and a Latin one (Augustine). Their writings not only illustrate the differences in thought between the Byzantine east and the Roman west, but they also show the various applications of literary rhetoric. The selection from St. Basil is from a treatise addressed to young Christians explaining that it is acceptable to read the classics because there is much good to be found in them. However, Basil warns that Christian schoolboys should not "imitate the orators in their art of lying" (4.43–44).

Basil's address has always been of interest to scholars because his rhetorical stance is so unique. Here is the father of Christian monasticism penning an apologia for pagan literature! Further paradoxes lie in the fact that during his lifetime, Basil was both ascetic and sophist, both a bishop and a teacher of rhetoric.

Like Basil, St. Augustine went from teaching rhetoric to preaching Christianity. Following one of the most dramatic conversions in history (narrated in the *Confessions*), Augustine resigned his chair of rhetoric in Carthage in 386 and was ordained bishop of Hippo less than ten years later. He then produced a voluminous amount of literature in an extraordinary variety of styles: autobiography, philosophical dialogues, polemics against heresies, letters, sermons, and commentaries.

Our selection is from Augustine's *On Christian Doctrine*, which explains how a Christian can use rhetoric as an aid both to discover scriptural meaning and to share this meaning via sermons. Our excerpts are taken from the last part of the treatise, in which Augustine gives an overview of Ciceronian principles and practices.

These three selections from the later period of ancient rhetoric illustrate the development from epideictic oratory to literature. We also chose them to demonstrate how the use of writing enlarged the scope of rhetoric from the second through the fifth centuries. Finally, the last two readings help to show the different ways in which both eastern and western forms of Christianity modified classical concepts of rhetoric.

Menander Rhetor

In Byzantine times the best authority on epideictic rhetoric was considered to be Menander of Laodicea-on-Lycus, who both practiced and taught rhetoric in the third century A. D. Two treatises that deal with epideictic forms (*Peri epideiktikōn*) have come down to us ascribed to him. However, D. A. Russell and N. G. Wilson do not think that Menander wrote these treatises, and they assign both works to the reign of Diocletian (died A. D. 316).[1]

These treatises were written for the professional speaker of the late empire who had to compose encomia on a variety of subjects for both public and private celebrations. The main topic of Treatise 1 is how to divide and subdivide forms of praise. Men praise gods with hymns. Book 1 discusses eight types of hymns and the degree to which they can be made suitable for prose. Men compose encomia to praise such mortal subjects as countries and cities. Books 2 and 3 point out the many divisions and subdivisions under which the orator can praise a country and a city.

Treatise 2 presents detailed instructions for composing seventeen types of encomia appropriate to many events. From Treatise 2 the orator would, for example, learn what to say in praise of the emperor or at a wedding, a birthday, a funeral, a departure of someone on a journey, and so on.

Our selection, *The Talk* (*lalia*) comes from Treatise 2. We have chosen *The Talk* rather than the theoretical sections of Treatise 1 or the more historically representative discussion of *The Imperial Oration* in Treatise 2 because the *lalia* has no clear classical ancestors but is a new form based on traditional foundations. Menander tells us that the *lalia* fulfills the requirements of both deliberative and epideictic rhetoric. The modern reader may note that in its apparent informality the *lalia* somewhat resembles the English essay.

The sign (?) has been placed by the translators wherever there is doubt about the word or sentence that immediately precedes.

---

1. For evidence for the authorship and date of these treatises, see *Menander Rhetor*, xxxiv–xl.

The Talk

The 'talk' form is extremely useful to a sophist. It seems to fall under two kinds of rhetoric, the deliberative and the epideictic, for it fulfils the needs of both. If we wish to praise a ruler, it yields abundant store of encomia: we can indicate his justice, wisdom, and other virtues in the form of a talk. We can also easily give advice in this form to the whole city and all our audience and (if we wish) to a governor who attends the delivery of the speech. Nor is there anything to prevent one revealing to the audience in a 'talk' some anger or pain or pleasure of one's own. It is possible also to give the whole thought a special slant by making a jest of it or trying to satirize (?) someone's character or finding fault with his way of life, or something like that.

We shall give examples of this and then endeavour to explain the other features of this kind of composition.

Let us assume we are to deliver an encomium of a provincial governor in 'talk' form. We shall investigate his attitude to the emperors, to the construction of cities and public buildings, to the trials of private individuals, and also what he is like in himself—whether affable and gentle, or severe and reserved. We shall find an example to illustrate this, an old story or one of our own invention, so as not to appear to be dealing in bare facts, in which there is no charm. The 'talk' indeed likes sweetness and the delicacy attained by narratives. A speech may be lent 'sweetness' by the insertion of examples making the speaker's intentions clear, and by the choice of stories which are very agreeable to the audience to learn, e.g. stories about the gods, showing how their nature is to take thought for mankind, or a reference to Heracles and how he always obeyed the commands of Zeus and laboured for the life of men, extirpating the unjust and setting up the good to care for cities; or again, how Agesilaus obeyed the Lacedaemonians' orders, ruled Ionia and the Hellespont brilliantly, and was so much admired that he was garlanded and pelted with flowers by his subjects when he visited the cities. Herodotus' history is full of pleasant narratives. In these, every kind of charm is added to the writing, not only by the novelty of the stories, but also as a result of a certain type of word-arrangement, when the style employed is not rough or periodic or argumentative, but simpler and plainer, like the casual and unelaborate manner of Xenophon, Nicostratus, Dio Chrysostom, and the Philostratus who wrote the *Heroicus* and the *Pictures*. One may also invent dreams or claim to have heard some report and want to pass it on to the audience: e.g. (i) dreams: suppose I were to say: 'Hermes appeared to me by night and bade me proclaim the best of governors; it is in obedience to his commands that I shall proclaim in the midst of the theatre what I heard him say'; (ii) hearing a report: one might say: 'someone from a neighbouring city told me of many wonderful qualities, which I should like to tell you about, if you have the time to listen.'

You can give advice in 'talk' form about concord to a city, to your audience, to friends, or to persons engaged in political opposition and disturbance, urging them to bring themselves together in mutual goodwill. You should sometimes advise them to be willing to listen to speeches, if you know them to have a distaste for literature and to be reluctant to meet. You may express your feelings, saying for example that audiences do

Menander Rhetor, *The Talk*, in *Menander Rhetor*, ed. and trans. D. A. Russell and N. G. Wilson, Oxford: Oxford University Press, 1981. Reprinted by permission of Oxford University Press.

not often invite you or make you speak; you can invent some such fable as this: 'Apollo was for ever prophesying at the tripods; he had seized Castalia and Delphi and was filling the prophets with the spirit of divination. But he was neglecting the Muses. The Muses were therefore distressed, and asked why he did not share in the dances on Helicon with them, but prophesied in his shrine apart [from the Muses] and longed rather for his tripods.' You can say also, with figurative reference to yourself and to your audience: 'Zeus blamed the Muses for not encouraging Apollo to dance with them and strike his lyre.' You should also make your pleasure obvious to the audience, when you accept their attention as critical hearers, by saying that you are pleased to see such an attitude, just as Isocrates was pleased when he read his *Panegyric* to the Greeks at Olympia and saw that they evidently appreciated the grandeur of the speech. You should often ridicule or find fault, but without mentioning names, sketching the personality, if you so wish, and criticizing the character. Just as in praising it proved possible to ground encomia on any virtue, so it is possible here to criticize and find fault on the ground of any vice, as desired. It is sometimes possible also to take a defensive line and make the hearer favourably disposed towards the public appearance one is about to make, often by speaking with disarming moderation—'the cicada mimics the singing birds'—but often also by asking pardon, alleging that one's work is extemporized, or that one is offering one's country and fellow citizens the first-fruits of a literary career, as farmers offer their harvest festival to Demeter and Dionysus.

It is also to be noted, as a general principle, that a 'talk' does not aim to preserve a regular order as other speeches do, but allows the treatment of the subject to be disorderly. You can put anything you please in first or second place. The best arrangement in a 'talk' is to avoid proceeding always on the same track, but to display continuous disorder. One moment, you may praise the subject on the basis of origin, the next on intention, the next on recent events that have affected him; sometimes again on the basis of fortune, sometimes on a single action. But enough of this; other points also may be made. (?)

You may also address your native city on returning after a long absence, and beholding it with great joy. In these circumstances, you should quote the lines of Homer—'he kissed the fertile ground', 'rejoicing in his native land'—and greet the audience in your speech both collectively and individually, though without mentioning names, and in such a way as not to give a name openly, but to express pleasure at seeing as old men those whom you left in the prime of life, as grown men those you left as students, and as youths those you left as children. Again: 'Nothing is sweeter than one's fatherland and parents.'

(We should note as a general rule about the 'talk' that we are able to express any subject we choose in this medium, without observing any technical rules of order, but taking things as they occur, so long as we aim to make each point at the proper time and understand what it is expedient to put in first or second place.)

You should also mention Athens itself, the place you are coming from: the hierophants and torch-bearers, the Panathenaea, the contests of literature, the Museums, the teachers, and the young people. These themes afford much 'sweetness'. You should also list outstanding lyre-players—Orpheus, Arion, Amphion—and notable flute-players and prophets, and indeed the successes of famous artists generally. You can mention famous mountains also—Olympus, Pieria, Ida, Helicon, Parnassus; these give much charm to the 'talk' form. There should also be a good deal about Dionysus and the Dances, Silenuses and Satyrs, the river of Ocean, the Nile, Ister, Achelous, Eurymedon, and Tiber, and other famous rivers. Very useful for the 'talk', as for many other and varied educational uses, are Plutarch's *Lives*. They are full of stories, apophthegms, and proverbs; it is useful to use these as ingredients of talks, so that we can get pleasure from them all. We should also look for metamorphoses of plants, birds[, and trees]. The poet Nestor and some sophists have written metamorphoses of plants and birds, and it is extremely profitable to read these writings. You must also remember the famous poets, Homer, Hesiod, and the lyricists. They deserve to be recalled for their own sake; but they have also praised and blamed many persons, from whom you will be able to draw examples. (Nor should you neglect Archilochus; he punished his enemies very adequately in his poetry, so that you will be able to make good use of him when you want to criticize people.) These poets are excellent as people—they always associated with kings and tyrants and gave very good advice; and quotations and reminiscences of their poetry are also excellent, because they have 'sweetness' and are very suitable for lending your writing charm.

I have now explained sufficiently how it is possible to praise, blame, [encourage, and] dissuade in the medium of the 'talk', and how this may also be used to express mental attitudes of one's own, such as pain, pleasure, anger, etc. The point has also been made that the type of style should be simple, plain, and unadorned. We have learned that the form allows no order laid down by rule. Let us add now that 'talks' must not be long, unless one intends that they should form the entirety of the performance. Proportion is a good thing, while the garrulous waste of words involved in piling historical instance on historical instance, myth on myth, and narrative on narrative, is acknowledged to be in bad taste.

There is also the 'valedictory talk' (*suntaktikē lalia*); e.g. if, being about to sail from Athens to our home city, or again from our home city to Athens, we express our distress at departure, indicating our (?) grief; we must then proceed to formal encomia of the city we are about to leave. For example, with reference to Athens: 'Who would choose to leave without a tear the mysteries, the sacred proclamations enjoining the march to Eleusis and back from Eleusis to the city? Who could endure to leave behind the beauty of that acropolis, the festivals of Dionysus, the Panathenaea, the chosen men, fosterlings of wisdom and virtue?' And so we can fit in all the glories of the city, the beauty of the buildings, the magnificence of the festivals.

It is also possible to deliver a talk on arrival, at the moment of landing in one's native city, as mentioned above in connection with the Homeric quotations. In such a talk, the speaker must at all costs display his love for the city, starting from the present moment, and saying how joyful and happy he is to have sailed into the harbour, how he has seen the beauty of the countryside, how he has gone up to the acropolis, how he has embraced his fellow citizens, one and all, in deed and in word, how he thinks all his contemporaries his brothers, and the rest his father's brothers, and the whole city one family, and how he never forgot his native city on his travels. Add also 'Let me now (?) describe its special glories, those which do not belong to other cities', and then proceed to an encomium of the governor if he is present, and to one of your father (?) or the political life of the city: 'Who would not long for a political life in which there is concord and friendship, and all men are joined in virtue . . .?' and so on.

The usefulness of the talk is indeed manifold: it can elaborate every subject appropriate to an orator.

Basil

As the father of eastern monasticism, St. Basil (A.D. 330–79) is honored in both the Orthodox and Catholic churches. Born in Caesarea in the province of Cappadocia, he taught rhetoric before becoming a Christian. Turning to a life of asceticism, he was ordained bishop of Caesarea in 370. Soon Basil was already being referred to as "the Great," and from his position at the center of both intellectual and ecclesiastical scholarship, he produced an enormous number of letters, homilies, theological treatises, and works on asceticism.

Basil transformed the rhetorical practices he had inherited from the second sophistic into a "theology of the literary *logos*." As George L. Kustas explains, Basil provided a religious foundation for epideictic rhetoric, thus establishing a "full Christian language that, no longer limited to genre, such as apology or historiography, could evoke and respond to the full beauty of the Christian message as a whole. It is this language that came to serve as a model for all subsequent cultivated Christian speech."[1]

St. Basil's address *To Young Men on Reading Greek Literature* became the "charter of all Christian higher education for centuries to come."[2] Written by Basil when he was an old man, it advises young Christians to read Greek literature not only as a preparation for studying the Bible but also for its inherent value. What we have reprinted below is the section of his essay that tells how to read the pagan classics.

1. 231.
2. Jaeger, 81.

To Young Men on Reading Greek Literature

4   But that this pagan learning is not without usefulness for the soul has been sufficiently affirmed; yet just how you should participate in it would be the next topic to be discussed.

First, then, as to the learning to be derived from the poets, that I may begin with them, inasmuch as the subjects they deal with are of every kind, you ought not to give your attention to all they write without exception; but whenever they recount for you the deeds or words of good men, you ought to cherish and emulate these and try to be as far as possible like them; but when they treat of wicked men, you ought to avoid such imitation, stopping your ears no less than Odysseus did, according to what those same poets say, when he avoided the songs of the Sirens. For familiarity with evil words is, as it were, a road leading to evil deeds. On this account, then, the soul must be watched over with all vigilance, lest through the pleasure the poets' words give we may unwittingly accept something of the more evil sort, like those who take poisons along with honey. We shall not, therefore, praise the poets when they revile or mock, or when they depict men engaged in amours or drunken, or when they define happiness in terms of an over-abundant table or dissolute songs. But least of all shall we give attention to them when they narrate anything about the gods, and especially when they speak of them as being many, and these too not even in accord with one another. For in their poems brother is at feud with brother, and father with children, and the latter in turn are engaged in truceless war with their parents. But the adulteries of gods and their amours and their sexual acts in public, and especially those of Zeus, the chief and highest of all, as they themselves describe him, actions which one would blush to mention of even brute beasts—all these we shall leave to the stage-folk.

These same observations I must make concerning the writers of prose also, and especially when they fabricate tales for the entertainment of their hearers. And we shall certainly not imitate the orators in their art of lying. For neither in courts of law nor in other affairs is lying befitting to us, who have chosen the right and true way of life, and to whom refraining from litigation has been ordained in commandment. But we shall take rather those passages of theirs in which they have praised virtue or condemned vice. For just as in the case of other beings enjoyment of flowers is limited to their fragrance and colour, but the bees, as we see, possess the power to get honey from them as well, so it is possible here also for those who are pursuing not merely what is sweet and pleasant in such writings to store away from them some benefit also for their souls. It is, therefore, in accordance with the whole similitude of the bees, that we should participate in the pagan literature. For these neither approach all flowers equally, nor in truth do they attempt to carry off entire those upon which they alight, but taking only so much of them as is suitable for their work, they suffer the rest to go untouched. We ourselves too, if we are wise, having appropriated from this literature what is suitable to us and akin to the truth, will pass over the remainder. And just as in

Reprinted by permission of the publishers and The Loeb Classical Library from Basil, *Address to Young Men on Reading Greek Literature* (4–7), trans. Roy Joseph Deferrari and Martin R. P. McGuire, in Saint Basil, *The Letters*, vol. 4, Cambridge, Mass.: Harvard University Press, 1950.

plucking the blooms from a rose-bed we avoid the thorns, so also in garnering from such writings whatever is useful, let us guard ourselves against what is harmful. At the very outset, therefore, we should examine each of the branches of knowledge and adapt it to our end, according to the Doric proverb, "bringing the stone to the line."

And since it is through virtue that we must enter upon this life of ours, and since much has been uttered in praise of virtue by poets, much by historians, and much more still by philosophers, we ought especially to apply ourselves to such literature. For it is no small advantage that a certain intimacy and familiarity with virtue should be engendered in the souls of the young, seeing that the lessons learned by such are likely, in the nature of the case, to be indelible, having been deeply impressed in them by reason of the tenderness of their souls. Or what else are we to suppose Hesiod had in mind when he composed these verses which are on everybody's lips, if he were not exhorting young men to virtue?—that "rough at first and hard to travel, and full of abundant sweat and toil, is the road which leads to virtue, and steep withal." Therefore it is not given to everyone to climb this road, so steep it is, nor, if one essays to climb it, easily to reach the summit. But when once one has come to the top he is able to see how smooth and beautiful, how easy and pleasant to travel it is, and more agreeable than that other road which leads to vice, which it is possible to take all at once from near at hand, as this same poet has said. For to me it seems that he has narrated these things for no other reason than to urge us on to virtue and to exhort all men to be good, and to keep us from becoming weak and cowardly in the face of the toils and desisting before reaching the end. And assuredly, if anyone else has sung the praise of virtue in terms like Hesiod's, let us welcome his words as leading to the same end as our own.

Moreover, as I myself have heard a man say who is clever at understanding a poet's mind, all Homer's poetry is an encomium of virtue, and all he wrote, save what is accessory, bears to this end, and not least in those verses in which he has portrayed the leader of the Cephallenians, after being saved from shipwreck, as naked, and the princess as having first shown him reverence at the mere sight of him (so far was he from incurring shame through merely being seen naked, since the poet has portrayed him as clothed with virtue in place of garments), and then, furthermore, Odysseus as having been considered worthy of such high honour by the rest of the Phaeacians likewise that, disregarding the luxury in which they lived, they one and all admired and envied the hero, and none of the Phaeacians at the moment would have desired anything else more than to become Odysseus, and that too just saved from a shipwreck. For in these passages, the interpreter of the poet's mind was wont to declare that Homer says in a voice that all but shouts: "You must give heed unto virtue, O men, which swims forth even with a man who has suffered shipwreck, and, on his coming naked to land, will render him more honoured than the happy Phaeacians." And truly this is so. Other possessions, in fact, no more belong to their possessors than to any chance comer whatever, quickly shifting now here, now there, as in a game of dice; but virtue alone of possessions cannot be taken away, as it remains with a man whether he be living or dead. It was for this reason indeed, as it seems to me, that Solon said this with respect to the rich: "But we will not exchange with them our virtue for their

5

wealth, since the one abides always, while riches change their owners every day." And similar to these words are those of Theognis also in which he says that God, whomsoever he means indeed by this term, inclines the scale for men at one time this way, at another that way, now to be rich, but now to have nothing.

And furthermore, the sophist from Ceos, Prodicus, somewhere in his writings uttered a doctrine kindred to these others regarding virtue and vice; therefore we must apply our minds to him also, for he is not a man to be rejected. His narrative runs something like this, so far as I recall the man's thought, since I do not know the exact words, but only that he spoke in general to the following effect, not employing metre. When Heracles was quite a young man and was nearly of the age at which you yourselves are now, while he was deliberating which of the two roads he should take, the one leading through toils to virtue, or the easiest, two women approached him, and these were Virtue and Vice. Now at once, although they were silent, the difference between them was evident from their appearance. For the one had been decked out for beauty through the art of toiletry, and was overflowing with voluptuousness, and she was leading a whole swarm of pleasures in her train; now these things she displayed, and promising still more than these she tried to draw Heracles to her. But the other was withered and squalid, and had an intense look, and spoke quite differently; for she promised nothing dissolute or pleasant, but countless sweating toils and labours and dangers through every land and sea. But the prize to be won by these was to become a god, as the narrative of Prodicus expressed it; and it was this second woman that Heracles in the end followed.

6   And almost all the writers who have some reputation for wisdom have, to a greater or less degree, each to the best of his power, discoursed in their works in praise of virtue. To these men we must hearken and we must try to show forth their words in our lives; for he in truth who confirms by act his devotion to wisdom, which among others is confined to words, "He alone has understanding, but the others flit about as shadows."

It seems to me that such harmony between profession and life is very much as if a painter had made a likeness of a man of quite wondrous beauty, and this same man should be such in reality as the painter had portrayed him on his panels. For brilliantly to praise virtue in public, and to make long speeches about it, but in private to rate pleasure before temperance, and self-interest before justice, resembles, as I would assert, those stage-folk who bring out plays and often appear as kings and potentates, although they are neither kings nor potentates, and perhaps not even free men at all. Again, a musician would not willingly consent that his lyre should be out of tune, nor a leader of a chorus that his chorus should not sing in the strictest possible harmony; but shall each individual person be at variance with himself, and shall he exhibit a life not at all in agreement with his words? But one will say, quoting Euripides, "the tongue has sworn, but the mind is unsworn," and the appearance of being good will be his aim instead of being good. Yet this is the last extreme of injustice, if we are to hearken to the words of Plato—"to appear to be just without being so."

7   As to the passages in literature, then, which contain admonitions of excellent things, let us accept this procedure. And since the virtuous deeds, likewise, of the men of old have been preserved for us, either through an unbroken oral tradition

or through being preserved in the words of poets or writers of prose, let us not fail to derive advantage from this source also. For example, a certain fellow, a market-lounger, kept railing at Pericles, but he paid no attention; and he kept it up all day long, he giving Pericles a merciless dressing of abuse, but he taking no heed of it. Then, when it was already evening and dark, though the man was scarcely desisting, Pericles escorted him home with a light, lest his own schooling in philosophy be utterly brought to naught. Again, a certain man, having become enraged against Eucleides of Megara, threatened him with death and took oath upon it; but Eucleides took a counter-oath, to the effect that verily he would appease the man and make him put aside his wrath against him. How very valuable it is that an example of this kind should be recalled to memory by a man who is on the point of being held in the grip of a fit of passion! For one must not put a simple-minded trust in the tragedy when it says "Against enemies anger arms the hand," but, on the contrary, we should not permit ourselves to be aroused to anger at all; but if this is not easy to achieve, we should at least apply reason to our anger as a sort of curb and not allow it to be carried too far beyond the bounds.

But let us bring our discussion back again to the examples of virtuous deeds. A certain man kept striking Socrates, son of Sophroniscus, full in the face, falling upon him unmercifully; yet he did not oppose, but permitted the wine-mad fellow to satiate his rage, so that his face was presently swollen and bruised from the blows. Now when the man ceased striking him, Socrates, it is said, did nothing except inscribe on his own forehead, like the name of the sculptor on a statue, "So-and-so (naming the man) made this," and only to that extent avenged himself. Since these examples tend to nearly the same end as our own precepts, I maintain that it is of great value for those of your age to imitate them. For this example of Socrates is akin to that precept of ours—that to him who strikes us on the cheek, so far from avenging ourselves upon him we should offer the other cheek also. And the example of Pericles or Eucleides is akin to the precept that we should submit to those who persecute us and gently suffer their anger; and this other one—that we should pray for blessings for our enemies instead of cursing them. For whoever has been instructed in these examples beforehand cannot after that distrust those precepts as utterly impossible to obey. I should not pass over the example of Alexander, who, when he had taken prisoner the daughters of Darius, although it had been testified to him that they possessed a marvellous beauty, did not think it fitting even to look upon them, judging it to be disgraceful for one who had captured men to be vanquished by women. Indeed, this example tends to the same purport as that well-known precept of ours—that he who looks upon a woman to enjoy her, although he does not commit adultery in act, yet in truth, because he has received the desire into his soul, is not free of guilt. But as for the action of Cleinias, one of the disciples of Pythagoras, it is difficult to believe that it is by mere chance that it coincides with our own principles, and not through its imitating them designedly. What was it, then, that Cleinias did? Although it was possible by taking oath to escape a fine of three talents, he paid rather than swear, and that too though it would have been a true oath that he would have taken. He must have heard, it seems to me, our commandment forbidding the taking of an oath.

Augustine

Augustine (A.D. 354–430) was already an accomplished teacher of rhetoric before he embraced Christianity. He became bishop of Hippo in 395 and authored a large number of treatises, dialogues, sermons, and refutations of heresies. In his most famous work, the *Confessions*, he explains his conversion from rhetoric and philosophy to Christianity.

On Christian Doctrine or *De Doctrina Christiana* contains Augustine's advice to preachers on how to interpret the scriptures. He feels that they should learn the art of rhetoric in order to equip themselves to instruct and strengthen the faith of their audiences. Unlike earlier Christian rhetoricians such as Tertullian, who were suspicious of pagan authorities, Augustine's scholarship grew out of continuous immersion in both cultures.[1] Thus the "great virtue of *De Doctrina Christiana* is that it made it possible for Christians to appreciate and teach eloquence without associating it with paganism."[2]

Augustine divided *On Christian Doctrine* into four books, but it is easier to follow his own advice and regard the treatise as consisting of two parts. The first part, Books 1–3, tells the preacher how to discover the truths that are in the Bible. In this section, Augustine touches upon such topics as semiotics, translation, ambiguity, and the rules of inference. His main concern is that such pagan "treasures" as history, the theory of tropes, and Platonic philosophy should be "seized and held to be converted to Christian uses" (2.40.60).

In Book 4, the second part of *On Christian Doctrine*, Augustine explains how the preacher should express the insights he has discovered from the scriptures or how he should teach what he has learned. The selections below reprint three keys excerpts from Book 4. The first, from the beginning of Book 4, justifies the use of rhetoric by the Christian preacher. The second explains why preachers should be guided by the three Ciceronian principles: to teach, to delight, and to persuade. The final excerpt, which is the conclusion of *On Christian Doctrine*, tells how the preacher should adapt his style to both his aim and his audience.

1. Hagendahl, 15.
2. Kennedy, *Classical Rhetoric*, 159.

On Christian Doctrine

This work of mine, entitled "Christian Teaching", I had, according to my first   4.1
arrangement, divided into a certain two parts. For after the introduction, in
which I answered those who were likely to be critical, I said: "There are two things
upon which every treatment of the Scriptures depends: the means of discovering
what the thought may be, and the means of expressing what the thought is. We
shall discuss first the discovery of the thought, then its expression." And so,
because we have already spoken at length on the discovery of the thought, and
have finished three books on this part alone, we shall, with the help of God, speak
in brief on the expression of the thought, so as, if possible, to include all in one
book, and to finish this whole work in four sections.

And so, first, in this introduction, I wish to put down the hopes of readers who,
it may be, think that I am going to set forth the rules of rhetoric which I learned
and taught in the public schools, and I wish to warn them not to look for this from
me, not because such things have no utility, but because, if they have any, it must
be got elsewhere if perchance a worthy person have time to learn even such things;
but this must not be required of me, either in this work or in any other.

For since through the art of rhetoric both truth and falsehood are pleaded, who   2
would be so bold as to say that against falsehood, truth as regards its own defenders
ought to stand unarmed, so that, forsooth, those who attempt to plead false causes
know from the beginning how to make their audience well-disposed, attentive,
and docile, while the others remain ignorant of it; so that the former utter their lies
concisely, clearly, with the appearance of truth, and the latter state the truth in a
way that is wearisome to listen to, not clear to understand, and finally, not
pleasant to believe; so that one side, by fallacious arguments, attacks truth and
propounds falsehood, the other has no skill either in defending the true, or
refuting the false; so that the one, moving and impelling the minds of the
audience to error by the force of its oratory, now strikes them with terror, now
saddens them, now enlivens them, now ardently arouses them, but the other in
the cause of truth is sluggish and cold and falls asleep! Who is so foolish as to be
thus wise? Since, therefore, there has been placed equally at our disposal the
power of eloquence, which is so efficacious in pleading either for the erroneous
cause or the right, why is it not zealously acquired by the good, so as to do service
for the truth, if the unrighteous put it to the uses of iniquity and of error for the
winning of false and groundless causes?

But, whatever the rules and precepts are on this subject, which, with the   3
addition of adroit oral practice in the use of a large vocabulary and rich diction,
result in what we term eloquence, or oratory, they must be acquired by those who
can do so quickly, outside of this treatise of ours, at a proper and fitting age, when
a suitable amount of time has been set aside for them. For even the very masters of
Roman eloquence themselves have not hesitated to say that no one can ever

Reprinted by permission of the publishers from Augustine, *On Christine Doctrine* (4.1–6, 4.9–19,
4.22–31), trans. Sister Therese Sullivan, Washington, D.C.: Catholic University of America Press,
1930.

acquire this art at all unless he do so quickly. What need is there to question the truth of this? For even if these rules can at length finally be mastered by the plodder, we do not consider them of such value that we wish the mature, or even the later years of life, to be spent in their acquisition. It is enough that this be the concern of the young, and not even of all whom we wish trained for service in the Church, but of those whose attention is not required by a more pressing duty, and one which ought unquestionably to take precedence of this study. For in the case of a keen and ardent nature, eloquence will come more readily through reading and hearing the eloquent, than through pursuing the rules of eloquence. Nor is the Church wanting in its own literature, even apart from the Canon which is with saving grace fixed in the place of supreme authority; and if a man of ability use this literature, although he has no further aim, but is occupied only with the matter which he finds there, even while he is attending to this alone, he becomes imbued with the eloquence of its diction. This is even especially the case if he adds practice in writing, or dictating, or too, even in speaking his views as guided by the rule of righteousness and faith. But if such ability be wanting, either the precepts of rhetoric will not be grasped, or if by dint of great labor they are grasped to some degree at least, they will be of no avail. For indeed even the very ones who have learned them, and express themselves fluently and elegantly, cannot all, when they are talking, think of these rules, in order to speak in accordance with them, unless the discussion be on the rules themselves. Nay more, I believe there are scarcely any who can do both things, viz., speak well, and in order to do so, think of the rules of oratory while speaking. For they have to be careful not to forget what they want to say, while they are attending to saying it according to theory. And yet, the rules of eloquence are found fully exemplified in the speeches and discourses of the eloquent, even though to arrive at that eloquence, or in the midst of that eloquence, these men did not think of them, whether indeed they had ever learned them, or whether perhaps they had not even slightly engaged in them. For they exemplify them because they are eloquent; they do not use them to become eloquent.

Wherefore, as children do not learn to talk except by listening to the talking of those who talk, why cannot men learn to be orators not by studying the rules of oratory, but by reading and listening to the orations of orators, and, in as far as it is possible, by imitating them? Is is not true that in actual experience we find that this is so? For we know many who are more eloquent without the rules of rhetoric than many who have learned them, but none who are eloquent without having read and heard the discussions and speeches of the eloquent. Children, for instance, would not even need the very rules of grammar, through which the purity of speech is attained, if they had the opportunity of growing up and living with men who talked correctly. For though ignorant of the names of mistakes in speech, they would recognize whatever was faulty in the language of another, and would, because of their own good usage, criticise it and guard against it; just as city people, even when unlettered, criticise country people.

4   It is the duty, then, of the student and teacher of the Holy Scriptures, who is the defender of the true Faith, and the opponent of error, both to teach what is right, and to correct what is wrong; and in this function of discourse, to conciliate the

hostile, to arouse the careless, and to inform those ignorant of the matter in hand, what they ought to expect. But when he finds his audience kindly disposed, attentive, and docile, or when he has himself made them so, the rest must be carried out as each case demands. If his hearers need information, the matter under discussion must be made clear by giving the history of the question, if indeed that is wanting. On the other hand, to make clear a doubtful matter, there is need of argument and the presentation of evidence. But if the audience needs to be aroused rather than to be informed, in order that they may not be slow in living up to what they already know, and that they may give their assent to what they are convinced is true, greater powers of oratory are required. In such a case, entreaties and reproaches, exhortations and compulsion, and every other means conductive to stirring the heart, are necessary. And indeed, every one of the methods which I have enumerated are continually made use of by nearly all men in their efforts in speaking.

But as some do this bluntly, inelegantly, and coldly, while others, with tact, elegance, and force, the important thing now is that the instruction of which we speak, be made the business of one who, even though he has no powers of eloquence, does possess *wisdom* in arguing and speaking, so that he may do good to his audience, even though that be less than if he could at the same time use eloquence in speaking. But a man who has merely an empty flow of eloquence, ought to be the more guarded against as he is the more pleasing to his audience in those matters which have no expedience, and as, since his audience hears him speak with fluency, it judges that he likewise speaks with truth. This view, indeed, did not escape even those who considered rhetorical training necessary, for they hold that wisdom without eloquence is of small avail to a country, but that eloquence without wisdom is generally a great hindrance, and never a help [Cicero *De Inventione* 1.1.1]. If, therefore, those who have given us the rules of oratory, in the very books in which they have treated this subject are forced through the urgency of truth to make this confession, ignorant as they are of the true, that is, of the supernal wisdom which comes down from the Father of lights, how much more are we, who are the children and the ministers of this wisdom, under obligation to hold no other opinion! But a man speaks with more or less wisdom as he is the more or less versed in the Holy Scriptures—I do not mean in the very copious reading and memorizing of them, but in the true understanding and the careful investigation of their meaning. For there are some who read them, but indifferently; they read them in order to memorize them, but they are indifferent to understanding them. There can be no question but that they by far deserve the preference who know them less, word for word, but who look into the heart of the Scriptures, with the eyes of their own hearts. But he is better than either of these, who both quotes them at will, and understands them as he ought.

And so, for one who should speak with wisdom, even for the very reason that he cannot do so with eloquence, it is absolutely necessary that he remember the words of the Scriptures. For in as much as he sees himself poor in his own resources, in so much the more does it behoove him to be rich in those of the Scriptures, that what he says in his own words, he may prove by the Scriptures; and that he who was of little importance in his own words may gain, in some

5

measure, from the authority of the great. For by his proofs he satisfies, even though he cannot satisfy by his bare statements. Furthermore, the man who wishes to speak not only with wisdom but also with eloquence, since indeed he will do more good if he be able to do both, I rather send to read or hear the eloquent, and to imitate them by practice, than advise to give his time to professors of rhetoric; on this condition, however, that those who are read and heard be recommended, in all truth, as men who have spoken and who speak not only with eloquence, but also with wisdom. For those who speak eloquently are listened to with pleasure; those who speak with wisdom are heard with profit. Wherefore, the Scripture does not say, "The multitude of the eloquent," but *The multitude of the wise is the welfare of the whole world.* But as often even bitter medicine must be taken, so always harmful sweets must be avoided. Still, what is better than wholesome sweets or sweet wholesomeness? For the greater the desire of sweets in such a case, the more readily does their wholesomeness prove beneficial. So there are churchmen who have expounded Sacred Scripture not only with wisdom, but also with eloquence; and for reading these, students and those at leisure have not sufficient time in which to exhaust them.

6   Here, someone perhaps may ask whether our authors, whose divinely inspired writings, with saving authority, make up the Canon for us, should be ranked merely as wise, or also as eloquent men. For myself, and for those whose opinions are the same as mine, this question is, of course, easily settled. For when I understand them, it seems to me that nothing can have more wisdom or even more eloquence. And I venture to state this also, that all who rightly understand what these writers say, understand too that they could not have spoken otherwise. For as there is a certain eloquence which is more becoming to youth, and a certain one to old age; and as eloquence does not deserve the name, if it be not in accord with the person who speaks, so there is a certain eloquence suitable to men especially worthy of the highest authority, and who are clearly inspired. With such eloquence have our authors spoken. No other is fitting to them, nor is theirs, to others; for it perfectly accords with them; but as it seems the more lowly, so it the more highly transcends others, not by its inflation, but by its solidity. Where, however, I do not understand these writers, then indeed their eloquence is less apparent to me, but still I doubt not but that it is such as it is where I do understand them. Indeed, that very obscurity of the divine and saving writings had, of necessity, to be mingled with such eloquence whereby our minds should profit, not only through the working out of their meaning, but also through the practice of their art.

All the merits and beauties of eloquence, about which those critics are puffed up, who, not because of its real greatness, but because of its bombast, prefer their own language to the language of our writers, I could, if there were time, point out in the Sacred Writings of those whom Divine Providence has provided to instruct us, and to bring us from this corrupt world to the world of the blessed. But it is not the points which they have in common with the pagan orators and poets that please me more than I can say, in their eloquence; what I admire and wonder at more, is that they so use our eloquence, through another kind of eloquence, as it were, of their own, that ours is not wanting to them, and still is not conspicuous in them, for it would not be fitting for them either to reject it, or to flaunt it. The former would be the case if they avoided it, the latter might be imputed to them if they made it too noticeable. And in those places where it happens to be recognized by scholars, the subject-matter is such that the words in which it is expressed seem not to have been sought out by the writer, but seem to belong naturally to the matter itself, as if, to express a comparison, wisdom came forth from its own dwelling-place, that is, from the heart of the wise man, and eloquence, its inseparable handmaid, followed, even though uninvited.

There are some matters, which in their true force are not intelligible, or scarcely   4.9
intelligible, no matter how great the eloquence, nor how extended nor how clear the speaker's explanation. Such matters should be put before a popular assembly either rarely, if necessity urges, or not at all. In books, however, which are so written that they, so to speak, hold the reader to themselves, when they are intelligible, or when they are not intelligible are still not a burden to those who do not wish to read them, and in conversations with others, the duty ought not to be neglected of bringing the truth—though it may be most difficult to understand, which we, however, have already grasped—to the understanding of others, no matter what the labor of discussion, provided that the listener or interlocutor have the desire to be informed, and that mental capacity be not wanting to enable him to receive the information in whatever manner presented, the instructor attending not to the degree of eloquence with which he teaches, but to the degree of clearness.

A studied leaning toward such clearness, at times neglects the more elegant   10
expression, and has no concern for what sounds well, but for what tells and explains well what one aims to point out. And so it is that a certain authority says, in treating of such kind of speech, that it possesses a kind of careful negligence. Still, while this discountenances florid expressions, it does not countenance vulgar ones. And yet good teachers have, or ought to have such care in teaching that a word which cannot be expressed in good Latin except obscurely and ambiguously, but which as given in the common idiom, has neither ambiguity nor obscurity, should be expressed not as the cultured, but rather as the uncultured are wont to express it. For if our translators have not hesitated to say, *I will not gather together their meetings for blood offerings*, since they consider that the subject matter called for the plural use of the noun in this place, though in good Latin this word is used only in the singular, then why should a teacher of righteousness when addressing the unlettered, hesitate to use *ossum* for *os* for fear lest this word might be understood as coming not from the same form as *ossa*, but from the same form as *ora*, since the African ear does not distinguish between short and long vowels? For what is good of correctness of speech if the understanding of the hearer does not follow it, since there is absolutely no reason for speaking if they for whose instruction we speak are not instructed by our speaking. And so, one who teaches will avoid all words which do not teach; and if in place of them he can use other correct expressions which are intelligible, he will choose these by preference, but if he cannot, either because they do not exist, or because they do not occur to him at the moment, he will use words even less correct, provided, however, that the matter itself be taught and learned correctly.

And this indeed must be insisted upon, that we may be understood, not only in conversations with one person or with several, but also much more when a sermon is being delivered before assemblies. For in conversations, each one has the opportunity of questioning; but when all are quiet, that one may be heard, and all are turned toward him with fixed attention, then it is neither customary nor proper for any one to ask about what he has not understood, and for this reason it should be the special concern of the speaker to assist the silent listener. But an assembly eager to learn generally shows by some movement whether it has understood, and until it does show this, the matter in hand ought to be presented in many different forms; but this they have not the power of doing who deliver word for word what they have prepared and committed to memory. However, as soon as it is clear that the matter has been understood, the discourse ought to be ended, or to pass on to other things. For though one gives pleasure when he clears up matters that need to be made understood, he becomes wearisome when he keeps hammering at things which are already understood, at least to those men whose whole expectation was centered in the solution of the difficulty in the matter under discussion. It is true that for the sake of giving pleasure, even well-known things are talked over; when, not the facts themselves, but the manner in which they are expressed, holds the attention. And if this itself also is now well known, and is popular with the audience, it makes almost no difference whether the man talking be a speaker or a reader. For generally, things which are attractively written are also read with pleasure, not only by those who come to know them for the first time; but even by those who have already made their acquaintance, and from whose memory they have not yet been effaced, are they reread not without pleasure; or they are listened to willingly by both classes. On the other hand, what a person has forgotten, when it is recalled to him, he learns again. But I am not now treating of how to please; I am speaking of how they are to be taught who desire instruction. That, indeed, is the best method, which results in the listener hearing the truth, and understanding what he hears. When this end has been attained, then there should be no further effort toward expounding the matter longer, as it were, but perhaps toward commending it, so that it may be fixed deep in the heart; but if it seem that this ought to be done, it must be done with such moderation as not to lead to weariness.

11   This, of course, is eloquence in teaching, whereby the result is attained in speaking, not that what was distasteful becomes pleasing, nor that what one was unwilling to do is done, but that what was obscure becomes clear. Still, if this be done in an unpleasing manner, its fruit falls to the very few zealous persons, forsooth, who are eager for the knowledge which is proposed for instruction, no matter how meanly and inelegantly it be explained. When they have once gained this end, they feast upon the truth itself with delight; and it is the fine characteristic of great minds that they love the truth in words, not just the words. For what is the use of a golden key if it cannot open what we want it to? Or what is the objection to a wooden one if it can do so, since we are asking nothing save that what is closed be opened? But as eating and learning have a certain similarity one to the other, because of the natural fastidiousness of most people, even the very food which is necessary for life's sustenance must have seasoning.

And so, a well-known orator has said, and has said truly that an orator ought to speak in such a way as to instruct, to please, and to persuade. Then he adds, "Instructing belongs to necessity; pleasing, to interest; persuading, to victory" [Cicero *Orator* 21.69]. Of these three, that which is given first place, the necessity of instructing, depends upon the things we say; the other two, upon our manner of saying them. Therefore, the man who speaks with the view to instructing, as long as he is not intelligible, should consider that he has not yet said what he wishes to say to the one whom he wishes to instruct. Because, though he has said what he himself understands, he should not be thought yet to have said it to him by whom he has not been understood; if, however, he has been understood, whatever the manner of his having said it, he has said it. But if his aim is also to please the one to whom he speaks, or to persuade him, he will not accomplish it by any manner of speaking whatsoever, but it is of moment how he speaks, in order to accomplish it. Moreover, as a listener must be pleased if his attention is to beheld, so he must be persuaded if he is to be moved to action. And as he is pleased if you speak attractively, so he is persuaded if he likes what you promise, fears what you threaten, hates what you censure, embraces what you command, grieves over what you emphasize as deserving of grief, rejoices when you say something should gladden, sympathizes with those whom you by your words set before his eyes as objects of pity, shuns those whom you with threats consider ought to be avoided — and so on in regard to whatever else in the way of moving the hearts of an audience is possible through powerful eloquence, not that they may know what they must do, but that they may do what they already know they ought to do.

But if they do not yet know this, instruction must, of course, precede persuasion. And perhaps, when the facts themselves have been learned, they will be so far moved, that there will be no longer need that they be moved by greater powers of eloquence. However, when there is need, this must be used; but there is then need when, although they know what they ought to do, they do not do it. And for this reason, instruction is of necessity. For men have the liberty of doing or not doing the things they know. But who would say that they ought to do what they do not know? And so it is that persuasion is not of necessity, because there is not always need of it if only the listener is in agreement with the one who is instructing, or also pleasing. But so it is that persuasion is of victory, because there is the possibility that a person may be instructed, and pleased, and still not give his assent. But what will the two former things avail if the third be lacking. For too, pleasing is not of necessity, since, indeed, when in a speech the truth is pointed out — a thing which belongs to instruction to do — it is not done by using eloquence, nor indeed is attention given to this, to please by the matter or the style itself, but the mere exposition of the truth gives pleasure through its very nature, since it is the truth. Whence it is that many times, even falsehood, when exposed and refuted, is a source of pleasure. For it does not please because it is falsehood, but because it is true that it is falsehood, the very explanation which shows that this is true, is a matter of pleasure.

But because of those whom by reason of their prejudice truth does not satisfy if it is put in any other way than that whereby the speaker's words also are attractive, no small place has been given in oratory even to the art of pleasing. And still,

12

13

when this is added, it is not enough for hardened natures who reap no profit from having understood and having enjoyed the instructor's speech. For what do these two things avail a person who both owns the truth and praises eloquence, but who does not give his assent, although it is for this alone that the speaker in an argument gives close attention to the matter which he is treating? For if the matters taught are such that knowledge of and belief in them are sufficient, agreement with them is nothing more than confessing their truth. But when a line of action is the matter of instruction, and that this be followed is the reason for the instruction, in vain is conviction that the words are true, in vain is the style of the speech pleasing, if action does not follow upon understanding. It is necessary, therefore, that the sacred orator, when urging that something be done, should not only teach in order to instruct, and please in order to hold, but also move in order to win. For indeed, it is only by the heights of eloquence that that man is to be moved to agreement who has not been brought to it by truth, though demonstrated to his own acknowledgment, even when joined with a charming style.

14   And for the sake of this charm, such an amount of trouble has been taken by men, that not only must we not follow, but even we must shun and detest the many abominably wicked and shameful deeds which are urged in this most elegant way by the evil and unjust, not to gain assent for them, but that they may be read eagerly for the mere sake of the pleasure in them. But may God keep from the church what the prophet Jeremias relates of the synagogue, saying: *Fearful and dreadful things have been done in the land. The prophets prophesied falsehoods, and the priests clapped their hands; and my people loved such things: and what will you do in the future?* O eloquence, so much the more terrible as it is so unadorned; and as it is so genuine, so much the more powerful! O truly, an axe hewing the rock! For it was in this similitude that God Himself through this same prophet spoke of His own word, which He has uttered through the holy prophets. Far be it, then, far be it from us, that priests should applaud evil-speakers, and that the people of God should be pleased thereat! Far be such great madness from us, I say, for what shall we do in the future! And assuredly let what is sad be less understood, less pleasing, less moving, but still let it be said; and let righteousness, not evil, gain a willing hearing! But this undoubtedly would not be possible unless it possess charm.

But in a strong people, such as are spoken of by God—*I will praise thee in a strong people*—that charm of style is not pleasing in which, though indeed falsehood is not involved, still, slight and unimportant truths are adorned with a foamy redundancy of expression, such as even great and enduring matters would not fittingly and worthily be adorned with. There is such an instance in one of the letters of the blessed Cyprian, which, I think, so fell out, or was thus done on purpose, in order that succeeding ages might know from what redundancy the soundness of the Christian teaching has recalled his style, and to what more dignified and reticent eloquence it has restricted him; which is such in his succeeding letters that he is safely admired, scrupulously copied, but with difficulty imitated. So he says in a certain passage: "Let us seek for that spot; the neighboring solitudes offer a retreat, where, as the wandering tendrils of the vine-shoots with overhanging interlacings creep along the trellis supports, the covering leaves have formed an arbor of vines." This is certainly expressed with marvellously flowing exuberance of language, but because of its excessive profuseness, it is not pleasing to the serious reader. However, those who admire this style think that of a certainty those who do not express themselves after this manner, but rather keep their eloquence within bounds, cannot thus be eloquent, and not that they avoid such language by preference. For this reason, this holy man shows that he *can* thus express himself, since he has done so in this place, but that he does not *wish* to do so, for nowhere does he do so afterward.

And so, that orator of ours, in speaking of justice, holiness, and a good life, the 15
subjects on which alone he should speak, strives, in as far as possible, when speaking on such subjects, to make his words understood, enjoyed, and persuasive; and this he should not doubt but that he can do if it is possible, and in so far as it is possible, more through the piety of his prayers than through his orator's skill, so that by praying for himself and for those whom he is going to address, he is a petitioner before a speaker. At the very time, then, when he is going to preach, before he loosens his tongue to speak, he should lift up his thirsting soul to God, in order to give forth what he will drink in, and to pour out what he will be filled with. For although one every topic which can be treated according to faith and love, there is much that may be said, and many ways in which it may be said by those versed therein, who knows either what is best for us on a special occasion to say, or what is best that others should hear from us, if it be not He who sees the hearts of all? And who can make us say what we ought, and in the manner we ought to say it, if not He in whose hands are both ourselves and our words? And for this reason the one who would both know and teach should learn, of course, all that he has to teach, and should acquire such skill in speaking as becomes an ecclesiastic; but indeed at the time of the sermon itself he should consider that admonition rather as befitting a good disposition, which the Lord utters: *Take no thought how or what to speak: for it shall be given you in that hour what to speak. For it is not you that speak, but the Spirit of your Father that speaketh in you.* And so, if the Holy Spirit speaks in those who are given over to persecution for the sake of Christ, why will He not do so also in those who give Christ to their disciples?

But if any one says there is no need to lay down rules as to what and how men 16
should teach, since it is the Holy Spirit who forms the teacher, he can say likewise that we do not need to pray, since the Lord says: *Your Father knoweth what is needful for you, before you ask Him,* or that the Apostle Paul ought not to have given instructions to Timothy and to Titus as to what or how to instruct others. Nay, he who has been given the role of teacher in the Church ought to have before his eyes three of the Apostle's Epistles. In the first Epistle to Timothy, do we not read: *These things announce, and teach,* that is the things which he explained above? Do we not read there too: *An ancient man rebuke not, but entreat him as a father?* In the Second Epistle does he not say: *Hold the form of sound words, which thou hast heard of me?* And does he not say to him in the same place: *Carefully labor to present thyself approved unto God, a workman that needeth not to be ashamed, rightfully handling the word of truth?* There too is this: *Preach the word: be instant in season, out of season: reprove, entreat, rebuke in all patience and doctrine.* And so too to Titus, does he not say that a bishop ought to be persevering

in that faithful word which is according to doctrine, that he may be able in sound doctrine to convince the gainsayers? There again he says: *but speak thou the things that become sound doctrine, that the aged men are sober,* and so on. There, too, we read: *These things speak, and exhort, and rebuke with all authority. Let no man despise thee. Admonish them to be subject to princes and powers.* What then should we think? Can it be that the Apostle holds contrary opinions to himself, since though he says that teachers are formed by the action of the Holy Spirit, he himself gives others instructions as to what and how they should teach? Or are we to understand that even with the outpourings of the Holy Spirit, man's help too is not to be dispensed with in the instructing of even the instructors themselves, and still, *neither he that planteth is anything, nor he that watereth, but God that giveth the increase?* And so it is that though, too, holy men themselves should help, or even the holy Angels should lend their aid, no one learns aright the things which pertain to life with God, if he becomes not through God, docile to God, to whom it is said in the Psalms: *Teach me to do thy will, for Thou art my God.* And therefore the Apostle says the like also to the same Timothy, speaking certainly as the master to his disciple: *But continue thou in those things which thou hast learned, and which have been committed to thee: knowing of whom thou hast learned them.* For as the medicine of the body, which is administered to men by men is of no avail except to those to whom God restores health, since He can cure even without it, though without Him, it cannot, and yet it is administered—and if this be done in kindliness, it is counted among the works of mercy or charity—so, also aids to learning, when given by men, are of help to the soul when God makes them of help, who could have given his Gospel to man even without man's agency or help.

17   He, therefore, who strives in speaking, to convince of what is good, since he is concerned with the threefold aim, viz., instructing, pleasing, and persuading, should pray and labor, as we have said above, to make himself understood, enjoyed, and persuasive. And when he accomplishes this rightly and fitly, he is not unworthily called eloquent, even though the agreement of his hearer does not follow him. For it is to these three points, viz., instructing, pleasing, and persuading, that the great authority on Roman eloquence himself seems to wish to apply those other three points in that place where he has said, "He therefore will be eloquent, who can speak in a subdued manner on unimportant matters, in a moderate style on things of greater importance, and in a grand style on great matters," as if he would add also those other three points given above, and would express one and the same idea, thus: "He, therefore, will be eloquent who, in order to instruct, can speak in a subdued manner on unimportant matters; in order to please, in a moderate style on things of greater importance; and in order to persuade, in a grand style on great subjects" [Cicero *Orator* 29.101].

18   Now our authority could have illustrated these three points, as explained by him, in legal cases; but he could not have done so here, *i.e.* in the instance of ecclesiastical questions, the type with which that form of discourse is concerned which we wish to describe. For in the former, those matters can be called unimportant where money questions are concerned; those are great where it is a question of the welfare and life of man; but where neither of these is concerned,

and it is not a matter of pleading or judging, but merely of pleasing the listener, such questions are midway between the two, and for that reason are called 'middling', that is 'moderate'. For 'moderate' gets its name from *modus*, 'measure', so we do not apply the term properly, but misuse it, when we say 'moderate' for 'small'. However, in these discourses of ours, since indeed everything, especially all which we address to the people from our high position, we must direct to man's welfare—and that not his temporal but his eternal welfare—where, besides, we must warn against eternal destruction, all that we say is of great importance, even to the extent that even money matters themselves, whether in regard to gain or loss, when put forth by the ecclesiastical teacher ought not seem of small importance, let the amount be great or little. For the matter of justice is not of small importance, and this surely we must safeguard even as regards a small amount of money, since the Lord says: *He that is faithful in that which is least, is faithful also in that which is greater.* And so a little thing is a little thing, but to be faithful in a little thing is a great thing. For as it is the nature of a circle that all the lines drawn from a point in the middle to the circumference are equal, and this principle is the same in a large disk and in a small coin, so when justice is administered even in a small matter, the greatness of justice is not diminished.

Therefore, when the Apostle spoke of worldly trials (and with what, truly, were these concerned unless with money matters?), he said: *Dare any of you, having a matter against another, go to be judged before the unjust, and not before the saints? Know you not that the saints shall judge this world? And if the world shall be judged by you, are you unworthy to judge the smallest matters? Know you not that we shall judge angels, not to speak of things of this world? If therefore you have judgments of things pertaining to this world, set them to judge, who are the most despised in the Church. I speak to your shame. Is it so that there is not among you one wise man, that is able to judge between his brethren? But brother goeth to law with brother, and that before unbelievers. Already indeed there is plainly a fault among you, that you have lawsuits one with another. Why do you not rather suffer wrong? Why do you not rather suffer yourselves to be defrauded? But you do wrong and defraud, and that to your brethren. Know you not that the unjust shall not possess the kingdom of God?* Why is it that the Apostle is so indignant, that he so upbraids, so reproaches, so rebukes, so threatens? Why is it that he calls the emotion of his soul to witness, with such numerous and harsh expressions? Why is it, finally, that he speaks in such a lofty strain on trivial matters? Is it that mere worldly questions deserved so much from him? Far from it! But he does so because of justice, charity, and righteousness, which no one in a sane mind can doubt but are great, even in things however insignificant.

Certainly, if we were to advise men how they ought to plead such worldly cases before ecclesiastical judges either for themselves or for their friends, we should be right in advising them to plead in a subdued manner, as of matters of small importance. But since it is a question of the eloquence of one whom we wish to be a teacher of those matters through which we are freed from eternal pains and brought to eternal happiness, it makes no difference where such things are treated, whether before the people or privately, whether with one person or with more, whether with friends or with enemies, whether in an unbroken speech or in a conversation, whether in tracts or in books, whether in letters, long or short, they are great; except perhaps that because a cup of cold water is a very little and unimportant thing, so what the Lord says is very little and unimportant, viz., that whosoever shall give one to his disciple shall not lose his reward; or, indeed, that when a preacher in the Church develops a sermon from this text, he ought to consider that he is talking on something of little weight, and so should express himself not in the moderate or in the grand style, but in the subdued style. Is it not true that when we chance to speak to the people on this text, and God's Presence is with us so that we speak not unfittingly, that a kind of a flame darts forth, as it were, from that cold water, which inflames men's cold hearts to the accomplishment of works of mercy, through the hope of heavenly reward?

19   And still, although our teacher is necessarily the spokesman of great subjects, he need not necessarily always speak in the grand style, but in a subdued manner when something is being explained, moderately when a thing is being criticised or commended; but when something ought to be done, and we are speaking to those who ought to do it, although they do not wish to, then the matter which is an important one, should be stated in the grand style, and in a manner adapted to move their hearts. But sometimes one and the same great matter is treated in a subdued way, if information is given; moderately, if commendation is made; and in the grand style, if adverse opinion is forced to change. For what is greater than God Himself? But is that a reason why He should not be studied? Or should one who teaches about the unity of the Trinity use other than subdued language if he wishes to make a matter difficult of distinction understood, in as far as it is possible? In such a case, are embellishments demanded rather than proofs? Is the listener to be persuaded to do something, and not rather to be instructed so as to learn something? But when God is being praised either for Himself or for His works, what a glory of beautiful and splendid language wells forth for one who can go to the very lengths of praise of Him whom no one fittingly praises, but whom no one fails to praise in one way or another. But if He be not worshipped, or if with Him or even before Him idols be worshipped, either demons or some other creature, the grievousness of this offense, and the exhortation to men to be converted from it ought certainly be expressed in the grand style.

4.22   No one should suppose that it is against the rule to mingle these three styles. On the contrary, as far as it can properly be done, one should vary his diction by using all three. For when a speech is surfeited with one style, it does not keep the listener's attention. But when a change is made from one to another, even if the discourse is stretched out to some length, it proceeds in a more pleasing fashion; although each style, too, has variations of its own in the language of the eloquent, which do not allow the attention of the audience to grow languid or to cool off. However, we can more readily bear the subdued style alone for a longer time, than the grand style alone. For the higher the pitch to which the feelings are to be excited in order to gain the assent of the audience, the shorter the time that this can be maintained once they have been sufficiently excited. And so we must take care lest desiring to lift higher what is already lifted high, there be rather a fall from the pitch of excitement already attained. But by interspersing matter which requires rather the subdued style, a pleasing return can then be made to the subject calling for grand expression, so that the flow of diction comes and goes like the tides of the sea. Hence it is that the grand style of diction, if it has to be continued for some time, must not be used alone, but must be varied by the interspersion of the other styles. The whole discourse, however, is attributed in kind to the style which predominates.

It is, therefore, a matter of importance to know what style should be interspersed 23 with what other style, and what kind should be used in definite, necessary places. For even in the grand style, properly the introduction should always, or nearly always be moderate. And the orator has the right in some places to speak in the subdued style, even when the grand style could have been used, so that what he expresses in the grand style may by comparison become even grander, and as it were, through the shadows of the other appear even more luminous. But whatever the style, if some knotty question demands solution, acumen is called for, and this the subdued style claims as its own. And for this reason, this style must be used even in the other two, when such questions arise in them; just as when something requires praise or censure, and it is not the question of the condemnation or the acquittal of anyone, nor of a person's assent to some course of action, no matter what the kind of style used when this occurs, the moderate style must then be taken up and interposed. And so in the grand style and in the subdued also, the other two find place. The temperate style, on the other hand, not indeed always, but still sometimes requires the subdued style if, as I have said, some question occurs whose difficulty demands solution, or when something which could be embellished is not embellished, but expressed in subdued language that it may furnish a more conspicuous place for certain bows, as it were, of embellishment. But moderate diction does not need the grand style, for it is used to please the mind, not to move it.

If a speaker get frequent and loud applause, it should not on that account be 24 imagined that he is talking in the grand style, for this is the effect of the acumen of the subdued style, and of the ornament of the temperate. But the grand style does generally silence all voices by its impressiveness, and calls forth tears. In fact, when at Caesarea in Mauritania, I was urging the people against civil strife or worse than civil strife, which they called *caterva*—for not only fellow-citizens, but also relatives, brothers, even fathers and sons, setting themselves into two divisions, fought each other with stones for several days at a time regularly each year at a certain season, and each killed whomever he could—I pleaded indeed in the grand style to the best of my power, to root out and dispel by my words so cruel and inveterate an evil from their hearts and lives; still, it was not when I heard their applause, but when I saw their tears, that I felt I had gained something. For by their applause they showed that they understood and were pleased, but that they were won, they made evident by their tears. When I saw these, I knew, even before they proved it by the actual fact, that that barbarous custom, handed down from fathers, grandfathers, and far back from their ancestors, which had obsessed, or rather possessed their hearts in so savage a manner, was conquered. And directly my discourse was ended, I turned their hearts and lips to offering thanksgiving to God. And behold, it is now almost eight or more years since, through the grace of Christ, anything of that kind has been attempted there. And there are also many other experiences through which I have found out that men manifest the effect of the grandeur of grave eloquence not by shouting, but rather by groans, sometimes by tears, finally by change of life.

But even by the subdued style many have been changed, but only to know what they were ignorant of, or to believe what seemed unbelievable to them, not, however, to do what they already knew they should do, and did not wish to do. For truly to bend stubbornness of this kind, the grand style is necessary. For even when praise and censure are expressed eloquently, though merely in the moderate style, some people are so affected that they are not only pleased by the eloquence with which the praise or censure are expressed, but they seek to live in a manner deserving praise, and they avoid living in one deserving censure. But who will claim that all who are pleased by a speech, model themselves on it, as all who are moved by the grand style act in accordance with it, and all who are instructed by the subdued style understand or believe the truth of which they are ignorant?

25   From this we may conclude that the end which the two last named styles aim to bring about is very important to those who desire to speak with wisdom and eloquence. But the end in view in the moderate style, namely, to please by eloquence, is not in itself worthy of being used, except, through the very pleasing quality of the expression, to gain a somewhat more willing assent or a firmer hold for a matter which is useful and good but which does not require explanation or persuasive eloquence, since it already has its audience well-informed or favorably disposed. For since the function of all eloquence, no matter in which of these three styles, is to speak in a way adapted to persuasion, and the end, that is, what you aim at, is to persuade by speaking, so, in whatever of the three styles indeed an orator speaks in a manner adapted to persuasion, unless he does persuade, he does not attain the end of eloquence. For instance, in the subdued style he persuades his audience that what he says is true; he persuades them in the grand style, to do what they now know they ought to do, but are not doing; he persuades them in the moderate style that he is expressing himself in beautiful and elegant language. But of what use to us is this end? Let them aim at it who glory in fine language, and who show off in panegyrics and such like modes of speech, in which the aim is not to instruct the audience, nor to move them to some course of action, but merely to please them. But as for us, let us turn this end to another end; for instance, to aim to bring about, even by this style, what we aim to effect in a speech in the grand style, that is, to make good morals esteemed or evil morals avoided, if the audience are not so hostile to this course of action as to seem to need urging to it by the grand style, or if they are now following it, to make them follow it with greater zest and to persevere in it with constancy. Thus it is that we use even the ornament of the moderate style not ostentatiously, but wisely, not content with its own purpose, namely, merely to please the audience, but rather striving for this, to help them even thereby to the good toward which our persuasion aims.

26   And so those three points which we named above as ends to be striven for by everyone who desires to speak with wisdom and with eloquence, namely, to make

one's words understood, enjoyed, and persuasive, are not to be so taken as to be applied only respectively to the three styles of speaking: being understood, to the subdued style; being enjoyed, to the moderate style; and being persuasive to the grand style; but rather in such a way that the orator ever aims at all three, and employs them all, in so far as it is possible, even when he is concerned with each one of them separately. For it is not our desire that even what we say in the subdued style be tiresome, but through this style we wish not only to make ourselves understood, but even enjoyed. And why do we enforce what we have to say in teaching, by quotations from Holy Scripture, but to make ourselves persuasive, that is, to make our audience believe us, with the assistance of Him to whom it is said, *Thy testimonies are become exceedingly credible?* What too does he desire except to be believed, who tells a story to an audience even though in the subdued style? But who would wish to give one his attention unless the latter could hold his listener by some charm of style? For who does not know that one who is not understood cannot make himself either pleasing or persuasive? For as to this subdued style, many times when it unravels very difficult questions, and proves them by an unexpected explanation, when it unearths and displays the most penetrating observations from obscure caverns, as it were, whence they were not expected, when it proves an opponent's error, and shows that to be false which seemed to have been stated as unassailable by him, especially if a certain grace accompanies it, not aimed at, but, in a certain measure natural and some use of rhythm in clausulae, not obtrusive, but, as it were, necessary, and, so to speak, drawn out of the subject itself, it excites such applause that one would scarcely believe it to be the subdued style. For from the very fact that it does not come forth adorned and armed, but stalks out stripped bare, as it were, for that very reason it does not fail to crush its opponent by its very sinew and muscle, and to overwhelm and destroy the resistance of falsehood by its own strong arm. But whence comes it that such speakers are so frequently and greatly applauded except that truth thus set forth, thus defended, thus rendered unassailable, gives pleasure? And, therefore, in this subdued style, that teacher and speaker of ours ought to strive not only to make his discourse understood, but also to make it enjoyable and persuasive.

The eloquence of the moderate type, too, in the case of the ecclesiastical orator is not left unadorned, and yet it is not unbecomingly adorned, nor does it only aim at giving pleasure, the sole end that it professes in the hands of others, but in holding up those things which it praises or censures, on the one hand as matters worthy of being sought for and firmly maintained, on the other, as deserving to be avoided and rejected, it also certainly aims at being persuasive. But if it is not understood, neither can it give pleasure. And so all three ends, viz., that the audience should understand, be pleased, and be persuaded, must be striven for even in this one style where giving pleasure holds first place.

But when it is necessary to move and convince a listener by the grand style—as it is when one's opponent grants the truth and attractiveness of what is said, but is unwilling to act upon it—one must without doubt express himself *grandly.* But who is moved if he does not understand what is said, or whose attention is held if he is not pleased? Wherefore, in this style also, when an obdurate heart has to be to be bent by the grand manner of speech, unless the speaker makes himself both understood and enjoyed, he cannot make himself persuasive.

27   But the life of the speaker has greater force to make him persuasive than the grandeur of his eloquence, however great that may be. For the man who speaks wisely and eloquently, but lives evilly, instructs indeed many who are eager to learn, though *he is unprofitable to his own soul*, as it is written. And so the Apostle says: *Whether by occasion, or by truth, Christ be preached.* Now Christ is truth and still, truth can be preached, even though not with truth, that is when by a mean and deceiving heart righteousness and truth are preached. Thus, indeed, Jesus Christ is preached by those who seek their own ends, not those of Jesus Christ. But since good Christians obey not any man whatsoever, but the Lord Himself, who says: *Whatsoever they say to you, do: but according to their works, do you not, for they say and do not*, therefore are they heard with profit, even though they themselves do not lead profitable lives. For they are zealous in seeking their own ends, but they dare not teach their own from the high place, forsooth, of ecclesiastical authority, which sound doctrine has established. For this reason the Lord Himself, before saying what I have just quoted about men of this kind, declared: *They have sitten on the chair of Moses.* That chair, therefore, which was not theirs but Moses', forced them to say what was good, even though they were not doing what was good. And so they pursued their own ends in their lives, but to teach their own, that, the chair which belonged to another did not allow them to do.

And so they do good to many by preaching even what they do not live up to; but far more would they do good to by practising what they preached. For there are many who seek to defend their own evil lives by their very superiors and teachers answering in their hearts, or even if they go so far, saying with their lips, "What you tell me to do, why do you not do yourself?" And so it comes about that they do not follow one who does not follow his own preaching, and they contemn the word of God which is preached to them, along with the preacher himself. Accordingly, the Apostle, in writing to Timothy, after saying, *Let no man despise thy youth*, adds how he would avoid being despised, saying, *Be thou an example of the faithful in word, in conversation, in charity, in faith, in chastity.*

28   Such a teacher, to render himself persuasive, may without presumption express himself not only in the subdued and in the moderate style, but also in the grand style, because his life is beyond reproach. For truly he so chooses to live a good life as not indeed to neglect a good reputation, but especially so as to forecast what is good before God and man, in as far as possible, by fearing God and by caring for man. Even in his very speech he should prefer to please through his matter rather than through his words, and he should consider that a thing is not well said unless it be truthfully said; nor should the teacher serve words, but words, the teacher. For this what the Apostle says: *Not in wisdom of speech lest the cross of Christ be made void.* Of the same purport, too, is what he says to Timothy: *Contend not in words, for it is to no profit, but to the subverting of the hearers.* This, however, is not said to the end that we should say nothing in defense of truth whenever opponents attack it. And where will be what, among other things, he said when he was showing of what character a bishop ought to be: *That he may be able in sound*

doctrine, also to convince the gainsayers? For to contend in words is not to care how error may be overcome by truth, but how your style may be preferred to another's. However, the man who does not contend in words, whether he expresses himself in the subdued, or in the moderate, or in the grand style, has this aim in speaking, that truth be made clear, that truth be made pleasing, that truth be made convincing; for not even love itself, which is the end of the commandment and the fulfilling of the law, can in any way be right if the objects of love are not true but false. For as one whose body is comely, but whose heart is depraved is more to be pitied than if his body also were deformed, so those who express falsehood with eloquence are more to be deplored than if they should express the same in an unseemly way. And so what is it to speak not only with eloquence but also with wisdom, except to employ words which are adequate, in the subdued style; striking, in the temperate style; and strong, in the grand style—in regard to truth, of course, which it is fitting should be heard? But if a person cannot do both, let him speak with wisdom, even though he cannot with eloquence, rather than with eloquence without wisdom. But if even this is impossible, let him so conduct himself as not only to deserve a reward for himself, but also to offer an example to others; and in his case, let his manner of life be, as it were, a flowing speech.

But there are, indeed, some men who can deliver a sermon well, but who cannot think out its matter. Now if they take what has been eloquently and wisely written by others, and commit it to memory, and deliver it before the people, if they assume this character, they do no wrong. For thus, as is certainly profitable, many become preachers of truth, though not many, teachers, if they all speak the same thing of one true teacher, and there are no schisms among them. Nor need they be frightened by the word of Jeremias the Prophet, through whom God rebukes those who steal His words, everyone from his neighbor. For those who steal take what belongs to another, but the word of God belongs to those who obey it; and that man rather speaks the words of another, who speaks well but lives badly. For whatever good sentiments he expresses seem to proceed from his own thought on them, but they do not belong to his way of living. And so God has said that those men steal His words who wish to appear good by speaking God's word, though they are evil in following a course of their own. And indeed it is not they themselves who speak the good that they speak, if you study the matter closely. For how can they express in words what they do not express in deeds? Truly not for nought does the Apostle say of such: *They profess that they know God: but in their works they deny Him.* And so in a certain sense they speak, and again in another sense they do not, since both these verses are true, because Truth itself utters them. For, again, speaking of such as these, He says: *What they shall say to you, do; but according to their words, do ye not.* That is, "What from their lips you hear, that do, but what in their works you see, that do not do." *For they say,* he continues, *and do not.* And so thought they *do* not, still they *say.* But in another place, rebuking such men, He says: *Hypocrites, how can you speak good things, whereas you are evil?* And from this it would seem that even what they say when they speak good things, they do not themselves say, since forsooth in will and in deed, they gainsay what they say. And so it may happen that an eloquent man,

29

though bad, may himself compose a sermon in which truth is set forth to be delivered by another who, though not eloquent, is good. And when this is done, the former gives as from himself what belongs to another, while the latter receives from another what is really his own. But when good Christians render this service to good Christians, both speak what is their own, because God is theirs, and to Him belong the words which they speak; and they make these, too, their own, though they were not able to compose them, if they compose their lives in accordance with them.

30   But whether a person is now making ready to speak before the people or before any other group whatever, or to compose something either to be delivered before the people or read by those who wish or can do so, he should pray God to put a fitting discourse upon his lips. For if Queen Esther prayed when she was about to address the king in regard to the temporal affairs of her people, that God might give her a well-ordered speech in her mouth, how much more ought he to pray to receive such a gift who labors in word and teaching for the eternal welfare of mankind? Those, too, who are to deliver what they receive from others, even before they receive it, ought to pray for those from whom they receive it, that what they wish to receive, may be given to them; and when they have received it, they should pray that they themselves may deliver it well, and that those to whom they speak may take it; and for the successful issue of their discourse, they should give thanks to Him from whom they cannot doubt but that they have received it, that he who glories may glory in Him in whose hand are both we and our words.

31   This work has turned out longer than I had wished, and than I had planned. But if it is interesting to one who reads it or listens to it, it will not be long; if, however, anyone finds it long, he should read it in parts if he still wishes to become acquainted with it; on the other hand, one who is not interested in making its acquaintance should not complain of its length. But for my part, I give thanks to God that in these four books, I have treated with whatever little ability I have, not of such a one as I myself am, for I have many deficiencies, but of such a person as he should be who in sound teaching, that is in Christian teaching, strives to labor not only for himself, but also for others.

Bibliography

Bibliography

Alcidamas. In *Artium scriptores (Reste der voraristotelischen Rhetorik)*, edited by Ludwig Radermacher, 132–47. Vienna: Rudolf M. Rohrer, 1951.

Aphthonius. *Progymnasmata*. In *Rhetores Graeci*, edited by Leonard Spengel, vol. 2, 21–56. 1853–56. Reprint. Frankfurt: Minerva, 1966.

———. *"The Progymnasmata of Aphthonius."* Translated by Ray Nadeau. *Speech Monographs* 19 (Nov. 1952): 264–85.

Aristotle. *The "Art" of Rhetoric*. Translated by John Henry Freese. Vol. 22. 1926. Reprint. Cambridge: Harvard University Press, The Loeb Classical Library, 1975.

———. *On Sophistical Refutations*. Translated by E. S. Forster. Vol. 3. 1955. Reprint. Cambridge: Harvard University Press, The Loeb Classical Library, 1978.

———. *Prior Analytics*. Translated by Hugh Tredennick. Vol. 1. 1938. Reprint. Cambridge: Harvard University Press, The Loeb Classical Library, 1967.

———. *Topica*. Translated by E. S. Forster. Vol. 2. 1960. Reprint. Cambridge: Harvard University Press, The Loeb Classical Library, 1966.

Augustine. *On Christian Doctrine*. Translated by Sister Therese Sullivan. Washington, D.C.: Catholic University of America Press, 1930.

Basil. *Address to Young Men on Reading Greek Literature*. Translated by Roy Joseph Deferrari and Martin R. P. McGuire. In Saint Basil, *The Letters*, vol. 4, 365–435. 1939. Reprint. Cambridge: Harvard University Press, The Loeb Classical Library, 1950.

Cicero. *Brutus*. Translated by G. L. Hendrickson. Vol. 5. 1939. Reprint. Cambridge: Harvard University Press, The Loeb Classical Library, 1971.

———. *De Inventione*. Translated by H. M. Hubbell. Vol. 2. 1949. Reprint. Cambridge: Harvard University Press, The Loeb Classical Library, 1960.

———. *De Oratore*. Translated by H. Rackham. Vol. 4. 1942. Reprint. Cambridge: Harvard University Press, The Loeb Classical Library, 1982.

———. *De Partitione Oratoria*. Translated by H. Rackham. Vol. 4. 1942. Reprint. Cambridge: Harvard University Press, The Loeb Classical Library, 1982.

Clark, Donald Lemen. "The Rise and Fall of Progymnasmata in Sixteenth and Seventeenth Century Grammar Schools." *Speech Monographs* 19 (Nov. 1952): 259–63.

Demetrius. *On Style*. Translated by W. Rhys Roberts. 1927. Reprint. Cambridge: Harvard University Press, The Loeb Classical Library, 1973.

Dionysius of Halicarnassus. *On the Arrangement of Words*. Translated by D. A. Russell. In *Ancient Literary Criticism*, edited by D. A. Russell and M. Winterbottom, 321–43. Oxford: Oxford University Press, 1972.

Dixon, Peter. *Rhetoric*. London and New York: Methuen, 1971.

Gorgias. *Encomium of Helen*. Translated by D. M. MacDowell. Bristol: Bristol Classical Press, 1982.

———. "The Ecomium of Helen, by Gorgias." Translated by LaRue Van Hook. *The Classical Weekly* 6 (Feb. 1913): 122–23.

———— . *Helen.* Translated by George A. Kennedy. 1988.

Grube, G. M. A. *A Greek Critic: Demetrius on Style.* Toronto: University of Toronto Press, 1961.

Guthrie, W. K. C. *A History of Greek Philosophy.* Vol. 4. Cambridge: Cambridge University Press, 1975.

Hagendahl, Harald. *Augustine and the Latin Classics.* Stockholm: Almqvist & Wiksell, 1967.

Hermogenes. *On Types of Style.* Translated by Cecil W. Wooten. Chapel Hill: University of North Carolina Press, 1987.

———— . *Progymnasmata.* In *Rhetores Graeci,* edited by Leonard Spengel, vol. 2, 3–18. 1853–56. Reprint. Frankfurt: Minerva, 1966.

Herodotus. Translated by A. D. Godley. Vol. 2. 1921. Reprint. Cambridge: Harvard University Press, The Loeb Classical Library, 1957.

Hock, Ronald F., and Edward N. O'Neil. *The Chreia in Ancient Rhetoric.* Vol. 1. Atlanta: Scholars Press, 1986.

Homer. *The Iliad of Homer.* Translated by Richmond Lattimore. Chicago: University of Chicago Press, 1951.

———— . *The Iliad of Homer: Books 1–12.* Edited by M. M. Willcock. New York: St. Martin's Press; Basingstoke and London: Macmillan Education Ltd., 1978.

How, W. W., and J. Wells. *A Commentary on Herodotus.* Vol. 1. Oxford: Oxford University Press, 1912.

Isocrates. *Against the Sophists.* Translated by George Norlin. Vol. 2. 1929. Reprint. Cambridge: Harvard University Press, The Loeb Classical Library, 1982.

———— . *Antidosis.* Translated by George Norlin. Vol. 2. 1929. Reprint. Cambridge: Harvard University Press, The Loeb Classical Library, 1982.

Jaeger, Werner. *Early Christianity and Greek Paideia.* Cambridge: Belknap Press of Harvard University Press, 1961.

Kennedy, George A. *The Art of Persuasion in Greece.* Princeton: Princeton University Press, 1963.

———— . *The Art of Rhetoric in the Roman World.* Princeton: Princeton University Press, 1972.

———— . *Classical Rhetoric and Its Christian and Secular Tradition from Ancient to Modern Times.* Chapel Hill: University of North Carolina Press, 1980.

———— . *Greek Rhetoric under Christian Emperors.* Princeton: Princeton University Press, 1983.

Kerferd, G. B. *The Sophistic Movement.* Cambridge: Cambridge University Press, 1981.

Kustas, George L. "Saint Basil and the Rhetorical Tradition." In *Basil of Caesarea: Christian, Humanist, Ascetic,* edited by Paul Jonathan Fedwick, 221–79. Toronto: Pontifical Institute of Medieval Studies, 1981.

Lang, Mabel L. *Herodotean Narrative and Discourse.* Cambridge: Harvard University Press, 1984.

Lanham, Richard A. *A Handlist of Rhetorical Terms.* Berkeley: University of California Press, 1968.

Lesky, Albin. *A History of Greek Literature.* London: Methuen, 1966.

Longinus. *On Great Writing (On the Sublime).* Translated with an introduction by G. M. A. Grube. Indianapolis: Bobbs-Merrill, Library of Liberal Arts, 1957.

Longus. *Daphnis and Chloe.* In *Three Greek Romances,* translated by Moses Hadas, 3–68. Indianapolis: Bobbs-Merrill, Library of Liberal Arts, 1964.

Menander Rhetor. *The Talk.* In *Menander Rhetor,* edited and translated by D. A. Russell and N. G. Wilson, 115–27. Oxford: Oxford University Press, 1981.

Nicolaus. *Progymnasmata.* In *Rhetores Graeci,* edited by Leonard Spengel, vol. 3, 449–98. 1853–56. Reprint. Frankfurt: Minerva, 1966.

Parry, Adam, ed., comp., and trans. *The Making of Homeric Verse: The Collected Papers of Milman Parry.* Oxford: Oxford University Press, 1971.

Patterson, Annabel M. *Hermogenes and the Renaissance: Seven Ideas of Style.* Princeton:

Princeton University Press, 1970.

Pausanias. *Description of Greece*. Translated by W. H. S. Jones. Vol. 1. 1918. Reprint. Cambridge: Harvard University Press, The Loeb Classical Library, 1969.

Philodemus. *The Rhetorica of Philodemus*. Translated by Harry M. Hubbell. *Transactions of the Connecticut Academy of Arts and Sciences* 23 (Sept. 1920): 243–382.

Philostratus. *The Lives of the Sophists*. In *Philostratus: Lives of the Sophists. Eunapius: Lives of the Philosophers and Sophists*, translated by Wilmer Cave Wright. 1921. Reprint. Cambridge: Harvard University Press, The Loeb Classical Library, 1968.

Plato. *Gorgias*. In *Plato: Socratic Dialogues*, edited and translated by W. D. Woodhead with introduction by G. C. Field, general editor, Raymond Klibansky. Walton-on-Thames: Thomas Nelson and Sons, 1953.

———— . *Menexenus*. In *Platonis opera*, edited by John Burnet. Vol. 3. 1903. Reprint. Oxford: Oxford University Press, 1968.

———— . *Phaedrus*. Translated with introduction and commentary by R. Hackforth. Cambridge: Cambridge University Press, 1952.

Quintilian. *Institutio Oratoria*. Translated by H. E. Butler. Vols. 1, 3, 4. 1921. Reprint. Cambridge: Harvard University Press, The Loeb Classical Library, 1976.

Rhetorica ad Alexandrum. Translated by H. Rackham. In *Aristotle: Problems*, vol. 2. 1937. Reprint. Cambridge: Harvard University Press, The Loeb Classical Library, 1981.

Rhetorica ad Herennium. Translated by Harry Caplan. 1954. Reprint. Cambridge: Harvard University Press, The Loeb Classical Library, 1981.

Russell, D. A., and M. Winterbottom. *Ancient Literary Criticism: The Principal Texts in New Translations*. Oxford: Oxford University Press, 1972.

Schein, Seth L. *The Mortal Hero: An Introduction to Homer's "Iliad."* Berkeley: University of California Press, 1984.

Sprague, Rosamond Kent. *The Older Sophists*. Columbia: University of South Carolina Press, 1972.

Tacitus. *Dialogue on Orators*. Translated by W. Peterson, revised by M. Winterbottom. 1914. Reprint. Cambridge: Harvard University Press, The Loeb Classical Library, 1980.

Theon. *Progymnasmata*. In *Rhetores Graeci*, edited by Leonard Spengel, vol. 2, 59–130. 1853–56. Reprint. Frankfurt: Minerva, 1966.

Thompson, Wayne N. "Dionysius of Halicarnassus: A Reappraisal." *The Quarterly Journal of Speech* 65 (1979): 303–10.

Thucydides. Translated by Charles Forster Smith. Vol. 2. 1920. Reprint. Cambridge: Harvard University Press, The Loeb Classical Library, 1965.

———— . *The Complete Writings of Thucydides: The Peloponnesian War*. Translated by R. Crawley, unabridged, with an introduction by John H. Finley, Jr. New York: Modern Library, 1951.

Patricia P. Matsen is associate professor of Greek and Chair of the Classical Studies Committee at the University of South Carolina. A graduate of Agnes Scott College, she received her M.A. from the University of Mississippi and her Ph.D. from Bryn Mawr College. She has previously published translations of Greek texts on allegory and related rhetorical figures.

Philip Rollinson is professor of English at the University of South Carolina. He has published scholarly works on Old English, Renaissance Latin literature, Milton, Spenser, and critical theory from classical antiquity through the Renaissance. He was born in Chattanooga, Tennessee and received his B.A. from the University of Chattanooga and his M.A. and Ph.D. in English from the University of Virginia.

A graduate of the composition/rhetoric program at the University of South Carolina, *Marion Sousa* received her Ph.D. in 1989. Her dissertation studies the development of literacy in ancient Greece, exploring the ways in which literacy affected classical rhetoric. She received her M.A. from the City College of New York in 1966. Since 1980, she has taught courses in English composition and literature, business writing, and ESL.